GEORGIAN

ABO

A Multidisciplinary Perspective From Québec

Edited by Gordon Christie

Theytus Books

Copyright © 2006 The Authors

Library and Archives Canada Cataloguing in Publication

Aboriginality and governance : a multidisciplinary
perspective / edited by Gordon Christie.

Includes bibliographical references and index.
ISBN 1-894778-24-3

1. Native peoples--Canada--Government relations.
2. Native peoples--Canada--Politics and government.
3. Native peoples--Legal status, laws, etc.--Canada.
I. Christie, Gordon

E78.C2A12 2006   323.1197'071   C2006-905666-8

Printed in Canada

Cover and interior by Suzanne Bates
Photograph by Nicolas Raymond

On behalf on Theytus Books, we would like to acknowledge the support of the following:
We acknowledge the financial support of the Government of Canada through the Book
Publishing Industry Development Program (BPIDP) for our publishing activities.
We acknowledge the support of the Canada Council for the Arts which last year in-
vested $20.0 million in writing and publishing throughout Canada.
Nous remercions de son soutien le Conseil des Arts du Canada, qui a investi 20,0 mil-
lions de dollars l'an demier dans les lettres et l'édition à travers le Canada.
We acknowledge the support of the Province of British Columbia through the British
Columbia Arts Council.

  Canadian Patrimoine
Heritage canadien
  Canada Council Conseil des Arts
for the Arts du Canada
 BRITISH COLUMBIA
ARTS COUNCIL

ABORIGINALITY AND GOVERNANCE

A Multidisciplinary Perspective From Québec

Edited by Gordon Christie

Introduction

Looking out over the broad, multidisciplinary landscape of Aboriginal studies from within an English-Canadian institution, one can easily overlook a vast body of research speaking to many of the same issues, debates and concerns. While I cannot speak to the degree to which scholars working within French-Canadian institutions are conversant with discussions and debates ongoing amongst English-speaking scholars, I can say that many scholars working within English-Canadian institutions are, by and large, removed from the rich dialogue ongoing within the Francophone community. This text is meant to play a small role in overcoming this problem, introducing English-Canadians to a selection of works produced by a group of researchers working in Québec. Thirteen papers, originally produced and published in French, have been translated and gathered into this one volume.

'Autochtonie et gouvernance' originated as a research partnership between (a) researchers from the University of Montréal, McGill University, Laval University, the University of Québec à Chicoutimi, and the National Institute of Scientific Research, and (b) the Assembly of First Nations of Québec and Labrador, the Avataq Cultural Institute, and the Makivik Corporation. Working within and between multiple disciplines, employing progressive modes of collaborative and respectful community-based research, and displaying new and exciting theoretical approaches and frameworks, these authors fruitfully explore many of the issues lying at the core of the fundamental problems facing Aboriginal peoples in Canada today as Aboriginal nations work toward regaining control of lands, lives and resources.

Research coordinators for this project describe it as seeking to, "circumscribe the characteristics of Aboriginal society that will provide guidance for the creation of governance models in the political, social, legal and economic spheres". Focusing on 'self-governance' (understood in a manner distinct from the conception offered by the federal government) the research team examined two sets of factors in relation to their influence on the creation of governance models. The first set:

> ... connects the present with the past. It deals with links between, on the one hand, myths and other traditional conceptions ... and, on the other hand, the numerous contemporary Aboriginal conceptions of ancestral rights. These factors also take into account the effects of the colonial form of the Canadian State and the historical relationship the State has had with ... Aboriginal peoples regarding the interpretation and the application of Aboriginal rights. ... These are some of the parameters that will guide the possibilities for the movement towards adequate macro-governance, particularly with regard to its elements of communitarianism, political control of the territory, and the status of individual Aboriginal persons, both on and off the reserves.

The second set:

To the extent possible, this volume follows this division – the first six articles look at connections between the present and the past, the last seven at recent and ongoing changes. Overlap, however, is unavoidable, as, for example, any examination of the historical relationship between the state and Aboriginal peoples will have much to say about the contemporary situation, just as a look into any transfer of authority and power must rest on an appreciation of the history lying behind and around Aboriginal peoples, the state, and dominant society.

In the following introductory comments I remark briefly on each paper – in an attempt to tease readers so as to invite them into these valuable texts – and then make some general remarks about the papers as a whole, about their status (which is certainly not unique) as explorations into vexing questions circling around the current situations facing both Aboriginal and non-Aboriginal societies in Canada.

The Articles

Sylvie Vincent's "The Uepishtikueiau Narrative: The Arrival of the French at the site of Québec City according to Innu Oral Tradition" explores oral narratives reaching back to the early period of contact between the Innu and the French at modern day Québec City. These narratives tell a tale of early agreements, subsequent trickery and conflict, and the eventual displacement of the Innu. Vincent, tellingly, includes comments about contemporary conflict, as this sequence of events seems destined to repeat:

> Today there are no longer any Innu inland. You see Whites there and they do not hesitate to build houses everywhere. They are making the backcountry into their land rather than that of the Innu, and yet the Innu are its masters. They act as if the backcountry was under their control. They cannot be satisfied with Uepishtikueiau, with what they were given. (Marie-Madeleine Kaltush, Nutashkuan, 1993)

Denys Delâge's "Aboriginal Influence on the Canadians and French at the Time of New France" provides an extensive accounting of the various ways by which Aboriginal peoples impacted on the lives of newcomers to Québec. While early sections provide exhaustive detail around such matters as food and transportation, equally fascinating are the later sections, exploring in great detail the role Aboriginal societies played in the rethinking of political, legal and religious beliefs that formed the core of French-Canadian identity. While Delâge identifies three factors that played into the eventual development of 'Canadian character' (the influence of Aboriginal peoples, various social factors, and an 'illusion' generated by the dominant class), suggestions are made about the vast subterranean impact 'Others' had on European peoples. With the growing influence of cultural relativism (emerging out of continued contact with the cultures of Others) and a move toward the 'objectification' of culture (emerging out of the study of Others), European culture was undercut from within, though this weakening of cultural pillars went hand-in-hand with the West's domination over non-European peoples.

Denys Delâge and Jean-Phillippe Warren's "The Meeting of *Bourgeois* and Aboriginal Ethics: Modernity, Postmodernity and Aboriginality" delves into certain oppositions that function to clearly set alongside one another *'Bourgeois'* (Western) ethics and Aboriginal ethics – oppositions around the concepts of guilt/debt and work. The authors construct a framework around the related notions of guilt and sin, a conceptual framework around *Bourgeois* ethics that ties into and underlies the emergence of the central notion of individualism. In contrast to this, they articulate a notion of transgression in Aboriginal societies that builds on the concept of debt, on the idea that all acts of transgression in this world are redeemable, with suitable compensation. Acts of an individual are transgressive in so far as they mark the breakdown of relationships, human and non-human, with compensation functioning to repair these bonds – the very conceptual lens for making sense of the actions of an individual plays, then, an essential role in strengthening communal bonds. In relation to 'work', the authors note that the activities falling under this concept come to be seen in the West as ends in themselves (if one *could* point to some other external end it would be outside one's life, indeed outside this world: one works for God), while within the Aboriginal world work is done for its enjoyment, and to meet 'personal' needs (where 'personal' is expansive in scope, pulling in various social obligations and responsibilities).

These sorts of oppositions are not merely present – in the meeting of *Bourgeois* and Aboriginal ethics we see a ground upon which these concepts can be tools for domination and resistance. The authors argue that:

> European peoples subjugated Aboriginal peoples in part through military strength, in part through the worldwide communication of disease, in part through deceit and treachery, but also through a new interpretation of man's place in the world, which left Aboriginals defenceless and confused.

Colonial powers used these 'new interpretations of man's place in the world' to certain ends – Aboriginal peoples were labelled 'lazy', and determined to be ignorant of the very concept of 'sin', which had the effect of firmly placing Aboriginal peoples in the distinct category of 'the Other'. So placed, colonial powers were able to justify programs of separation, domination, and conversion. On the other hand, building on notions of debt, Aboriginal peoples came to rely heavily on notions of state responsibility and compensation, thereby playing their own role in the creation of a system of ward-ship and dependency.

Much of this piece focuses, however, on the passage of time, on movements away from 'feudal' and religious groundings of Western ethics, first toward modern (secular) frameworks, and then most recently toward postmodern sensibilities. How can Aboriginal peoples (and the ethical systems they live through) respond to these movements? Living within or through a postmodern sensibility, for example, citizens in Canada come to conceive of themselves as essentially removed from guilt and responsibility, individually (and to some degree collectively) as 'innocent' and as potential victim(s). How can Aboriginal societies respond to these times and conditions? Delâge and Warren suggest that while placing themselves as 'victims' has 'worked' for certain elements of Aboriginal societies, a more powerful move toward the strengthening of 'traditional' Aboriginal culture (visible through the growing resistance of Aboriginal peoples to the replacement of Aboriginal ethics with an individualist ethics), coupled with a drive toward greater political control, can move us all forward.

Bernard Saladin d'Anglure's "The Construction of Shamanic Identity among the Inuit of Nunavut and Nunavik", "The Inuit 'Third Gender'", and "The Whale Hunting among the Inuit of the Canadian Arctic" form an impressive trilogy exploring both past and present practices connected to aspects of Inuit identity. The two articles exploring the construction of shamanic identity and whale hunting look at two activities lying at the core of Inuit life, exploring their development through periods of immense upheaval, as Inuit went through periods of religious conversion and economic turmoil. The article exploring an Inuit 'third gender', on the other hand, is interesting in its focus on the impact of careful study of Inuit society on theoretical discussions around gender. Arguing that 'classical thought' (formed around the pillars of Judeo-Christian ideology and scientific rationalism) has trapped the West in a dualist conception of gender, d'Anglure argues that it "would be wise to look to hunter-gatherer societies for the right questions to ask in our own society and for a better concept of the gender system."

Mylène Jaccoud's "Aboriginal Criminal Justice: From Imposed Justice to Power Transfer" examines the history around the interaction of the Canadian justice system and Aboriginal peoples. The focus, however, is the present context, as talk has built recently around the transfer of power from the central state to local Aboriginal communities. This notion of 'power transfer', however, admits of quite a range of possible instantiations. We see, for example, recent policies aimed at the 'indigenization' of the Canadian justice system (fundamentally by incorporating more Aboriginal peoples into the apparatus of this system, as court workers, lawyers, judges and such). Jaccoud notes, however, that:

> While the indigenization policy is one way of changing government institutions, or at least those institutions' relationship to minorities, what is of course at stake is the assimilation of Aboriginals into the state justice system.

Jaccoud notes as well that the current move toward transfer of power to Aboriginal communities could be understood within the general movement in Canada toward a communitarian vision of justice management. She asks, however, whether "transferring responsibilities to a community [is] the same as transferring powers?" Which way, then, are we going? Is power actually being transferred to Aboriginal communities, or are we really in the midst of a movement toward greater incorporation of Aboriginal peoples into the imposed, dominant system?

Ghislain Otis' contributions, "Elections, Traditional Aboriginal Governance and the *Charter*" and "Aboriginal Governance with or without the Canadian *Charter*?" explore two contentious issues facing contemporary Aboriginal communities, as control over how governing bodies are established, and how they function, are vested more completely in the hands of these communities. How might we expect various constitutional instruments to operate, given the challenges the existence and exercise of these powers will unavoidably generate?

In the context of elections and democratic rule, Otis sets out certain parameters within which we might reasonably expect debates and experiments to occur. Aboriginal communities will continue to move toward systems that attempt to effect a return to traditional ways of selecting leaders, all the while cognizant of the impact the *Charter* may have on the range of possible alternatives deemed reasonable. Otis argues – as he does more fully in his companion piece in this volume – that section 25 of the *Charter* (ensuring that the *Charter* 'shall not be construed so as to abrogate or derogate from any aboriginal, treaty or other rights and freedoms that pertain to the aboriginal peoples of Canada') protects the *existence* and *core features* of Aboriginal rights from *Charter* interference, but that actions taken in *exercise* of these rights may not be immune from challenge. Clearly the *Charter*, he argues, will be a factor in the development of innovative modes of selecting leadership. How all this plays out is still unclear, as Aboriginal communities strive to regain control over leadership selection through the invention of institutions that, "… foster cultural dignity and meet the aspirations of present and future generations."

In the second more general (and far-reaching) piece, Otis examines in great depth the inter-relationship between emerging Aboriginal forms of governance and the *Charter*. Several themes and arguments introduced in the piece on elections are carefully developed and examined – the notion that current thought around 'good governance' will impact on models developed, and that the *Charter* will play a role in channelling models in certain directions. Otis argues (in opposition to many other current commentators) that Aboriginal governments will fall under the *Charter*, and that section 25 offers at most partial or limited immunity to *Charter* challenge. Otis notes that Aboriginal governments regaining political control will be taking upon themselves power in the context of the modern legal and political landscape, a landscape dominated by notions of good governance and the protection of individual rights and freedoms. Otis argues that this will not, however, pose insurmountable problems, for he sees (again contrary to much of the commentary on this issue) no clear indication or evidence of, "a fundamental tension, or even opposition, between Aboriginal cultures and the modern culture of fundamental individual rights and freedoms."

In "Legal Pluralism at Kahnawake?" Andrée Lajoie, Henry Quillinan, Rod Macdonald and Guy Rocher explore conceptions of pluralism in relation to the social and political milieu marking the complex and dynamic situation on the Mohawk reserve of Kahnawake. The emphasis is on forms of pluralism that posit, "… institutions [in the community] that were sufficiently formal to be identified by the stakeholders in the community and that set out, interpreted and applied norms that were claimed to apply to all members of the community living on the reserve." The authors set out to test the hypothesis that legal pluralism could describe the recent past on the reserve, not only in the sense that the Canadian state might have devolved significant power to the reserve's band council (a form of 'intra-state' pluralism), but in the sense that in reaction to the imposition of state power a form of 'popular' law might have emerged, a legal regime formed outside the state apparatus (embodied in various Longhouses that began to openly assert their presence on reserve, beginning in the 1970's). This would be, "... a new creation, at least partially, in which traditional law is reinterpreted in a completely new context." Complicating the already complex narrative that emerges in the course of this study is a movement in the mid 1990's by the Band Council to itself shift toward the traditional precepts and principles of the *Great Law of Peace*.

Andrée Lajoie, Eric Gélineau, I. Duplessis and Guy Rocher's "The Integration of Aboriginal Values and Interests Into Canadian Judicial and Normative Discourse" is an exploration of the extent to which Aboriginal values and interests have worked their way into jurisprudence and negotiated agreements around Aboriginal issues. The authors first identify values and interests that can be read out of the discourse of groups bringing claims to the courts, and explore the paths by which such values might work their way both into the courts and to negotiating tables. They also attempt to identify values that appear to animate judicial discourse and that appear on the state side of negotiations. The analysis culminates in an examination into the degree to which one can then verify that Aboriginal values and interests have been integrated into either the discourse of the courts or the nature of agreements entered into.

In some respects the results are not surprising ("... the Aboriginal values most notably absent from the Court's discourse are political self-determination and control of land"), while in other respects they may be startling to some ("... the consistency of both bodies [courts and political actors] over so many years, and especially the refinement and complementarity of their approaches, does seem surprising, even to the best informed.") This is an important piece for those who have a sense that 'progress' is being made, but have a nagging suspicion about what that progress might amount to.

Carole Lévesque's "Aboriginal Peoples' Quest for Identity and Self-Government" also explores some of the values and interests Aboriginal peoples have pursued in various arenas over the last few decades. Lévesque explores three (distinct but complementary) quests around identity and autonomy in which Aboriginal peoples have recently been engaged: the assertion of an inherent right to self-determination, demands for full recognition of land claims and ancestral and treaty rights, and the abolition of discrimination against Aboriginal women.

In the course of her overview of these struggles Lévesque identifies many of the difficult questions these quests invite. For example, around the project of asserting an inherent right to self-determination one must ask:

> Will the future political foundations of Aboriginal peoples' forms of government be ethnic or territorial? Will they be regional or provincial? Will Aboriginal peoples have two nationalities in the future, one Canadian and the other Aboriginal? Will the Canadian *Charter* of Rights and Freedoms coexist in the future with a *Charter* of Aboriginal Rights?

Her piece concludes, however, with words about other developments that point the way toward the resolution of many of the most vexing problems facing Aboriginal communities. In talking about the struggles around the plight of Aboriginal women she notes:

> Not only were they speaking up for the first time, but their struggle ... was particularly difficult within the Aboriginal milieu. Consequently, awareness was triggered, first among Aboriginal women but also with time among Aboriginal men, of the need to improve relations with one another and to promote family and community integration.... This movement, which attracted much less media attention than the big legal battles, has also helped to consolidate a collective identity with a more social than political scope.

Finally, in "Aboriginal Peoples' Right to Self-Government: A Phoenix that Will Rise from its Ashes" Alain Bissonnette tackles, as so many of the collaborators in this volume do, perplexing problems swirling around the project of transferring legal and political power to Aboriginal communities within the context of a larger political society, one built on precepts of individual rights and freedoms. These two facts, Bissonnette argues, account for the rejection of the Charlottetown Accord by Aboriginal peoples in Canada: some within the Aboriginal world were concerned with the ways in which the Accord would have effectively maintained power in the hands of the larger political society, while some in the Aboriginal world (particularly Aboriginal women) were concerned with the threat to their rights and freedoms that might have followed on the transfer of *some* degree of political and legal power to Aboriginal governments.

In relation to the first concern, Bissonnette notes that Aboriginal peoples would prefer to have their own legal notions function to define and describe the new legal regime that a transfer of power might have generated. In fleshing out these points Bissonnette makes use of some of the same tools of analysis employed by other authors in this collection, specifically notions about and around legal pluralism. For example, in concert with a number of other authors in this text, Bissonnette makes use of a particular vision of the very nature of 'law' Noting the great diversity in legal and political systems that we can see around the world and through time, he notes:

.... [D]iversity and difference can themselves be interpreted in many different ways. Here, we will evoke only one possibility: an approach that has been developed over the last 20 years by researchers at the *Laboratoire d'anthropologie juridique* in Paris. According to the *Laboratoire's* researchers, law should not be approached as a concept but as a phenomenon. Thus, instead of trying to define what law is, we should study juridicization phenomena in various societies. ... Anthropologists of law ... look at law as a juridicization phenomenon, rather than as a concept. For them, law is less a specific type of social relation than a specific description that each society chooses to give to certain social relations. In other words, while legal facts are social facts, not all social facts are legal facts. Social facts become legal only by passing through a specific social filter or control designed to ensure the cohesion and perpetuation of the group in question. From this point of view, law is not a set of specific rules, but an inter-normative process ... Of course, social facts can vary over time within a society. Likewise, the kind of control can also vary, as can what a semi-autonomous group considers necessary for its cohesion and perpetuation. Naturally, what a society considers to be legal facts will vary in consequence.

The second half of this piece looks at the question of how we might build up a notion of Aboriginal self-governance from the notions of human and 'peoples' rights (both fairly recently emergent on the international scene, though the notion of the rights of peoples is much more recently emergent). Bissonnette looks first at some who have written about the notion of the rights of peoples, and ends with a look into the *Indigenous and Tribal Peoples Convention (ILO no. 169)* and the still-nascent draft *Declaration of the Rights of Indigenous Peoples*. As promising as these documents may be, some of the same problems identified earlier still arise – some Aboriginal peoples will see in these instruments values and principles that do not reflect their own legal notions (a problem with 'cultural diversity' that is tied to the problem of controlling 'symbols and ideas', and of having access to resources to be able to exercise this control). Such problems, Bissonnette suggests, seem capable of resolution only through the creation of "intercultural dialogue" directed at designing "... new mechanisms for reconciling the parties" and fostering "the emergence of new shared legitimacy".

An Observation

As editor of this collection of translated articles, it has been understandably difficult for me not to grow close to them. I have come to see in them a fantastic store of historical information (issuing from a wonderful mix of different kinds of narrative), innovative modes of argumentation and theorizing, and a wealth of insights and suggestive comments. But with greatest respect and fondness, I must acknowledge the place of such studies within our larger understanding of the role of 'knowledge production' vis-à-vis the relationships between the Canadian state (and Canadian society) and Aboriginal peoples.

These articles themselves deploy structures and strategies that speak to an appreciation of this understanding – either overtly, or more subtly, the reader can find in these texts acknowledgement that as much as 'history' is the record of movements, of conflicts and conquests, of the sharing of technology and other moments of assistance, it is also a record of ideological conflict.

This insight, however, flows up and over us, for full appreciation of it entails that we recognize not only the role discourse – the production of 'knowledge' – has played in the subjugation of colonized peoples around the world, but also that we recognize that the *production of history itself* (historical discourse, the production of historical knowledge) is one ground upon which such ideological conflict is unavoidably waged. No scholar *today* can rest content in the unreflective cocoon of 'neutrality' and 'objectivity'.

In their piece "The Meeting of *Bourgeois* and Aboriginal Ethics: Modernity, Postmodernity and Aboriginality" Delâge and Warren describe the emergence of a postmodern sensibility, forged partly in response to the shift in power dynamics in our late industrial, capitalist world:

> The individual is no longer guilty of what happens to him, and for good reason: most of the time the changes that affect him result from decisions in which he was not involved. He drifts in the stream of upheavals caused by structures over which he has no control.

While this captures a sense of the 'innocence' of the individual in our modern world, buffeted by forces over which she has no control, it does not adequately capture the way in which the modern academic is now acknowledged to be clearly implicated in 'politics', no matter how remote their production of knowledge may be – or seem to be – from the larger forces determining our individual and collective fates. The modern academic – even the postmodern academic – cannot outrun the responsibilities now clearly recognized and understood as befalling all scholars. We are all now aware of the role our academic studies can have on the representation of reality, the impact we thus can have on policy, and the impact this may, then, have on the very lives of people written about.

Consider this summary of the social, political, legal and economic context within which contemporary Aboriginal peoples exist:

> Contemporary Aboriginal life is made up of more than the legacy of pre-Columbian ancestors. It also has irrefutably modern characteristics such as sedentary lifestyle, growing individualism, increasingly formal economic relations, urbanization, integration into the bureaucratic structure of public services and government financial transfers, aspirations to economic development through the marketing of land and resources, quests for salaried employment, consumerism, subjection to mass media and technologies, promotion of education and technical training, existential crises among youth lacking direction, and painful reworking of re-

      lationships between men and women. [from Otis, "Elections, Traditional
      Aboriginal Governance and the *Charter*"]

This is a fair description of the reality facing Aboriginal peoples in contemporary
Canada, a description of a reality that itself is to a significant degree the result of
representations of Aboriginal peoples historically made. How will representations
made today impact on future realities? How will such summations look a generation or two hence?

So much depends on this critical juncture we find ourselves in during the early
years of the 21st century. The transfer of power that we hear so much about, the
apparent movement toward a strengthening of political control in the hands of Aboriginal communities, has the promise of reducing the power of dominant society
to use the power of the word to control and subjugate Aboriginal peoples. With
the transfer of political power comes an increase in the power to self-identify, to
regain control over the very power of representation, to tip the scales back to the
point where Aboriginal communities are able to dream their own futures.

The challenges inherent in such a project are immense, and we see as well in
these texts appreciation of the nature and scope of these challenges. Aboriginal
peoples do find themselves existing in the sort of reality summarized in the above
quote. The key challenge, however, is not the physical environment, nor even the
economic, legal or political environment – it lies with the effects of the diminishment of cultural legacies. Aboriginal peoples are faced with the daunting task of
trying to work themselves out of the absolute devastation of cultural instability
wrought by colonialism. Even *beginning* to think about how to 'decolonize' is a
daunting task.

Naturally, one thing we also come to appreciate in reading the studies in this text
is the symbiotic relationship – built on a bedrock of identity – that has come to
envelop both Aboriginal and non-Aboriginal societies in Canada. While for generations non-Aboriginal elements have deployed aggressive strategies of all stripe
and variety aimed at controlling the lives and thoughts of Aboriginal peoples, they
have also thereby been engaged, unavoidably, in a process of building their own
'Canadian character'. A transfer of power to Aboriginal communities, then, must
be seen as not only playing a fundamental role in opening the door to possible futures for Aboriginal peoples, but also as playing a role in the ongoing development
of Canadian character. How do non-Aboriginals want to see themselves? What
character do they want to vest in themselves? How do they want to see themselves,
and how do they want others to see them? Do non-Aboriginals not want to also
engage in a process of 'decolonization' (this is not, after all, a project that only
Aboriginal peoples must – or can – engage in)?

Finally, let me inject a comment about the future of this research. The texts in this
volume were for the most part originally made possible by a grant from Valorisation Recherche Québec (VRQ). As this text goes into publication, thanks to a Major Collaborative Research Initiative grant from the Social Sciences and Humani-

ties Research Council of Canada (the result of tremendous organizational efforts by a core team at the University of Montréal), the project is entering a new stage of development, becoming national in scope. The dialogue between researchers within and without Québec is broadening and strengthening, the results of which will be certainly positive and progressive.

This book has its genesis in the mind and spirit of Andrée Lajoie, of l'Université de Montréal. Others were quite helpful in its development: I would like to thank David Milward, Carissa Browning, Caleb Toombs, and Ardith Walkem – the time and energy they spent in working on this project is much appreciated. Anita Large, publishing manager at Theytus Press, was unwavering in her support and excessively patient as this collection slowly came together, and Suzanne Bates' work on producing the volume is most appreciated.

Gordon Christie
Faculty of Law
University of British Columbia

The Uepishtikueiau Narrative: The Arrival of the French at the site of Québec City according to Innu Oral Tradition[1]

Sylvie Vincent
With the collaboration of Joséphine Bacon

The Uepishtikueiau Narrative is not a myth, tale or legend. It is a historical narrative transmitted by the Innu oral tradition.

As we commemorate an alliance reported in Samuel de Champlain's 1603 travelogue, here is how generations of the Innu have been telling the story of the arrival of the French in their lands.[2]

1. Introduction

The Innu are one of the eleven Aboriginal nations of Québec. While they live today in nine communities, most of which are scattered along the North Shore,[3] their ancestral lands cover almost half of the Québec-Labrador peninsula. Given their geographic location, they were among the first to come into contact with the Europeans who, in the sixteenth and early seventeenth centuries, ventured into the Gulf of St. Lawrence and then upstream to the future site of Québec City.

The arrival of the French in Innu lands is recounted by oral tradition in what can be described as a founding narrative in that it explains a number of aspects of the present situation and, more specifically, relations between the Innu and French-speaking Québeckers. This is the narrative printed here. It is not a myth, tale or legend, but a historical narrative. It contains the Innu version of events that occurred in a not-so-distant past which are also reported, though in a different fashion, in the Québec version of the history, which is based on writings from the seventeenth century. Since the time the events occurred, the Innu have recited what happened, passing the narrative down from generation to generation, each generation attentive to transmitting what the previous generation had entrusted. Indeed, just as historians must identify and evaluate the sources they use, Innu narrators say from whom they heard the narrative and do not recite narratives from sources that they do not consider reliable, or at least not without warning their listeners.

Since the mid-twentieth century, however, Innu oral tradition has encountered many obstacles caused by the adoption of a sedentary way of life, education in French, and changes in social roles. Maintaining the tradition is a real challenge because even though the elders can talk about the narratives that they have heard,

1

comment on them and recite passages, very few can still recite the narratives as they were transmitted.

I became aware of this narrative in the early 1970s, but it was only at the end of the 1980s and in the 1990s that I was really able to gather elements from many people (around 40 living on the North Shore between *Pessamit* and *Pakua-shipit*). The text that follows has been constructed out of a narrative recorded in 1975 and recordings of 18 people from *Pessamit, Mani-Utenam, Nutashkuan* and *Unaman-shipit*. The goal was to deliver the common core of the Innu tradition as I heard it while showing some branches that, while not completely divergent, do not seem to be shared by all.

In 2003, there was a commemoration of the apparent 1603 alliance between Samuel de Champlain and the Innu chief whom he calls *Anadabijou* in his writings. The Innu have their own version of the events and agreements that marked their first contact with the French. As we will see, the Innu version is different from the "official" version. When one lives in a tradition dominated by writing, one generally tends to want to establish links between what we hear and what we read in historical documents. However, oral traditions have their own logic and therefore deserve to be apprehended on their own, at least initially. This is not easy to do. For example, there are neither dates nor names in the Uepishtikueiau Narrative. Yet we know that the people who appear in the narrative are the ancestors of the Innu and the first French people to visit their lands. From the issues and behaviour described, the narrative also sheds light on, by analogy, what is happening today between the descendents of the people mentioned. While it is important for the Innu to convey their own version of their history, it is just as important for those who are now their neighbours to be able to understand what the Innu version contains.

2. Uepishtikueiau

It is said that the ancestors of the Innu used to frequent a placed called Uepishti-kueiau. It was located at the extreme west of their lands, on the banks of a river, at the exact spot where, as the name indicates, the river narrowed.[4] The river is called *Uepishtikueiau-shipu*, but is known in French as the *Fleuve Saint-Laurent* and in English as the St. Lawrence River. The name "*Uepishtikueiau*" has been kept to refer to the city that the French call "Québec" and that they have built on the ancient site where the Innu's ancestors used to stay.

After having spent most of the year inland, it is said that the Innu used to come down the rivers in the spring and stay in small groups at the river mouths. They also used to go to *Uepishtikueiau*, which was their main gathering place before the French arrived.

Why go to the coast in late spring and early summer? It is said that it was because at that time the game inland is not good to eat. Moreover, in olden times as today, it was important to leave the animals the time to raise their young "in peace, far from noise" (William-Mathieu Mark, Unaman-shipit, 1988).

The Innu have always been in the backcountry. [...] They used to spend time at Uepishtikueiau to wait for the animals inland to reach maturity. [...] The Innu take care of what is found inland. They are quiet so that everything grows well, for example so that the young animals do not run away. While they are at the seaside [...] in the spring and summer, the animals inland give birth to their young. The Innu do not go into the backcountry at that time; they leave those areas and they do not hunt there. They go there only in the winter, and in the summer they wait on the coast. [...] In the winter, the animals are good to eat; those that were born that year have grown big. That is when the Innu go into the backcountry. [...] In the olden days, they used to go down to Uepishtikueiau when they went to the coast, but it was only one place among others. They stayed in various places along the St. Lawrence River. (William-Mathieu Mark, Unaman-shipit, 1993)

When they got to the coast of the Gulf of St. Lawrence or to the bank of the river, especially at *Uepishtikueiau*, the Innu found the food they needed. They lived mainly off of hunting migratory birds and fishing. In August, when the animals inland became edible again, the Innu left the St. Lawrence River area and did not come back again until the next year. Of course, some families stayed near the lakes in the backcountry in the summer and ate mainly fish, but many went to the coast in late spring and early summer.

The Innu could choose from among a number of destinations along the St. Lawrence River and Gulf. They preferred *Uepishtikueiau* because, it is said, there was a lot of game there and also the bark needed to make canoes.

The Innu must have been at Uepishtikueiau, naturally, because there is a river there. It was surely a good river, given its width. There must have been everything in terms of resources. There must have been geese there. The Innu must have gone there every spring and probably stayed there to hunt the animals that ensured their subsistence. (Délima André, Mani-Utenam, 1999)

They used to go to Uepishtikueiau to make their canoes. It was the only place where there was good bark for making canoes, the kind that is thick, bark that is very thick. That was the only kind of bark they used to make their canoes. [...]

In those days there were not yet any French people at Uepishtikueiau and it is said that it was the only place where the Innu took bark. They must have made their canoes right there. [...] Here [on the Middle North Shore] they would not have been able to get bark. The birch trees are too thin and would have given them too many little pieces of bark. It is said that it was possible to make a canoe with the bark from a single tree. It is also said that, when they could not make their canoes there, they used to carry the bark away with them. [...]

> Once they had harvested the bark, they used to travel towards the Gulf and make their canoes in places where there were rivers. They made their canoes in places where there were lots of fish in the rivers, and then they used to go back inland. (Joseph-Bastien Wapistan, Nutashkuan, 1992, 1993)

It is said that the bark could be harvested only in spring and summer.

> It is said that the Innu did not touch birch trees in the winter. They did not use them. It was only in the spring, when it was warm, that they were able to harvest the bark. [...] They chose a tree that did not have too many knots so that there would not be too many in the canoe. (Joseph-Bastien Wapistan, Nutashkuan, 1992)

It is said that in olden times, before the French arrived, there were many Innu at *Uepishtikueiau* in the spring and early summer. Of course, they stayed in many different places along the river, at the mouths of rivers and in places where they knew they would be able to find game and fish, but "they liked being at Uepishtikueiau" (Pierre Mesténapéo, Nutashkuan, 1993), especially on a point there, where they used to stay. They used to arrive one after another, in little groups, and in the end there were quite a few people there.

> The Innu must have been very numerous in the past. And at Uepishtikueiau there must have really been a lot of people. [...] The Innu must have gone there mainly when they were coming down to the coast after spending autumn and winter inland. (Jean-Baptiste Bellefleur, Unaman-shipit, 1993)

The oral tradition indicates that *Uepishtikueiau* was one of the favourite places of the ancestors of the Innu. It was a meeting and assembly place: an "Innu land".

Before the French arrived, the Innu used to live inland and their real gathering place was Uepishtikueiau. (William-Mathieu Mark, Unaman-shipit, 1988)

> Uepishtikueiau is said to be Innu land. It was called the land of the Innu. At least, that is what the Innu used to call it. It is said that it is their land. (Pierre Mesténapéo, Nutashkuan, 1992)

But who really were the people who met at the place where the river narrowed? According to the main branch of the oral tradition, they were the ancestors of the Innu only.

> It was Innu like us who were there, at Uepishtikueiau. [...] It was our ancestors who were there. (Jean-Baptiste Bellefleur, Unaman-shipit, 1993)

> We all come from Uepishtikueiau, all of us, we come from Uepishtikueiau. That is where the Innu began to become really numerous. (Pierre Courtois, Nutashkuan, 1992)

> The people of Uepishtikueiau, those who live there today [the Huron-Wendats] would not have come from there. [...] It seems that there used to be Innu like us there. It's as if the Innu were at Uepishtikueiau at that time. Then other Indians arrived, perhaps it was [...] the Iroquois or the Hurons. (Desanges Saint-Onge, Pessamit, 1994)

> The people of Uepishtikueiau were our ancestors, we all come from there. They are the ancestors of all of the Innu who are here [on the North Shore]. We are all descendents of the few Innu who must have been there. (Joseph-Bastien Wapistan, Nutashkuan, 1992)

The Innu living today on the Upper, Middle and Lower North Shore, in the Saguenay-Lake St. John area and even in Labrador are thus considered descendents of the people of *Uepishtikueiau*.

A less often heard branch of the oral tradition says that *Uepishtikueiau* was also frequented by representatives of other nations, in particular the Micmacs and Huron-Wendats.

> There were a lot of Innu at Uepishtikueiau at that time, and Micmacs too, as well as Huron-Wendats. (William-Mathieu Mark, Unaman-shipit, 1988)

> There were Indians from several nations there. That is where they must have met, where they could get to know one another, learn one another's names and the lands they roamed. [...] The Innu were everywhere but it was at Uepishtikueiau really, it was mainly there, that they used to stay in the summer. Other Indians must have come there too. [...] It was as if they visited one another at Uepishtikueiau. That must have been what happened. [...] That was where all the nations used to gather. (Jean-Baptiste Bellefleur, Unaman-shipit, 1993)

While part of the oral tradition says that members of other nations, in particular the Huron-Wendat nation, came to *Uepishtikueiau*, the majority claims that when the French arrived, only the Innu were there.

However, whether they were alone or not, it is claimed that the ancestors of the Innu used to frequent the place called "*Uepishtikueiau*" and that they used it as a major meeting place.

Then everything changed.

3. The arrival of the French

The Innu who had gathered at *Uepishtikueiau* and were staying on the point saw one or more sailboats arrive. The boats were made of wood, which is why those who built them were called "*Mishtikushuat*."[5] Later it was learned that those people

made things out of wood and that they used wood as one of their major raw materials. The narratives do not really describe the new arrivals, aside [from] their
hats.

> The French must have worn fabric clothing as we do today. That is how
> they must have been dressed. It is not said what their clothing was like,
> but they certainly must not have been wearing caribou skins. They had
> to be wearing fabric. The Innu wore clothing made from caribou skins.
> [...] Maybe the French people's hats looked like those really big hats that
> were seen in the past. At least, that is what was said about their hats. It
> was said that the one who met the Innu at Uepishtikueiau had a broad hat.
> (Joseph-Bastien Wapistan, Nutashukuan, 1993)

However, the tradition does say why the French suddenly appeared at *Uepishtikueiau*.

> It was said that in the past the French traveled looking for land. They
> sailed their ships in search of land. They used to roam the seas looking for
> land, it is said. [...] They did not just come to Uepishtikueiau; it is said
> that they also visited other places. However, the Innu saw only the French
> who came to Uepishtikueiau. It is said that they were not very numerous
> when they arrived. (Jean-Baptiste Bellefleur, Unaman-shipit, 1993)

> The French were looking for something that they could own. They were
> looking for a place where they could be the masters. [...] They must
> have come here for that reason. They were looking for a place of their
> own. They came because they were looking for a place to live. (Charles
> Kaltush, Nutashkuan, 1993)

Aside from the fact that they came from the east in sailboats, the French are thus
defined essentially as people who were looking for land. When they arrived by
chance near *Uepishtikueiau*, they saw that the Innu land seemed good and so they
went closer to shore.

> There must be a point at Uepishtikueiau. The shore of the St. Lawrence
> River curves back in on itself, thereby creating a point. It is said this was
> the part of Uepishtikueiau where the French arrived the first time that
> they came. (Jean-Baptiste Bellefleur, Unaman-shipit, 1993)

What did the Innu do when they saw the French put a rowboat in the water and
approach the shore? There are several versions of the oral tradition on this point.
The most frequently heard one says that the Innu chief went towards the French
and invited them to come ashore.

> When the French arrived at Uepishtikueiau, the Innu were very surprised
> to see the sailing ship. The French took a rowboat towards the shore and
> got out. They could not understand one another at all. The Innu would

have said: "Come ashore." They must have said *"kapaku"* to the French, and the French understood that the Innu were telling them "Québec". And they called Uepishtikueiau "Québec" because that is what they understood that the Innu were telling them when the Innu were telling them to come ashore. (Desanges Saint-Onge, Pessamit, 1994)

It is said that there used to be Innu everywhere, and that there were some here too, downstream along the St. Lawrence [on the North Shore]. They used to be everywhere that there were rivers, it is said, and they must have also gone by canoe to Uepishtikueiau. It is said that this is where they gathered. The Innu really used to gather at Uepishtikueiau. Then the French came to them by the sea. They were in sailboats, big boats with sails, the olden days sailboats. So the Innu said to them: *"Paka!"*[6] ["come ashore"] and Uepishtikueiau is called "Québec" because that is what the French understood when the Innu told them to come ashore. [...] They are the ones who called it "Québec." But "Uepishtikueiau" is the real Innu toponym. It is the term used in Innu when we talk about it. It is because the French understood "Québec" when the Innu invited them to get out of their boat that the place came to be named in that way. It is said that this is why Uepishtikueiau is still called "Québec" today. (Joseph Bellefleur, Nutashkuan, 1992)

However, the Innu were fearful. They did not understand the French people's language, just as the French could not understand theirs, and they were not sure what the foreigners were planning to do on their land. Moreover, the French were armed.

I do not know what the Innu thought the first time they saw the French. They must not have been on good terms with them. In addition, they did not understand them. Since they could not understand them, they must have wondered when they saw them what they were going to do. They must have wondered, "What are they planning to do here?" As for the French, they must have left their boat with the intention of living according to their customs and staying here forever. And that is what happened: they stayed at Uepishtikueiau. (Joseph Bellefleur, Nutashkuan, 1992)

The Innu must have hidden when the French arrived and came ashore. Then the French went and saw them and must have told them that they were going to stay there. They also asked them who they were. The Innu did not understand and must have told them that the place where they were was called Uepishtikueiau and that the river got narrower upstream. They were talking about the St. Lawrence River. Then the French probably set up camp on the other side of the river. [...] When you start having friendly relations with people who have just arrived, you do anything you can to make them as comfortable as possible and make sure they do not need anything, right? You do everything possible so that the people are at ease and really as comfortable as possible. Anyway, you are afraid of them if you see that they have guns. The Innu had no guns. They had only bows and arrows. That made them afraid in the past. They were afraid that the others would shoot at them or attack them. (Pierre Mesténapéo, Nutashkuan, 1993)

The French showed the products that they had brought with them, including food that the Innu were not familiar with and guns.

When they met, they did not understand one another. The Innu were afraid of the French. The French unloaded food and all the things that they had brought with them. We had never seen such food and were familiar only with meat. We ate only animals. (Paul Benjamin, Pessamit, 1995)

It is said that the French went and made contact with the Innu. They must have shaken their hands. [...] Then they asked them how they survived. The Innu must not have understood, naturally. The people at Uepishti-kueiau would not have understood the French when they spoke, [...] they did not understand French, just as we do not understand it. It must have been the same as today. They probably used gestures to understand one another. [...] Then the French showed them flour, baking powder... They showed them everything they had and gave them some. Then they showed them guns. (Pierre Mesténapéo, Nutashkuan, 1993)

According to another version of the oral tradition, when the French tried to get close to shore, Innu arrows stopped them.

The French could not get off of their ship because the Innu were attacking them. It took a long time before they got off. [...] The Innu were hidden, so the French did not know where the arrows were coming from. They could not hear anything, but the Innu could hear the French's gunfire. [...] That is why it took so long for the French to come ashore. [...] They could not do so until they had beaten the Innu. At first, they could not get off their boat because they could not conquer the Innu. That is what prevented them from getting off. [...] It was only after defeating them that they were able to come ashore. The Innu had attacked them. You get to do what you want when you win a war. Once they had won that war, the French were able to get off their boat. Then they went to see the Innu. (William-Mathieu Mark, Unaman-shipit, 1993)

When the French arrived the very first time, the Innu must not have agreed to leave. So, when they came back, they fought them. [...] There must have been a cliff and it was from there that the Innu fought. That is where the French boat must have been anchored. It is said that those who fought the Innu were aboard a ship while the Innu must have been in the forest. It is said that the women also shot arrows at the French. They were also using bows and arrows. Women used a different kind of bow than the men, it is said. They mainly used a kind of crossbow. That is what it is said they used. When the battle ended, all the men were dead. The only people left must have been women. They must have run away and hid in the woods. Later, when the hostilities were over, the women came back to the coast and stayed there, it is said. Then the Innu population started growing again, little by little. It is said that in the past there used to be many Innu. If the French had not killed them, there would be many Innu today. [...] There was only one battle. It is said that the French had guns, while the Innu had bows and arrows, according to what is said. They killed all the men and there were only women left. Only the Innu who were inland when this happened survived. Later, they must have gone down to Uepishtikueiau and married some of the women who were there. (Joseph-Bastien Wapistan, Nutashkuan, 1992)

Whether they were welcomed or not, the oral tradition says that the French were faced with the Innu's distrust. However, they finally landed and began negotiations with them. What they wanted was clear: they were barely ashore when they asked the Innu to give them *Uepishtikueiau*.

I do not know how the French lived over there, on their own land; I don't know anything about it because no one saw how they did it. When they arrived at Uepishtikueiau, they saw how the Innu met their needs by using lakes and rivers. That is why, after seeing that it was possible to live well there, they asked for the land; that is why their chief asked the Innu for the land. (Charles Kaltush, Nutashkuan, 1993)

The oral tradition says that the Innu were reluctant to grant the request of the French.

The French must have come from the east, from the direction where the sun rises, and they came to Uepishtikueiau. When they arrived, the Innu were making their canoes as was the custom in the olden days. That is what the Innu must have been doing when the sailboat arrived. So they went down to meet it and their chief told the French chief to come ashore. He invited the Frenchman to come ashore and it is said that the Frenchman understood that the Innu were telling him "Québec". That is the origin of the location's name. So the Frenchman got out of his boat. They started negotiating on the shore. I wonder what the Innu looked like while he was talking with the Frenchman. The Frenchman asked for his land. The Innu listened to him while making his canoe and nodding his head. [...] Then the Frenchman asked him for the land: "Give it to me," he said. (Pierre Courtois, Nutashkuan, 1993)

Some say that the French had to try two or even three times before they obtained Innu permission to settle at the place called *Uepishtikueiau*. It is said that they made an offer as well as a promise.

3.1. Request and promise

Finally having got off their boat, the French said that they wanted to be allowed to settle and live on Innu land. They had seen how the Innu themselves lived on their land and they thought that it could be farmed. That is why they planned to produce their own food, which, according to the oral tradition, was based on flour and typically took the form of bread.

> The French must have studied the Innu land because they are people who plant all sorts of things. They must have seen how fertile the land was. (Délima André, Mani-Utenam, 1999)

> The French saw that Uepishtikueiau was good land, that it would be good for growing wheat and other things – like potatoes – and that it was fertile enough for all of them to live there. [...] The French chief said to the Innu: "I am going to grow wheat and other things and that way everyone will have what they need, including the Innu." It is said that this is what he said to them. (Joseph Bellefleur, Nutashkuan, 1993)

If the Innu agreed to let the French settle at *Uepishtikueiau*, they would receive in exchange a share of the wheat that would be grown and that way they would no longer have to fear the difficult periods of famine that they sometimes suffered. It is said that this is what the French promised.

> The French chief came from the east when he asked the Innu to give him Uepishtikueiau. However, the Innu did not give it to him right away. It was when he asked a second time that they gave it to him. After the first request, the French planted a little wheat and after a small amount of wheat had grown, the French chief asked them for their land again. He told them: "Later there will be a lot of wheat and, if the Innu are in need, if they have no food, we will be able to use the wheat to feed them at any time. The Innu will never be in want. You will no longer have to worry that your descendents will go hungry." It is said that this is what he said. (Mathieu Menikapu, Nutashkuan, 1971)

> After disembarking, the Frenchman acted as if the land belonged to him. He grew wheat on it. When he asked the Innu for their land, he told them: "It is thanks to this wheat that you will survive. Thanks to it, you will always have something to eat. This is where we will give you money so that you can buy food and have flour." (Pierre Courtois, Nutashkuan, 1992)

> It is said that the French chief met with the Innu chief and asked him for his land, which it is said was at Uepishtikueiau. [...] And it seems the Frenchman said: "I will give you food of all kinds and you will eat really very well." That is what he said, according to the what they say. He would have said: "I will make sure that you will always have what you need, and in sufficient quantities." (Marie-Madeleine Kaltush, Nutashkuan, 1993)

The promise that the French would always give the Innu enough food to survive extended to future generations.

> The French chief said to them: "As long as you live, it is because you left us Uepishtikueiau that you will find all you require to meet your needs." He also told them: "Your children also will never experience hunger, it is thanks to this that they will also find the food they need." (Pierre Courtois, Nutashkuan, 1993)

The French planted wheat and it is said that the first harvests were good.

> It is said that everything grows well at Uepishtikueiau. That is why the French asked the Innu for the land. They told them that they would be very good to them, in exchange. [...] It is said that the land was very good. It is said that things grew well. (Michel Bellefleur, Unaman-shipit, 1988)

Another branch of the oral tradition suggests that the French also showed the Innu other products. And, without the Innu realizing it, the promise to help them by providing food turned into an offer to trade.

> It is said that there were no French there, in Uepishtikueiau. There were only Innu. So trading company bosses went to the Innu. They met with the Indians. They asked: "Can we settle here?" They talked about Uepishtikueiau. They said: "We will build a warehouse." The bosses said: "If ever you are in need in the future, we will be able to help you." So, according to what is said, the Innu agreed. Then the French built a warehouse at Uepishtikueiau. And then they became numerous. (Michel Grégoire, Nutashkuan, 1975)

> They came from very far away; they came from Europe. More and more of them came and they brought all they needed with them. They brought from their lands, from France, what they would need at Uepishtikueiau. Then they sold all sorts of things to the Innu: food, guns, and other goods that the Innu might need. And the Innu must have finally accepted the French who sold them guns. The Innu had nothing like all that. They had neither flintlocks nor muskets. They must have been happy. When they were given some, they must have thought that they had good guns and that they would never have had any if the French had not come. They used the guns for hunting. They must have been useful for hunting and shooting animals. Before, they had only their bows and arrows. If they could not get close enough to the animals, they could not kill them. However, with guns they could kill from afar, no matter what kind of animal, and they must have appreciated the new possibility. So in the end they liked the French who were there, and the French sold them all sorts of things. (Joseph Bellefleur, Nutashkuan, 1992)

Won over, according to the narrative, by the products and economic assistance offered, the Innu allowed the French to settle at *Uepishtikueiau*.

> The Innu left Uepishtikueiau to the French because they would no longer have to search for food since everything necessary would be available at Uepishtikueiau. (Pierre Courtois, Nutashkuan, 1993)

The permission is sometimes presented as a requirement.

> The Innu who was in charge of Uepishtikueiau must have been like a chief. So the French chief must have asked that Innu for the land. When he arrived, he must have asked him for it [...] It is said that he submitted a request to the Innu; it was their land that he asked for. After the Frenchman made the request, the Innu chief would have told him: "I will let you have my land but in exchange you must never refuse to give me anything that I may ask of you in return." (Marie-Madeleine Kaltush, Nutashkuan, 1993)

There was also a discussion concerning land. The French apparently suggested that the Innu live along the riverbank whereas the French would go and develop the land in the interior. However, the Innu rejected the arrangement.

> After they got off their boat, the French went to see the Innu to tell them that they could keep control of the coast and the French would go inland. However, the Innu did not accept the proposal. They continued to live inland and let the French have only the coast. They let them use the coast along the salt water so that they would not gain control of the inland areas. (William-Mathieu Mark, Unaman-shipit, 1993)

The oral tradition thus reports that there was an agreement between the French and the Innu. The Innu agreed that the French could come ashore, sow wheat and build a warehouse, but the permission covered only *Uepishtikueiau*. In exchange, the French promised the Innu that they and their descendents would from then on have access to food aide, essentially in the form of wheat flour, and that at *Uepishtikueiau* they would always find manufactured goods that could be useful to them, such as guns.

However, it is said that this is not exactly what happened.

3.2. Enticement, trickery and bushfighting

The oral tradition contains two versions of the events that followed the French promise. One places the emphasis on the fact that the new arrivals used their products to entice, and then trick, the Innu. In particular, it is reported that the flour and rifles, which were particularly attractive to the Innu, ended up being a kind of trap into which the Innu fell without realizing it.

Everything happened because of food. The French acted friendly. They gave the Innu food and the Innu were happy to be able to feed their children. Since their children had enough to live on, why would the Innu have had anything bad to say? They did not know that they were being given all those things in exchange for their land. Land had not been mentioned when the French, out of apparent generosity, gave them their goods. [...] The Innu must have been happy to accept the food. It satisfied them. They must have been happy to be treated that way and that is how the French were able to trick them. If the French had not given them the goods, they would never have managed to trick them and the Innu would have kept their land. [...] The French knew that they were going to lay hold of the Innu's river [the St. Lawrence River], and they knew it because they had already built their houses. They had it in mind. [...] The Innu must not have paid attention to what the French were doing because they were happy with the things they had been given. [...] The Innu must not have paid attention to them because they thought the land was theirs. They never imagined that in the end they would be forced to move and that their land would be taken away. But the French knew that they would displace the Innu as soon as there were enough of them. (Pierre Mesténapéo, Nutashkuan, 1993)

The first time the French came to Uepishtikueiau, they were in a boat, a sailboat. That is how they arrived in Innu lands. They came ashore and started selling their goods to the Innu. At the time there were not the same things as we find today. Moreover, the French must have had food that they also traded. Then, from that time on, they continued bringing those products. [...] When the French gave guns to the Innu, they told the Innu that there were no better guns. [...] So the Innu thought that the guns that came from France were better than all the others. They took the French's word for it. [...] They thought that by accepting the guns they were receiving help from the French; they did not see that this was how they were being displaced. [...] By bringing all those things for sale and tempting the Innu with them, the French succeeded in quietly driving the Innu away, almost without giving battle. That is how they were able to take possession of the land because they knew how they would use it. (Paul Benjamin, Pessamit, 1993)

Thus initially, the French made presents of what they harvested and of their technology. However, they soon began to sell them.

The French would have said to the Innu: "I will grow wheat, it will be very beautiful, your land will be magnificent!" It is said that the French said: "We will till the earth and send you the products." But in fact, they farmed the earth for themselves, in order to later sell what they harvested. [...] The French also had guns. [...] They had brought some with them and they gave some to the Innu. And then in the end they sold them to them. (Joseph Bellefleur, Nutashkuan, 1993)

Thus, having demonstrated the usefulness of their goods, the French, who, it is said, were quite aware of what they wanted, managed to make the Innu dependent on their goods, so much so that the Innu would even trade their furs for them. The relationship then stopped being friendly and became commercial.

But even worse: the French gradually set down roots.

Initially, the Innu were not worried. Above all, they knew they were on their own land and did not think they had anything to fear.

> The Innu must have believed that their land would always be their own. That is why they did not need to hate the new arrivals. (Jean-Baptiste Bellefleur, Unaman-shipit, 1988)

Then, since they used to spend most of the year inland, they were not immediately aware of what was happening. However, every time they came back to *Uepishti-kueiau*, that they saw that the French were expanding their "garden."

> After a year living there, the French must have grown wheat. They would have made their own flour and they would have grown wheat at Uepishti-kueiau. It is said that their garden was not very big then. At first, they did not plant very much. [...] They must have grown only what they needed to feed themselves. [...] They probably enclosed their garden with a wooden fence. Then, while the Innu were not there, while they were gone inland, they must have expanded it. They must have increased the land on which they grew wheat. Some Innu would have remained there to see what the French were doing, to watch them. They must have seen what they were doing. They must not have understood anything about it. They neither spoke nor understood French. They must have been afraid of the French; they must have simply watched them and seen what they were doing. The French must have done as they pleased and that way they finally managed to push the Innu off their land. It is by their agriculture that they must have succeeded. They must have extended their fence depending on what they were growing. They must have made it bigger and bigger, and the Innu must have ended up leaving Uepishtikueiau. (Jean-Baptiste Bellefleur, Unaman-shipit, 1993)

As time went by, not only did the farmed land get bigger, but the foreign population also increased considerably.

> The French came by boat and disembarked. After the first ship, more came and the French became more numerous. Then they became innumerable. After the first came ashore there, at Uepishtikueiau, after the Innu told them to get off of their boats, the French became extremely numerous. [...] This was how they were able to get the Innu to move away from Uepishtikueiau and how they came to control that land. (Joseph Bellefleur, Nutashkuan, 1992)

The French must not have been very numerous at the very beginning.

> Their numbers grew at Uepishtikueiau. [...] Once they had become numerous, then they must have driven the Innu away. (Jean-Baptiste Bellefleur, Unaman-shipit, 1988)

According to this branch of the oral tradition, this is how the French insidiously settled and soon behaved as if they were at home. As they covered more and more space with their homes and farms, the French displaced the Innu from *Uepishti-kueiau.*

Another version of the oral tradition, which seems more widespread, relates instead that there were fights between the Innu and the French. Though, of course, at the beginning the new arrivals respected the Innu because they needed their help.

> At first the French must have held the Innu in esteem. It was thanks to them that they had things to eat, thanks to them that they had food. They ate what the Innu themselves ate. The Innu gave them food that they brought from inland. Then, after the Innu had saved them from famine, the French began to hate them (Jean-Baptiste Bellefleur, Unaman-shipit, 1988)

> It was the Innu who must have taught the French how to survive inland. They taught them everything and, once they knew everything, the French had no more consideration for the Innu. (Joseph Bellefleur, Nutashkuan, 1993)

Indeed, it is said that soon after they arrived, the French became very numerous, got organized and, in particular, established a government. The government seems to have been placed under the authority of a young female ruler and a decision was then made to take over the Innu's land and drive them away when they tried to return.

> The French formed a government, and that is how their population was able to grow at Uepishtikueiau. This is what they did to appropriate the land, to appropriate Uepishtikueiau. They must have decided that they were going to set up a government, and that is when they began acting as if Uepishtikueiau belonged to them. From then on, they no longer had to pay attention to the Innu, they did whatever they wanted with them. (Joseph Bellefleur, Nutashkuan, 1993)

> It must have been because of the land that the French fought the Innu. They must have wanted to take it. (Joseph-Bastien Wapistan, Nutash-kuan, 1992)

After the French had come ashore, they appointed a young female ruler. And the young ruler asked that the men be killed but the women be spared. [...] The men were killed when they came down to the coast and the French saw them. The Innu and the French killed each other. You could say that they were at war. They killed each other. [...] The ruler feared that Uepishtikueiau would be taken away from her. She feared that the Innu would take possession of it again, but she thought that if there were no more men, then Uepishtikueiau could belong to her. (William-Mathieu Mark, Unaman-shipit, 1993)

In short, the French feared that the Innu would try to take *Uepishtikueiau* back, while the Innu fought not only to keep it but also because they feared that the French would spread beyond Québec City and try to take over the areas inland.

The Innu must have been afraid of the French because they thought that the French would drive them off their land, of course. They feared that they would force them off the land where they hunted in the backcountry. (Joseph Bellefleur, Nutashkuan, 1993)

The Innu fought for their land. They must have wanted to stay at Uepishtikueiau because in the past it was they who were there. [...] The French drove them out, they drove them off their land. Perhaps they would not have been able to do it if they had not fought them. They killed the Innu and that is how they gained control of Uepishtikueiau. If there had been no war, the Innu would not have let them have Uepishtikueiau. They must have loved that land when they went there in the olden days. They came there from very far away. (Joseph-Bastien Wapistan, Nutashkuan, 1992)

The Innu must have tried to protect themselves, but the French attacked them. [...] They must have gotten killed and they must have killed French people also. There must have been a lot of casualties, among both the Innu and the French. (Joseph-Jacques Fontaine, Pessamit, 1994)

The French killed the Innu who were at Uepishtikueiau, and then they took their land. Otherwise the Innu would be numerous today. The French killed them to take their land, that is why they harassed them. (Délima André, Mani-Utenam, 1999)

The oral tradition shows the Innu were attached to *Uepishtikueiau* and always wanting to return to it, especially to harvest the birch bark needed to build canoes. Apparently, that important raw material was later delivered to them from Québec City by boat and they had to buy it.

It is said that the Innu returned to Uepishtikueiau because they wanted to see their land again. [...] It is said that they went there to get bark. They must have been afraid when they went to get it; they must have just passed through and not stayed. They must have just passed by in canoe without spending time there. (Joseph-Bastien Wapistan, Nutashkuan, 1993)

The Innu and the French engaged in bushfighting when the Innu came down from inland and approached *Uepishtikueiau*. It is said that the French killed only the men. They spared the women.

> There, at Uepishtikueiau, they killed the men. They did not kill the women because they took them as wives. [...] If they had not killed the men, perhaps they would have been killed themselves. And it is said that the women taught them how to hunt. In the olden days, the French must not have hunted inland. Innu women showed them how. Innu women also made their moccasins and snowshoes. (Joseph-Bastien Wapistan, Nutashkuan, 1993)

During the battles between the French and the Innu, the Innu were decimated because the French had an advantage in weapons.

> The French must have shot at the Innu because they had guns and the Innu had only bows and arrows. It is said that the Innu and the French were not on good terms at the time. They were always killing each other (Joseph Bellefleur, Nutashkuan, 1992)

> It is said that the French wanted to hurt the Innu. They attacked the men and took the women. [...] The Innu could not do anything. They had nothing and perhaps they were not as numerous as the French or perhaps the French were better organized to attack them. [...] They must have had something that the Innu did not have to protect themselves, and that is why the Innu were defeated. (Thommy Canapé, Pessamit, 1993)

The Innu were also less numerous.

> Since they were growing more and more numerous, the French did not want the people who used to come to Uepishtikueiau to keep coming there. They killed the men and kept the women for themselves. [...] Every time the Innu came down to the coast, the French were waiting for them. Every year when the Innu came down to the coast, the French killed the men and took the women to keep them for themselves. (William-Mathieu Mark, Unaman-shipit, 1996)

The oral tradition thus says that the French made it clear to the Innu that they were not welcome at *Uepishtikueiau*, which had become Québec City. The agreement, which had seemed to be based on friendship and generosity, changed into a commercial relationship and the French behaved as if they owned the land. It is said that, as they increasingly expanded, they made their hosts uncomfortable and even in fear for their lives when they visited what they considered their land.

So, tired of resisting and the danger involved, the Innu avoided *Uepishtikueiau*.

4. The Innu avoid Uepishtikueiau

It was becoming more and more clear to the Innu who used to visit *Uepishtikueiau* regularly that they would have to remove that destination from their itineraries. Thus, they avoided returning there and when they used to come down from the backcountry, they used to set up camp downstream from *Uepishtikueiau*, at the mouths of rivers that flow into the St. Lawrence River and the Gulf.

> The Innu had to leave Uepishtikueiau. They were afraid that the French would attack them again, that they would shoot at them. It is said that in the olden days, the Innu were not given guns for fear they would engage in a new battle to retake Uepishtikueiau. [...] It took a long time before they were given any. [...] So, since they themselves were afraid of being shot at, the Innu went elsewhere. (Joseph-Bastien Wapistan, Nutashkuan, 1992)

The news spread that it was better to avoid *Uepishtikueiau* from then on. Those who had fought told groups they met inland, and others learned it first hand when they went there in later years.

> After they left, they must have met other Innu who came from elsewhere, and they told them what had happened. They told them that they had been forced away from Uepishtikueiau. So they lived in other areas of their lands. (Pierre Mesténapéo, Nutashkuan, 1992)

> The men had been killed during the attacks by the French. And it is said that then the population was able to rebuild because the Innu who were inland came down to the coast and, seeing the women, took them as their wives. It is said that they made some of them their wives. And the Innu population of Uepishtikueiau was able to grow back. [...] Those men must have come from inland. It was when they were coming down to the coast that they must have learned that the others had been killed. It must not have been until they saw the women that they knew that the men had been killed. When there was the war, there must have been only some of the Innu on the coast. The others were inland. (Joseph-Bastien Wapistan, Nutashkuan, 1992)

As we saw at the beginning of this narrative, *Uepishtikueiau* was not the only place where the Innu could find food in spring and summer. Many rivers full of fish empty into the St. Lawrence River and the Gulf of St. Lawrence, and the Innu were already used to staying near the river mouths. Thus, they maintained their cycle of activities, spending part of their time inland and part on the coast. What was important, of course, was to have access to game and fish.

In greater number and more often, they spent time on the Upper, Middle and Lower North Shore, depending on their preferences and kinship relations since, it is said, like the Innu today, they had relatives more or less everywhere.

When, after giving up the idea of going back, they left Uepishtikueiau, they went to other places along the coast and also continued living inland. (Marie-Madeleine Kaltush, Nutashkuan, 1993)

The Innu must have liked the things that they had been sold and that they were using. However, they were exiled from Uepishtikueiau, their land. So they did not stay there. They ran away and came to the North Shore. They scattered and went where there was game, where they could hunt. (Joseph Bellefleur, Nutashkuan, 1992)

It is said that the French attacked the Innu in the olden days; they must not have liked them. So the Innu apparently left Uepishtikueiau because their population dropped. [...] They ran away and that is how there came to be more and more Innu on the North Shore. (Joseph-Bastien Wapistan, Nutashkuan, 1992)

Then the Innu left; they went towards the place where we are now [Upper North Shore]. That is what seems to have happened. They came here in little groups, and went even further to the east. (Roméo Rousselot, Pessamit, 1994)

It is said that there used to be Innu on the exact site of Québec City today. But they were forced to leave, they were displaced. [...] It is said that the French displaced them and that is why they no longer felt like staying at Uepishtikueiau. Since the Whites forced them to leave, they did not want to stay. [...] They were so afraid that they preferred to go away and leave Uepishtikueiau. They did not give them the land; they were evicted from it. [...] They would have stayed if they had not been afraid. [...] We do not know what the French said to them to make them so afraid. [...] They came to the North Shore, and each group decided to stay along the river that it liked. (Philomène McKenzie, Mani-Utenam, 1999)

The movement towards the east explains why all Innu, no matter what community they belong to today, can say that their ancestors frequented *Uepishtikueiau* before the French arrived.

The French sometimes attacked the Innu when the latter came down to Uepishtikueiau. [...] So the Innu came here [to the Lower North Shore]. They went downstream. The Innu who live here now are the descendents of those who were at Uepishtikueiau. [...] We are all from Uepishtikueiau. (William-Mathieu Mark, Unaman-shipit, 1993)

Then Uepishtikueiau was taken away from the Innu. [...] The Innu must have moved to Nutashkuan and then to Unaman-shipit, and all the way to Pakua-shipit and Sheshatshiu. And the furthest they went was Utshimassit. (Pierre Courtois, Nutashkuan, 1992)

Those who are here now must be descendents of those Innu. We must come from that generation. (Délima André, Mani-Utenam, 1999)

The loss of *Uepishtikueiau*, which was a gathering place, also explains, it is said, why different dialects and accents can be heard in the Innu language.

It was at Uepishtikueiau [...] that we separated, so we speak differently from one another today. The people at Pessamit speak in a certain way and those from Uashat have a different accent. Those at Unaman-shipit also speak differently, and it is the same with the people from Ekuanitshit and from Nutashkuan. It was there, at Uepishtikueiau, after we became separated, that our language broke apart. [...] Everyone must have spoken the same language in the past [...] when we were at Uepishtikueiau. (Pierre Courtois, Nutashkuan, 1993)

The arrival of the French and the atmosphere of fear created by the war had repercussions that extended even to the relations among Aboriginal peoples.

After the Innu were killed by the French, we all distrusted one another. The French killed the Innu. So, from then on, when the Innu, those who spoke the same language as us, came down to the coast, they were always careful. There were battles between the Innu and other Aboriginal peoples. We probably distrusted one another, and feared that the French were being helped by the members of other nations. (William-Mathieu Mark, Unaman-shipit, 1988)

The war, in which many men were killed, also explains why the Innu are not very numerous today.

It was the French who attacked the Innu. It is said that they killed a lot and that otherwise the Innu would be very numerous today. It is certain that they must have been numerous in the olden days because there were Innu everywhere. (Délima André, Mani-Utenam, 1999)

It is said that a man used to spend spring and summer on an island located close to *Uepishtikueiau*. Despite the fear that the French inspired in the Innu, the man continued to go there with his family.[7]

The Innu no longer went to Uepishtikueiau, except for brief trips to get bark and make canoes. It is said that an old man had been living there for a long time on an island. That was where he must have been sometimes. [...] So, when the Innu went to get bark, they would have had to pass by there in canoe. [...] They must have visited the old man on the island. [...] He would have lived close to the coast in the winter, and when the summer came he would have set up camp on the island. He would have fished there and that is also where he must have made his canoe. [...] He was there with his wife and children, with the whole family. [...] He must have had a lot of children. [...] He must have belonged to the same nation as us. [...] The last time that this Innu was heard of, he was living on that island. And then no one heard about him again. So it was thought that the French had killed him. [...] He must have wanted to fight to keep his land. [...] It was said that he had certainly been killed. He must have refused to give up the island; he must not have wanted to give it up, and that is why he would have been killed. (Joseph-Bastien Wapistan, Nutashkuan, 1992, 1993)

It is said that this man was the last to live in the *Uepishtikueiau* area and the last to be killed there.

However, the unfortunate *Uepishtikueiau* episode provided food for thought. Indeed, it is said that some time later, when the French tried to displace the Innu again, the latter managed to dissuade them.

There were Innu everywhere, all the way to Tadoussac and in other places too. They were everywhere. The French wanted to displace them. The Innu already had villages. They did not have very many, but they had some. So the French wanted to displace them. They probably wanted to attack the Innu, but the Innu told them: "You will not come here. Go elsewhere, you will not take this land, we are using it." They wanted to attack them, but the Innu had probably already begun to defend themselves a bit. So the French left them alone, it is said. [...] The Innu seem to have told them: "This land belongs to us and we are using it, we do not want you to go into the backcountry, go somewhere else." [...] Those Innu had to be on good land [...] it was a little settlement, perhaps like Pessamit or Uashat. At that time, there were not as many Innu as there are today. [...] The French left them alone because there was enough land for them to go and settle somewhere else. [...] They left them alone, and since then there have been no major attacks on the Innu. They keep trying to displace them, but they no longer do what they did in the past when the French attacked them as soon as they arrived. (Thommy Canapé, Pessamit, 1995)

While they had not given it up, it is said that the Innu had to stop visiting *Uepishti-kueiau* and later they kept their guard up because today, as in the past, and even though there is no war, the Whites still want their land.

5. Testimony from afar

This narrative originates with those who witnessed the events. It was conveyed by many generations to finally come to us today.

There must have been Innu there, at Uepishtikueiau, and they are the ones who must have told what happened. We have heard the same story generation after generation. [...] The Innu were everywhere, all over the whole area. And naturally there must have been some at Uepishtikueiau too. There were some here, on the North Shore, and there were also some there. Otherwise, how would we have heard about all that? The Uepishti-kueiau Narrative comes from Uepishtikueiau. [...] The words that tell of these events do not come from here but from there. (Pierre Mesténapéo, Nutashkuan, 1992)

It was those who were at Uepishtikueiau who told what happened there. They reported it to those who later related what I am telling you my-self. The narrative has existed for a very long time, it goes back very far in time. [...] It is known as the Uepishtikueiau Narrative. There must have been a large number of Innu at that place. Their ancestors must have been there too, and that must be why they could not leave their land. [...] The first generations died, and it was their descendents who stayed at Uepishtikueiau when the area was abandoned. And the story of Uepishtikueiau has reached our generation. For us, those people were the *Tshiashinnuat*, the Ancients, those whom we did not know, the ancestors of those we have not seen ourselves, those who, for our own ancestors, were the fathers of the Ancients whom they themselves had not seen. (Jean-Baptiste Bellefleur, Unaman-shipit, 1988)

The memory of the event is not specific to a family or community. It is shared by the whole Innu nation.

It was my grandfather who told me what happened at Uepishtikueiau. My father also told me. They themselves were reporting what they had been told and those words came to me. [...] What I tell, I did not believe it before. I did not really believe what was said about Uepishtikueiau. [...] But the Elders all tell the same story, even those who live upstream from the Gulf of the St. Lawrence, like those at Pessamit and Uashat. [...] That is why I believe in the truth of this narrative. (William-Mathieu Mark, Unaman-shipit, 1993)

It is a narrative that the Elders consider important because it explains the present situation, which it is said reproduces that at *Uepishtikueiau*. It is important to keep reciting it if we are to understand not only how *Uepishtikueiau* was taken from the Innu but also how they risk losing the land in the backcountry today. Indeed, the French were not content with *Uepishtikueiau*. Little by little, they settled all along the North Shore and today the Whites act as if they owned the land in the backcountry as did their own ancestors at *Uepishtikueiau*.

Sometimes the Elders said what was going to happen, they predicted what would happen. When they told their children things, they told them what the future would be like. They are the ones who thought about the turn that events would take and today we are experiencing what they predicted. [...] They must have already had an inkling of what was going to happen. They must have known what the future had in store. It was when they were still there, at Uepishtikueiau, that they must have started suspecting that there would always be a desire to take their land away from them. [...] The Innu who ran away from Uepishtikueiau must have been careful to observe how things happened. They must have thought that what they were experiencing would always repeat itself. And they always said so. They always said what was going to happen. Today we can see that their predictions and words are coming true. (William-Mathieu Mark, Unaman-shipit, 1988)

Today there are no longer any Innu inland. You see Whites there and they do not hesitate to build houses everywhere. They are making the backcountry into their land rather than that of the Innu, and yet the Innu are its masters. They act as if the backcountry was under their control. They cannot be satisfied with Uepishtikueiau, with what they were given. (Marie-Madeleine Kaltush, Nutashkuan, 1993)

In the olden days, there were never any French inland. [...] They were only at Uepishtikueiau. In the backcountry, you did not see them very often. There were none. Now, however, they are the only ones in the backcountry. They are about to force all the Innu out. They are going to hurt them. They are going to send them to the coast. Already there are a lot of things built by Whites in the backcountry. They are going to try and build more. They are going to want to control the whole backcountry. They are going to do to the Innu the equivalent of what they did at Uepishtikueiau. [...] The French did not want the Innu to keep visiting that place. It is said that they attacked them and succeeded in making sure that there were no more Innu at Uepishtikueiau. The Innu were attacked at Uepishtikueiau, and then they were chased away, and then the French took their land. So the Innu went elsewhere. And now the Whites want to ban them from the backcountry. Already they have almost succeeded in expelling them from the interior as they did at Uepishtikueiau. (Joseph-Bastien Wapistan, Nutashukuan, 1992)

Such is the Uepishtikueiau Narrative and the teachings of past generations passed down to the present generation.

Map of Innu communities
Innu Communities (2003)

*At the end of 2002 and beginning of 2003, the community of *Utshimassit* moved to *Natuashish*, a newly built village some 15 km away.

People quoted

Pessamit
Paul Benjamin, 1993
Thommy Canapé, 1993
Joseph-Jacques Fontaine, 1994
Roméo Rousselot, 1994
Desanges Saint-Onge, 1994

Mani-Utenam
Délima André, 1999
Philomène McKenzie, 1999

Nutashkuan
Joseph Bellefleur, 1992, 1993
Pierre Courtois, 1992, 1993
Michel Grégoire, 1975
Charles Kaltush, 1993
Marie-Madeleine Kaltush, 1993
Mathieu Menikapu, 1971
Pierre Mesténapéo, 1992, 1993
Joseph-Bastien Wapistan, 1992, 1993

Unaman-shipit
Jean-Baptiste Bellefleur, 1988, 1993
Michel Bellefleur, 1988
William-Mathieu Mark, 1988, 1993, 1996

---

[1] First, I would like to thank all those who, from *Pessamit* to *Pakua-shipit*, received us and spent many hours speaking with me and then with Joséphine Bacon and I between 1971 and 1999. While not everyone is quoted here, it was with the help of all of their remarks that I was able to piece together the Uepishtikueiau Narrative as it appears in this publication.

Second, I have to express my warm gratitude to Joséphine Bacon, who acted as an assistant, interpreter and translator over the years, and who provided the French translation of all of the passages cited from recordings. However, she is not responsible for any errors in the choice of passages, their arrangement or the overall design of this document.

I would also like to thank Gloria Vollant from the ICEM, who was immediately receptive to the idea of publishing a text on the Uepishtikueiau Narrative and who never stopped believing in it, despite the many obstacles encountered along the way.

With respect to the design and writing stages, I would like to give special thanks to Diane Lemieux, who was Québec Minister of State for Culture and Communications at the time, Danielle Bilodeau, one of Ms Lemieux's political advisors, and Carole Lévesque of the *Institut national de la recherche scientifique (Urbanisa-*

tion, culture et société). In addition to the financial support of their respective institutions, the personal interest that they expressed in the project encouraged me to complete it.

For their kindness and speed, thanks must also be given to Marcelle Roy, who did the final proofreading to identify errors in French, spelling mistakes and punctuation problems, to Serge Ashini-Goupil, Director and Yannick Labbé, Geomatician of Ashini-Goupil Inc., who produced the map of Innu communities, and especially to François Girard, painter in watercolour, who created the cover for the original publication.

Finally, this work would never have seen the light of day without the technical assistance, unflagging support and time provided by Thierry, Nadine and Gaëlle Vincent. They know how much they contributed to this project, and how grateful I am to them.

[2] This short text was sponsored by the *Institut culturel et éducatif montagnais* (ICEM). Parks Canada (Saguenay-Lake St. Jean Marine Park) provided funding for translation from Innu to French. The writing was funded partly by the *INRS-Urbanisation, Culture et Société* and by the cultural initiative fund administered by Diane Lemieux, who was Québec Minister of State for Culture and Communications at the time.

The excerpts of the Innu oral tradition that are quoted here were recorded and first translated into French between 1971 and 1999 in the course of various contracts and on personal initiative, but mainly with the help of a grant from the Social Science and Humanities Research Council of Canada (1987).

[3] Two other communities of the same nation are located in Labrador. See the map of Innu communities included at the end of this work.

[4] "An ancient form of this toponym, '*Ouabichtigoueiakhi*,' appeared in 1634 in Father Paul Le Jeune's writings, and means literally 'where the river gets narrow'"; see Charles Martijn, "Gepèg (Québec): un toponyme d'origine micmaque," (1991) XXI (3) *Recherches amérindiennes au Québec* 59 [our translation].

[5] In the singular: "*mishtikushu*"; the word is formed out of "*mishtik^u*" (wood, tree) and "*ush*" (boat, canoe).

[6] At *Betsiamites*, "come ashore" is said "*kapak^u*" rather than "*paka*", which is used on the Middle and Lower North Shore. In terms of sound, the former resembles "Québec" more closely.

[7] The fact that the Île d'Orleans is the island closest to Québec City (for example, compared with the Île aux Grues or the Île aux Coudres) leads us to think that it is the island in question, though we cannot assert this as a fact.

Aboriginal Influence on the Canadians and French at the Time of New France[1]

Denys Delâge[2]

1. The Meeting

A Jesuit missionary, probably Father Louis Nicolas, spent ten years living and travelling with Aboriginals to gather their knowledge of plants and animals for his book, *Histoire naturelle des Indes Occidentales*, which unfortunately remains unpublished. Around 1685 he wrote,

> I have often found great pleasure in seeing and hearing new arrivals from France protesting that they could never live like Indians, and that even just seeing Indians' dirty way of eating way disgusts them. But finally, under the circumstances, they grow accustomed to it out of pure necessity, like the other old habitants and inseparable companions of Indians.[3]

Were habitants and Aboriginals inseparable companions? Yes, certainly, though to different degrees. Interaction was closest in Aboriginal settlements, where *coureurs de bois* married Aboriginal women. Depending on the location and circumstances, such marriages led to either complete assimilation into Aboriginal society,[4] or the creation of mixed communities that were themselves culturally very close to those of Aboriginals.[5] The cultures also had a strong influence on each other in French settlements located near large Aboriginal communities, such as Baron de St. Castin's colony in Abenaki territory in the north of Maine, and that of the Canadians who left Montréal in the early eighteenth century to farm land at Detroit and at *Cahokia* on the banks of the Mississippi.

A third situation was that of settlers living in the St. Lawrence parishes and farming land where the initial sedentary occupants had disappeared at the end of the sixteenth century. While their interaction with Aboriginals was less intense, it was nonetheless not negligible, much to the contrary. The history that we will describe concerns mainly the first and third types of community, for we will not be able to extend the study to the case of the American Midwest. For the time being, we should keep in mind that there was a lot of interaction between Aboriginals and French Canadians in every location, including Montréal, Trois-Rivières, Québec City and rural parishes.

2. European Borrowings from the Aboriginal World

2.1. The Country and Its Name

As foreigners in North America, the Europeans first had to get to know the continent. As others have already pointed out, Europeans discovered only the ocean routes to America. Once they got there, the Aboriginals taught them the way around. There are many texts showing this, for example, the passage from *Histoire de l'Amérique* by Bacqueville de la Potherie concerning Nicolas Perrot's trip to *Baie des Puants* (now known as Green Bay).[6]

> The curiosity of the French sent by Mr. De la Barre was piqued by everything the Indians told them. At the Bay, they kept hearing about new nations unknown to us. Some said that they had been in a country to the southwest, and others had just come back from there, where they had seen beautiful landscapes. They brought back blue and green stones that looked like turquoise and that they attached to their noses and ears. Some had seen horses and men similar to the French there; they must have been Spaniards from New Mexico. Others said that they had traded hatchets with people who were in a house that walked on water at the mouth of the river of the Assinibouels, which is at the Northwest sea. The river of the Assinibouels leads to Hudson Bay to the north; it is close to Fort Nelson.[7]

The people around the Great Lakes who spoke to Perrot had therefore travelled to (or at least heard of) the Gulf of Mexico and Hudson Bay, and it seems they were also familiar with the Prairies. They provided Perrot and his men with verbal information on the continent's geography. The information was only general and could not contain many details or particulars. La Hontan, like Father Lafitau,[8] tells us that Aboriginals also had maps

> ...that are the most accurate of the lands they know and that lack only lines of latitude and longitude [which are European scientific inventions]. They mark the true north according to the North Star, and show ports, harbours, rivers, coves and shores of lakes, paths, mountains, forests, marshes, fields, etc. They count distances by days, warriors' half-days, each day equivalent to five leagues [24 kilometres].[9]

However, this should not lead one to believe that another village might have maps of all of North America. The maps must have shown areas travelled by members of the community, and sometimes the areas would have been very large. It is certain that they did not have maps of lands that they knew about only through hearsay. Aboriginals also taught their guests techniques for orienteering in the forest, and about the peoples, animals, plants and other resources, such as minerals. For example, they showed them where there were copper and lead mines.[10]

According to La Hontan, on this continent, every port, harbour, river, marsh and prairie already had a name, or even several. Explorers therefore usually transcribed them phonetically, and the accuracy of the transcription depended on their far from uniform knowledge of the language of the people with whom they were speaking. In 1847, an Iroquois chief and interpreter from Sault Saint Louis (*Kahnawake*) pointed out the etymology of some names that are now considered European: "*Hochelaga*" from "*Ohserake*" for "beaver dam"; "Ontario" from "*Onontario*" for "beautiful lake"; "Erie" from "*eri*", meaning "cherry tree"; "Niagara" from "*Jaonniaka-re*" for "noisy point or portage"; "Ohio" from "*Ohioonhua*" for "mistress or main river"; "Kentucky" from "*Keintake*" for "in the prairies"; and "Toronto" from "*Thoronhionko*" (perhaps) for "he shocks you under the heavens."[11] Another word of Iroquois origin is "Canada", which means "village." Among current place names with Aboriginal origins, those with Algonquin roots are the most widespread in Canada and the eastern United States, which is not surprising given the vast area over which nations belonging to that linguistic family are scattered. "Québec" probably comes from the Micmac word "*gepèg*", which means "the narrowing of the river." [12] "*Outaouais*" or "Ottawa" comes from "*Odawa*", which designates the nation by the same name and means "traders".[13] "*Yamaska*" comes from the Abenaki word "*Mamaska*", which means "toad"; and "*Missisquoi*" comes from the Abenaki word "*Massipscoubie*", which means "silex water". [14] "Romaine" comes from "*orumen*", which means "red earth" in Montagnais. Manitoulin Island and Manitoba both take their names from "*manitou*". In the north, *Inuktituut* was transcribed into English. Thus, the Koksoak River is a deformation of "*Kuu Juak*", which means "large river".[15]

But are not most North American place names French and especially English? Of course. They almost always replace Aboriginal place names that may nonetheless still be used in parallel by Aboriginals, though those with European roots are officially imposed. This is a symbolic appropriation of land that obscures the prior presence of Aboriginals. The practice therefore belongs to the process of conquest. Colonial powers came to America to create a new Holland, Sweden, England or Spain. Generally, when Europeans found that they were immigrants in Aboriginal societies or that they and the Aboriginals were highly interdependent, such as in the fur trade, Aboriginal place names took precedence. However, in areas where the Europeans cut down the forest, occupied the land and chased away the Aboriginals, place names tend to be European, and most often have no Aboriginal roots. This can be seen clearly in maps of areas where the French and Aboriginals were allied. Place names in French seigneurial lands tend to sound French, whereas Aboriginal languages dominate everywhere else. Thus, even the French finally gave up the name "Fort Frontenac" (Kingston) and called the post "Fort Cataracoui", which means "clayey earth dredged from water".[16] A significant exception was that missionaries in Aboriginal areas always gave Christian names to Aboriginal villages, but the villages themselves kept their Aboriginal names and used the Christian name to refer to the mission only.

Within the present boundaries of Québec, outside of the old farming and seigneurial areas, almost all place names were still Aboriginal in the nineteenth century.

This can be seen, for example, on a map from 1829 accompanying a notarized treaty between the Algonquins and Hurons concerning two communities sharing Montagnais areas, and the delineation of hunting areas in the Laurentians. The map contains very few French names, though they are omnipresent on maps today.[17] Anne Antane Kapesh notes that the same is true of the Lower North Shore. So, who turned the past into a blank slate? It was the Québec Geography Commission. Beginning in 1912, it eliminated thousands of Aboriginal names.[18]

Indeed, was it not necessary to erase from memory the prior presence of Aboriginals, who had to be expropriated so that the land could be settled, logged and mined? Naturally! However, the justification simply obscured the dispossession. Listen to Eugène Rouillard, who was Secretary of the Société de géographie at the time:

> Are we aware of the harm that this mania for Indian names does us abroad? Ladies and Gentlemen, take a look at the geographical maps of our country and of our province in particular: would one not believe it was an immense camp of redskins? Leaf through the timetables of railroad companies […] and you will be shocked to see that the majority of the stations are decorated with the most repulsive and unattractive Indian names.[19]

The fear that French Canadians in the nineteenth and twentieth centuries had of "being mistaken for Indians" seems to have been a fundamental aspect of their identity, though this is a subject for debate that we will not enter into here.

2.2. Transportation

> Are all the rivers navigable? I would say yes with Indian canoes, but not with our ships.[20]

From Québec City, you can canoe to Hudson Bay, the Prairies or New Orleans. All you have to do is paddle towards the *Pays d'en Haut* or the *Pays d'en Bas* (upper and lower countries), as in traditional songs. Canadians did not take long to learn how manoeuvrable and agile canoes were, and how useful for navigating lakes and rivers, threading through rapids and riding waves. They were soon as skilful as the Aboriginals who had taught them.[21] They began practicing "when they were still wearing bibs" according to Father Charlevoix.[22] Thus, three Canadians alone, without any Aboriginals, travelled by canoe from Hudson Bay to Québec City in 1693.[23] That required not only knowing how to use a canoe like an Aboriginal but also how to repair and waterproof it using bark, roots and resin.[24] Settlers learned to build canoes and Trois Rivières became a major production centre. They were made of birch bark, which was abundant at the time along the banks of the St. Maurice River, and cedar or fir struts. The bark was sewn together with spruce roots covered in fir gum.[25] In 1752, the engineer Louis Franquet watched the construction of an eight-person canoe that was 33 feet (10 meters) long.[26] Both the French and the Aboriginals built canoes large enough to carry two-ton cargos.[27] It was in the same area that *rabaskaws* (extra large canoes designed for travelling to the west) were built in the first half of the nineteenth century. In the colony itself, as in France, coastal trade employed *pirogues* dug out of red elm or large softwood trees. They could carry up to 20 people. Birch bark canoes were also used, though less frequently.[28] In the north, the British used Inuit kayaks instead of canoes.

But what about in winter? How did they deal with the "frightening quantities of snow that fall in Canada"? Mother Superior Marie-Andrée Duplessis, in charge of the hospital at Québec City, explained that it was thanks to "one of the Indians' best inventions": snowshoes.[29] They made it possible to hunt in the wintertime, in particular to hunt moose. While it seems there were hardly any in the homes on the Ile d'Orléans, for they appear in only a quarter of estate inventories,[30] a pair was sent to Versailles for the Dauphin[31] and they were used both for going to church and for fetching wood.[32] Used with a sled, they made it easy to transport goods. Toboggans were made of wood laths that curved upwards at the front. They were about a foot (30 cm) wide and up to 8 or 10 feet (2.5 to 3 meters) long.[33] Further north, where there is less snow and a crust forms on top, the Aboriginals and Inuit instead used sleighs with runners to which one or more dogs were harnessed. The English and French also borrowed this technology.

Long-distance travel was made possible by loading the toboggan or sleigh with supplies: mainly corn flour, a blanket, a firearm, ammunition, gun powder and the indispensable cover for a "teepee", which was initially rolls of birch bark but later oil cloth. Bark had the advantage of being light, but oil cloth that of strength. The Sulpician Priest Galinée describes the winter tents as follows:

> The Algonquins carry with them thin pieces of birch bark that have been sewn together so that they are 4 fathoms [20 feet or 6 meters] long and 3 feet [1 meter] wide. They can be rolled very small, and 8 or nine men can easily fit under three such pieces of bark suspended on poles [to make a summer shelter]. They can even be used to make winter cabins that are warmer than our houses. You arrange 20 or 30 long poles so that they are all touching at the top, and you spread the bark over the poles with a little fire in the middle. I have spent days and nights under such bark when it was very cold out and there were 3 feet of snow on the ground, and I was not particularly uncomfortable.[34]

The snow had to be shovelled away using snowshoes in order to reach the frozen ground, which was covered with fir boughs, except for a central circle of stones, where a fire was maintained. Indeed, C. Lebeau tells us that the *coureurs des bois* "learned from the Indians the best way to keep warm."[35]

This made it possible to undertake winter expeditions lasting several months. A French soldier (J. C. B.) described in his diary his departure from Québec City on January 15, 1754 with 500 troops and militiamen. They travelled over ice and snow, and reached Montréal 11 days later, on January 26. They left Montréal for Fort Niagara on February 3 with reinforcements of 300 militiamen and 2 months of supplies. Every man pulled a sleigh, but some, such as J.C.B., had a dog that they harnessed. The hardest part was crossing swift-running rivers, which involved "getting undressed and carrying one's clothes on one's head, and after getting to the other side, getting dressed again very quickly and running to warm up, which happened about three times a day".[36] They took advantage of the bare ice on Lake Ontario, and made trains of 7-8 sleighs that were pulled by ice skaters. On February 25, they reached Fort Niagara at the mouth of the river by the same name. Aside from around 100 men who stayed there, the group continued their trip in boats and canoes. On April 4, they arrived at the site where Pittsburgh is located today, and prepared to build Fort Duquesne.[37]

2.3. Clothing

Naturally, since appropriate clothing was essential, *coureurs de bois* in particular learned how to dress "Indian style".[38] Habitants, who were often conscripted into the militia for expeditions, brought aspects of Aboriginal clothing back to their sedentary lives. Moccasins proved indispensable because rigid European shoes could not be adapted to snowshoes.

Canadians learned how to make moccasins[39] and used almost no other kind of shoe.[40] They created an adapted version for everyday life called *le soulier du pays*, *le pichou* or *le soulier ou botte du pays*, in other words, "country shoes". Cowhide, sheep skin and calf leather were commonly substituted for moose hide, cariboo skin, deerskin and sealskin.[41]

Instead of shirts and pants, the *coureurs de bois* wore a breechcloth, in other words, "a piece of leather one foot by four that they straddle and tie around their waists". They covered their legs with leggings, which were kind of like long footless boots, wore a tunic with a decorated belt, to which removable sleeves could be added, and generally sported headbands. Rather than of leather, their clothing was usually of European cloth, but the cut, fringes and motifs were based on Aboriginal designs.[42] Militiamen had no uniform, but they seem to have been more inclined to keep European-style clothing. The government sometimes provided them with a few items, especially in winter, including "Indian shoes", leggings and blanket coats.[43] Finally, *voyageurs* in the interior of the colony wore moccasins, beaver skin coats and marten hats. While they kept European styles, the Canadians followed the Aboriginals' example and turned the fur towards the inside rather than the outside.[44]

Pehr Kalm noted that in their homes during the week, habitants dressed partly in French and partly in Aboriginal style: "the same stockings, shoes and garters, the same belts around the waist".[45] We should not conclude from this that there was a style that was half old and half new because the description of the clothes of peasants and tradesmen in thousands of estate inventories does not mention Aboriginal clothing and ornaments. French fashion dominated Canadian dress.[46]

The *ceinture fléchée* (arrow sash) married Aboriginal tradition (bison hair, porcupine needles and beads) with European (Scandinavian, Basque, Acadian and Scottish) customs. Initially, it was not loom but finger woven. It was part of the student uniform at the *Séminaire de Québec* in the seventeenth century, but did not become characteristic of Métis and habitant dress until the nineteenth century, when it was produced on a large scale, particularly in Assumption Parish.[47] In his account of college days after the Conquest, Philippe Aubert de Gaspé describes his companions' winter dress. Note the mittens, arrow sash with beads, moccasins and porcupine needle decorations:

> Their dress is the same: blanket coats with hoods, scarlet leggings edged with green ribbons, blue knit wool garters, wide, bright, many-coloured belts decorated with beads, Iroquois-style caribou skin shoes with uppers embroidered with porcupine quills, and finally real beaver hats folded down over the ears with a red silk scarf knotted at the neck.[48]

In the eighteenth century, Canadian women wore large woven wool shawls when they travelled by sleigh. According to Robert Lionel Séguin, the shawls resembled the dress of Aboriginal women, who wore square fur or leather blankets with fringed edges and measuring around 5 by 7.5 feet (1.5 meters by 2 meters). Until recently, the fur blanket for a sleigh was still called a "robe".[49] The wealthier classes remained less influenced by the Aboriginals than the habitants, but a trace can perhaps be seen in the export to France of hummingbird feathers for earrings, and swan skins, which Louis Nicolas hoped to see worn by the king.[50]

2.4. Hunting and Fishing

The settlers came from a country where they were generally forbidden to hunt and fish, since those activities were reserved for lords, nobles and the king. Of course, that does not mean that they were strangers to poaching, but they did not normally have firearms. In America, hunting and fishing were democratized. They were used as a way to attract colonists and make it easier for them to settle, but in any case it would have been unthinkable to prohibit hunting in an economy based on the fur trade. Freedom to carry weapons was required because of Iroquois raids. Yet not all men owned weapons. In the seventeenth century it was estimated that one in three had firearms, but in the following century only one in five.[51] Not all hunting required guns: migratory birds could be netted, and fur-bearing animals could be caught in wooden traps. All in all, however, fishing was much more common than hunting because of the incredible wealth of fish in the river. For the Intendant Jean Talon to have issued an order in 1671 requiring all unmarried men to marry or else lose their fishing, hunting and fur trading rights, those rights must have been highly prized![52] Almost all writings from New France include passages on the distribution and habits of wildlife, hunting techniques (lures, bait, traps, blinds, firearms, bird and animal calls, etc.) and on how Aboriginals used them. The largest document on this is the *Histoire Naturelle des Indes occidentales*, the author of which lived with Aboriginals for many years and accompanied them when they were hunting, fishing and gathering plants. The author made detailed notes on everything he saw and learned while he was with the Aboriginals. Baron de La Hontan also went on many long hunting expeditions with his hosts. Since he spoke Algonquin, he was able to learn how to make duck blinds and decoys, hunt turkeys and ice fish.[53] Species that were unknown in Europe, such as the wood duck, were sent to the Versailles menagerie.[54] Passenger pigeons were also released in France.[55]

When it came to hunting and fishing, Aboriginals and Canadians of all classes were in contact with one another. Champlain learned about the longnose gar (*lepisosteus osseus*),[56] Charlevoix described the habits of muskrats and beavers,[57] and officer J. C. B. described traps in the shape of the number four.[58] At Sillery, where the Montagnais' fishing camp used to be located, eel was fished and considered the colony's "manna".[59] An anonymous memoir describes an occasion when "over 50 French and Indians" worked together to push a weir across the Famine River, where they took "300 hooked snout salmon in less than two hours".[60] Similar fish weirs (perpendicular to the current and removed at low tide, unlike fish traps, which could remain in place) seem to have been used on both continents before contact.[61] Torch fishing, however, seems to have been invented in America.

Coming from a world where hunting and fishing were reserved for the rich and noble, most settlers had never engaged in the activities before, unless they had been ready to face the punishment for poaching. Thus, when they arrived in America, they hunted to excess. One killed 30 to 40 moose in the winter of 1660.[62] As early as 1664, Pierre Boucher noted that "hunting is not as plentiful now as it used to be near Québec City: the wildlife has withdrawn 10 to 12 leagues from there".[63] A century later, in the winter of 1776–1777, two officers posted at Batiscan wrote that big game hunting was no longer possible because

> ...the habitants have already exterminated the big game around the settlements...In order to experience real hunting, with real excitement, you have to join the Indians [according to the officers]. In fact, many Canadians and Englishmen [note the introduction of a third player] go hunting with them. They speak and live like them, in the middle of the forest for many years.[64]

There were still many passenger pigeons, but while they could be killed "in the gardens of Québec City" in 1664, Pehr Kalm noted that in 1749 they no longer came near Québec City but lived a bit further away "to the northeast, in the forests along both sides of the St. Lawrence". He wrote that where they nest, "the ground is covered in a layer of droppings that can be one or two feet thick."

Settlers were not content to net large numbers of them during their migrations. They hunted them even during nesting season, which shocked the Aboriginals. According to Pehr Kalm,

> American Indians never shoot at or kill pigeons when they are nesting or when they are young. They do not let others do so either and say that to

kill the parents would be very cruel to the baby birds, for they would die of hunger. Some Frenchmen told me that they went out with the intention to kill some at that time of the year, but the Indians first nicely, and then by threatening them, prevented them from doing so because they could not tolerate that kind of thing.[65]

2.5. Medicinal Plants

In his *Histoire naturelle des Indes occidentales*, Father Louis Nicolas placed as much importance on plants as on wildlife. He described the main species and how they were used by the Aboriginals. While his quest for knowledge fit scientific goals (such as to know and classify all the plants in the world), it also met practical, and particularly therapeutic, needs. There was a desire to discover the "Indians' secrets" of their remarkable remedies.[66] From 1685 to 1734, Michel Sarrazin was responsible for gathering plants and fruit from Newfoundland to the Great Lakes, not to mention ore and insects, samples and specimens of which he sent to France. Sarrazin was followed in 1741 by Jean François Gaultier, who completed his findings. At the request of the colonial authorities, he wrote a memorandum to local commanders to get them to collect plants and pay attention to the medicinal plants (then called "simples") of the various nations. In Louisiana, Le Page du Pratz, historian and inspector of the Compagnie des Indes from 1718 to 1734, loaded over 300 plants into willow baskets accompanied with Aboriginals' comments on their properties. The samples were sent to France, where they were planted in one of the Company's botanical gardens.[67] Catherine Jérémie (1664–1744), midwife and herbalist, worked as a clerk for the King's Posts at Hudson Bay, and also sent plant specimens with notes of the same kind to the *Jardin royal des plantes médicinales* in Paris. Intendant Hocquart wrote in 1740 that she had long been dedicated to "learning the secrets of Indian medicine". At other times, governors and intendants sent from Québec not only minerals but also plants, or at least their roots, seeds, pollen and leaves, with properties unknown in France.[68] In the same period, the surveyor Joseph-Laurent Normandin explored the *Domaine du Roi* starting at Tadoussac, and was also made responsible for asking Aboriginals about the medicinal plants that they used.[69] In short, to Montréal and Québec City were sent all sorts of plant species from Acadia and the gulf, the Great Lakes and "Indians even further away". The samples were transplanted into the gardens of the Jesuits and the Intendant. They were identified, catalogued and labelled. For example, it was noted that annual mercury (*mercurialis*) contains "balsamic juices that the Indians use on wounds". Many plants were put on ships to end up, if they did not die of drought or salt water, in royal gardens.[70]

In 1749, the botanist Pehr Kalm, who collaborated with the great scientist Linne and Sweden's Royal Academy of Science, brought back from his trip to Canada "a number of roots and remedies used by the Indians".[71] A Huron (of English origin, who had been captured and adopted as a child some thirty years before) guided him around the countryside and forests near Québec City, and pointed the plants' uses out to him.[72] On his trip to Baie Saint Paul, Kalm also spoke with a man named Cartier on Baie Saint-Paul Road. Cartier had "gone to 'Labrador Land' many times and spent quite a lot of time with Indians".[73] Among other things, he told Kalm about the virtues of cloudberries: the Aboriginals boiled their roots and leaves in the spring to fight against scurvy.[74] It was just as important to know how to identify poisonous plants and tell them apart from plants that looked similar, which could otherwise be confusing. At several points in Jean François Gaultier's writings, he noted, concerning specific parts of such plants, that "it is said that the Indians use them when they can no longer endure their unhappiness".[75]

The interest "in the rare plants the properties of which Indians are very knowledge-able" was shared by the English in their colonies.[76] For example, in the seventeenth century Quinine bark of Incan origin was introduced into Virginia, and the potency was taken out of the malaria that used to kill one settler out of five.[77] In all colonies, non-Aboriginals eventually made medicinal use of local vegetation. In the writings of Sarrazin, Vaillant and Gaultier, we find mention of sassafras from which cam-phor is made, the balsamic juices of the honey-locust "that Canadians call 'green balm' and which is used successfully by Indians and others to heal wounds and ulcers", the decoction of the bark of red wood (dogwood or *cornus*) used against gout, and osmunda "that our French Canadians who go deep into the woods call the rattlesnake herb [in other words, rattlesnake antidote]".[78] Apparently, a certain Abbey Gendron gained a great reputation in Paris for "curing small cancers" with mashed leatherwood (*Dircus palustris*) bark.[79] There was also goldthread (*coptis groënlandica*), sarsaparilla (*aralia*), Labrador tea (*Ledum groënlandicum*), win-tergreen (*Gaultheria*) and choke cherry (*prunus virginiana*). For many American plants that are similar or related to, and distributed like European plants, it is impos-sible to know whether settlers adapted their own traditions or borrowed ideas from Aboriginals. This is the case for noble yarrow (*Achillia millefolium*) and mountain ash or dogberry (*sorbus*).[80]

Even today, modern medicine uses around 50 pharmaceutical products the me-dicinal properties of which were identified by Aboriginals from North or South America, for example, cinchona bark, which is the source of quinine used against malaria; and ephedrine, which is used as a nasal decongestant.[81]

Some of the plant products that came to be used in the seventeenth and eighteenth centuries gained wide renown. First, there was fir gum that was gathered by the bucketful, used to waterproof canoes and considered the supreme remedy for healing cuts.[82] The *Hospitalières* at Québec City's hospital bought it from "Indians who gather it" and Mother Duplessis de l'Enfant Jésus had it imported to the hospital in Dieppe.[83] According to Brother Marie Victorin, it was one of the "essentials of French Canadian home medicine, and used, with good reason, to prevent scurvy, as an antiseptic on wounds and in poultices for burns".[84] The same went for spruce, which as also called a "universal medicine", considered a source of "canoe tar" and provided the indispensable fine roots for sewing pieces of bark together. It was also used to make spruce beer, but perhaps this was not learned from Aboriginals.[85]

In the eighteenth century, American ginseng was exported to China via France. As its scientific name (*panax*) indicates, it was considered a panacea. Aboriginals thought, wrongly, that it increased fertility. Settlers and Indigenous people, mainly the Lorette Hurons, Iroquois, Algonquins and Nipissings in the *reductions* (i.e., conquered areas), gathered large quantities of it.[86]

Maidenhair fern (a fern with fine leaf stalks and the Latin name of *adiantum pedatum*) was considered to have curative virtues that led to it being exported to Europe. Aboriginals (in particular the Lorette Hurons) sold a lot of it to the French.[87]

Means of inducing abortion were more controversial. Doctor Jean François Gaultier noted that "Indians and ill-intentioned French women" used bloodwort (*sanguinaria canadensis L.*) and juniper (*Joniperus virginia*).[88] Pyrite sulfide also seems to have been used.[89]

Animals were also sources of medicinal ingredients, and beaver "kidneys" (in fact, musk glands) and moose hooves (preferably the left back hoof as a remedy for epilepsy) were especially popular. Aboriginals sold them to settlers for local consumption and export to France.[90] Finally, some protection had to be found against mosquitoes and other biting insects. They were kept at bay with smoke and by covering the body with grease, in particular, with bear and pig fat.[91]

Initially, many French people challenged the worth of Aboriginal traditional medicine, which they associated entirely with witchcraft.[92] However, experience soon forced them to acknowledge its superiority in some areas, such as with respect to healing wounds and setting broken bones. Some Aboriginals were opposed to bleeding as a remedy, though it was the Europeans' panacea.[93] In Louisiana, French people who were dissatisfied with their doctors went to see Natchez healers.[94]

European medicine borrowed from that of the Aboriginals, but the opposite was also true. Aboriginals went to the colony's hospitals. However, though the two traditions interpenetrated, each continued to operate according to its own rules. Neither was a science at the time. In other words, neither proceeded by identifying variables, formulating hypotheses, assessing relations of cause and effect, testing with control groups, etc. They were based on knowledge acquired empirically by trial and error. Each tradition explained the causes of illnesses according to its own general belief system and the way it interpreted the world. According to Aboriginals, illness resulted from something that was missing or dissatisfied desires. Thus, it had to be healed by the opposite, such as by providing an excess in the form of large quantities of food, much dancing, music-making and socializing, and the fulfilment of desires expressed in dreams. On the contrary, Christian Europe thought that disease resulted from listening to one's desires too much, in other words, from being in a kind of state of sin. Therefore, the patient had to be isolated and kept at a distance. Reserve and restraint were required. The sick were given weak broth to drink, those nearby walked softly, visiting was kept to a minimum and people had to speak quietly. Patients were bled to draw the evil out. This is how missionaries cared for Aboriginal patients when there were epidemics. Since the illness came from their barbarism and paganism, they had to be healed using the signs of civilization and true religion, such as small quantities of sugar and European fruit, and of course baptism. The two traditions were thus too antithetical to merge into a single system despite occasional borrowing on both sides. However, they did share the same conviction that there was a need for reconciliation with the spiritual universe in order to heal. In the end, Aboriginals were probably better off than the Europeans in terms of health care, for they had a vast repertory of medicinal plants and the tradition of sweat lodges, which were a kind of sauna, while at the time Europeans did not bathe at all.[95]

2.6. Other Uses of Plants

The French learned how to use birch bark at the beginning of the colony. In addition to the canoes, tepees and shelters[96] that we have already mentioned, it was used to make recipients for collecting maple sap, and continued to be employed in that way until around the 1870s, when the recipients were replaced with tin vessels.[97] Birch bark was also used for insulation: houses were sheathed in it before being covered in shingles. Its use "as a wind break or steam-break seems to have come from Amerindian customs".[98]

Nuns used the bark to make "wallets, small baskets, toiletry cases, etc., decorated with designs embroidered using moose fur that they dyed in bright colours. They also make models of Indian canoes and weapons".[99] The Mother Superior at Québec City's Hôtel Dieu sent the apothecary Féret in Dieppe "an Indian box and a few little *orogans* [work baskets]" with a note saying that they had been made by a French woman who had copied Aboriginals' work.[100] Some vegetable dyes used for such objects (and more generally for fabric) had been learned from Aboriginals. For example hemlock was used to produce red dye and goldthread to produce yellow. Cochineal red, which was used widely in the British textile industry, came from Mexico.[101]

Habitants used elm and ash bark to make baskets and chair seats. Though it is not certain, there may have been some Aboriginal influence on these activities.[102] Other borrowings include ropes and straps made of leatherwood (*Dirca palutris*) and, in the southern parts of New France, candles made of vegetable oil.[103]

2.7. Food

Father Louis Nicolas saw his hosts gather birch sap.[104] He wrote that from the white ash there flows "in season a liqueur much milder and sweeter than that of the maple tree [...] and it is made into syrup that has much more body than that made with the sap that comes out of the maple tree".[105] His description of maple sap made into syrup by boiling it "until it reduces by half"[106] corroborates Father Charlevoix's comments on how the Aboriginals and Canadians influenced each other:

It seems that the Indians, who were very knowledgeable about all the virtues of their plants, had always used the sap as they do today, but it is certain that they did not know how to turn it into sugar, as we taught them. They simply boiled it two or three times to thicken it a little and make a kind of syrup that is quite pleasant. What we have added is how to turn it into sugar by leaving it to boil until it is thick enough.[107]

Apparently, Aboriginals did not make maple sugar until they had metal pots. Father Chrestien Leclerc first described this in 1676.[108] Settlers stocked up on birch bark to make recipients to collect maple sap.[109] Maple products were consumed widely:

Local medicine and country candy, maple sap is eaten less as a syrup than in loaves of sugar. It is used in all cooking to such an extent that some people lose their teeth![110]

Naturally, local guides were not required to gather nuts, berries (strawberries, raspberries, blackberries, mooseberries, etc.), fruit (small apples, pears, plums, etc.), wild onions and garlic because they or closely related varieties also grew in Europe. However, it is likely that information was frequently sought on where they grew. Samples of unknown trees and shrubs, such as staghorn sumac, were sent to the King's gardens,[111] and settlers discovered cranberries, groundnuts (*apios Americana*), blueberries and milkweed shoots, which did not grow in Europe. They used dogtooth violets, wild ginger, devil's club and sweet gale to make substitutes for, respectively, garlic, ginger, anise and pepper.[112] Outside of the colony, travellers and *coureurs de bois* certainly learned from the first inhabitants how to survive when they were faced with famine.[113]

Over the last five centuries, world agriculture has benefited enormously from species originally cultivated by Aboriginals. After the discovery of America, over 50 new varieties of edible plants were introduced into Europe, and today those species account for around half of the world's food production.[114] Plants that come to mind include corn (also known as "Indian corn"), potatoes, manioc (from which tapioca is made), beans, squash, pumpkins, tomatoes, peppers, sweet potatoes, peanuts, cacao, chicle (used in chewing gum), artichokes, avocados, and pineapples. It is hard to imagine a western-style dinner that does not contain at least one component based on Aboriginal food.

In northeast America, agriculture was based on corn, beans and squash, which were known metaphorically as the "three sisters". Before coming to America, the first settlers may have already been familiar with these crops, and may have even grown them, particularly beans and squash. The plants had spread across Europe from Spain. When the settlers arrived in America, they found many more varieties (largely unknown to them) grown on large scale.[115] Unlike the British and Dutch settlers, who originally gave up farming wheat in favour of corn but later returned to wheat, the settlers in New France grew little corn.[116] However, favoured with a warmer climate, the people in Montréal grew more of the Aboriginal cereal. There was a small market for it among the *voyageurs* from the *Pays d'en Haut*, who, unlike the settlers, ate *sagamite* (corn porridge with meat or fish) as their staple.[117] The account books of Montréal outfitters in the eighteenth century show that men travelling by canoe took wheat flour biscuits on their travels. However, beyond Detroit and *Michilimakinac*, they ate more corn. It was eaten as corn on the cob, boiled and roasted, as flour and cornmeal for *sagamite*, more rarely in unleavened bread (bannock), and as a snack (popcorn). Canadians loved "flowering corn", which they popped over the fire and "ate like pralines".[118] Observers noted that settlers' vegetable gardens contained beans, melons, squash, sometimes Jerusalem artichokes, and pumpkins with a shape and taste different from those in France.[119] Not all of the plants were necessarily borrowed directly from the local Aboriginals because, as we have already mentioned, many plants had already spread from America to Spain and France in the sixteenth century. Therefore, the food eaten in New France was not necessarily much different from that eaten in France, except that more meat was consumed in the colony. In both cases, the diet was based on bread and milk products.[120]

Marie de l'Incarnation sent her brother a recipe for *sagamite* and her son in France pumpkin seeds that she had obtained from Hurons.[121] If they did not grow what they needed, for example if they lacked sunflower seeds, the settlers bought them from the Aboriginals. The Iroquois from Sault St. Louis sold their surplus harvest at Montréal.[122] Many Canadians ate wild rice as a celebratory dish. These grains were abundant upstream from Montréal and around the Great Lakes, where people assigned to outposts ate large quantities of them.[123] Under the French regime, South American potatoes were not eaten in Canada. They were introduced by the English after 1759.

Local cereals and vegetables were of course supplemented by game and fish. Pehr Kalm assures us that Canadians had no lack of words to praise beaver meat, "which they classify as fish, thereby enabling them to eat it during lent, on Fridays and on other days of abstinence".[124] Canadians learned from the Aboriginals how to turn bear fat into oil. This was often used in *sagamite* and was an essential ingredient in the *voyageurs'* pemmican. Settlers used it instead of butter for frying and on salads.[125]

In addition to new kinds of fresh food, the Canadians' borrowings from the Aboriginals included various methods for preserving food. Corn was often kept in Aboriginal-style braids until it was stored in the granary.[126] It is possible that it was in North America that Canadians learned how to bury fruit and vegetable in root cellars.[127] However, Indigenous methods for drying and smoking meat were adopted only rarely. Canadians used such processes only for fish.

These various borrowings added new components to the farming and cooking of the new arrivals, but they did not change the structure. They were simply new ingredients to be used in pickles, soups, jellies, jams, desserts and puddings.[128] Farming techniques remained European, as did ways of preparing and combining ingredients in recipes and, of course, table manners.

However, one local product did introduce new behaviour: tobacco, which was called "*pétun*" at the time. Canadians adopted it immediately. Pehr Kalm said that the common folk smoked and chewed a lot, and that he had even seen boys as young as 10 or 12 walking about with pipes in their mouths.[129] Tobacco was grown in every garden, and men had snuffboxes and clay pipes or, more frequently, calumets decorated in Indigenous style. Like the Aboriginals, they carried tobacco pouches, generally made out of otter skin.[130] Unlike Aboriginal women, Canadian women smoked only exceptionally, though they frequently took snuff. Even today, some common expressions in French Canada show how widespread tobacco use was. For example, "*reste fumer*" ("stay and smoke") and "*viens fumer*" ("come and smoke") are used instead of "stay for a drink" or "come for a coffee", and people say "*être réduit à manger sa pipe*" ("to be reduced to eating one's pipe") instead of "to be reduced to eating shoe leather" and "*mets ça dans ta pipe*" ("put that in your pipe and smoke it") after stating a strong argument.[131]

2.8. Culture

Both the French and the English adopted thousands of Aboriginal place names, as we have already noted. However, many other words were borrowed to refer to things that were specific to the Americas, such as indigenous food, animals and plants. A few examples of French borrowings are *manitou*, *totem* and *mackinaw* (Algonquin), *pemmican* (Cree), *babiche* (Micmac), *igloo* and *kayak* (Inuit), *wawaron* (Huron), *carcajou* (Montaignais), *ouananiche*, *achigan* and *maskinongé* (Algonquin), *atoka* (Huron-Iroquois), *pacane* and *pimbina* (Algonquin). Examples of English borrowings include words as common as chipmunk, hickory, moose, raccoon, skunk and squash.[132] While it is probable that the syntax of Aboriginal languages influenced the syntax used in French by bilingual *coureurs de bois*, there does not seem to have been any lasting effects on the language spoken by sedentary settlers. In this respect, there seems to be a parallel between linguistic borrowing and borrowing of other types. Many components were assimilated but the original structure did not change. To this general observation, we can add a note on the selective nature of the exchanges. Generally, borrowings occurred more in areas of activity dominated by men because they were more often in contact with Aboriginals. The women who came into contact with Aboriginals were generally nuns who received Aboriginal students in their convents. They lived in a world where very few women came to school; over 90% were illiterate. Aboriginal slaves serving rich families in the colonies may have had more influence on their mistresses.

Since Canadian women were the primary conduits of culture, Aboriginal influence did not penetrate very far. Another filter, if not to say dam, was religion. The settlers belonged to an exclusive religion based on dogma. They therefore rejected their allies' religion and considered it to be on the side of the forces of evil and pagan superstition. Moreover, in so far as Aboriginal religions infused social life to a higher degree than Christian religions, many of the Aboriginals' routine practices seemed unacceptable, such as rituals associated with farming, fishing, hunting, sculpture, painting, music and dancing. Of course, the Aboriginal "theme" appeared in the arts, but only treated according to the European canon. We can see this in the many engravings where the subject is in *contrapposto*, in André Ernest Modesto Gretry's opera *Le Huron*, and in the opera *Les Indes Galantes* (1735), the title of which says much about Rameau's optic. There seem to be few Aboriginal traces in traditional French Canadian dances, except perhaps in the Mauricie, where the *makusham* was still danced until recently.[133] Yet, the first Ursulines danced "Indian style" with the residents of their school,[134] and Canadians danced in the villages of their allies. In Montréal also, three Canadians danced Aboriginal-style at the Great Peace celebrations in 1701.[135] Later, when they received Pehr Kalm at their convent in La Chine, the sisters of the Congregation had four young Canadian residents whose parents lived among Aboriginals perform Aboriginal dances for him.[136] In the end, however, the imperialist relationship and plan for conquest at the very foundation of every colony carried with it the conviction of its own superiority.

More generally, except with respect to religion, where Christianity's superiority was absolute for its faithful, things were borrowed in the same way everywhere: they were reinterpreted and used in new ways consistent with the borrower's culture. Material borrowings are always the most easily integrated, and resistance increases as one "rises" towards the realm of mentalities and beliefs.

Let us look at religion. As we have seen, official Catholicism adopted almost nothing from Aboriginal religions, while the syncretic nature of the latter was conducive to borrowing. Marius Barbeau has found in the narratives of many Aboriginal nations medieval stories told long ago by *coureurs de bois*, but Aboriginal narratives and myths barely penetrated French Canadian folklore in Québec. The *chasse galerie* (flying canoe) is not an Aboriginal story but simply the borrowing of an Aboriginal canoe to make it fly in the sky. The story's prototype is European. Celebrating hunters travelling in the firmament became in North America *voyageurs* and later loggers travelling by canoe to see their girlfriends.[137] Settlers' folktales were enriched by features of Aboriginal culture and sometimes even by episodes borrowed from the history of interactions with Aboriginals or from Aboriginal stories.[138] The apparition of a burning black vessel sailing on the waves sometimes seen by sea fishermen seems to date back to when Aboriginals in the Gaspé area set a ship on fire by shooting flaming arrows into its sails. The attack was in revenge for having got their brothers drunk and made them captive to be sold as slaves in Europe.[139] In the Bic, the legend is that Massacre Island's name refers to a massacre by traditional enemies of Aboriginals who were travelling from Donnacona and had stopped on the little island. The high tide forced them to come out of the cave where they were hiding. The tragic event would have occurred a little before Jacques Cartier arrived.[140] A beautiful Basque princess desperately searching for her future husband was sometimes seen by *voyageurs* above Eboulements Bay. This refers to the story of a Basque fisherman on the north shore of the St. Lawrence who had promised his only daughter to an Aboriginal chief. However, she was in love with an English trapper. The couple had to hide to escape the vengeance of the gods: the forest caught fire and the earth shook.[141] Perhaps this is the explanation for the earthquake in 1663? There are a few exceptional cases in which Aboriginal mythology affected the structure or content of the narrative, but Christianity remained dominant in the end. For example, let us look at the story of Ile Verte.

> At the beginning of the world, all the elements of nature were tangled together, and thunder, water, glaciers, wind and rocks created a hellish noise. God was busy creating humans, animals and plants, so he asked Lucifer to put some order into the St. Lawrence River. Satan agreed to take care of digging the river and placing islands on the condition that he could reign there later. After setting up the North Shore and planting capes Trinity and Eternity (on the Saguenay), he proudly challenged God do to as good a job. However, God caused a great wind to arise that blew Lucifer down below the capes. He fled to the south, and every time he took a step in the river, an island rose up. Finally, he settled on Ile Verte, and the people worshipped him to thank him for having created such beautiful land, plants and animals.

> Basque whale hunters arrived on the island one evening, and raised a large white cross. The people living nearby ran to Satan and asked him to chase away the intruders, or else to worship the Basque's god with them. A great storm arose and in the middle of the lightning and thunder, Satan turned to stone.

> Since that time, on some nights when the sea is calm, it is possible to see the silhouettes of women singing praise to the creator on a stony part of the island across from the cross. On a rock, the devil's footprints can still be seen.[142]

This creation narrative is related to Aboriginal myths in that instead of there being one creator, there were two presiding over the creation of the universe. It concerns the principle of the good and easy, versus that of the evil and difficult. Here, Satan represents the trickster. Of course, the story might also be about the archaic opposition between the good God and the demon, which dates back to the Babylonians and remains in popular Christianity. In either case, the narrative explains Christianity's superiority over the Aboriginal religions associated with devil worship. A final example of how borrowings were incorporated into the Catholic tradition is the legend of the Iroquois woman. It was published in 1827 and tells the story of wars between mission Indians of the Ottawa nation and the Iroquois of the League of Five Nations in the seventeenth century. It relates how a young Iroquois woman who had converted to Christianity preferred to die at the stake rather than renounce her faith.[143]

Folksongs also took on an American flavour (underlined): *mon père n'avait fille que moi, encore sur la mer il m'envoie, le marinier qui m'y menait...canot d'écorce qui vole qui vole. M'en revenant de la jolie Rochelle j'ai rencontré trois jolies demoiselles, c'est l'aviron qui nous mène, qui nous mène...* Like the many songs and laments that beat time for the paddles of the *voyageurs* and *coureurs de bois*, these classic refrains take us "to the *pays d'en haut* among all the Indians". There, in those foreign lands where one is exposed to enemy warriors, one can come to know the "Indian tribes and their different languages", and discover love on the shores of the Great Lakes and the banks of the Mississippi.[144]

The opposite is expressed in the sad ballad of Lisa, the "young Indian slave", which reminds us of the condition to which were reduced around 2400 of her compatriots for the benefit of the settlers in New France.[145] Perhaps some of our grandparents remember weeping as they hummed the couplets telling the story of how René Goupil's mother was informed that he had been made prisoner of the Iroquois? However, the song was a written only at the beginning of the twentieth century.[146]

In French Canada, children were neither found in the cabbage patch nor brought by storks. Was it because there were no storks in America? In any case, no local bird got the job. Instead, children were brought by "Indians". Does the association of Aboriginals and birth suggest the opposite relation of children born out of wedlock and given to Aboriginals for adoption? Or, instead of an exchange of children, perhaps there was an exchange of spouses? When European-Canadian men left for the *pays d'en haut*, they often acquired a wife there. In the meantime, did Aboriginal men come and visit the Canadian women who had been left behind? This fantasy would mean that Aboriginal men would take advantage of the departure of the European men, and impregnate the women left behind. On another level, perhaps the image instead connotes the wish for an easy delivery because Aboriginals gave birth more quickly and with less pain? Not excluding any of these paradigms and considering that several could be at work at the same time, can we at least take for certain the association of Aboriginals and children with nature and the forces of evil, in opposition to the culture that a child enters through christening, which was the path to the community of men and saints? A variant of this perception is perhaps the use of a threatening Aboriginal face to keep children away from the house when it was time to give birth.[147]

Canadians borrowed the great American team sport of lacrosse,[148] though Scottish shinny or field hockey, not lacrosse, seems to have been the origin of hockey. Finally the game of knuckle-bones or sticks that have to be picked up one at a time without moving the others is of Aboriginal origin. It was one of the games played by the Ursulines' students.

2.9. Diplomacy and War

Canadians methodically learned Aboriginal diplomatic rules and rituals.[149] It was the only way to conduct negotiations. They learned the metaphors and were careful to express themselves using only porcelain necklaces (wampum), which they knew how to make.[150] They complied with the opening rituals that required that one mourn the other's dead, clear one's throat so as to speak clearly, and clean one's ears so as to hear well. They also followed the closing rituals. However, these borrowings were used only in dealings with Aboriginals and never became part of the diplomatic methods used among Europeans. This means that they were used to manipulate Aboriginals. All that remains of them are a few colourful expressions, such as "bury the hatchet" and "smoke the peace pipe".

It was very different with respect to war. The Canadians completely assimilated the guerrilla tactics of their allies, though they used them for purposes and in accordance with an overall strategy that corresponded to the interests of their own society. As for agriculture, business, art, diplomacy, etc., Europe and America each had its own traditions when it came to war. In Europe, war involved large armies that lined up hierarchically facing each other on immense battlefields. Infantrymen, cavalrymen and artillerymen fought according to a strategy based on the movement of the various army corps rather than on the actions of individuals. Armies were stratified according to caste. Leadership and cavalry positions were reserved for nobles, and the fact that paid mercenaries were recruited limited the development of the soldiers' sense of belonging to their army, which in any case had no trouble sacrificing them as cannon fodder to win short-term victories. The strength of European armies was therefore based on the state's ability to recruit, pay and supervise a large number of men. The weakness of these armies was the absence or fragility of the soldiers' loyalty to the institution and its goals. This was one of the reasons that soldiers were dressed in bright colours: blue for the French and red for the British. Not only did it make it possible for the noble generals mounted on horses at the back of the lines to see the movements of their troops, but it also prevented enlisted men from hiding to escape the fight. Honour in war was thus limited to nobles and resulted less from personal courage than from the victory of one apparatus over another. It was only under Napoleon, after the French Revolution, that soldiers went to war for a national cause that they made their own.

The French colonial power was unable to transpose all of this way of waging war onto its operations in America. First, at the time, British settlers were on average twenty times more numerous than the French, which made direct confrontation difficult. Thus, they had to avoid situations in which the match was too unequal. More importantly, how could they deal with Aboriginal enemies, who did not assemble armies and tended instead to use guerrilla tactics? Also, how were they to deal with their Aboriginal allies, who refused any form of conscription and maintained their own sovereignty? Aboriginal military might was based on warriors' independence and mobility, rather than on concentration of power and mechanical discipline. Left to himself, an Aboriginal warrior would not avoid battle but rather camouflage himself to fight more effectively. The risks that a warrior took thus depended more on himself than on a superior's decisions. This made it possible for Aboriginals to defeat larger European armies by avoiding direct confrontation in the open and instead setting traps for the troops when they were travelling through the forest. In such situations, European generals lost control of their soldiers while Aboriginal warriors used their skills to maximum effect. However, Aboriginal war traditions did not permit the sacrifice of wave after wave of attackers against a stronghold until victory was finally won. The relative strength of warriors trapping an enemy army in an ambush at a bend in a river had its relative weakness in the same warriors before an even mediocre stockade around a fort.

Europeans had to learn from their Aboriginal enemies, who evaded grouped troops, chose their own terrain for combat and counter-attacked in small parties. Europeans were particularly constrained by the fact that they could not conscript their allies; they therefore had to adapt. Since the French were less numerous than the Aboriginals, they were especially dependent on their military support. We could even say that the Aboriginals' military support was the primary strength of French power.[151] The colonial fur-exporting society created a new type of man: the *voyageur* and *coureur de bois*, who escaped colonial control, at least partially, and lived in contact with Aboriginals.[152] Another new type of person was the habitant, who was different from the French peasant in that he had not only the right to bear arms, but also overall greater social weight and status, which translated into greater self-confidence and freedom. Since Iroquois guerrilla warriors threatened both farmers and *voyageurs*, both had motives to enlist. This was also a departure from European wars. Thus, new social conditions combined with pressure from and the tactics of Aboriginal friends and enemies led Canadians to wage war Aboriginal style. The Iroquois, Hurons, Abenakis, Algonquins and Mahicans living in the *reductions* "teach Canada's soldiers and habitants how to wage war against the League of the Iroquois as they wage it against us."[153]

This is the style of war that the French Canadians employed against the British invaders, Hudson's Bay Company employees at trading posts and civilians in villages on the border of New England. Iberville led joint raids by French Canadians and Aboriginals that took fishing villages by surprise.[154] The new way of fighting made it very easy to tell the difference between French troops fresh off the boat, and Canadian militias, and to a lesser extent between soldiers from Québec City and those from Montréal, who were more "used to the Indians".[155] In 1759, Bougainville wrote that that Canadians "are brave; their kind of courage, like that of the Indians, is to expose themselves very little and use ambushes. They are very good in the woods, shoot skilfully, scatter and take cover behind large trees when they fight.[156] While [Aboriginals] remain the best, French Canadians are by far superior to the French who are not yet familiar with the country."[157] Though we have to consider his remarks with some distance, Louis Franquet said:

> In war time, the habitants are the only ones we can arm to defend the colony and attack or harass the English because they are the only ones who can travel by canoe in the summer and snowshoes in the winter, survive on a little flour, fat and suet, do forced marches through the woods for three to six months at a time, resist the cold, and live from the end of their guns, in other words, from hunting and fishing alone.

French soldiers, not being accustomed to this kind of life, are unable to go on military expeditions in the winter or even the summer, or if they do it is only with a great deal of difficulty and many are lost because of the cold.[158]

Franquet overlooked a few things. There were two French army corps: the marine corps, which arrived in 1685, and the army corps, which arrived later (1755–1760). In the seventeenth century, the former were just as used to the country as the French-born Canadian militiamen, and also participated in war parties.[159]

Finally, this kind of war showed the difference between French Canadian settlers and their British counterparts. In 1756, the sub-lieutenant Parscau du Plessix wrote that the latter "are neither as alert nor as brave, and allow themselves to be surprised because they do not wage war in the woods like our Canadians, which will always place us in a position of superiority because there is no choice but to fight in the woods that cover the whole expanse of this country, unless one stays enclosed in forts, as the English do."[160] The assertion was well founded, but exaggerated since the British had created the Rangers, who were skilful in guerrilla warfare. In sum, there were differences in the ways war was waged, depending on how close one lived to Aboriginals, though the differences were not as great as suggested by authors at the time. Thus, thirty years earlier, the historian Charlevoix said that "the English Americans do not want war because they have a lot to lose, and they do not cultivate their relationships with the Indians because they think they do not need them. For the opposite reasons, young French people hate peace and live happily with the natives of the land, whose esteem they never have any trouble winning."[161] In his passion for military exploits, the historian seems to have confused young people with *coureurs de bois*, thus obscuring the efforts of Canadian settlers to create a farming society. He perpetuates the false idea that French Canadians built nothing, lived from day to day and preferred fighting to working. Yet it is certain that French Canadians had a lot to lose from war. This is exactly what Bougainville said in his 1759 report: "Naturally, the peoples of Canada must be very tired of war. Many have died in it, they have taken on the hardest kinds of work, [and] they have no time to increase their wealth or even to rebuild their homes."[162] What can we conclude from this? Did the Canadians' war tactics become "Indianized" and was this process stronger in Canada than in the American colonies? The answer to these questions has to be yes, but we should also look at other indicators.

Governor Frontenac had a prisoner tortured at Québec City using Iroquois methods, and danced a war dance while waving a tomahawk in order to persuade his allies to take his side.[163] Canadians told stories of their war exploits in Aboriginal villages,[164] scalped enemies, tortured enemy warriors in Aboriginal style in the *Pays d'en haut* and at Québec City,[165] and finally, may even have engaged in cannibal practices by eating "Aboriginal or English soup" with Aboriginal warriors for whom it was not taboo.[166]

Like their allies, the French kept captives and adopted them. For example, in 1703 when she was six years old, Esther Wheelwright was captured at Wells, Maine and adopted by the Abenakis. Later she was given to the family of Governor Vaudreuil, who named her Louise. She became an Ursuline nun despite opposition from her adoptive family, gained a reputation for skill in embroidering on birch bark, became her community's Superior and acted as an ambassador to the English after Québec City fell in 1759.[167]

However, the French colonial empire did not renounce all of its military traditions. It incorporated the guerrilla warfare practised by Canadians and its Aboriginal allies, but the troops from Europe maintained some of their regular practices. The result was an amalgam of the two approaches.[168] French military expeditions against Aboriginal enemies combined a core of regular troops led into combat in well-supervised regiments, and Canadian or Aboriginal soldiers, who acted as scouts until they arrived at the battle, where they added mobility and surprise to the strength in numbers and heavy artillery. The relative weight of each strategy generally depended on the relations between the French and Canadians. Thus, when the English attacked in 1759, France relied on Montcalm, who fought European-style rather than using the guerrilla tactics of the Canadians and Aboriginals of Vaudreuil. This contributed to the French defeat.

In conclusion, on the surface, it seems that the reasons for going to war did not change. Aboriginals went to war to avenge their dead and acquire prestige, while the French did so to increase their markets and empire. More fundamentally, however, traditional Aboriginal war was adulterated in that it was turned into an instrument used to achieve the goals of an empire. Thus, the shadow of the mercenary began to extend behind the warrior ally.

3. Values, Symbols, Identity

In Champlain's time, the King of France agreed to recognize every converted Aboriginal as a subject. The policy was based on the postulate that after coming to know the French, the "Indians" would desire nothing more than to become French also. Missionaries thought in the same manner, and imagined that a colony of good Catholic immigrants guided by the clergy could impose its example on the pagans, who would quickly abandon their satanic rituals. Persuaded of the material, cultural and spiritual superiority of their civilization, the French colonizers thought they were doing the right thing by trying to assimilate backward peoples who were living in the dark. These expectations did not come true, so an explanation was sought in Aboriginals' natural distraction and laziness. The colonizers never imagined that the opposite scenario could be true, though it was to a certain extent. Many Canadians, *coureurs de bois* and *voyageurs* were assimilated into Aboriginal societies. In contrast, the Canadian assimilation policy largely failed, despite the fact that Aboriginal children were sent to live in convents and monasteries.[169] All observers agree on this. For example, Father Charlevoix reported on the trip of a group of Iroquois to Paris, where they were shown "all the royal homes, and all the beauties of the great city". Apparently, the visitors admired nothing but the boutiques where meat was roasted, and "preferred their villages to the capital of the richest kingdom in Europe."[170] Rather than adopting a simplistic explanation of the sort "they know nothing of the comfort of our way of living" the great Jesuit historian of New France advanced an unexpected hypothesis:

> Quite a large number of French have lived like them [the Aboriginals], and found it suited them so well that many have never felt the need to come back, though they can be very comfortable in the colony. On the contrary, not a single Indian has been able to get used to our way of living. We have taken their children when they were still babes in arms, we have raised them with a great deal of care, we have left out nothing to

remove from them any knowledge of what their parents were doing. All these precautions have amounted to nothing. Blood has triumphed over education. As soon as they are set free, they tear their clothes to pieces and disappear into the woods to find their compatriots, whose life appears to them more pleasant than the life they lived with us.[171]

Replace their blood by their culture, education and identity, and it is easy to understand the return to nature. However the situation was still more grave: even Christians exposed to Aboriginal life did not want to come back. The botanist Pehr Kalm wrote about this:

> It is also remarkable that most European prisoners who have been taken in war and mixed with the Indians, especially if they were captured when they were young, never want to return to their original country later, even when their father and mother or close relatives come to see them to try to persuade them and they have complete freedom to do so. They find the independent life of the Indians preferable to that of Europeans. They have adopted Indigenous clothing and do everything in the same manner as the Indians, to such a degree that it is difficult to tell them apart, except that their skin and colouring is slightly lighter. There are also several examples of French men who have voluntarily married indigenous women and adopted their way of life. On the contrary, there is not a single example of an Indian man who has married a European woman and adopted her lifestyle. If an Indian man is made prisoner by Europeans during war, he always looks for a chance to get back home, even when he has been held for many years and enjoyed all the freedoms of a European.[172]

While the age at which the prisoners were captured has to be taken into account, as well as the strong pressure that Aboriginal communities could have exercised over their captives to oppose their departure after the conclusion of peace treaties, it remains that Kalm's observations were accurate. They are confirmed by many other accounts, including from the British colonies.[173] Even in the *reductions* near French settlements, the Aboriginals, though they had been converted, seemed to assimilate more of their French allies than the French assimilated of them. Governor Denonville complained of this in 1685:

> We long praised the fact that Indians were drawing near our settlements as a very significant means of accustoming them to our way of life and teaching them our religion. However, Monseigneur, I see that the exact opposite is occurring because instead of getting them used to our laws, I assure you that they are conveying to us all of their most evil habits, and are themselves adopting only what is bad in us.

Certainly, the administrator was very disappointed because he dreamed of regulating the cultural exchange in accordance with his king's desires. In fact, the Aboriginals were acquiring European habits, though the Governor did not see it, and the settlers were acquiring Aboriginal habits, which the Governor did not want.

Worse, the whole process escaped bureaucratic control, even in the area peopled by the French. Thus, the Governor's frustration did not stop there. Imagine that even nomadic Aboriginals corrupted the people living on the seigneuries?

> You would not believe, Monseigneur, the harm that it does to the colony, for not only do the children of the seigneurs become accustomed to libertinage like them, but they even take advantage of the Indian girls and women that they keep with them, and go on their hunts in the woods, where they often go so hungry that they eat their dogs.[174]

These brief words mask great fears: that of shaking up the French social and conjugal order (through libertinage), and, even worse, that of a return to barbarism, for it was taboo for a European to eat dog meat. It seemed better to excuse poor behaviour by putting it down to evil Aboriginal influence than to blame it on the French people's desire for freedom. At carnivals and festivals, the French "dressed as naked Indians", which the Governor saw as "customs that only encourage young people to live like Indians, communicate with them, and be eternally libertine like them."[175] Fear led him to exaggerate the Aboriginal influence, but he did not invent it. Denonville wrote to the Minister: "Monseigneur, I do not know how to describe the attraction that all young people have for the Indians' lifestyle, which involves doing nothing, having no restraint, following all one's inclinations and setting oneself beyond correction."[176] The Governor was talking nonsense when he wrote that Aboriginals lived without work, without constraints and simply in accordance with their desires, but he was right to say that there was no correction, especially none by the colonial authorities. What would this mean for the *coureurs de bois* who, as we have seen, sometimes became completely "Indianized", and escaped the control of colonial authorities? The official views on them were particularly biased. It was said that "most Canadian youths have abandoned farming the land and gone into the [fur] trade generally to live a libertine life."[177] Yet, only a minority of the population, mainly in the Montréal area, participated in the fur trade. And libertine life? This refers to the absence of Catholic sacraments[178] (and often the celebration of marriages *à la mode du pays*, in other words, in accordance with Aboriginal customs). It was said that the men who paddled from Montréal to *Michilimakinak* were lazy, lived in the woods, and were "bestial like the Indians with whom they consort, and like whom they become."[179]

A number of administrators also pointed out the danger that the Indianization of the French posed to agriculture. It was said that once they got used to life as *voyageurs* and *coureurs de bois*, "young Canadians find it hard to get interested in farming the land",[180] lose their taste for work and become unable to accept the slightest constraint.[181] Canadian society was thus apparently in danger of becoming disorderly and nomadic. The fur trade and travel discouraged agriculture and the Aboriginal influence encouraged mobility and freedom. As a priest at a seminary in Louisiana pointed out, Canadians kept a taste for building and solving problems, but they found it difficult to tolerate the routine of rural life:

...for we have had only Canadians here. They are truly skilled mechanics and builders, but since they are accustomed to travelling, they are more suited to making discoveries than to cultivating the earth. Thus, we need good labourers from France here.[182]

According to the administrators, the Aboriginal influence eventually affected all of the values and personalities of Canadians. The family, the foundation of society, was the first to be shaken. Apparently, parents no longer knew how to discipline their children, who were raised too freely, "like Indians." From the beginnings of the colony, missionaries had remarked on the less authoritarian nature of Aboriginal families, and suggested disciplinary measures to raise children with the fear of God and their parents.[183] Apparently, the opposite was achieved. According to Intendant Raudot, Canadian fathers and mothers were besotted with their children, behaviour they had acquired from the Aboriginals. Without discipline, youngsters became stubborn, a character trait that became clear in the disrespect they showed for their parents, superiors and priests.[184] Soon a distinction was made between the permissive, Canadian way of raising children, and the more authoritarian French manner. Thus, a subversive Aboriginal influence was suspected: "the worst thing that our French acquire from living near Indians is that our young children become accustomed to their example of having no subjection or obedience, and always being the masters of their will, and doing nothing but walking about together without any purpose."[185]

Canadians had a reputation for being proud, haughty, insolent, self-assured, difficult to control and full of independence.[186] According to Father Charlevoix, the faults of the French Canadians were also those of the Aboriginals, and he added:

It is as if the air that one breathes on this vast continent contributes to it, but the example and company of the natural inhabitants, who place all their happiness in freedom and independence, are more than sufficient to produce this character.[187]

Since they were difficult to handle, Canadians made very poor valets, and they also did not have European refinement. However, they were warriors able to take on difficult and dangerous tasks that could win the esteem of the "natural people of the country."[188] The neo-Americans were very sharp, particularly the women, according to Father Charlevoix. They proved able to conduct major business undertakings. Apparently, these strong women were more numerous in Canada in every social stratum.[189] Pehr Kalm echoes these comments concerning the women in Montréal, who were supposedly "Indianized." An analogy can be made with the supposedly more Americanized nature of Montréalers today, compared with the provincials living in the old capital:

The women born in Montréal are accused by many of the immigrant French born in France of largely lacking the good French education and manners of their origins. They are said to be motivated by pride and contaminated by the imaginative minds of American Indians. Those who do not like them call them "half-Indians." On the contrary, it is said that the women from Québec City perfectly resemble French women in their style, education and manners. In this respect, they greatly surpass the women of Montréal.[190]

As they formed their identity, the settlers adopted the combination of qualities and defects that the European imagination associated, half rightly and half wrongly, with Aboriginal influence. They began by adopting the name. At the beginning of colonization, the terms "Acadians", "Canadians" and "Americans" designated only the first inhabitants and excluded Europeans. By the second half of the seventeenth century, they included the "habitants", in other words, the children of immigrants born on this side of the Atlantic.[191] The proximity of Aboriginals was a determining factor in the construction of the Canadian identity. Aboriginal cultural transfers distinguished settlers from the French. In contrast with the French, Canadians and Acadians paddled to the *pays d'en haut*, hid behind trees to engage in guerrilla warfare, hunted and fished in the winter, made maple sugar, knew Aboriginals and traded, drank and smoked with them, but also feared, envied and talked about them.

In their works on plants, Michel Sarrazin, Sébastien Vaillant and Jean François Gaultier sometimes indicate the Latin or French name of a plant, as well as the Aboriginal or Canadian name. Thus, we find "*opulus canadensis*...in Indian and Canadian, *pain-mina* [in other words, pimbina]", and "*oxicocus*, in French *canneberg* and in Indian and Canadian, *atoca*... The Indians and Canadians call it *atoca*, which means 'good fruit'".

The ironwood is a beautiful, large tree that is called *charme* in French and can be found everywhere in Canada. Its wood is very hard and quite compact, which is why the Indians and Canadians call it ironwood. The latter use it for farm tools and various other things. The Indians make their bows out of this wood. They used it a lot in the olden days.[192]

Until now, we have talked about Aboriginal influence on Canadian values and identity in terms of ideas and imaginings. Should we take the documents literally and therefore find the sources of every feature of "Canadian character" in Aboriginal influences? Of course not. A more rigorous analysis shows that there were two series of factors that came into play concurrently. There were certainly cultural influences, for example, Aboriginal influence is undeniable, but they were also social influences, specifically, changes in the class structure in America. In addition to these two series of factors, there is also an illusion created by the point of view of the dominant classes at the time. We will look at these three aspects, beginning with the last one.

4. Illusion or Reality?

The themes of independence and insubordination, sloth and especially idleness were omnipresent at the time in the discourse of nobles concerning the lower classes. Likewise, the poor were considered to lack modesty and good manners, and to raise their children poorly by giving them too much freedom, which led to libertinage and insubordination later. Is it possible that in America old prejudices were simply repeated and adapted to the local colours of the winter and "redskins"? Quite certainly, but not only. While it is impossible to measure them, two kinds of factors, namely social and cultural, certainly affected the values of the colonial community and helped to form its personality.

The most important social factor was the scarcity of labour. Overall, this led to higher salaries, greater control over working and living conditions, and thus better working and living conditions. In America, it was as if lords and merchants were elbowing one another away at the gate to hire or sign contracts with tenant farmers, artisans, labourers and servants. In the countryside, the Canadian seigneurial system never managed to subjugate peasants as thoroughly as it did in France. Indeed, it was to mark their freedom from servitude that the citizens here called themselves "habitants" instead of "peasants."[193]

Moreover, in America, the distinctive signs of nobility were democratized. This began with the right to carry arms. While in France the fear of popular revolution prohibited the ruling classes from allowing peasants and poor people to carry arms, in America, the smaller gap between the upper and lower classes and the need to arm the habitants in case of war against the Iroquois made it necessary to lift the embargo. Moreover, to attract settlers, hunting and fishing rights were offered that had traditionally been reserved for the nobility in France. Canadians took to these activities with a passion. In his *Mémoires*, La Galissonnière deplored the fact that Canadians "cannot give up the lifestyle to which they have been accustomed since their childhood, namely hunting and fishing."[194]

Next, there was the language. In France, there were still many regional dialects and patois. What we now call French was spoken really only in the *Ile-de-France*, the court and surrounding area. However, it became the common tongue of immigrants to Canada from various regions in France. This occurred two centuries before it spread throughout the mother country. All observers noted that "people speak perfectly well here, without a bad accent."[195] Finally, the ownership of a horse, which was so useful for telling the difference between a noble and rogue in France, became widespread in the colony, and habitants bred many more than the administrators wished. In short, commoners riding horses, armed with guns and carrying purses could address lords in French and look them in the eyes. What insolence! The way that the land itself was divided into ranges of long thin lots allowed the settlers to use the river's resources, but also to escape government control easily. Here again, Father Charlevoix wrongly believed that even this could be explained by the "spirit of the Indians" and he again added that "it is breathed in with the air of their country."[196] Indeed, was the colony not on Aboriginal land, and was it not possible to leave the colony in any direction and go to an Aboriginal village? The colony did not live in a closed system. None of its borders could be shut. If there was too much pressure inside it, one could leave. This was also a constraint on social coercion.

Simply because they existed, Aboriginal societies changed the rules of the game for every European society with a settlement in America. Naturally, they provided refuge for dissidents, and they could inspire new attitudes and forms of behaviour. While it cannot be measured, their more flexible and less hierarchical social stratification, and less coercive decision-making processes, must have influenced Canadians, given the extent of their interactions. This was obvious from the very beginning of the colony. For example, the Urselines learned the local languages from the students in their convent, thereby transforming the pedagogical relationship. Moreover, with a language comes a culture. Without being "untrue to oneself", one has to adapt. Marie de l'Incarnation, who "noticed" parents' extraordinary love for their children, found that she could not keep them by force. She allowed her little Aboriginal students to circulate more freely. They were also allowed to wear their moccasins in the convent, where one was clearly more likely to freeze than in a tent. For the time, she took a rather soft approach. In today's terms, we would say that she was open to intercultural exchange.[197]

Overall, the strongest influence certainly came from cultural relativism and the distance from culture that results from the cohabitation of two societies with different structures. Societies were no longer able to see themselves as natural and eternal. Customs and institutions came to be seen as cultural variations and therefore products of history.

5. Institutions

We would be barking up the wrong tree if we tried to find a direct link between Aboriginal institutions and the reforms and revolutions that occurred in societies in America and Europe. Thus, despite the views of many authors as well as what many Iroquois believe and argue, it seems that the American constitution was not modelled after the much older constitution proclaimed by Deganawida and Hiawatha. Naturally, the fathers of the American constitution had gathered documentation available at the time on the constitutions of earlier republics since the time of Rome, including those of Venise, the United Provinces and the Iroquois, to which Franklin referred. However, the key principles on which they agreed belonged to European tradition and thought. The principles included majority rule rather than unanimity, the right to use coercive power to enforce laws rather than dissidents' right to withdraw if there was no consensus, democracy based on the citizenship of men rather than on a kinship system managed by women, and the concentration of military power rather than its dispersion among private clans. Finally, the constitution also provided for the establishment of a central government with power divided into three branches, namely, the legislature, executive and judiciary, rather than a single body as under the Iroquois constitution, which established the League Council and gave it the formal authority to exercise all three functions though the real power remained in the member villages and nations.[198] It would be even more extravagant to believe that the Iroquois were at the origin of the Russian Revolution, though one of Marxism's founders, Friedrich Engels, was greatly inspired by the work of the American anthropologist Lewis Henry Morgan when he wrote *The Origin of the Family, Private Property and the State*.[199] Lewis H. Morgan had spent several decades with the Iroquois, studying their kinship system.

It would also be mistaken to believe that in Europe criticism of institutions and reflection on society resulted only from outside influences. The debate over social change began in the Renaissance with the emergence of critical distance and the first steps towards desacralization of tradition. It was at work in the many peasant revolts, the Reform movement, utopist ideologies and later the democracy of colonial societies in New England. European society was thus the origin of doubt about and distance from itself, and the age of discovery helped to increase the critical distance. Of course, Europeans were ethnocentric, and when they went out to conquer the planet, they were armed with a complete ideological system that justified expansion and conquest. As unshakeable as it may have seemed, the system nonetheless contained weaknesses and ambiguities. First, it was based on a religion that, since it was not specific to a given ethnic group, claimed universality. Next, the tradition of questioning and analysis could be applied to colonialism, as can be seen in the Dominican Las Casas' great fight against the spirit of conquest. However, it has to be noted here that colonial expansion created even greater critical distance from the colonizers' own society as well as other societies. Indeed, simple contact with other societies alone was sufficient to introduce aspects of cultural relativism and turn culture into an object to some degree.[200] For example, let us look at the link between monarchy and patrilineal systems. Was it not at the heart of the political system in France? In Louisiana, French explorers encountered a society, that of the Natchez, in which a Sun Queen reigned with absolute power, which was transmitted from mother to daughter. They found the analogy with the Sun King, Louis XIV very intriguing and recognized as legitimate the ruler of their Natchez allies.[201] However, this did not revolutionize the French monarchy: France declared war on Austria in 1744 because a girl, Maria Theresa, had inherited the throne.

Though it was still widespread at the beginning of the seventeenth century, the idea that in America everything was backward, barbarous and reigned by the Devil did not concord with reality. The missionaries who learned an Iroquois or Algonquin language were enthusiastic about the experience. Soon it was admitted that cultural features are always relative. In the Jesuits' *Relations* dating from 1658, there is a superb chapter entitled "Of the diversity of the actions and approaches of the French and Europeans, and the Indians."[202] The author, Father Le Jeune, began by explaining that the senses perceive nothing in nature as beautiful or ugly, or good or bad in itself, and that what we sense is nothing but raw material that our birth and habits train us to love or hate. This is why what is sweet to some is bitter to others, and this is also the origin of the great differences between the senses of the Aboriginals and the French, which the missionary illustrates at great length. For example, the French liked the musky smell of the muskrat, but Aboriginals detested it. However, the latter anointed their heads and faces with oils that they considered precious but that smelled like rotten meat to the French. Aboriginals chanted when there was danger, in time of turmoil and when death was near, whereas the French maintained a deep silence in such frightening circumstances. One group preferred to smoke food, the other to salt it. The former wore little in winter, whereas the latter put on as many layers as they could. Painting one's face with various colours made it look like one was wearing a hideous mask in

Europe, but it was to be at one's best in America. In France, a beard made a man look distinguished, whereas it was considered very ugly in Canada. Their jewellery, various shapes of clothing and ways of dressing made it difficult for French women to do without chairs, but their allies prefer to squat. Next, Le Jeune considered social relations. A European artisan would agree to work before being paid, but an Aboriginal would demand an advance. A European had no trouble giving his name to anyone who asked, but an Aboriginal found the question sensitive and would ask someone else to identify him. The dowry paid by the father of the bride in France was contrasted with that paid by the father of the groom in some Aboriginal societies. Patrilocality (in which the man brings his new wife into his house) was frequently replaced by matrilocality in America.

After making these and many other comparisons, the author concluded that it was not so bad if instead of bequeathing one's property to one's children, one left it to one's sister's sons, or if instead of punishing and insulting people who get angry, one gave them presents to remove bad ideas from their minds. Europe had been drawn into such an excess of ceremonies and compliments that sincerity had been banished. In America, sincerity was naked. This led him to the extraordinary reflection that "In the end, it is better to live in a straightforward, truthful manner than to wander in wind and smoke, with offers of assistance that are full of lies." European civilization appeared false. Thus, everything could be different and Europe itself could have reason to envy America. Only God remained:

> The world is full of variety and inconsistency. We never find solid ground. If someone climbed up a tower high enough to see all the nations of the earth, he would not be able to say which are wrong and which are right, which are crazy and which are wise among the variety and strange patchwork. In fact, God is the only constant. He alone is unchanging and invariable. It is to this that we must hold fast in order to avoid change and instability.[203]

The expansion of the French-Aboriginal alliance to cover half of the continent confronted the French with very great cultural diversity, in which even time was a variable. In Illinois country, the Canadians found forests made up of fruit trees planted in rows, the remains of houses, and mounds that yielded jars and stone artifacts when excavated.[204] These were the remains of the great urban civilizations of the Mississippi. The general framework of the French-Aboriginal alliance, in which the partners were interdependent and had frequent interactions of all sorts, was conducive to the acquisition of knowledge about other cultures, as well as to interpenetration. Some real or imagined features of northeast Aboriginal societies were major inspirations for the European movement towards taking distance from and having a critical view of society, but relativism did not feed only on America. All around the world, Europeans encountered different societies. However, for reformers, the Chinese and Aztec empires could not provide a justification for the dream of a less hierarchical society governed in a less authoritarian manner, except in the form of a negative example. Thus, attention focused on less hierarchical societies. Already in the sixteenth century in France, Montaigne had read stories of travels in Brazil, and was reflecting on societies that he believed were guided by "natural law" and less corrupt. The English humanist Thomas More had read the accounts of the explorer Amerigo Vespucci on "free and classless societies" before he wrote *Utopia* in 1516. In the seventeenth and eighteenth centuries, writings by missionaries and explorers of New France were very influential in the debate over alternatives to the social order of the time. Indeed, the philosophers of the Enlightenment read the accounts by the Récollet, Sulpicien and especially Jesuit missionaries who had lived with the nations in America. They read *Moeurs des Sauvages Américains*, by J. F. Lafitau, who lived as a Jesuit priest and missionary at Sault St. Louis (Kahnawake) and is now considered one of the founders of anthropology. They also read the history of New France and letters by Father Charlevoix, who was a professor at the Jesuit college in Québec City. Charlevoix had questioned many travellers and missionaries about the peoples of America, and also travelled by canoe from Québec City to New Orleans. The philosophers also read works by lay writers, such as the accounts on Acadia by Marc Lescarbot and Nicolas Denys; the memoirs of the interpreter Nicolas Perrot, who had carried out several missions to nations in the Great Lakes area; *L'Histoire de la Nouvelle France* by Bacqueville de la Potherie, whose sources were missionaries, travellers and material in the archives of the Governor's palace; and finally the memoirs, dialogues and accounts of travels from Newfoundland to the Great Lakes by Baron de La Hontan. In the United States, the writer Thomas Paine, who took part in both the American and French revolutions, frequently used Aboriginal examples to denounce poverty and, especially, autocratic power.

Other philosophers used Aboriginal societies as illustrations, in the "bad Indian" paradigm, of the woes of primitiveness and barbarism. This can be seen in *Leviathan* by Thomas Hobbes and in Voltaire's work, though the latter used a Huron character to criticize *Ancien régime* society.[205] However, most reformers thought of Aboriginals as "noble savages." Now, did Aboriginal social organization inspire Western reformers or is this a biased or even false image? Perhaps Aboriginal (generally Huron) characters were simply borrowed to put a subversive discourse in their mouths when it would have been too risky for the author to assert it in a straightforward manner? Was the "noble savage" just a device? Yes and no! Social criticism and more generally thought about society in the seventeenth and eighteenth centuries was based less on fictional data than on selected information. For example, certain groups were chosen as typical of the various Aboriginal societies, and selected features were described outside of their cultural context. Finally, the criticism of European society that was put into the mouths of Aboriginal characters was more than just an artifice of style designed to circumvent censure. We know that the Aboriginals who came into contact with Western civilization were critical of many aspects of it. Let us try to untangle what was fictional from what was selective and what was real.

We will begin with Baron La Hontan's supposed conversations with a Huron named Adario, whom, it was claimed, had visited France and spent a lot of time with Canadians. They discussed religion, law, medicine, marriage and happiness.[206] La Hontan argued in favour of social order whereas Adario systematically criticized French society, and identified its fundamental vice in the idea of "yours and mine", in other words, private property. From it follow venality, cunning, injustice, disdain for the poor, dependency, etc. To these vices, Adario opposed the much more just and reasonable world of the Hurons.[207]

There is no doubt that the narrator was creating a fictional character to incarnate Enlightenment thought and systematically criticize society. It is also clear that much of the argumentation relied on the tradition and vocabulary of Enlightenment thinkers. This is the case for Adario's position in favour of merchants and, indirectly, against nobles.[208] Yet, the criticism was not completely fictional. La Hontan spent a lot of time with Aboriginals. He was able to speak Algonquin at least, and had long hunted with that nation. He had also been one of Frontenac's protégés, attended missions, and frequently eaten at his table, where Aboriginal chiefs were often invited, such as Kondiaronk, the Huron chief who was perhaps the inspiration for Adario.[209] Thus, La Hontan knew Aboriginals, talked with them, and very probably heard their criticisms of European society. We have already pointed out with respect to trade and religion the Aboriginals' criticisms of the behaviour and ways of the people from across the sea. Therefore, La Hontan did not invent everything. The archives contain many passages in which Aboriginal lifestyles and civilization are defended, as well as passages recording Aboriginal criticism of European civilization and resistance to colonialist ideology.

In 1632, Savignon became the first Huron to visit France. He was scandalized to see misery and wealth side by side, the omnipresence of gallows and especially the ways that children were punished.[210] Around 1680, the Recollet Chrestien Leclerc, who was acting as an interpreter, reported a Micmac chief's answer to gentlemen from Ile Percée, who had come to tell him that they wanted his people to live and build homes in the French style. At that time, the Micmacs and Europeans had been in contact for over a century for reasons that included fishing in the Gulf. The following is part of Leclerc's report.

> "I am very surprised that the French have so little intelligence, at least as appears in what you have just said on their behalf, as to try to persuade us to trade our poles, bark and cabins for houses made of stone and wood that are as high and tall, according to what they say, as trees!" He continued, "Why would men who are five or six feet tall need houses that are sixty or eighty feet high?…my brother, do you have as much skill and intelligence as the Indians, who carry their houses and cabins with them so that they can live where they please, independent of any lord whatsoever? You are neither as brave nor as strong as us because when you travel, you cannot carry your buildings and edifices on your shoulders… Indeed, my brother, if you do not yet know the real feelings that we Indians have for your country and all your nation, it is right that I teach you about them now. Thus, I beg you to believe that as miserable as we may appear to you, we consider ourselves much more happy than you because we are very content with the little we have, and believe, once again I beg you, that you are very mistaken if you think you can persuade

us that your country is better than ours, for if France is, as you say, a small Heaven on Earth, were you smart to leave it and why did you leave your wives, children, relatives and friends?...Now, tell me a little, if you are intelligent, who is wiser and happier: he who works all the time and only manages to gather what he needs to live after much labour, or he who rests pleasantly and finds what he needs through the agreeable activities of hunting and fishing." ...He finished his speech by saying that an Indian was able to live anywhere, and that he could say that he was the lord and king of his country because he lived where he wanted as long as he wanted, with all sorts of rights, such as to hunt and fish, without any worries, a thousand times happier in the woods and in his cabin than in a palace or at the tables of the greatest princes in the world.[211]

Here, we are very far from Adario's discourse in which he criticizes European social order in the hope of seeing reforms emerge. The Micmac speaker defends his own way of life as a hunter-gatherer, which in his time, given the Atlantic economy, had become archaic. The criticism targets less European civilization than sedentary civilization. If the circumstances had been appropriate, it could just as well have targeted the "high houses of stone and wood" of the Incas or Mayans. When a nomad in his own country judges a civilization that is spilling over its borders, his discourse does not differ from that of a peasant or artisan in the periphery facing Alexander the Great, Genghis Kahn or an Aztec emperor. Likewise, if it were addressed to the Natchez of Louisiana, the denunciation of class-based society would be just as relevant. The speaker is thus not a critic of modernity, but an Abel reproving a Cain.[212]

How did the Recollet missionary react to the discourse, which greatly surprised the gentlemen from Percé, despite the fact that it was delivered very patiently?

Whatever one might say about this line of reasoning, I have to admit that to me they looked incomparably happier than we, and that the lives of these barbarians could make one jealous if they had the education, enlightenment and same means of salvation that God has given to us to save ourselves, because he prefers us to so many poor infidels and thanks to his mercy. For, after all, their lives are not afflicted with a thousand woes like ours. They have neither responsibilities nor work such as judging and going to war, which we seek with so much ambition. They own nothing personally, and thus have no arguments or law suits about their inheritances from their parents. The titles of sergeant, lawyer, clerk, judge and president are unknown to them. Their ambition is limited to surprising and killing large numbers of beavers, moose, seals and other wild animals so as to take meat from them to feed themselves and skin to make clothing. They live in a very unified manner, and never quarrel or fight except when they are drunk. On the contrary, they help one another to meet their needs with great charity and no interest. Their cabins are always happy places. Their many children do not trouble them for, far from finding them a burden, the larger their family is, the happier and richer they consider themselves. They do not try to ensure that their children's riches are greater than those of their fathers, so they do not have the worries that we give ourselves when we try to amass goods and bring our children up in luxury. Thus among them nature has maintained conjugal love whole, which must never change between husband and wife because of a fear of having too many children, which in Europe is a burden considered too heavy, but that our Indians see as very honourable, advantageous and useful...[213]

Thus, the missionary takes this culture's side against that of the French, except, of course, with respect to religion. Note that this criticism of Whites by a White is based, in a negative form, on what the Aboriginals *were not*. It mythologizes the harmony: "nature has maintained conjugal love whole" to denounce modern egoism that reduces the birth rate.[214] However, it is clear that he could have delivered the same discourse from the point of view of a village of peasants in Brittany to denounce the mercantilism and values of Paris. His criticisms of Europe thus target more the modern values of his time and those who convey them. As he takes the Micmacs back to the lost paradise of the first days of the world, Father Leclerc associates civilization with artificiality, excess and egoism. Here, we see how resistance to colonialism was expressed by Aboriginals: they asserted their sovereignty, defended their lifestyle and customs, and criticized the invading society. In the minds of Europeans who lived with Aboriginals, the argument was placed in the evolutionary paradigm of the beginnings of humanity, when life was simple and happy in comparison with modern, civilized humanity, in which there is competition, hierarchy and sophisticated manners. Elsewhere, it was not missionaries but travellers and philosophers who recommended the "simpler" society out of empathy with the men and women with whom they spent their days. This point of view could also have been inspired by Christian values, which might have been seen as more authentic in a society where community values and sharing were more predominant than in a society governed by the state and market capitalism. The result of this was a reversal of the nature-culture paradigm. While the missionary continued to place his own society on the side of progress and modernity, he judged as artificial all of the symbols and forms of behaviour that characterized not only his original society in relation to others, but also all of the European ranking that divided the world between those with titles and money, and those without. "Natural" came to be contrasted with "artificial."

While we will not cite many more examples, we will note that there was a critical Aboriginal discourse, and that it was heard despite distortion and reinterpretation. Did the discourse target European civilization specifically? Generally not, since it focussed on the city, sedentary lifestyles, social classes and the accumulation of wealth, depending on the circumstances. La Hontan, Rousseau and their successors reinterpreted the remarks as criticism of the *Ancien régime* in order to promote modern society. This was not the point of view of Aboriginal discourse, though it could be seen as similar to and a confirmation of that of the common people in French colonial society, who were sometimes scandalized by the excessive wealth and arrogance of their superiors. Nicolas Perrot said that the allies considered the French to be "miserable valets and the most unhappy people in the world", and that French interpreters take the Aboriginals' side "because of the unjust leaning they generally have for them."[215] French Canadians, such as missionaries and interpreters, who lived with Aboriginals learned their languages and often adopted their hosts' point of view, at least in part. Overall, the situation in North America, where colonial power was dependant on the economic and military plans of its Aboriginal allies, helped to open ears and make the Other heard. Snatches of speeches and conversations thus filtered through, helping to undermine the infallibility of dogma and spread doubt. The certainty of belonging to the civilized world rather than to barbarism was thus shaken. Of course, this did not stop the empires from advancing, particularly since the movement was infused with the spirit of discovery and free inquiry, but it introduced doubt and social criticism. However, once again, we have to qualify our remarks. Doubt did not spring exclusively from contact with Aboriginals, as we have already pointed out. Study of classical antiquity and other factors also contributed. French dependency on Aboriginals was also not a condition *sine qua non*. Las Casas' criticism did not come out of a context in which the Spanish were dependent. We should remember, however, that interaction between the cultures was intense in the French-Aboriginal alliance, which allowed greater ethnographic knowledge to be gathered, as well as cultural relativism to emerge as a source of perplexity and fascination.

To the French administrators who believed that they were the rulers of America, Aboriginals always answered that they were the masters of their own home. For example, when he was travelling on the Ottawa River in 1650, Father Lalemant refused to pay the Algonquins from Allumette Island for right of way.

> Father Lalemant made them understand that since the French owned the land, they were not required to do that and persuaded them to take the small channel. Le Borgne (the chief of the village on the island) was soon notified of this, and sent his warriors… [and] had Father Lalement caught and hung from a tree by his arms, telling him that the French did not rule his country, that he alone was recognized as chief and that on his land all were under his power.[216]

Settlers believed they were superior, but they were faced with Aboriginals who were just as arrogant and considered them inferior and dependent.[217] In short, both sides were completely ethnocentric, and there was conflict. Europeans who thought that on the edges of civilization humans were like animals covered in fur found themselves confronted with peoples of Asian origin and very little body hair. Indeed, Aboriginals found facial hair ugly, and some said that the French were related to bears because they had beards. Given their esteem for the animal, attributing its totem to the French may have been an expression of approval.[218] Instead of meeting deformed beings, as had been anticipated, the French rubbed shoulders with Aboriginals who were taller than they and in better physical condition.[219] On top of it all, the supposed barbarians thought the French were savages. First, they found that they stank, and in this respect the feeling was mutual,[220] that their villages also stank and that they were dirty (here again there was reciprocity!). In 1645, an Iroquois diplomat visited Québec City, and said:

> Our country is full of fish, game and hunting; there are plenty of deer, elk and beavers everywhere. Leave…these smelly pigs that run here between your houses eating only garbage, and come feast on good meat with us; the way is clear, there is no longer any danger.[221]

Aboriginals who practiced cannibalism thought that French and English flesh tasted bad because it was too salty.[222] Aboriginals also considered many things that the French did barbarous. In addition to the ways that the French treated the poor, prisoners and children, which we have already mentioned, the Aboriginals disapproved of duels, the venality of those who went so far as to steal the furs and burial objects of the dead, the high murder rate, pettiness, the lack of hospitality, and the impoliteness of always cutting one another off when speaking.[223] Of course, Aboriginals also admired Europeans, but less for their values and behaviour than for their technology.

Many religious and lay French and Canadians were receptive to and shouldered the criticism, as did Father Louis Nicolas, who wrote that contrary to the customs of "our Indians", Europeans oppressed the poor "with violence that makes good people shudder."[224] However, others were less receptive and continued to see Aboriginals as barbarians. While it was not a rule and did not always occur, the long cohabitation promoted openness to the other and a critical regard on oneself. Enough authors listened to what Aboriginals had to say for their discourse to feed the challenge to the social order in Europe.

The interaction between the partners in the alliance led many to become interested in learning about Aboriginal societies, and the interest soon developed into fascination. Jesuits often reminded their European correspondents that they were not exaggerating. "Many people…believe that the *Relations du Canada* attribute more intelligence to Indians than they really have."[225] "Yet they are men," we are reminded, and belong not only to a "common humanity" but also to a model humanity in some respects. As the alliance network extended to the Mississippi and Prairies, the French met yet other nations, and thus learned about other aspects of Aboriginal societies, such as the couvade ritual in which men mimicked the pain of childbirth,[226] the relative importance of young girls and boys and the manners in which they were educated,[227] coming of age rituals, polygamy, divorce,[228] the homosexual practices of berdaches,[229] abortion and contraception.[230] The descriptions all emphasize freedom. If a society accepts such and such behaviour, which is prohibited in ours, why should we not do like them? Are our society's prohibitions natural or arbitrary? If they are natural, should they not be universal? And what about if they are not? Behind the descriptions we can see the shadows of debates. Some, such as La Hontan, emphasized the premarital sexual freedom in most Aboriginal societies, while others, such as Father Charlevoix, insisted rightly on the importance of sexual taboos after marriage (e.g., long periods of breastfeeding, and preparatory periods for hunting and war). The former highlighted the absence of constraints, the latter their necessity.[231] Interest in customs led to ethnography. Observers went beyond fascination with the exotic to describe the rules and components of kinship systems. They compared societies with one another, and sought constants.[232] This was an objective, scientific approach to societies and their rules of operation. Indeed, the purpose behind juxtaposing and comparing the customs of different American societies was to show that customs were neither natural nor eternal, and consequently that it was possible to question those of Europe. Such relativism was not the product of any Aboriginal society, each of which considered its way of doing things to be the right one. It was instead the product of comparison. Note that observers frequently described customs out of context. Let us go back to the example of premarital sexual freedom, which was frequent in many societies. It was used as an argument against the sexual ethics of the Catholic Church, but obscured the many post-marital taboos. In this case, it was the choice to describe certain forms of sexual behaviour, and not reality, that drove the arguments. The resulting biased picture was based less on false observations than on the way features were selected and reconstituted. In the end, European debates determined the issues raised as well as the development of new fields of interest. For example, consider the theme of Aboriginal religions. At the beginning of the seventeenth century, missionaries placed no importance on knowledge of religions deriving from Satan's work. The growth in agnosticism in Europe at the end of the seventeenth century, along with the idea that religion and God were invented by the Catholic church to subjugate people and amass wealth, led missionaries to try to demonstrate that religious feeling was universal and natural in man. While he was not an atheist but rather a deist, La Hontan attacked missionary activity and promoted religious freedom.[233] The debate was at the origin of major ethnographic writings on religion.

Descriptions of the legal system in America, which was based on the principle of compensating the victim rather than punishing the guilty, provided weapons for those who opposed the ordeal of the question chamber and the torture of prisoners in Europe. Indeed, in America, most disputes were resolved by the guilty person and his family giving gifts to the victim and his family. Here, as elsewhere, it would be a mistake to believe that Europeans "borrowed" criticism of torture from Aboriginals, and that otherwise they would not have been able to challenge it. What is certain, however, is that the Aboriginal example fed and reinforced a criticism that had already begun.[234]

Political systems also came under scrutiny, and here also the increase in information made it possible to consider alternatives.[235] The Aboriginal diplomatic tradition was an enigma for men and women who came from societies dominated by absolute power. They found it difficult to understand the operation of councils, the polite and respectful manner of debate and deliberation, consensus-making, the participation of women and, above all, despite the lack of coercion, the enormous moral authority of elected chiefs.

It was also an enigma how such societies could be managed when "subordination is not a rule among the Indians." This was true in the family and in military and political operations, but it did not lead to anarchy.[236] Thus, gradually, *through* description and questioning, Aboriginal political systems came to be seen as republics. Of course, the form of government had been known since the time of the Greeks, and philosophers had been arguing about it for centuries, but suddenly it was possible to see components of it at work in neighbouring societies. Even an eighteenth-century Jesuit like Father Charlevoix wrote that "independence does not eliminate subordination and often free and voluntary obedience is that on which one can count most surely."[237] While in truth this remark concerned warriors, the same author wrote the following with respect to politics:

> It is true that they request or suggest rather than command, and never exceed the limits of the small authority that they have. Thus, it is reason that governs and the government is all the more effective because obedience is more free and there is no fear of degeneration into tyranny.[238]

If Father Charlevoix and Baron La Hontan[239] were right that Aboriginal politics were based on reason instead of the arbitrariness and petty play of interests characteristic of European governments then one would be led to suggest that Aboriginal methods be adopted as political models. However, the description of Aboriginal reality was not accurate. The authors projected onto Aboriginals their dream of a society in which an elite enlightened by God and reason would govern for the greatest good of the society. This was not the nature of politics among Aboriginals, at least in sedentary societies. Rather, the councils sought to manage tension and conflict, and sought consensus through the expression of different points of view and interests. This was done in the name of not reason, but compliance with tradition.

In addition to freedom, another ideal was at work in the writings that came out of New France, where the French and Canadians studied Aboriginal societies: equality. Whereas it was thought that Aboriginals would be impressed by displays of European wealth, they were instead scandalized by the contrast between extreme poverty and extreme luxury.[240] This introduced some doubt in European minds about the race to obtain distinctions and the need for ostentation. The egalitarian living conditions of Aboriginal societies in northeastern America reinforced the doubt, which was also fed by a myth of perfect equality resulting from an under-evaluation of Aboriginal symbolic hierarchies. Generally, however, the less hierarchical nature of Aboriginal societies in the northeast challenged the extreme hierarchy in Europe. Father Charlevoix wrote that "inequality of wealth is not necessary for the maintenance of their society, and therefore they are less ambitious"[241] and less self-interested. He said that one only rarely encountered "those haughty persons who, full of their greatness and merit, almost imagine that they are a species apart, and disdain all other men, and who therefore never inspire trust or love in others."[242] In this country, Charlevoix continued, in a marvellous admission of virtually agnostic humanism,

> All men believe they are equally men, and what they value most in man is man. No difference in birth, no prerogative of rank that infringes on

the rights of individuals, no pre-eminence attached to merit that inspires pride and makes others feel their inferiority. There is perhaps less delicacy of sentiment than among us, but more directness, fewer manners and what can make them ambiguous, less soul-searching.[243]

Let us begin by pointing out the extraordinary lucidity of the most famous teacher at the Jesuit college. As he compared societies, he identified the reflexivity and self-consciousness ("soul-searching") at the heart of modernity.[244] Next, let us see how the encounter with Aboriginals fed European thought on the equality of men. This leads to questions about the sources of the social problems in Europe (the egalitarian societies of America did not give rise to theft[245]) and to question the *Ancien régime* society divided into three classes according to birth. However, the effect on Europe of the encounter with American cultures was even deeper, and contributed to a deritualization and deformalization of society. I say "contributed to" because once again there was no exclusive causal relation. Think of the Italian philosopher and historian Vico, who found in the ancient Greeks all that was necessary to deformalize society.

Europe was marked by quarrels over precedence, and unbridled quests for the distinctive signs of rank and status (clothing, decorations, architecture, titles and codes of etiquette), but suddenly all the objects of discord appeared contingent, artificial, superficial and even false, and contact with Aboriginal societies seemed to confirm this perception.

Next, the nature–culture relation was shaken. Whereas perfection had meant the maximum of refinement, suddenly there was the idea that a simple, hard life was much more true and authentic, and led to more happiness and freedom than the existences of the *superbes* who "never really enjoyed the pleasures in life."[246] Even Aboriginal food, which was considered more simple, was associated with what was thought to be the "superior quality of their blood."[247] Finally, in addition to being associated with the search for happiness and the simplicity of nature, the idea of equality was also linked with brotherhood since the absence of "defects" such as cupidity and envy, "which dilute the pleasure of life", favour mutual assistance and co-operation.[248] The observer was struck by the respect accorded to elders[249] and the primacy of sociability over hierarchies. Nicolas Perrot noted that "the greatest and wealthiest chiefs walk with the lowest commoners and even with children; they confer with them as with very wise people."[250] Here again, fascination wins Father Charlevoix, who follows La Hontan in a criticism of property as the ultimate cause of domination and inequality:

> But what is most surprising in men whose exteriors announce nothing but barbarism is that they deal with one another with a gentleness and consideration that are never seen among the people of the most civilized nations. This is probably partly because the "mine and yours", those cold words, as Saint Grégoire Pape says, that damp the fires of charity in our hearts while lighting those of envy, are not yet known among the Indians. One is no less charmed by the natural, unadorned gravity that infuses all of their

actions, and even most of their entertainment. Likewise for the honesty and deference that appears in their dealings with their equals, and young people's respect for older people, and the fact that one never sees them quarrelling or using indecent words or swearing, as is so common among us. This is all proof of well-formed minds and good self-control.[251]

The great Western ideals of freedom, equality and brotherhood, and the search for happiness in a more "natural" life thus result partially *but not exclusively* from the shock that resulted from observing Aboriginal societies and inserting the observations into a humanist framework of thought. The philosophers of the Enlightenment were very familiar with the Jesuits' writings, La Hontan's memoirs and works on New France in general. They viewed Charlevoix as the greatest historian of the New World, and the highest authority on primitive peoples.

Ethnographic writing on Aboriginals appeared along side that on peoples in the Antiquity and on other continents, which led, through comparisons, descriptions and analyses, to an objectivization of culture. All sorts of social models and organizations were juxtaposed, and attempts were made to describe and understand them. Everything became a subject for discussion, except for religion, as we have said. However, we should specify that the exception was in fact only *Christianity*, for rational explanations were sought for the religions of others. Father Charlevoix described shamanic rituals and explained the shaman's ambivalent discourse and self-fulfilling prophecies. He deconstructed the shaman's prestige and explained the social foundations of his power.[252] Indeed, he proved an excellent sociologist of the religions of others. All that remained was for the philosophers who read his work to apply the same rules to Christian religions by extending the rational-critical analysis to all areas of human activity, without exception.

While Europeans' ideas about Aboriginal cultures served as inspirations and models for reform movements, and even for the birth of the social sciences, we may wonder what kind of a fate the reformers and thinkers reserved for real Aboriginal societies. In fact, there was never any question of adopting the ways of the "model" societies. This was because certain positive features had been consciously selected, but no one wanted to endorse others, such as torture, cannibalism, superstition, vulnerability to the forces of nature (e.g., famines), the hard work of women who often carried very heavy loads, or even, to highlight an aspect that we consider progressive today, the participation of women in politics and diplomacy.[253]

Missionaries thought that the simple societies of the first period of humanity had to be preserved by creating *reductions*. Thus, thanks to segregation, religion could be used to "perfect what these people have of good and correct what is bad."[254] The fervour of nascent Christianity would be able to blossom sheltered from the perverse influences of bad Christians.[255]

Lay thinkers who were interested in Aboriginal societies were instead in favour of assimilating them into European colonial societies. Why? In the name of work. Did not the Aboriginals' "happiness and simplicity" go hand in hand with laziness and sloth? In other words, all the authors endorsed imperialism and held that Aboriginals had to be either segregated or assimilated.[256] Alone at the time among the authors published in French, La Hontan criticized imperialism. He did so implicitly in his dialogues with Adario, when he placed the two speakers on equal footing, and also explicitly when he noted that "the French have usurped the country that belonged to the [Aboriginals] since time immemorial."[257]

The parameters of the colonial policy with respect to Aboriginals were thus set in the seventeenth and eighteenth centuries, and remain in effect to this day. In order to implement them, the colonial societies used the intellectual distance acquired through ethnological discourse to manipulate the cultures, which at the same time fascinated them.[258] The accumulation of knowledge about Aboriginals thus contributed to knowledge of the Other and a questioning of one's own society. Greater distance was taken from society and culture but, as we have seen, objectivization of culture was not accompanied by questioning of colonial relationships.

Aboriginals were also led to adopt a degree of cultural relativism. Generally, an Aboriginal did not criticize his own culture in front of a White man. This was a fatal weakness. Aboriginals did not see themselves as separate from their culture or turn it into an object, while this is precisely what the Europeans did. Changes in Renaissance ways of thinking had already prepared them for this, and their societies were also the most exposed to cultural variations because they were at the centres of empires. Thus it was the Europeans more than any other people who manipulated cultures for their own purposes. Two contradictory processes were thus at work at the same time. Cultural relativism and objectivization of culture undermined the West while facilitating its domination.[259]

Clearly, not all of the Aboriginals' cultural transfers to the settlers have survived today. Many disappeared with traditional ways of life and folklore. However, the transfers were not confined to a single milieu. Some transfers affected the lower classes most, others religious communities, and others intellectual circles. The doctor-botanist Jean François Gaultier, who inventoried plants in New France as a correspondent for the Académie Royale des Sciences, considered that Canadians were "so little educated that they do not know what is in their country."[260] This was certainly an exaggeration, but it is clear that no settler knew as much about plants as Jean François Gaultier. Geography was also relevant, and borrowings were more numerous as settlers moved upstream and when they lived close to Aboriginal communities. However, we have learned to use the sources carefully, particularly those that discuss "Indianization." They all have the defect of equating Canadians with *coureurs de bois* who prefer adventure to hard work on the land. Thus, we must not lose sight of the fact that most settlers were habitant-farmers.

Finally, the things that were borrowed, including both material objects and ideas, were decontextualized, selected and reinterpreted. Over time, the borrowings have been assimilated and often carry no traces of their origins. This process is crystal-clear in botany. Father Louis Nicolas was a missionary and did fieldwork. He gathered all of his information directly from Aboriginals. Thus, his writings constantly mention his hosts and their knowledge. At the end of the seventeenth century and beginning of the eighteenth century, Michel Sarrazin compiled a collection of 800 plant specimens, and while he had contact with Aboriginals, his interactions with them were not as close as those of his Jesuit predecessor. Nevertheless, he described many species that were until then unknown to botanists, and he "kept the vulgar Canadian or Indian names that have been given to each of the trees." He kept a critical distance by withholding judgment on uses of plants so long as he had not used them. Finally, in Jean François Gaultier's *Description de plusieurs plantes du Canada*, which was published at the end of the French regime, there are as in Sarrazin's writings, many traces of borrowings from Aboriginals. The botanist and advocate of the development of knowledge later wrote a treatise entitled *De l'explication des vertus des plantes*, in which botanical sorting is replaced by medical classification. Under every illness we find appropriate plants, such as plants that prevent scurvy, act as antivenins or treat stomach or liver ailments. However, there is nothing in the text that explicitly identifies borrowings from Aboriginal nations, aside from the adjective "Indian" attached to "grass", "chicory" and "cucumber." Moreover, the whole classification is infused with the theory of humours, which was current in European medicine at the time.[261] In short, one might believe that there had been no Aboriginal contribution at all.

---

[1] I would like to thank Louise Dechêne, Andrée Fortin, Nicole Gagnon and Jean Jacques Simard for their comments. I would also like to express my gratitude to Hélène Bédard, who gathered the preliminary data.

[2] Department of Sociology, Laval University

[3] Attributed to Louis Nicolas (circa 1685), *Histoire naturelle des Indes*, Manuscript (Folio 100), Paris: Bibliothèque Nationale, fond français 24 at 255 [our translation].

[4] F. X. de Charlevoix, *Histoire et description générale de la Nouvelle-France avec le Journal historique d'un voyage fait par ordre du Roi dans l'Amérique septentrionale 1744*, Paris: Nyon Fils Librairie, Reprinted at Ottawa, Éditions Élysée, 1976, Vol. 1 at 532, Vol. 3 at 89; Nicolas Perrot, *Mémoire sur les moeurs, coutumes et religions des Sauvages de l'Amérique septentrionale,* Edition established by R. P. J. Tailhan, Montréal: Éditions Élysée, 1973 at 130–131.

[5] M. Giraud, *Le Métis canadien, son rôle dans l'histoire des provinces de l'Ouest*, Paris: Institut d'éthologie, 1984 at 379–383, 405–419.

[6] Marcel Trudel, *Atlas historique du Canada Français*, map 47, La région des Grands Lacs au dix-huitième siècle (1755 map by Bellin conserved in Public Archives of Canada), Québec City: Presses de l'Université Laval, 1961 at 178.

[7] Claude Charles Le Roy Bacqueville de la Potherie, *Histoire de l'Amérique septentrionale 1722*, Vol. 2, J. L. Nion and F. Didot at 178 [our translation].

[8] Joseph-François Lafitau, *Moeurs des sauvages américains*, Vol. 2, Paris: Maspéro, 1983 at 51–52.

[9] L. A. de Lom D'Arce, Baron de La Hontan, *Oeuvres complètes*, (Edition established by R. Ouellet and A. Beaulieu), Vol. 1, Montréal: Presses de l'Université de Montréal, 1990 at 645 [our translation].

[10] Bacqueville de la Potherie, *Supra* note 7, Vol. 2 at 260; *F. X. de Charlevoix, Vol.*

3, supra note 4 at 304, 393; *L. Nicolas, supra* note 3, Folio 8.

[11] F. Verreau, Reg. 037 No. 19, "Étymologies sauvages" in *Archives du Séminaire des missions étrangères (A. S. M. E.)*, Québec City.

[12] Charles A. Martijn, "Gepèg (Québec, un toponym d'origine micmaque)", (1991) XXI (3) *Recherches amérindiennes au Québec*, at 51–64; *F. X. de Charlevoix, Vol. 3, supra* note 4 at 70.

[13] Ludger Beauregard and Jean-Yves Dugas, *Dossier Toponymique de la région de Montréal*, Commission de toponymie, Government of Québec, 1980 at 29.

[14] Pierre Paré *et al.*, *La toponymie des Abénaquis*, Dossiers toponymiques, No. 20, Government of Québec, 1985 at 51–52.

[15] Henri Dorion with the collaboration of Christian Morissonneau, *Les noms des lieux et le contact des langues. Place Names and Language Contact*, Centre international de recherches sur le bilinguisme et groupe d'étude et de terminologie, Québec City: Presses de l'Université Laval, 1972 at 270–282.

[16] *F. X. de Charlevoix, Vol. 4, supra* note 4 at 195.

[17] Marguerite Vincent Tehariolina, *La Nation Huronne. Son histoire, sa culture, son esprit*, Québec City: Éditions du Pélican, 1984 at 138–139.

[18] Donald B. Smith, *Le Sauvage pendant la période héroïque de la Nouvelle-France (1534–1663) d'après les historiens canadiens-français des XIXe et XXe siècles*, Montréal: Hurburtise HMH, Cahiers du Québec (Collection Cultures amérindiennes), Ottawa, 1974; National Museums of Canada, National Museum of Man, 1979 at 82; Jean Poirier, "Regards sur les noms de lieux", *Études et recherches toponymiques 3*, Commission de toponymie, Government of Québec, 1982 at 60–62, 123–128.

[19] Quoted in *H. Dorion, supra* note 15 at 274 [our translation]; see also D. B. Smith, *Ibid.* at 82.

[20] Pierre Boucher, *Histoire véritable et naturelle des moeurs et productions du Pays de la Nouvelle-France vulgairement dit le Canada (1664)*, Paris: Florentin Lambert, Reprinted by the Société historique de Boucherville, 1964 at 146.

[21] *F. X. de Charlevoix, Vol. 3, supra* note 4 at 173.

[22] *Ibid.*, Vol. 3 at 193.

[23] *Ibid.*, Vol. 2 at 134; *Ibid.*, Vol. 3 at 172–173; *Baron de La Hontan, supra* note 9 at 294–295; Ivanhoë Caron, *Journal de l'expédition du chevalier de Troyes en 1686*, Beauceville: L'Éclaireur, 1918 at 51.

[24] Pehr Kalm, *Voyage de Pehr Kalm au Canada in 1749*, Translated and annotated by Jacques Rousseau, Guy Béthune and Pierre Morisset, Montréal: Pierre Tisseyre, 1977, Folio 916–917.

[25] Jean-François Gaultier, based on notes by Michel Sarrazin annotated by Sébastien Vaillant, *Catalogue des plantes du Canada*, after 1707, Part Two, *Les Arbres*, Fonds privés 91, Archives Nationales du Québec (A. N. Q.) at 11–12; Jean-François Gaultier, *Description de plusieurs plantes du Canada* (1749), Fonds privés 91, Archives Nationales du Québec at 143–144.

[26] Louis Franquet, *Voyages et mémoires sur le Canada*, Montréal: Édition Élysée, 1974 at 17.

[27] *F. X. de Charlevoix, supra* note 4, Vol. 3 at 193.

[28] Robert Lionel Séguin, *La civilisation traditionnelle de l'habitant aux XVIIe et XVIIIe siècles*, Montréal: Fidès, 1973 at 581–587; *Pehr Kalm, supra* note 24, Folio

840, 916, 933; *J. F. Gaultier, Description, supra* note 25 at 574, and "Mémoire sur quelques espèces de pin" in *Catalogue, supra* note 25.

[29] *Monumenta Novae Franciae (M. N. F.),* Lucien Campeau S. I., Ed., Québec City: Presses de l'Université Laval, 1967 ss, in APUD Roma, "Monumenta Historica Soc. IICSU", 4 volumes published, others forthcoming [our translation].

[30] Bernard Audet, *Le costume paysan dans la région de Québec au XVIIe siècle,* Montréal: Leméac, 1980 at 60.

[31] *Louis Nicolas, supra* note 3, Folio 82.

[32] *Baron de La Hontan, supra* note 9 at 324–329; Gabriel Théodat Sagard, *Histoire du Canada et voyages,* Vol. 1, Paris: Librairie Toss, 1866 at 299; *R. L. Séguin, supra* note 9 at 587.

[33] *G. T. Sagard, supra* note 32, Vol. 1 at 248–249; *Archives du Séminaire des missions étrangères* (F. Verreau), Reg. 037, Québec City.

[34] Brehant de Galinée and Dollier de Casson, *Ce qui s'est passé de plus remarquable dans le voyage de MM. Dollier et Galinée (1669–1670),* in James H. Coyne, Ed., *Exploration on the Great Lakes 1669–1670,* Ontario Historical Society Papers and Records, Vol. IV, Part I, Toronto, 1903 at 12 [our translation].

[35] Claude Le Beau, *Aventure du Sr. C. Le Beau, avocat en parlement ou voyage curieux et nouveau parmi les sauvages de l'Amérique septentrionale,* Amsterdam: Herman Hytwerf, 1738, Reprinted at New York: Johnson Reprint, 1966, Vol. 1, pp 64–65 [our translation].

[36] J. C. B., *Voyage au Canada fait depuis l'An 1751 à 1761,* Paris: Aubier-Montagne, 1978 at 81; *Pehr Kalm, supra* note 24, Folio 760.

[37] J. C. B., *Ibid.* at 80–83.

[38] *Pehr Kalm, supra* note 24, Folio 929 [our translation].

[39] *Ibid.,* Folio 812.

[40] *Rapport de l'archiviste de la Province de Québec* (R. A. P. Q.) 1923–1924, Québec City: King's Printer at 57; Mémoire Bougainville.

[41] M. A. Bluteau, J. P. Charland and M. Thivierge, *Les cordonniers artisans du cuir,* Montréal: Boréal Express, 1980 at 38–39; *Bernard Audet, supra* note 30 at 56.

[42] *Pehr Kalm, supra* note 24, Folio 929; *Claude Le Beau, supra* note 35, Vol. 1 at 64–65 [our translation].

[43] Louise Dechêne, personal correspondence; *R. A. P. Q. 1923–1924, supra* note 40 at 29: Mémoire sur le Canada 1759.

[44] *L. Franquet, supra* note 26 at 131.

[45] *Pehr Kalm, supra* note 24, Folio 812 [our translation].

[46] Sophie Laurence Lamontagne, *L'hiver dans la culture québécoise XVIIe-XIXe siècles,* Québec City: Institut de recherche sur la culture, 1983 at 58–60, 73.

[47] Marius Barbeau, *Ceinture fléchée,* Montréal: Éditions de l'Étincelle, 1973 at 16–17, 28–36, 55; Cyril Simard, *Artisanat québécois,* Vol. 1, Montréal: Éditions de l'homme, 1975 at 194; S. A. Freed, *La grande aventure des Indiens d'Amérique du Nord,* Montréal: Sélection du Reader's Digest, 1983 at 46.

[48] Philippe Aubert De Gaspé, *Les Anciens Canadiens,* Montréal: Beauchemin, 1931 at 15.

[49] *R. L. Séguin, supra* note 28 at 6–7.

[50] *Louis Nicolas, supra* note 3, Folio 130, 163; *P. Kalm, supra* note 24, Folio 748,

833.

[51] Louis-Paul Martin, *Histoire de la chasse au Québec*, Montréal: Boréal Express, 1980 at 41.

[52] Pierre-Georges Roy, *Ordonnances, commissions, [...] des gouverneurs et indendants de Nouvelle-France, 1639-1706,* Archives de la Province de Québec, Vol. 1, Beauceville, l'Eclaireur, 1924 at 104–105.

[53] *Baron de La Hontan*, *supra* note 9 at 330–340, 357–361, 370, 375–383.

[54] *L. Nicolas*, *supra* note 3 at 148.

[55] *Pehr Kalm*, *supra* note 24, Folio 749.

[56] *F. X. de Charlevoix, Vol. 3, supra* note 4 at 153.

[57] *Ibid.*, Vol 3. at 94, 103–107.

[58] *J. C. B., supra* note 36 at 75.

[59] Reuben G. J. R. Thwaites, Ed., *The Jesuit Relations and Allied Documents*, Cleveland: The Burrows Brothers Co., 1869–1901, Vol. 6 at 308–310; *L. Nicolas*, *supra* note 3 at 155.

[60] C11A-122, A. P. C., Archives coloniales, Folio 290–291 [our translation].

[61] Marcel Moussette, *La pêche sur le Saint-Laurent, Répertoire des méthodes et des engins de capture*, Montréal: Boréal Express, 1979 at 126–151.

[62] *Relations des Jésuites*, Reprint of the 1856 edition, Montréal: Éditions du Jour, 1972, Vol. 5 at 4.

[63] *Pierre Boucher*, *supra* note 20 at 16 [our translation].

[64] Willian L. Stone, *Letters of Brunswick and Hessian officers during the American Revolution* at 36, 63–64 in *P. L. Martin*, *supra* note 51 at 53 [our translation].

[65] *Pehr Kalm*, *supra* note 24, Folio 749 [our translation].

[66] *F. X. Charlevoix, Vol. 3, supra* note 4 at 365; C11A, Vol. 33, Folio 213R, Mémoire Catalogne 1712 [our translation].

[67] M. Le Page Du Pratz, *The History of Louisiana*, London: T. Beckett, 1774, Translated from French, republished at Baton Rouge: Claitor's Publishing Division, 1972 at 44–53, 234.

[68] C11A, Vol. 65, Folio 140; Vol. 70, Folio 113; Vol. 72, Folio 63, quoted in *Dictionnaire biographique du Canada* (D. B. C.), Vol. 3 at 338–339.

[69] *Archives nationales du Québec*, P 195/1, Diary of J. L. Normandin.

[70] J. F. Gaultier, *Catalogue, Supra* note 25, Part One, *Histoire des plantes du Canada*, Fonds privés 91, *Archives Nationales du Québec* at 57, 76–79, 91, 135–136, 140–141, 144–145, 165–166; Part Two, *Les Arbres* "Alkiminis févier" [our translation]. See also his *Description, supra* note 25 at 443; Brother Marie-Victorin, *Flore laurentienne*, Montréal: Presses de l'Université de Montréal, 1964 at 214.

[71] *Pehr Kalm*, *supra* note 24, Folio 898.

[72] *Ibid.*, Folio 726.

[73] *Ibid.*, Folio 804 [our translation].

[74] *Ibid.*, Folio 801–804.

[75] *J. F. Gaultier, Catalogue, Sspra* note 25, Vol 1 at 5, 155, 173; Vol 2 angelica, citronnier, carotte [our translation].

[76] *R. A. P. Q.* 1923–1924, *Supra* note 40 at 56; Bougainville, *Mémoire*, 1758.

[77] Jack Weatherford, *Indian Givers: How the Indians of the Americas Transformed the World*, New York: Crown Publishers, 1988 at 178–179.

[78] *J. F. Gaultier, Catalogue, supra* note 25, Vol. 1 at 76–79, 140–141; Vol. 2: Bois

rouge, cornus, févier; and *Description, supra* note 25 at 167, 263.

[79] *J. F. Gaultier, supra* note 25, Vol. 1 at 130; Vol. 2: *Thymeliaca*; *Description, supra* note 25 at 463.

[80] *F. X. de Charlevoix, supra* note 4, Vol. 3 at 163, 454; *Brother Marie Victorin, supra* note 70 at 230, 319, 322, 391, 412–413, 438, 444, 518–520, 592, 656–567; Bernard Assiniwi, *La médecine des Indiens d'Amérique*, Montréal: Guérin Littérature (*Nature et Mystères* collection), 1988 at 13–19; *J. F. Gaultier, Catalogue, supra* note 25, Vol. 2: *aralia.*

[81] Barrie Kavasch, *Medicinal Plants in American Indian Life,* Pamphlet accompanying the exhibition *Native Harvest: Plants in American Indian Life*, (Washington: Smithsonian Institution Traveling Exhibition Services, 1984), see the Introduction; Susan Hamilton and Ritchie Marion, "Les contributions autochtones au monde moderne" in *Oracle*, Ottawa: National Museum of Man, National Museums of Canada at 3.

[82] *L. Nicolas, supra* note 3, Folio 30; *P. Boucher, supra* note 20 at 49; *Pehr Kalm, supra* note 24, Folio 768.

[83] "Lettre de Mère Duplessis à Féret", 1733, *M. N. F., supra* note 29, Vol. 6 at 114.

[84] *Brother Marie Victorin, supra* note 70 at 146 [our translation].

[85] *J. F. Gaultier, Catalogue, supra* note 25, Vol. 2: *Baume; Description, supra* note 25 at 13–16; *Brother Marie Victorin, Ibid.* at 143–144.

[86] *Pehr Kalm, supra* note 24, Folio 607, 707, 718, 819; *F. X. de Charlevoix, supra* note 4, Vol. 3 at 316; *Louis Franquet, supra* note 26 at 212; *Mère Duplessis à Féret*, 1733, *M. N. F., supra* note 29, Vol. 4 at 120; *J. F. Gaultier, Catalogue, Ibid.*, Vol. 2: *araliastrum.*

[87] *Pehr Kalm, Ibid.*, Folio 707.

[88] *A. N. Q.* at 91/1; *J. F. Gaultier, supra* note 25, Vol. 2 at 73, 217 [our translation]; *Journal étranger*, "Mémoire sur les coutumes et usages des cinq nations iroquoises du Canada (a) de leurs gouvernements" C11A-125, April 17, 1762.

[89] *Pehr Kalm, supra* note 24, Folio 897.

[90] C11A-122, Folio 311, *Mémoire sur la chasse et la pêche*; "Mère M. A. Duplessis à Féret", Dieppe *M. N. F., supra* note 29, Vol. 4 at 119–122, 375; *L. Nicolas, supra* note 3, Folio 103–105.

[91] *J. C. B., supra* note 36 at 126; *Pehr Kalm, supra* note 24, Folio 604.

[92] *Relations des Jésuites, (R. J.), supra* note 62, at 30–31.

[93] *Baron de La Hontan, supra* note 9 at 690–691.

[94] *Le Page du Pratz, supra* note 67 at 44; *F. X. de Charlevoix, supra* note 4, Vol. 3 at 365; *P. Kalm, supra* note 24, Folio 739; *Journal Étranger*, "Suite de Mémoire sur les coutumes et usages des cinq Nations Iroquoises du Canada" C11A-125, May 1762.

[95] Claire Gourdeau, *Marie de l'Incarnation et ses pensionnaires amérindiennes (1632–1672): transferts culturels et acculturation*, Master's thesis in History (draft version), Laval University, Québec City, 1992 at 80.

[96] *P. Boucher, supra* note 20 at 54–55.

[97] Jean Provencher, *C'était l'été: La vie rurale traditionnelle dans la vallée du St-Laurent*, Montréal: Boréal Express, 1982 at 151.

[98] *Ibid.* at 152.

[99] Isaac Weld, *Voyage au Canada dans les années 1795, 1796 et 1797*, Volume 2, Paris: Imprimerie du Munier, P. 172; see also *J. F. Gaultier, Catalogue, supra* note 25, Vol. 2: *Betula*.

[100] "Mère M. A. Duplessis à Féret", *M. N. F.*, Vol 4 at 246–247; and *J. Provencher, supra* note 97 at 148.

[101] *I. Weld, supra* note 99, Vol. 3 at 103; *L. Nicolas, supra* note 3, Folio 39; *P. Kalm, supra* note 24, Folio 614–625; *J. Weatherford, supra* note 77, 1988 at 45.

[102] *Jean Provencher, supra* note 97 at 152–153 and *C'était l'hiver: la vie traditionnelle dans la valée du Saint-Laurent*, Montréal: Boréal Express, 1986 at 31; Paul-Louis Martin, "Chaises et chaisiers québécois", *Ethnologie québécoise 1*, Cahiers du Québec 7, 1972 at 149–150.

[103] *J. F. Gaultier, Catalogue, supra* note 25, Vol. 2: *Gale americana*, bois de plomb; *Brother Marie-Victorin, supra* note 70 at 362–363.

[104] *L. Nicolas, supra* note 3, Folio 43.

[105] *Ibid.*, Folio 39 [our translation].

[106] *Ibid.*, Folio 36 [our translation].

[107] *F. X. de Charlevoix, supra* note 4, Vol. 3 at 122 [our translation].

[108] J. F. Pendergast, *The Origin of Maple Sugar*, National Museum of Natural Sciences, Syllogeus No. 36, Ottawa, 1982 at 8.

[109] Serge Saint-Pierre and Muriel Pouliot, *Cueillettes d'hier et d'Aujourd'hui*, under the direction of Marcel Moussette for the association of French-Canadian civilization research centres, Québec City: Laval University (CELAT research reports and theses), 1990 at 12.

[110] *P. Kalm, supra* note 24, Folio 873; *J. F. Gaultier, Catalogue, supra* note 25, Vol. 1 at 158; Vol. 2: *Acer, syrop d'érable*.

[111] *L. Nicolas, supra* note 3, Folio 22.

[112] Marie de l'Incarnation, *Correspondance*, Solesme, Abbaye de Solesme, 1971 at 833; *J. F. Gaultier, Catalogue, supra* note 25, Vol. 1 at 125–126, 143–144; Vol. 2: *Aralia, Azarum; Description, supra* note 25 at 77–79, 371, 391; Marthe Faribault, "L'Apios tubéreux d'Amérique: histoires de mots," in *Recherches amérindiennes au Québec*, Vol. XXI, No. 3, Fall 1991 at 65–69.

[113] *J. F. Gaultier, Catalogue, supra* note 25, Vol. 2: *Quercus; Description, supra* note 25 at 406.

[114] *Susan Hamilton and Marion Ritchie, supra* note 81 at 2.

[115] *Lepage Du Pratz, supra* note 67 at 202–206.

[116] *P. Kalm, supra* note 24, Folio 962; Louise Dechêne, *Habitants et marchands de Montréal au XVIIe siècle*, Paris and Montréal: Plon, 1974 at 301.

[117] *P. Kalm, supra* note 24, Folio 875–876.

[118] *"Lettre de Mère M. A. Duplessis de Saint-Hélène à Mme Hecquet, 30 octobre 1751", M. N. F., Vol. 4, January 1, 1929 at 40; F. X. de Charlevoix, supra note 4, Vol. 3 at 331.*

[119] *P. Boucher, supra* note 20 at 88; *P. Kalm, supra* note 24, Folio 703, 707, 833; *Baron de La Hontan, supra* note 9 at 369, 596, 602–603; C11A-33, Folio 213R – Mémoire Catalogne; *J. F. Gaultier, Description, supra* note 25 at 231.

[120] Louise Dechêne, personal communication.

[121] *Marie de l'Incarnation, supra* note 112 at 113; Anonymous, *Les Ursulines de Québec, depuis leur établissement jusqu'à nos jours*, Vol. 1, Québec City, 1863

at 270.

[122] C11A-33, Folio 220R – *Mémoire Catalogne*; P. Kalm, *Supra* note 24, Folio 875–876.

[123] P. Kalm, *Ibid.*, Folio 658 [our translation]; François Rousseau, *L'Oeuvre de chère en Nouvelle-France. Le régime des malades à l'Hôtel-Dieu de Québec*, Québec City: Presses de l'Université Laval (Cahiers d'histoire de l'Université Laval, No. 29), 1983 at 389; *J. F. Gaultier, Catalogue, supra* note 25, Vol. 2: *Avena*.

[124] P. Kalm, *supra* note 24, Folio 613, 876, 878 [our translation].

[125] P. Kalm, *Ibid.*, Folio 934; C11A-122, Folio 314 – *Mémoire sur la chasse*.

[126] R. L. Séguin, *supra* note 28 at 166.

[127] J. F. Lafitau, *supra* note 8, Vol. 1 at 229; Jean Provencher, *C'était l'hiver*, *Supra* note 97 at 47; Jérémie Noël, "Relation du détroit de la Baie d'Hudson", in P. Carle and J. L. Minel, *L'homme et l'hiver en Nouvelle France*, Cahiers du Québec, Hurtubise HMH (coll. Documents d'histoire), 1972 at 79.

[128] J. F. Gaultier, Catalogue, *supra* note 25, Vol. 2: *Cerasus*.

[129] P. Kalm, *supra* note 24, Folio 787, 833, 940.

[130] *Ibid.*, Folio 940, 787.

[131] Georges Fortin, personal communication.

[132] Letitia Humphreys Wrenshall, "Algonkian Words in American English: A Study in the Contact of the White Man and the Indian" in *The Journal of American Folklore*, Vol. XV, 1902 at 240.

[133] Jean Duberger, personal communication.

[134] *Marie de l'Incarnation, supra* note 112 at 962–963.

[135] *Bacqueville de la Potherie, supra* note 7, Vol. 4 at 252–253; *F. X. de Charlevoix, supra* note 4, Vol. 2 at 283; C11A-19, Folio 117; Gilles Havard, "La grande paix de Montréal de 1701: les voies de la diplomatie franco-amérindienne", Montréal: *Recherches amérindiennes du Québec No. 8* (collection: Signes des Amériques), 1992 at 152.

[136] P. Kalm, *supra* note 24, Folio 896.

[137] Jean-Claude Dupont, *Légendes amérindiennes*, St. Foy: Éditions Dupont, 1992 at 7.

[138] *Ibid.* at 8.

[139] Jean-Claude Dupont, *Légendes du Saint-Laurent II, de Montréal à Baie Saint-Paul*, St. Foy: Éditions Dupont, 1986 at 49.

[140] *Ibid.* at 33.

[141] *Ibid.* at 11.

[142] *Ibid.* at 29.

[143] Guildo Rousseau, Ed., *The Iroquoise, A North american Legend/L'Iroquoise, une légende nord-américaine*, Sherbrooke, Québec City: Éditions Naaman, 1984 at 37–77.

[144] Madeleine Béland, *Chansons de voyageurs, coureurs de bois forestiers*, Québec City: Presses de l'Université Laval, 1982 at 137–142, 315, 406–407.

[145] Roger Paradis, "Lisa, The Ballad of a Young Indian Slave", University of Maine, a paper presented on the occasion of the *Nineteenth Conference of the International Folklore Commission,* May 3–6, 1986, Freiburg, West Germany, 1989.

[146] Abbey Charles Émile Gadbois, *La bonne chanson*, St. Hyacinthe: Éditions de

la bonne chanson, 1939–1951, Vol. 1 at 7.

[147] Andrée Gendreau and Guy Rocher, personal communication.

[148] *Bacqueville de la Potherie, supra* note 7, Vol. 2 at 126–127.

[149] *Ibid.*, Vol. 3 at 244–246.

[150] *R. J., supra* note 62, Vol. 48 at 188.

[151] *L. Nicolas, supra* note 3, folio 117–118; *N. Y. C. D.*, E. B. O'Callaghan, Ed., *Documents Relative to the Colonial History of the State of New York 1856–1877*, Vol. 4, Albany: A. Weed at 206; *Rapport de l'archiviste de la Province de Québec (R. A. P. Q.)*, Nelson Memorial 1696, Parscau du Plessix, Québec City: King's Printer, 1928–1929 at 221–223.

[152] Papiers La Pause, *R. A. P. Q.*, 1933–1934 at 212; C11A-15, Folio 124R – Champigny au Ministre, October 1697.

[153] C11A-125, force des Iroquois [our translation]; F. X. de Charlevoix, *Supra* note 4, Vol. 2 at 353.

[154] *Bacqueville de la Potherie, supra*, Vol. 1 at 25, 29–35, 45, 65, 173; *F. X. de Charlevoix, supra* note 4, Vol. 2 at 74, 86, 134, 165, 166, 181, 189–191, 336; Vol. 3 at 87.

[155] *P. Kalm, supra* note 24, Folio 665, 689, 771, 776, 833, 838, 852, 858, 860, 904, 927, 941.

[156] Mémoire 1759, *R. A. P. Q., supra* note 40, 1923–1924 at 58.

[157] C11A-13, Folio 328–361.

[158] *L. Franquet, supra* note 26 at 193 [our translation].

[159] Louise Dechêne, personal communication.

[160] *R. A. P. Q., supra* note 40, 1928–1929 at 221 [our translation].

[161] *F. X. de Charlevoix, supra* note 4, Vol. 3 at 80 [our translation].

[162] *R. A. P. Q., supra* note 40, 1923–1924 at 28 [our translation]. Discussion with Louise Dechêne.

[163] C11A-22, Folio 381V; *F. X. Charlevoix, supra* note 4, Vol. 2 at 60.

[164] M. B. Anderson, "Relation of the Discovery of the Mississippi River (1898)," 19–21, in George Sabo III, "How did they see it? Interpreting Native American Views of Contact with Europeans", paper presented at the *American Society for Ethnohistory Annual Meeting*, Nov. 11–13, 1988, Williamsburg, Virginia, Department of Anthropology, University of Arkansas, 1988 at 3.

[165] *Bacqueville de la Potherie, supra* note 7, Vol. 3 at 135; *P. Kalm, supra* note 24, Folio 952; *J. F. Lafitau, supra* note 8, Vol. 2 at 98.

[166] *J. C. B., supra* note 36 at 110 [our translation].

[167] James Axtell, *The Invasion Within. The Contest of Cultures in Colonial North America*, New York: Oxford University Press, 1985 at 297–299.

[168] *Bacqueville de la Potherie, supra* note 7, Vol. 2 at 171–173, 270, 282.

[169] C11A-33, Folio 135V – Bégon au ministre, November 8, 1712.

[170] *F. X. Charlevoix, supra* note 4, Vol. 3 at 322 [our translation].

[171] *Ibid.*, Vol. 3 at 322; see also Vol. 1 at 344, 497.

[172] *P. Kalm, supra* note 24, Folio 726–727; see also *Bacqueville de la Potherie, supra* note 7, Vol. 4 at 150–151.

[173] *J. Axtell, supra* note 167 at 303.

[174] C11A-33, Folio 90–92V [our translation].

[175] *Ibid.,* [our translation].

[176] *Ibid.,* [our translation].

[177] C11A-122, Folio 302 [our translation].

[178] C11A-11, Folio 262R.

[179] C11A-11, Folio 262R, *Mémoire Champigny* 1691; Louise Dechêne, Ed., "Vauban à Maurepas 7 janvier 1699" in *La correspondance de Vauban relative au Canada,* Québec City: Ministère des Affaires Culturelles, 1968 at 29.

[180] C11A-11, Folio 262R, *Mémoire Champigny* 1691.

[181] *F. X. de Charlevoix, supra* note 4, Vol. 3 at 89; C11A-122, Folio 312R, *Mémoire Raudot,* around 1720.

[182] Letter R, No. 77, *Sauvages,* November 1705, A. S. Q. [our translation].

[183] *R. J., supra* note 62, Vol. 2, (1639) at 55.

[184] "Lettre de Jacques Raudot à Pontchartrain", Québec City, November 10, 1707, *R. A. P. Q. supra* note 40, 1940–1941 at 406; *F. X. de Charlevoix, supra* note 4, Vol. 3 at 174–175, 303, 306.

[185] "Denonville au Ministre, 10 novembre 1686", C11A-8, Folio 146R; C11A-7, Folio 90–92; see also *Journal étranger, supra* note 94, "Iroquois", May 1762; *Marie de l'Incarnation, supra* note 112 at 735, 802, 202, 164, 139–140.

[186] *Bacqueville de la Potherie, supra* note 7, Vol. 1 at 26.

[187] *F. X. de Charlevoix, supra* note 4, Vol. 3 at 79–80, 138, 173 [our translation]; see also *R. A. P. Q. supra* note 40, 1923–1924, Folio 29, *Mémoire sur le Canada* by Bougainville, 1759.

[188] *F. X. de Charlevoix, supra* note 4, Vol. 3 at 80, 172–175; *Bacqueville de la Potherie, supra* note 7, Vol. 1, Introduction and at 26, 311, 365–367.

[189] *F. X. de Charlevoix, Ibid.,* Vol. 3 at 173.

[190] *P. Kalm, supra* note 24, Folio 689; see also J. C. B., *Supra* note 36 at 43.

[191] *L. Nicolas, supra* note 3 at 112; *F. X. de Charlevoix, supra* note 4, Vol. 1 at 149; *Bacqueville de la Potherie, supra* note 7, Vol. 1 at 198.

[192] *J. F. Gaulthier, Catalogue, supra* note 25, Vol. 1 at 76–79; Vol. 2, *opulus, oxicocus,* bois dur; see also *Ibid.,* Mémoire sur quelques espèces de pins, *citrullus, rubus, toxicodendrum, lilium; J. F. Gaulthier, Description, supra* note 25 at 2, 29, 152, 231, 395, 491, 498.

[193] *R. A. P. Q. supra* note 40, 1923–1924, Folio 58, *Mémoire sur l'état de la Nouvelle-France* de Bougainville, 1757; *F. X. de Charlevoix, supra* note 4, Vol. 1 at 371; *Marie de l'Incarnation, supra* note 112 at 219.

[194] Marquis La Galissonnière, "Mémoires sur les colonies de la France dans l'Amérique septentrionale", *Bulletin de Recherches Historiques, (B. R. H.) 1895–1925,* Vol. XXXVI, May 1930, No. 5, Beauceville: Léclaireur at 360 [our translation].

[195] *Bacqueville de la Potherie, supra* note 7, Vol. 1 at 179 [our translation]; *F. X. de Charlevoix, supra* note 4, Vol. 3 at 79–80; Philippe Barbaud, *Le choc des patois en Nouvelle-France. Essai sur l'histoire de la francisation au Canada,* Sillery: Presses de l'Université du Québec, 1984 at 125–185.

[196] *F. X. de Charlevoix, supra* note 4, Vol. 1 at 497.

[197] *Marie de l'Incarnation, supra* note 112 at 177, 202, 230, 718, 802, 962–963; Archives des Ursulines du Québec (A. U. Q.), Annales du Monastère des Ursulines at 11; Registre des recettes et dépenses de 1672 à 1750 in *Claire Gourdeau, supra* note 95 at 84, 139, 140.

[198] Elisabeth Tooker, "The United States Constitution and the Iroquois League", *Ethnohistory*, Vol. 35, No. 4, 1988 at 305–336.

[199] Friedrich Engels, *The Origin of the Family, Private Property and the State*, 1884.

[200] Discussion with Jean-Jacques Simard.

[201] *Le Page Du Pratz, supra* note 67 at 79–80, 299–300, 306–315, 326–330.

[202] *R. J., Supra* note 62, Vol. 5 at 27–35 [our translation].

[203] *R. J., Ibid.*, Vol. 5, Chap. 7, pp 27–34 [our translation].

[204] *P. Kalm, Supra* note 24, Folio 877, see also Folio 679.

[205] *Jack Weatherford, supra* note 77 at 117–131.

[206] *Baron La Hontan, supra* note 9 at 801–885.

[207] *Ibid.* at 816, 850, 851, 858–865 [our translation].

[208] *Ibid.* at 860–865.

[209] Antoine Roy, "Les Indiennes de Chateaubriand" in *Cahiers des Dix*, No. 19, 1954 at 99–109.

[210] *Gabriel Théodat Sagard, supra* 32 at 320 (344), 332 (357).

[211] Father Chrestien Leclerc, *Nouvelle relation de la Gaspésie*, Paris: Amable Auroy, 1691 at 75–85 [our translation].

[212] Discussion with Jean-Jacques Simard.

[213] *Father Chrestien Leclerc, supra* note 211 at 85–89 [our translation].

[214] Discussion with Jean-Jacques Simard.

[215] *Nicolas Perrot, supra* note 4 at 150 [our translation].

[216] *Ibid.* at 95.

[217] *Ibid.* at 96; see also *F. X. de Charlevoix, supra* note 4, Vol. 1 at 131.

[218] *L. Nicolas, supra* note 3, Folio 78; *F. X. de Charlevoix, supra* note 4, Vol. 3 at 311; *J. C. B., supra* note 36 at 169; *J. F. Lafitau, supra* note 8, Vol. 1 at 66.

[219] *J. F. Lafitau, Ibid.*, Vol. 1 at 67; *Baron La Hontan, supra* note 9 at 632–637.

[220] *L. Nicolas, supra* note 3, Folio 19.

[221] *R. J., supra* note 62, Vol. 3 at 26.

[222] *F. X. Charlevoix, supra* note 4, Vol. 3 at 311.

[223] *J. F. Latifau, supra* note 8, Vol. 2 at 99; *F. X. Charlevoix, supra* note 4, Vol. 2 at 32; Vol. 3 at 353; *Gabriel Théodat Sagard, supra* note 32 at 320 (344), 332 (357); Sagard, *Le Grand Voyage du pays des Hurons*, Cahiers du Québec, Montréal: Hurtubise HMH, 1976 at 57, 77, 186; Le Page Du Pratz, *supra* note 67 at 348; *N. Y. C. D., supra* note 151, Vol. 13 at 109; *Baron La Hontan, supra* note 9 at 638.

[224] *L. Nicolas, supra* note 3, Folio 90 [our translation].

[225] *F. X. de Charlevoix, supra* note 4, Vol. 3 at 129 [our translation].

[226] *J. F. Lafitau, supra* note 8, Vol. 1 at 51.

[227] *Bacqueville de la Potherie, supra* note 7, Vol. 2 at 32; *Journal étranger, supra* note 94, "Iroquois", May 1762.

[228] *Nicolas Perrot, supra* note 4 at 22–23; *Baron La Hontan, supra* note 9 at 668–682.

[229] C11A-122, Folio 274V; *F. X. de Charlevoix, supra* note 4, Vol. 3 at 303; J. F. *Lafitau, Supra* note 8, Vol. 1 at 52.

[230] *F. X. de Charlevoix, supra* note 4, Vol. 3 at 303; *Baron La Hontan, supra* note 9 at 801–829, 876–885.

[231] *Baron La Hontan, supra* note 9 at 876–885; *F. X. de Charlevoix, supra* note 4,

Vol. 3 at 326–327, 286–288.

[232] *F. X. de Charlevoix, Ibid.* at 283–286, 287.

[233] *Baron La Hontan, supra* note 9 at 623, 630–632, 653–668, 801–828.

[234] *J. F. Lafitau, supra* note 8, Vol. 1 at 95–102; *Nicolas Perrot, supra* note 4 at 73–75, 117; *F. X. de Charlevoix, supra* note 4, Vol. 3 at 272–275; *R. J., supra* note 62, Vol. 3 at 41; *Baron La Hontan, Supra* note 9 at 829–848.

[235] Jean-Marie Therrien, *Parole et pouvoir. Figure du chef amérindien en Nouvelle-France,* Montréal: L'Hexagone, 1986 at 83.

[236] *Nicolas Perrot, supra* note 4 at 83 [our translation].

[237] *F. X. de Charlevoix, supra* note 4, Vol. 3 at 269 [our translation].

[238] *Ibid.,* Vol. 3 at 268 [our translation].

[239] *Baron La Hontan, supra* note 9, Vol. 2 at 829–831.

[240] *F. X. Charlevoix, supra* note 4, Vol. 3 at 321–322.

[241] *Ibid.,* Vol. 3 at 341.

[242] *Ibid.,* Vol. 3 at 341–342 [our translation].

[243] *Ibid.,* Vol. 3 at 342 [our translation].

[244] Discussion with Jean-Jacques Simard.

[245] *Baron La Hontan, supra* note 9 at 672.

[246] *F. X. de Charlevoix, supra* note 4, Vol. 3 at 321–322, 340–342; *Baron La Hontan, Supra* note 9 at 849–865 [our translation].

[247] *F. X. de Charlevoix, Ibid.,* Vol. 3 at 311 [our translation].

[248] *Ibid.,* Vol. 3 at 340.

[249] *Journal étranger, supra* note 94, "Iroquois", May 1762.

[250] *Nicolas Perrot, supra* note 4 at 72.

[251] *F. X. de Charlevoix, supra* note 4, Vol. 3 at 308 [our translation]. See David M. Haye, "Charlevoix," in the *Dictionnaire biographique du Canada,* Vol. III (Québec: Presses de l'Université Laval, 1974) at 111–118. See in particular page 116 concerning the reception of Charlevoix's work.

[252] *Ibid.,* Vol. 3 at 117–118; see also *Bacqueville de la Potherie, supra* note 7, Vol. 2 at 42.

[253] *Marie de l'Incarnation, supra* note 112 at 72–73; *J. R., supra* note 62, Vol. 6 at 234, Vol. 7 at 87.

[254] *F. X. de Charlevoix, supra* note 4, Vol. 3 at 342.

[255] *Ibid.,* Vol. 3 at 342.

[256] *J. F. Lafitau, supra* note 8, Vol. 1 at 45, 69; Annie Jacob, "Révolution française, essor ou blocage économique?" in *Histoires et géographes,* 1990 at 69, 289–290.

[257] *Baron La Hontan, supra* note 9 at 287, 831 [our translation]; *Annie Jacob, Ibid.,* at 291–296.

[258] *F. X. de Charlevoix, supra* note 4, Vol. 3 at 341.

[259] Discussion with Jean-Jacques Simard.

[260] *J. F. Gaultier, Catalogue, supra* note 25, Vol. 2, *calceolus* [our translation].

[261] *J. F. Gaulthier, supra* note 25, Vol. 1 at 29, 88–89; Vol. 2: *Acer,* Mémoire sur quelques espèces de pin at 449, 495; *De l'explication des vertus des plantes,* Fonds privé 91, A. N. Q., undated at 64, 65, 87, 90; *D. B. C., Supra* note 68, Vol. 3 at 735.

The Meeting of *Bourgeois* and Aboriginal Ethics: Modernity, Postmodernity and Aboriginality[1]

Denys Delâge[2]
And
Jean-Phillippe Warren[3]

By seeing the process of modernity as a mechanical, predetermined, fateful phenomenon, most authors in both economics and sociology have avoided close examination of cultural underpinnings. Particularly in economics, modern society is too often reduced to a system separated from the contingencies of history and values.[4]

In this essay, we will adopt the opposite perspective. We will try to gain a better understanding of modernity's links with the new configuration of values that appeared in the wake of the rupture at the end of the Middle Ages. Max Weber's most famous book, *The Protestant Ethic and the Spirit of Capitalism* (Weber 1930)[5] provides a brilliant illustration of this attempt from the rather narrow point of view that is also ours, namely, that of religion and beliefs. "The question of the motive forces in the expansion of modern capitalism is not in the first instance a question of the origin of the capital sums which were available for capitalistic uses, but, above all, of the development of the spirit of capitalism." (Weber 1930: 68) There was in fact a background of moral ideas, a foundation of new meaning on which capitalism grew. Even if we were able to describe all of the historical necessities involving the interplay of economic structures, we would be unable to explain the emergence, consolidation and then expansion of the capitalist system in Europe at the end of the Middle Ages. We would still be lacking the worldview on which the ideologies were based and which gave meaning to people's intentions as they created history.

Our goal here is to identify how this "background of moral ideas" is related to the background of moral ideas of Aboriginal peoples at the time of confrontation with Europeans. It is true that today's political correctness obscures real differences between primitive thought (which is primitive only in that Western thinkers remained ignorant of its complexity for so long) and the Western way of thinking (which is Western only with respect to its theoretical and practical development). No matter how much it may dismay humanists, their arguments will not persuade "Indians" to think in accordance with the theorems of Enlightenment philosophers. Claude Lévi-Strauss got around this problem by postulating that human thought has basic universal structures. Rapid reconciliation of all members of the human race was an underlying hope for the author of *Race and History*, but he did not focus on the diversity of anthropological beliefs and systems. This diversity is the subject of this essay. The questions that we will try to answer flow from acknowledgement of the cultural incompatibility of Aboriginal and European peoples when the two worlds met. Is it possible that the culture shock was so violent and terrible partly because there was a clash of ethics, ethics that followed primarily from the world-view determined and mediated by religion? If so, is it possible that the confrontation continues to obscure the future of Aboriginal peoples, though this time in a new way that corresponds to the emergence of a new form of social regulation? We will not have enough room here to answer such questions, for the topic is vast and has complex ramifications and major consequences. In this essay, we will simply identify a few avenues, formulate a few hypotheses and open the debate. We do not hope to find final and conclusive answers to such sensitive questions.

1. Aboriginal Ethics and Guilt

1.1. Primitive Religions and Modernity

Our first shortcut (and unfortunately not our last) will be to boil the moral beliefs and principles of Aboriginal peoples down to an ideal type or generalization, and to do the same thing with the moral beliefs and principles of European peoples. Our goal is to identify the basic principle of a complex set of inter-related ideas and attitudes, and not to provide a phenomenological, historical or accurate description of reality. Max Weber described his method in detail and it has been covered in so many books that we do not need to weigh ourselves down on this point. No one can deny that it has its advantages and disadvantages, but it allows us to lay the groundwork for deeper, more detailed research. Thus, the purpose of the proposed approach is to delimit an area of research, and we will apologize in advance for the generalizations that will have to be made rather than try to proceed from a faithful reproduction of the complex structures of primitive and modern systems. To begin with, note that here we will lump together Protestant and Counter-Reformation ethics, despite the obvious major differences, including in the form that colonization took under the Dutch, French and English. These two systems of ethics will be reduced to one, which we will call "Reformation ethics" or "*bourgeois* ethics." In parentheses, the differences partially explain why the Catholic and Protestant religions were received in different ways by Aboriginals. While it was more authoritarian, Catholicism was less strict than Protestantism, and the Church's many forms of mediation provided greater freedom for popular pagan animist, magical, mystical or simply Aboriginal cultures. Likewise, in Canada, the Anglican Church, namely the most authoritarian and least individualistic version of Protestantism, came to be adopted by Aboriginal peoples, and this was for reasons that were not uniquely political. Note also that both of these churches had distinct, unique leaders, namely the Pope in Rome, who had armies of missionaries, and the British king, who was the head of the Church of England. This facilitated the adherence of Aboriginals because they saw an analogy with what was for them a familiar idea of an authority with real protective, redistributive power on Earth and in Heaven. At the time this was true of both the Pope and the King of England, who had real power on Earth and also in Heaven. Moreover, believers attributed to God Almighty (Christ the King) the attributes of the monarchy, including a veritable court.

Finally, we will also note, though it probably goes without saying, that by making generalizations about different Aboriginal ethics under the name of "Aboriginal ethics", we obliterate for the purposes of argument the great differences among, for example, the ethics of nomadic hunter-gatherer societies such as the Algonquins and Athapaskans, and those of semi-sedentary farming societies, such as the Iroquois, where a structured political power was starting to emerge, and thus the capacity to institutionalize norms. Indeed, the weakness of this paper is probably that it does not indicate clearly enough the differences in the relationships with Europeans depending on whether the Aboriginal culture was animist or involved beliefs in which the sacred was an institutionalized sphere. It goes without saying that shamans already embody a form of power at the limits of mythology, and are thus signs of a tear in the "totalizing" fabric of a so-called primitive society. Among other things, for the purposes of this paper, we will make no distinction between morals and ethics, which is in any case a distinction that is reformulated differently by virtually every author who spends time on the issue. We will also not distinguish between "worldview", "sphere of meaning" or "background of moral ideas." Later studies can make distinctions and describe typologies, though even detailed schematics have to make generalizations about the amazing complexity of real life. For, just as the notion of rights is initially negative in myth-based societies (where it is made up of obligations and reciprocal prestations), the notions of morals and ethics do not have the formal, individual, independent features that they have in modern societies. The ethic specific to the Aboriginal cosmology thus appears in a depersonalized form, is not assumed by individuals but collectively, and is situated in a debate over meaning that is for a large part that of destiny. *Bourgeois* ethics and Aboriginal ethics are so different that we have to wonder whether the term "ethics" can apply in cases in which individuals do not interpret their actions in subjective terms. However, the alternative would be to say that Aboriginals have no morals and thereby, despite the centuries that have passed, repeat the missionaries' old prejudices about beings "without laws, faith or king."

We will reduce the comparison between primitive and (Counter) Reformation religion to two key oppositions: the presence or absence of guilt and the attitude to work. We will look at each of these oppositions in turn to show their scope and implications in modern society. By "modern society" we mean society as it was at the time the New World was discovered, and not our present society, though we will come back to the latter to show how it has adopted a radically different form of regulation since the end of World War II. Modern society was emerging at the time of the conquest of the New World, and was partly a product of doctrine and practices that originated outside it. This is why we will return several times in this essay to the medieval and pre-modern nature of the subjugation of Aboriginals in the first centuries of European colonization, though we will try to polish the typology, which is still too rigid and rough. By "oppositions" we mean the key points on which there were incomprehension, criticism and misunderstandings when modern (and post-modern) society came in contact with Aboriginal societ-

81

ies. Indeed, the difficulty that Aboriginal peoples have in adapting to the modern world does not result only from Whites' evilness, armed violence and political subjugation; it is perhaps equally owing to a cultural system that historians have to examine in order to put the drama of contemporary Aboriginal peoples into perspective. Animist ideas and the omnipresence of spirits in the world and in myths indeed entail submission to destiny rather than mastery of the future. This affects the relationship to time, community, work and education. In short, it has an impact on the relation to the world.

1.2. Guilt and Debts

It is difficult to reduce to a common core the many variations of the beyond held by the so-called primitive peoples of North America without simultaneously erasing the nuances of each view's originality and depth. Yet, despite the societies' numerous different ways of portraying the afterlife, anthropologists have noted a unanimous rejection of the idea of eternal damnation. The dead lead an existence quite similar to that of the living in a world most often described as a copy of the world here below, aside from the relatively common reversal of the normal course of life on Earth (day for the living is night for the dead, the right hand of the living is the left hand of the dead, the taboos of the living are broken by the dead and vice versa, etc.). Evil people are sometimes excluded in a manner similar to Christian purgatory, but only temporarily. No matter what the casuistry and mythological acrobatics of primitive religions, the omnipresence of occult forces never produces a result that includes the idea of hell. For example, reincarnation makes it possible to think of death as part of the continuity of life according to the system of eternal return analysed by Mircea Eliade (1989), and avoids questions about the conditions in heaven for those who have lived a good life. Moreover, even when an attenuated kind of damnation is posited in the form of dissipation of the body or fading of the soul, it is almost impossible to see it as corresponding to Christian damnation because it is suffered by outcasts and not by those who have done evil. Exclusion from paradise can strike murderers, those who commit suicide, people who are (physically or mentally) handicapped, and people who die from a spectacular illness or accident (for example, from being struck by lightening). Clearly, this conception of life after death is completely foreign to that suggested by Christian religions. An illustration of this can be seen in a dialogue with an Aboriginal reported by Gabriel Sagard:

> They believe that souls are immortal and that when they leave the body, they immediately go to dance and rejoice before *Dyoscaha* and his grandmother *Ataensiq*, who control the path and road of the stars [...]. They say that the souls of dogs go there too [...] and they told us that souls are immortal, but that in the other life they have the same need to drink and eat, wear clothes and work the land as they did when they were wearing their mortal bodies. This is why they bury or enclose biscuits, oil, skins, hatchets, pots and other tools with the bodies of the dead so that the souls of their relatives will not be poor and needy in the other life for lack of tools. They imagine and believe that the souls of the pots, hatchets, knives

and everything they dedicate to the dead person, especially at the great celebration of the dead, will go into the other life to serve the souls of the dead...

To this, Sagard replied with the zeal of a proselyte and the conviction of the Catholic faith that "Indians" had neither the intelligence to grasp theology nor the faculties necessary to understand that

> ...there is a paradise above us, where all the blessed are with God, and a hell below with devils and a fiery abyss underground, where all the souls of the evil and their dead relatives and friends are tortured along with those of their enemies because they did not know and love God our creator and because they led such bad lives with such dissoluteness and so many vices. (Sagard 1990: 255–257 [our translation])

This evangelist added that the Aboriginals were nonplussed and impressed by this discourse. No doubt, especially since the preaching was accompanied by a collection of icons portraying scenes each more terrible than the next. (Gagnon 1975)

While Aboriginals did not really feel a need to invent a tribunal responsible for punishing bad people or establishing redistributive justice after death, Christianity used the theme of eternal damnation as a central pillar of its dogma and preaching, especially after the Reformation and Counter-Reformation. While the former believed in earthly justice and immanent divine justice in order to maintain order in the tribe, the latter produced a huge literature on the tortures and agony of hell, with burning flames, inextinguishable thirst, torturers disguised as devils and sulphurous fumes. While the former did not carry evil into the hereafter, the latter were not content with earthly punishment, in which they had only weak belief (even after Job's trials), and added infernal retribution. Perhaps Dante's descriptions still provide the most striking images of the fear of death rooted in the heart of Christians in medieval times. Among the terrible pictures of the pain and punishment of the damned that the Italian author included in *The Divine Comedy*, there is that of a man slit open like a cracked barrel, from his chin to his hips, with his intestines hanging out of his body all the way to the ground. Elsewhere Dante mentions a sinner whose atrocious cries filled his eyes with tears, and he then goes on to pity all of the others crowded into the shadows. (Alighieri, 2003) This description was echoed many times in the following centuries.

In the fourteenth century, hell became a common theme of sermons, preaching and homilies. However, it had little effect on the consciences of the masses and proved rather ineffective despite the use of rhetorical and visual devices. It was not until the Counter-Reformation that it was transformed into an instrument of virtue and spur of moral conscience, the formidable power of which is clear in the doctrine of the Council of Trent. Ignatius of Loyola, for one, used it to frighten the soul in his *Spiritual Exercises*.[6] In the first half of the seventeenth century, a new mentality confirmed this dogmatic turn, among both Catholics and Protestants. Hell was a terrifying place where sinners experienced indescribable, fearful bloody tortures with no chance of reprieve.

> [T]heologians and men of the Church carefully delimited hell and gave it a very specific role: that of terrorizing Christians in order to keep them away from evil and help them to progress in religion. Hell was a part of the great plan for human salvation; it became an essential component in moral life. (Minois 1991: 242 [our translation])

This can be explained by the growing importance of the feeling of guilt in Reformation thinking. Hell appeared as such a strong, terrible instrument of divine retribution and justice because men had to pay for their sins, and the amount they had to pay was in accordance with a very *bourgeois* evaluation. In a dialogue written by the Priest of St. Sulpice in 1736 (Minois 1991: 243–244), it is asserted that the soul leaves the body at death and rises to heaven, where God presides over a court waiting to pass judgment. God weighs the soul's good and bad actions with "rigor", "severity", "implacability" and "measure." This is no longer a god but a grocer adding up his clients' payments and debts. The calculations (which are what count here, much more than the act of judgment itself) determine whether the soul appearing before God will fly to heaven or descend to the eternal prison of hell.

Sermons designed to create guilt complexes fed on the vague fear of the beyond, thereby creating the perfect conditions for the emergence of a super-ego strangely similar to that conceptualized by Freud in Vienna at the beginning of the twentieth century. Indeed, hell was important not because it divided the elect and the damned, the saints and the sinners into two clear camps, but because it was the means of radically internalizing the feeling of sin. Eternal torture of souls quickly became the most terrifying means of policing behaviour because the Christian God has "hawk eyes", and to think about committing a crime is to have committed it already. By infiltrating the soul, God takes complete possession of it. The soul trembles before him like a leaf in the slightest breeze. This plays a bigger role among Protestants than among Catholics because the latter have the pressure valve of confession for unloading sins and receiving the pardon accorded to men, and also because they have purgatory, which alleviates the inexorability of hell. However, in Protestant sects, particularly among American Puritans, God watches what men do just as much as in the Catholic Church, and, as Victor Hugo wrote, continues to watch them through the walls of cities, masonry of prisons, iron of armour and wood of the tomb.

Historians of Christianity have spoken of a veritable theology of sin that was always latent in the writings of the Fathers of the Church and that crystallized at this time. There were annotations on the consequences of Adam's fall, mortification became atrocious in its sophistication, and divine vengeance became a reality so terrifying that today we have difficulty imagining the degree of fear that it created. The world was considered corrupted and described as a valley of tears. Many books and essays were devoted to distinguishing between venal and mortal sins, and to establishing a clear gradation of evil. Scholasticism established the dogma of the seven deadly sins (pride, greed, lust, gluttony, envy, anger and sloth). It is no exaggeration to say that sin played a central role in the theology of the time, as in consequence did sermons on penitence and atonement. Vice was seen as a stain on the soul and defiance of God. It therefore had to be punished by insisting on morals that held believers responsible for everything they did, said and felt. To appease the anger of an omnipotent, severe, distant and authoritarian god, believers fasted and mortified their bodies. Thus everything was related (sin, fear and hell), and it should be noted that the internalization was particularly violent in Protestantism. As Jean Delumeau notes, despite the fact that even the most terrifying condemnations resulting from the theology of sin include a perceptible discourse of consolation, discourse invoking laws and threats predominated in the West from the end of the Middle Ages to the beginning of the Renaissance. It was based on a pessimistic and negative conception of human beings. (Delumeau 1983: 551–564)

Jean de Brébeuf, the first saint of the colony of New France, is a classical example of a man whose faith was in accordance with the Council of Trent and the Reformation. Educated at the Society of Jesus school, he absorbed the Society's austere spirit composed of submission to authority and desire for penitence. The Christ of his prayers was the crucified Christ: "Turn yourself to Jesus Christ on the cross, and from now on let him be the base and foundation of your thought." (Brébeuf 1640, quoted by Latourelle 1999: 277 [our translation]) The vocation he adopted was that of martyr. These were values that Aboriginals were not willing to endorse, except with very natural distaste.

There was nothing similar in the religious universe of so-called primitive peoples. Unlike the Christian religion, which focussed on life after death, Aboriginal religions focussed on the present. (Charlevoix 1975, 3: 353; RJ 1972 [1634], 1: 78–79) Guilt, if it even existed in the sense that we understand it, played a very small role. The admonishments of missionary priests seem to have had very little effect on Aboriginals' consciences when they were based only on the idea of sin. This was not only because their teachings breathed a different culture and paid little attention to situations considered sinful according to Christian dogma, but also because the idea of sin itself made little sense to them. At Québec City in 1634, when he was preparing to baptize a dying Aboriginal, Father LeJeune wrote "I was at great pains to get her to feel pain for the sins she had committed; Indians have neither a word for nor customs pertaining to sin." (RJ 1972 [1634], 1: 9 [our translation]) Reciprocally, since the missionaries could not find a moral order based on the feeling of personal guilt, they came to believe in the barbarism of Aboriginals: "...the problem is that in this country there is no...punishment for any wrongdoing; this is why everyone lives in freedom and each does as he pleases..." (Sagard 1990: 208 [our translation])

Gabriel Sagard's criticism would have been more sensitive if he had taken the notion of debt instead of that of guilt as a premise. Indeed, the notion of debt is necessary to an understanding of the operation of moral sanction in Aboriginal nations. In this respect, Aboriginals are not very different from the Nuers studied by Evans-Pritchard. The British anthropologist said he was surprised to find that, far from feeling fear when they committed a crime against the gods, the Nuers felt the same emotion as a debtor feels to a creditor (Evans-Pritchard 1968). They knew that they would have to pay the debt some day, sooner rather than later, but this did not bother them much and they sometimes even tried to strike a bargain to reduce what was owed. This means that the relationship uniting the Nuers and their gods was an alliance. This analysis applies *mutatis mutandis* to Aboriginal peoples. In 1844, when Father Chazelle told his hosts that Jesus Christ had come to teach and save all men, Ojaouanon, a chief from Walpole Island, responded that the Great Spirit's son had gone to the missionary's island (i.e., Europe) because the people there had rejected the ancestors' blessings, and not to America because the people there had not defied the traditional customs. In other words, Christ was trying to save only those who had betrayed the original alliance. (Chazelle, January 24, 1845 in Cadieux 1973: 256)

The notions of alliance and debt are related to the logic of exchange in archaic societies. There is no need to review the well-known theses of Marcel Mauss[7], which Lévi-Strauss so brilliantly expanded, to grasp the movement of gift–counter-gift in Aboriginal societies. According to these theses, what is accepted must be rendered. Well aware of Mauss's arguments, Cazeneuve said with respect to guilt and law in archaic societies: "Primitive law is generally based on the principle of reciprocity, and is thus related to the great system of exchange, prestations and counter-prestations, which regulates the economy and marriages." (Cazeneuve 1967: 269 [our translation]) Legislation is based on a vast system of reciprocal obligations, which maintains the cohesion of the group and social order. Guilt has little place in such an organization, for to refuse to pay a debt is to place oneself on the margin of society, inspire the disdain of others and compel one's own ostracism. People who do not pay their debts can and will eventually put an end to the service to which they subscribe. The same applies in Aboriginal societies, where wanting to cut oneself off from the group virtually means wanting to commit suicide.

Pagan Aboriginals are just as responsible as Christian Europeans, except that their responsibility is not perceived in the same manner and is therefore experienced differently. A rough sketch of the differences might portray guilt as experienced from the inside, whereas debt would be seen as coming from the outside. Between the two emotions, there is a difference as wide as that separating sin from taboo. Jean Cazeneuve spent many years studying the Zuni Indians. His research led him to see taboo as an aspect of rites, and rites themselves as kinds of dramatizations of myths. (Cazeneuve 1971) Ritualization of life would be a solution to man's constant infringement of the boundaries set by moral injunctions, if indeed such things exist. Dread would be the price of human freedom, and it would be all the more consuming and vivid in that it embraces the indetermination that underlies existence. Rudolf Otto called such apprehension "mystical" and described it as flowing from the fear inspired by *numina*.[8] Here, the word "*numina*" designates what mysteriously escapes the order of society, goes infinitely beyond it, and wanders around the world like a patient, elusive animal. Two main attitudes can be adopted with respect to *numina*; Cazeneuve divides them into the categories of magic and taboos. Taboos are everything unusual, and include the rules of both hygiene and morals. A dog that is too lucky a hunter, a deformed baby and twins are all taboo; incest, adultery and murder are also taboo in so far as they are anomalous. A new event or rare phenomenon, for example, birth and especially death, menstruation, initiations, inaugurations and rites of passage, can set off a series of taboos. Magic refers to an attempt to control the forces freed by the sacred. Instead of fearing the extraordinary, a sorcerer or magician seeks it out systematically. A sorcerer's potions are made of blood of toad, bent fingernails and snake spit; he gathers plants at the full moon, on stormy days and at the summer solstice; his home is at the edge of the village, at the end of a winding path. Apprentice magicians manipulate occult powers in full knowledge that they are playing with fire. They do not commit sins because fault is not subjective and is not shouldered by an individual. Even if a sorcerer's experiments have unfortunate results, the individual's guilt stops at criminal negligence, and the worst he can suffer is banishment from the village, just as one would fire a dangerous employee, especially when the *numina*, which are contagious evils, have entered into him. The same applies to men and women who break taboos. The stain resulting from the transgression can be washed away by ablutions, libations, sacrifices and quarantine, or by exile as if the person had the plague. An exaggeration of the way Aboriginals feel might be that they use a hygienic or medical approach to cure society of its vices. The consequence is that Aboriginals very rarely moralize in order to ensure compliance with ethical rules. Guilt does not have the control over them that it had over Christians in the sixteenth to nineteenth centuries.

We have just said that guilt is a rare emotion in Aboriginal nations. Let us add once again that responsibility itself is shared and more diffuse. It is shared because the misfortunes of one individual have an impact on the whole nation, since every member feels solidarity with every other member. It is diffuse because it is possible that the misfortune that strikes one individual was caused by magic or by a whim of the gods. Here we hear echoes of Oedipus in Sophocles's *Oedipus at Colonus*: "...my deeds. Deeds of a man more sinned against than sinning..." The gods sometimes give meaning to human actions, and sometimes they lead and guide, as in Homer's tale of the war of Troy. What follows from this is that, in the minds of Aboriginals, responsibility takes the form of a debt, and the debt is neither personal nor specific. The example of the sale of alcohol to Aboriginals is a good illustration of this kind of moral passiveness. Church authorities, who considered it morally wrong, and colonial authorities, who feared its concrete devastation, outlawed the sale of alcohol to Aboriginals. The Church threatened excommunication, and the state fines. However, except for a few exceptions, the law did not prohibit the consumption of alcohol by Aboriginals. Conscious of the noxious effects of alcohol, Aboriginals called for a ban of the sale of spirits, but did not really shoulder the responsibility for their conduct when they were inebriated.[9]

The principle of diffuse responsibility at the heart of Aboriginal tradition can be seen clearly in the history of law relating to Aboriginal peoples. We should therefore discuss it briefly. Indeed, it is not true that the colonial legal system was applied without adaptation to and mixing with the traditions of the peoples who were subject first to the French empire, and then to the English. Colonization instead led to a degree of legal pluralism, and the two traditions existed in parallel for many years. It was only after the war of 1812–1814 that the British legal system was enforced, and the process was gradual. In the ambiguity between the two legal systems, there is a clear opposition between the underlying values of European and Aboriginal law. Throughout French rule in the *Pays d'en haut*, the Aboriginal nations' dominance forced the French to make accommodations in the French legal system to match Aboriginal views. For example, if a Frenchman was killed by an Aboriginal, the latter was brought before one of the colony's commanders to be sentenced to prison. However, when examined carefully, the ceremony that followed was less that of punishment than of pardon. The French ritual, which was a kind of hybrid of two traditions, remained all in all very close to Aboriginal traditions, according to which murders concerned a family or line, and justice's purpose was to make reparations or pay compensation for the loss suffered by the victim's kin. Indeed, Aboriginals always favoured compensation over punishment (White 1991: 82–93). For example, near Keweenam Bay, on the south shore of Lake Superior, two Frenchmen were killed in fall 1683. The French authorities were deaf to the offer of slaves in compensation and to the invitation to smoke the peace pipe, and decided to capture the guilty parties and punish them according to the letter of the law in effect in the colony. The traditional dispute resolution process was set aside, and a tribunal was formed to hear witnesses and admit evidence. It seems that a Menominee and two Aboriginals who were sons of an important leader in Keweenam Bay had committed the act. The tribunal had to rule on the responsibility of each party, and charged not only the murdering sons but also the father because he was morally responsible for his children, even though he was in no way involved in the murder. The Aboriginals were offended by the idea that the blood of three of theirs would be spilled for that of two French. Justice did not consist in punishing the guilty but in compensating losses. Its purpose was to restore balance to the order of things, beings and the world. Presents and services had to be offered to make up for what had been taken by force (this was known as "covering the dead"), or people, slaves, children or women had to be given to replace those who had been killed (this was known as "raising the dead"). (Tanner and Sioui 1994: 77–79) The rest of the story and the many negotiations to which it gave rise are not relevant here. Note for now the friction and misunderstanding caused by contact between two systems of values with diametrically opposite foundations. (Stone 2000: 65–78)

Generally, colonial justice adapted to Aboriginal traditions. Aboriginal murderers were more easily pardoned than French assassins, and had to pay back the debt contracted with respect to colonial society by good conduct in war. When an Aboriginal murderer was nevertheless sentenced to death, negotiations between the village council and colonial authorities would lead to a sentence involving a warrior's honourable death by clubbing or shooting, and not hanging. In short, Aboriginals in America were treated like nobles in Europe, where scoundrels and the poor were hung, but nobles had their throats slit or were run through with a sword. Rather than punishing sin with a fall from grace, debts were repaid: an eye for an eye and a tooth for a tooth.

Finally, it has to be said that among Aboriginals, responsibility was indirect, in other words, it was not immediate as in the Christian religion since it did not address one's conscience but took the form of material repercussions suffered by the guilty party for the crime committed. Incest is a serious, even terrible crime in primitive societies, but only because of the concrete consequences that it can have on an individual's life and on order in the village. Take the case of a man who has had sex with his little sister. The thing comes to be known in the village, and a jealous suitor even declares the crime in the central meeting place. At first sight, the violation of the taboo is unforgivable. Yet, what happens? Nothing. Nothing happens. In order to prevent divine punishment, the guilty party can always use superstitious means of separating himself from his crime. (Malinowski 1980: 51–93) In a writing by the Jesuit Lejeune, there is a telling description of this conception of responsibility. Having broken customary prohibitions and given bones to dogs to eat, the missionary was immediately accused of a major crime against the nation. The men got angry and the women were upset. Yet this is as far as things went at the time. However, Lejeune feared for his life; everything depended on whether the hunt would be successful. Fortunately, a moose was killed a few days later and made everyone forget about the debt resulting from having shown disrespect to the remains of animals. Lejeune wrote that he was lucky, for otherwise it would have been the end of him. The little band was in debt to the animal spirits, but the latter seemed to have pardoned the crime, or at least there was nothing to show that they held a grudge. Thus everyone could consider himself out of debt. (RJ 1972 [1634], 1: 71, 77–78, 80)

Given Aboriginals' different conception of guilt and responsibility (and thus of law and citizenship), the French and English, in their rush to justify the invasion of American land and subjection of Aboriginals, generally interpreted Aboriginal ways of thinking as immoral and irresponsible. They were quick to see this as proof of childlike behaviour. In the medieval imagination, a child was a person whose morals were not sure and whose behaviour was erratic, and who therefore had to be educated about sin and prohibitions, by the whip if necessary. By placing children and "Indians" in the same category, European powers could see themselves as fathers laying down the law and shouldering responsibility. At the same time, this reduced Aboriginals to infantile individuals who had to be gradually educated to be adults, in other words, they were persons (or communities) subject to the "father's" law. The absence among Aboriginals of a guilt-based moral system reinforced, justified and legitimized domination by an order that looked down on, repressed, alienated and crushed Aboriginals with the assurance that it was helping them to rise and progress.

1.3. *Beruf* and Work

The way that crime and punishment are viewed depending on whether the society is archaic or Western reveals another feature that distinguishes Aboriginal from *bourgeois* ethics, for the deep unity of the nation, which was reflected in the rejection of the idea of hell, was broken in Christianity. In the afterlife, a small number of elect will be eternally separated from the mass of the damned. This means that there is no deep solidarity amongst all members of society, and this undermines the system of reciprocal prestations in primitive societies. Believers walk their paths alone, particularly in Protestantism where there is no support from a Church or clan. Authors, such as the ethnologist Louis Dumont, have shown the distance separating the individualism of *homo hierarcicus* from the holism of *homo aequalis* (Dumont 1977 and 1979) by focussing on the things that modern individualism owes to Christian principles. Dumont could have illustrated his demonstration using the example of missionaries who, when trying to convert Aboriginals, had trouble getting the prospective Christians to imagine an afterlife in which not all dead people would be reconciled. Dying Aboriginals refused the services of a priest if it meant that they would be prevented from joining their ancestors. Parents feared entrusting their children to missionaries because they would be separated from their offspring, who would enter the heaven of European peoples whereas they would go to an Aboriginal afterlife.

Primitive peoples' distrust of liberal individualism has repercussions on their definition of work. Among Aboriginals, work is an eminently social activity that, like any other activity, is regulated by and subject to the law of exchange. Aboriginals would never work directly and exclusively for themselves, for that would be to risk breaking the symbolic and concrete chain linking them to one another and create the danger of a solitary death. The story of Thomas Arakwente, a rich Iroquois merchant at *Caughnawaga* (Kahnawake) at the end of the eighteenth century and beginning of the nineteenth century is instructive. According to custom, the woods surrounding the village were collectively owned, governed by the chiefs and could be used by all to gather firewood, maple sap, etc. Instead of going and cutting firewood himself for his own personal use, Arakwente hired workers to cut many cords of wood and sell them outside of the reserve. Next, he tried to make a communal maple tree grove his own private property. He was also involved in many disputes over fences. In short, Arakwente turned the whole community against him, and he was finally exiled from the village in 1807.[10] While he would have died if he had been rejected by his community a century earlier, Arakwente's trials after his ostracism by the nation were not very hard, which probably explains his arrogance and shows the deep changes that had occurred in the internal organization of Aboriginal societies by then. In archaic societies, work is subject to a complex system of prestations and obligations that prevents it from ever being done in itself or for itself. This is how it was in Aboriginal societies before the arrival of European conquerors and merchants.

The Christian mentality born of the Reformation and Counter-Reformation belongs to a world very foreign to the one that has just been described. In it, work is experienced as a vocation, which Weber called "*beruf.*" We will quickly sketch out its main characteristics. Naturally, precapitalist economies and the rudiments of capitalism existed in Aboriginal societies. No one would dream of claiming otherwise. Greed and the desire for material benefits have also always been present in Aboriginal minds. However, capitalism as the legitimization of profit and a rational system for organizing free work is an invention that dates from medieval Europe, and one of its features is specifically that it breaks with the balance of myth-based societies. Claude Lévi-Strauss spoke of "hot societies" and "cold societies" to illustrate the operation of modern and primitive societies. Whereas the latter create little disorder and function in a closed circuit, the former are in constant disequilibrium, a dynamic unbalance that produces order, though it requires an infinitely greater expenditure of energy. (Lévi-Strauss 1961: 35–48) How have we come to prefer disorder over balance, entropy over harmony? In order to answer this question, we have to return to the ethos that, by revolutionizing the ancient beliefs and traditions of cold societies, led, in combination with many other factors, to the emergence of hot societies.

The economic mentality specific to the Christian world in the sixteenth century saw the role and place of believers on Earth in a new way (see Weber 1930). The question of asceticism dominates the pages of *The Protestant Ethic* because Weber was essentially using a new notion of work to trace the prodromes of the spirit of capitalism and "rationalization of the world." Calvinism's "worldly monks" exert self-control in the form of strict regulation of behaviour and personal planning, which involves rationalization of daily life, moral rigor and an utterly new investment in an occupation. Work is not only a source of physical and moral discipline, but also provides Puritans with the certainty of salvation. It erases irrational thoughts, impulsive emotions and useless amusements. The principle of sober efficiency became virtually the sole, imperative measure of human relationships. (Groupe de recherche sur la culture Weimar 1997) Formerly associated with suffering and torture, and the exile of men and women from paradise, work became a source of accomplishment and freedom.

> [These writings] will testify to the world on my behalf that I have not led an idle, lazy, or dronish life, not spent my time wantonly, fruitlessly or in company-keeping as some have been too ready to asperse me, or that I have had in my whole time either in Old England or New many sparse hours to spend unprofitably away or to refresh myself with recreations, except reading and writing hath been a recreation to me, which sometimes is mixed with pain and labour enough. Rather I have studied and endeavoured to redeem my time as a thing most dear and precious to me and have often denied myself in such refreshings that otherwise I might lawfully have made use of. (*The Apologia of Robert Keayne. The Self-Portrait of a Puritan Merchant.* Bernard Bailyn, Ed., New York: Harper & Row: 73–74, quoted by Disselkamp 1994: 155)

Protestant circles in particular adopted an attitude that was frankly favourable to economic rationalism. The influence of Reformation ethics (which certainly did not exempt France) on the consciences of financiers and merchants cannot be overlooked. It had the curious characteristic of blending a virtually absolute detachment from the pleasures of the world with an insatiable desire to accumulate wealth. Sects known for the austerity of their customs and repression of desires accumulated immense fortunes, as if one's nose for business were not dulled but sharpened by the new faith. Speaking of the English in *L'Esprit des lois*, Montesquieu said: "They know better than any other people upon earth how to value, at the same time, these three great advantages — religion, commerce and liberty."[11] It seemed obvious to him to link success in business, the development of democratic institutions and piety, but not just any piety: the Anglo-Saxon version born of the ethics specific to the Reformation.

Reformation ethics were not a means of procuring always more goods and enjoying life, but instead made profit an objective that was valid in itself. Earning money was the sign of successful exercise of an occupation, and Reformation ethics attached primary importance to such success. This is why English capitalists at the time seemed so grasping, unscrupulous and greedy. This kind of behaviour can be seen in every country and in every period, but in Europe at the time of the Reformation, it took on a new aspect because the self-interested egoism and fierce desire for profit were not seen as excuses for stealing or dishonesty, but were oriented towards meticulous, upright exercise of one's occupation in order to *make* money.

Clearly, the new desire for profit was largely foreign to Aboriginal thinking. For example, when the fur companies tried to encourage Aboriginals to bring more furs to the trading posts, they thought that the best way to do so would be to increase the price. However, this had exactly the opposite effect. Instead of producing more, Aboriginals spent less time hunting simply because their needs were stable and they were happy with the amount of merchandise they usually received from trading. In economic terms, Aboriginal demand for fur trade merchandise was inelastic. Rigidity of demand was a major factor in the companies' decision to expand their areas of fur supply because they were unable to increase local production as they wished. (Ray 1974: 140–162) The idea of accumulating wealth for personal non-use (!) seemed to Aboriginals to be the summit of the absurd and contemptible. In their eyes, earning money was only a means of performing exchanges and increasing one's comfort within reasonable limits. Thomas Aquinas would have agreed with them, for he called the quest for wealth *turpido*, i.e., base, as would all peoples on Earth, since the Protestant action appears empty, irrational and derisory when laid bare.[12] In conclusion, let us cite the riposte reported by an explorer: when you offer money to an Aboriginal, he says "I'm not hungry."

In this respect, let us examine a statement of Aboriginal philosophy:

> Indeed, my brother, if you do not yet know the real feelings that we Indians have for your country and all your nation, it is right that I teach you about them now. Thus, I beg you to believe that as miserable as we may appear to you, we consider ourselves much more happy than you because we are very content with the little we have, and believe, once again I beg you, that you are very mistaken if you think you can persuade us that your country is better than ours, for if France is, as you say, a small Heaven on Earth, were you smart to leave it and why did you leave your wives, children, relatives and friends?…Now, tell me a little, if you are intelligent, who is wiser and happier: he who works all the time and only manages to gather what he needs to live after much labour, or he who rests pleasantly and finds what he needs through the agreeable activi-

ties of hunting and fishing." ...He finished his speech by saying that an Indian was able to live anywhere, and that he could say that he was the lord and king of his country because he lived where he wanted as long as he wanted, with all sorts of rights, such as to hunt and fish, without any worries, a thousand times happier in the woods and in his cabin than in a palace or at the tables of the greatest princes in the world. (Leclerc 1691: 79–86 [our translation])

The poverty of Aboriginals shocked Europeans:

To wish to be poor was, it was often argued, the same as wishing to be unhealthy...Especially begging, on the part of one able to work, is not only the sin of slothfulness, but a violation of the duty of brotherly love according to the Apostle's own word. (Weber 1930: 163)

This association of ideas is also found in the writings of explorers and settlers. While the frugality of Aboriginal peoples was praised as one of their greatest virtues, many explorers' reports equated poverty with Indianness. "The concept of poverty is essential...The Indian is he who lacks everything." (Gagnon and Petel 1986: 99 [our translation])

The way that Catholics, particularly the clergy, viewed the poverty of Aboriginal peoples was at least as ambiguous as that of Protestants. For example, when Father Chrestien Leclerc denounced European civilization for being quarrelsome because craving material possessions, he contrasted it with the pleasant lifestyle of the inhabitants of the New World, and their brotherly unity, disinterested charity and uncomplicated manners. He said that they do not have "the worries that we give ourselves as we try to accumulate goods." Indeed, how could a priest not be charmed by poverty that he himself has taken a vow to embrace? Of course, a nomadic lifestyle might make men more like animals and maintain them in a pagan state (owing to an association between the forest and lack of civilization), and work prevents vice born of laziness. However, the quest for wealth subverts Christian ideals. In short, the missionary was in favour of work as a means of protecting virtue, but opposed to it if its ultimate goal was the accumulation of wealth. This is a restatement of the opposition between what is necessary and what is superfluous. What is necessary is the minimum needed for decency, and what is superfluous is the beginning of self-indulgence. Far from stating an original argument, the missionary was simply repeating the core paradox of *bourgeois* ethics: it accuses poverty of being a sign of barbarism but assails wealth as a cause of vice. This already makes it easier to understand how Europeans could stigmatize Aboriginals for their apparent nudity, but at the same time salute their simplicity as a noble quality. The *Bourgeois* and Puritans were not supposed to enjoy poverty, but to refuse to spend money. In order to grasp the deep logic of the dialectic between frugality and poverty, we have to go back to the *bourgeois* conception of work.

Bourgeois ethics make work a good in itself, valid in itself, and justified through its very performance. Work is at the top of the list of moral obligations. Benjamin Franklin remains for posterity a shining example of the new attitude to work. He extolled three virtues: temperance, order and industry.[13] Temperance, because it prevented people from falling into excess, giving into debauchery and savouring lowly material pleasures. This attitude can be seen in the paintings of Flemish artists, in which subjects stand out against black backgrounds, and which show rooms in *bourgeois* homes with naked walls bathed in an atmosphere of contrition and renunciation. Protestants' moral rigor went hand-in-hand with simple clothing, few furnishings and a constant rejection of ostentation. Franklin also recommended order. For Protestants, the exercise of an occupation should not be left to routine. An honest employee is an efficient man. There is a veritable work ethic (which includes the principle of fair play) in Protestant countries. The ethic is used as a basis for rationalizing work and subjecting it to technical imperatives. Otherwise it would not be possible to make a profit, and profit is constantly subject to improvements in management and performance of work. Finally, Franklin praised industry at the same time that he condemned laziness and idleness. Franklin belonged to the race of Englishmen for whom time is money. Indeed, he lectured his son about the principle that a day of labour was more pleasing to God than a day of prayer, and Sunday was the only day when one should pray. Moreover, work is a means of not being guilty of dispersing one's energy and not giving into the temptations of luxury. In Franklin's three ethical rules, we can see the idea that work is the goal of human existence, its alpha and its omega. This was to such an extent that religious writings in his time considered laziness to be an absence of grace. Thus one must always work, and work always with a view to wealth that, because it is a sign of occupational accomplishment, can no more be spent than a train ticket, unless one decides to give up the trip.

Here as elsewhere, we have to specify the historical differences between Catholicism and Protestantism. Colonization by the British was different enough from that by the French that there is no danger of mixing them up. A Puritan farmer in Massachusetts had a work ethic that had nothing, or very little, in common with that of French *coureurs de bois*, who, to quote Indendant Champigny:

> ...live in the woods like Indians, and can go two or three years without sacraments, living idly and often in extraordinary poverty. Once they are used to the lifestyle, they have difficulty devoting themselves to farming the land and remain in extreme poverty, spending much money when they come. (Champigny 1916: 278 [our translation])

Cavalier de la Salle, who was an adventurer without any real scruples, would have been in strange company with Pastor John Williams, who was taken prisoner with his wife and children during Deerfield's attack on Massachusetts and brought to Kahnawake where, with integrity and courage, he survived what he described as a "purging" and "purifying" captivity. (Demos 1999: 68–70) Catholic missionaries evangelized by teaching the catechism; they did not think of doing as their Protestant counterparts, who tried to completely transform the customs of so-called savages. Catholics believed that it was necessary to adapt rites and cultural practices, which was unpardonable in the eyes of English Puritans for whom orthodoxy did not mean dogma and hateful scholasticism, but a measured and regulated life. Nonetheless, there are enough similarities for sociologists to be able to contrast the so-called primitive mentality with the general point of view of these branches of Christianity.

The Reformation conflated occupation with vocation, and the exercise of an occupation became the performance of a duty. In a way, Luther tore down the walls of monasteries only to expand them to enclose the whole nation, except that God would then be pleased by the performance of duties in the world, and not by mystical contemplation or ruminations on the mysteries of the universe. Once the faithful became monks and nuns in the world, they applied ascetic ideals to their occupational lives. Likewise, in the Catholic world, the station of monk was rethought according to criteria that resembled those used in the work world. This can be seen, for example, in Loyola's spiritual exercises. In both cases, the ethic tends to turn sanctification of life into a commercial undertaking, or at least a rational and strategic enterprise. Calvin and the sects issuing from Calvinism were more revealing of society's development in this direction than was Luther, the great German reformer. Calvinism, Pietism, Methodism and the Baptist sects in Germany, England, Holland, France and America strengthened Lutheran investment in the world. Through his doctrine of predestination, Calvin made life on earth subject to irrevocable decree. By divine decision, individuals were damned to hell or elected to heaven for all eternity. This theology left people before the terrible question of whether they were among the damned or the elect. How can I know whether I am doomed to damnation or promised to enter paradise? Calvin's followers found two ways of answering this question. One could live as a saint, in other words, repress one's feelings, internalize the law and be a man of steel, or one could work unceasingly in order to accumulate in this life the signs of divine election. The latter point is important because it implies that the certitude of salvation is acquired by proof of objective results. Good works do not change a believer's destiny. Everything has already been decided since the dawn of time, but perhaps one can guess or glimpse the future through one's undertakings. The proverb says that the Lord helps he who helps himself, and to believers in the Reformation and Catholic followers of the Council of Trent, it meant that God helps those who do not need help. Through his doctrine of God's infinite supremacy over man, Calvin called on the elect to increase the glory of God in this world. Man had no other duty but to follow the Commandments and ensure that social life in general was organized in accordance with them. He therefore had to work, and work in a rational, methodical, systematic and useful manner. This reasoning had so much influence that in utilitarian philosophy, the words "good" and "utility" are conflated for all practical intents and purposes.

The Protestant "*beruf*" was completed and perfected in English Puritanism. Admiration for self-made men, in particular for their diligence, temperance and good *bourgeois* sense, spread to different degrees throughout all classes of society. American religious fanaticism, which was a mixture of German, Dutch and English ethics, magnified this aspect to the point of condemning even the smallest signs of frivolity (for example, with respect to clothing) and used the imperative of utility to break the aristocratic ideal of the superfluous. In his general description of Protestantism, Weber described the lifestyle in which one devotes oneself to managing creation in a rational manner, increasing one's possessions and wealth through cold mercantilism and work, and controlling consumption while being racked with acquisitive desires. In short, this meant turning useful and necessary work into a way of practicing asceticism.

> [T]he religious valuation of restless, continuous, systematic work in a worldly calling, as the highest means to asceticism, and at the same time the surest and most evident proof of rebirth and genuine faith, must have been the most powerful conceivable lever for the expansion of that attitude toward life which we have here called the spirit of capitalism. (Weber 1930: 172)

A caricaturist of the *bourgeois* could probably not have found better models than the members of the most orthodox and puritan circles that landed on American soil in search of a new Eden where they could live by the strictures of their faith. Though their wealth was to grow to colossal sums, the customs and lifestyle to which they aspired were simple and old-fashioned.[14]

The religious ethos of toil and the *bourgeois* view of labour made work a vocation, in other words, a form of asceticism. This attitude persisted until recently in America, despite the gradual diminishment of the religious feeling that gave rise to it. In the nineteenth century, it was clear that the Reformation ethic was weakening while capitalism was developing and consolidating on the surface in Europe and everywhere in America. However, the Reformation ethic of *beruf* took distance from religion without losing strength. On the contrary, it seems it became secular naturally as the *bourgeois* spirit predominated. The capitalist *fact* was accepted and recognized: there was a need to rationalize work to avoid being crushed by one's competitors and to work hard and diligently in order to avoid starvation. In a world where solidarity was conveyed through work, industry became a universal law and prophecy whether or not one was religious and perhaps *a fortiori* when one was not religious, since the refusal to count on heavenly retribution led to much greater value being given to earthly acquisitions, which only participation in the society of production and consumption could provide.

Now that we have painted this rough sketch of the *bourgeois*, perhaps we can advance a thesis that should be interpreted in a neutral, anthropological sense: European peoples subjugated Aboriginal peoples in part through military strength, in part through the worldwide communication of disease, in part through deceit and treachery, but also through a new interpretation of man's place in the world, which left Aboriginals defenceless and confused. A crystal goblet can be broken by a hammer, but it can also be shattered by a voice. Thus, our thesis is that the economic and political subjugation of Aboriginals can be partly explained by a mentality that resisted the modern capitalist ethos. An Aboriginal never would have written the lines by a Protestant author quoted by Weber (1930: 162):

> If God show you a way in which you may lawfully get more than in another way (without wrong to your soul or to any other), if you refuse this, and choose the less gainful way, you cross one of the ends of your calling, and you refuse to be God's steward, and to accept His gifts and use them for Him when He requireth it: you may labour to be rich for God, though not for the flesh and sin.

This discourse would have seemed absurd to an Aboriginal. He worked to live, did not live to work and certainly did not work to acquire wealth that was absolutely useless and desperately evil, since it was the cause of excess and debauchery!

The Aboriginal thinking that resisted the *bourgeois* work ethic made Aboriginals look lazy to Europeans. Lafitau wrote, "Indians are almost always sitting with their arms crossed, holding meetings, singing, eating, playing, sleeping and doing nothing." (Lafitau 1983, I: 183) Alcohol consumption very often revealed the economic repercussions of idleness. In 1668, in his instructions to the Intendant concerning a request for an inquiry into the sale of alcohol to Aboriginals, the King described the opposing points of view of the missionaries and merchants.

> The Bishop and Jesuits claim that these beverages inebriate the Indians, that they are unable to consume them in moderation, and that drunkenness makes them too lazy to go hunting, and gives them all sorts of bad habits with respect to both religion and the state. In contrast, the leading habitants and merchants claim that the desire to acquire alcohol, which is traded for a high price, forces Indians to spend more time hunting. (ANQ-Q, B, Vol. 1, Folio 86v, *Instruction pour le sieur Bouteroue s'en allant intendant de la justice, police et finances en Canada*, April 5, 1668 [our translation])

Clearly, the moral problem of too much alcohol was no obstacle to merchants, for the resulting impoverishment was an incentive to go hunting. However, in both cases, it seems that consumption of alcohol was always assessed and judged in relation to the work of hunting.

Yet, many witnesses rightly expressed their surprise as to the valiance of Aboriginal peoples and did not hesitate to admit that they were enterprising and hard-working people. Indeed, it would be difficult to accuse of laziness men and women who covered astonishing distances under the hardest conditions such that they exhausted the missionaries, interpreters and merchants who accompanied them. There are many examples of situations in which their resistance and endurance were admired. Yet, curiously, the impression of laziness remained:

> Nevertheless, one hardly ever sees Indians running about like that, for their days are filled with nothing but pleasant pastimes. They are never in a hurry, much unlike us, who cannot do anything without rushing and, I should say, oppressiveness, because our desires tyrannize us and banish peace from our actions. (RJ 1972 [1611], 1: 11 [our translation])

The hitch is that *bourgeois* ethics add the virtue of accumulation to the idea of work. Both values are equally important, and we have examined their religious roots above. A *bourgeois* works to keep getting richer and not to pay back a debt or increase expenditures. Whether or not Aboriginals work therefore does not matter if they do not accumulate goods so that outside observers can recognize the *value* of their work. However, accumulation was something that Aboriginals simply did not care about.

It is not surprising that Lejeune made many comments on the food and eating and drinking habits of those he called "savages." They certainly involved customs that could disgust and astonish a Christian trained in the spirit of the Council of Trent. One was that meals were divided into two kinds: those where one ate what one wanted, and those where one had to eat everything. The latter in particular shocked Lejeune.

> For their feasts where nothing may be left, they deserve severe criticism, and yet these are among their most important ceremonies, for such feasts are held to ensure good hunting. They are very careful to make sure that the dogs taste not even a little bit, for if they did then all would be lost and the hunt would amount to nothing. Moreover, the more they eat, the more effective the feast. Thus they give a single man what I would not want to try to eat with the help of three big eaters. They would rather die, so to speak, than leave anything...He who eats the most is esteemed; you hear them telling stories about how much they can eat, specifying the quantity and parts of the beast that they have eaten. (RJ 1972 [1634], 1:38 [our translation])

Such waste was probably just as absurd to Lejeune as *bourgeois* accumulation of wealth was to an Aboriginal. It confirmed the European prejudice about the irrational behaviour of so-called savages. It completely devalued the results of work: for a Reformation Christian, there was no merit in working to live a dissolute life. In a way, work did not exist if it was always lost.[15] Christians could go even further, and express a common-sense moral hypothesis that the drunkenness of Aboriginals was caused partly by their ethics: they drank like they ate. Father Lejeune certainly noted the transformation of feasts where everything was eaten into parties where everything was drunk. (RJ 1972 [1634], 1: 31–32, 38)

European observers believed that the solution to the problem of the poverty and laziness of Aboriginals was to settle them into a sedentary way of life and have them become farmers. (RJ 1972 [1636], 1: 34–36, 52–53) Naturally, the association of "savageness" with a nomadic way of life ("savage" has the same root as "*sylvan*") was routine at the time of the conquest of the New World. Forest dwellers escaped the Catholic institution of the sacred, which was associated with village life. Of course, a "savage" was also someone who remained outside of the three levels of society in the Middle Ages: he was not a farmer, lord or priest, and had no role in the system of civilization. He was a strange stranger. In thinking that still contained a background of moral ideas from the Middle Ages, the purpose of having Aboriginals lead sedentary lives was to get them used to working the land. Modern thinkers were no less convinced of the need to achieve this, though by slightly different means.

In European Renaissance law, land ownership was linked to use. Land title could be refused to a person who did not make his property productive or cultivate the earth. Today, land ownership can be symbolic or non-agricultural, but this has not always been the case. European settlers were faithful to a physiocratic vision, and linked insufficient farming of the land with savageness. This enabled them to withdraw Aboriginals' right to use their land. In European languages, work is indeed associated with labour and *labourer*, which means "to till" in French. Fieldwork was seen as the nation's source of wealth and a stable means of feeding its inhabitants. It therefore represented both the first (needs) and last (luxury) occupations in the scale of human activities. This can be seen in comments by explorers and missionaries on Aboriginals' work, which anticipated the theories and discourse of physiocrats. They wrote that the women were the only ones who did any work, and that the men did nothing. Biard, a missionary in Acadia, wrote, "Once they have set up their tents, they become lazy and do not want to do any work. They depend entirely on their wives." (Quoted by Jacob 1994: 209 [our translation]) Women worked because they were responsible for farming the fields and other agricultural activities. Indeed, agriculture remained the best civilizing activity in the eyes of European settlers. Missionaries, who were known as Christ's workers, frequently used metaphors that evoked an abundant harvest of souls, the field of Aboriginal peoples, the fruits of proselytism, the seeds of the Gospel and preaching, the sheaves of missionary harvests, etc. Father Brébeuf spoke of "workers" who came to the New World to "cultivate the vines" that "already seem to be turning white for the harvest." Real work was that of the farmer, and this could be seen even in the vocabulary used to describe the religious undertaking of conversion. In the next century in the United States, in the discourse of both intellectuals and preachers, farming remained associated with civilization, whereas hunting, which was closely linked to Aboriginals in *bourgeois* imaginations, remained associated with animals. In the desire to settle Aboriginals and confine them to reserves, there were probably several ideas at work, and certainly the following one: this would allow Aboriginals to become real men by performing real work, namely that on the land, and to become civilized by practicing the civilizing activity *par excellence.*

In her book, Jacob shows clearly that the moral accusation of laziness levelled against Aboriginals was later combined with another criticism that has its source in an eighteenth-century economic theory, namely that Aboriginals had no needs. Not only did they not till the land, but they did not seem to consume, and were therefore unable to increase their production above the strict minimum needed for subsistence. From the point of view of a modern state, Aboriginals were useless or even harmful because they did nothing to increase wealth. Capitalist economic theory long rested (and still rests today) on ideas about the primary and secondary needs of humans. People work to meet their needs, except when work is a need in itself. Everyone aspires to get richer, invent more efficient means of production, and accumulate wealth. Everyone, except it seems Aboriginals, according to explorers. Curiously, Aboriginal needs seemed to be simple, rudimentary and almost animal. They did not seem eager to acquire the material prosperity of settlers or to join them in accumulating wealth. Aboriginals seemed to be happy to live idly: "...the sight of our conveniences, wealth, magnificent did not impress them very much." Worse, when they were brought to Europe, taken to see the most beautiful sights in France, shown French gardens, invited to worldly evenings where ladies danced in shiny sequined ball gowns, welcomed into royal mansions and shown the splendour of Paris, Aboriginals remained indifferent. They

> ...admired nothing and would have preferred their villages to the capital of the most flourishing kingdom in Europe, if they had not seen the rotisseries in the stores on Rue de la Huchette, which they always found full of meat of all kinds and which captivated them. (Charlevoix 1976, 3: 322 [our translation])

Charlevoix (who admitted that justice and brotherhood were stronger and better among Aboriginals than in the kingdoms of Europe and who was surprised to find that he envied their lifestyle) felt that there was only one possible explanation: Aboriginals were not "slaves to ambition and interest." His description thus repeats features of that of the "good Indian" who is happy with little, has the Spartan virtues of Antiquity, is philosophical in his temperance and has little desire to acquire material wealth.[16]

In both the United States and Canada, Aboriginal "civilization" and assimilation policies always consisted in expropriating land and then settling Aboriginals on reserves and "teaching" them to farm. Once again, the goal was to fit them into the practical and symbolic order of society (traditional society through binding to land and farming, and modern society through productive work). This undertaking quickly met virtually insurmountable obstacles. Not only was the land reserved for Aboriginals often inappropriate for agriculture because it was too dry or stony, or the climate was too cold (when it was good for farming, Aboriginals were evicted rather quickly), but farm "work" was an activity habitually reserved for women in the societies, which in any case had not waited for European settlers to work the land and discover agriculture. In contrast, in Europe, aside from the vegetable garden next to the house, fieldwork was reserved for men. In America, women were in charge of planting, weeding and harvesting while men hunted, fished, traded and made war. Moreover, agriculture was practiced on communal lands in a semi-sedentary manner. Thus, three challenges faced the ideologues who sought to assimilate Aboriginals into Western civilization: they had to turn women's work into men's work, privatize land and institute permanent ties to land. Enclosure on reserves certainly forced Aboriginals to become sedentary. However, this draconian policy did not succeed in turning Aboriginals into farmers, except for a few exceptions. Until recently, in areas where it was feasible, women continued to care for family vegetable gardens, and that is all.[17]

Men's refusal to farm is constant throughout Aboriginal history, and there are many examples of it. For instance, the Lorette Hurons, who lived near Québec City, were first settled on the *seigneurie* of Sillery, which they owned and which, officially, was simply managed by the Jesuits. Then, behind the Hurons' backs, the Jesuits became the owners. Of course, the Hurons have been protesting the loss of Sillery for two centuries, but surprisingly they have never asked for agricultural land in compensation. They demand an income. It is also because they received an income and not because they had access to farmland that Québec Aboriginals were jealous of the Iroquois of Kahnawake and Akwesasne and the Abenakis of Odanak, three communities that owned *seigneuries* where taxpayers paid rent to Aboriginal councils.

According to the precursors of anthropology, Aboriginals led idle, libertine, lazy and lascivious lives. They therefore had to be gluttonous, greedy, demanding and thieving.

> They [Aboriginals] are proud of their idleness. Laziness, indolence and sloth are in their tastes and at the foundation of their nature…they work less than any other people in the world…they almost always have their arms crossed, and never do anything but hold meetings, sing, eat, gamble, sleep and do nothing. (Lafitau, quoted in Jacob 1994: 213–214 [our translation]).

There is no point in reviewing the vast literature made up largely of racial prejudices, cultural misunderstandings, and, occasionally, religious otherworldliness. Jacob has already inventoried the best and the worst of these writings. Note only that the general gist is almost always "their life was truly idle and lazy." Since idleness and laziness were the mothers of vice, poverty and barbarism on the moral, economic and social levels, it followed that a lazy man could be only a sinner and vagabond. In contrast, converted Aboriginals took on the qualities and virtues of Europeans, and shared the values of sobriety, endurance and industry. Thus, in his 1639 report, Lejeune described a new convert as "a man of great skill and industry, far from the idleness and laziness natural to Indians." (JR, 16: 84 [our translation]) In missionaries' reports the expression most often connected with work is probably "laziness", just as that linked with morality is "lack of discipline." Sometimes European observers were astonished and exasperated by this because they believed strongly that "man is born to work and languishes and becomes bored with resting. He needs work, and if he has none, he seeks and finds it for himself." (Lafitau quoted in Jacob 1994: 213 [our translation]) A people that does not live wholly for work and devote itself to a life regulated by work runs the risk of falling into vice, corruption and wantonness. Yet colonial observers said that Aboriginals led a simple life. They therefore lacked only regulated, rational work to achieve happiness.

Clearly, as trade with European merchants increased, Aboriginals did not become wealthier, but there is no point in laying the blame on the greediness of the Whites or unequal trade. Why would an Aboriginal want to become rich if the foundations of his culture and his most inner self did not allow him to see wealth as an ideal? It did not play the same role or carry the same value as in the Western world. While Europeans considered Aboriginals to be poor or even miserable vagabonds living in unimaginable destitution, Aboriginals thought completely differently. In a 1611 letter to the Provincial of France, Father Biard said of the *Etchemins* that "…they are extremely proud and consider themselves braver than us, better than us, more ingenious than us, and, though it may be hard to believe, richer than us." (Quoted in Jacob 1994: 209 [our translation])

What was perhaps the most important implication of the absence of a sense of guilt among Aboriginals at the time of European colonization of America and the encounter between Aboriginal and *bourgeois* ethics was the social disintegration of a world based on unity of all with all, and not on personal internalized responsibility. It is useful to remember Émile Durkheim's concept of *anomie*.[18] The conquest of the New World resulted in a weakening of traditions and abandoning of certain roles in the shared culture, which could only have tragic consequences in a society where individuals were not supported by an internalized superego but rather directly by a meaningful "whole" that preceded them. It is important to grasp this to fully understand the thesis of this article. Among modern peoples, the collapse of customary rules is compensated by the internalization of abstract principles that are constantly used as bases from which we can deduce rules for handling the wide range of experiences with which we are faced. From a still very schematic point of view, it might be appropriate to follow David Riesman (1964) and contrast the "inner-directed" type with the traditional type. For example, compare Robinson Crusoe's industrious career on his island, where he works constantly and sets up a strict calendar from the time he first washes up on shore, with the anomie of life on some reserves isolated in the middle of a civilization that is either hostile or *a priori* contradictory. From the time of the first contact between Europeans and Aboriginals, it was possible to foretell Aboriginal demographic, economic and political subjugation not only by measuring the military might on each side or by predicting the epidemics that would decimate whole populations, but by foreseeing the breakdown of a social order in which each individual's activities and status were given basic meaning. On the fringes of the economy and excluded from the political status of citizen, in other words, as slaves to some extent, Aboriginal peoples suffered the same fate as European workers, who were condemned in the nineteenth century to learn the utilitarian standards of industry according to a constant, regular schedule foreign to the seasonal cycles of intermittent handicraft work.

> These labourers also had to learn to be tempted by money. British employers of that time, like those of South Africa today, constantly complained of the "laziness" of their workers and of their tendency to work until they had earned what for them was a week's salary, and then stop. The solution was draconian discipline at work (fines, master-slave codes, use of legal authority by employers, etc.), and especially, whenever possible, the institution of salaries that were so low that labourers had to work all week to earn the minimum necessary to survive. (Hobsbawm 2000: 89 [our translation])

Aboriginals' history thus resembles that of any people thrown into an industrial world after having lived according to traditions and meanings passed down through the ages. Yet they were also unprepared for the changes because their society had not even begun the transition towards *bourgeois* ethics and because they unfortunately had the luck (the wordplay is intentional) to be part of a colonial relationship, which allowed them to escape what Weber called the modern "iron cage." Aboriginals' lack of *beruf* consummated their exclusion from the new order of a society based on *bourgeois* and industrial work ("work is freedom"!). In nineteenth century Canada, not working was more than weakness; it was neither more nor less than to cut oneself off from civilization and participation in society. Aboriginals thus committed themselves to becoming the "beggars" of the colonial empire in a world where hunting was virtually impossible.

2. Primitive Ethics and Contemporary Society

In the first part of this article, we tried (too) briefly to identify two oppositions between Aboriginal and Reformation ethics. We also showed, in conclusion, the historical repercussions of these differences on the development of Aboriginal nations after their land was expropriated and they were excluded from the world of work. With a destabilized social organization and living in isolation on reserves, Aboriginals did not have the moral support of Reformation ethics and were in consequence beaten, so to speak, both militarily and culturally.

The analysis could remain there, but this would be to fail to ask what is happening now. Aboriginal ethics did not stop being retranslated and reproduced after conversion to Christianity and settlement on reserves. Aboriginals do not deny their heritage when they embrace the world created out of colonization. It is a cultural avatar carried by each generation, and loses nothing of its power. This is all the more true and important when we consider that the Aboriginals' situation in the Canadian political system over the last two centuries has, under the cover of rendering justice and improving living conditions, only deceitfully reinforced the causes of their misery and broken attempts to heal. Colonialism is a system that grinds down Aboriginal nations efforts to recuperate because it is blind to the Aboriginal ethics that motivate individuals and partly determine their destinies. Projected into a Christian universe, where the notions of occupational vocation and guilt play a central role, forced to operate in a culture with which they used to have only slight contact, and located on land that they cannot leave unless they choose to deny a part of themselves, Aboriginals have experienced aid, sympathy and philanthropy that have perhaps hindered more than helped their emancipation. Good intentions sometimes result in the worst policies.

2.1. Aboriginal Ethics and Victim Ideology

Aboriginal ethics do not include guilt as it is expressed in the Christian religion. Thus, full responsibility for one's destiny is impossible because accountability is always diffuse, shared and involves forces beyond one's control. If a man dies in strange, unsettling circumstances, the people of his nation immediately invoke a sorcerer's action, a violation of a taboo or a supernatural curse. His death is not entirely his own fault. If he drowned while trying to cross a swift-flowing river, then we have to ask why, why him when someone else could have done it; why then, when he had been able to cross in the past? Why was he not strong enough, and why was the current so strong that day? Someone must have wanted him dead, visited a sorcerer's hut, and performed the incantations to persuade the evil spirits. This is often (but of course never exclusively) how traditional Aboriginal thinking works in such circumstances.

This explains why Aboriginals find it so easy to see themselves as victims. When the mythical narrative is upset, the world order broken and the universe incomprehensible, one has to find meaning elsewhere than in myth and tradition. One knows that one is a victim of a situation as ineluctable as a curse, and as irrevocable as a divine decree. One feels one is the plaything of transcendent powers, and note that in the case of Aboriginals, this was objectively true for a long time. For example, consider the epidemiological shock, which had a greater impact than the worst catastrophes in medieval Europe. However, unlike Christians whose Reformation ethics allowed them to submit to external powers with the joy of martyrs or try to profit from the new developments in order to bounce back, Aboriginals felt that the world's equilibrium had been upset with respect to debt. This made them very different from Christians with *bourgeois* ethics, for whom the natural world is mute, has no soul, operates mechanically, and cannot and should not be expected to provide anything, and for whom other people are egotistical, self-interested and greedy. Those with *bourgeois* ethics seek salvation alone, through perseverance and abnegation. Adam Smith took these ethics to what may be their most inhuman degree.[19] He wrote that when a baker offers bread, it is not out of charity or goodwill, but out of material interest, and it is out of material interest that he buys shoes from the shoemaker. In such a world, no one should expect anything from anyone. Man is a wolf to man. In the Aboriginal world, debt, even if it is symbolic and in a sense especially if it is symbolic, must always be honoured. When the balance is upset, it must be re-established and injuries compensated. Traditional Aboriginals live in a world that is a totality, where beings are real and belong to the order of the world, or are swallowed up by nothingness. In other words, as long as an individual is not accepted by the nation, he is worse than a stranger: his existence is similar to that of a dog. However, as soon as he is integrated into the community, he becomes a man and receives the right to participate in the nation's symbolic and material system.

Unlike French Canadians, who, though they were conquered, demanded rights as citizens and not simply as subjects, Aboriginals' relationship to the British was based on a system of alliance and debt. Aboriginals never saw themselves as conquered peoples, even when they had lost all of their land and were reduced to living on reserves. For example, the Iroquois invoke the two-row wampum metaphor to express their relationship with the Canadian government. According to the metaphor, at the time of first colonization, the Iroquois signed a treaty with the Dutch at Albany in which each party promised to take a path parallel to the other without ever crossing. There are no documents to prove that such a treaty exists, and its late appearance in Aboriginal claims in Canada (around 1920, see NAC, RG10, 1919) makes it extremely suspect. However, it reveals an Aboriginal attitude to history, and more plausibly to their history in the United States, where American Indians really did take a separate, parallel and perfectly Euclidian path (see Marienstras 1976: 157–183). The most radical proponents of the two-row wampum metaphor give it an interesting interpretation: they see themselves as allies of the British Crown, and not as subjects of the Canadian parliament, and even less as citizens of Canadian provinces. Nostalgic for the historical alliance, they tend to deny the whole process of colonization. They obscure not only the Conquest and the expropriation that took place, but also the integration of Aboriginals into state structures and Canadian society. So doing, they show a vision of the world that is very old in Aboriginal imagination. There are many traces of it in all archives, in particular in petitions dating as far back as 1760 and addressed to the colonial government by Aboriginals living in Québec. The oldest type of narrative, a kind of summary of the Aboriginal interpretation of colonial history, is that of hospitality and the obligation to reciprocate. There are many variations. They can be summarized by a discourse that takes the following form: "When we, the people of the First Nations, were powerful and prosperous, you, Europeans, came to our lands. You were miserable, vulnerable, reduced to starvation. We had pity on you. We fed, clothed, healed and housed you with generosity. Gradually, you became stronger. Then you seized our lands and wealth. Now you are rich and prosperous and we are poor. See our suffering. Have pity! Be generous in turn! Acknowledge your debt and repay it!"

For example, on November 28, 1833, representatives of the Iroquois, Abenaki, and Nipissing at *Lac des Deux Montagnes* complained to Governor General Aylmer that the gifts they were given each year had been reduced. They also mentioned land claims that brought them into conflict with the Sulpicians. Admitting that they had been dispossessed and that they were not knowledgeable, they implored him to have pity and be charitable.

> Tell Our Father, the Good King, that there was a time when his Red Children at Lac des Deux Montagnes were rich in land. That their Good King at the time gave it to them and even guaranteed it in a Proclamation in 1763. Then there was no need to pity them! They took enough pelts to clothe their families... [and once a year] they all went to the late General to salute their Father and receive the gifts that he had the Great Kindness to send them. Everything has changed now. Our Lands have been taken away. By what authority we do not know. Be Charitable My Father, help your Children...We kneel down before you My Father to beg you for your help...We know that you are Just and Charitable and we are persuaded that You will do everything in your power so that your Children receive the justice that they have the right to hope for. And Your Children will continue praying for you. (NAC, RG10, 1933b [our translation])

Note that this was in 1833, on the eve of the 1837 Rebellion, in the years when the Patriots of Upper and Lower Canada denounced the high-handedness of the King and local authorities, and demanded ministerial accountability. Canadian rebels wanted to reduce the King's power, while those who presented the petition to Aylmer were instead asking the King to use his power to render justice in accordance with the system of alliance and debt. A number of petitions repeated the theme, but with respect to Aboriginal participation in colonial wars: "We fought for you, our "father" and King, now protect us." In this father-child relation (see Delâge 2001), Aboriginals played the role of creditor and the English king that of debtor. The latter was indebted to his Aboriginal allies because they had saved the colony from attacks by enemy Aboriginal nations, and the French and American armies. Without them, the King's possessions would have fallen into other hands. The King had thus created eternal obligations to Aboriginal peoples: he owed them "life."[20]

At the same time that the ethics of Aboriginals encouraged them to expect compensation for injuries inflicted by those who now wanted to call themselves their allies, both the French and English monarchies had long operated through favours and gifts. In diplomatic relationships, Samuel de Champlain had systematized the traders' practice of sealing commercial alliances with trinkets and small items, and with military expeditions. This practice continued throughout the seventeenth and eighteenth centuries. An ambassador's mission had to begin with a feast, an alliance had to be sealed with presents and a treaty had to be concluded with an exchange of wampum. It was enshrined enough in nineteenth century customs to become a kind of income that was all the more impatiently anticipated by Aboriginals because it was increasingly becoming their sole source of revenue. A Huron-Wyandot legend gathered in the early nineteenth century said that the Great Serpent told the mischievous Wolverine: *"Tu es fier et orgueilleux; je te couvrirai de soie, d'écarlate et de cercles d'argent comme un grand-chef qui rend visite à Ononthio."* (quoted by Barbeau 1994: 321) In return for military services that were often decisive in war, the kings of France and England gave presents to warriors and their families. The gifts were not limited to the officers' jackets and medals that Aboriginals wore with pride, but also included pensions, in particular to widows of warriors who had died in combat. (NAC, RG10, 1816) The Aboriginal warrior tradition, which valued marks of honour, accepted the presents not only for their material value but also as signs of prestige from a more powerful chief. The relationship was far from without consequences. With no other role but the defence of a nation of which they were not citizens, and with no prestige aside from that of dying in combat for a system from which they were radically excluded, Aboriginals looked more and more like mercenaries. But of course, they never saw themselves that way. On the contrary, they believed themselves to be associated with what was most noble and elevated in the English political structure: the monarchy. The cultural proximity of European aristocrats, who were often military officers or at least saw themselves in terms of medieval military culture, and Aboriginal chiefs can be seen in their love of pageantry, and in the military exploits, sports and hunting in which they engaged. Aboriginals prided themselves on this association. Unfortunately for them, the aristocracy was declining, condemned by history and increasingly parasitical on a society that would either cut off its head with the guillotine or turn it into a kind of quaint eccentricity.

The military treaties between European empires and Aboriginal nations were conducive to maintaining the formal status as allies until the end of the 1812–1814 war, and, to a lesser extent at least, until Canada was created in 1840. Aboriginals then came under the authority of a government that was civilian rather than military, and suddenly the British administration saw gifts and presents as superfluous. Aboriginal nations resented the breaking of the military alliance, which was linked to the cessation of presents and seen as an abandonment and failure to fulfill a paternal duty. "What will become of us if our good Father the King stops clothing us as he used to?" (NAC, RG10, 1933a [our translation]) The quest for independence continued to focus paradoxically on increased dependency. In the minds of the colonized, Aboriginal socio-economic autonomy required that the central government take control.

It is impossible to understand Aboriginal history, and therefore the relationships that were established between the Aboriginal nations and colonial powers, without analysing the father-child metaphor. The original system of relationships between Aboriginal and European peoples has ramifications even today. Is Tocqueville not there to remind us that societies long remain marked by the circumstances of their birth? In the case of Aboriginal society, we can say, without playing on words, that it is born of a kinship relationship. This relationship is so fundamental that we have to trace its history in order to fathom the four centuries of colonialism. Both hunter-gatherer and sedentary Aboriginal societies were based on kinship in the sense that it covered all social relationships. Even in the most institutionalized societies, such as among the Iroquois, politics hardly ever extended outside of family lines. When they arrived in the New World, the French thus had to negotiate their position within pre-existing alliances, which were themselves expressed within kinship relationships and symbols. This explains why the French were initially received as brothers (or cousins) in the alliance, in other words, as partners that were the others' equals.

The French-Aboriginal alliance was seen as a brotherly relationship until 1660. At that time, the French Governor, whom Aboriginals called "*Onontio*" (which means "big mountain", in reference to Governor Montmagny), became a "father" and Aboriginal nations his "children." On August 13, 1682, Kondiaronk (Saretsi) described the change in the relationship and its consequences:

> Onontio, Saretsi your son used to call himself your brother, but no longer. Now he is your son and you have given birth to him through the protection that you have given him against his enemies. You are his Father and he knows you as such. He obeys you as a child obeys his father. He listens to your voice, and he does only what you want because he respects his father, whom you are. (C11a-6 Folio 7v, words exchanged between Frontenac and his allies [our translation])

By providing them with military protection, which became necessary after the wars with the Iroquois League and the terrible epidemics in the first half of the seventeenth century, the French governor had managed to raise himself above the

Aboriginal nations that were his allies. However, we should note the misunderstanding with respect to the obedience of a "child" to his "father" that could arise when one society was patriarchal European, and the other matrilineal Aboriginal. In Huron societies, the maternal uncle has much more moral authority over his sister's children than does their father. The father's role is limited to that of a protector and provider. The title of father therefore led Europeans to imagine that they played the role of maternal uncle, while Aboriginals thought they were under the protection of an Aboriginal father when they agreed to comply with his authority. This misunderstanding is the key to fully grasping French-Aboriginal diplomatic relations. In the end, it involved a degree of Aboriginal subordination to the French colonial power. Conquest was lying in wait under the system of alliance. When they agreed to be "children" born out of their "father's" protection, Aboriginals believed they were placing their nations under the benevolent care of stronger nations (by paying in blood when necessary), but for the French this meant reproducing the feudal hierarchies of the king above his vassals (the Sun King was the metaphor for royal absolutism). In the colonial context at the time of "progress", the father-child metaphor was a continuation of the well-known theme of civilization, which was associated with adulthood (see Kant's famous essay, *What is Enlightenment?*[21]), in contrast with Indianness, which was associated with childhood. Thus, power and responsibility were concentrated in the hands of the representative of the Crown, while irresponsibility was the lot of the colonized.

During the French regime, the "father's" authority over his "children" was limited by grim resistance that resulted from the dependency of the French on Aboriginals with respect to trade and war, and from competition from a powerful rival, the King of England. After the Conquest of Canada, the British copied the relationships established by the French, and took advantage of the elimination of colonial rivalries to increase their authority. Former allies became "allies and dependants."[22] In particular, to borrow Jean-Jacques Simard's accurate expression, Aboriginal nations were subject to a "reduction."[23] As in the seventeenth century, this meant reducing the nomads' freedom and mobility, making them sedentary, and "reducing" their pagan beliefs to control their unreasonable impulses. The only difference in the nineteenth century was that the "reduction" took on a totalitarian meaning. It meant reducing the geographical area occupied, closing the political forum and eliminating cultural differences. Aboriginals, who used to be child-warriors fighting for the king of France or England, were from then on seen as "backward children" belonging to the past and hanging onto outdated customs. The goal was to teach the children, and force them if necessary, to grow up and become "adults." So long as they remained "children", the king had the duty to protect them from others and from themselves, provide for their needs and keep them under his guardianship. The colonial family metaphor should not mislead us into thinking that the king-father loved both his red and white children equally and did not discriminate amongst them. This idyllic image is a lie. The real "children" were the ones whom the "father" could imagine as adults, in other words, the "white children." Those who were stubbornly called "children", but who were destined to always remain dispossessed of everything, were in fact servants. (Until 1960, educated Aboriginals lost their legal status as "Indians" because the status was associated with a primitive, and therefore not cultivated, state, which gave Aboriginals only one means of progressing, namely, assimilation through the status and culture of English Canadians.) Yet, sometimes with blind determination, Aboriginals never dared break with the father–child metaphor. In 1833, the Algonquins, Nipissings, and Iroquois at Oka (in Kanesatake) certainly noted the loss of their lands, yet they continued, in a pathetic manner, to ask for pity and beg the King to rise to the role of father. (Likewise, Black Americans in the civil rights movement did not accuse America of being built on racism, but racists of betraying America's founding principles. Martin Luther King's dream was the American Dream.) Cut off from their traditional means of subsistence and their military functions, these Aboriginals implored the king's indulgence, and asked him to maintain the annual distribution of gifts. There was no dependency in their eyes. The gifts were only the just repayment of a debt. They were no longer military allies, and were prevented (and restrained themselves to some extent) from becoming European settlers. They begged the King to take care of them, as his "children." However, the presents, which were initially signs of the alliance, simply legitimized colonialism.

By voluntarily submitting to colonial management, Aboriginals probably hoped to be able to profit from the government's generosity according to their own logic and not that of their Western counterparts. For, among Aboriginal peoples, a chief, hunter or warrior accumulates wealth in order to redistribute it later. Prestige is acquired through sacrifice and gifts rather than through ostentation and accumulation. "The personal motive for trade was not for a man or his family to possess an inordinate amount of exotic goods but to be able to acquire prestige by giving them away." (Trigger 1992: 269) Thus, they held potlatches, in other words, rituals in which chiefs increased their glory by destroying as many goods as possible in order to humiliate their adversaries. Clearly, the colonial government did not see things this way, and its reasoning was basely economic and political when it came to dealing with Aboriginals. The Iroquois, Algonquins and Nipissings of *Deux Montagnes* (Oka), who originally owned the banks of the Ottawa River, finally lost everything, including their village. This was how their "father" demonstrated his generosity.

One might have thought that Aboriginal ethics would have been exhausted with respect to its relationship to responsibility. Aboriginals might have gotten tired of always begging for what they were due from a distant, deaf power with malevolent policies. They could have finally had enough of playing a game in which they had to humiliate themselves and beg without ever receiving anything in return, except leftovers that no one else wanted. Curiously, far from tending towards a change in attitude similar to that of Reformation ethics, in recent decades they seem to have reinforced the victim discourse that they have been putting forward for two centuries. Submitting claims to various levels of government, they demand compensation and reparations. Some want land, others want reserves expanded and better supported, some want "Indian" status preserved, others want free circulation between Canada and the United States, some want the promotion of Aboriginal culture, and others want stronger assistance programs. All of this is to compensate for the death and disaster caused by the French and British presence. We are seeing the emergence of a corporate discourse based on the ancient discourse. The placards that Aboriginals wave are their suffering, alienation and dispossession.

Jean-Jacques Simard has shown this in admirable articles, as well as a recent book that provides a synthesis of his work. We will limit ourselves to noting the key theses relevant to this article. Simard says that Aboriginals have been able to play the role of victims so well only because Whites have slowly internalized guilt with respect to the peoples of the First Nations. This is expressed in the (relatively recent) transformation from "bad Indian" into "good Indian." While Aboriginals used to be considered greedy, deceitful, barbarian thieves, relegated to the obscurity of history by the march of progress, and cut off from humanity by those who were the most racist, they have become in the eyes of many "good Indians." This occurred in the very movement by which life in the West has come to be seen as alienating and disillusioned. Lévi-Strauss said, "Western Europe may have produced anthropologists precisely because it was prey to strong feelings of remorse..." (Lévi-Strauss 1976: 509) Thus, the range of qualities describing Whites is opposed to that of those describing Aboriginals. Since the former are thieving, vile, greedy, basely material, blind, sectarian, exploitative, raping, murderous, persecuting dominators, "Indians" can only be happy, innocent, hospitable and in communion with nature. (See Ohl 1991) Colonization's influences have corrupted Aboriginals, but within the limited freedom granted to them by ferocious White insatiability, they still struggle to be "real Indians." The more Whites are guilty of creating the "Indian's" condition, the more "Indians" are passive victims of Whites' evil. The more they are victims, the more compensation they can win. This is why the discourse of some Aboriginal leaders focuses on misery. While in the past they threatened to return to the warpath, pity has now become one of their only means of gaining acknowledgment (and therefore money) from the authorities. This involves recalling the conquerors' crimes, such as systematic massacres of so-called savages, breaking of treaties, merchants' unbridled greed, wars, and the "genocide" caused by epidemics. Why such denunciation and indictment? To get grants from governments. Clearly, the greater the indictment and crimes, the more innocent the victim, and the more dependency increases. In consequence, Aboriginal peoples increasingly depend on the feeling of guilty condescension that they create among federal and provincial authorities.

2.2. The Standard of Governmental Solicitude was Formed in the Mould of Paternalism

[T]o different degrees, the state makes up for the lack of a natural labour market by creating and increasing jobs within its own programs. It has often been said that the primary effect of White society's massive intervention in Aboriginal economics is the creation, after Aboriginal societal structures are eliminated, of a dependency that increases the need to intervene to support employment, even artificially. This intervention in turn increases dependency and leads to greater intervention in a vicious circle that requires more and more public money. (Drouilly 1991: 88 [our translation])

At the time of the Royal Commission on Aboriginal Peoples ("RCAP" 1996b), there were around 500 000 registered and unregistered "Indians" in Canada. The federal and provincial budgets that were set aside for them totalled around $13 billion, which amounted to $26,000 per capita. Simard *et al.* (1996, 1: 51–52) confirmed these numbers in a study on total per capita expenditures between 1983 and 1989 by all governments combined. Government spending averaged $7,710 per capita in Québec, but $15,094 per capita for the Cree. In New Québec, the per capita average for status "Indians" was $21,117, in the Northwest Territories $23,258 and for the Inuit $29,369. These impressive figures are partly misleading. Per capita expenditures are necessarily higher in the North because of the distances, isolation and climate, and Aboriginals and Inuit live mainly in the North. However, even when they are weighted to take into account the "northern factor", per capita expenditures on Aboriginals and Inuit are approximately twice that spent on Québeckers and Canadians in general. The RCAP found that "…the amount spent per person for Aboriginal people is 57 per cent higher than for Canadians generally." (1996b: 138) The governments are therefore generous to Aboriginal nations, and the primary explanation for the visible poverty of many Aboriginal communities cannot be an absence of financial resources (though it is clear that more will have to be provided in years to come). The quest for concrete solutions therefore has to target less new financial resources than new responsibilities. (We will discuss the new responsibilities in greater detail below, but here we would like to point out immediately, so as to prevent the reader from going off in the wrong direction, how far we are from wanting to insinuate that the solution simply requires the moral regeneration of Aboriginal peoples.)

The state (which includes legal and administrative frameworks, sovereignty, and policies and procedures for managing the Aboriginal "problem") is a kind of unavoidable limitation on Aboriginal destiny. On one hand, it is responsible for the interminable expropriation of the first inhabitants. On the other hand, it is in consequence responsible for compensating the expropriation by providing paternal protection and confirming a special status. Together, these two responsibilities (which entail Indian status, recognized Aboriginal rights, the resulting services and budgets, etc.) are still the best means of protecting Aboriginal birthrights in Canada against assimilation and negation by the popular majority. Out of force of habit, when Aboriginal solidarity is not based on permanent, immemorial cultural evidence, it tends to come from the state itself. Solidarity becomes an epiphenomenon of the fact of being placed in a legal and administrative category and, once it is swallowed in that way, collective claims confirm and perpetuate the secondary state (which becomes the first) of a special "clientèle" of state patronage. It is as if oppression and emancipation attracted one another, as if Aboriginal identity was literally created by legislation and therefore by the special state structures responsible for keeping former "savages" in their place while at the same time ensuring that their place is not too uncomfortable. The contemporary Aboriginal movement reproduces this contradiction, for it can be said to spring both from the thigh of the Minister of Indian Affairs and from the belly of the First Nations. (Simard 1985: 15 [our translation])

While the reserve framework remains unchanged, and even tightens around Aboriginal communities, some Aboriginals dance ancestral dances before television cameras, like trained bears imprisoned in zoos. This is why we have to worry about a situation that has been constructed out of the materials of colonial history, in which the state is the eternal provider and to which some Aboriginals abandon their primary social responsibilities and limit themselves to playing the role of beggar.

> In order to save their collective identity and dignity, some Aboriginals believe they are forced to have a discourse that draws on nostalgia for victimization (even among the Inuit, for whom the White "invasion" occurred mainly after 1955 and coincided with all the paternalistic indulgences of a welfare state). This can be seen as a particularly insidious form of colonial alienation, which condemns such peoples to exist truly only in so far at their status as victims is recognized and confirmed in the eyes of the Other. (Simard 1991: 131 [our translation])

Aboriginals are victims, first because of colonization but also because of the humiliations that they had to suffer throughout colonial history. In this respect, even though it was not really a genocide in Canada, the conquest of the New World reinforced, through brutal exclusion and expropriation measures, the self-image of Aboriginals as passive victims. Unfortunately, enclosure in the logic of the victim can only feed dependency.

Let us take the example of residential schools, which Aboriginals see as a major source of unhappiness. We cannot underestimate the trauma suffered by young children taken away from their families, or the systematic policy of assimilation, or the intolerable sexual abuses. However, we have to recognize that Aboriginal discourse sometimes tends to exaggerate and generalize. Most importantly, we have to admit that the criticism is wide of its target, for by obsessing about the harm done by residential schools and members of the clergy who worked there, it fails to attack colonial history and political institutions. It prevents a challenge of the ethnocentric and racism of the majority. It limits itself to assailing Catholic and Anglican institutions that are in decline and that are largely only (bad) memories in Aboriginal lives.

However, we have to take the analysis further by noting, with Simard, the imprisonment in a paternalistic bureaucratic system that leaves little room for Aboriginal initiative and the development in contemporary society of an identity precisely based on the feeling of being a victim. Erasing 200 years of colonial history requires more than taking control of one's life and breaking free of the yoke of state paternalism, or shouldering responsibilities overnight. On top of it all, Aboriginals are not the only ones who adopt the attitude of victims with respect to authority today. Reformation ethics are shrinking away to nothing in the face of the rise of a new ethic, which has no Aboriginal features, except perhaps distrust of individual responsibility. With the monstrous development of anonymous bureaucratic and organizational powers, features that used to fall under individual responsibility become areas outside of the system's jurisdiction, with the result that people look less able to take action and more like powerless subjects.

Freud thought he could link the feeling of guilt to the development of civilization. He saw the repression of impulses as the condition for artistic and scientific sublimation, as well as for the effectiveness of moral prohibitions. "Cultural renunciation" of satisfaction of instincts, such as aggressive or sexual instincts, requires fear of public authority and of the private authority that is, in a way, the superego. According to Freud, this explains the inevitability of the feeling of guilt. He portrays "the sense of guilt as the most important problem in the development of civilization" and tries to show that "the price we pay for our advance in civilization is a loss of happiness through the heightening of the sense of guilt." (Freud 1961: 102) Such guilt is no longer part of discourse and no one would think of arguing that it is worthwhile to endure unhappiness in order to achieve humanization. This is because society is now less something created by men and women, but more, and increasingly, a puppet of major organizations that pull the strings of history in the shadows offstage. Thus it is no longer the individual's responsibility. It is becoming a more plural, complex, hostile environment, as well as less easy to trust, and individuals have to protect themselves against it. Major organizations have a powerful impact on society but outside of cooperative human objectives, for their only criteria are efficiency and profitability. It pushes onto the fringe the subject's ability to interpret the world, participate in it and play a leading role. We will not discuss in further detail the change from modernity to postmodernity, which is not an integral part of this article. Instead we refer the reader to authors who have dealt with the topic better and in greater detail than we. To save time, we will simply quote a long passage from a forthcoming book on the way a citizen's identity has changed in contemporary society.

> In their dreams, individuals can identify with powerful organizations and imagine that they share their influence. I call such people "organization people." When their own world suddenly changes out of the blue, such people may imagine that their hardships are punishments, that the so-called punishment is proof that they are guilty and that their powerlessness proves it. In both cases, however, harbouring such illusions is a pure waste of time. Individuals do not have to agree to constraints that are established in the name of nothing and without their consent. Likewise, there is no reason to identify with a mega-machine of which one is, in a way, the lubricant and medium. Individuals seem thus to oscillate like manic-depressives between the two positions. Sometimes they feel included in society's mode of production, such as when they feel they belong to the organizations in question, and sometimes they feel excluded when they feel they have fallen back into the mass on which the organizations operate. In any case, what we call "social" operates whether or not individuals subjectively assume its capacity for change. Without

> an explicit law that they can endorse, individuals go off in all directions seeking intersubjective meaning, but their actions have no impact on the system. At the same time, individuals no longer have to worry about encountering a Big Brother in the form of a single, tyrannical person or centre of power. Thus they can freely seek one another out, and tend towards intimate relations. This does not concern the system, only the world of experience. Should we now call out: "Free the world of experience"? Yet, this has already been done! Given the way society has evolved and the world has changed, we are all, taken individually, perfectly innocent, in the dual sense of individuals fundamentally incapable of responsibility and guilt. Impersonal powers change society simply by reproducing their technical ability to do so. Each power's reasons for action, if it has any, are its own and specific historical societies, which are foreign to the forces that control and literally feed them, no longer dare to say in what name they exist, if they exist. (Gagné 2005 [our translation])

The individual is no longer guilty of what happens to him, and for good reason: most of the time the changes that affect him result from decisions in which he was not involved. He drifts in the stream of upheavals caused by structures over which he has no control. Now who will be responsible for the perverse effects of the development of capitalist society, and who will pay the cost? Major organizations, certainly, when they can and if they can be proven responsible. However, now that such proof is fading and becoming less clear, we have to turn to the state as the last hope for levels of society excluded from general prosperity. In other words, society's outcasts, failures and misfits will become the state's responsibility. The rapid growth of the welfare state after WWII coincided with a new awareness of collective responsibility for what used to be individual faults.[24] The state now solves social problems, makes up for the deficiencies of civil society, supports families, takes care of mentally handicapped people, funds young entrepreneurs, organizes amateur sports, takes care of those hurt in traffic accidents, etc. What do we say about its jurisdiction and duties? Yet, when the state's solicitude is not justified by efficiency or competitiveness, it is always inspired by the concrete hardships of groups or companies that lobby it because, now that they have discharged upon the state their responsibility for the market, the groups and companies are simple victims of fate's blows. In the end, the state gives public recognition only in accordance with the suffering to which an individual can lay claim.

> When we are faced with a state that has to take charge of the concrete conditions of the pursuit of happiness, our best arguments become our hardships. Let us take the argument to its final conclusion: since we are innocent of the constraints imposed on us by change, it is natural that we should be their victims. Social rights thus come together to create victims' rights, and we no longer have to worry about victims, big or small, as soon as they all have equal social rights. (Gagné 2005 [our translation])

According to this view of postmodern society, individuals cannot be responsible for their irresponsibility, but they are victims of their innocence. This applies to Aboriginals like everyone else, and every individual brandishes his or her hardship in an effort to move public opinion enough to get the state to mobilize the maximum resources. For Aboriginal peoples, this system is even more perverse and determining than for the rest of the population. This is because Aboriginals submit claims to the state based on the fact that they are substantially victims of history and not the random functional victims of a system. Aboriginals take on the identity of victims as "Indians" (in other words, biologically and by blood) not to confront a foreign, usurping state, but to ask it for help and beg for assistance. Thus, what other people do in today's society is quite different from the actions of Aboriginals.

> Except for very rare exceptions, [the Lorette Hurons] have not...acquired a taste for farm work or an aptitude for land ownership. They have no ambition to become individual owners of plots of land. Moreover, they do not wish to be emancipated at either the public or private levels. Indeed, they even fear emancipation. Those with whom I spoke about this were frankly hostile. Many of them were so discontented with the current state of things and unhappy about the way in which business was managed by the chiefs, agent and Department of Indian Affairs, that they refused to attend meetings and take part in elections. However, they did not see emancipation as a remedy for their woes. They simply wanted new guardians. They said that they needed the protection of someone powerful. If they were emancipated, they might lose all they owned to dishonest Whites, and they would have to pay heavy taxes. Under the current system, the government pays for religion and education, and even the roads are maintained by the Whites in parishes neighbouring Lorette in exchange for right of passage on the Huron reserve. According to them, emancipation was a danger in private life and a burden in public life. (Gérin 1902: 341 [our translation])

The only hitch is that when one is the private victim of a public order, one forgets to think about public responsibility for the private level. However, we have no intention of ending this section by reducing the demand of collective rights for Aboriginals to an attempt to manipulate public opinion to get money from the state. In this respect, we have to commend the actions of a number of Aboriginal groups that are requesting full political responsibility, and all the rights and duties that go along with it. There have been rapid changes in the last ten or fifteen years. Aboriginals are becoming more aware that a discourse intended to attract pity cannot replace combat that is both more general and more fundamental against the state's paternalistic power, that the pity-based discourse is better at maintaining dependency than providing a springboard to self-government, and that by being only a passive victim of history, one undermines oneself. In other words, Aboriginals' political struggle for recognition requires that they agree to have rights and duties. We will try to explain our position more clearly in the conclusion.

2.3. Aboriginal Ethics and Work[25]

Government assistance is not improving the general situation of Aboriginal peoples. On the contrary, it seems to get worse in direct proportion to the amount of solicitude shown, though in the last 40 years there has been notable progress in terms of life expectancy and education. Various new services and government attention may have raised the overall standard of living, but they have not checked the social problems in Aboriginal communities, far from it. In Québec, Aboriginal communities have the highest death rates and are in brutal disarray, and this leads to problems such as family break-up, domestic violence, homicide, alcoholism, trauma, obesity and respiratory problems among children. The low morale may be better expressed by a few statistics. The Dussault-Erasmus Commission gathered them systematically, and the picture that emerges is all the more pathetic since the Commission's report has more or less been shelved.[26] The life expectancy of registered "Indians" is ten years less than that of other Canadians; 57% of the former have not finished high school, compared with 37.8% of the latter; other Canadians (11.4%) are four times more likely to complete a university degree than are Aboriginals (3%); the unemployment rate from 1981 to 1991 was 30% for registered "Indians", but only 9% for Canadians in general[27]; in 1991, the average income of an Aboriginal was $14,561 compared with $24,000 for the general population; in Canada as a whole, around .63% of children were apprehended by social services, but 4.1% of registered "Indian" children were taken into care (which means that over seven times more were removed from their homes!); the suicide rate for men is ten times higher among registered Indians than among the population in general (5.15 per 100,000 against .49 per 100,000). In short, in all of the statistics related to social or socio-economic problems, Aboriginals are scandalously over-represented. Consequently, Aboriginals account for 17% of the people in federal and provincial institutions. Aboriginal dependency on the government is so well documented that there is no point in insisting on it. How can this be explained without resorting to racist theories (whether they are based on the "good" or "bad" Indian) or colonialist ideas (whether they involve Whites' civilizing mission or a wide-ranging accusation of Western imperialism)? Every year, the federal Department of Indian Affairs puts billions of dollars into improving the situation in Aboriginal communities. Should we blame bureaucratic muddles or the negligence of the Aboriginal elite for the fact that so much money does not seem to have had the beneficial effects that we might expect, though clear improvements have been made since the 1960s?

Once again, the history of the social decline of Aboriginal peoples can be understood by invoking the fact that the social equilibrium was broken as sectoral and operational state intervention replaced ancient ties within the community. Some do not hesitate to explain the high level of incest by a system of exchange that was perverted when tribes withdrew to their reserves and by the disintegration of not only traditions but also Aboriginals' original social pact. Since social networks were dismantled and collective ties broken, the overall symbolic order was blown away forever, and Aboriginal peoples found themselves thrown into a system that was not their own and that tended to gradually take over all social and cultural space. The debt of meaning has thus been projected onto a social level, namely that of the bureaucratic state, over which Aboriginals have little control and that also obeys requirements of technical efficiency that help to further erode living solidarity. (Leroux 1995: 51–69) This leads to both economic and symbolic subjugation, clear signs of the alienation of Aboriginal peoples and symptoms of not only the specific exploitation of which Aboriginals were recently the victims, but also of a confrontation between two contradictory ethical systems.

Duhaime has pointed out that the behaviour of contemporary Aboriginal employees resembles that of European workers at the dawn of the Industrial Revolution. Note also the degree to which this behaviour resembles that of French Canadians in the nineteenth century according to descriptions by Léon Gérin and Étienne Parent, who strongly believed that idleness was the cause of the economic inferiority of their compatriots. "While it is not an absolute rule, the tendency to be absent from work, ignore work schedules, and quit jobs is widespread in Inuit lands, as in other traditional societies that are entering modernity." (Duhaime 1991: 114 [our translation]) In cases as different as the Irish, Polish, Russians and various African groups, observers have always believed that traditional peoples have greater difficulty adapting not to modernity as Duhaime believes, but to the capitalist system of work, which is very different. What Duhaime says of the Inuit is true of Aboriginals in general. If we limit our study to Canadians of Aboriginal origin living off-reserve and participating in the labour market, we find that only 39% work full-time year-round. The figure for Canada as a whole is 60%. Canadians of Aboriginal origin who live on reserves have a labour market participation rate of 43%, in comparison with 67% for the rest of the population of Canada. In 1986, the census showed that nearly 60% of Aboriginals said they were unemployed and not looking for work. Unemployment is twice as common in the Aboriginal labour force than among that of Canadians in general. Their family incomes were the lowest, and 45% of Aboriginals were living on government grants and allocations in 1985, a jump of 12% compared with 1980. In short, the situation is dramatic and seems to be getting worse.

Anthropologists and historians have been trying to explain these statistics for years, and their many hypotheses have ranged from so-called primitive peoples' native laziness to colonial alienation.

Duhaime suggests a different reading of the Inuit's tendency to change jobs:

> We are suggesting that, while it may be a lifestyle, it is not based on a natural tendency towards laziness or dislike of work, but on the fact that collectively the Inuit are able to meet their needs with what they have and economic pressure is not sufficient to drive them to adopt a different approach. The situation was different for the English masses at the turn of the eighteenth century, when they were forced off their land by fences, sent to growing cities, and led by hunger to the doors of factories. (Duhaime 1991: 115 [our translation])

This explanation is attractive, and above all it has the advantage of looking beyond the ethnocentrism and moralizing of earlier anthropological judgments. However, it is false to claim that hunger has not been available as a motive for conversion to capitalist thinking when we know of the disastrous scarcities of which the Inuit were the victims in the twentieth century. The Inuit have been living below the poverty line for too long for a social dynamic of needs to be plausible. Moreover, the other explanations in Duhaime's text (great diversification of possible sources of revenue and institutional acceptance of worker mobility) are at least as likely to be the consequences as the causes of the phenomenon. We have to look else-where for a rational and hermeneutic understanding of the abandonment of stable employment.

Duhaime probably provides the key to the enigma when he writes that the Inuit manage to meet their needs collectively and that the "ancient networks of solidar-ity still operate as mechanisms for redistribution of wealth." The fact that people switch jobs, which entails that part-time, temporary and seasonal jobs are four times more numerous than the Inuit labour force, cannot be linked primarily to in-come or the institutional structure of employment (though seasonal work increases greatly in the summer), but to the work culture.

On one hand, capitalist work, which has strict rules, compartmentalized tasks and roles, and purely operational purposes, is foreign to the traditional symbolic sys-tem. Duhaime highlights the incompatibility of Western work values and tradi-tional values, which would force the Inuit to keep jobs for relatively short periods since they would be unable to see them as sources of esteem or accomplishment. The capitalist description of work reveals the mechanical, absurd nature of the act itself, which has no meaning when it is compared with its immediate purposes. Manufacturing makes it possible to artificially create continuous working condi-tions that are broken down into units of time. This is why it developed as it did in the nineteenth century. The work cycle is that of a machine, and workers live to the rhythm of factory whistles. Concretely, it designates the process of appropriation of work by the capitalist regime and its total decomposition in order to create a production code with no symbolic meaning in life, and at a time when leisure and consumerism had not yet been established as the flip side of alienated work.

On the other hand, Duhaime notes the degree to which the ancient custom of shar-ing income and the products of labour continues in northern Québec culture.

> Required generosity, which is governed by a series of rules that take into account the degree of participation in productive activities and the needs of family units, for example, seems to be one of the key foundations of reproduction of social relations. Networks of forced solidarity, the prin-ciple of reciprocity and the system of gifts have survived recent upheav-als and still operate. However, as people have become sedentary, ancient bands have been reunited in single locations, which has created a need for new socio-political structures and forms of solidarity. While sharing drinking water and heating oil, for example, was not part of ancient soli-

darity because it belonged to political rights rather than domestic duties, sharing in itself existed and is still based (though not exclusively) on the extended family, the living remains of band solidarity and new neighbourly links. (Duhaime 1991: 120–121 [our translation])

Duhaime believes he can find the logic of the gift at work in the way people find others to take over their jobs. Inuit people quit jobs when they consider that they have fulfilled their duty to their extended family circle. They see that they are replaced by relatives, which creates broad circulation of employment. Duhaime reports that a cook at a local hotel said he hardly ever worried about absenteeism because if an assistant did not come into work, she would send her daughter, cousin or sister. The work culture coupled with state organization of Inuit people's occupational lives leads to a special situation. An Inuk may have several temporary jobs at the same time, go lightly from one part-time job to the next, receive transfer payments from different levels of government, sometimes receive employment insurance, welfare, training allowances and family allowance and old-age security cheques, as well as hunt and sculpt for profit. When the infinite combinations of sources of income are added up, a family's budget and comfort can be secure. Duhaime is therefore quite right to see Aboriginal "sporadic employment" as an economic system very different from that of the West. He is all the more right to point this out given that it sometimes strikes Western capitalist thinking as a sign of anomie, debauchery and laziness.

The mandate of the *Horizon 1986–1996* program was to train 150 Cree over 10 years so that they could have permanent jobs (as mechanics, electricians and office clerks). The program lasted nine years and 47 Aboriginal workers were trained, of whom around 10 got permanent jobs. The experiment showed that Aboriginals were not very career-oriented. They had little ambition to achieve professional success in the Western sense. Family life was suggested as an explanation, as was the possibility of combining traditional activities and capitalist economic occupations through temporary jobs. However, there is also the fact that for the Cree, use value is more important than exchange value and, more generally, consumption more important than accumulation. "For the Cree, it seems that work is more a use value than an exchange value, in which the work itself becomes what is exchanged." (Bernard 1997: 66 [our translation])

Research should be conducted in this direction because everywhere in Canada there are many counter examples of the socio-economic difficulties experienced by Aboriginals and, to a lesser extent, the Inuit, who do not all subscribe to the American dream or self-made man ideologies. By emphasizing the poverty and drama of the Aboriginal situation, we risk painting Aboriginals as to be pitied. Our intentions in this article are of course completely different. Thus, as we conclude this section, we will return to two examples of successes that provide fresh looks at ways of resolving the current crisis. First, we will look at the Wendake (Lorette) Hurons. Their community is prosperous, has long had full employment and provides jobs for non-Aboriginals in the area. The first entrepreneurs appeared in the village around 1840, and have never ceased their activities. The businesses have had impressive levels of activity, first thanks to supply contracts with the British army, then owing to exports throughout North America of traditional products (which today include outdoor sporting equipment), and finally thanks to the expansion of tourism. Many educated Hurons have been hired as professionals and managers in a wide range of Aboriginal institutions. Sociological explanations for the Lorette Hurons' success include traditions (such as a farming tradition rather than that of hunting and gathering), history (such as long contact with Europeans, which has resulted in a high rate of mixing), attitudes (such as great pride, which results from their position in the division of labour) and diplomatic factors (such as their proximity to "VIPs", including the court of the Governor General and the Lieutenant Governor). The Oneidas of Wisconsin are in a similar position, and share with the Hurons a long history of contact and proximity to a large city. They too are considered refugees (they originally came from New York State), though they never suffered the violence of deportation. The Lorette Hurons successfully entered the modern world through unusual but perfectly legitimate means (and in this they resemble French Canadians when compared with the English, at least in the nineteenth century). Their means were handicrafts (which have resulted in dynamic, international businesses), women's work (through the sweating system), commercialization of outdoor tourism, hunting and fishing in continuity with their status as hunters, maintenance of diplomatic relations with senior military and representatives of the Crown, development of tourism at the village itself, etc. A whole people cannot survive on the proceeds of handicrafts alone in the industrial age, but the little community at Lorette has been able to use its expertise in the industry to exploit a niche and develop prosperous businesses.[28]

Our second example is an educational experiment among young Aboriginals. We know that young Aboriginals are over-represented among school dropouts. Guillaume Carle and Mireille St-Jean, who are both Algonquins, established a computer programming school open to Aboriginals from anywhere in Canada. At first, the school, called "Night Hawk", had only two or three graduates after a year and a half of intensive study, despite the fact that there were around 15 students enrolled. Concerned by this, the school's management decided to amend a regulation. Only one. However, it completely changed the graduation rate. From then on, in order for a student to graduate, the whole class had to graduate. In other words, a student's personal success was linked to the success of the group as a whole. Everyone had to pass the exams, or no one would. This radically changed the way the school operated. Today, Guillaume Carle and Mireille St-Jean can be proud of exceptional success rates. In the midst of the educational stagnation among Aboriginals in Canada, in the face of constantly growing dropout rates, their school is a small miracle. In the end, its recipe is very simple: introduce a sense of community into school, rather than relying, as did the Jesuits in their colleges and residential schools, on emulation, competition, exclusion and discrimination. The tradition of community, far from being an obstacle to educational success, becomes a necessary ingredient of it.

We should also mention, though we lack space and it has already been done by *Le Devoir* in its summer 2001 series on Aboriginal peoples, the commitment of people like Tamusi Qumak, who have helped to form cooperatives, furthered self-government and assisted in municipal administration.

Our culture, he said, cannot be reduced to traditional elements alone. Our culture provides a foundation for and cohesion to routine activities. In the past, we used to hunt with dog sleds; today, we build cooperatives, and tomorrow we will run our government and institutions... (quoted by Filotas 2001 [our translation])

However, no matter how great they are, these specific success stories should not lead us to believe that there is no need for reform at a more general political level. If there is no minimal state or government recognition, in other words, if collective territorial self-government is not negotiated, there can be no hope for either long-term rebirth of Aboriginal communities or severance of the colonial links that persist through current federal government programs. We will devote the conclusion to a discussion of this difficult issue.

2.4. Ancient Ethics and New Policies: Necessary Political and State Control

The French long believed that sedentary, educated Aboriginals would form a single people with them. They spontaneously encouraged mixed marriages and gave the status of "natural subjects" to all converted Aboriginals. (We should note in passing that the Iroquois had the same plan, except that they thought they would assimilate the French.) The colonialist plan failed in general because mixed marriages and the peoples' proximity favoured "Indianization" of the settlers rather than "Gallicization" of Aboriginals with respect to language (which was not crucial at the time), government and religion. By the eighteenth century, the French colonial state had stopped encouraging mixed marriages, and in the end it completely prohibited them. It then unsuccessfully tried to pressure the Jesuits to not only convert "residents" but also to "Gallicize" them. These efforts, which bespeak a standardization policy specific to modernization of the French state in the eighteenth century, failed because of New France's military and economic situation. The French were too dependent on Aboriginal nations for assimilation and integration to be possible. Thus, the French policy on Aboriginals was limited to leading them "little by little with prudence and care" to become "citizens."[29]

In general, the history of New England is strewn with more massacres, social exclusion and legal inflexibility than that of New France. The reason for this is not, as claim some historians, that the Kingdom of France was more modern, or at least closer to a modernity defined in terms of openness to others and reciprocal tolerance, but for exactly the opposite reason. Of course, the government of New France was modernized long before that of New England, since the latter remained at the communal stage of medieval history, unable to imagine power other than in arbitrary terms and tempted by an ideal of elected representatives and equals in the formation of civil society. New France was part of a centralized bureaucracy and rationalized legitimacy, namely that of the *Ancien Régime*, which Tocqueville was to analyse (1952). However, in relations with Aboriginals, the French authorities continued to emphasize allegiance to the King, and promoted a political structure of subjection rather than of citizenship. The following discussion must therefore be understood to apply to Aboriginals, and Aboriginals only.

Modernity means recognition of the infinite diversity of cultures and the relativism of values, but it was imposed, paradoxically, through what were perhaps the most barbarian massacres in the history of humanity, namely anti-Semitic pogroms and the slave trade. Michel Freitag's theory of social regulation (1992: 1–55) can explain this contradiction. Traditional societies (as opposed to myth-based communities) are established and governed by an institutionalized authority. The justification for authority flows from a transcendent power, such as in the case of royalty by divine right. Such societies do not base their internal balance on mythical narratives or the immanence of ancestral traditions, and they cannot do so because, under a hierarchical system, they subsume various irreducible customs, beliefs and practices. The customs, beliefs and practices relate not only to orders, castes and social classes, but also to regional communities and ethnic groups scattered across the land. For example, the France of Henri IV did not achieve linguistic and cultural unity, and since it was still a traditional power, it did not try to do so. It limited itself to enforcing specific arbitrary and historical rights, strictly defining the freedom entailed by exercise of those rights (and their reciprocal duties), and collecting taxes. The King was literally the emperor in his realm because his status was above that of his subjects, who did not see themselves directly in him, and because he incarnated a unity beyond concrete social and cultural divisions. The status of royal subjects was always specific (commoner, vassal, *seigneur*, woman, peasant, etc.), and always entailed privileges in that it was based on arbitrariness of custom or the Crown, which were always external to the subject since he or she had no say in them. This form of recognition of identity also applied to foreigners, whose status defined them as the subjects of another power. This had two consequences. First, subjects belonged to a common humanity in that they were the subjects of a power. Next, it was possible to interact with foreigners and accept them within the borders of the kingdom, which means that they were accepted with their differences. Always persecuted, Jews were tolerated in medieval times, as were, *a fortiori*, the inhabitants of other European kingdoms. Thus, traditional power was able to cover very different areas so long as subjects obeyed a single master, namely Christ with respect to religious power (which was at the time also in part basely temporal) and the King in that he had the divine right to determine and enforce laws. France had long begun its transition towards modernity and rationalized its power. However, by playing on royal legitimacy, it was still able to situate itself in this traditional view of power when America was discovered. At the beginning of the colony, a few high-placed persons, including Samuel de Champlain, asked that converted Aboriginals be treated as natural subjects of the King of France. These notables felt that it was sufficient for Aboriginals to pledge allegiance to the King of France, convert to Catholicism and enrol in the French army for them to become French subjects (perhaps with different rights and privileges, but that was true of every status in the Middle Ages, including peasants, seigneurs, aristocrats, and Jews). The illusion was complete and made it possible to include Aboriginals without having to assimilate them. However, this did not last long, and it is possible that, if the Conquest had not occurred, the changes would have been the same as those under the English regime after 1760.

The treaties signed with Aboriginal peoples are very instructive. In 1665, four of the five Iroquois nations (the Mohawks, did not sign) went to Québec City to make peace with the French. The French version of the treaty says that peace was granted in the name of the King, who had sent his subjects, in his own name and in that of Christ, to discover and conquer the Aboriginal nations. It goes without saying that the Iroquois nations' interpretation was different from that of the French and that they did not see their alliance as "subjection or vassalage." (Delâge *et al.* 1996: 2–9) However, the 1701 peace treaty, which was nonetheless signed under the same king, Louis XIV, no longer employed feudal imagery. In it, there was no mention of right of discovery or right of conquest, but of a family in which the King was the "father" and Aboriginal nations the "children." In contrast, it was of their own free will, after long negotiations, that the nations buried the hatchet and became "brothers." Naturally, the *Ancien Régime* system still applied, but a new aspect was introduced because of the impossibility of establishing absolute power over Aboriginals and settlers in North America. Just as ancient European patriarchal control disintegrated in America where land and work were plentiful, and young people could quickly escape the control of their fathers, so the weakness of the French colony and its dependency on Aboriginals forced the King to abandon the system of strength and right. Louis XIV, the Sun King, had to take into account the world view of those he wanted to make his subjects. (ANQ-Q, C11A, vol. 19, Folio 41–44, *Ratification de la paix faite au mois de septembre dernier*)

Colonial rivalries generated ambiguities in the process of imposing European sovereignty in America. The French considered their Aboriginal allies to be subjects whereas the Aboriginal allies of the English maintained their sovereignty and were not the subjects of anyone. (Naturally, the English saw the situation in completely opposite terms.) In these circumstances, the French invited ambassadors of the Iroquois (aside from the Mohawks) to sign a declaration of independence with great pomp and ceremony at Québec City on November 2, 1748. The Iroquois ambassadors solemnly affirmed that they were not the vassals of the English Crown and that they had never given up their lands to anyone. They said they had received their lands from heaven. (ANQ-Q, C11A, Vol. 91, Folio 252–253; Delâge *et al.* 1996: 9–20) By doing this, the French Crown encouraged the Iroquois to reject the legitimacy of the claims of a rival crown. Things were different in the treaties signed with the English and Dutch. The Netherlands, which was probably the country closest to the communal ideal in the seventeenth century, at least with respect to law, was the first to introduce land transfer treaties in North America. Having won independence from Charles Quint, and denouncing the Spanish conquests in both Europe and South and North America, they promoted contractual relations among peoples. Thus, before settling, they solicited clear title of full ownership. By cutting North America up into parcels of privately owned land, the Dutch could force Aboriginals to move outside of the borders of the land purchased (and the price was quite reasonable!). One need not be a Marxist to see that respect for Aboriginal property was a powerful instrument for social exclusion on the basis of birthright. When they bought Manhattan Island, the Dutch not only made a good deal but they legally expelled all foreigners. In contrast, the French tried to annex the land with the people living on it. After the conquest of New Holland, the English copied this policy in the *Royal Proclamation of 1763* and in later treaties. The *Proclamation* was based on the principle of transforming every form of collective ownership into private property. While it recognized three types of property (private, *seigneurial* and collective) on the land over which the King reigned, the *Proclamation* provided for transfer, in exchange for compensation, of Aboriginals' collectively owned land to settlers as private property. Unlike the English, the French feudal tradition accommodated all sorts of rights over land and forms of land ownership. The English instead aimed for standardization of private property, which meant, since collective land ownership concerned Aboriginals, the disappearance of the latter either physically (from disease) or culturally (through assimilation). The future predicted by the *Proclamation* was that there would be a homogenous population in the colony. In the meantime, until their individual inclusion was achieved through conversion to the supposedly civilized lifestyle, Aboriginals lived collectively on the fringes of society, on the scraps of land called reserves. The law thus changed, from French to English (and there was evolution even within the tradition of those laws). Combined with Aboriginals' military minorization and settlement on reserves, this changed the power relations with the colonial authorities.

Modernity requires a radically new definition of law and political identity. In traditional societies, subjects' status is recognized in accordance with traditional privileges and an unchanging order of beings, things and the world. In modern society, special, hierarchical and inherited privileges are abolished, and the legal system is based on equal rights. Because of their irreducible, natural subjectivity, individuals are not the subjects of a king but of reason, and they are free and equal before reason, in other words, before all. Every individual has two roles: he or she is free to govern and be governed, obey and act, because he or she is politically and legally subject to the general will as to his or her own will. In other words, every individual is a citizen, and it is as citizens that modernity emancipates them from tradition, divests them of privileges and makes them brothers before universalist shared law. The individuals that make up society are freed one after the next, in other words, in concentric layers of which rich land-owning white men are the first, then believers of other religions, then workers, then women, and finally ethnic minorities, according to a system that involves arbitrary features of tradition (e.g., religion), education (e.g., the unschooled), nature (e.g., the weaker sex), and race (e.g., inferior ethnic groups). Consequently, the Other of modernity is no longer the foreigner as in traditional societies. The modern, institutional state tends to embrace all of humanity as human, so otherness becomes for it the kinds of societies that are still subject to ancestral traditions and customary irrationality. In other words, the otherness of modernity is its own past in so far as the former represents progress with respect to the latter.

> Let us say schematically that the new otherness is the negative point of the historicist conception of the Progress of Reason and Civilization with which modern society, states and the abstract universal collective subject identify ideologically. Otherness thus takes the irremediable form of "the garbage heap of history" or "shadows of the past" to which are consigned

not only outmoded points in the development of modern Western societies [...] but all societies that have remained structurally premodern,
whether traditional or primitive, and that still coexist for a time in the
empirical world with the "enlightened", "rational" modern state. (Freitag
1992: 25 [our translation])

Freitag rightly points out that there are reasons for the worst excesses of colonialism and the organized and rationalized acculturation of premodern societies. In the
eyes of Westerners, primitive societies seemed to have no history. They therefore
had to be parachuted directly into modernity by settlement on reserves. Traditional
societies appeared to be delayed, and they therefore had to catch up (as in the expression "developing countries") to the Western societies that had preceded them
on the path of progress. In the first case, assimilation and in the second, acculturation is suggested as means of achieving modern universalism and common humanity, which is based on the universality of reason (universal because is it shared by
all human beings and delimits a single rational, institutional, formal and irrefutable
culture). This means nothing less for barbarian, primitive and traditional societies
than to reject their own social order and abandon their culture, beliefs, prejudices,
traditions and even identity. The passage from an otherness of the foreigner to an
otherness of the "primitive" or "traditional" has had terrible repercussions on the
fates of traditional and myth-based Aboriginal societies. The effects have been as
terrible as was the incarceration of the insane, who were stripped of their political
and citizenship status, as Michel Foucault has described so well. In the seventeenth century, "exclusion" and "re-education" gradually became interchangeable
words in Western political and cultural vocabulary, when they were not replaced
by repression pure and simple. Madmen were individuals considered incapable
of reason, as were also Aboriginals. It is possible to trace a lumping together of
Aboriginals and the insane in the American political tradition. Since Aboriginals
were considered the complete opposites of the civilized, they could not participate
in the American political system and civilization except if they were completely
assimilated by it. As Marienstras notes, "if he converts to the ways of the Whites,
in other words, if he loses what makes his identity [...] In such cases, some authors such as Jefferson, consider the possibility of admitting him into the nation."
(Marienstras 1976: 208 [our translation]) Otherwise, Aboriginals were left on the
sidelines of progress. They remained on the fringes of a civilization now defined
by the function of citizen and the possibility of being a reasonable, rational voice
in a democratic undertaking.

Despite its accuracy, let us not remain at this relatively abstract level of analysis.
If Aboriginals were considered savages unable to see the light of reason, then we
have to ask what forms of behaviour made it possible to pass such a judgment in
the eyes of Western settlers, and what characteristics rendered Aboriginals temporarily or permanently outside of modernity's history? Aboriginals were parked in
areas that were enclosed and politically marginalized (they received the right to
vote in federal elections only in 1960) for reasons that did not always have to do
with a formal conception of rational state universalism. What concrete accusations
were made against Aboriginal peoples to prevent them from becoming citizens?

Of all the charges, there seems to be one in particular that was the key because of the role it played in missionary and bureaucratic discourse: we have called it laziness, of which the opposite is work. Work, and especially rational work, is certainly one of the major pillars of the modern ethic, and perhaps the one that makes it easiest to discriminate in practice between the modern and the primitive.

> Between labour and idleness in the classical world ran a line of demarcation that replaced the exclusion of leprosy. The asylum was substituted for the lazar house, in the geography of haunted places as in the landscape of the moral universe. The old rites of excommunication were revived, but in the world of production and commerce. It was in these places of doomed and despised idleness, in this space invented by a society which had derived an ethical transcendence from the law of work, that madness would appear and soon expand until it had annexed them. (Foucault 1965: 73)

Like the insane of modern madness, Aboriginals would have to shoulder everything that Western society had invested in the new ethic of guilt and work specific to the *bourgeois* system.

We hope the nature of Aboriginals will always remain the same, eternally identical to what it was before Europeans arrived, eternally adapted to the great spaces of America and the traditional organization of the tribe. Unfortunately, as Nietzsche said, eternity can be fatal. However, unlike some authors, it seems, we acknowledge that improving the Aboriginal situation is impossible if the spirit of their culture and customs is lost. Replacing Aboriginal communitarian ethics with European individualistic ethics (according to the typology developed by Demolins in 1927), if such ethics still exist in the vicissitudes of contemporary history, will not magically solve the very real problems facing Aboriginal peoples today. It is very likely that this will simply make them worse. Forcing the destiny of a culture into that of another has never had anything but dubious results, if history is any guide. In famous studies on European nations, Demolins, a disciple of Frédéric Le Play, concluded that an individualistic family system was better that a communitarian system, and he preached France's conversion to British family traditions, believing that Great Britain's economic domination was a result of its individualistic education. Fortunately, we have gone beyond this. Economic success does not necessarily depend on the elimination of organic ties of solidarity, and we now know that it is sometimes compromised when those ties are broken.

Does this mean that the only way to repair the situation of Aboriginals today is through moral regeneration? Of course not. As paradoxical as it may seem after an article devoted to ethics and the horizon of meaning of Aboriginal peoples, we continue to believe, as we have noted in the section on political control,[30] that Aboriginals' future is linked to their taking charge of politics, where politics means first, specifically and precisely refusing to see one's life as destiny.

Appendix

A Look at Some Reserves in the American West, Travelogue, spring 1999 (extracts)

This narrative is based on six weeks of shared experiences and encounters during a trip to Native American Indian reserves in the United States by Denys Delâge and Jean Jacques Simard, who were both professors in the Department of Sociology at Laval University. However, the narrative is by Denys Delâge alone.

Located at the confluence of the Missouri and Mississippi rivers, the city of St. Louis has always been a gateway to the American West. Under the leadership of the Chouteau family, it was the centre of the American fur trade, and the point of departure for many exploratory expeditions, the most famous of which is Lewis and Clark's. The *rabaskas* and canoes that used to glide silently down the river have been replaced by floating casinos with twinkling lights that shine on ships in the port. Most American states prohibit casinos, and Missouri is no exception, but the Mississippi River is under federal jurisdiction and so gambling is permitted.

Cahokia, Illinois, on the other bank of the Mississippi facing St. Louis, is the site of a prehistoric city where nearly 20,000 people once lived. Their homes were grouped around a number of earthen mounds and pyramids, the largest of which took three centuries to build. Cahokia's interpretive centre is remarkable. Its sober architecture employs natural colours, and it has a roof that makes it look like a mound in which treasures are hidden. The exhibition is educational, and the reproductions of works of art impressive. Overall, the design is impeccable except for one thing: the political correctness of the accompanying texts. Two texts accompany every work, one by a woman archaeologist and one by a "traditional Aboriginal storyteller" who uses common-sense discourse full of stereotypes, such as the eternal great circle of love and respect for Mother Earth. Thus, concerning the burial rituals for priest-kings, in which servants were put to death, the storyteller emphasizes the relationships of exchange and balance with nature and the gods. Likewise, there is barely any mention of war even though the city was strongly fortified, or of the relationships among the classes that led to construction of the main pyramid.

The road that we took crosses the State of Missouri and leads to northern Kansas. In the nineteenth century, this is where members of the Sioux-speaking Iowa tribe were settled after they had been deported from the state that bears their name. The Potawotamis and Kikapoos, former allies of the French and signatories of the Great Peace of Montréal in 1701, were also brought to northern Kansas from Michigan and Wisconsin.

Mr. DeRoin, a descendent of a French Canadian like so many others in Aboriginal nations, is the chief of a small reserve of 500 Iowas near White Cloud, a village with run-down western facades. The décor lacked nothing: there was even a big yellow dog sleeping in front of the general store. Most of the reserve's Iowas live elsewhere in the United States, and the tribe actually owns only a small part of the land that it was granted. We learned that in the United States one should never confuse the borders of "Indian" land with those of a reserve. Indeed, after American Indians had been expropriated and forced onto reserves, the US Congress passed the *Dawes Allotment Act* in 1887, which expropriated most of the good uncultivated land on the reserves so that it could be redistributed to settlers. Today, American Indians often own only small pieces of their original reserves. In order to create jobs on the Iowa reserve, the Band Council borrowed a few million dollars and opened a casino. However, for many different reasons, of which the primary is probably the casino's distance from large cities, success has been mitigated. An effort is being made to attract people by holding fighting events and showing action films.

In order to get to the nearby Kikapoo reserve, you have to drive down a road along the Missouri with plastic bottles and garbage of every kind all along the shoulders. A primary and secondary school run by the Bureau of Indian Affairs teaches young Aboriginals who have difficulty in regular public schools. Despite the often long commute by school bus, the school offers such children a second chance. It institutes a kind of segregation that allows young people to escape the discrimination they suffer elsewhere. The Vice Principal, Napoleon Cruise, is a Black American who has clearly invested a lot in his school and wants his students to succeed. He told us that Aboriginal parents do not yet have the pride of Black Americans. Aboriginal parents want their children to do well, but are convinced that the school alone has to shoulder full responsibility for making sure they succeed.

A little further south, near Mayette, the Potawotamis' reserve is larger than those of their neighbours but it too has had its best land amputated. This is why the Potawotamis are a minority on their reserve, and the rest of their nation is scattered elsewhere. Their casino's success has eliminated unemployment, but some people see it as a source of social problems. At the community centre, a free lunch is offered to elders every day. Many attend, and others join them for as little as $3.50. There were chicken livers, vegetables, fresh-picked mushrooms, and attention and friendliness for everyone. Two old ladies, one of whom was among the very last Potawotami speakers, were chatting in English, railway employees were sipping coffee, three young skilled labourers had decided not to go to work and were playing cards, and a retired soldier was proudly recounting his career in the army. Life on the reserve is slower, calmer.

Much further south, as we entered New Mexico, it seemed like we had crossed a real border. The colour of the houses shifted to ochre. Taos is a completely gentrified small town with boutiques and art galleries. Pueblo-style architecture is everywhere, and tourists can visit a pueblo dating back to prehistory. It is magnificent, with five stories, adobe walls and a large square. However, despite the crowds of tourists, it is as lifeless an historical monument as the Place Royale in Québec City. The Taos live nearby in pretty little modern homes. Old-style pueblo homes had only one room and no creature comforts at all.

More to the west, a reserve belonging to 220 000 Navahos straddles New Mexico, Arizona and Utah. It is of unimaginable beauty: immense desert plains shadowed by mesas and the Shiprock rising out of the sand like a flame. However, the tribal council has often decided that Navahos' homes are to be built along the highway. The reserve is larger than Belgium, which is probably because it is located in the middle of a desert, in other words, on land that was completely unusable at the time the borders were drawn. All around the reserve, hotels, motels, restaurants and pawn shops have sprung up like mushrooms. The hotels, which are always run by Whites, depend on the huge flow of tourists who come to see the breathtaking scenery. The pawn shops take cars and pick up trucks on consignment from Aboriginals when they are having financial problems. The Navaho had a long tradition of raising goats and sheep. The men used to sell the wool while the women used to trade their magnificent carpets for next to nothing. Mass production has now replaced handweaving, and the most beautiful motifs have become the trademarks of outside companies. Navahos now make jewellery using semi-precious stones and silver, and sell beaded knickknacks from roadside stalls. Stores, souvenir and handicraft shops, restaurants and hotels inside and outside the reservation only rarely belong to Navahos. However, Navahos do own their newspaper, the *Navaho Times*, and a radio station that broadcasts in their own language. Need we mention that English is used in every aspect of day-to-day communication?

To the west of Arizona, near the California border, there is the Poston reserve, which belongs to Indians of various origins who are grouped together under the appellation "Colorado River Indians." Major irrigation networks crisscrossed the reserve, and as usual the houses were small and there seemed to be little urban planning. We were surprised not to see any agricultural buildings in the middle of the irrigated fields. In the middle of the village, there was a little corner store that sold alcohol, which is rare on a reserve. The "Head Start" program was advertised in large letters. It is a program designed to provide schooling as early as possible for children who are especially underprivileged, such as those in ghettos and on reserves. Aside from one slightly wealthier enclave, all the houses looked alike, though a third of them were empty, boarded up and often vandalized. In the general store there was nothing but junk food, and extremely obese people could be seen everywhere.

There is a commemorative monument in the middle of Poston in memory of the 18,000 American citizens of Japanese origin who were interned there in camps between 1942 and 1945. The camp was located on the reserve, thus on federal land, in the middle of a desert. In order to improve their situation, the Japanese began farming despite the impossible conditions. Seeing their determination, the camp authorities dug an irrigation canal, and the prisoners turned the desert around their barracks into a garden After the war, the Aboriginals on the reserve did not take over the Japanese farms. The federal government therefore brought Hopis and Navahos onto the reserve, but finally, the land was leased to farmers in the area. Thus, the Aboriginals receive rent for their land, but do not work there, aside from a few who have small vegetable gardens.

The Hoopa Valley Indian Reservation near Willow Creek in northwest Washington State is about 30 miles from the sea. It is about 10 miles square, and leaves a very different impression from other reserves. It is one of the ten reserves in the United States where self-government has been most successful. The difference was striking at first sight. First, the roadsides were tidy and cleaned by residents. Next, the village had all the normal services one might expect, such as a grocery store, hardware store, bank, restaurants and motel. There was excellent service everywhere, and everything was clean. For the first time, we saw a store selling outdoor plants. Indeed, many homes had beautiful landscaping. There also did not seem to be many overweight people in the village, and there seemed to be a lot of work available, mainly in forestry. Naturally, there is a small casino on the reserve, as well as a very simple museum located between it and the grocery store. The museum essentially contains small collections of objects from the Hoopas and even Whites in the area. There is a great deal of basketry, as well as drums, tikamagens and jewellery. Families can take back the objects that they have lent, and they do so, particularly when there are celebrations. The museum also sells local handicrafts, such as jewellery and basketry made on the reserve. The reserve itself has a small primary and secondary school, as well as a Head Start program as on other reserves. Some young people can speak their own language, but not all, which means that English is the language of communication. A number of students study off-reserve, but many come back and raise their families on the reserve, which is an indication of good living conditions. The reserve is thus completely self-sufficient, and the site along the Trinity River is magnificent. There are fishing and tour guides available right on the reserve, canoeing instructors, and inflatable rafts for riding the rapids. What is the reason for this success? Naturally, life is easier on the coast than in the desert, but what is perhaps more important is the fact that the Aboriginals in Hoopa Valley were never deported, and had the advantage of being able to stay on their own land. In fact, this is rather exceptional in the United States, and even more so in California, which was marked by pogroms against Aboriginals during the Gold Rush in the nineteenth century. Detachments of armed men raided villages to capture people whom they turned into slaves or prostitutes. Nearby, at Eureka on an island near the coast, a tribe was massacred for no reason by people who, it seems, simply hated "Indians". The crime remains unpunished, which is not surprising since in the nineteenth century testimony by a person with a quarter or more Indian blood was not admitted in court.

In Montana, the Crows are proud of their college, and rightly so, for it is an exception because the US Bureau of Indian Affairs is much less generous than Canada's Department of Indian Affairs, and does not pay for college-level education. The community built and operates its college on a budget of $2000 per student (whereas the state average is three times higher). Jeannine Pease-Pretty On Top, recipient of one of the MacArthur "Genius" Awards, manages to stretch the college's budget through grants from foundations and private donations. Women control the college, and in fact two thirds of the students are female. Boys seem to resist certain kinds of sedentary work, in particular that involving classrooms and offices, and prefer outside activities, such as construction, forestry and other work involving risk. However, prejudice against those who study has disappeared on the reserve. What is the source of this progress? It is Chief Plenty Coups, who said at the beginning of the twentieth century, "Education is your most powerful weapon. With education you are the white man's equal; without education you are his victim." Progress has also been achieved through combativeness, as well as the generosity of professors and leaders who are devoted to a cause, ready to accept salaries far below the norm and determined to put in the time required (normally two full years) to bring students with high school diplomas up to the normal college admissions level.

Pine Ridge in North Dakota is a large reserve with several villages. The Sioux have a few stores there, but they were all a little run down when we visited. Most people were living in mobile homes or very small bungalows. At Pine Ridge, one middle-class neighbourhood had a sign saying "We call the Police", and a wealthier quarter was enclosed behind a barbed wire fence. Life is thus dangerous in the little village, and criminality high. Despite its historical importance, the site of the battle at Wounded Knee had no buildings, no guide and only one text panel. A few Aboriginals were selling knickknacks. In short, the Sioux have put no effort into promoting a historical site that should attract thousands of tourists a year. Yet they have a very high level of unemployment. The reserve had many scrap yards full of old cars, and many houses were surrounded by rusting car bodies. The roadsides were covered in garbage and a dump marked the entrance to the reserve. In the shops, there were many books on Aboriginals and titles such as "Mother Earth and Indian Spirituality", "The Teachings of…", and "Medicinal Plants of…."

We will end our narrative at the Oneida reserve in the suburbs of Green Bay, Wisconsin. The reserve has 4500 inhabitants, and is relatively prosperous thanks to a bingo hall and two casinos. The profits have been reinvested in post-secondary school scholarships for students, a health centre, an old age home, the repurchase of lost lands, business creation and bus services. There are no poor areas, only pretty homes, gardens, trees and a few wealthier quarters. In a more industrial area, scrap cars are gathered and hidden behind a high fence. In addition to the tribal office, which is called the "Business Office," there are small repair shops, public works and stores. What is the secret of the Oneidas' success? Is it the same as for the Hurons: a society with sedentary traditions and a proto-state, a long history of contact and the proximity of a city? Or is it because they were not deported and managed to keep a little control over their destiny? During the American Revolution, the Iroquois Confederation split into two camps: one pro-British, and one in favour of revolution. The Oneidas, along with the Tuscaroras, the sixth Iroquois nation, fought on the side of the Americans. To thank them for their support, the Continental Congress guaranteed them full title to their lands in the Treaty of Fort Stanwix, which was signed in 1784. However, New York State dismissed the treaty and pursued a policy of expropriation and eviction. Like other Aboriginals, the Oneidas were gradually dispossessed, which led a few hundred of them to move to Wisconsin. They bought some land from the Menominees (whom the French called the "wild oats" people), and moved there in 1820–1832. They thus migrated before the 1830s, when the US policy to deport Indians to the west of the Mississippi was implemented.

Everywhere, the traditional cultures of American Indians are rapidly disintegrating, and most of their languages are dead or dying. What is striking is that no matter what the location, original culture or history, there are similarities among all of the reserves, which is an indication that they were governed by the same colonial regime. However, there are two different general trends. The most widespread is that of under-development, ghettos and high unemployment, where the vestiges of tradition are now mixed with a culture of poverty, which includes rejection of regular work and regular working hours, a *laissez-faire* approach to the education of children and resignation to fate. Rather than remaining trapped in that world, young couples who aspire to something better leave the reserve. The other possibility is development, when the land has resources, and promotion of education and independence, when oppression and destiny have not crushed all initiative.

Denys Delâge

Archival documents

NAC = National Archives of Canada, Indian Affairs, RG10 Series.
—, 1794: Réponse de Lord Dorchester aux Sauvages des Sept Villages du Bas-Canada, Montréal, August 28–29, 1794, bob. C-10999, Vol. 8: 8677–8678.
—, 1816: Louis de Salaberry aux Sept-Nations du Canada, Beauport, October 1, 1816, bob. 13499, Vol. 785: 181461–181464.
—, 1833a: Tiiom Sagaonong8as à Matthew, Lord Aylmer, Sault St. Louis, November 27, 1833, bob. C-11466, Vol. 87: 34840–34843.
—, 1833b: Sharo Kanasato, p. s., Constant Pénesse et Frens8e Pabennon à Matthiew, Lord Aylmer, Lac-des Deux-Montagnes, November 28, 1933, bob. C-11466, Vol. 87: 34847–34848.
—, 1919: Joseph K. Gabriel et Mitchell Martina Arthur Meighen, Oka, November 19, 1919, bob. C-8106, Vol. 6750, dossier 420-10.
ANQ-M = Archives nationales du Québec à Montréal, TL Series, Archives juridiques, Tribunaux inférieurs.
ANQ-Q = Archives nationales du Québec à Québec
—, Series B: Lettres envoyées du ministre de la Marine aux administrateurs des colonies.
—, Series C11A: Correspondance générale, Canada.
—, Series TL: Archives judiciaires, Tribunaux inférieurs.

Works cited

- Alighieri, Dante, 1927: *The Divine Comedy.* Trans. John Ciardi. New York: New American Library.
- Aquinas, T., *The Summa Theologica of St. Thomas* Aquinas (New York: The Benziger Bros., 1947) (trans. by Fathers of the English Dominican Province).
- Barbeau, Marius C., 1915: *Huron and Wyandot Mythology. With an Appendix Containing Earlier Published Records.* Ottawa, Government Printing Bureau.
- Bernard, Nick, 1997: "La formation professionnelle en milieu autoch-

tone. Le cas d'Hydro-Québec et des Cris de la Baie James." *Recherches amérindiennes au Québec* XXVII(2): 61–74.

- Besnard, Pierre, 1970: *Protestantisme et capitalisme, la controverse post-weberienne.* Paris: Armand Colin.
- Cadieux, Lorenzo, s.j., 1973: "Lettres des nouvelles missions du Canada 1843–1852." Montréal: Bellarmin.
- Cazeneuve, Jean, 1967: *Ethnologie.* Paris: Larousse.
- —, 1971: *Sociologie du rite.* Paris: PUF.
- Champigny, 1916: "Mémoire instructif sur le Canada, Québec, 10 mai 1691." *BRH (Bulletin de recherches historiques)* XXII(9).
- Charlevoix, François-Xavier de, 1976 [1744]: *Histoire et description générale de la Nouvelle France, avec le Journal historique d'un Voyage fait par ordre du Roi dans l'Amérique Septentrionale, Vol. 3: Journal d'un voyage.* Montréal: Élysée.
- Delâge, Denys, 2001: "Mauvais 'pères' et faux 'enfants'." In *Le Devoir*, June 30 and July 1, A-9.
- Delâge, Denys and Jean-Pierre Sawaya, 2001: *Les Traités des Sept-Feux avec les Britanniques. Droits et pièges d'un héritage colonial au Québec.* Sillery: Septentrion.
- Delâge, Denys *et al.*, 1996: "Les Sept Feux, les alliances et les traités. Autochtones du Québec." In *L'Histoire pour Sept générations.* CD ROM Ottawa: Libraxus.
- Delumeau, Jean, 1983: *Le Péché et la peur. La culpabilisation en Occident (XIIIe–XVIIIe siècle).* Paris: Fayard.
- Demolins, Edmond, 1927: *A quoi tient la supériorité des Anglo-Saxons?"* Paris: Firmin-Didot.
- Demos, John, 1994: *The Unredeemed Captive: A Family Story from Early America.* New York: Vintage Books.
- Disselkamp, Annette, 1994: *L'éthique protestante de Max Weber.* Paris: PUF.
- Drouilly, Pierre, 1991: *Profil sociopolitique des Amérindiens du Québec.* Québec City: Bibliothèque de l'Assemblée national, Bibliographie et Documentation No. 40.
- Duhaime, Gérard, 1991: "Le pluriel de l'Arctique. Travail salarié et rapports sociaux en zone périphérique." In *Sociologie et sociétés* XXIII (2): 113–128.
- Dumont, Louis, 1977: *Homo aequalis: genèse et épanouissement de l'idéologie économique.* Paris: Gallimard.
- —, 1979: *Homo hierarchicus: le système des castes et ses implications.* Paris: Gallimard.
- Durkheim, E., *The Division of Labor in Society*, (Trans. by George Simpson) (New York: The Free Press, 1947).
- Eliade, Mircea, 1989: *Le Mythe de l'éternel retour.* Paris: Gallimard.
- Evans-Pritchard, E. E., 1968: *The Nuer.* Oxford: Clarendon Press.
- Filotas, Georges, 2001: "Portrait d'un précurseur: Tamusi Qumak." In *Le Devoir*, September 1 and 2 A-9.
- Foucault, Michel, 1965: *Madness and Civilization.* Trans. Richard How-

ard. New York: Vintage Books.

- Franklin, B., *The Autobiography* (with an Introduction by Daniel Aaron) (New York: Vintage Books, 1990).
- Freitag, Michel, 1992: "L'Identité, l'altérité et le politique." In *Société* 9.
- Freud, Sigmund, 1961: *Civilization and its Discontents.* Trans. James Stachey. New York: Norton.
- Gagné, Gilles, 2005: *De la société au système social. Essai sur la transition postmoderne.* Unpublished manuscript.
- Gagnon, François-Marc, 1975: *La Conversion par l'image. Un aspect de la mission des Jésuites auprès des Indiens du Canada au XVIIe siècle.* Montréal: Bellarmin.
- Gagnon, François-Marc and Denise Petel, 1986: *Hommes effarables et bestes sauvages. Images du Nouveau-Monde d'après les voyages de Jacques Cartier.* Montréal: Boréal.
- Gérin, Gérin, 1902: "Le Huron de Lorette. A quels égards il s'est transformé." In *La Science sociale* XXXIII: 319–342.
- Groupe de recherche sur la culture de Weimar, 1997: *L'Éthique protestante de Max Weber et l'esprit de la modernité.* Paris: Éditions de la Maison des sciences de l'homme.
- Hobsbawm, Éric J., 2000: *L'Être des révolutions.* Paris: Éditions complexe.
- Jacob, Annie, 1994: *Le Travail reflet des cultures. Du sauvage indolent au travailleur productif.* Paris: PUF.
- JR = Thwaites, Reuben G., Ed., 1896–1901: *The Jesuit Relations and Allied Documents.* Cleveland: Burrows Brothers.
- Kant, I., "What is Enlightenment?", (1784), available online at: http://www.fordham.edu/HALSALL/MOD/kant-whatis.html.
- Lafitau, Joseph-François, 1983: *Moeurs des Sauvages américains comparés aux moeurs des premiers temps.* Paris: Maspero.
- Latourelle, René, 1999: *Jean de Brébeuf.* Montréal: Bellarmin.
- Leclerc, Chrestien, 1691: *Nouvelle Relation de la Gaspésie.* Paris: Amable Auroy.
- Leroux, Jacques, 1995: "Les métamorphoses du pacte dans une communauté algonquine." *Recherches amérindiennes au Québec* XXV(1): 51–69.
- Lévi-Strauss, Claude, 1976: *Tristes Tropiques.* Trans. John and Doreen Weightman. New York: Penguin Books.
- —, 1961: *Entretiens avec Lévi-Strauss.* Paris: Julliard and Plon.
- Malinowski, Bronislaw, 1959: *Crime and Custom in Savage Society.* Paterson, N.J.: Littlefield, Adams & Co.
- Marienstras, Elise, 1976: *Les Mythes fondateurs de la nation américaine.* Paris: Maspero.
- Marshall, Gordon, 1982: *In Search of the Spirit of Capitalism: an essay on Max Weber's protestant ethic thesis.* New York: Hutchinson.
- Mauss, M., *The Gift: Forms and Functions of Exchange in Archaic Societies* (London: Routledge, 1990).

- Minois, Georges, 1991: *Histoire des enfers*. Paris: Fayard.
- Montesquieu, *De L'Esprit des Lois* (1758). A modern edition has been produced by Laurent Versini (Paris: Éditions Gallimard, 1995).
- Ohl, Paul, 1991, "Les 500 ans d'un massacre." In *Le Devoir*, November 14.
- Otto, Rudolph, *Mysticism East and West. A Comparative Analysis of the Nature of Mysticism* (New York: Macmillan, 1932).
- Poggi, Gianfranco, 1983. *Calvinism and the capitalist spirit: Max Weber's "Protestant ethic."* Amherst: University of Massachusetts Press.
- Ray, Arthur J., 1974: *Indians in the Fur Trade. Their Role as Hunters, Trappers and Middlemen in the Lands Southwest of Hudson Bay 1660–1870.* Toronto: University of Toronto Press.
- Riesman, David, 1964: *La Foule solitaire*. Paris: Arthaud.
- RJ, 1972: *Relations des Jésuites*. Montréal: Éditions du Jour.
- Royal Commission on Aboriginal Peoples, 1996a: *People to People, Nation to Nation: Highlights from the Report of the Royal Commission on Aboriginal Peoples.* Supply and Services Canada, Ottawa.
- —, 1996b: *Report of the Royal Commission on Aboriginal Peoples.* Supply and Services Canada, Ottawa.
- Sagard, Gabriel, 1990: *Le Grand Voyage du pays des Hurons*. Réal Ouellet, Ed. Montréal: Bibliothèque québécoise.
- Simard, Jean-Jacques, 1985: "Préface." In Richard Dominique and Jean-Guy Deschênes. *Cultures et sociétés autochtones du Québec. Bibliographie critique.* Québec City: Institut québécois de recherche sur la culture.
- —, 1991: "Les structures contre la culture." In *Liberté* 196–197.
- —, 1993: "La Réduction des Amérindiens. Entre l'Envers-du-Blanc et l'avenir pour soi." In J. Lafontant, Ed. *L'État et les minorités.* Saint-Boniface: Presses universitaires de Saint-Boniface et Éditions du Blé.
- __, 2003: *La Réduction: l'autochtone inventé et les Amérindiens d'aujourd'hui.* Québec, Editions du Septentrion.
- Simard, Jean-Jacques, *et al.*, 1996: *Tendances nordiques. Les changements sociaux 1970–1990 chez les Cris et les Inuit du Québec. Une enquête statistique exploratoire.* Québec City: GÉTIC, University Laval.
- Simard, J., "La réduction des Amérindiens: entre l'Envers-du-Blanc et l'avenir pour soi», in J. Lafontant, (ed.), *L'état et les Minorités* (Saint-Boniface, Manitoba: Éditions du Blé et Presses Universitaires de Saint-Boniface, 1993).
- St. Ignatius, *The Spiritual Exercises of St. Ignatius of Loyola*, (trans. from the Autograph by Father Elder Mullan) (New York: P.J. Kennedy & Sons, 1914).
- Smith, A., *An Inquiry into the Nature and Causes of the Wealth of Nations*, (London: Dent & Sons, 1904).
- Stone, Helen, 2000: "Les Indiens et le système judiciaire criminel de la province de Québec: les politiques de l'administration sous le Régime britannique." *Recherches amérindiennes au Québec* XXX(3).
- Tanner, Helen Hornbeck and George E. Sioui, 1994: "Personal Reactions

of Indigenous People to European Ideas and Behavior." In Jaap Lintvelt, Réal Ouellet and H. Hermans. *Culture et colonisation en Amérique du Nord.* Sillery: Septentrion.

- Toqueville, Alexis de, 1952: *L'Ancien Régime et la Révolution.* Paris: Gallimard.
- Trigger, Bruce G., 1985: *Natives and Newcomers Canada's "Heroic Age" Reconsidered.* Kingston and Montréal: McGill-Queen's University Press.
- Weber, Max, 1930: *The Protestant Ethic and the Spirit of Capitalism.* Trans. Talcott Parsons. London: Unwin.
- White, Richard, 1991: *The Middle Ground, Indians, Empires and Republics in the Great Lakes Region, 1650–1815.* Cambridge: Cambridge University Press.

---

[1] We would like to thank the following people for their valuable comments: Gilles Bourque, Gilles Gagné, Bogumil Jewsiewicki-Kos and an anonymous referee at *Recherches amérindiennes au Québec.*

[2] Department of Sociology, Laval University, Québec City

[3] Department of Sociology and Anthropology, Concordia University, Montréal

[4] In order to gain a greater understanding of the relevance and scope of this article, we suggest the reader begin with the appendix at the end, which provides some concrete descriptions of Aboriginal living conditions today.

[5] Justice has to be done to Weber's book despite the constant criticism with which it is bombarded. For an overview of the debate, see Disselkamp, Annette, *L'éthique protestante de Max Weber,* Paris: PUF, 1994; Besnard, Pierre, *Protestantisme et capitalisme, la controverse post-weberienne,* Paris: Armand Colin Besnard, 1970; Marshall, Gordon, *In Search of the Spirit of Capitalism: an essay on Max Weber's protestant ethic thesis,* New York: Hutchinson, 1982, and; Poggi, Gianfranco, *Calvinism and the capitalist spirit: Max Weber's "Protestant ethic",* Amherst: University of Massachusetts Press, 1983. While Weber's thesis postulates that the very content of Protestant doctrine expresses and explains the formation of the capitalist spirit, we will limit ourselves to positing a correspondence between Protestant ethics and the capitalist spirit, and not a historical causal relation or a direct or indirect explanatory link. We will assume simply a heuristic relationship and exemplary value. In other words, Protestant ethics are with respect to asceticism of work a valid illustration of the dissolution of the traditional symbolism of "work." In a dense book that is persuasive at least with respect to the general thesis, Disselkamp (1994) shows that Weber's evidence was insufficient and that it encounters historical difficulties when it comes time to understand the precocious industrial boom of some European peoples, with the exception of the English. In this article, we will not try to match Aboriginal ethics with a rejection of capitalism and see *bourgeois* ethics as a larval form of capitalism. Instead, we will try to understand how both are illustrations of different means of social regulation in which capitalism may or may not be legitimized. That "Puritanism conveyed a specific culture of work" is sufficient for now, and we will not try to go further, for the purpose of this article is not to shore up Weber's fruitful thesis.

[6] St., Ignatius, *The Spiritual Exercises of St. Ignatius of Loyola,* (trans. by Father

Elder Mullan) (New York: P.J. Kennedy & Sons, 1914).

[7] Mauss, M., *The Gift: Forms and Functions of Exchange in Archaic Societies* (London: Routledge, 1990).

[8] Otto, R., *Mysticism East and West: A Comparative Analysis of the Nature of Mysticism* (New York: Macmillan, 1932).

[9] ANQ-Q, TL 999, evidence from files of the *Cour du Banc du Roi* 1764–1793. Proceedings against Charles Nichau Noite, Malecite. ANQ-Q, TL 999, *Juges de paix et sessions de la paix*, 1765–1802. Application by Louis Hataretsin, Lorette Huron requesting to be freed from prison. (See Delâge, Denys and Sawaya, Jean-Pierre, *Les Traités des Sept-Feux avec les Britanniques. Droits et pièges d'un héritage colonial au Québec,* Sillery: Septentrion, 2001 at 78–79.)

[10] ANQ-M, TL 19, S4, SSI, case file 155, October 1799 and case file 48, April 1803; ANQ-M, TL 32-SS 11, case file October 1803–July 1806; ANQ-M, TL 19, S4, SS1, case file 89, April 1807; ANQ-M, TL 19, S4, SS1, minutes book of hearings, February–October 1807.

[11] Montesquieu, *De L'Esprit des Lois* (1758). A modern edition has been produced by Laurent Versini (Paris: Éditions Gallimard, 1995). This is available online at: http://classiques.uqac.ca/classiques/montesquieu/de_esprit_des_lois/de_esprit_des_lois_tdm.html

[12] Aquinas made these remarks in *Summa Theologica*: Aquinas, T., *The Summa Theologica of St. Thomas* Aquinas (New York: The Benziger Bros., 1947) (trans. by Fathers of the English Dominican Province). This is available online at: http://www.newadvent.org/summa/.

[13] Franklin, B., *The Autobiography* (with an Introduction by Daniel Aaron) (New York: Vintage Books, 1990).

[14] The lesson of *bourgeois* ethics is set out explicitly in *Robinson Crusoe*. The hero of the novel is absolved of his sins through work even though accumulation and storage of goods in a cave is absurd and useless on a desert island. In the author's eyes, work has a timeless, eternal value, namely, redemption. The pages of the book in which he records the actions and deeds of the hero are a living sermon that is both a defence of the civilizing mission of the British Empire's conquest and a recommendation that one should labour to ensure divine election.

[15] Note that according to the *bourgeois* ethic contained in the saying "time is money", inaction is already a form of waste of work. Work is thus a reified form of social activity or labour. Work is a good in itself because it is simply worthwhile. Crossing half the continent by canoe, braving snowstorms, going hunting for many days in difficult conditions and performing the exploits of a warrior are not "work" in the *bourgeois* sense, for work emerges only in a society that has rationalized and functionalized its relationship to time and productivity. Even today, the Pope in the Vatican does not work.

[16] Baron de Lahontan, whose views were in the end rather analogous, tried to use a fictional Huron character named Adario to prove that man had a natural tendency towards good, in other words, towards freedom, equality, brotherhood and happiness, rather than towards artifice, luxury and the vices maintained by an insatiable desire for money, the "demons of demons." Through the pen of Lahontan, a ruined aristocrat, we discover a criticism of *bourgeois* ethics and the association of a certain conception of Aboriginal life (idleness, hunting, warrior

spirit, etc.) with an idealized view of the lives of nobles. De Lahontan's original manuscript was published as *Nouveaux Voyages de Mr. le baron de Lahontan dans l'Amérique septentrionale* (La Haye: Les frères l'Honoré, 1703) and in English as *New voyages to North America: containing an account of the several nations of that continent, their customs, commerce, and way of navigation upon the lakes and rivers, the several attempts of the English and French to dispossess one another ... to which is added a dictionary of the Algonkine language which is generally spoke in North-America* (London: H. Bonwicke, T. Goodwin, M. Wotton, B. Tooke, and S. Manship, 1703). An online version in English can be found at: http://www.canadiana.org/ECO/ItemRecord/37429?id=64cbf77ff496795c.

[17] While Aboriginals do not consider farming to be men's work, they do not consider regular, repetitive work to be for men either. This was not true of women. Housework, the preparation of skins and today handicrafts are described in various ways as the kind of work that men reject. This may be why on many reserves it is more often women than men who "take care of business", manage institutions and do the work. Since agriculture was reserved for women, Aboriginals forced into reserve-ghettos reacted a little like Jews, but in completely different occupations. They became loggers on reserves where forestry was possible. They also raised livestock. In the nineteenth century, a third of the cowboys were Aboriginals! Today, many Aboriginals join the army and succeed remarkably well—as warriors.

[18] Durkheim, E., *The Division of Labor in Society*, (Trans. by George Simpson) (New York: The Free Press, 1947).

[19] Smith, A., *An Inquiry into the Nature and Causes of the Wealth of Nations*, (London: Dent & Sons, 1904).

[20] Note the address, which is one among many, by Governor Dorchester to the ambassadors of the Sept Feux of Lower Canada in 1794: "*Mes enfants / C'est avec bien du plaisir que je vous ai entendu hier déclarer votre fidélité et attachement envers le Roi votre père, et que vous étiez prêts à combattre pour lui lors qu'il seroit attaqué, et en conséquence je m'y fierai.*" (RG10, 1794)

[21] Kant, I., "What is Enlightenment?", (1784), available online at the Modern History Source at: http://www.fordham.edu/HALSALL/MOD/kant-whatis.html.

[22] "Report of a Committee of the Executive Council", Québec City, June 13, 1837, LaBouchere, [June 17, 1839], 1973: 27. (A handwritten copy of the report is available: NAC, RG10, bob. C-13499, Vol. 992, at 283–252).

[23] Simard, J., "La réduction des Amérindiens: entre l'Envers-du-Blanc et l'avenir pour soi", in J. Lafontant, (ed.), *L'état et les Minorités* (Saint-Boniface, Manitoba: Éditions du Blé et Presses Universitaires de Saint-Boniface, 1993).

[24] There are radical differences between the welfare state in the period after WWII and the contemporary technocratic state. The welfare state system is like insurance, in other words, it provides help for those who are injured or victims of a system for which they are not individually responsible. We are quite certain that this system has been corrupted to benefit a cybernetic system.

[25] This section is rather tentative because of a lack of research on this issue, which is in itself particularly revealing. We hope that future work will eliminate this lack.

[26] In the following data, the term "Aboriginal" refers to a person who self-identifies as such, whether or not he or she is a registered "Indian".

[27] Royal Commission on Aboriginal Peoples, *Report of the Royal Commission on*

Aboriginal Peoples, Ottawa: Supply and Services Canada, 1996, Vol. 2: 135, 139, 266; Vol. 3: 141, 159, 175, 191, 497; Vol. 5: 33, 34, 51.

[28] The theme of the 2000 Gala of Aboriginal business people in Québec (*Mishtapew*), the purpose of which has been for some years to highlight innovation and success in Aboriginal businesses, was "it's time to come out of our tents." At the Gala, prizes were awarded to an aviation company, a trucking company, and a restaurant, and for achievements in culture, the arts, publishing, education, etc. In short, it celebrated the idea that it is possible to appropriate modernity without denying one's Aboriginal origins. It also celebrated the fact that Aboriginals were ready for this and had the tools needed, which was revealing of social and economic changes.

[29] ANQ-Q, B, v. 36 (6), Folio 28–29, Mémoire du Roy au Sr Le Marquis de Vaudreuil et Bégon, Versailles, March 19, 1714; C11A, Vol. 53, Folio 216V, lettre de l'intendant Hocquart au Ministre, 1730 [our translation].

[30] Until now, the historical heritage of Aboriginal peoples has always been portrayed as destiny. Historically, "Whites" have often meant inevitable dispossession, fatal illnesses and irreversible loss. The expulsion of Aboriginals onto reserves was explicitly segregationist and marginalizing. Even modernized, the *Indian Act* still entails that the Aboriginal nations are under the guardianship of the government. No matter how you look at it, invoking the clauses of old treaties before the courts, though it may be an opportunistic way of promoting Aboriginal rights, is a very poor strategy because the treaties were signed in a colonial system that prohibited any attempt by Aboriginals to take charge of their own future. To invoke the old treaties is to agree to remain the subjects of colonial/federal power, and not the subjects of law, responsible and committed to appropriating politics. This is why we think that the rights enshrined by the treaties should someday be traded for new rights negotiated in new treaties, which would give Aboriginal nations land and resources over which they could exercise their sovereignty fully.

The Construction of Shamanic Identity among the Inuit of Nunavut and Nunavik

Bernard Saladin d'Anglure[1]

Based on accounts gathered in Nunavik and Nunavut since the mid-1950s, I have tried to show how Inuit individual identity (*inuuniq*) was gradually constructed from birth (*inuulirniq*) to the time of marriage (Saladin d'Anglure 2000, 2001b). The process involved learning and performance, which was celebrated collectively by rites of passage. This developed an individual's independence, and made him into a productive man (*anguti*), or her into reproductive woman (*arnaq*), while inexorably submitting the individual to the group's collective interests as expressed by the elders' will. The elders, whether they belonged to the same generation (*angajuit*) or an earlier generation (*angajuqqaat*), had to be respected and obeyed. This was the condition for having a long life, successful hunts and many children. It was dangerous to transgress regulated social life.

In a more recent collective work (Saladin d'Anglure 2001a), I adopted a broader perspective in an analysis of a number of conversations on cosmology and shamanism recorded with elders during ethnographic research at *Igloolik* in 1972 and while teaching a course on the theme at Nunavut Arctic College in *Iqaluit* in 1998.

This article is a continuation of these publications. Here, I will discuss identity, but focus on that of shamans (*angakkuit*) and show that construction of shamanic identity (*angakkuuniq*) requires deconstructing individual identity (*inuuniq*), transgressing social rules and crossing cosmological barriers. The construction process is based on tangible signs from the invisible world of the dead and spirits, highlights unique and extraordinary experiences, and requires social recognition by the group.

This is a complex problem, for shamanism has been gradually eradicated in the Arctic ever since the power relations between the local population and Western immigrants turned in favour of the latter. This occurred after a long period of intermittent contact with European-Americans and gradual settlement by missionaries belonging to various Christian churches.

Very few authors witnessed shamanic rituals, and those able to speak with shamans in their own languages were even more rare. Knud Rasmussen's work (1929, 1930, 1931) is thus indispensable, even though it is lacking in many respects, at least concerning the topic of this article. The number of Inuit informers is decreasing every year. They have all been converted to Christianity and very few are willing to speak about shamanism, which was long condemned as satanic by Christian evangelists, priests, pastors and catechists. I will therefore use data from fieldwork that I did in Nunavik between 1961 and 1971, and in Nunavut since 1971. I will also use unpublished data gathered in *Kivalliq* by Svend Frederiksen between 1946 and 1961 (see Saladin d'Anglure and Hansen 1997).

While, as we have just suggested, a child's identity was constructed in a cumulative manner as he or she acquired new skills under the watchful eye of his or her midwife, close relatives and the community's elders, the opposite process occurred in the case of a boy or girl whose shamanic destiny had been foretold by a shaman. If the prediction was made at the time of birth or in infancy, the shaman prescribed many prohibitions and obligations that set the child apart, and made him or her different from his or her peers. If the prediction was made when the child was an adolescent, the future shaman was required to undergo training under the supervision of one or more shamans. He or she had to regress, symbolically die, sometimes come back as a foetus, and be reborn as a different person in order to acquire shamanic clairvoyance, assistance from auxiliary spirits and the ability to travel beyond the limits of the visible world.

Shamanic identity was constructed outside the group and outside of the habitat, in places where there were no footprints (*tumitaittuq*) and spirits lived, but also within the group, through public demonstrations. Thus, shamans were characterized by culturally controlled marginality and by a crossing of boundaries that gave them access to all forms of mediation. Their marginality was expressed in various ways, such as by marks on their bodies or clothing, unusual sensory and psychic abilities, and exceptional physical feats. It was also expressed in their relations with other members of the group, and with cosmic and non-human entities.

1. Shamanic Identity and Personal Names

The importance of personal names in the construction of Inuit identity has been the subject of much recent work (Saladin d'Anglure 1998a, 1998b; Kublu and Oosten 1999). Names also play a major role in the construction of shamanic identity, though this theme has been overlooked in ethnography. I believe that among the few to have studied this are myself and Frederiksen (1960, 1964). Frederiksen was a pioneer in the field, and had the luck to be able to talk about this with many older shamans. In order to explore a few possibilities and open the way for future research, I will look at a number of hypothetical situations. The first is that of a child who is named after the auxiliary spirit of a shaman; the second is that of a shaman who receives as an auxiliary spirit a human or non-human entity whose name was among his or her names; and the third is that of an individual who receives the name of a shaman as a personal name.

1.1. An Auxiliary Spirit (*tuurngaq*) as a Personal Name (*atiq*)

If a birth was difficult or the newborn would not stop crying, it was attributed to a failure to satisfy the desire of a dead person who wanted to live again in the child through his or her name. In such cases, clues were sought, in particular in the dreams of close family members, to identify the dead person so that his or her name could be given to the child. However, in extreme cases, when the baby was in danger of dying, a shaman's services were sought. The shaman would give the baby the name of one of his or her auxiliary spirits. This practice was considered a last resort. Among the Inuit at *Igloolik*, I gathered a number of examples of this type.

The first is from *Qatiktalik* (Cape Fullerton), and dates from just after the turn of the twentieth century. It is the case of Iqallijuq. After five stillborn children, Nuvvijaq finally gave birth to a daughter who was very weak and lost consciousness several times. Her father, the shaman Ittuliaq, therefore decided to give her extra life (*inuuliksaut*) by naming her after one of his main auxiliary spirits, "Iqallijuq", the mythical creator of salmonids. The child regained consciousness, and the name remained her principal name for all of her long life.[2]

My second example dates from the 1920s and comes from *Sagliq* (Southampton Island). It concerns Qaumajuq, the son of the shaman Kappianaq. One evening, the young child was seriously ill, and began spitting up blood. His frightened parents asked for help from a local shaman, Manaapik, who came to the child's bedside and decided to rename him Ijiraq, which was the name of one of his invisible but human-shaped auxiliary spirits. The child got better and still has the name.[3]

My third example comes from Aupilaarjuk (Saladin d'Anglure 2001a), whose younger brother Kukigaq was very sick when he was young. He was saved by a powerful shaman, Alakannuaq, who gave him the name of his auxiliary spirit, Kakiarnuit. The child survived and gains great mental strength from his name.

Thanks to Frederiksen, we have a manuscript of a very special account from *Igluligaarjuk* (Chesterfield Inlet): that of the great shaman Qimuksiraaq, who spoke of his auxiliary spirits' desire to share their names with young children.

> *Tuurngara, Pisuktikuluk atiqarpuq Aivilimmi arnamik, angakkuugama, suli inuujuq nutaraulluni; arnaq tainna anigami atiqaqtitauvuq Pisuktikulummik tuurngara Pisuktikuluk atiqatigiquullugu* (Qimuksiraaq 1946: 135–136).

> (My tuurngaq, Pisuktikuluk, shared his name with an Aivilik woman who was a child when I was a shaman. When the woman was born, she was named Pisuktikuluk in order to share the name of my tuurngaq, Pisuktikuluk.)

Another of his three auxiliary spirits also shared its name with a child. The third one had had a namesake long before, and it was jealous of the other two and strongly desired to have one again.

My hypothesis is that giving such a name to a dying child increased the likelihood that the child would become a shaman if he or she survived. Indeed, he or she would later be able to use the eponymous spirit as an auxiliary spirit. In Frederiksen's terms, in this case the word *inuulikaut* (additional life) would become *angakkuksaqtuq* (that which leads to shamanism). Iqallijuq told me that she agreed with this interpretation, but in her case the family's conversion to Christianity thwarted her shamanic destiny. This was also what happened in the families of Ijiraq and Kakiarniut.

1.2. A Personal Name (*atiq*) as an Auxiliary Spirit (*tuurngaq*)

At a time when, on average, one out of every two children died at birth or in the first year, people sought means, even when the child was still in the womb, of countering the lethal powers that threatened them (Saladin d'Anglure 1998b). A foetus was considered to be able to think and to have emotions, like the anthropomorphized entities in the invisible world. A newborn could be tempted to join his or her stillborn siblings waiting in the beyond. If a child survived a nearly fatal loss of consciousness, it was interpreted as a sign of shamanic election, and led to all sorts of restrictions for the child and his or her close relatives. This made the child a being apart, different from the others. The case of Ava, reported by Rasmussen (1929), is an example of this.

Ava's mother, Ataguarjugusiq, had lost all of the children that she had conceived one after the other, and feared that once again she would not be able to bring the child to term. Thus, when the foetus began to kick her violently in the stomach, she sought out Aarjuat, a shaman woman from a neighbouring camp. With the help of the elders, Aarjuat determined that the foetus was very sensitive to all of his or her parents' failures to follow the rules prescribed during pregnancy. They all predicted that the child would have a great future as a shaman.

When the pregnancy came to term, the child was born strangled with its umbilical cord. Aarjuat was called again, and it took her a long time to reanimate the child. She prescribed very severe prohibitions for the child and his mother. They were to last until he reached adulthood, had killed one of every kind of game and conceived his first son. Rasmussen tells us that the child was given the names Kaujjajjuk, Uriuqtuq and Ava, which is the name of a small female coastal spirit. Ava later became the man's primary auxiliary shamanic spirit, which he invoked by chanting:

> Joy, joy, joy, joy, I see a little spirit of the beach, a little ava, I myself am an ava, the spirit's namesake, joy, joy (Rasmussen 1929: 119–120).

Though Rasmussen does not say so, there is every reason to believe that the name "Ava" was chosen by Aarjuat and that it was one of her auxiliary spirits, which would bring us back to the cases mentioned above.

In Balikci's list of the auxiliary spirits of the shaman Netsilik Iksivalitaq (1963), there is "*Iksivalitaq*", the eponym of the shaman. However, the ethnographer did not notice this detail and we do not know whether the name came from a deceased relative or the auxiliary spirit of another shaman, who would have given it to him to help him survive at birth.

One of the problems encountered when interpreting old data on Inuit shamanism is that ethnographers most often failed to note the secondary personal names of the shamans they interviewed. Yet, for our purposes, we need not only a list of all the auxiliary spirits of every shaman, but also a list of all their personal names. The latter list shows whether there are links between the two systems (personal names and auxiliary spirits). The recent republication by Laugrand *et al.* (2001) of Rasmussen's detailed lists of the auxiliary spirits of six shamans (1929, 1931) highlights this lack.

Frederiksen describes another example of a personal name that became an auxiliary spirit. Qimuksiraaq carried the name Nanuq (polar bear) until the death of his eponym, a cousin on his father's side. The death of his cousin was a terrible ordeal for Qimuksiraaq; it was as if he had died also. His soul left his body for four days. No one had the right to use his former name. It was then that Quttik, an old shaman, went into the dream world to look for a new name for him in the world below, where Nuliajuk, the goddess of sea mammals lives. He found the name Qimuksiraaq, which was very old and had not been used for a long time. The new name (*illuqqitaat*) was ritually given to him and his old name, Nanuq, became his first auxiliary spirit. The old shaman saw the expression of a much more general rule in his personal example. Here is how he explained it to his friend Frederiksen:

> ...The shamans changed their first name, which became the name of their auxiliary spirit... The shaman's first soul-name starts being his auxiliary spirit... My auxiliary spirit, Nanuq, received my first name as its name... (Saladin d'Anglure and Hansen 1997: 54–55).

The change of identity makes our Western heads spin because we are used to rigid boundaries between the real and imaginary. In this case we no longer quite know who is who. The individual called Qimuksiraaq, formerly called Nanuq, is easily recognizable by his features, character and behaviour, but as soon as he changes his name, we are not so sure what he has become. The auxiliary spirit Nanuq is not the deceased eponym, who has left for the beyond. It is a namesake and therefore a kind of double, but with a very specific function: to serve the new shaman. Qimuksiraaq says:

> *Angakkut attiuqpaktut atirmut aippaanut angakkuuliqtumut ajuqiqtuivakkut ukiunik sitamanik nalliraangat ajuqiqtuilirlutit* (Qimuksiraaq 1946: 256. 6 p., 189).

(The angakkut who gave the second names were the ones who educated the novice angakkuts for the four winters necessary.)

The change therefore corresponds to the beginning of Qimuksiraaq's initiation as a shaman. He lost his original personal identity, which he shared with his eponym, and took on a shamanic identity with a new name chosen by the entities in the invisible world. It is as if his name and self became dissociated, died in the social reality of human life, only to live again in a much stronger and dynamic relationship, namely that which unites a *tuurngaq* with its shaman. However, this relationship belongs to the invisible world, the world of spirits.

In the new reality, the name Nanuq loses the anthropomorphic and classificatory connotations that it had as a proper name in human reality, and takes on a "religious" connotation, since it now designates an auxiliary spirit belonging to a shaman. Paradoxically, the new connotation is related to a word in ordinary language, *nanuq*, which means "polar bear". However, it is not just any polar bear, but an abstract entity: the master-spirit of polar bears. This detail becomes even more meaningful when we learn that when he was a teenager, Qimuksiraaq was attacked by a polar bear, but he managed to fight it off and chase it away using only a stick.[4] We will look at the various roles of this shaman's auxiliary spirits below.

1.3. A Shaman's Name as a Personal Name

As in the case of ordinary people, shamans' names were passed down to their descendants. Sometimes shamans chose to pass on their names while they were still alive, sometimes after their death. In the latter case, a shaman sometimes appeared in a dream and said that he or she wished to live again in a specific family, and sometimes a shaman's family decided to give his or her name to a newborn in order to maintain his or her presence in and close links with the family.

There are few very old genealogies available to assess the possible links between the transmission of a name and the transmission of shamanic power. Perhaps a close examination of the unpublished genealogies gathered by Father Van De Velde could shed some light on this. The table prepared by Cornélius Remie based on these genealogies (Oosten and Remie 1997) indeed shows that the shaman Iksivalitaq had a grandson and namesake, but we know little more. However, this link exists among other Arctic peoples with shaman traditions, such as the Yukaghirs and Evens in Siberia, among whom we have found a few cases.[5]

My Inuit data, which straddle the pre-Christianization–post-Christianization period, are fragmentary, but still shed useful light on the effects of an eponymic link between a shaman and his or her descendants. The following are a few examples of this.

Memory of the female shaman Arnatsiaq is still strong in the *Igloolik* area because she died of natural causes at a very advanced age. Her name was given to her great grandson, the son of the shaman Ikyuksarjuat, whom she had adopted and in whose home she lived the last years of her life. When Arnatsiaq Junior became an adult, before his family converted to Christianity, he did not become a shaman. However, it is said that he had inherited from his eponymous shaman grandmother the remarkable clairvoyance of a shaman that enabled him to find lost hunters, such as those who had been carried out to sea by currents while they were hunting on the banks.

Iktuksarjuat often accompanied Arnatsiaq when her services were requested by patients living in distant camps, carried the old shaman on his back and sat her in his sled to take her where she needed to go. Family tradition says that she transferred her shamanic power to him and Iqallijuq says that after her death, she became one of his auxiliary spirits (personal communication).

The case of Piluqtuutialuk, one of the last great shamans in the *Tarramiut* (Nunavik) area, is a little different. Towards the end of his life (he died in 1927), upon learning that his adoptive daughter was pregnant, he expressed a wish to have a namesake. When the pregnancy came to term, the newborn was named Piluqtuuti (or Pilukallak, "little Piluq"), but she was a girl. The old shaman was upset and said that he did not want to menstruate (namely, by living again in the body of a woman). As we have described elsewhere, the hex was later seen in the fact that his great granddaughter namesake had amenorrhea and died when she was an adult without ever having menstruated.

Eugène Amarualik of *Igloolik* provides another example. His eponym, Amarualik, was a famous shaman whom he never met, and also the first husband of his mother, Iqallijuq. It was a custom to give the first child of the second marriage the name of the deceased spouse. Since the shaman had died under strange conditions, after having been attacked by *ijiqqat* (invisible spirits shaped like humans), his widow did not want to continue the practice. However, she nonetheless named her third child after her deceased husband after he had appeared to her in a dream and threatened to kill the child if she did not give him or her his name.

It has to be said that before marrying Iqallijuq, the shaman had experienced a great deal of distress. His first wife had died, and he had developed a relationship with two invisible *ijiqqat* women, which his shamanic powers enabled him to see. They had approached him and convinced him to live with them. In exchange, they brought him many caribou. However, the relationship had a very special aspect in that the shaman regularly felt the need to go back and live among his own people, and each time he did so, he completely forgot his relationship with the *ijiqqat* women. Then, depending on what happened when he was out hunting caribou, he suddenly found himself back with them, without knowing how he got there.

During one of his returns back among his own people, his mother decided to marry him to young Iqallijuq, who had been christened in the Catholic Church when she was a child. For a time, the couple lived peacefully, but then while the newlyweds were on a trip into the backcountry, the shaman's two invisible wives came to him to try to bring him back to their home. They tormented him so much that he died. On his deathbed, he remembered everything that had happened and told the whole story to his wife.[6]

Some 30 years later, Amarualik Junior, who was christened Eugène, got married. Suddenly he had a dream: two beautiful young Inuit women dressed in traditional clothing came to him and very explicitly expressed their desire to have sex with him. When he told me the story, his wife was beside him and he told me that he had always rejected the advances of the two women. He said that it was quite certain that they were the *ijiqqat* companions of his eponym and that they were mistaking him for the earlier Amarualik. In order to punish him for refusing, the *ijiqqat* caused several of the children that he later had to fall seriously ill.

At the end of his account, Eugène Amarualik added that he had inherited strong mental powers from his shaman eponym, in particular the power to turn evil spells back on those who cast them on him.

These examples show that it was not sufficient to receive the name of a shaman to become one oneself. However, special powers were transmitted along with an eponym's name. The power was negative in the case of Pilukallak's amenorrhea, but in Eugène Amarualik's case the power was defensive and in Arnatsiaq's beneficial. Moreover, in cases where a shaman himself or herself chose to transmit his or her own name to a grandchild, and the child showed an early predisposition towards shamanism, it seems likely that there was special transmission of shamanic powers, which is probably what happened in Iksivalitaq Junior's case.

1.4. Shamanic Identity (*angakkuuniq*) and Auxiliary Spirits (*tuurngait*)

Frédéric Laugrand's discovery of Reverend Peck's notes on *tuurngait* in the archives of the Anglican Church of Canada, and their recent publication (Laugrand *et al.* 2001) has breathed new life into discussions on this theme, which were initiated by the work by Thalbitzer and Rasmussen in the first half of the twentieth century (Weyer 1932; Thalbitzer 1910, 1930; Rasmussen 1929, 1931). The 347 terms qualifying *tuurngait*, which were gathered by Peck and probably also by Bilby, likely came from the mouths of old shamans who had converted to Christianity. The adjectives and accompanying comments provide considerable new information but at the same time raise innumerable questions about the methodology employed in their collection, transcription and meaning of the terms, identity of the informers, distinction between names of auxiliary spirits and shamanic terms designating animal species, and finally the number and identity of the shamans who had the auxiliary spirits. These questions have yet to be answered.

In addition to the confusion created by the very wealth of the corpus, there is also that surrounding the illustrations of *tuurngait* published by Rasmussen, partially reproduced by Carpenter (1973) and taken up again in the work by Laugrand *et al.* (2001). The reports of the Fifth Thule Expedition are abundantly illustrated by photographs taken on the expedition and by drawings, often of excellent quality and astonishing realism, that were done by various Inuit in the groups visited. However, contrary to shamans' narratives describing their auxiliary spirits, which are precise and mention all sorts of anthropomorphic details, we have to admit that the six shamans who drew their auxiliary spirits for Rasmussen produced drawings of disarming poverty, if not to say of disconcerting confusion.[7] They remind one of the drawings that the Inuit at *Igloolik* did at the request of captains Parry and Lyon in 1821, which was the first time those Inuit had ever come into contact with Whites.[8]

Of course, we can admire their "primitive" and "original" nature, and see them as examples of "first art" giving access to the collective Inuit imagination, but we have to cast a skeptical eye on the judgment by Carpenter (1973: 189), who is nonetheless an experienced anthropologist. He comments on the shaman Anar-qaq's drawings, which have an important place in Rasmussen's corpus:

> Such drawings do what neither waking reality nor the world of dreams can accomplish alone: they give dreams a waking reality and waking reality a freedom comparable to that in a dream. They make a human universe possible.

Yet, Carpenter has the honesty to tell us about the conditions in which Rasmussen asked the shaman to draw his visions of spirits:

> At first he hesitated, for fear of offending the spirits, but then after some bargaining, I promised to pay him enough to satisfy his auxiliary spirit. He agreed on the condition that I not try to show them to his people, though I could do what I liked with the drawings in the White man's lands. He had never before drawn with a pencil on paper, but it has to be said that he employed the new tools with all the humility of an artist... he did not erase or retouch in a disorganized manner; he remained for hours with his eyes closed, concentrating on fixing his ideas in his memory, and it was only once he had succeeded in doing so that he tried to record their form. Sometimes, the memory of an event affected him so strongly that his whole body began trembling and he had to stop what he was trying to do (Rasmussen cited in Carpenter 1973: 181).

Here we see attitudes that could be observed relatively often only 50 years ago in the Canadian Arctic, when adult Inuit were questioned or asked for information by Euro-Canadians. It is also possible to see in the shaman's attitude a refusal or incapacity to translate into an image a reality as esoteric and subjective as auxiliary spirits were for him or her.

Coming back to the lists of spirits, the same things can be said about them as we said earlier about the lists of names of persons. They will have only limited docu-mentary and historical interest so long as we do not have more information on the contexts, which alone can provide their meaning and function.

So, how can we contribute to the debate over the role of *tuurngait* in the construc-tion of shamanic identity? I will do so here by focussing on three corpuses of data: one that I found in the Greenland Archives at *Nuuk* (1997), thanks to K. G. Hansen; and two that were gathered in the field, one in *Inukjuak*, Nunavik (1968), and one in 1998 in *Kangiqtugaapik* (Clyde River, Nunavut).

The exceptional quality of the first corpus, which was gathered at *Igluligaarjuk* (Chesterfield Inlet) in 1946, is a result of its age, Frederiksen's talent as an ethnographer and the abilities of the great shaman Qimuksiraaq (who had converted to Catholicism around 1924).

2. Qimuksiraaq, His Masters (ajuqiqtuijiit) and Auxiliary Spirits (tuurngait)

In an earlier work (Saladin d'Anglure and Hansen 1997), I presented extracts in *Inuktitut* of Qimuksiraaq's accounts of his entry into shamanism and his auxiliary spirits. Here, I will review some relevant aspects and complete them with unpublished passages from the manuscript transcribed by Frederiksen (1946).

> When my eponym Nanuq died, my soul (*tarniq*) and I became very sick. For four days I no longer had a shadow (*tarraq*)...I almost died on the second day. For a whole week I had no breath (*anirniq*). For four days I no longer had a soul. It was forbidden to say the name (Nanuq) because if someone had said it, I would probably have been really dead. I stayed in a tomb (*iluviq*) and began dreaming that I was going into igloos that I did not usually enter... (Qimuksiraaq 1946 in Saladin d'Anglure and Hansen 1997: 53–54).

In order to fully understand this account, we have to look at the Inuit conception of death (*tuquniq*), which is difficult to translate into European languages because it designates both numbness of the body or a limb, and unconsciousness or fainting. A dog that is beaten by its master falls unconscious. It is then said to be dead. But a few minutes later it staggers to its feet; it is no longer dead. The same thing is said of someone who is numb from the cold, and of a drowned person before reanimation. This is the reason for Qimuksiraaq's clarification. If the prohibition on saying his name had not been respected then he would be "really dead" (*tuqummarigajaqpunga*). Yet here again we have to note that death is seen much more as a passage than as a state, if one takes the point of view of the soul and life energy, as Inuit most often do. The "death" of the apprentice shaman has to be considered in this way.[9]

Let us go back to Qimuksiraaq's narrative. Unable to find the exit of the igloo that he had entered, the future shaman was guided by a baby who led him out. This is when a first master-shaman, Quttik, gave him his new shaman name, Qimuksiraaq, as we have described above. There was the symbolic death of the novice shaman (*angakkuksaq*), then recreation, symbolic rebirth in a dream and finally the giving of a new name in the visible world. This was followed by the astonishing ritual breastfeeding of Qimuksiraaq by his own mother, Tinnualluk, who was herself a shaman. She participated in his initiation for four winters:

> When Quttik repeated the formula "He shall be called Qimuksiraaq!", my mother offered me her breast. When she offered it to me I told her

that I was no longer a baby and that I did not want to suckle milk. "You who will not suckle milk, put it in your mouth!" and I put it in my mouth (Saladin d'Anglure and Hansen 1997: 54).

The cycle was then complete. The novice had a new life, a new youth and a new apprenticeship with his masters, based on the image of a suckling baby.[10] However, everything occurred in a manner opposite to empirical human reality. Whereas young children were constantly thrust into the adult world, where they learned by being made to believe that they already performed like adults, the apprentice shaman was sent back to the womb and then into the neonatal world. Whereas children were given the names of their most prestigious ascendants, or of those who had been closest, such as those who are recently deceased, an apprentice shaman was given a very old name that had not been carried for a long time and was chosen by the spirits. Whereas a child was encouraged from the time he or she was very young to gradually eat mostly meat, an apprentice shaman who was already a young adult was asked to suckle the breast of his mother, who had probably not had any milk for a long time.

In addition to his mother, Qimuksiraaq had no less than five master shamans, each of whom played a specific role in his training. Only those shamans had access to the igloo built specially for his training. Quttik gave him his new name and first auxiliary spirit (*tuurngaq*), Nanuq (polar bear). Sauri, who died before the end of his apprenticeship, provided him with a second auxiliary spirit, *Pisuktikuluk* (little walker).[11] Kamimmalik, his mother's cousin, gave him his third *tuurngaq*, *Nuvak&iq* (jellyfish).

The auxiliary spirits, particularly the principal one, deeply marked the shaman's personality. During trances (*sakaniq*), it was as if an auxiliary spirit possessed him. When Qimuksiraaq went into a trance, the white canines of the polar bear could be seen in his mouth and he began growling like a bear.[12]

A fourth shaman, Urpitijik, helped in Qimuksiraaq's training. Finally, the last was Inirnirunasuaq, whose contribution is said to have lasted only two days:

> *Tuququjiqattarmat Inirnirunasuaq tuninngilara. Ullut marruinnaat pia-nimmata ilinniarunnairpara* (Qimuksiraaq 1946:264.2, p. 163).

> (Since Inirnirunasuaq wanted to kill often, I did not give him a gift (*tuni-jjuuti*) and after the end of the second day I stopped all training with him.)

We know from other accounts that master shamans often shared their auxiliary spirits with their apprentices. In such cases, the auxiliary spirit divided into two in order to carry out its new duties. This is how Qimuksiraaq later shared *Nuvak&iq* with the young shaman Anarraq. The link between the master shaman and his or her student was acknowledged by gifts (*tunijjuutit*) given by the student to the master's auxiliary spirits. Throughout his or her life, the master remained linked with former students, who were sometimes asked to help perform certain collective rituals. The new shaman's various masters, auxiliary spirits and patients created a framework for his or her identity. He or she became part of a veritable shamanic space-time and cosmology.[13]

In Qimuksiraaq's case, we know that his first (female) auxiliary spirit, *Nanuq*, came from a tomb very early in the morning. She was the specialist of sea mammals. His second spirit, *Pisuktikuluk*, arrived during the day from inland. It was the intermediary with the moon spirit. Finally, during the night and from the sea, came the third auxiliary, *Nuvak&iq* (jellyfish), who was the intermediary with Nuliajuk, the goddess of sea animals at the bottom of the sea.

The socio-cosmological environment that gradually formed around the shaman was a kind of guarantee of his or her legitimacy, but it also exercised a degree of control over his or her behaviour and effectiveness. The shamanic belt was like the visible expression of that environment. It showed the shaman's status, power and original identity. For, while the gradual integration of children into adulthood entailed the adoption of culturally standardized clothing, in the case of shamans, original distinctive marks, such as the shamanic belt and motifs sewn on the coat, were not only possible but promoted.[14] When he visited the Caribou Inuit, Rasmussen recorded interesting comments on the belt of the female shaman Kinaalik (Rasmussen 1930: 56–58). Attached to the belt there were:

> ...a piece of a rifle because her master shaman had shot her during her initiation; - a piece of braided tendon that had been used during divination (probably her first time); - a ribbon that had been used to tie up a packet of tobacco that she had received as a present from a patient and that therefore had miraculous powers; - a piece of a bonnet that had belonged to her deceased brother, who had become her principal auxiliary spirit; - the paw of a polar bear, her second auxiliary spirit; - a piece of white caribou skin that a patient had given her; - a piece of a knitted vest that had belonged to a White and that she had received as a present from a patient; - a caribou tooth that a patient had given her; - caribou skin mittens that were a gift from a patient.

Note that her master shaman had shot Kinaalik with a cartridge filled with a round stone during her initiation. She had remained unconscious for several days. Among the same Caribou Inuit, Rasmussen also noted another form of "initiation death" for novices: death by drowning (1930).

While all of the rites of passage marking the gradual integration of children into the world of adults highlighted the production of the material conditions for survival and reproduction (Saladin d'Anglure 2000, 2001b), shamanic initiation rites insisted on the need to die in the visible world so as to be reborn in the invisible world and possibly find there infinite regeneration, as we will see in the following example.[15]

3. Qursulaat, a Shaman Woman Who Left to Live With the Spirits (tuurngait)

The following example illustrates a specific facet of the shamanic identity, which is related to the spirit world and revealed when the shaman leaves the society of humans to live in the spirit world. The case described below occurred during the period of transition to Christianity among the *Qikirtait Inuit* (Belcher Island) in the early 1930s. It was recounted by Akuliaq, an *Inukjuak* elder who had spent his youth at *Qikirtait*.[16] Akuliaq remembered that one day on the islands, after an Anglican service led by Uumajualuk, a young man in the assembly named Qarvik made the following public confession:

> *Piulijaugumajunga arnaqaqpakami inuunngitumik inuugumagamali piulijaulunga" taimaak uqaqtuq qiatsunilu arnangalu inuummat qiturngangillu sitamat asianik arnaqarsunilu inuunngitumik upinnarani qulaqtuq imminik qanimamuummgituq niparumagani taikani arnamik nuungunnangijjanguursuni Inuunginnaaluni arnangalu inuutillugu qiturngangillu inuutillugit uqarumanngikaluarsuni uqanngikuni piulijaugajannginami uqaajuq tanna nakuqtuq inuunginnasuni* (Akuliaq 1968).

("I want to be saved when I die, but because I have had relations with a non-human woman, I will not be able to be saved. I want to live and be saved later," he said, with tears in his eyes. He had an Inuit wife and four children, but also a non-human wife. It was normal for him to be worried, not that he was sick, but he feared that if he continued to see the non-human woman, he would not be able to see his wife anymore. He wanted to live with his wife and four children and remain an Inuk. If he had not made that confession, it would have been impossible for him to be saved. It was good that he confessed while he was still a human.)

Qarvik was faced with a dilemma. He had to choose between continuing his affair with a non-human woman, which would mean passing over into the world of spirits (*tuurngait*) and never seeing his human family again, or breaking off the affair, remaining an *Inuk* (human) and living again with his family. The human–*tuurngaq* opposition is very clear here, not only with respect to identity but also with respect to life (brief vs. regenerated). This is probably because there were no longer any shamans to guide Qarvik and teach him how to use shamanic practices to divide his life between the invisible non-human world and the visible human world. Indeed, his experience closely resembles that of election by spirits, which is the first step in a calling as a shaman.

The conversion to Christianity of most of the families in the Belcher Islands a few years prior to the confession probably tipped the scale towards the human world. The last practising shamans in the area had to give up their auxiliary spirits under pressure from Anglican missionaries and catechists living in nearby villages where the inhabitants of the islands went for imported supplies.

The next part of the confession shows how others before him had made the opposite choice and decided to remain with the spirits. Qarvik explained that one day when he was walking on the land, he met a man who he had never seen before. They walked and talked together for a time, until a passage opened before them in a rock face. It was the entrance to the home of the stranger, who was a *tuurngaq*. He looked like a man in his prime, and was very tall with big eyes. The inside of his home closely resembled the comfortable homes of Whites built near northern counters. It had many lamps, a wood stove with an oven, a washroom, and several rooms. The *tuurngaq*'s wife lived there. Her name was Qursulaat and she was very old. Their two children, a young man and a young woman, were also there. The woman listened very closely to Qarvik's description of his own home and the members of his camp, and she told him about herself. She had lived among the Inuit long ago and she told him the names of people she had known.

At the end of the day, the *tuurngaq* took Qursulaat into the washroom and when they came out, she had been turned back into a young woman. The man devoured his wife whenever she got too old and then expelled her young again. He did the same thing with his four sled dogs. When it was time to go to sleep, their daughter lay down in Qarvik's bed, made love with him and spent the night there. Neither her parents nor her brother objected.

On the third day, Qarvik wanted to see his Inuit family again and the *tuurngaq* let him go, despite his daughter's objections. However, Qarvik came back two weeks later and for a time divided his life between the two families. The *tuurngaq* had a brother who lived with his wife and children on the mainland. They were the last survivors of a non-human people that had been very numerous in the area in the past.[17]

In his commentary on Qarvik's confession, old Akuliaq provided a few details on Qursulaat, whom his grandmother had known very well. The two women had lost their husbands and been abandoned by the other members of their camp, who had left in dog sleds. Akuliaq had young children with her, but no dogs. Qursulaat had dogs but no children. The two women had to work together to capture seals. Qursulaat had more luck hunting than her companion, and also shamanic powers. When the former members of their camp decided to come back and get them, they could not find Qursulaat and, fearing her power, gave up the search. No one had heard about her since then, though Akuliaq's grandmother was regularly provided with game by the *tuurngait* at the request of her former companion in misfortune.

In 1932, when they established a Hudson Bay Company counter in the Belcher Islands, the Whites asked people about someone named Qijuapik, who had ordered a lot of imported products from the company. There was no one by that name in the Belcher Islands, but all the Inuit understood that the person in question was the son of Qursulaat and her *tuurngait* husband.

This examination of Inuit ideas associated with a period of major economic and religious change sheds interesting light on the relationships shamans had with non-humans. Since spirits are not mortal, it is easy to see how the ageing process would be a problem if a human were to live with a non-human. A periodic return to youth solves the problem. It is not unlike the way that the first humans, who lived before death existed, got younger by leaning forward head first over the edge of the platform in the home.

The technique of eating a person and expelling him or her by excretion or regurgitation is seen in shamanism when an apprentice shaman is initiated, and in some rituals in which the shaman was eaten and then expelled, transformed by his or her auxiliary spirit. The latter practice is confirmed by many of the last great shamans in *Nunavik*, such as Pilurtuutialuk, who was devoured by a lion, and Arnaitualuk, who was eaten by a Miqqiajuk.

Whether what is in question is renewed youth or regeneration, there is symbolic death and rebirth, which, as we have seen above, is at the very heart of accession to the position of shaman. Qursulaat's story shows how a shaman without human descendants, since she had lost her spouse and was in conflict with her community, allowed herself to be attracted into the non-human world of auxiliary spirits (*tu-urngait*), where she found everything she was missing: husband, descendants, as well as periodic renewal of youth. Her original group's conversion to Christianity was probably one of the reasons that she sought refuge with the spirits.

The story of the shaman Amarualik from *Igloolik*, which was cited in the first part of this article, has a number of similarities with the stories of Qarvik and Qursulaat. Solicited by non-human women (*ijiqqat*) while he was in mourning after having been widowed and was hunting outside the areas where humans went, Amarualik lived a double life for a time. Then he decided to stay with his new human wife, which unfortunately did not please his non-human companions, who tormented him to death.

We could also mention the case of the shaman Qinngaq, who also came from *Igloolik* and maintained relationships with *ijiqqat* even after his conversion to Catholicism. He had made a pact with them: they would provide him with caribou when he needed them, and he would live with them when the time came for him to die. He confessed this to his wife on his deathbed, and added that he would stay with the *ijiqaat* until the end of the world, and then he would join his family in Heaven (Saladin d'Anglure 1983, Saladin d'Anglure and Morin 1998).

The theme of marriage and society with non-humans is one of the least documented in ethnographic writings on the Inuit. However, the many examples gathered in places as different as *Inukjuak* in Nunavik, Clyde River and *Igloolik* in Nunavut, and the Inuvialuit area show its importance in the past.[18]

4. Nuajarlaaq, Whose Non-human Family Merged With His Human Family

Another example that I would like to examine comes from *Kangiqtugaapik* (Clyde River). It is the story of an old man, Nuajarlaaq, who developed family ties with another category of non-humans, the *tarriaksuit* I interviewed him at length in 1998 after he had been the subject of a television news story in Inuktitut on Radio Canada (northern program) in the mid-1990s. In relation to the two preceding cases (Qarvik and Qursulaat), Nuajarlaaq's case shows an original solution to the same problem: how can a relationship with spirits be reconciled with a relationship with humans? Nuarjarlaaq's solution is mid-way between the two preceding ones. It is again a question of shamanic identity in the context of a transition to Christianity.

When he was still a child, Naujarlaaq often accompanied his grandfather, who was a shaman, on seal hunts. One day, his grandfather introduced him to a hunter whom the child had never seen before. He was accompanied by a young boy Naujarlaaq's age. They were spirits in human form, *tarriaksuit,* who lived in the cliffs near the seashore. The *tarriaksuit* are normally invisible to ordinary humans, except when they want to be seen. Shamans, however, see them and often take them as auxiliary spirits (*tuurngait*). This was the case with Nuajarlaaq's grandfather. Nuajarlaaq told me that the old man was trying to introduce his grandson to the world of spirits to turn him into a shaman. Nuajarlaaq became friends with the young *tarriaksuit.* They often hunted on the same land and grew up together, until the day that the shaman grandfather died.

By then, Nuajarlaaq was old enough to get married. His *tarriaksuit* friend introduced him to his sister, with whom Nuajarlaaq fell in love. They even had a daughter together. At the same time, Nuajarlaaq's parents decided to marry him to an Inuit girl, with whom he also had a daughter.

At that time, Nuajarlaaq's Inuit community decided to convert to Christianity. The *tarriaksuits* also converted, but since they feared that Nuajarlaaq might be criticized by the Inuit because he had family ties with them, they came to get him one day with an invisible snowmobile that made no sound and left no tracks in the snow. They took him to their new church, which was invisible to humans. The whole *tarriaksuit* community was waiting for him to celebrate his marriage in a Christian church. At the end of the ceremony, his *tarriaksuit* wife told him that they would not see each other any more. Shocked, Naujarlaaq looked at her without understanding. She explained that she had visited his Inuit wife in a dream and that she was going to merge with her, so that they would be one. The same thing would happen with their daughter, who would be one with his Inuit daughter. Thus they would be reunited again.

This original solution, which was chosen by the spirits, enabled Naujarlaaq to keep a special relationship with the invisible spirit world, a relationship that had been initiated by his shaman grandfather, while at the same time adhering to the values and lifestyle of the Inuit community that had converted to Christianity.

What is striking in this example, as in the preceding examples, is the non-human spirits' ability to adapt. They are able to integrate novelty and change faster than humans. The *tuurngait* in the Belcher Islands lived in homes with all the comforts of those of Whites. The *ijiqaat* in Igloolik were both very traditional and very modern, and the *tarriaksuit* understood the White's language and had technology that was further advanced than that of Inuit communities. Do we not see here one of the characteristics of shamanism and shamans, namely the ability to assimilate difference and change in order to better manage adversity and unpredictability?[19]

5. Conclusion

At the end of this case study of Inuit shamanic identity, we can begin by stating the following rule: personal names (PN) are to individual identity (II) as auxiliary spirits (AS) are to shamanic identity (SI): [PN:II::AS:SI].

These two systems of identity are necessarily related to each other, since in order to become a shaman one first has to be a socially recognized individual, therefore going from one system to the other requires passing by death. For a child to receive the name of an auxiliary spirit, he or she has to be on the threshold of death. For an apprentice shaman to receive his or her own personal name as an auxiliary spirit, he or she has to die symbolically, lose the name and receive a new one chosen by the spirits.

We can now come back to the hypotheses made at the beginning of this article, such that the construction of shamanic identity requires a deconstruction of individual identity, transgression of social rules, and crossing of cosmological boundaries.

5.1. Deconstructing Individual Identity to Construct Shamanic Identity

Ordinary individual names, in other words, ones from dead ascendants, were seen as like clothing or envelopes for the child (Rasmussen 1931). They constituted his or her identity as prescribed by the group. The child acquired the sum of all the experiences and skills of the long line of people who had carried the name. Names were given at birth and gave the child a genealogical status equivalent to that of the last person to have had the name, which helped to tighten the child's social ties with his or her family (Saladin d'Anglure 1998a).

If a child's names (which were often numerous) were not sufficient to protect him or her against the forces of death that began attacking at birth, then the services of a shaman were sought. He or she exorcized the child by giving him or her the name of one of the shaman's auxiliary spirits (*inuuliksaut*, which means "additional life"). The child's original names became secondary. We saw above that shamanism could result from this type of name (*angakkuksaqtuq*, which means "that which leads to shamanism"*).

In addition to the identity prescribed by the child's name, an identity was acquired through socialization between birth and marriage. Formation of the latter identity was punctuated with various rites of passage that marked the learning of rules and skills required by the group under the elders' authority. Respect for the elders, exchange and reciprocity were the foundations.

At more or less the same time, some girls and boys were apprenticed to shamans. While most adolescents were integrated into the producer–reproducer group, a few became apprentice shamans and were subject to a reverse process, namely the deconstruction of the individual identity prescribed by their names. We studied this in detail in the case of Qimuksiraaq, who died symbolically, had his former name removed from circulation, was reborn and was renamed with a very ancient name (*illuqqitaat*) that had not been used for a long time. The name was chosen by a spirit and conveyed by Qimuksiraaq's shaman teacher. The *illuqqitaat* (shamanic name), which neither evoked nor created links with living members of the group, was a sign of recognition in the world of the spirits that had chosen it.

Unlike ordinary name-envelopes that enable a child to "stand" physically and symbolically, as Rasmussen (1931) has shown clearly, auxiliary spirits sometimes devoured shamans (or apprentice shamans) in order to give them power or regenerate them. The spirits were sometimes incorporated into the shamans or merged into them to appear to humans during trances of possession at public and private rituals, as we have seen above.

5.2. Transgressing Human Rules and Complying with the Spirits' Prescriptions

A shaman's role was unique in other ways also. Unlike young adults, who had to dress in accordance with the rules for their sex, age and family status, and for whom originality was not appropriate, shamans were encouraged to wear the distinctive signs of their power, such as a shamanic belt or any other sign sewn on their clothing or worn as an ornament. Their travels in the human and spiritual worlds fed their creativity and led them to innovate and open new paths for managing misfortune, unforeseen events and change.

In short, the shaman had a separate status, which was related to his or her power to communicate with the invisible world, and to travel in the circular space-time of myths, dreams, the dead and spirits. On behalf of his or her auxiliary spirits, the shaman received certain advantages in the form of both material and sexual prestations (*tunijjuti*) from clients.

When other members of the group were required to share and engage in reciprocal exchange of game, children and spouses, the shaman was often in a dominant position that enabled him or her to have first pick (Saladin d'Anglure 1989). However, any abuse of power by the shaman exposed him or her to ostracism by the group or, in extreme cases, execution. A shaman's life was not without danger, particularly for those who entered into shamanism without an apprenticeship. It was said that their power was often excessive and could absorb their strength and shorten their lives.

Young shaman had to perform public demonstrations of their power and the help they received from auxiliary spirits. They thereby gained prestige and clients.

5.3. Crossing the Cosmological Barriers Between Humans and Spirits

Elsewhere, I have evoked the symbolic and psychological value of footprints (Saladin d'Anglure 1988; Saladin d'Anglure and Morin 1998), and the Inuit distinction between "space marked by footprints" (*tumitaqaqtuq*), which is the secular, safe space of humans that surrounds their homes and the lands they generally use and cross, and "space without footprints" (*tumitaittuq*), which is the sacred space of non-human beings, where shamanic initiation takes place and spirits are invoked (*qingarniq*).

Children and adults who were in mourning or afflicted with misfortune were told never to venture outside of the spaces marked by footprints. Otherwise, they would be easy prey for non-human spirits that would try to lure them into their world by offering affection and comfort. Many forms of behaviour that are called "irrational" by the Inuit and "pathological" by Euro-Canadian health authorities are attributed to the transgression of this rule. They result in a loss of identity. This was the case in particular for individuals possessed by incubuses and succubuses, in other words, sexually possessed by spirits encountered in spaces without footprints. The fatal consequences of such experiences could be avoided only through confession.[20]

Sacred spaces, which laypersons had to avoid, were exactly what shamans sought. There, they could communicate with their auxiliary spirits and find the causes of their clients' misfortune. For them, such spaces were where they could develop and consolidate their shamanic identities.

Likewise, if a layperson transgressed the prohibition against zoophilia, death would result. There could be no confusion between game and spouses, or animals and humans. For a shaman, on the contrary, an alliance with animal spirits able to take human form could be a conjugal relationship. Shamans' auxiliary spirits were often animal spirits.

The shaman's multi-faceted identity gave him or her the ability to cross the cosmological barriers between visible and invisible, space and time, thereby enabling him or her to act as a mediator and conduit among the various components of the cosmos.

References

- Aigle, Denise, Bénédicte Brac de la Perrière and Jean-Pierre Chaumeil, Eds. 2000. *La politique des esprits. Chamanisme et religions universalistes*. Nanterre: Société d'Ethnologie.
- Akuliaq. 1968. Handwritten manuscript in syllabary. Inukjuak: B. Saladin d'Anglure Fonds.
- Balikçi, Asen. 1963. "Shamanistic Behaviour among the Netsilik Eskimos" in *Southwestern Journal of Anthropology*, 19(4): 380–396.
- Blaisel, Xavier. 1986. *Analyse sociologique de trois rites d'initiation chamanique esquimaux (Ammassalik, Iglulik, Caribou)*. Master's thesis. Department of Sociology, University of Montréal.
  -- 1993. "Du sacrifice des hommes aux esprits selon la règle des initiations chamaniques chez les Inuit" in *L'Ethnographie*, 89(1): 113–147.
- Burch, Ernest S. Jr.1971. "The Nonempirical Environment of the Arctic Alaskan Eskimos" in *Southwestern Journal of Anthropology*, 27(2): 248–165.
- Carpenter, Edmund.1973. *Eskimo Realities*. New York: Holt, Rinehart and Winston.
- Chaumeil, Jean-Pierre.2000. "Chasse aux idoles et philosophie du contact" in D. Aigle *et al.*, Ed. *La politique des esprits. Chamanisme et religions universalistes*. Nanterre: Société d'Ethnologie: 151–164.
- Dehouve, Danièle.2000. "La mort symbolique dans l'initiation chamanique et la conversion chrétienne (Mexique, XVe–XVIIe siècles)" in D. Aigle *et al.*, Ed. *La politique des esprits. Chamanisme et religions universalistes*. Nanterre: Société d'Ethnologie: 165–186.
- Descola, Philippe.1996. "Les cosmologies des Indiens d'Amazonie" in *La Recherche*, 292: 62–67.
- Erasmus, Didier.1981 (1532). *La correspondance d'Érasme*. Translated and annotated by P. S. Allen, H. M. Allen and H. W. Garrod. Brussels: Brussels University Press, Vol. X:1532–1534.
- Frederiksen, Svend.1960. "The "primitive" Eskimo conception of souls" in *Actes du VI Congrès International des Sciences Anthropologiques et Ethnologiques*. Vol. II. Paris: 383–387.
  -- 1964. "Some Preliminaries on the Soul Complex in Eskimo Shamanistic Belief" in *Journal of the Washington Academy of Sciences,* 54: 109–112.
- Geertsen, Ib.1990. *Kârale Andreassen eqqumiitsuliortoq Tunumiu, en østgrønlandsk kunstner*. Nuuk: Atuakkiorfik.
- Gessain, Robert.1975. "Uizerk, l'amant, un personnage de la mythologie des Ammassalimuit (Côte Est du Groenland)" in *Objets et Mondes*, XV(3): 319–330.
- Hallendy, Norman.1985. "Reflexions, shades and shadows" in M. Patterson, R. Janes and C. Arnold, Eds. *Collected Papers on the Human History of the Northwest Territories*. Yellowknife: Prince of Wales Northern Heritage Centre, Occasional Paper No. 1: 125–167.
- Hamayon, Roberte.1990. *La chasse à l'âme. Esquisse d'une théo-*

rie du chamanisme à partir d'exemples sibériens. Nanterre: Société d'Ethnologie.

-- 2000. "Avant-propos" in D. Aigle *et. al.*, Ed. *La politique des esprits. Chamanisme et religions universalistes.* Nanterre: Société d'Ethnologie: 7–13.

• Kublu, Alexina and Jarich Oosten. 1999. "Changing Perspectives of Name and Identity among the Inuit of Northeast Canada" in J. Oosten and C. Remie, Eds. *Arctic Identities.* Leiden: Leiden University, Research School CNWS: 56–78.

• Laugrand, Frédéric, Jarich Oosten and François Trudel. 2001. *Representing Tuurngait, Memory and History in Nunavut.* Iqaluit: Nunavut Arctic College.

• Nappaaluk, Mitiarjuk Salomé. 1997. "Un témoignage inédit de Mitiarjuk sur les Mumitsimajut de Baie aux Feuilles et sur les uirsaliit et nuliarsaliit du Nunavuk" in *Études/Inuit/Studies*, 21(1-2): 249–254.

• Oosten, Jarich and Cornelius Remie. 1997. "Angakkut and Reproduction. Social and Symbolic Aspects of Netsilik Shamanism" in *Études/Inuit/Studies*, 21(1-2): 75–100.

• Ouellette, Nathalie. 2000. *Tuurngait et chamanes inuit dans le Nunavik occidental contemporain.* Master's thesis in Anthropology. Québec City: Laval University.

• Pouchelle, Marie-Christine. 1986. "Le corps féminin et ses paradoxes: l'imaginaire de l'intériorité dans les écrits médicaux et religieux (XIIe–XIVe siècles)" in *La condicion de la mujer en la Edad Media.* Madrid: Universidad Complutense.

• Qimuksiraaq. 1946. *Interviews recorded and transcribed by Svend Frederiksen.* Igluligaarjuk: Frederiksen Fonds. Nuuk: Greenland National Archives.

• Rasmussen, Knud. 1929. *Intellectual culture of the Iglulik Eskimos. Report of the Fifth Thule Expedition.* 1921–1924, 7(3). Copenhagen.

-- 1930. *Iglulik and Caribou Eskimo texts. Report of the Fifth Thule Expedition.* 1921–1924, 7(3). Copenhagen.

-- 1931. *The Netsilik Eskimos: Social life and spiritual culture. Report of the Fifth Thule Expedition.* 1921–1924, 8(3). Copenhagen.

• Saladin d'Anglure, Bernard. 1983. "Ijiqqat voyage au pays de l'invisible inuit" in *Études/Inuit/Studies*, 7(1): 67–83.

-- 1988. "Penser le féminin chamanique ou le "tiers-sexe" des chamanes inuit" in *Recherches Amérindiennes au Québec*, 18(2–3): 19–50.

-- 1989. "La part du chamane, ou le communisme sexuel inuit dans l'Arctique central canadien" in *Journal de la Société des Américanistes,* 75: 131–171.

-- 1992. "Pygmées arctiques et géants lubriques, ou les avatars de l'image de l'autre, lors des premières rencontres entre Inuit et Blancs" in *Recherches Amérindiennes au Québec*, 22(2–3): 73–88.

-- 1998a. "La parenté élective chez les Inuit du Canada, fiction empirique ou réalité virtuelle" in A. Fine, Ed. *Adoptions, la parenté choisie.* Paris: Éditions de la Maison des Sciences de l'Homme: 121–150.

-- 1998b. "Entre forces léthales et forces vitales, les tribulations du foetus et de l'enfant inuit" in F. Lonabend and C. Le Grand Sébille, Eds. *Le foetus, le nourrisson et la mort.* Paris: L'Harmattan: 55–76.

-- 2000. *"Pijariuniq.* Performances et rituels inuit de la première fois" in *Études/Inuit/Studies,* 24(2): 89–113.

-- 2001a. *Cosmology and Shamanism, Interviewing Inuit Elders.* Iqaluit: Nunavut Arctic College.

-- 2001b. *"Pijariuniq.* Performances and Inuit Rituals of the First Time" in *Inuit Identities in the Third Millenium.* Québec City: Association Inuksiutiit Katimajiit: 34–59.

• Saladin d'Anglure, Bernard and Klaus Georg Hansen. 1997. "Svend Frederiksen et le chamanisme inuit, ou la circulation des noms (*atiit*), des âmes (*tarniit*), des dons (*tunijjutit*) et des esprits (*tuurngait*)" in *Études/Inuit/Studies,* 21(1–2): 37–73.

• Saladin d'Anglure, Bernard and Françoise Morin. 1998. "Mariage mystique et pouvoir chamanique chez les Shipibo d'Amazonie péruvienne et les Inuit du Nunavut canadien" in *Anthropologie et Sociétés,* 22(2): 49–74.

• Thalbitzer, William. 1910. "The heathen priest of East Greenland (Angakut)" in *XVI Amerikanisten-Kongress (held in Vienna 1908):* 447–464.

-- 1930. "Les magiciens esquimaux, leur conception du monde, de l'âme et de la vie" in *Journal de la Société des Américainistes,* Nouvelle série XXII. Paris.

• Victor, Paul-Émile and Joëlle Robert-Lamblin. 1993. *La civilisation du phoque. Légendes, rites et croyances des Eskimos d'Ammassalik.* Bayonne: Éditions Raymond Chabaud.

• Viveiros de Castro, Eduardo. 1998. "Cosmological Deixis and Amerindian Perspectivism" in *Journal of the Royal Anthropological Insitute,* 4(3): 469–488.

• Weyer, Edward M. Jr. 1932. *The Eskimos: Their environment and folkways.* New Haven: Yale University Press.

---

[1] Department of Anthropology, Laval University, Québec City, Québec, Canada.

[2] It is important to make a distinction between two anthroponymic uses: the first was the use of a personal name as such, which is what is in question here; the second is the use of a kinship term that designated the person's epynom. The two uses could co-exist. In other words, Iqallijuq's close relatives spoke to her using the kinship terms that linked them to the dead people who had carried her other names, while "Iqallijuq" was how she was best known in her community and neighbouring villages (see Saladin D'Anglure, "La parenté élective chez les Inuit du Canada, fiction empirique ou réalité virtuelle" in A. Fine, Ed., *Adoptions, la parenté choisie,* Paris: Éditions de la Maison des Sciences de l'Homme, 1998, 121–150; Kublu, Alexina and Jarich Oosten, "Changing Perspectives of Name and Identity among the Inuit of Northeast Canada" in J. Oosten and C. Remie, Eds., *Arctic Identities,* Leiden: Leiden University, Research School CNWS, 1999, 56–78).

[3] In the 1980s, Canadian Inuit generally adopted family names. Most Inuit chose their father's personal name as a family name. However, Ijiraq chose his own

personal name, "Ijiraq", as his family name. The brother of Aupilaarjuk, Kukigaq, (mentioned in the next paragraph) did the same, and chose "Kakiarniut".

[4] Personal communication with Qaq&iq (1998), the grandson and adoptive son of Qimuksiraaq.

[5] During an ethnographic mission in northeast Yakoutia-Sakha.

[5] This is a relatively frequent occurrence in old accounts. Contact with non-human entities is obliterated from the memory of humans until just before they die, when the memories come back. We will see another example of this below.

[7] Their poverty contrasts strangely with the richness of the drawings of *tuurngait* by Greenland artists such as Kârale Andreassen (Geertsen, Ib, *Kârale Andreassen eqqumiitsuliortoq Tunumiu, en østgrønlandsk kunstner,* Nuuk: Atuakkiorfik Geertsen, 1990).

[8] The drawings are conserved at the Scott Polar Research Institute in Cambridge, England.

[9] Dehouve presents very similar data on the conception of death and shaman initiation death among Mexican Indians at the time of the Conquest [Dehouve, Danièle, "La mort symbolique dans l'initiation chamanique et la conversion chrétienne (Mexique, XVe–XVIIe siècles)" in D. Aigle *et al.*, Ed., *La politique des esprits. Chamanisme et religions universalistes,* Nanterre: Société d'Ethnologie, 2000, 165–186].

[10] The breastfeeding metaphor is probably universal. It was very frequent in Europe in the Middle Ages, when there was devotion to "Jesus our Mother" and whose words were drunk like milk from his breasts (Pouchelle, Marie-Christine, "Le corps féminin et ses paradoxes: l'imaginaire de l'intériorité dans les écrits médicaux et religieux (XIIe–XIVe siècles)" in *La condicion de la mujer en la Edad Media,* Madrid: Universidad Complutense, 1986). In the sixteenth century, Rabelais wrote a letter to Erasmus containing the following "...I called you 'father', I would even call you 'mother', if your kindness would permit me to say so...you have ceaselessly fed me with the immaculate and rich milk of your divine wisdom..." (letter dated November 30, 1532 in Erasmus, Didier (1532), *La correspondance d'Érasme.* Translated and annotated by P. S. Allen, H. M. Allen and H. W. Garrod, Brussels: Brussels University Press, Vol. X:1532–1534, 1981, 169–170).

[11] This name was sometimes given to the white fox in shaman language, but it can also designate other small land animals.

[12] One of the other animal auxiliary spirits that could cause such metamorphoses and was often mentioned by elders was the walrus. It made two ivory tusks appear in the shaman's mouth, and the shaman would cry out like a male walrus in rut: "uurk uurk". The caribou was also mentioned. A shaman possessed by a caribou imitated a male in rut with a kind of dance and very special cries.

[13] The study of Aboriginal conceptions of the soul, spirits and cosmology has recently led to interesting theoretical debates, in particular concerning the inhabitants of the Amazon (Descola, Philippe, "Les cosmologies des Indiens d'Amazonie" (1996) 292 *La Recherche* 62–67; Viveiros de Castro, "Cosmological Deixis And Amerindian Perspectivism" (1998) 4(3) J. of the Royal Anthropological Institute 469-488) and Siberia (Hamayon, Roberte, *La chasse à l'âme. Esquisse d'une théorie du chamanisme à partir d'exemples sibériens,* Nanterre:

Société d'Ethnologie, 1990). We will have to wait until similar comparative research is done among the Inuit in order to add Inuit data to the discussion.

[14] See in particular the coat decorated with the unique signs of the shaman Qingailisaq from *Igloolik*, which is conserved at the American Museum of Natural History, New York, and described in Saladin d'Anglure, Bernard, "Ijiqqat voyage au pays de l'invisible inuit" (1983) 7(1) *Études/Inuit/Studies* 67–83.

[15] See Blaisel's analysis of shamanic initiation rituals, based on ethnographic publications: Blaisel, Xavier, *Analyse sociologique de trois rites d'initiation chamanique esquimaux (Ammassalik, Iglulik, Caribou)*, (1986) Master's thesis, Department of Sociology, University of Montréal, and; "Du sacrifice des hommes aux esprits selon la règle des initiations chamaniques chez les Inuit" (1993) 89 (1) *L'Ethnographie*, 113–147.

[16] Components of this text have been analysed in Saladin d'Anglure, "Pygmées arctiques et géants lubriques, ou les avatars de l'image de l'autre, lors des premières rencontres entre Inuit et Blancs", (1992) 22 (2-3) *Recherches Amérindiennes au Québec*, 73–88, and; Saladin d'Anglure and Morin, Françoise, "Mariage mystique et pouvoir chamanique chez les Shipibo d'Amazonie péruvienne et les Inuit du Nunavut canadien", (1998) 22(2) *Anthropologie et Sociétés*, 49–74. See also, with respect to Alaska, Burch, Ernest S. Jr., "The Nonempirical Environment of the Arctic Alaskan Eskimos" (1971) 27(2) *Southwestern Journal of Anthropology*, 248–165.

[17] In recent research by Nathalie Ouellette on *tuurngaq* in the Inukjuak region, her informers told her about many other clues to the presence of *tuurngaq* in the area (Ouellette, Nathalie, *Tuurngait et chamanes inuit dans le Nunavik occidental contemporain,* Master's thesis, Department of Anthropology, Québec City: Laval University, 2000).

[18] Ouellette, *supra* note 17, reports that at Inukjuak, a number of adults who had gone missing while travelling inland were said to have been kidnapped by *tuurngait* or to have decided to go and live with the *tuurngait*.

[19] See the recent work edited by D. Aigle [*La politique des esprits. Chamanisme et religions universalistes*. Nanterre: Société d'Ethnologie, 2000] on the relation between shamanism and universalist religions, in particular the chapters by J. P. Chaumeil ("Chasse aux idoles et philosophie du contact") and R. Hamayon ("Avant-propos").

[20] See Mitiarjuk Nappaaluk's account (Nappaaluk, Mitiarjuk Salomé, "Un témoignage inédit de Mitiarjuk sur les Mumitsimajut de Baie aux Feuilles et sur les uirsaliit et nuliarsaliit du Nunavuk", (1997) 21 (1-2) *Études/Inuit/Studies*, 249–254) concerning the *uirsaliit* (people possessed by an incubus) and *nuliarsaliit* (people possessed by a succubus) in Nunavut. See also the interesting remarks by Gessain [Gessain, Robert, "Uizerk, l'amant, un personnage de la mythologie des Ammassalimuit (Côte Est du Groenland)" (1975) XV (3) *Objets et Mondes*, 319–330] and Victor and Lamblin [Victor, Paul-Émile and Joëlle Robert-Lamblin, *La civilisation du phoque. Légendes, rites et croyances des Eskimos d'Ammassalik,* Bayonne: Éditions Raymond Chabaud, 1993] on this theme with respect to eastern Greenland, where possession by a *uizerk* (incubus) led to death when the person was a layperson but to the acquisition of a new auxiliary spirit in the case of a shaman. Hallendy gathered comparable accounts on Baffin Island [Hallendy, Nor-

man, "Reflexions, shades and shadows" in M. Patterson, R. Janes and C. Arnold, Eds., *Collected Papers on the Human History of the Northwest Territories*. Yellowknife: Prince of Wales Northern Heritage Centre, 1985, Occasional Paper No. 1: 125–167].

The Inuit 'Third Gender'

Bernard Saladin d'Anglure[1]

In the human sciences, sexual categories were long considered to be a natural fact: two sexes, male and female, are responsible for reproduction of the human species. It was also thought that the sexual division of labour was related to biological features. Men were responsible for productive activities and difficult tasks requiring physical strength, speed and intellectual powers (hunting, war, etc.). Women were in charge of reproduction, simple tasks and service (gathering, domestic chores, childcare, etc.). Menstruation, pregnancy and breastfeeding were invoked as physiological constraints to explain why women were confined to the home. Power relations between the sexes, which were most often reduced to this kind of "naturalist" logic, thus also remained outside of the social realm. Aside from a few precursors (such as Fourier, Engels and Freud), the anthropologist Margaret Mead was the first to try free the relations between the sexes from biological determinism. In the 1930s, using examples from fieldwork in Oceania, she showed that the sexual division of labour differed from one society to the next, and was related more closely to culture than to nature.[2] However, her dualist approach to the sexes stopped her from accounting for individuals who did not fit into the traditional division of labour. With Simone de Beauvoir, the socio-cultural definition of the sexes became much more sophisticated. Yet, the dualist perspective that can be seen in her essay "The Second Sex" (1949) prevented her from analysing her own situation as a non-traditional woman, except by contemplating a future utopia in which the social borders between the sexes/genders would be eliminated and boys and girls would be educated together. Forty years later, Élisabeth Badinter (1986) took up this hypothesis again from an evolutionary point of view. I will come back to this in the conclusion.

The feminist renewal in the 1970s resulted in major advances in theoretical reflection on social relations between the sexes, particularly in work by English-speaking anthropologists.[3] Questions were asked about the origin and universality of male domination, and, in an attempt to find answers, studies were undertaken of the last hunter-gatherer societies, which were believed to be living as our ancestors did in prehistoric times. The ethnographic data on these societies generally showed that men were dominant and controlled hunting and war, whereas women were more or less confined to gathering and domestic work. However, these facts were interpreted in highly divergent ways, resulting in very different positions.[4] Proponents of sexual equality, faithful to Engels' thought on precapitalist societies, rallied behind Eleonor Leacock, who saw male domination as either a result of Western influence or an expression of ethnologists' masculine prejudices.[5] Others supported the idea that male domination in public life was matched by female domination in private life. Yet others acknowledged the power of women and complementarity of the sexes in many activities, but concluded that technology and ideology were dominated by men. Every camp held fast to its position, which caused interest in origins and even in the power relations between the sexes to dwindle in the 1980s.

At the same time, there was growing interest in gender studies,[6] the study of which was a precondition for research on social relations between the sexes. The categories were still always defined in dualist terms despite new ethnographic data indicating that a different approach we needed and a few attempts,[7] including my own,[8] to open up the field. By 1992, the concept of "gender" was standard in the human sciences, though it was often confined to feminist academic writing. Research on the topic is still marginal and far from the forefront in the human sciences in general and anthropology in particular, and in France it is even falling behind. Reasons for such low interest include the confusion that remains in many researchers' minds between gender and biological sex, which has already been noted with respect to earlier ethnography. A flagrant example of this is the incorrect use of the term *"berdache"*, which has strong homosexual connotations, to refer to the gender-crossing phenomena seen among American Aboriginals even though many *"berdaches"* are not homosexual and many Aboriginal homosexuals are not *"berdaches"*. It should also be noted that barriers between disciplines, areas of knowledge and themes make it very difficult to study gender because it is an interdisciplinary topic. For example, the same phenomenon could be called androgyny in religious studies, inversion in structural anthropology and marginality in sociology. This does not aid comprehension. Given the theoretical stagnation, I think it would be wise to look to hunter-gatherer societies for the right questions to ask in our own society and for a better concept of the gender system. This shift in perspective requires an epistemological analysis of the dualist conception of the sexes in which we are imprisoned by classical thought, Judeo-Christian ideology and scientific rationalism.

It may seem paradoxical to look to the Inuit for fresh data to renew the theoretical approach to Western sexual categories and relations, for that "exotic" Aboriginal people has always been absent from theoretical debates in anthropology. One of the reasons for the absence is probably the glorification of Inuit technology given that it took Westerners four centuries to learn to adapt to Arctic conditions. As more was learned about the Inuit, Europeans marvelled at their ability to survive in such a hostile environment, and imagined that survival was their only concern and took up all their energy. Their name also long remained based on imagination. First they were called "hyperboreal pygmies", then they were taken for Tatars, then they gradually came to be known as *"Eskimos"* (an Algonquin term), until finally their own name was imposed: Inuit.

Preconceived ideas about the Inuit influenced generations of ethnologists and led them to avoid close examination of the Inuit's social, economic, political and religious structure. The prevailing restrictive definition of Inuit society is summed up nicely, if baldly, by C. Lévi-Strauss: "The Eskimos, while excellent technicians, are poor sociologists…"[9] He goes on to compare them with Australian Aboriginals, whom he describes as the opposite.

The only theoretical interest that has really been shown in the Inuit comes from Marcel Mauss, yet curiously he never set foot in their lands. At the beginning of the twentieth century, he published an essay on seasonal variations in the social life of the Inuit, which he described as oscillating between two extremes: summer individualism based on the nuclear family, the private, non-religious life of couples, and individual production; and communal living in the winter, when economic, sexual and religious activities involve sharing and general exchange of goods, children and spouses, and there are major collective rituals.[10] At the time, this was called "primitive communism". While Mauss's essay is interesting and unique because of its global perspective, it does not contain exhaustive information on the sexual division of labour or on sexual categories, and it remains enclosed in a reductionist, dualist and seasonal explanation of their social life.

Another attempt to use the Inuit as an example to support a theory was that of L. Spier, who took up the idea that L. H. Morgan had suggested 50 years earlier, according to which Inuit kinship terms formed a system with the same structure as that of kinship terms used in western Europe and among the Yankees in New England.[11] Spier extended his analysis and typology to the rules of filiation and residence after marriage, in short to what is known in anthropology as the kinship system. He thus described an "*Eskimo*" kinship system that was shared by the Inuit, the pygmies of the Andaman Islands and Westerners. The typology was taken up by G. P. Murdock,[12] who extended it to the whole social structure. Thus, it was claimed that on both ends of the "scale" of human technological and economic development, namely among both hunter-gatherers and Westerners, there was the same kinship system and same type of social organization. However, recent ethnographic research on Inuit kinship systems challenges the scope of the data that were used to define the "*Eskimo*" system. It shows that there are many different systems and so much variation in kinship customs that a number of authors have concluded that the defining feature of Inuit social structure is great flexibility.

Aside from Naomi Giffen's interesting 1930 work on the sexual division of labour among the Inuit,[13] it is clear that ethnologists studying the Inuit have written little on the relationships between the sexes. Moreover, if we look at only research resulting from fieldwork, we go from studies of technology and myths, to cultural ecology, to the psychology of emotions, and then to ethnographies of villages, with a focus on kinship and social change. In the 1960s, many anthropologists still harboured the hope that the "*Eskimo*" kinship system would hold the key to Inuit social organization. Sexual categories appeared only accessory. The rapid interpenetration of Inuit society and our own has only increased the haze that the first stereotypes produced around Inuit social organization.

Finally we come to symbolic anthropology, which is my field of study. My first ethnographic research among the Inuit began in the early 1960s on the general theme of kinship, and more specifically on fictive kinship or pseudo-kinship, which is highly developed among them. I thus studied the relationships created by adoption (30% of Inuit children are adopted) and the quasi-kinship relationships between newborns and the midwives who deliver them. A midwife is thought of as a cultural mother, and helps and guides the child until adulthood. In return, the child gives the midwife presents at each new stage in his or her life.

I also looked at the effects of given names on identity and on how kinship terms are used. I found that with respect to the attribution of kinship status, Inuit society operated in an order that was the inverse of the generations concerned. Children who receive the name and identity of their deceased grandparents have a symbolic status that is greater than that of their parents, until they themselves become parents, at which time they are symbolically subordinate to their own children. The circular and cyclic Inuit conception of time can be seen clearly in these practices. Moreover, since names are not linked to gender, they can be given to either sex, which can lead to reverse socialization when the sex of the ancestor whose name is given is not the same as that of the child who becomes the namesake. My research soon revealed the central position of human procreation in the Inuit conception of the world: the various components of the universe are articulated around the foetus. The male component, represented by the man's sperm, blocks the uterine passage, begins the reproductive process, and then mixes with the mother's blood to give the embryo its form, structure and wholeness. The female component, represented by the mother's blood, coagulates, becomes part of the embryonic egg, and then forms the foetus's blood. The animal component, represented by meat eaten by the pregnant woman, is consumed by the foetus and becomes its flesh. Finally, the supernatural component is represented by the souls of deceased ancestors who are reincarnated in the child about to be born and expect to be recognized by the living.

Thus, inside the little uterine igloo, a microcosm of the universe, the emergence of life is replayed. Cosmogenesis and ontogenesis are thought of in the same way, like the cycle of life, the cycle of the seasons, and the cycle of day and night. The first humans lived on earth in quasi-uterine obscurity before having access to the light of day, just as later humanity, struggling with the growing complexity of rules for living and many spirits, lived in a dangerous obscurantism before gaining access to the light of shamanism. The active principle of all shamanic power is clairvoyance, the Inuit word for which is *Qaumaniq*, which means "the light".

An in-depth study of myths of origin also revealed that sexual differentiation was the first major differentiation in Inuit cosmogenesis. Moreover, differentiation is seen as a key event in human reproduction. Many narratives illustrate these beliefs. The Inuit think that a foetus can change sex at birth. Individuals who are thought to have changed sex at birth are called *sipiniit* (from the verb radical *–sipi*, which means "to crack"). Two thirds of the time, a boy turns into a girl. The signs of such transsexuality include a long, difficult delivery, a genital oedema with some genital ambiguity in the newborn (in other words, it is difficult to tell the child's sex), and genitals that are blocked by mucous, thereby making it difficult to urinate in the moments following birth. A number of Inuit midwives say that they have seen the penis and scrotum of newborns retract and turn into a vulva in the perineum. Thus, according to Indigenous theory, it is important to stabilize the organs by looking at them and touching them to prevent the transformation if one wishes the newborn's sex to stay that way. Otherwise, one should let the process take place.

It is difficult to know how many cases of perinatal transsexuality there are, but an oral survey in a village of 900 people, where I did my research, showed that it occurred in nearly 2% of cases. There are a number of hypotheses, yet unverified, that could explain the belief. The first is that such cases involve genetic inter-sexuality, adreno-congenital hyperplasia or damage to the adrenal glands, which results in female pseudo-hermaphroditism. This has been found to be 10 times more frequent in some Inuit areas, such as in southern Alaska, than in Caucasian populations. While this genetic feature in the central Canadian Arctic,[14] which has not to my knowledge been studied, may have contributed to the formation of the belief, it cannot explain all of the cases because pseudo-hermaphroditism is normally accompanied by sterility, which is not the case of most of the *sipiniit* studied.

The second hypothesis has to do with the birthing technique and the position of the foetus when it is expelled. For example, a breech birth often gives the newborn a genital oedema. Whether or not there is a link between this kind of "abnormal" birth and a presumed sex change remains to be verified in the field, for despite the publication of many works on Inuit childbirth, there are no exhaustive data on the position of the foetus at the time of delivery. However, my own research and that of others shows that if a child is in an "abnormal" position at birth, then the family may reverse socialize the child, or invert the direction of the fur on some of his or her clothes or change the direction of some movements in certain rituals.

The intrauterine memories of Iqallijuq, an Inuit woman from *Igloolik* who says she changed sex at birth, shed interesting light on *sipiniit*. Her memories date back to before her conception. In the form of the invisible soul of her maternal grandfather, Savviuqtalik, of whom she is the namesake and who died just before her story begins, she came out of the grave and went to his daughter (Iqallijuq's mother), who was squatting nearby to relieve herself. She touched her mother's unknotted belt and found herself in her uterus, which looked like the inside of a small igloo (Figure 1). In the uterus, she ate white-coloured food that a dog regularly came and regurgitated, and changed from a soul to a male foetus. The foetus grew rapidly and when the igloo became too small, it decided to come out. At first, it picked up the male tools but, remembering how hard, cold and dangerous life had been as a hunter, it changed its mind and decided to live in a woman's body instead. So, it put down the male tools, picked up the female tools, and was violently ejected. Iqallijuq's penis immediately retracted and perineum cracked, and she was born a girl.

These kinds of memories are not rare among the Inuit. They are found in various groups and their credibility is supported by a very well-known myth: the story of a woman who is beaten by her husband, transforms into a dog and then into various species of game, until she finally becomes a foetus in the womb of the wife of her own brother, and is reborn a boy.

Another myth related to perinatal transsexuality describes Inuit cosmogenesis and the first sex change. It tells the story of how the first two humans came out of two small mounds of earth as two adult males. They soon wanted to multiply and one of them got the other pregnant. However, when the pregnancy came to term they realized that the pregnant man was unable to deliver. So, his companion performed a magic chant that caused the pregnant man's penis to retract and an opening to form in his perineum, thereby changing him into a woman, the first woman. She soon gave birth to a son. It is said that all Inuit come from the first two men. Thus, at the infrahuman level of life, namely the passage from life in the uterus to human life, sex is unstable and its borders can easily be crossed in both directions, from boy to girl and from girl to boy. The instability existed at the origin of human life and is still present at every delivery.

I mentioned above how the identity of a newborn was determined by the names it was given. The child's ascendants chose the names in order to allow the dead to live again among their loved ones. The ascendants chose the names of relatives or friends whose absence affected them the most. If a newborn had trouble surviving the first few days following his or her birth, it was a sign that a deceased person wanted to live again in him or her. The desire had to be fulfilled to ensure the child's survival. Dreams were another way to learn the desires of the dead. If someone dreamed that a dead person had come to visit or was asking for something to drink, it was a sign that he or she wanted to be reborn in the family.

The random and unpredictable nature of death, and thus the sex of the next person to die, combined with the unforeseeability of a child's sex at birth and the sex of children not yet born, led to a relatively high number of newborns (15–20%) being named after an ancestor of the opposite sex. Such cases often led to symbolic expression of various forms, which are referred to here collectively as sex-role reversal (which includes kinship terms, hairstyle, clothing and jewellery, tools and skills, gestures and body position normally associated with members of the opposite sex). Since children often received more than one name and therefore several identities, they could be the namesakes of people of different sexes and live with multiple identities that co-existed or alternated in time. They coexisted when the attributes of both sexes were present at the same time, and they alternated when the attributes of each sex were present in different circumstances.

The extent and duration of sex-role reversal depended on a number of factors, such as the presence near the child of those who had named him or her after someone of the other sex, the emotional closeness of those individuals and the eponymous ancestor, and the proportion of the child's names that were in memory of ancestors of the opposite sex. If all of a child's names came from ancestors of the opposite sex, the sex-role reversal was stronger and could continue beyond adolescence.

There was also a fourth factor: the family sex ratio. It came into play when the newborn's sex was not what the parents had hoped. Their expectations were based on the child's birth rank and the existing sex ratio among the children in the family. In families without sons or without daughters, it was not rare for children to undergo sex-role reversal and be raised as if they were of the opposite sex in order to assist the parent of that sex. This has been noted by a number of authors, including

J. Briggs, Memorial University, Newfoundland, and J. Robert-Lamblin, CNRS, Musée de l'Homme,[15] who have tried to explain the phenomenon in terms of demographic, economic and psychological adjustment. They see it as either a chance exception to the sexual division of labour, or a sign of the system's flexibility. In their comparative essays on the sexual division of labour among hunter-gatherers, P. Tabet, University of Siena, and A. Testart, CNRS,[16] both interpret cases of female hunters among the Inuit as exceptions. Because of their dualist framework, these interpretations all seem to me to impoverish the Inuit reality.

In order to find a more satisfactory understanding of reverse socialization, I have suggested that it be related to an ideal underlying the Inuit social organization and ideology (and inspired by Claude Lévi-Strauss's "atom of kinship"): the "family atom" made up of a male-female couple (spouses) and a brother-sister pair (the spouses' children), who assist them. A conjugal family aspires to balance and symmetry in the sexual division of labour, which is expressed as the desire to have at least one son to assist the father and one daughter to assist the mother. This microcosmic model, which mirrors the order of the universe and reproduction, is however often frustrated by the unpredictability of life and great variation in the sex ratio at birth. Indeed, while it is more or less balanced at the level of most of the world's populations, birth sex ratio varies greatly at the level of the family. When there was an imbalance, the Inuit resorted to adoption or reverse socialization, particularly when the firstborn children were girls. In such cases, the namesake tradition was used to the hilt, a girl's sex role was reversed and she was taught male tasks. The oldest or youngest girl was often reverse socialized until her first menstruation, which was celebrated as if she had killed a large animal (whereas normally it would have been celebrated as if she had given birth to a son). From that day on she was required to wear female clothing. Symmetrically, if a family had only sons, the youngest was often cross-dressed and socialized as a girl, until he killed his first large animal. Then he had to cut his hair short and dress like a boy. In cases in which the determining factor for sex role reversal was not an imbalance between the sexes, more symbolic and affective reasons were invoked to determine the degree. The *sipiniit* described above were generally reverse socialized to the highest degree.

If we go now from forms of reverse socialization to its effects on those subject to it, we find unanimity on the difficulties and emotional suffering experienced by those who underwent sex-role reversal or were reverse socialized and then at puberty required to adopt the clothing, tools and tasks habitually assigned to those of their biological sex. They were rarely helped by their close relatives, who were the very people who had decided to reverse socialize them, participated in their socialization, and indeed continued to use the kinship terms required by eponymy. The fact that they had to conform to a reality different from that of their childhood created real crises for such teenagers, and resulted in conflict and rebellion. They were able to acquire the skills of people of their sex only slowly and progressively, and for the rest of their lives they remained marked by their first education and by the way they had crossed over the border between the sexes. The crossover became a component of their personalities and put them in a separate category, which I have suggested be called the "third gender". In general, such people were esteemed for their polyvalence and independence, as well as special mediation abilities, particularly in religious contexts.

K. Rasmussen, the authority on Inuit shamanism in the central Arctic, and later authors, such as Mircea Eliade, who used Rasmussen's data,[17] never considered Inuit shamans from the angle of gender or more specifically sex-role reversal and androgyny. Yet Rasmussen's work is still valuable because he provides one of the best descriptions of Inuit spiritual life, based on the testimony of the last shamans still working in the 1920s. No one since him has dared to do field work in this area, even though in his seminal study on Siberian peoples published in 1914,[18] Czaplicka clearly showed the importance of Siberian shamanic sex-role reversal (Figure 2). In the preface, R. Marett does not hesitate to speak of the "third sex" in relation to the shamans described. Sternberg added important ethnographic support,[19] with an explanation of sex-role reversal based on the selection of the shaman by a protective spirit of the opposite sex. Moreover, he cites J. G. Frazer, who was also interested in religious sex-role reversal and sex change with respect to data from classical Antiquity and various Aboriginal peoples.[20]

In fact, since the ethnographers had never met Inuit adults whose sex roles were reversed or who were homosexuals, and because they had preconceptions about Aboriginal "*berdaches*" (based on travel writing that portrayed them as kinds of perverse homosexuals), they completely overlooked childhood sex-role reversal and the symbolic androgyny of shamans. This was probably because they did not make a clear distinction between sexual orientation and gender.

In 1983, when I was doing research on a shaman's coat from *Igloolik* that had been acquired at the turn of the century and conserved by the American Museum of Natural History in New York, my attention was drawn to its decorative motifs, which were feminine in style. I had the shaman's descendants make three replicas of the coat so that I could conduct surveys on the decorations inspired by an *Ijiraq* or shaman's female protective spirit. Such spirits can be of either sex and look like humans with caribou nostrils. They have great powers, can be seen only by shamans and play an important role in Inuit myths and beliefs. They are still greatly feared at *Igloolik*. Since museums have very few Inuit shaman coats, and shamans usually took off their upper garments when they performed a major ceremony, it is easy to see how such details could have been overlooked.

Already aware of eponymic sex-role reversal, I saw in the motifs another sex-role reversal, this time resulting from the protective spirit's sex, and it quickly became clear to me that the two systems were closely linked. On one hand, it was frequent for shamans to have their eponymous ancestors as protective spirits, and on the other hand it was not rare to give a newborn the name of a shaman's protective spirit in order to strengthen the child. Just as an individual could have several names, a shaman could have several auxiliary spirits, one of which was the main protector. My hypothesis was therefore that symbolic sex-role reversal was one of the components of shamanism, that sex-role reversal was related to the acquisition of a protective spirit of the opposite sex by analogy with the eponym system, and that the vocation of shaman came to individuals who had experienced sex-role reversal and been socialized as the opposite sex. A rapid survey of seven ancient shaman life histories (five men and two women from *Igloolik*) showed that each of them had at least one auxiliary spirit of the opposite sex. The other part of the hypothesis, concerning sex-role reversal, cannot be validated in these seven cases because there is not enough data, but I have gathered other more recent life stories that provide ample support for it.

If, as we saw above, Inuit cosmogonic belief sees sexual differentiation as primordial and uses it to think about other forms of differentiation, then an individual who is socialized to straddle the divide from the time he or she is a baby becomes a crosser of borders and able to pass over them all when he or she is an adult. Is this not the definition of a shaman, who has to know how to cross over not only the barrier between the sexes, but also that between humans and animals, and between the natural and supernatural worlds, as has shown R. Hamayon of the École Pratique des Hautes Études (Fifth Section)?[21] Reverse socialization would therefore be a necessary, if not sufficient, condition for the vocation of shaman.

For a child who had been reverse socialized, entrance into the adult involved a symbolic death, and a deep identity crisis, with suffering and disarray. Likewise, for an adolescent, election as a shaman also resulted in a deep identity crisis, suffering and disarray. One had to fast alone in the cold, and suffer a symbolic death until the Moon spirit, the mythical and incestuous brother of his sister-Sun, filled the novice with shamanic light.

At the end of our travels through the Inuit social and belief systems, we see a guiding line, that of the "third gender" (Figure 3), a veritable "total social fact". It is rooted in Nature, in the infrahuman reality of biological disorders and intersexuality seen in obstetrics. It is based in the culture and family atom, where it provides a solution to the problem of symbolic and real imbalances in the sex ratio that are caused by death and birth, and makes it possible to ensure that the sexual division of labour operates smoothly. It blossoms in the shamanic mediation by which it manages crises, conflicts, changes and the group's social relations and interactions with the natural world and animal kingdom. Finally, it is the intermediary with the suprahuman world of the dead, stars and spirits, and finds its strength and limitations in the natural disorder of the apparent imbalance in celestial bodies, which is translated by eclipses and the lunar and solar cycles. Thus, natural disorder, in the form of the biological overlap between the sexes and the celestial overlap of heavenly bodies, is the foundation of the social order and the third gender, which maintains order, particularly when unexpected events, catastrophes, disorder and social change occur. Perhaps this notion of crossing a barrier is a key to the Inuit social system and could lead to further research in dynamic structural anthropology. By extending its application to the exchange of children (adoption) among households and generations, exchange of game, exchange of spouses between couples, migratory exchange in terms of camps, and exchange of names between the living and dead and humans and spirits, perhaps we will discover the structure so desperately sought by anthropologists studying Inuit social organization.

Binary thought and dualism have been questioned recently in anthropology, in particular by L. Dumont,[22] who has taken a ternary approach to hierarchical levels with respect to castes in India, by S. Tcherkezoff,[23] who uses the same model to rework dualist classifications, and by G. Berthoud,[24] who uses "métis" and ternary thought to analyse African beliefs, not to mention Lévi-Strauss's earlier criticisms of dualism and A. Leroi-Gourhan's theses about the role of the "third animal" and "third sign" in the dynamics of the sexual system of prehistoric cave art. [25] These authors' research seems to converge towards what the exact sciences call fuzzy set theory. In other areas of the human sciences, Michel Serres is not far from the "third gender" when he praises the "cultivated thirds": those who cross borders, such as left-handed people who have been forced to use their right hands, people who are somewhat androgynous, and travellers, immigrants and polyglots.[26] Sandra Bem of Stanford University uses the concept of "psychological androgyny" to explore the psychosocial components of this.[27] Based on tests in which people are assessed for male and female characteristics, she finds that 30% of Americans are psychologically androgynous. This concept could also be compared with the idea of the "marginal man", who is a mediating immigrant and cultural hybrid. This idea was developed in Chicago in the 1930s by Park and Stonequist,[28] and has some affinity with the more recent idea of "cultural intermediary", which is used in France by historians and to describe the role of some immigrants. E. Badinter,[29] who believes she has found the historical advent of androgyny, in fact sees the history of society from the point of view of the third gender without realizing that such a category cannot exist without a structural relationship of coexistence with the two others. Society is not becoming androgynous; it is the third gender that is becoming more visible as Judeo-Christian values weaken.

Will the third gender finally give the Inuit their rightful place in theoretical debates on social ties, gender relations and links with the world? Perhaps, if the first uses of the Inuit model in studies on Québec women who have taken non-traditional jobs or entered into religious service are any indication. These studies reveal the importance of birth-rank and sibling sex ratio with respect to choice of career path. Perhaps our societies, in which family sex ratio is also random, employ reverse socialization too.

Note that they too transmit identity from one generation to the next by choosing given names, the gender of which can also be changed. Recent work on atypical career paths of French women[30] could probably benefit from using the Inuit model to analyse the way families create individual destinies. In light of the Inuit custom of marrying a third gender "masculinized" woman to a third gender "feminized" man (figure 4), should we not take another look at the case of the "*héritière*" in Pyrenean families, who is a woman made masculine by her role and married to a younger, feminized, man, who is required to move into her home and take her family name? Or is it only an exception as asserted by H. Lefebvre and P. Bourdieu?[31] Does not the *héritière* model also come into play in distaff noble houses, and in royal lines, when a woman ascends to the throne and marries a prince consort? Look again at how the destinies were shaped of great mediators, founders of religious orders, strategists and heads of state, charismatic and ambiguous masculinized daughters and femininized sons, artists, writers, researchers and therapists, the new shamans of the twentieth century. Sartre, Condorcet and many others, such as the youngest children of royal families, were dressed as girls until they reached adolescence. Is this unrelated to their destinies and unlinked to a ternary approach to gender? This is an open question. However, by going back to Frazer's intuitions when he saw sex-role reversal as one of the keys to religious mediation, and by bringing the study of the sexual system back into the social field, even if it means infringing a little on the psychoanalytic monopoly, we would certainly be able to take a new anthropological, structuralist and dynamic look at the social construction of gender in various cultures.

---

[1] Professor, Laval University, Québec City

[2] Mead, M., *Sex and Temperament in Three Primitive Societies*, New York: William Morrow, 1935.

[3] Reiter, R., Ed., *Toward an Anthropology of Women*, New York: Monthly Review Press, 1963.

[4] Mathieu, N.C., "Études féministes et anthropologie" in P. Bonte and M. Izard, Eds., *Dictionnaire de l'ethnologie et de l'anthropologie*, Paris: Presses universitaires de France, 1991.

[5] Leacock, E., "Women's Status in Egalitarian Society: Implications for Social Evolution" (1978) 19 *Current Anthropology* 247-255, 268-275.

[6] Mathieu, N.C., *Anatomie politique, Catégorisations et idéologies du sexe*, Paris: Éditions côté-femmes, 1991.

[7] Ortner, S.B. and Whitehead, H., Eds., *Sexual Meanings: The Cultural Construction of Gender and Sexuality*, Cambridge University Press, 1981, and McBroom, P., *The Third Sex. The New Professional Woman*, New York: William Morrow and Co, 1986.

[8] Saladin d'Anglure, B., "Du foetus au chamane, la construction d'un troisième sexe inuit", (1986) 10(1-2) *Études Inuit Studies,* 25-113, and "Penser le feminine chamanique, ou le tiers-sexe des chamanes inuit", (1988) 18(2-3) *Recherches Amérindiennes au Québec,* 19-50.

[9] Lévi-Strauss, C., *Anthropologie structurale*, Paris: Plon, 1958.

[10] Mauss, M., "Les Esquimo" (1904), reproduced in: Mauss, M., *Oeuvres 3: Cohésion sociale et division de la sociologie* (Paris: Les Éditions de Minuit, 1969) at 68.

[11] Spier, L., "The Distribution of Kinship Systems in North America" (1925) 1(2) *University of Washington Publications in Anthropology* 69.

[12] Murdock, G.P., *Social Structure*, New York: Macmillan & Co., 1949.

[13] Giffen, N.M., *The Roles of Men and Women in Eskimo Culture*, University of Chicago Press, Chicago, 1930.

[14] Hirschfeld, A.D., and Fleschmann, J.K., "An unusually high incidence of salt-losing congenital adrenal hyperplasia in the Alaskan Eskimo", (1969) 75 *Journal of Pediatrics,* 492–494; Pang, S., Murphy, W., et al., "A Pilot Newborn Screening for Congenital Adrenal Hyperplasia in Alaska" (1982) 55 *Journal of Clinical Endocrinology and Metabolism*, 413–420.

[15] Briggs, L., "Eskimo Women: Makers of Men" in *Many Sisters. Women in Cross-*

Cultural Perspective, C. J. Matthiasson, Ed., New York: Free Press, 1974; Robert-Lamblin, J., (1981) 5(1) *Études Inuit Studies*, 117.

[16] Tabet, P., "Les mains, les outils, les armes" (1979) 19 (3-4) *L'Homme*, 5. Testart, A., *Essai sur les fondements de la division sexuelle du travail chez les chasseurs-cueilleurs*, Paris: Éditions de l'école des hautes études en sciences sociales, 1986.

[17] Eliade, M., *Le chamanisme et les techniques archïques de l'extase*, Paris: Payot, 1951.

[18] Czaplicka, M.A., *Aboriginal Siberia. A Study in Social Anthropology*, London: Oxford University Press, 1914.

[19] Sternberg, L., "Divine Election in Primitive Religion", *XXIst International Conference of Americanists*, Göteborg: Göteborg Museum, 1925.

[20] Frazer, J.G., *Adonis Attis Osiris: Studies in the History of Oriental Religion*, London, Macmillan, 1906.

[21] Hamayon, R., "Des chamanes au chamanisme" (1982) 87-88 (1-2) *L'Ethnographie* 13.

[22] Dumont, L., *Essai sur l'individualisme. Une perspective anthropologique sur l'idéologie moderne*, Paris: Le Seuil, 1983.

[23] Tcherkezoff, S., *Le Roi Nyamwezi, la droite et la gauche, Révision comparatiste des classifications dualistes*, Cambridge, Paris: Cambridge University Press and Éditions de la Maison des Sciences de l'Homme, 1983.

[24] Berthoud, G., "La pensée métisse" in Horton, R., et al., Eds., *La pensée métisse*, Geneva: Presses Universitaires de France and Cahiers de l'Institut Universitaire d'Études du Développement, 1990.

[25] Lévi-Strauss, C., *Anthropologie structurale*, Paris: Plon, 1958; *Anthropologie structurale 2*, Paris: Plon, 1973; Leroi-Gourhan, A., *Les racines du monde, entretiens avec Claude-Henri Rocquet*, Paris: Belfond, 1982.

[26] Serres, M., *Le Tiers-Instruit*, Paris: Gallimard, collection Folio, 1991.

[27] Bem, Sandra L., "The Measurement of Psychological Androgyny" (1974) 42 *Journal of Consulting and Clinical Psychology* 155-62.

[28] Park, R. E., & Burgess, E. W., *An Introduction to the Science of Sociology*, Chicago: University of Chicago Press, 1921; Stonequist, E. V., *The Marginal Man: A Study in Personality and Culture Conflict*, New York: Charles Scribner's Sons, 1937.

[29] Badinter, E., *L'un est l'autre: des relations entre hommes et femmes*, Paris: Odile Jacob, 1986.

[30] Chaudron, M., "Sur les trajectoires sociales des hommes et des femmes: stratégies familiales de reproduction et trajectoires individuelles" in *Le sexe du travail*, Grenoble: Presses Universitaires de Grenoble, 1984; Daune-Richard, A.M., "A propos de la reproduction du rapport social entre les sexes et de l'articulation des rapports sociaux: réflexions à partir d'une enquête en cours" in *Atelier production-reproduction*, Vol. 1, 1988; Flament, C., "Du garçon manqué à la fille réussie: catégorisation sociale de sexe, problèmes de frontières," in *Catégorisation de sexe et constructions scientifiques*, Aix en Provence: Collection CEFUP, 1989.

[31] Lefebvre, H., *Du rural à l'urbain*, Paris: Anthropos, 1970; Bourdieu, P., "Célibat et condition paysanne" (1962) 5-6 *Études rurales* 32; Assier-Andrieu, L., *Coutume et rapports sociaux, étude anthropologique des communautés paysannes du Capcir*, Éditions du CNRS, 1981.

The Whale Hunting among the Inuit of the Canadian Arctic

Bernard Saladin d'Anglure[1]

Thanks to political will and their elders' knowledge, the Inuit have succeeded in reconnecting with a millenary tradition that had been abandoned for decades. With the help of ritual injunctions, they have relearned how to reconcile themselves with the whale spirit and re-establish the alliance that united it with Inuit hunters. Sometimes as a very virile husband, sometimes as a very considerate wife, sometimes as a son who is a diligent provider, the whale plays a major role in Inuit mythology.

1. Introduction

Never in the last 80 years has subsistence hunting of bowhead whales been so present in political debates and the imagination of Canadian Inuit as it is at the end of the twentieth century. Beginning in the mid-nineteenth century, the hunt, which had been carried out for hundreds of years by the Inuit's ancestors, was gradually replaced by commercial whaling in which Inuit hunters worked for European and American whalers. The new industry, which employed much more elaborate and deadly technology, was completely unregulated and led to a drastic decline in the bowhead population in the Canadian Arctic.[2] The collapse of the market for whale products, which coincided with World War I, put an end to the commercial bowhead fishery in the area in 1915.

In the following decades, some of the mammals were occasionally caught by the Inuit for subsistence use in various locations in the central Arctic. During the Fifth Thule Expedition (1921–1924), which was led by K. Rasmussen, the Inuit killed several whales at Repulse Bay and Pond Inlet. More recently, in the 1960s, in the *Igloolik* area, an experienced hunter named Piugaattuq (who was in his 60s at the time) caught one using a traditional harpoon and an improvised lance. Another was taken in 1971 in Repulse Bay. However, in 1977, despite the noticeable growth in the whale's numbers in the north of Hudson Bay, Canada supported the International Whaling Commission's year-long moratorium on whale hunting.[3] The purpose of the moratorium was to suspend hunting of northern right whales (including bowhead whales) for one year (1978), and then prohibit it altogether. Alaskan Inuit were affected immediately, as were those in Greenland. In Canada, the Inuvialuit, who live adjacent to the northern part of Alaska, felt they were being oppressed. Like their cousins in Alaska, they felt it was very important to be able to continue the hunt, even though they had not gone whaling for over ten years. The last time they had requested and received permission to take a northern right whale was in 1966, though in the end the hunt had not taken place. (Rodon 2003)[4] Since then, they had constantly asserted their desire to return to the hunt.

2. Identity at Stake

In 1977, the Circumpolar Inuit Conference was established to defend the interests of all Inuit in the Arctic. One of its earliest actions was to study the whale hunt considered as a traditional subsistence activity in Alaska, Greenland and Denmark, and on a smaller scale in Canada. It succeeded in gaining a seat as an observer at International Whaling Commission meetings. The Alaskan Inuit were the first to react, and their opposition to the Commission's moratorium was very strong. The Commission, heavily influenced by environmentalist organizations such as Greenpeace and the American Cetacean Society, had based its decision on a scientific study that had concluded that the northern right whale was in danger of extinction in the western Arctic. The study claimed that the Alaskan Inuit had killed twice as many whales annually in the 1970s as in the 1960s and that the animal stock had been reduced to around 600.

2.1. An Inuit Whaling Commission in Alaska

These findings in no way matched the much more optimistic observations by Alaskan Inuit in hunting areas.

In 1981, in order to persuade the Commission that it was mistaken, the Inuit created their own commission, the Alaskan Eskimo Whaling Commission, with the material assistance of the North Slope Borough regional corporation, which funded an independent research program with revenue from petroleum operations. (Rodon 2003) The new research proved that the species was not endangered at all and that the stock numbered over 4000. Finally, after lengthy negotiations, the American government agreed to allow them to manage Inuit whale hunting in Alaskan waters and to support their request that the International Commission recognize their right to hunt whales. In 1982, the Commission both completely prohibited commercial hunting of right whales, and agreed to establish a special category of hunt, namely Aboriginal subsistence hunting, for groups that traditionally held hunts involving the whole community and provided the whale was for local consumption only. It also gave the Alaskan Inuit an annual quota, and the right to employ unused portions of the quota the following year.[5] In the mid-1980s, the quota was on average 26 whales a year. It reached 40 in the mid-1990s. (Rodon 2003)

Canada blocked the Canadian Inuit's hopes to return to the whale hunt, particularly those of the Inuvialuit (Mackenzie Inuit), for fear of economic retaliation by the United States. However, the position of the Canadian delegation within the International Whaling Commission was becoming increasingly uncomfortable. It was trapped between growing environmental pressure from its partners and Aboriginal demands. In 1982, it therefore decided to give up its status as member of the Commission and become an observer on the pretext that there was no longer any whale hunting in Canada. (Rodon 2003)

However, at that time, the Inuvialuit were in the process of negotiating their territorial rights with Canadian authorities, which placed them in a strong position to demand that they, like their Alaskan cousins, be given joint control and management of the stocks and the right to hunt whales for subsistence.

2.2. The Rebirth of Whale Hunting by the Inuvialuit of Canada

Every spring and fall, more and more whales were being seen in the old hunting areas in the western and central Canadian Arctic. Their number was constantly growing and hunters often saw them. I remember seeing them when I was travelling by canoe with an Inuit family to a narwhal hunting camp in early July 1985. We were crossing a narrow passage when suddenly the long black expanse of a bowhead broke the surface only a dozen meters from the canoe, along with the whistle of its breath from its blowhole. My companions cut the motor immediately so that it would not frighten the animal, which could have resulted in a dangerous swipe of the tail. In the half-light of the midnight sun, the whale's gigantic form glided for a long time at the surface of the water. The Inuit immediately invoked *Takannaaluk*, the goddess of marine animals who lived at *Igloolik* at the dawn of time, and they meditated for a few minutes, until the whale disappeared. When we got back to the village, old Piugaattuq, who was then 85 years old, gave us a very detailed account of the time he caught a whale 25 years earlier.

In 1991, the Inuvialuit negotiated with their Alaskan cousins in order to acquire the unused part of the Alaskan whale quota for the previous year. The United States and Canadian governments were not against this and the Canadian Department of Wildlife even offered to supervise the operation. The Inuvialuit were not to kill any baby whales or females with babies. A leader of the hunt who would be accountable to the Department's officer had to be named by the hunting associations. The hunting plan had to be approved by a joint committee. If the hunters lost a whale that had been wounded or killed, all possible effort had to be made to bring it in, and no useable part of the whale was to be wasted.

On September 3, 1991, the Inuvialuit whale hunters were able to proudly announce on their short wave radio station that a whale had been successfully harpooned and killed. It was then towed to be butchered at a site chosen and prepared in advance. Hundreds of Inuit made their way to the site, by whatever means available. And the celebration began. Every family received its share of *maktak* (edible whale skin) and tongue, and when everything edible had been removed, a great drum dance was held, punctuated by thanksgiving prayers and chants. In the following weeks, every Inuvialuit village received its share of the meat and participated in the celebration in one way or another.

Schoolchildren who had been made aware of the preparations for the hunt composed stories and chants about the capture and soon all of the Inuit in the Canadian Arctic were informed of the success, which was seen as a return to tradition and a new contract with the forces of nature.

2.3. An "Exemplary" Case of Whale Poaching by the Inuit of Igloolik

At *Igloolik*, old Piugaattuq was not the last to rejoice. He was then over 90 years old and in declining health. He had taught many of those close to him the whaling secrets that he had learned from his forefathers. His son-in-law, Simiumi Quannaq, had paid close attention to the teachings. When on the radio in the summer of 1994 the old man expressed his desire to eat bowhead one last time before dying, everyone in the area endorsed his wish. By strange coincidence, his son-in-law was hunting with two other Inuit on September 19 a dozen kilometres northwest of *Igloolik* when they suddenly saw a small bowhead that seemed to be having trouble swimming. It was a four- or five-year old female and eight meters long. They immediately decided to capture it and managed to harpoon it. Then, following Piugaattuq's instructions, they made a lance using a long hunting knife tied to the end of an oar. They delivered a mortal blow to the animal using their improvised weapon, and then towed the body to the shore of the nearest island, *Imilik* (the name of which means "the place where there is drinking water").

The next day, when the news got to Igloolik and began to spread, there was general excitement. Despite being 94 years old and under medical care, Piugaattuq decided to go with his nurse to *Imilik*, where the animal was being butchered. Everyone who had a boat prepared to go and help cut up the animal. According to Georgia (1996: 12–15), who was there in person, at 7:00 in the morning on Wednesday, September 21, boats of all kinds took advantage of the high tide to sail to *Imilik*. By the afternoon there were up to 30 boats, including that of the wildlife and fisheries officers who were responsible for investigating the hunt, taking samples of various organs of the whale and ensuring that none of the edible parts were wasted. The atmosphere was festive.

At the site, everyone was working hard. Some were cutting wide strips of skin off the carcass, some were making caches of meat and blubber for dogs under the stones on the shore, and others were carrying the valuable shares of *maktak* and tongue to the boats, all the while taking breaks to snack on cubes of delicious *maktak*. Inuit reporters armed with video cameras interviewed the hunters. Piugaattuq had a new lease on life and mixed traditional chants with religious hymns. In the evening the festivities began again, but this time in the village. In the days that followed, visitors flowed in by plane and boat from neighbouring villages, some of which were several hundred kilometres away, to join in the celebrations and eat *maktak*. The news reached the local and regional media. Piugaattuq was sated, satisfied and happy. He lived for one more year before passing away in fall 1995, mourned by all.

However, many things had changed in the Canadian Arctic since the Inuvialuit were first authorized to kill a whale in 1991.[6] A new regional entity, Nunavut, had come into being in 1992, and covered all of the Inuit lands that used to be part of the Northwest Territories. The leaders of the new entity had been promised political independence. The right to practice traditional subsistence hunting was part of the agreement and a Nunavut Wildlife Management Board had been created to watch over wildlife resources, participate in international meetings on wildlife protection, ensure compliance with agreements with Canadian authorities, etc.

Now, the hunters who had killed the whale near *Igloolik* did not have a hunting licence, had not consulted a committee ahead of time, and had contravened Canadian law. They had committed an offence. A territorial court sitting in *Igloolik* in spring 1995 notified the three hunters of this. The trial was set for fall 1995. However, the charges against the three Inuit soon gave rise to a strong solidarity movement in the Inuit community, to the point that the Inuit authorities in Nunavut decided to support the three accused and help them with their defence. The best lawyers were selected and pressure on the Canadian government increased until it finally decided to abandon the proceedings. All northern media reported the ups and downs of the case, and it was even possible to follow it on the Internet.

The right to hunt bowhead whales in Arctic waters had become a symbol of cultural identity and ethnicity for the Inuit. The 1992 agreements that had established Nunavut (on April 1, 1999) had also led to the creation of a Wildlife Office with the power to assign a quota of one whale, which could be killed in territorial waters. At the same time, a four-year research project was to be conducted on whale hunting in various Nunavut villages. The unpremeditated capture of a whale by the *Igloolik* hunters upset all of the Office's plans, but the huge publicity surrounding the hunt also provided a powerful argument in favour of re-opening subsistence hunting of the animal.

2.4. The Misadventures of Inuit Chosen to Hunt a Whale

The first research carried out under the Wildlife Office's initiative in the northwest of Hudson Bay and North Baffin showed an increase in the number of whales visiting those areas and a general desire in the various communities to begin subsistence hunting again. The Office decided that a hunt would be held in summer 1996. At first the hunt was to be held in the *Pangnirtung* area in East Baffin, but later the location was changed to Repulse Bay. Hunters were chosen by the hunting associations in the various areas, and many local, regional and even national media prepared to cover the event. A harpoon with an explosive head was procured to kill the whale with a minimum of suffering, as requested by the International Whaling Commission. A leader of the hunt was designated, and harpoons and floats, as well as a lance for the kill, were prepared. In short, there was detailed preparation. But at the same time there was bald-faced improvisation. No one knew how to use a harpoon with an explosive head, the organizers forgot to include the Repulse Bay community in the hunt, and the fact that the hunters came from many different places limited their stay at Repulse Bay to one week because every one had to get back home on the scheduled flight. The hunt was supposed to be the beginning of a new era in the self-management of large marine wildlife by the Inuit of the central Canadian Arctic and raise international visibility. Instead, because of the improvisation, it almost turned into a catastrophe and complete failure.

Despite technical assistance from a ship belonging to the Canadian government, there were pieces missing for the explosive head harpoon, which no Inuit there had ever used before. On August 15 at around noon, a whale was finally sighted by local hunters near the village at Repulse Bay. The team of designated hunters, who had been criss-crossing the coastal waters in search of a whale for several days, was 75 kilometres to the south. Their leader radioed the local hunters and asked them to try to push the whale towards the coast and keep it there in order to make it easier to capture later. It would take two hours for the designated hunters to make their way there.

On shore, groups of people had been following the nearby whale's movements since noon, and were openly encouraging the local hunters to kill it with no further ado so as to shorten the hunt and reduce the risk of losing it. However, the local hunters had received the order to leave the catch to the designated hunters. When the leader of the hunt finally got to the whale, he missed with the harpoon three times. On his fourth try, he succeeded and everyone applauded. Other designated hunters also managed to plant their harpoons in the animal.

Now that the whale was dragging a cluster of floaters designed to slow it down and prevent it from sinking later, an attempt had to be made to kill it with a deep stab of the lance before it swam too far out to sea. One of the designated hunters brandished the long lance that had been prepared for the purpose and tried to strike a mortal blow to the animal, but he missed, the lance broke and the whale kept diving at regular intervals. Total confusion followed. Gunfire was heard the next time that the whale reappeared. The shots probably came from local hunters who were frustrated because they had been left out of the hunt and wished to kill the whale as quickly as possible. Then everyone began shooting. Bullets were flying in all directions, endangering the lives of everyone in the area. After two hours, the pursuit was bordering on the grotesque. The mortally wounded whale blew out bloody water and dove into deep water. Consternation filled the participants in the boats and spectators on the shore. Around 6:00 in the evening, the designated hunters returned to the village with their tails between their legs and met behind closed doors with representatives from Nunavut's Wildlife Office in order to decide whether a hunt would be held for a second whale. In the meanwhile, the old hunters in the village were not sparing in their criticism. They said that the hunters had insulted the goddess of sea animals by arguing on the hunting grounds, which was traditionally forbidden. They had not been able to keep the whale in the shallow coastal waters before killing it, as had been the technique of their forefathers. However, the government boat later found the animal's body using radar. It was in mid-water, at a depth of 80 meters. The government boat tried to dredge the whale using a trawl net, but in vain. The media were also unrestrained in their criticism and sarcastic comments about the painful scenes that they had witnessed.

Finally, on Saturday, August 19, the day before the departure initially planned by the team of designated hunters (though a new hunt had just been decided upon for the following Monday) village women reported that the whale had risen to the surface and could be seen in the open sea. Hope and pride returned immediately.

The boats used for the hunt went back out with new harpoons and floats. They found the floating corpse, which was full of gas after spending 46 hours in deep water. They made it fast and hauled it towards the village and onto the shore, where the outgoing tide gradually revealed the 15 meter-long, 45-ton animal.

Joy was at its height and people's appetites also, for while much of the meat had become unfit for human consumption, the *maktak* and tongue were still delicious. There was general disorder as people began cutting and carrying away strips of skin and blubber, which they planned to take back to their communities. It was decided that the butchering would stop and continue the next day because people wanted to celebrate the event on that very evening. However, the next day was when the designated hunters had decided to leave. They woke up late after having partied into the wee hours, and the plane flew them away before the butchering began again. A third of the *maktak* was still on the carcass when the plane took off. It flew over the animal before continuing on its way to the northern villages. The local people took their share of the abandoned whale, and the putrefied remains long remained on shore, a reminder of the unfortunate adventure.

In response to criticism from government observers, the media and ecologists, representatives of Nunavut's Wildlife Office said that it was unfair to criticize the hunters. They had not had the benefit of a proper initiation to the millenary tradition of whale hunting by their parents or grandparents because the species had almost disappeared owing to over hunting by European and American whalers at the turn of the century.

At noon on a Sunday in February 1997, the national television station, Radio Canada, showed a film on the tumultuous hunt in Repulse Bay. The prime time documentary tried to show both sides: it paid homage to the Inuit's right to subsistence hunting in accordance with their beliefs, food needs and traditional skills, but it criticized the improvisation that marked the hunt in August 1996.

If we have to draw conclusions from the three recent whale hunts by Canadian Inuit, we could note the success of the 1991 hunt by the Inuvialuit in the western Arctic, who are closely related to the Alaskan Inuit. The Inuvialuit have never been completely cut off from seasonal subsistence hunting of the animal, if only through their relations with their Alaskan cousins, and they were able to easily acquire the knowledge and know-how needed for successful hunting. The 1991 hunt was carried out using modern technology, such as the explosive "bomb" rifle, which is widely used now in Alaska, but with a traditional social organization involving collective preparation, general distribution of the meat and fat, and a very strong spiritual dimension.

The illegal *Igloolik* hunt may have attracted the most sympathy because hunters who were familiar with ancient hunting techniques had decided it on the spot, and the whale was already in difficulty. It was carried out masterfully, and followed by collective sharing. Its political and symbolic repercussions provided strong impetus for a renewal of Inuit identity in that part of the Arctic. It was controversial, but in the end it was entirely to old Piugaattuq's credit, for in his long life as a hunter, which began at the time when harpoons, lances and bows and arrows were the Inuit's only weapons, he was always a strong advocate for the environment and endangered species. Through his narratives and teaching, he greatly helped to convey the secrets of a harmonious relationship with the forces and spirits of nature.

In order to correctly assess the Inuit's point of view and actions, the purpose of which was to gain recognition of their hunting rights, we have to go beyond western notions of environmental protection, endangered species and subsistence hunting, which flow from a new world order embodied by the International Whaling Commission and environmentalist NGOs. We have to take into account the social and economic value of the traditional hunt that prevailed before European industrial hunting perverted its spirit and objectives. We have to identify the symbolic and cosmological dimensions of the hunt, which are very important to the Inuit. I will attempt to do this below.

3. Social and Economic Value

Among the many sea mammals living in the Arctic seas surrounding Inuit lands, the bowhead or Greenland whale (*Balaena mysticetus*) plays a special role because of its huge size (up to 20 meters long and 60 tons), the danger involved in hunting it, and the immense economic gain when it is captured. A whale carcass can provide several dozen tons of meat, around 20 tons of subcutaneous fat, and a few tons of *maktak* (edible skin), which is enough to feed a camp of 50 people and all their dogs for the whole winter. In earlier times, it could also provide enough oil for the soapstone lamps that were used for light, heat and cooking in the community's igloos.

Bowhead baleen,[7] which can be up to two meters long, were highly prized for their flexibility and strength. They were used to make the edges of the round wooden plates on which boiled meat was served and the skin-covered hoop (*nuitaq*) that was attached with the float to the harpoon line used in whaling. The hoop helped to slow the wounded animal down after it had been harpooned. Baleen was also used to cover the bottoms of dog sled runners, and baleen fibres were used to make snares. Bowhead ribs were used to support the turf roofs of semi-subterranean winter houses and to make the peaks of skin tents in summer. The whale's vertebrae were used as blocks for adze work.

Like all big game (walruses, beluga whales, polar bears, bearded seals, etc.), a bowhead was the occasion for systematic sharing among the hunters who participated in its capture. J. Vanstone (1962: 49) gives a very detailed description of this for the Point Hope area in northern Alaska. (See Figure 1: Shares of a whale) The sharing he describes closely matches the rules that we observed with respect to beluga and narwhal sharing in Hudson Bay and Hudson Strait. At Point Hope, where whaling involves collective chases with up to a dozen boats and crews, the first share goes to the captain of the boat that harpooned the whale first. The second share is divided among the members of his crew. The third and fourth shares go to the members of the second and third crews, the fifth and sixth shares go to the members of the fourth and fifth crews, the seventh and eighth shares go to the sixth and seventh crews, and the ninth share, which is a 30-centimeter wide strip of skin circumscribing the whale's body, goes to the ninth crew. The tenth share is the upper part of the head, and all the remaining boats share it. The eleventh and twelfth shares are set aside for the spring whale hunt celebration, and the fifteenth share is kept for another celebration that can take place in either the spring or fall. The last two shares are two strips of skin going from the navel to the sexual organs of the animal, and they belong to the captain of the first boat, who gives one to the first harpooner and, in olden times, one to the shaman who advised him.

In the north of Hudson Bay, every large animal killed was the occasion for a communal banquet and ritual consumption, as we will see below. A very large animal, which was truly dangerous to hunt, was the object of all sorts of attentions, prescriptions, prohibitions and beliefs.

4. Symbolism and Cosmology

The bowhead played an important role in the Inuit imagination, myths and rites. To begin with, its very size placed it above humans, in the same realm as giants and great spirits and shamans.

4.1. Disproportion, Hunting and Sexuality

A legend gathered on the east coast of Hudson Bay illustrates the disproportion:

> Inuit were chasing a bowhead in a kayak, when a giant looking for bullhead entered the sea not far from there. He was naked and had a fish club for stunning his prey. He was so big that he was walking on the bottom of the sea, but the water came up only to his waist. When he got to the place where the Inuit were hunting, he stopped and examined the surface of the water to see whether there were any bullhead. In fact, the Inuit and the giant were hunting the same prey, but what was a whale to the Inuit was only a bullhead to the giant. Suddenly, he saw a form (*puiji*[8]) break the surface of the water and it looked to him like a bullhead, so he immediately struck it violently with his club. But then he fell unconscious in the water. He had become so excited by the hunt that his penis had become erect. When it broke the surface of the water, he had mistaken it for a bullhead and hit it with his weapon.

The Inuit love such stories for the misunderstandings they involve, the clumsy use of excessive force, the stupidity attributed to giants or suprahuman forces, and the sexual symbolism that is expressed by transforming various things associated with production into phallic symbols, such as the kayak (the prow of which is called *usuujaq* in Inuit), the harpoon (which is called *naukkuuti* in some regions, the same word used for "penis" in other areas) and sea animals, such as the surfacing whale in the story. In the story, the phallic symbolism refers to the periodic surfacing of marine mammals to breathe, which is compared to the movement of an erect penis. Some Inuit compare the tension felt by the hunter when he is about strike his prey to the sexual excitation of a man having relations with a woman. The symbolism also refers to a special characteristic of some mammals: the male bowhead has a baculum,[9] or penis bone that can be several meters long.

The story is a good illustration of the Inuit conception of the world: like a set of Russian dolls, it is divided into levels of different scales, such as the suprahuman level (that of giants), the human level and the infrahuman level (that of dwarves). Every level is homologous with the other levels, and also operates in a parallel manner. Problems, ambiguity and confusion arise when two beings of different levels meet and interact. From the human point of view, the bullhead is a small animal of infrahuman proportions, like a man's penis. In contrast, for humans, the whale is the largest animal known and hunted in the natural world. Given the disproportion and real danger involved in whale hunting, Inuit thought uses humour and derision by inverting the perspective. Indeed, the story suggests taking the point of view of the giant, who represents extreme disproportion in the story because he is in the same disproportion as the whale with respect to the men. Seen from a suprahuman level, the whale is reduced to the size of a bullhead, which is easy for Inuit to capture, or to the size of the hunter's own erect penis, which is very expressive of the disproportion if it is compared with its size in its familiar flaccid state. Note that the bowhead, bullhead and erect penis all have one thing in common: a head disproportionately large in relation to the body compared with most of the animals that the Inuit routinely encounter. It should also be noted that in the analogy language of shamans, the bullhead and the whale are designated by the same term *taakslaingiq* of the radical "*taaksla*" (to mention), the privative "*i*" and the substantive suffix "*ngiq*", in other words, "he who must not be mentioned" (K. Rasmussen 1929: 79). Rasmussen adds that the Inuit consider the Greenland sculpin to be a degenerate bowhead.

In the above legend, the chance encounter of a giant, a bowhead and Inuit hunters in kayaks allows the narrator to change scale easily, and to create confusion among types of things (bullhead/bowhead/human penis; the prow of the kayak/the giant's erect penis/a bowhead surfacing), which makes the narrative charming and very funny. Confusion with respect to scale is possible in the narrative because, in Inuit thought, there is a prevailing belief that the form and scale of objects and beings is not set and unchanging, but unstable and variable. Thus, in mythical times, dwarves could grow larger and rise to the scale of their adversaries, just as animals belonging to the suprahuman scale could shrink to infrahuman size if a prohibition was broken. If a woman miscarried, she was required to be careful about where she looked for a long time. She was forbidden to look at large game because if she did, the animals could shrink down to the next scale. A bowhead (or sometimes a walrus) could be reduced to the size of a bullhead, and a polar bear to that of a fox. The more important the hunt, the greater the precautions to ensure success and guard against such effects.

4.2. The Whale-husband: a Sexual Animal

Another myth told by the Inuit of *Igloolik* attributes great sensuality to a bowhead in his relations with a young Inuit woman:

> Four young women, who were almost of marriageable age, were pretending to wish for husbands. The first, upon seeing a male *arvik* (bowhead) surfacing in the sea, cried out and her wish became true. The second chose a bullhead, the third a pretty pebble, and the fourth an eagle. The whale carried the first woman away to an island. There, he built her a house out of his own bones, and gave her pieces of his own flesh and *maktak* (edible skin) to eat. He was so infatuated with his wife and so afraid of losing her that he never let her go out, even when she wanted to relieve herself. He kissed her (by rubbing his nose against hers) and made love to her so often that the skin of the young woman's nose and genitals started to turn into *maktak*. The parents of the young woman knew that she was on the island and visited regularly in an *umiaq* (large communal boat made of skin) to try to bring her back home. But they always came back without her because she was confined inside the house. When she asked to go outside to relieve herself, her whale husband said, "You can urinate in my mouth, but for your other needs use my flipper". One day, however, he allowed her to relieve herself outside, but on the condition that she would be tied to one end of a long line and he would hold the other end. As soon as she got outside, she untied herself and attached the line to a whale bone that was lying on the ground. She told the bone that if her husband called from the house to see if she was finished, it was to imitate her voice and tell her husband "No, I'm not finished yet!" Then she quickly ran to her parents, who were waiting for her with their boat to take her back home. In the meantime, the whale was getting impatient and kept asking his wife whether she had finished. Then he pulled on the line and discovered that there was a bone at the end of it instead of his wife. So he ran outside, and gathered all his bones together to regain his whale form, but in his haste he forgot to take his pelvic bone. He dove in the sea and pursued the fugitives, whom he caught up to easily. But then he realized that he had forgotten his pelvic bone, so he went back to get it, which allowed the occupants of the boat to get a little further ahead. When the whale caught up to them again, they tossed him the young woman's coat. He threw himself at it while they got a bit further away. Then they threw him her boots, one after the other, to slow him down a bit more, and finally her skin pants, which were still full of the smell of her body, and that stopped him for a long time. The people in the boat took advantage of this to reach the other shore and get on land as fast as they could. The whale also arrived and in a rage he threw himself onto the shore. But then found himself on dry land, where he immediately died and became a bone again.

This myth shows the hyperactive sexuality, exaggerated jealousy and olfactory eroticism attributed to the whale husband. When she becomes the unwilling prisoner of the whale's passionate love, which she had imprudently provoked by her wish, the heroine begins to turn into an animal as a result of the erotic olfactory and sexual relations that the whale imposes on her. The external signs of the transformation can be seen in the skin of her nose and genitals, which takes on the consistency of whale skin (*maktak*). Without her family's intervention, which saves her *in extremis*, the young woman would have gradually lost all of her human features.

In mythical times, marriages with animals that had metamorphosed into humans were frequent. It was the time of undifferentiation. For example, in the preceding myth, there is a confusion of types: the whale is simultaneously the young woman's husband, house (his bones support the roof) and food (his flesh and *maktak*). There is confusion of scale and of the animal and human kingdoms, through the marriage of the young woman with the whale. Note that in the Inuit language there is also some semantic confusion between alimentary and sexual consumption. Moreover, the term *mamarpuq*, which designates both deliciousness and sexual pleasure, is constructed out of the radical "*mamaq*", which designates the particularly delicious flesh of a whale's gums. While the time of metamorphoses and marriages with animals is portrayed in mythology as belonging to a primordial past, we must not forget that mythical space-time is circular and remains accessible to spirits and shamans.

4.3. The Whale-wife: a Considerate Hostess

In the mythology of the Mackenzie Inuvialuit (H. Schwarz 1970), there is the sad narrative of a bowhead and a raven:

> Once upon a time there lived on Herschel Island, a silly raven that imagined himself to be one of the cleverest creatures alive. He used to fly around the island and proclaimed to everyone that he was the wisest of them all. Then all must listen to him and take note of his wise sayings. But no one ever did, and all the animals and all the people on the Island called him a silly old raven, which indeed he was.
>
> So the raven was frustrated and irritated and he cackled and raved at everybody's stupidity but never his own. One day it occurred to him that on the mainland things might be a bit better, that there the creatures would probably be more intelligent and that they would treat him with more respect. So disgusted with everybody, he left Herschel Island and took off in the direction of the mainland. But being a very silly raven, he misjudged the distance, and to make matters worse, he flew right into a hail storm which swept the Beaufort Sea from the north. Pretty soon the raven lost his way completely. Tired and dispirited, he bitterly regretted having left his cozy nook on Herschel Island. He was flying lower and lower over the sea, and once was almost swept away by a particularly large wave. He was almost ready to give up when all of a sudden he noticed a black rock in the boiling sea.

In a last desperate effort, the raven flew straight towards the rock. Great was his surprise when he found himself in the mouth of a large bow-headed whale. In panic the raven flapped his wings which only carried him further inside, until he arrived at the whale's stomach. And there right in the whale's stomach the raven was amazed to see a large comfortable cabin. Inside it a lamp was burning brightly, and its walls and floor were covered with soft hides. Along the wall there was a spacious skin platform covered with furs. And there resting on the skin platform was the most beautiful young woman the raven had ever seen! On seeing the soggy and pathetic raven, the young woman bade him welcome and invited him inside. She made room for him on the soft skin platform, and from the larder produced delicious crabs, mussels, and small fish, which the starved raven devoured with great appetite. In the warm and friendly cabin, he soon recovered his spirits. He strutted and squawked a bit, and then as he was tired, he fell asleep. When the raven woke up, the beautiful girl was not in the cabin.

But she soon re-appeared, and brought some more fresh food, which the raven consumed with great gusto.. However, the girl was very restless and from time to time she stepped outside the cabin, only to return shortly afterwards. This irritated and upset the raven and finally, unable to hold his ill temper, he asked her: "How come that you leave this comfortable cabin so often?" And she replied, "I leave it in order to live – breath is my life." And the raven, being a very stupid one, tried to argue with her and begged her to stay with him all the time on the comfortable skin platform. But she would not listen to him. "You must let me go whenever I have the need to leave, and what is more, I warn you never to touch the lamp in the centre of the cabin. If you do, it will bring bad luck to us all!" So for a while the raven was content and, in his own selfish way, was grateful to the beautiful girl who was so good to him. She catered to all wishes, brought him delicious food, and made him comfortable on the skin platform. In the course of time he grew fat and lazy and spoiled. He strutted and squawked in the cabin, as if it were his own; he kept most of the skin platform to himself and became very arrogant and bossy.

It happened that one day the girl was on one of her frequent absences from the cabin, and the raven was bored and irritated. He tried to get to sleep, but the brightly burning lamp in the centre kept him awake. So he became very annoyed, hopped out of the skin platform and extinguished the flame which has burned so brightly before. As soon as the flame was out, the cabin became full of blood and blubber, and the raven felt suffocated for want of air. Too late did he realize that the bright light flame was the spirit of the whale and the beautiful girl the soul of the whale which had to leave the cabin from time to time in order to breathe. By not obeying her wishes he had killed the spirit and the soul of the whale. And as the raven was trying to make his way out of the stinking mess, bitterly did he regret his folly. Eventually, covered with blubber and blood, the raven emerged outside and perched himself on top of the dead whale as it was tossed about by the waves. And as it happened the whale was tossed right into the bay in Herschel Island. Soon enough its carcass was surrounded by the Eskimos in their kayaks to cut it up for meat and blubber. To their great surprise they saw the old raven sitting on top of the dead whale. And the raven hopped up and down and spread his wings and strutted and proclaimed to all people around him, "You see, it is I who am the wisest and cleverest of you all. Single handed I killed this giant whale." And the people on Herschel Island believed this stupid old raven; and from that time on, they held him in great esteem.

4.4. Women and the Whale Hunt

In Inuit thought, the relations between whales and women are ambiguous. They both attract and repel each another, and resent and seduce each other. Another *Igloolik* myth provides us with more details on this:

In the olden days, the whales used to move along the coast quite close to the shore, so the men always had their hunting implements ready on the beach, with the harpoon line fastened to a big stone and the harpoon close by. But one night when two men were going to change wives, and their wives, while all were asleep, went to the men they were to lie with, they saw a whale coming along by the shore, quite close to the beach; and in their eagerness, they ran to a harpoon and harpooned the whale. They got it, but since then the whales never move along close inshore, as they feel degraded at one of their number having been harpooned by a woman.

This major infraction of the rules governing the relations between hunters and their spouses, and between the hunters' spouses and game, probably highly displeased the whales because from that time on they stopped coming so close to shore. They became very wary and especially feared the presence of pubescent girls. It has to be said that in Inuit beliefs, the productive relations between hunters and game are considered analogous to the reproductive relations between men and women. Game is seen as being either like a woman in that it is the object of man's desire, or like a foetus that, after the woman is fertilized by a man, comes out of the woman's womb attached to the umbilical cord, just as an animal that has been harpooned is attached to the harpoon's line. Thus, it is dangerous to break rules and return to the mythical confusion of types. For example, if a hunter gives into a bestial desire with a female animal, there could be serious consequences, including the disappearance of all the game in the area.

Blood plays an important role in both the symbolism and the regulation of production and reproduction. An animal's spilled blood is a sign of its capture as game, and a woman's retained blood is a sign of pregnancy. This can be seen in rituals and beliefs surrounding the puberty of young women. A girl's first menstruation is celebrated as if a son were born, in other words, the first menstrual blood is seen in a positive light, as a sign that the girl has become a reproductive woman. In contrast, later menstrual blood is considered in a negative light because it is a sign of non-pregnancy, in other words, non-reproduction.

However, it should be noted that Inuit sexual identity was eminently social and could be different from an individual's biological sex. Thus, if at birth a girl was named after a close male relative, she was considered the reincarnation of that relative, and dressed and educated as a boy until she reached puberty. When she menstruated for the first time, the event was celebrated as if she had killed or butchered a bowhead, and the blood with which she was marked was considered to be the blood of the animal she had captured, in particular the largest game. As part of the celebration, she was required to visit each home and every one had to give her a little water to drink and congratulate her.

The inversion of roles ended after the girl's right of passage. She then took on the female roles assigned by the culture, such as caring for and raising children, preparing food and making clothes. Transgressing the rule after beginning reproductive life could endanger the group's survival, as in the case of the two women in the myth who switched the roles usually assigned to women for both the spouse exchange and the whale hunt, thereby challenging the relationship between hunters and game.

It is claimed that since that transgression, pubescent women have been required to wear a headband with a white stone on it to indicate their presence at whale hunting time. In order to inspire trust in the whales, men must not spit or urinate in the sea when on a hunting expedition.

If a woman was the first to spot a bowhead, she had to point at it and cry out until the men saw it and began the chase. As soon as the whale was harpooned, the whole group participated symbolically in its capture. Pubescent women were required to return home, undo all the ties on their clothing, remove their pants and lie down on the platform that was used as a bed as if they were offering themselves. They had to act as if they wanted to seduce the whale, or simply get it to imitate them and give in to the hunters who were trying to bring it to the shore. Indeed, it was not rare for whales to drag boats and hunters out into open sea.

Pursuing a harpooned and wounded animal could be perilous and result in injury, shipwreck, drowning or mutilation. In order to make it easier to tow the whale to shore, the harpooner's wife had to thread a needle and sew, pulling hard on the thread at each stitch. Her needle represented the harpoon, her thread the line, and the piece sewn the whale. It was as if she were drawing the whale towards her by pulling on the thread. Young boys were required to get into pairs and tie their legs together as if they were going to have a three-legged race. Then they had to run inland away from the shore, tripping as much as possible. This was supposed to hinder the whale's resistance to the hunters. Similarly, women who had reached menopause had their ankles tied together, and they too had to hop and trip away from the water in order to slow the whale down. In both cases, the effect was to be produced by imitative magic.

When the whale had finally been towed into the shallow water of the foreshore, the women put their pants back on and came out with their hearts filled with joy. Young mothers with sons had to run out in front of the whale and go in as deep as possible so that their sons would later become great whale hunters. When the animal's body was moored on the beach, the children were lined up with the boys on one side and the girls on the other, and they were thrown chunks of *maktak*. Each tried to be the first to eat a piece. The winner was thought to become the best in everything. Later the real butchering began, and those who did it had to get completely covered in the whale's fat and blood. This greatly pleased the whale, whose soul would seek reincarnation in the body of another bowhead in order to offer itself to the hunters again.

In a meeting area (*qaggiq*) made up of a circle of large stones, a banquet of meat and *maktak* was then held, to which all men and older women were invited. Young women with children were not allowed to participate because of the above-mentioned mythical transgression by two young women. They had to wait until all of the whale's vertebrae had been cut apart in order to cook their share of the meat in separate pots. It was important to avoid offending the whale's soul so that future hunts would go well. Dances followed that could last the whole night and celebrated the success of the hunt and the resulting wealth of food. Shamans also intervened before and after the hunt to win the whale's cooperation, gain the favour of the great spirits and create harmony between the whole group and the game. In case of failure or misfortune, causes and culprits were sought.

4.5. The Goddess of Sea Mammals

So far, all of the examples are the same in that the whale hunt is not portrayed as a purely technical operation, but always has a social, religious and even cosmological dimension. A very well known myth in the central Canadian Arctic tells the story of how a woman is at the origin of all sea mammals. Her name is Uinigumasuittuq, "she who did not want to marry":

> She rejected every suitor who tried to ask for her hand, but one day, a very insistent stranger came by kayak and, under pressure from her mother, she agreed and left with the stranger, lying down in the back of the kayak. It was in fact a petrel (sea bird) who had metamorphosed into a human. She soon discovered who he was, and saw his horrible eyes and small size, but it was too late and he brought her into his tent. She stayed there, dejected, until one day her father came to visit her in his skin boat. The petrel was not there and she begged her father to take her back with him. They fled but the bird soon found out. He started chasing them, using his wings to raise a violent storm and calling to the father to give him back his wife. The father had hidden his daughter under some skins, but since the bird kept chasing them, he threw the girl's clothes into the water piece by piece to make the petrel think that they were her. The storm continued and finally he ended up throwing overboard his own daughter, who clung to the side of the boat. To make her let go, the father cut off

her fingers, which immediately changed into sea mammals, such as ringed seals, bearded seals and according to some versions from East Baffin, beluga whales and bowheads. Next, he blinded his daughter in one of her eyes, and she sank to the bottom of the sea. He made it to shore, but was so full of despair that allowed himself to be drawn back into the sea by the tide and went to join his daughter at the bottom of the sea. From there they watch over the actions of humans and if rules are broken, they keep the sea animals that came from the daughter's fingers in their home.

Hunting puts the whole social order in question, beginning with the need for a young woman to agree to marry in a manner that is socially acceptable, in other words, in compliance with her parents' wishes. One must not marry relatives who are too close, or people one does not know, or who are too foreign, or *a fortiori* metamorphosed animals. It is important to comply with the sexual division of labour and maintain a clear separation between the production of meat and reproduction of life, even though the two processes are symbolically homologous. The most important distinctions in every rite related to whale hunting are among productive or reproductive individuals, other individuals, prepubescent children and women who have reached menopause. However, Inuit culture leaves open the possibility of an overlap between the sexes in the case of prepubescent children, who can be treated as the opposite sex because of their namesake. This is also possible among shamans, whose function is specifically to cross over the various borders between the sexes and between humans and animals, and humans and spirits.

4.6. The Whale Hunt: Cross-dressing and Sex Change

Shamanic cross-dressing normally resulted from the fact that the shaman's auxiliary spirit or namesake was of the opposite sex. However, a myth also tells how a shaman in the *Igloolik* area had his genitals cut off by the line of his harpoon after it had struck a whale. In despair, he decided to dress and live as a woman. A myth from St. Lawrence Island, Alaska, in the Bering Strait, which is peopled by Inuit from Siberia, provides an example in which the links between sexual identity, the sexual division of labour, whale hunting and procreation are challenged. It should be noted that in some areas of Alaska and northeastern Siberia, it was not rare for adults to cross-dress and sometimes engage in homosexual practices, particularly in the case of shamans. Here is the narrative transcribed by G. Slwooko (1979):

> For us, in the Eskimos' belief, there is another sex between man and woman. ...Inuit here in this area of Siberia and St. Lawrence have great consideration for this kind of person because he can't help his nature.

> When a man with a moustache is dressed like a woman, we are careful not to make fun of him as instructed by our elders. The elders would say that such people were protected by the Maker of All. So to laugh at him would bring a curse to the thoughtless ones. So when we see a man dress like a woman he is showing respect to his nature and we are not to laugh at him or hurt his feelings.

So there was one like that in this story. The man in this story dressed like a woman and never wanted to go hunting, but stayed home and sewed. He was the eldest of four brothers. It happened that the younger men, when they got whales and walruses out on the ice and sea, would get upset about meat taken to the eldest brother who didn't go out hunting at all. The younger brothers would complain, "Why do we have to take meat to our eldest brother when he doesn't work out on the cold moving ice and sea like us?"

When the strange acting man heard about this, he went out to the shore. He buried his face in his parka sleeves and the large ruff which were made like women's clothing, and cried because the brothers hurt his feelings. There he cried and cried. Soon a voice was heard asking, "Why is the woman crying?" It was the voice of the Maker of All. In answer, the strange man said, "My brothers complained about me not being out on the ice and sea with them at the hunts. I am unable to go. I can't! I can't! I am like a woman. How can I when I'm made like this?" He sobbed on as he poured out his grief. So the voice answered, "All right, I'll see to it that you'll get something". So, very much comforted, the strange man went home. It wasn't long when he felt that he was getting big like a woman that was going to have a baby! He got bigger. Boy, the poor strange man was frightened. "If I'm going to have a baby, how will it ever be delivered?" he moaned to himself. But the voice soon talked to him again asking, "Why is the woman crying again?" For an answer, the strange man asked, "If I'm going to have a baby, how is it going to be delivered?"- "You go down to the sea and bury your face in your sleeves and ruff and rest there on the sea. You won't sink." The voice answered. So the strange man hurried down to the sea in his parka made like that of women's and got on the sea and buried his face with his sleeves and large ruff made of black dog skin. This was the women's original parka. There he floated around as he cried. Somehow a little whale was born. When his baby was born, it was not like the humans. Instead, it was a little whale.

The strange man picked up the tiny whale and took it home. He loved it so dearly that he carved a large wooden bowl and put water in it for the whale to swim in. The whale was getting big fast so that in no time he had to carve another bowl. When the whale got too large to be kept in the house, the man took him to the sea. He stayed at the waves for some time. While he was at the waves, the little whale would come ashore many time to be with his mother. When he was grown up, the strange man made a marker for his son. He made holes at his nose and put a reddened baby seal skin on his nose to mark him. So the little whale would play out in the sea. There were times when he got as far as the horizon. He got to going so far away that he would bring another whale along when he came home. So the younger brothers of the strange man would go out and kill the one he brought. He brought home many whales and the brothers were getting rich. The people of the village also became good whalers because the whales which followed the man's special whale given him by the Maker of All. They were not short of meat and oil. They had plenty of bones for housing poles and for other uses. That was the way the strange man was comforted.

Then one day, his whale didn't come home. The strange man waited at the shore very anxiously and he was very worried. He waited and waited, but no whale came. Another day passed on, still no sign of his whale. Then finally he got into his parka and buried his face in his sleeves and the large ruff and cried. He cried and cried, and soon he heard a voice asking why the woman was crying. The strange man poured out his sorrow in answer. So the voice said to him, "You go out to the sea in your parka as you always do until you stop but you will still be moving." The man did as he was told. Out there on the ocean he moved along but he did not see where he was going. When he stopped moving, he got his head up from his parka and what a strange place he was coming to! Where was He? The strange man wondered and tried to figure out. Soon he found out that he was coming to a different village. As soon he came to the coast he skipped along to the shore. He walked up to the beach. At the beach, what tragedy met his eyes! There was the marked head of his son! Just the head. Where was his body? In vain he ran around the large head to see the body, but it was gone. His son was killed! He could see that there was a village close by. He followed the path to a house. When he got there, he found out that it was the home of a crew that got his son. The people were getting together there to tell stories to celebrate the event or honour the catch. The people humbly welcomed the strange man and asked him a story to tell as they were doing to show their thankfulness for a great event that had been given to them. The strange man replied, "I am coming to tell a story for I certainly have one. He started, "There is a man who was born to be unable to go hunting for whales and all animals like others do. When he was accused, he cried to the Maker of All and he was given a strange and powerful son, a whale. What a heart lifter he was. He got many whales for the village so the man, or his parent, was not helpless anymore. Very proudly he raised his son. He was a joy to him. So he put a marker on him, a beautiful piece of work on him, a reddened baby seal skin of great prize. To the parent's great sorrow, however, his son was killed when the poor ambitious child got too far from home. They should have left him alone as he had markings, but they have killed him anyway. This is a tragedy to his parents. That is my story." With this, the sorrowing mother left the place in tears. There was a terrible silence after he left. The people tried to understand what he meant and they thought about killing a whale with reddened skin on his nose.

A terrible and horrible thing happened after the strange man left the place. The crew of the boat that killed the whale with the reddened baby seal skin on its nose started to sweat! The men sweated and sweated. Terrified by their appearance, the men looked at each other. They got smaller and smaller until they all turned to liquid. They say that every time someone got a seal or some other animal which looked strange, usually some sorrow would come to the family that happened to get it. I guess this was because that animal was marked as belonging to someone and that it should never have been killed.

This narrative should be seen in light of the fact that at Igloolik a young woman dressed as a man was supposed to have butchered a whale when she was stained with her first menstrual blood. Her new procreative ability was thus translated into the language of male production, whereas in the story told above, a young man dressed as a woman is supposed to have given birth to a whale-son. He provided his human family with many whales for capture.

The many references to whale hunting in Inuit myths and rites prove how ancient the hunt is. Many prehistoric vestiges in the Inuit Arctic also show this. It was carried out on a grand scale by the Thule, the direct ancestors of today's Inuit, who spread across the North American Arctic beginning in Alaska in the twelfth century. In historical times, there are many records of whale hunting on the south shore of Hudson Straight and the west coast of Hudson Bay. In the former area, the *Kangirsujuaq* territory was famous for whale traps in the sea (*tinujjivik*). The traps were in fact small bays that, because of the very high tides, became saltwater lakes (*tasiujaq*) at low tide. Hunters tried to herd their prey into the traps because it was much easier to harpoon and kill the animals there than in deep water. Hunters generally used kayaks, but it is possible that the people in Hudson Strait sometimes used *umiaqs* (large skin boats with oars and sails) like the Inuit in Labrador, Greenland and Alaska.

Aside from the very special situation in which sea traps were used, capturing an adult whale in the sea was rare and exceptional enough to give one the right to receive a special tattoo on the shoulder or forearm commemorating the occasion. Rooted in a distant past, these customs, rites and myths reveal a concept of nature that is much more anthropomorphic than the corresponding concept in the West. Indeed, for the Inuit, nature and the human world are an indivisible whole, in which the components are as closely linked as man and woman in everyday life. However, the visible world is not controlled by humans but by spirits: the great master spirits of game and cosmic powers, and also the spirits of the dead. The world of the spirits is a veritable virtual world that gives meaning to and determines the real world. Taking it into consideration is indispensable for understanding today's Inuit's desire to resume subsistence hunting of bowhead whales. This supports and strengthens the Inuit demand to begin subsistence hunting bowheads again, though of course under the control of the International Whaling Commission and in compliance with international regulations. However, they should not be suspected of threatening an endangered species, for they have always had a symbiotic relationship with sea animals that implies mutual respect and even a degree of attraction.

By making whale hunting a political stake and test case, they are actually going even further. They can count on the support of a number of NGOs, such as the International Work Group for Indigenous Affairs (IWGIA)[10] and Indigenous Survival International, which represents Arctic hunters. Together, they challenge the very Western-centred ideology dominating the International Whaling Commission, calling it emotional, paternalistic and romantic because based on a conception of nature and animals that subordinates them to humans. Humans are thus their superiors and have to intervene in the natural order to protect them. Behind the International Whaling Commission, there are environmental NGOs that, encouraged by the success of the anti-fur movement, have made the prohibition of whale hunting a major issue, though often using arguments containing incoherencies. For example, under the same term, "whale," they indiscriminately include at least 75 different species of marine mammals, some of which are endangered but others not. They also speak as if all the species shared the characteristics that are attributed to right whales, such as huge size, superior intelligence and peaceful behaviour, in short, as if they were all extraordinary animals that hark back to ancient mythological gods of the sea. The Circumpolar Inuit Conference calls for greater realism. In 1995, at its General Assembly in Nome, Alaska, its Vice-President (Greenland) suggested the creation of a circumpolar Inuit whaling commission, which would co-manage subsistence right whale hunting by various Inuit groups in the Arctic, in collaboration with the various government agencies that govern the groups and are already members of the Arctic Council. The Inuit's expert, pacifist approach, which has served them so well in the past with respect to recognition of land rights and regional political autonomy, could soon allow them to participate with national and international authorities in a new form of co-management of subsistence bowhead whale hunting.

5. Epilogue

On July 20, 1998, two boats, each manned by four Inuit hunters, managed to locate a bowhead whale in *Pangnirtung Fjord*, on Baffin Island. Jaco Evic, an experienced hunter who was 75 years old and had participated with his father in the last capture of a whale in the area in 1946, and Simeonie Keenainak, a 48-year old hunter, led the two crews. Assisted by 16 other Inuit, they captured the whale and then brought it to shore in a couple of hours. Jaco had the honour of harpooning it, and Simeonie the responsibility for killing it using a harpoon with an explosive tip. The Government of Canada had approved the hunt, as had the Nunavut Wildlife Management Board.

Everything had been prepared locally, without the media publicity that had so marred the unfortunate incident at Repulse Bay in 1996. The gun and explosive-tipped harpoon were of the same type as those used in the nineteenth century. They had been offered to the hunters, who had prepared meticulously for the hunt. The traditional ritual injunctions were complied with, and the whale's *maktak* was shared with all Inuit communities in the Canadian north. Even Inuit living in Ottawa received a share. In Nunavut, there was euphoria. They had reconnected with the knowledge of preceding generations, been able to reconcile themselves with the whale's spirit, and re-established the alliance that linked it with Inuit hunters.

Bibliography

- Freeman, Milton M. R., Eleanor E. Wein and Daren E. Keith. 1992. *Recovering Rights: Bowhead Whales and Inuvialuit Subsistence in the Western Arctic.* Edmonton. Canadian Circumpolar Institute and Fisheries Joint Management Committee.
- Georgia. 1996. "La baleine franche d'Igloolik", *Eskimo*, New series, No. 50, 12–15.
- Lowenstein, Tom. 1994. *Ancient Land: Sacred Whale. The Inuit Hunt and Its Rituals.* New York: Farrar, Strauss and Giroux.
- Rainey, Froelich G. 1947. *The Whale Hunters of Tigara.* Anthropological Papers of the American Museum of Natural History. Vol. 41. Part 2. New York.
- Rasmussen, Knud. 1929. *Intellectual Culture of the Iglulik Eskimo.* Report of the Fifth Thule Expedition, 1921–1924. Vol. 7. No. 1. Copenhagen.
- Randa, Vladimir. 1994. *Inuillu uumajuillu. Les animaux dans les savoirs, les representations et la langue des Iglulingmiut (Arctique oriental canadien)"* Paris, Ph.D. thesis, École des Hautes Études en Sciences Sociales.
- Rodon, Thierry. 1997. *Cooption ou autonomie: L'expérience de cogestion des ressources renouvables des autochtones du Canada.* Doctoral thesis. Laval University.
- Rodon, Thierry. 2003. *En partenariat avec l'État. Les expériences de cogestion des Autochtones du Canada.* Québec. Les Presses de l'Université Laval.
- Schwarz, Herbert T. 1970. *ELIK and other stories of the MacKenzie Eskimos.* Illustrated by Mona Ohoveluk. Toronto: The Canadian Publisher, McClelland and Stewart Limited.
- Slwooko, Grace. 1979. *Sivuqam ungipaghaatangi II. St. Lawrence Island Legends II.* From stories written by G. Slwooko. Illustrated by J. Leslie Boffa. Anchorage: National Bilingual Materials Development Center, Rural Education Affairs, University of Alaska.
- Slwooko-Carius, Helen. 1979. *Sevukakmet. Ways of Life on St. Lawrence Island.* Anchorage: Alaska University Press.
- Vanstone, James. 1962. *Point Hope: An Eskimo Village in Transition.* University of Washington Press.
- Victor, Anne-Marie. 1987. "Éléments symboliques de la chasse à la baleine". *Études/Inuit/Studies*, Vol. 11. No. 2, 139–164.
- Wilkin, Dwane. 1997. "More planning needed for next bowhead hunt." *Nunatsiaq News.* April 14, 1997.

[1] Professor, Laval University, Québec City

[2] Until the First World War, the political status of the Canadian Arctic was controversial, at least with respect to the archipelago in the high north and the surrounding maritime waters. Indeed, the United States still does not recognize Canadian sovereignty over the Northwest Passage. The British Empire unilaterally declared sovereignty over the archipelago and surrounding waters in 1880, and transferred the area to its new dominion, Canada. This action flowed from an old geopolitical conflict between Great Britain and the United States involving American whalers (and explorers travelling to the North Pole). At the end of the nineteenth century, their increasingly visible presence in the waters and the business they did with Aboriginals worried the Canadian authorities. A number of major Canadian sea expeditions were thus sent, including A. P. Low's 1903–1904 expedition in Hudson Bay, those of J. E. Bernier in the Arctic Archipelago between 1906 and 1911, and that of V. Stefansson in the western Arctic, in 1913–1916.

[3] The International Whaling Commission (IWC) was established in 1946 to correct whale hunting excesses during the Second World War.

[4] Rodon, T., *En partenariat avec l'État: les expérences de cogestions des autochtones du Canada*, Québec City: Les Presses de l'Université Laval, 2003. [Rodon]

[5] In fact, there are limits on both the number of animals killed and the number struck but lost during the hunt. (Rodon, *Ibid.*)

[6] Later, they requested and received a permit to kill one northern right whale a year, but they did not manage to kill another one until 1996. (Rodon, *Ibid.*)

[7] A single whale has several hundred baleen, with a total weight of around a ton.

[8] The term normally designates a sea animal appearing at the surface of the water.

[9] Numerous mammals, including dogs, polar bears, many sea mammals, and some men, have a baculum.

[10] See in particular the interesting article by Oreskov, C., and Sejersen, F., "Arctic: The attack on Inuit whale hunting by animal rights groups," *IWGIA Newsletter,* 1993.

Aboriginal Criminal Justice:
From Imposed Justice to Power Transfer

Mylène Jaccoud[1]

The administration of the justice system within Native communities has gone through several transformations in Canada. Under the pressure of First Nations' claims, the model of imposition has left room for others based on adaptation of practices, participation, consultation and partial power transfers towards Native communities. Such power transfers within the justice field, which started in the 1990s, are part of a more general movement of communitarization of the penal system and diversion of some conflicts. They are not specific to native communities and are limited by several factors, particularly by the founding premises of the relations between the state and First Nations, namely the principle of incorporation of Native Peoples into the law of the state and the socio-economic conditions of Native communities.

1. Introduction

Criminal justice practices and policies in Aboriginal circles have undergone many changes over the last 30 years. At present, the accent is placed on a (professed or implemented) will to establish initiatives inspired by the philosophy and principles of negotiated or even independent justice. In this paper we will discuss power transfers concerning criminal justice in Aboriginal communities to see what has begun and how far it has progressed, and to identify and draw out the forms of power transfer and the issues that are being raised.

2. The imposition of Colonial Legal Systems

Legal anthropologists have gathered much documentation on the existence, vitality and effectiveness of social regulatory practices in Aboriginal communities before and at the time of first contact with European-Canadians. While we will not review in detail pre-colonial practices and ordering of transgressions, it is clear that Aboriginal communities generally applied the principles of negotiated and often restorative justice. They generally reserved punitive and exclusionist practices for extreme cases and serious transgressions, in particular those that threatened the survival of the group.[2]

Colonization and its "logical" outcome, namely the establishment of the Canadian nation-state, deeply disrupted traditional legal systems. The disruption was the result of both a complex, unequal power struggle, and a concomitant and deliberate policy of reducing and neutralizing Aboriginal customary practices in order to achieve colonial ends.[3] Since the process of colonization took different forms depending on the geopolitical conditions, it took several centuries to curtail traditional dispute resolution methods and practices. The process was fastest in Aboriginal nations and communities located close to colonial metropolises.[4]

Note[5] that the curtailment, neutralization and, probably in some places, dismantling of Aboriginal communities' regulatory processes began and developed at speeds[6] that depended on the circumstances and various issues.

Initially, the processes arose out of a nascent nation-state's political and symbolic desire to assert its identity and its sovereignty over land. The state was less concerned by forms of deviance and problem situations that were clearly only marginal at the beginning of colonization. These issues, coupled with a virtual absence of pressing social problems, helped to gradually impose Canadian criminal law. Indeed, from the beginning and especially in the seventeenth century, the colonizers were inclined to tolerate traditional Aboriginal justice systems when the conflict in question remained within the community. However, the full weight of the colonizer's justice system came down on any member of an Aboriginal nation who attacked a French or British subject.[7] Thus, the law was a political and symbolic reassertion of colonial power. This observation is consistent with conflict theories of the role of the criminal justice system in maintaining and reproducing the social and economic order of the governing classes.[8] Reinforced assertion of identity and emerging economic interests helped to strengthen and accelerate the imposition of Euro-Canadian law. The political and identity-related stakes remained intrinsically linked to changes in the power relations between the Aboriginal nations and the government. Thus, it is very difficult to dissociate the Euro-Canadian criminal law imposition policy from the rest of the government's policies and practices respecting the Aboriginal nations and especially the consequences of those policies and practices.

Indeed, the incorporation of Aboriginals into the nation-state with respect to politics, economics and identity necessarily reduced and neutralized local powers. That was the point. The balance of power and consequently the (unequal) economic relations helped to produce profound and rapid changes in all aspects of social life in Aboriginal societies. Colonialism and the resulting changes shook up and destabilized local powers, helping to undermine Aboriginal communities' independence and especially Aboriginal mechanisms for controlling the new social disorder, which was caused largely by the changes and dispossession. Social disorganization and its many accompanying problems (such as criminality and violence) also helped to legitimize the intervention of the state legal system. This is probably the key to the complexity of the development of the criminal justice system in Aboriginal communities. The development was non-linear, and always determined by fluctuations in the power relations between Aboriginal nations and the state. The dialectical incorporation of Aboriginals into the nation-state and the resulting diminishment of power have produced forms of and practices pertaining to resistance, and therefore sparked a process of decolonization in which, paradoxically, the government has participated. The dialectic, intrinsic to the development of criminal justice in Aboriginal circles, makes it more complex to analyse the power transfers that are now said to have begun. In fact, it would probably be a mistake to see the power relations between Aboriginals and colonizers with respect to criminal law as pure coercion.[9] Alliances between Aboriginals and colonizers have also favoured the incorporation of Aboriginal nations into the colonizer's legal system through acculturation.[10] Moreover, some observers note that Aboriginal nations had greater understanding of the legal system of French settlers than of that of the British, which facilitated the Aboriginals' acculturation in relation to the colonizer's law.[11]

3. Key Developments in Aboriginal Criminal Justice

Those responsible for enforcing criminal law, namely police officers and judges for the most part, will experience moral, social and political dilemmas that will translate into some ambivalence in the way that they apply criminal law in the next 100 years. While colonialism saw criminal law as an instrument of integration, a political lever for ensuring the submission of conquered peoples, and a civilizing and pacifying tool, it was also applied in a moderate manner on the basis of racist or race-based considerations. For example, in 1941, following the Belcher Islands case,[12] the officers of the court questioned the way that justice was administered, and more specifically its scope. Aboriginals' inferiority was then invoked to explain the limits of criminal justice enforcement. Various solutions were considered, such as amending the *Criminal Code*, applying it in a minimal, flexible manner, creating new sanctions,[13] increasing police supervision, and educating Aboriginals about the law. Combined with the principle of equality before the law, legal education for Aboriginals and flexible application of criminal law were the foundations for the administration of justice in Aboriginal communities in the twentieth century. Thus, the principle of equality before the law gathers citizens into a nation; it is a principle that consecrates the subjection of citizens to the state.

Our hypothesis is that, paradoxically, the race-based criteria invoked to justify differences in the application of criminal law created the conditions not only for the survival of customary dispute resolution principles among Aboriginals, but also for the transfer of powers to handle legal issues. In fact, it is on the basis of such survival that leaders legitimize their claims to powers with respect to criminal justice.

In Canada, the Trudeau government's 1969 White Paper suggested the abolition of special status for Aboriginals. This was the impetus for the organization of a pan-Canadian Aboriginal self-government movement, which was institutionalized and strengthened by the creation of local and national associations.[14] In consequence, Aboriginal nations have made major political gains: not only were the recommendations in the white paper never implemented but, in addition, section 35, paragraph 1 of the *Constitution Act, 1982* now recognizes and affirms "The existing aboriginal and treaty rights of the aboriginal peoples of Canada".[15]

In parallel with the movement to acknowledge the legal status of the Aboriginal nations, there was also a movement to identify and raise awareness of social and criminality problems in Aboriginal communities. As we will see, the movement is crucial to understanding the policies and guidelines concerning criminal law enforcement in Aboriginal communities.

In 1967, an initial report on criminal justice enforcement in Aboriginal communities identified a number of problems and difficulties, including the over-representation of Aboriginals in prisons and penitentiaries across Canada[16] and the extension of police services into reserves and "Indian" bands. [17] Applying the law in Aboriginal communities was considered difficult because of the political, social, economic and legal context. Solutions suggested by the authors of the report included the establishment of "special and decentralized" police forces, and also the participation of Aboriginals in such forces. In 1971, the Department of Indian Affairs and Northern Development[18] obtained approval from the Treasury Board to set up a program designed to increase the number of police officers on reserves. The position of band police officer was created, with a primary mandate to assist regular police officers. It was not until the Department of Indian Affairs and Northern Development filed a report in 1973[19] that the question of police officers in Aboriginal communities arose again. Even though a number of avenues were explored (including the development of "independent" police forces), the recommendation adopted at that point was the development of an Aboriginal police force (through a "special" constable program) within the Royal Canadian Mounted Police ("RCMP"). The RCMP's Native Special Constable Program began that very year, opening the way to the institution of similar programs in other Canadian police forces in the 1970s.[20]

The reasons for the creation of a "special" constabulary are part of a logic that seeks to reconcile two extremes in power relations between the state and Aboriginals. On one hand, the state's interest (and more specifically the interest of government law enforcement officials) lies in alleviating tensions between police forces and Aboriginal communities, reducing criminality, lowering the alarming rates of Aboriginal over-incarceration, promoting legal education for Aboriginals and curtailing the racism and prejudices of "white" police officers. On the other hand, the Aboriginal nations' interest (at least as reconstructed by government authorities) lies in obtaining better police services that are more adapted to their cultural traditions and in encouraging the participation of Aboriginals in government institutions. Thus we can consider that Aboriginal constabularies were designed to pacify (respond to Aboriginal claims and reduce disputes), prevent problems (reduce Aboriginal criminalization and over-criminalization) and enhance culture (strengthen Aboriginal traditions). Indeed, there is a parallel between the development of Aboriginal constabulary programs and the multiculturalism policy. In 1970, the Canadian government implemented a multiculturalism policy based on recognition of Canada's diversity. The policy encourages police forces to actively recruit representatives of minority groups in order to "reflect Canadian diversity". The same type of argument is invoked in the various reports and studies praising the advantages of recruiting representatives of minority groups to join the forces of state order.[21] Aboriginals are thus the reflection of such diversity, except that their historical relationship with the Canadian nation-state turns Aboriginal groups into legitimate claimants of rights and powers.

In the Aboriginal police force movement that began in the 1970s, band police officers and special constabulary forces had minimal powers. They enforced local regulations (municipal by-laws), had powers only on reserves and were allowed to investigate only petty offences. Since the policing policy agreements have been under the responsibility of the Solicitor General (1992), Aboriginal police programs have been standardized.[22] However, at present, some Aboriginal police officers still do not have the status of peace officer (for example, the officers serving the Dakota-Ojibwa tribe in Manitoba), and even when they have greater powers, they still have to enforce the legislation and regulations adopted by the state and answer to two separate authorities: the band council and the government.[23]

In the 1980s, as Aboriginal constabularies were developing, various initiatives were undertaken to adapt the justice system to the "particularities" of Aboriginal nations. Two forms of action were considered: providing non-Aboriginal state justice officers with training on the realities faced by Aboriginals (through awareness courses and programs) and adapting Aboriginals to the state justice system (through training on the justice system and the creation of intermediary services, such as paralegal counsellors responsible for advising and informing Aboriginal offenders). These initiatives are still in effect.

In 1991, the federal government adopted a policy known as the Aboriginal Justice Initiative[24] in order to find solutions to recurring problems (over-representation in prisons and penitentiaries, and Aboriginal incomprehension of and resistance to the state justice system). In 1996, the policy was extended as the Aboriginal Justice Strategy.[25] It mandates the Department of Justice to develop the administration of justice under the Aboriginal self-government policy.[26] The recommended approach is to strengthen initiatives that promote Aboriginal participation and self-policing, and are designed to reduce crime and incarceration rates among young and adult Aboriginals. The "national strategy" is strongly coloured by many reports and task forces[27] on administration of justice in Aboriginal communities recommending the total or partial transfer of justice powers to Aboriginal peoples. It is in this spirit that the appointment of Aboriginal justices of the peace is encouraged. Indeed, the *Indian Act* contains provisions for such appointments that predate Confederation.[28] For example, section 107 provides for the appointment of special justices of the peace and the creation of courts on reserves.[29] The Mohawk communities in Ontario and Québec were first to use the provision to request the creation of an Aboriginal court.[30] However, it should be noted that the provisions stipulate that the powers of justices of the peace are limited to violations of municipal by-laws and *Criminal Code* provisions concerning cruelty to animals, common assault, breaking and entering, and vagrancy. Moreover, band councils do not appoint justices of the peace. Instead, this is the prerogative of the Department of Indian Affairs, which takes the band council's recommendations into account. In order to expand the powers of Aboriginal justices of the peace, public authorities in Aboriginal communities have relied on provincial provisions concerning courts of law.[31] Thus, justices of the peace can hear pre-trial proceedings, sentence a person found guilty by summary procedure under the terms of the *Criminal Code*, set bail, release people on bail, receive criminal information and issue arrest warrants.

Adapting sentencing practices to the specificity attributed to Aboriginal peoples is an approach that has always been favoured by administration of justice in relations with Aboriginal nations. While, as we mentioned above, adaptation was initially motivated by racist considerations, it was later promoted on the basis of respect for cultural uniqueness. Thus, though they were forced to respect the constitutional principle of civic equality, judges working in the first itinerant courts tried to take into account the specificity of Aboriginals by handing down sentences that did not constrain freedom (such as community work) or by consulting, for example, a council of elders before sentencing. In the early 1990s, judges implemented a process of community consultation and participation with respect to sentencing, better known as circle sentencing.[32] Such means of adapting sentencing to the culture were formalized on September 3, 1996 by the adoption of section 718.2(e) of the *Criminal Code*. It stipulates "all available sanctions other than imprisonment that are reasonable in the circumstances should be considered for all offenders, with particular attention to the circumstances of aboriginal offenders".[33] In 1999, the Supreme Court of Canada rendered the first decision in which section 718.2(e) was interpreted. It said, "judges should pay particular attention to the circumstances of aboriginal offenders <u>because those circumstances are unique</u>, and different from those of non-aboriginal offenders".[34] Two types of "unique circumstances" were identified: distinct systemic and historical factors (systemic discrimination) and Aboriginal heritage. Section 718.2(e) is designed to alleviate the endemic problem of Aboriginal over-representation in prisons and penitentiaries while asking judges to sentence in a manner more respectful of Aboriginal traditions.

This survey of the development of criminal justice with respect to Aboriginals would be incomplete if we failed to mention the many restorative justice initiatives. Many dejudicialization programs (for both adults and minors)[35] have been established and are different from those for non-Aboriginals because they are less restrictive. For example, dejudicialization initiatives for Aboriginals tend to cover a wider range of offences. They are part of the Canadian criminal justice system, in particular the alternative measures provided for in the *Young Offenders Act*[36] and more recently (1997) in the *Criminal Code*. However, the programs remain discretionary. Justice committees have also been set up, particularly in Québec, to transfer dispute resolution and (generally minor) offence management powers to Aboriginal communities while promoting mechanisms such as mediation and dispute resolution circles.

Finally, the *Corrections and Conditional Release Act*[37] is the only piece of corrections legislation that contains provisions promoting the delivery of specific services to Aboriginal clients. Canadian correctional services have hired Aboriginal liaison officers and offer spiritual services in their institutions. Correctional centres[38] and transition houses for Aboriginals have also opened in some provinces. The National Parole Board recently created "releasing circles" and "community assisted hearings".[39]

4. Towards a Power Transfer?

According to Morse,[40] the result of mixing the colonizer's law with that of the colonized can range from simple *rejection* of Aboriginal systems of law and justice, to the *incorporation* of Aboriginal law in the colonizer's law or a degree of *cooperation* between the two, or to complete separation. While Morse considers that Canada embodies the cooperative model, we believe that the development of criminal justice with respect to Aboriginals shows that Canada is oriented towards the rejection of Aboriginal legal principles because none of those principles has changed the content of Canada's criminal law. However, it has to be admitted that Canada's criminal law has been deeply and constantly torn between the necessity of maintaining legal and political borders and the need to recognize that Aboriginal nations have a unique status, which Aboriginal peoples have acquired through political, legal and social struggle. This pair of constraints is the reason for Canada's political choice to *adapt the implementation of criminal law* with respect to Aboriginals rather than to amend the content. The exclusion of the principles of Aboriginal peoples' law thus remains moderated or limited in so far as the government has agreed to the expression of certain particularities. Moreover, LaPrairie[41] identifies four principles that structure the enforcement of justice with respect to Aboriginals: equity, equality, the "right of Aboriginals to participate in justice proceedings" and "cultural distinctiveness". Rouland[42] notes three types of innovation that flow from the government's will to adapt the legal system and judicial apparatus. The first consists in assigning new roles to "para-traditional" bodies,[43] the second in assigning traditional roles to new bodies,[44] and the third in creating institutions described as "assimilatory mediation systems". [45] According to Rouland, under the cover of adaptation, these innovations have precipitated the assimilation of Aboriginals into the state legal system.

In fact, the way that the relations between the state and Aboriginals have developed in the criminal justice sector indicates that the incorporation of Aboriginals into the colonizer's law is the basic premise of every initiative so far. This premise has also been behind the adaptation policies and practices that have been employed. As we have seen, the reasons for setting up such initiatives have changed over the last 100 years. The adaptation of criminal law procedures was initially motivated by racist ideas that Euro-Canadians had about Aboriginals, whom they considered too "primitive" to understand the colonizer's legal system. Next it was long motivated by a culturalist view of Aboriginals (for example, the principle of cultural distinctiveness of which LaPrairie speaks). It was only recently that adaptation policies and practices were infused with a more structural perspective. The amendments to the part of the *Criminal Code* encouraging judges to consider Aboriginal status as a differentiating criterion in sentencing are eloquent, particularly following the Supreme Court decision. Sentencing must be distinct (in other words less punitive and excluding) because of the prejudice that the Aboriginal nations have suffered and that must now be reduced or remedied.

Note also that the policy of adapting state criminal law and institutions works in two ways because the government hopes to influence the actors at both ends of the relationship. There are initiatives designed to adapt Aboriginals to the state justice system (in particular through the training and appointment of para-legal counsellors) and other initiatives intended to adapt non-Aboriginal law officers to the lifestyle and principles of Aboriginal communities (through training and awareness courses on Aboriginal mores and customs and by including Aboriginals in the justice system, which is better known as "indigenization"). While the indigenization policy is one way of changing government institutions, or at least those institutions' relationship to minorities, what is of course at stake is the assimilation of Aboriginals into the state justice system.[46] Note that the indigenization policy has proceeded in two ways: by the insertion of Aboriginals into the state apparatus, and by the creation of parallel institutions that are controlled by the state. Indeed, the initiatives to include Aboriginals in the state apparatus can be separated into two types depending on the kind of power because Aboriginals have decision-making authority in some cases (for example, special constables and Aboriginal corrections staff), and consultative powers in others (such as sentencing and release circles). Initiatives that involve the creation of parallel institutions confer decision-making powers (for example, in the cases of Aboriginal police forces and courts, Aboriginal justices of the peace, and justice councils) or hybrid decision-making and consultative powers (for example, when healing circles and sentencing circles are juxtaposed).[47]

In this context, should we conclude that the state has adopted a policy of transferring criminal justice powers to Aboriginal communities? Adaptation policies are not power transfer policies but principles for managing relations between the state and Aboriginals so as to soften the effects of the incorporation and assimilation of Aboriginals. Aboriginal resistance and claims are an integral part of the effects that the state seeks to contain in order to maintain the cohesion of its legal and national borders. In contrast, adaptation that proceeds by indigenizing the criminal justice system (through the insertion of Aboriginals in state apparatus and the creation of parallel institutions) has made it possible to define the parameters for a partial power transfer. Indeed, even integrated into the state legal system (and therefore bound to apply the state's legal standards), an Aboriginal police officer, justice of the peace, court or justice committee has a margin of manoeuvre and real decision-making power. However, such powers are limited by the basic premise of the legal and national incorporation of Aboriginals, particularly with respect to Aboriginal peoples' ability to establish their own legal standards (since their margin of manoeuvre is limited to the preparation of municipal by-laws, which have to comply with the charters and other legislation and regulations). The powers are also limited by the nature of the offences that Aboriginal communities are empowered to manage. Indeed, all of the initiatives that give Aboriginal communities power to deal with crime are oriented towards relatively minor offences.

Even though it is consistent with or meets the political agendas of Aboriginal leaders and government actors, the power transfer process with respect to criminal justice that began in the 1990s is part of a more general movement towards the communitarianization of criminal justice and decriminalization of certain disputes, which are to be handled by more or less formal authorities in the community. The stakes in such transfers are eminently economic and belong to a strategy for reducing public expenditures, increasing citizen responsibility in the fight against crime and deploying prevention strategies that the state delegates and/or shares with the community. However, does making the community responsible for managing crime really help to empower it? Does a community that is responsible for managing disputes really have authority? In the end, is transferring responsibilities to a community the same as transferring powers? In the case of Aboriginal communities, the transfer of the management of (minor) disputes and offences is clearly part of a process of reconstruction of identity and political status that promotes Aboriginal traditions and values with respect to dispute resolution. However, as some observers have noted, do such transfers of responsibility not involve some problems?[48] The absence of human and financial resources, and the size of the social problems limit the ability of Aboriginal communities to regain control over their destinies. The exhaustion, discouragement and rate of turnover of personnel (paid and volunteer), and the lack of training also limit communities' potential to implement the criminal justice powers transferred or conceded. Resistance from Aboriginals themselves, in particular from women, also presents a serious obstacle to the repatriation of powers by communities. National associations of Aboriginal women have publicly denounced the violence and insecurity in their communities. During the Royal Commission on Aboriginal Peoples, they opposed the development of independent Aboriginal justice systems so long as legal protection (in particular that provided by the charters) was not guaranteed.[49] Add to this what Bottoms calls the "twin track policy",[50] which establishes two parallel means of managing criminality in which the state tends to relegate the management of various forms of rudeness and petty crime to communities while maintaining and strengthening its intervention with respect to crimes that are considered serious. The result is preservation of confusion as well as the state's legendary paternalism with respect to the Aboriginal nations. Objective borderlines between minor offences and major crimes can certainly be drawn, and yet they still remain very subjective. The criteria for seriousness established by the state do not always coincide with those of Aboriginal communities, and they in no way provide an indication of a community's ability to resolve a dispute. Indeed, depending on the circumstances, a minor offence could be difficult to handle in a community whereas another crime, even a serious one, could be easy.

At this point, it is difficult to determine whether the policies that emerged in the 1990s for transferring powers to Aboriginal communities reflect a clear trend because they have been developing in parallel with those focussing on adaptation of law and judicial practices, as well as participation of Aboriginals. They remain dependent on the principle of incorporating Aboriginals into the state system of criminal law. Yet, they are essentially based on very different principles. Adaptation, participation and incorporation are ways of assimilating Aboriginals, even though the effects are attenuated by the adoption of principles and practices by which Aboriginal cultures are promoted. By reducing structural conflicts to cultural disputes, the state manages to deflect Aboriginals' political claims by recognizing culture and, sometimes, folklore. Under such circumstances, how can we understand and reconcile the development of policies that are apparently based on diverging principles: the state concedes powers, incorporates Aboriginals, maintains its legal borders, promotes some cultural principles, consults Aboriginals and adapts. Is it consistent to simultaneously develop participatory, independent and imposed justice? Some distance has to be taken to better assess the impact of these apparently contradictory policies.

---

[1] Professor, Centre international de criminologie comparée, Université de Montréal, Montréal, Québec

[2] Rouland, N., "Les modes juridiques de solution des conflits chez les Inuit" (1079) 3 *Études inuit* 171; Jefferson, C., *La conquête par le droit*, Collection sur les Autochtones, Ottawa: Attorney General of Canada, 1994. [Jefferson].

[3] Jaccoud, M., "Le Droit, l'exclusion et les Autochtones" (1996) 11:2 *RCDS/CJLS* 217–234; Jaccoud, M., "Processus pénal et identitaire: le cas des Inuit au Nouveau-Québec" (1992) 24:2 *Sociologie et Sociétés* 25–43.

[4] Aboriginal nations (in particular the Ojibways, Iroquois, Hurons and Micmacs) were confronted with the (French or English) colonizer's criminal justice system mainly beginning in the seventeenth century, while northern communities, because of their geographical distance from the metropolises, faced it later. For example, the Inuit of Nunavik did not come into contact with the police system until the twentieth century. See Jaccoud, M., *Justice blanche au Nunavik*, Montréal: Méridien, 1995.

[5] *Supra* note 3.

[6] The French were less distant than the British with respect to the Aboriginal nations, and mixed with their Aboriginal allies. Consequently, the traditional Aboriginal justice system conflicted with the French system earlier than with the English system. See Jefferson, *supra* note 2.

[7] Aboriginals were often sentenced more harshly than the French or British (when the offender belonged to the same group as the colonizer), *ibid.*

[8] See in particular crucial theses in criminology, such as in Quinney, R., *Critique of Legal Order*, Boston: Little Brown, 1974; Quinney, R., *Class, State and Crime*, New York: David McKay, 1977; Turk, A..T., *Criminality and Legal Order*, Chicago: Rand McNally, 1969 and Vold, G.B., *Theoretical Criminology*, New York: Oxford University Press, 1958.

[9] Smandych and Lee report a change in theoretical perspective in the 1980s among the proponents of legal pluralism in which the study of the relations between Europeans and Aboriginals is more subtle and the focus is less on the coercive and insidious imposition of European law and more on Aboriginal peoples' forms of resistance and accommodation. See Smandych, R., and Lee, G., "Une approche de l'étude de droit et du colonialisme: vers une perspective auto historique amérindienne sur le changement juridique, la colonisation, les sexes et la résistance à la colonisation" (1995) 28:1 *Criminologie* at 55–79.

[10] Rouland, N., "L'acculturation judiciaire chez les Inuit au Canada," Part 1, (1983) 13:3 *Recherches amérindiennes au Québec* 179–191, and "L'acculturation judiciaire chez les Inuit au Canada," Part 2, (1983) 13:4 *Recherches amérindiennes au Québec* 307–318.

[11] Jefferson, *supra* note 2.

[12] The Belcher Islands case involved religious fanaticism in which nine Inuit died. According to A. Goyette, the main reason why the justice system wished to impose itself was because of the major publicity that the series of murders received. The justice system was seeking to reassure public opinion by intervening. See Goyette, A., *L'administration de la justice au Nouvelle-Québec inuit: de l'évolution d'une justice imposée*, Master's thesis, Laval University, 1987 (unpublished).

[13] The creation of new punishments was studied by Cory, an administrator in the north, and was suggested to the Deputy Minister of Justice on June 22, 1945. Cory recommended that offenders be punished by humiliating them in front of the community; for example, a murderer could be whipped in public. In the case of minor offences, the family allowance could be suspended, *ibid.*

[14] For example, Femmes autochtones du Québec was founded in 1974, the Assembly of First Nations in 1980 and the Metis National Council in 1983.

[15] *Constitution Act, 1982*, Schedule B of the *Canada Act 1982* (U. K.), 1982, c.11.

[16] The over-representation has been constantly reported and confirmed ever since, and has been the main focus of research, policies and practices pertaining to criminal justice. This has been supplemented with a considerable number of studies highlighting the family violence, alcoholism, drug abuse and suicide problems that Aboriginal communities routinely experience.

[17] Canada, Canadian Corrections Association, *Indians and the Law*, Ottawa, Queen's Printer, 1967.

[18] The Department of Indian Affairs and Northern Development was mandated to monitor agreements concerning police services until 1992. In 1992, the mandate was transferred to the Department of the Solicitor General. See the Royal Commission on Aboriginal Peoples, *Bridging the Cultural Divide: A Report on Aboriginal People and Criminal Justice in Canada*, Ottawa: Supplies and Services Canada, 1996 [hereinafter the Royal Commission on Aboriginal Peoples].

[19] Canada, Policing on Reserves, Oshawa, Ontario: Indian Affairs and Northern Development Canada, 1973.

[20] Some examples of such programs are the Ontario First Nations police officer program (1975), the Sûreté du Québec special constable program (1978), the Amerindian Police of Québec (1978) and the Kahnawake Peacekeepers (1979). See Depew, R., *Les services de police aux Autochtones du Canada: examen de la question*, Ottawa: Solicitor General of Canada, 1986; see also the Royal Commission on Aboriginal Peoples, *supra* note 18.

[21] See Jaccoud. M., and M. Felices, "Ethnicization of Canadian Policing" (1999) 14:1 *RCDS/CJLS* 83–100.

[22] In June 1991, the federal government adopted the First Nations Policing Policy. The program has been administered by the Department of the Solicitor General since 1992 and is based on a partnership model. Tripartite agreements are negotiated (between the federal, provincial and local Aboriginal governments) to

establish and develop police forces in Aboriginal communities.

[23] Royal Commission on Aboriginal Peoples, *supra* note 18.

[24] Justice Canada, Ottawa: Supplies and Services Canada, 1991.

[25] Justice Canada, Ottawa: Supplies and Services Canada, 1996.

[26] Canadian Criminal Justice Association, *Aboriginal Peoples and the Criminal Justice System*, Ottawa: Canadian Criminal Justice Association, 2000.

[27] See, among others, the Royal Commission on Aboriginal Peoples, *supra* note 18; Law Reform Commission of Canada, *Aboriginal Peoples and the Criminal Justice System*, Ottawa: Supplies and Services Canada, 1991; Québec, Report of the Comité consultatif sur les Autochtones et la justice au Québec, *La justice pour et par les Autochtones,* Québec City: Bibliothèque nationale du Québec, 1995; and Hamilton, A.C., and C. M. Sinclair, *The Justice System and Aboriginal People: Report of the Aboriginal Justice Inquiry of Manitoba,* Vol. 1, Winnipeg: Queen's Printer, 1991.

[28] S.C. 1876, in particular 39 Victoria, c. 18, s. 70.

[29] Originally, this provision was designed to facilitate the assimilation of Aboriginals by having the government appoint an Aboriginal justice of the peace who would be responsible for enforcing order when Aboriginals were settled on the reserve. See the Royal Commission on Aboriginal Peoples, *supra* note 18 at 113.

[30] The Kahnawake court has been in existence since 1974, *ibid.* at 114.

[31] Some provinces and territories have adopted specific laws for developing Aboriginal justice of the peace programs. In Québec, this kind of initiative is still very limited because the province has less than ten justices of the peace, including those in Inuit territory.

[32] Concretely, participants (members of the community) sit in a circle with the judge, the accused and the victim to express and share their points of view on the conflict before coming to a decision (recommendation) that can guide the judge in sentencing. Usually the circles involve the participation (or presence) of 20 to 30 people. For a more detailed analysis of the principles and conditions of circle sentencing, see Jaccoud, M., "Cercles de guérison et cercles de sentences: une justice réparatrice?" (1999) 32:1 *Criminologie* 79–105 [hereinafter Cercles de guérison et cercles de sentences].

[33] This section is in the new Part XXIII of the *Criminal Code*, R.S.C. 1985, c. C-46, concerning sentencing.

[34] *R.* v. *Gladue*, [1999] 1 S.C.R. 688 [hereinafter *Gladue*].

[35] For example, forestry camp programs for young offenders, healing circles and family conferencing.

[36] 1985, c. Y-1.

[37] 1992, c. 20.

[38] The first detention centre for Aboriginal women under federal responsibility is the Okimaw Ohci Centre at Maple Creek, Saskatchewan; 60% of its staff are Aboriginal.

[39] Experiments have been conducted with at least six circles of this type in the Prairies. Circle participants convey information intended to inform Parole Board members when making decisions on the ideal conditions for release. See Canada, National Parole Board, *Pushing the Envelope of Human Rights through Innovation and Creativity in Aboriginal Corrections*, online: http://www.npb-cnlc.gc.ca/

infocntr/aborig_e.htm, 2001.

[40] Morse, B.W., "Indigenous Law and State Legal System: Conflict and Compatibility" in Morse, B.W., and G. R. Woodman, Eds., *Indigenous Law and the State,* Dordrecht: Foris Publications, 1988, 101–120.

[41] LaPrairie, C., "La justice pénale chez les Autochtones du Canada. Principes et pratiques" (1989) 13:1 *Anthropologie et Sociétés,* 143–154.

[42] Rouland, *supra* note 10 at 310.

[43] Local authorities in communities would act as filters with respect to the state justice system, and would use traditional dispute resolution mechanisms in some situations. In case of failure, they would refer the situation to government legal authorities. See Rouland, *supra* note 10.

[44] Thus, Aboriginal police forces, which are relatively new institutions, use their discretionary power to dejudicialize some situations. *Ibid.*

[45] An example of this can be seen in the para-legal counselors who were made official in the 1980s and act as legal advisors to offenders. Para-legal counselors thus foster the assimilation of the principles and operation of Euro-Canadian law. *Ibid.*

[46] See Haveman, P., "The Indigenization of Social Control in Canada", in Silverman, R.A., and M. O. Nielson, Eds., *Aboriginal Peoples and Canadian Criminal Justice,* Toronto: Butterworths, 1992, 111–119.

[47] See *Cercles de guérison et cercles de sentences, supra* note 32.

[48] See in particular LaPrairie, C., "The 'new' justice: Some implications for aboriginal communities" (1998) 40:1 *Canadian Journal of Criminology,* 61–79, and Linden, R., and D. Clairmont, *Making it Work: Planning and Evaluating Community Corrections and Healing Projects in Aboriginal Communities,* Ottawa: Solicitor General, 1998.

[49] Royal Commission on Aboriginal Peoples, *supra* note 18. See in particular the report by the Pauktuutit Inuit Women's Association, *Report on a Sentencing Circle in Nunavik,* Ottawa: Pauktuutit, 1994.

[50] Bottoms, A., "Reflection on the Renaissance of Dangerousness" (1977) 16:2 *Howard Journal of Penology and Crime Prevention* 88.

Elections, Traditional Aboriginal Governance and the *Charter*

Ghislain Otis[1]

"We are greatly concerned that Aboriginal people are increasingly equating 'democracy' with the act of voting."[2]

1. Introduction

The implementation of Aboriginal self-government raises the central issue of the role of elections as a means of devolving power among Aboriginal peoples. Do political modernity and good governance dictate that Aboriginal peoples always choose their representatives through the electoral system that gradually evolved in the Western state system? Is the democratic imperative of consent of the governed as strong and does it operate in the same manner in the Aboriginal context? Can this imperative be satisfied through non-electoral procedures or highly distinctive electoral operations fashioned in accordance with present-day interpretations of Aboriginal traditions?

These questions would probably not arise if Canadian law had irrevocably dissolved traditional Aboriginal political institutions into the state electoral system. However, while the state's domestication of Aboriginal political organizations has been taken very far, it still remains imperfect. Indeed, recent draft legislation by the Government of Canada has breathed new life into the debate because, if approved by Parliament, the new statutory framework would have accentuated Aboriginal cultural specificity and attenuated the role of elections in the choice of community leaders.

In this article, I will provide a brief overview of how the traditional political institutions of Canada's Aboriginal peoples have been changed by the gradual introduction of elections as the means of choosing community leaders. I will also analyze current criticism of the electoral model based on Aboriginal difference and argue that the state cannot legitimately cling to a dogmatic conception of democracy and set aside all alternatives to elections as a means of expressing the consent of the governed in the Aboriginal context. Finally, I will also try to identify the constitutional constraints bearing upon non-electoral democracy, in particular, those flowing from the *Canadian Charter of Rights and Freedoms.*[3]

Singularly Canadian in some respects, the issues discussed in this article are known in other countries facing the challenge of reconciling tradition and modernity or confronted with the need to heal the painful legacy of colonization.[4]

2. State Domestication of Aboriginal Government in Canada

It is not easy to trace the history of the political organization of pre-Columbian societies. Generally, the first European observers either took John Locke's approach,[5] and therefore doubted that there was any genuine political organization in pre-colonial Aboriginal societies, or described Indigenous customs in an ethnocentric manner that was more suited to their "civilizing" goals than an accurate assessment of reality.[6] Aboriginal oral tradition itself does not always clear the fog surrounding the political systems operating at that point in Americas' history.

Historians have shown that the great cultural diversity of pre-Columbian communities was reflected in the ways that they were governed and thus legitimized and devolved power. Sedentary and semi-sedentary chiefdoms on the northwest coast were very hierarchical and clan chiefs acceded to their positions in accordance with a strict conception of blood right.[7] Among a number of semi-sedentary peoples who practiced agriculture on a large scale, such as the Iroquois, the *sachems* designated by the "clan mothers" came from families that customarily had hereditary titles.[8] Generally, groups of Algonquian hunter-gatherers chose their leaders according to a consensual procedure in which elders played special roles as mediators.[9] It seems that in many societies, a chief's real power had its source in his or her exemplary conduct and ability to muster support, rather than in an institutionalized sanction of authority.[10]

These ancestral institutions have been largely eroded by the combined effect of state coercion and inevitable cultural change. The colonial containment of Aboriginal political communities was conducive to the gradual incrustation of state sovereignty. The relative equality that initially characterized the relationships between Indigenous peoples and European powers in North America was followed by the enclosure of Aboriginal societies in the grip of the state. From the state's point of view, this resulted in the "internalization" of Aboriginal issues, in other words, in the confining of Aboriginal status and rights within the exclusive reach of the domestic legal regime.[11]

While regarding the Crown's colonial assertion of sovereignty as unchallengeable, Canadian government is increasingly inclined to admit that some Aboriginal political prerogatives derived from pre-colonial systems may have survived the assertion of Crown sovereignty.[12] According to the "inherent right" doctrine, pre-colonial self-government powers was originally continued by British colonial law as an Aboriginal right,[13] and have therefore been affirmed and recognized by the *Constitution* in 1982.[14] Such an aboriginal right to self-government could, in theory, be exercised in a completely autonomous manner, in other words, without any implementing legislation or treaty. However, no community has yet unilaterally established or reactivated a purely inherent government through which it claims to totally and completely displace the *Indian Act*,[15] which has governed Aboriginal lands and communities since the nineteenth century.

While a growing number of communities have established institutions founded on unique regimes that sometimes protect a substantial degree of political autonomy,[16] the government of a very large majority of communities remains organized and implemented through the *Indian Act*. Under the *Act*, every Aboriginal community is governed by a collegial body called a "band council",[17] which the federal parliament invests with the responsibility of governing the community. Owing to its origins and colonial purposes, this responsibility is fulfilled in many respects under the control or supervision of the federal government.[18] Thus, the state bends and uses community structures to make them a tool for managing Aboriginals and reserves.

3. The Spread of Elections in Aboriginal Communities

In its efforts to take charge of and organize Aboriginal government, the state has focussed on how chiefs are chosen to serve on the politico-administrative body known as the band council. In 1869, the *Act for the gradual enfranchisement of Indians* authorized the government to decree that the chiefs of any tribe, band or body of Aboriginals would be elected by the male members of the community under the supervision of federal authorities, who also had the power to remove elected chiefs from office under certain conditions.[19] All subsequent legislation concerning band government has contained similar provisions, including the present *Indian Act*, in which we find at subsection 74(1):

> *Whenever he deems it advisable for the good government of a band, the Minister may declare by order that after a day to be named therein the council of the band, consisting of a chief and councillors, shall be selected by elections to be held in accordance with this Act.*

Subsection 78(2) of the Act states the reasons for which a position on a band council can become vacant or a chief or band councillor can be declared unfit to hold office. Pursuant to section 76 of the Act, the Governor in Council has established a regulation on band council elections in communities made subject to *Indian Act* electoral provisions by a ministerial order. This regulation deals with in particular the nomination of candidates, the conduct of elections and appeal mechanisms.[20]

In other words, from the beginning, state authorities intended to use the electoral system for selecting Aboriginal leaders. The system was modeled on the Westminster one-round, first-past-the-post system, and was a key feature of the strategy to assimilate Aboriginals into the majority culture.[21] However, the government refrained from suddenly imposing its own electoral practices everywhere. Instead, it "temporarily" maintained customary mechanisms for choosing chiefs in some communities. This transitory arrangement was to be maintained until Aboriginals had "developed" sufficiently to switch to the electoral system. Consistent with the British system of indirect rule, the colonizers' purpose was not to mark their respect for Aboriginal ancestral political culture,[22] but rather to instrumentalize traditional legitimacy until its effectiveness was dissolved through political acculturation.

219

Nonetheless, a significant number of communities had the *Indian Act* electoral system forced on them,[23] sometimes despite strong controversy.[24] Until 1951, implementation of elections remained slow and difficult. It was successful only in a minority of bands.[25] The difficulty sprang both from communities that resisted the "white-man's law", and from federal officials themselves, who were reluctant to act because they thought that the communities were not sufficiently "evolved" to make good use of the electoral mechanisms set out in the *Indian Act*. The federal government preferred to exercise close *de facto* control over the practices of communities to which the *Indian Act* electoral provisions were not applied. Bands were informally led to gradually adapt their customs to electoral practices, which were not necessarily in compliance with the prescriptions of the state electoral regime.[26]

Elections gradually spread, even to the so-called customary practices of the communities. This was probably a result of conscious planning by federal officials, as well as the constant influence of the institutions of the majority culture, in which Aboriginals were belatedly permitted to participate as voters after a long period of discriminatory exclusion.[27] This apparent democratic normalization probably explains why the designation of leaders according to a band's "customs" is still recognized in section 2 of the *Indian Act*,[28] and why formal implementation of the electoral regime dictated by the legislation has not been decreed for many communities.[29]

In 1971, over 70% of bands chose their councils in compliance with the *Act's* electoral provisions.[30] Today, only 50% do so because a number have since been exempted by the Minister from compliance with the *Act* so that they can apply their own "customary" electoral codes. This is often described as a "return" to custom.[31] Today, only 11 communities still appoint their leaders according to traditional non-electoral hereditary customs.[32]

According to the Federal Court, the "custom" referred to in the *Indian Act* is "a practice established or adopted as a result of the individuals to whom it applies having accepted to be governed in accordance therewith".[33] The courts have confirmed the validity, with respect to custom, of any rule that is "generally acceptable to members of the band and upon which there is broad consensus".[34] The party who invokes the custom has to prove its existence and content.[35]

In this context, the adjective "customary" does not refer to the *jus non scriptum* archetype used by legal anthropologists. Here, a rule is considered "customary" simply because it is originally developed outside of the formal state apparatus. The term therefore carries no *a priori* conceptions about how the rule is developed, the formal manner in which it is stated or the compliance of its content with any pre-colonial or traditional standard. While to a certain extent it authorizes an Aboriginal group to mark its cultural difference with respect to political organization, custom is not necessarily synonymous with tradition. Instead, it is a consensual and community-based means of producing law that, while not materially constrained by ancestral practices, enables contemporaries to find their own path between tradition and modernity.[36]

The *Act* does not impose any conditions as to the form of the rules resulting from a customary process. The community could therefore maintain an unwritten law,[37] or it could codify its practices in a manner similar to legislated state law.[38] In fact, it is not rare for a community's code to contain provisions that are practically identical to the electoral provisions of the *Act* and regulations. Electoral codes are amended as often as necessary to take changing circumstances into account.[39] However, it is possible that an effective, constant practice generally accepted by the community does not correspond to the rules set out in the code. In such a case, the courts have ruled that the customary rule was the one followed in practice, and not the written one.[40]

Not all customary rules of political organization are validated by the Federal Court, since only those pertaining to the composition and formation of the band's leadership body are recognized under the *Indian Act*. However, there is no reason to adopt a strict interpretation of the customary competency recognized in this manner. The customary regime could include a wide range of rules governing not only the formation of the leadership body, but also its structure and composition. The field covered by custom would thus extend to the method for choosing leaders, the duration of their mandates, the conditions under which such people are removed from office, as well as the whole administrative apparatus for enforcing the rules.

Since customary requirements are incorporated into federal law, Canadians courts, in particular the Federal Court, have jurisdiction to provide remedies for breach of custom.[41] Indeed, it is well established that a band council, individual or authority acting in accordance with the band's customs constitutes a "federal board, commission or other tribunal" within the meaning of the *Federal Courts Act*.[42] The courts have often been called upon to rule on the customary validity of action taken with respect to electoral issues, and to award redress appropriate to the circumstances.

4. The Differentialist Critique of Elections among Aboriginal Peoples

At the heart of the dominant line of political thought in Canada, there is the conviction that "elections are the basic principle of representative democracy. They provide leaders with political legitimacy."[43] The Supreme Court of Canada recently noted that:

> Democracy, of course, is a form of government in which sovereign power resides in the people as a whole. In our system of democracy, this means that each citizen must have a genuine opportunity to take part in the governance of the country through participation in the selection of elected representatives.[44]

In the discourse of constitutional modernity, democracy, political representation and elections are an indivisible trinity and the universal condition for just government.[45] Yet, based on cultural difference and tradition, a radical critique of the state model of electoral democracy sometimes appears in Aboriginal circles and in scholarly analysis. The state electoral system is criticized essentially for having broken down the traditional system of leadership without honouring the promise of just government.

For those Aboriginals whose ancestors employed consensual mechanisms to choose chiefs in pre-colonial times, the plurality system can prove hierarchical, a source of conflict and arbitrary because it can exclude from the process many, if not the majority, of the community's members.[46] In other words, elections can be experienced as a step backwards rather than as an advance in community democracy.[47] The ancestral consensualism of some Aboriginal peoples is in fact of undeniable modernity and relevance from the point of view of Western practices, in which "*consensualism* is a recent notion referring to a political culture that gives a primary role to the agreement of individuals".[48] The consensualist approach "opposes reification of debate to deliberation protected from partisan struggles, which is expected to promote prudent and moderate solutions".[49]

The changes that have occurred in Aboriginal societies have not eliminated the role of family circles as focal points of socio-economic and political solidarity. The persistence of this cultural singularity in many communities could explain why a culturally inappropriate electoral system would appear illegitimate. It would, by its very nature, destroy the balance customarily ensured by consensual inter-clan deliberation. The arithmetical logic of "one person, one vote", combined with a one-round, first-past-the-post system, will in many cases ensure that the families or clans with the most members will have lasting control over the reigns of power. Paradoxically, such forms of electoral democracy may produce dynasties, whereas traditional structures tended to ensure broadest possible community support for authority and did not recognize a "reigning family". In addition to failing to reflect the living sociological composition of the communities, this situation opens the way to nepotism and can make those who are excluded become cynical and lose their trust in institutions.[50]

It is also self-evident that the formally egalitarian logic of universal suffrage has undermined the traditional prerogatives of hereditary chiefs and specific groups, such as elders and "clan mothers".

The Assembly of First Nations ("AFN") says that we need to "encourage the establishment of Aboriginal governments based on the traditions of the Aboriginal nations, in particular hereditary systems, clan systems and other government structures."[51] However, the AFN refrains from recommending a simple archaeological reconstitution of political structures that have disappeared forever. Instead, it expresses a desire to see "innovative institutions reflecting tradition and contemporary needs with respect to government."[52] Indeed, alternatives to the Westminster system can be infused with traditional values without excluding elections. For example, the Huron-Wendat community recently adopted an electoral code based on an updated version of ancient lineage-based groupings.[53] The members of the community have been grouped into eight family circles, each with the right to be represented on the nation's council by a "family chief". Chiefs are elected using a double ballot system. In the first round, the voters belonging to each family circle hold a family assembly and vote on the nomination of candidates for the position of family chief. Candidates can also be nominated through a petition from at least 10% of the family clan. In the second round, all of the community's voters can vote on the family chiefs who were nominated in the first round. The vote is based on the principle of preferential majority. The Grand Chief is chosen by universal suffrage from a list of candidates nominated by each family circle at nomination meetings. This original procedure prevents the government body from being taken over by a family, prevents voters from being enclosed within their clans and gives elected chiefs dual legitimacy: that conferred by their families, and that by the community.

Some Aboriginals are however of the opinion that elections are not necessary for democracy and that consensual decision-making is more respectful of pluralism and diversity of opinion.[54] Still others go so far as to repudiate all democratic assumptions, and consider that legitimacy of authority can be based on traditional culture. In particular, this is the discourse of those who argue that Western conceptions of equality and representative democracy should not be obstacles to the maintenance and revitalization of hereditary institutions.[55]

5. The Legal Framework for Challenging the Electoral Model

The spread of elections in customary systems for choosing band chiefs is not irreversible in law. Indeed, this is what makes it interesting and pertinent to reflect on the conditions for adapting and challenging the electoral system to better reflect Aboriginal difference. Communities that are not subject to the electoral regime of the *Indian Act* can change their "customs" to modify or eliminate elections and replace them with another procedure that they consider better adapted to their situation. While such normative autonomy can in theory be displaced at the Minister's discretion pursuant to paragraph 74(1) of the *Indian Act*, the political context of current relations between the government and Aboriginals would be an obstacle to excessive unilateralism by federal authorities. This is why half of all the bands can still choose between electoral democracy and other means of selecting band council members.[56]

The potential for reducing the role of elections would have increased if Parliament had adopted the bill concerning reform of Aboriginal government institutions. Under Bill C-7, the *First Nations Governance Act*,[57] every Aboriginal community in Canada would have been able to hold a referendum to adopt a code concerning leadership selection.[58] Communities currently governed by the legislation's electoral provisions could then have adopted hybrid systems in which the majority of council members would be elected whereas others would be appointed using other means.[59] For such communities, election would have remained the primary process, but it would no longer have been the only means of selecting political leaders.

Communities currently following customary regimes would have been required to codify the rules and provide for appeal mechanisms and procedures by which the code could be amended.[60] Communities currently following electoral regimes could have adopted amendments wholly or partially changing their regimes.[61] Communities operating under non-electoral regimes could have kept their procedures, in accordance with the community's wishes.[62]

Thus it is clear that this reform of Aboriginal governance would have made it legally possible for the electoral principle to lose ground in Aboriginal communities in Canada. Communities that are now wholly subject to the state electoral system could have changed to a regime that would have been only partially electoral, whereas communities governed by custom would have kept their freedom to employ means other than elections to choose chiefs. For Aboriginal peoples, the draft legislation highlighted more than ever the relationships between tradition, democracy and elections.

However, Aboriginal chiefs have challenged the political legitimacy and constitutional validity of the proposed *First Nations Governance Act* because they considered that it would infringe on Aboriginal peoples' inherent right to self-government.[63] The arrival of a new Prime Minister at the end of 2003 has adoption of the reform envisaged in the bill unlikely.

But a very important issue that must now be addressed is whether the *Canadian Charter of Rights and Freedoms* will impact on the quest for alternatives to the state electoral model.

6. The Canadian Charter's Impact on the Development of Alternatives to the State Electoral System

The cultural validity of the liberal ideology of fundamental rights in Aboriginal societies is far from unanimously accepted. Many consider that the individualism celebrated by modern charters of rights cannot legitimately be grafted onto Aboriginal culture, which is reputed to be communitarian and consensual. For those who hold this view, requiring Aboriginal communities to comply with *Charter* rights and freedoms like other Canadian government institutions would be to perpetuate the cultural colonization of Aboriginals.[64]

However, it cannot be assumed that protecting fundamental rights using an instrument such as the Canadian *Charter* is by definition a violation of the integrity or dignity of Aboriginal culture. Those who argue that *Charter* rights and freedoms do not allow the culturally adequate articulation of group and individual rights often questionably conflate Aboriginal difference and ancestral tradition. They do not take seriously the hypothesis that Aboriginals could express a unique, strong and legitimate culture beyond pre-colonial references and traditional values.

Contemporary Aboriginal life is made up of more than the legacy of pre-Columbian ancestors. It also has irrefutably modern characteristics such as sedentary lifestyle, growing individualism, increasingly formal economic relations, urbanization, integration into the bureaucratic structure of public services and government financial transfers, aspirations to economic development through the marketing of land and resources, quests for salaried employment, consumerism, subjection to mass media and technologies, promotion of education and technical training, existential crises among youth lacking direction, and painful reworking of relationships between men and women.

As government bureaucracy, a structure with no equivalent in the traditional world, has become omnipresent in the lives of Aboriginal communities, the ability of public powers to affect the socioeconomic interests, security and freedom of Aboriginals has reached a degree unprecedented in the history of these societies.[65] Moreover, where there is broad institutionalized control of individuals, there is also the risk of abuse of power. This situation will not disappear with self-government because Aboriginals generally demand that their autonomous governments have at their disposal legislative and executive powers equivalent, although perhaps not identical, to that of state institutions.[66]

Despite the perennial cliché of societies that regard as culturally alien individual rights and freedoms as defined in modern charters,[67] contemporary Aboriginal peoples do not appear viscerally opposed to fundamental rights as they are known in contemporary legal systems. While the unwavering commitment to the Canadian *Charter* professed by some Aboriginal women's associations is well known thanks to its high-profile media coverage, it is also clear that Aboriginal individuals hardly ever miss an opportunity to demand that federal and provincial authorities respect their rights and freedoms.[68] There is every indication that they will expect no less of their own authorities, who are often accused by Aboriginal plaintiffs of violating the Canadian *Charter*, particularly with respect to "customary" elections.[69] It is especially relevant to note that individual rights and freedoms are sometimes invoked by Aboriginals against community institutions, such as "sentencing circles" in criminal law cases, which are generally seen as rather strong expressions of Aboriginal difference.[70]

When we see the living culture that infuses the behaviour and discourse of contemporary stakeholders, we have to admit that Aboriginal difference cannot be reduced to any traditionalist dogma or static truth impermeable to multiple interpretations of identity and culture.

In any case, there is little doubt that, even though the courts have yet to deliver a clear ruling on the issue,[71] the Canadian *Charter* applies as a matter of law to the "customary" procedure for selecting band council members who exercise the powers set out in the *Indian Act*.

Parliament, the executive and every authority and public body belonging to the federal government are required to comply with the rights and freedoms set out in the *Charter*. The Supreme Court of Canada applies the *Charter* to every body exercising a delegated power to implement government policy.[72] The subjection of band electoral customs to the *Charter* cannot, however, be grounded on the theory of delegated power. Case law shows that a band's power to choose its leaders according to custom is "inherent", in other words, does not have its original source in legislation but in the historical existence of the community along side state law.[73]

Yet, while a band's customary prerogative may not originally spring from governmental action, the way that it is employed by the government could suffice to render *Charter* guarantees applicable. The *Indian Act*, which clearly is targeted by 32(1)(a) of the *Charter*, makes customary rules effective as federal law.[74] By using the community's normative procedures for its own purposes, the federal Parliament makes it an essential cog in the implementation of its legislative policy with regard to "Indians", "Indian bands" and reserves. Formation of band councils according to custom, which Parliament itself makes a prior condition for the council's ability to exercise the powers conferred by the *Indian Act*, becomes an integral part of government policy. By incorporating community rules into federal law in this way, Parliament sufficiently integrates custom into the state regime to make it subject to the *Charter*.

Because they have failed to acknowledge that band custom has been functionally integrated into federal legislative policy, some authors have insisted on the inherent nature of electoral custom and have thus considered that it could not fall under section 32 of the *Charter*.[75] The mere fact that custom has its primary source outside of the state's law is not sufficient to give *Charter* immunity to rules formally appropriated by Parliament to implement its *Indian Act* governance policy. If it were, then the legislator would be able to avoid the *Charter* by adopting rules from bodies that cannot be classified as governmental within the meaning of *Charter* section 32. If the government borrows rules developed by a body not covered by section 32, those rules should then be subject to the prescriptions of the constitutional instrument. This is a corollary of the much more common opposite situation in which government powers are delegated to an otherwise non-governmental body.[76]

We also have to note that if the *Charter* were inapplicable to bands governed by custom, then there would be a fundamental inequality among Aboriginal Canadians whose constitutional rights and freedoms would vary depending on whether or not they belong to a band subject to a ministerial order under section 74 of the *Indian Act*.[77] In other words, by exercising his or her discretion to authorize a band to return to a customary system, the Minister would deprive all the members of the community of *Charter* protection with respect to the process for selecting their leaders. If this were the case, we would expect federal authorities to be more hesitant to set aside the electoral regime provided in the *Act*.

Of course, section 25 of the *Charter* provides that it "shall not be construed so as to abrogate or derogate from any aboriginal, treaty or other rights and freedoms that pertain to the aboriginal peoples of Canada..." Since a band's right, recognized in the *Indian Act,* to select its leaders according to custom is probably protected by this provision, it follows that the very existence of the right, as well as its distinctive features as a special right of the Aboriginal peoples, are immune from challenge based on an alleged violation of a *Charter* right or freedom.[78] However, the immunity does not shield each and every action taken in the exercise of a section 25 right. Only *Charter* challenges that threaten the very existence or the defining characteristics of such a right are blocked by section 25. This is the conclusion that can be drawn from Supreme Court of Canada decisions on provisions and principles of the same type as section 25.[79] Thus, in most cases, the customary process for establishing a band council within the meaning of the *Indian Act*, will have to comply with the *Charter*. Likewise, if it had been passed, the *First Nations Governance Act* would have been subject to *Charter* rights and freedoms, and the same would have applied to rules for choosing band leaders adopted in compliance with the legislation.

How will the *Charter* impact on an Aboriginal community's search for alternatives to the state electoral model? While it is true that the *Charter* does not require band council members to be elected,[80] it is difficult to see how certain basic rights could effectively exist without democracy. Could the consent of the governed be completely bypassed without discrimination with respect to political rights?[81] Blood rights, and matriarchal and gerontocratic prerogatives could be considered prima facie discrimination based on civil status, sex, age or family origin. To be considered discriminatory under *Charter* section 15, differential treatment based on enumerated or analogous grounds must violate essential human dignity.[82] In order to determine whether there has been a impairment of human dignity, the courts take into account various contextual factors, including pre-existing disadvantage experienced by individuals or groups excluded from a benefit, the correlation between the differential treatment and the actual situation or needs of the excluded individuals or groups, the ameliorative purpose of the impugned distinction and the importance of the interest affected by such distinction. So far, when it has applied these contextual criteria, the Supreme Court of Canada has given great weight to Aboriginals' right to participate in the political life of their communities.[83] Contextual analysis should thus lead the courts to rule that total negation of political rights because of civil status, sex, age or family origin constitutes a prima facie violation of section 15.

Of course, according to section 1 of the *Charter*, a limit on a right or freedom can nonetheless be found constitutionally valid if it is "reasonable" and can be "demonstrably justified in a free and democratic society". However, if a system for selecting Aboriginal leaders were, for example, exclusively hereditary, it could not be justified under section 1 because it would be totally at odds with the values of a democratic society.[84] Yet this does not mean that the *Charter* renders constitutionally invalid every form of special participation by customary actors, such as elders, hereditary chiefs, and clan mothers, in modern leadership bodies. While such participation may initially be seen as contrary to the right to equality under section 15 of the *Charter*, it could in several cases be saved using section 1. Giving such traditional actors special political rights would serve an important and legitimate purpose by creating unity, as well as historical and cultural continuity in the community's government. Indeed, traditional members could act as a kind of senate, and inform the elected members of the best ways to maintain the group's harmony, ensure its stability and create a dialogue between the past and present.

Consider a case in which the traditional authorities on an Aboriginal council have only a consultative role, that is, no formal decision-making power that enables them to block the will of the elected council members. Should such an arrangement face a *Charter* challenge based on equality rights, the court would probably find that the inclusion of non-voting individuals who are not elected but selected in a traditional manner can be justified in a democratic society open to Aboriginal difference. This kind of bipartite body would make it possible to coordinate modern and traditional authority in an original way, without contradicting the democratic principle.

Moreover, while respect for fundamental rights cannot really be imagined in the absence of democracy, it may be asked whether elections are a condition *sine qua non* of compliance with democratic principles. Perhaps consent of the governed can be obtained through consensual procedures in accordance with Aboriginal tradition. However, in addition to meeting the need for effective decision-making and taking into account present Aboriginal demographics, a consensus-based system for devolving power would have to respect freedom of expression, freedom of association and the equality rights of individuals. Protection of these individual rights and freedoms would be especially vital in order to ensure equality with respect to nomination and minimize intimidation or reprisals against participants in discussions intended to reach consensual decisions.

It was suggested above that section 1 of the *Charter* authorizes a partially elected government controlled by elected members but integrating customary actors. If this is so, then the same goes for a non-elected government controlled by members appointed by democratic consensus but also including full members who represent traditional powers.

These reflections on non-electoral solutions should not obscure the fact that compliance with the Canadian *Charter* is required even of a fully electoral regime for selecting band chiefs. Freedom of association in political organisations independent of lineage-based obligation, candidacy rights and equality in the composition of the electoral body are very sensitive issues. For example, the Supreme Court of Canada has ruled in *Corbiere*, that it would be discriminatory and thus unconstitutional to deny off-reserve band members the right to vote.[85]

7. Conclusion

This study shows that the federal policy of allowing bands to return to custom only if the community agrees to adopt an electoral code flows from a dogmatic conception of democracy, which excludes means of selecting leaders that may be legitimate and effective even though they do not fully conform to the state electoral model.

Moreover, at the dawn of the twenty-first century, many Aboriginals wish to move beyond the *Indian Act*. Most chiefs also want the federal government to stop trying to revamp the old *Act*, which still shows the imprint of Victorian evolutionism.

Aboriginals are calling for a new era in their relationship with the state, a period of egalitarian and effective political autonomy enshrined in Canada's basic law. For the new order of self-government, they hope to invent institutions that foster cultural dignity and meet the aspirations of present and future generations.

When they define the role of democracy and elections in the constitutions of future Aboriginal governments, the communities concerned will assess the electoral practices that have become commonplace under the *Indian Act*. In treaty and self-government negotiations, they will also have to deal with the federal government's "democratic requirements" aimed at promoting "good governance" values and principles that are supposed to be the inalienable heritage of all Canadians.

There is no reason to think that Aboriginals plan to reject democratic ideals or repudiate fundamental rights. However, it seems clear that many will ask whether Western-style democratic electoral procedures are compatible with their culture. The debate is perfectly appropriate and necessary, but it may lead to confrontation between certain traditional practices and *Charter* rights. The application of the *Charter* will affect the search for alternatives to electoral democracy, but it will not be an obstacle to innovative adaptations of the electoral system. Moreover, elections are not *in se* a *Charter* right that proscribes consensual practices inspired by custom.

Individual rights and freedoms necessarily convey the seeds of democracy and will thus prevent a return to ancestral practices that failed to generate the legitimacy flowing from consent of the governed. But the future will tell whether Canada's Aboriginal peoples will make an original contribution to the political development of mankind by conceiving of and achieving democracy without elections but also without denying fundamental rights.

---

[1] Professor, Faculty of Law, Laval University. Research for this article was conducted under the "Autochtonie et gouvernance" project funded by Valorisation recherche Québec.

[2] Council of Elders, *A Negotiation Process for Off-Reserve Aboriginal Peoples in Ontario*, 1993, p. 5, quoted in the *Report of the Royal Commission on Aboriginal Peoples, Vol. 2, Restructuring the Relationship,* Part I, Ottawa: Canada Communication Group, 1996 at 149. [Royal Commission on Aboriginal Peoples].

[3] Schedule B, *Canada Act 1982* (U.K.), 1982, c. 11, [hereinafter "the *Canadian Charter*" or "the *Charter*"].

[4] Africa has experienced many problems resulting from the fact that a colonial state apparatus was simply superimposed over indigenous forms of authority. See, for example, C. N. Mback, "La chefferie traditionnelle au Cameroun: ambiguités juridiques et obstacles à la démocratie locale", in *Ethnicité, identités et citoyenneté en Afrique centrale*, Cahier african des droits de l'Homme, No. 6-7, March 2002, 211; F. M. D'Engelbronner-Kolf, M. O. Hinz and J. L. Sindano, Eds., *Traditional Authority and Democracy in Southern Africa*, Windhoek : New Namibia Books, 1998.

[5] A critical analysis of John Locke's thought on North American Indigenous peoples can be found in J. Tully, *Strange Multiplicity: Constitutionalism in an Age of Diversity*, Cambridge: Cambridge University Press, 1995 at 70–82.

[6] See *Relations des Jésuites*, Éditions du Jour, 1972, 6 volumes (reprint of the 1858 edition).

[7] O. P. Dickason, *Les premières nations du Canada,* Sillery: Éditions du Septentrion, 1996 at 65–66.

[8] T. Porter, "Traditions of the Constitution of the Six Nations" in L. Little Bear, Ed., M. Boldt and J. Anthony Long, *Pathways to Self-Determination: Canadian Indians and the Canadian State*, Toronto: University of Toronto Press, 1984 at 14–21.

[9] See, among others, the Royal Commission on Aboriginal Peoples, *Supra* note 2 at 145–149.

[10] *Ibid.* at 149–152.

[11] Concerning internalization, see M. Morin, *L'usurpation de la souveraineté autochtone*, Montréal: Boréal, 1997; I. Schulte-Tenckhoff, "Reassessing the Paradigm of Domestication: The Problematic of Indigenous Treaties" (1998) 4 *Rev. Const. Stud.* 239.

[12] In 1995, the Government of Canada adopted an official policy of recognition and negotiated implementation of the inherent right to self-government. See *Aboriginal Self-government: Federal Policy Guide*, Ottawa: Public Works and Government Services Canada, 1995. Most commentators consider that such an aboriginal right exists and should be recognized by the Supreme Court of Canada. See in particular B. Slattery, "First Nations and the Constitution", (1992) 71 *Rev. du Bar. Can.* 261; K. McNeil, "Envisaging Constitutional Space for Aboriginal Governments", (1993) 19 Queens L. J. 951; P. Macklem, *Indigenous Difference and the Constitution of Canada*, Toronto: University of Toronto Press, 2001 at 107–131. [Macklem]. For the opposite view, however, see A. Émond, "Le sable dans l'engrenage du droit inhérent des autochtones à l'autonomie gouvernementale", (1996) 30 *R. J. T.* 89. The Royal Commission on Aboriginal Peoples argues in favour of such a right in its report entitled *Partners in Confederation: Aboriginal Peoples, Self-Government, and the Constitution*, Ottawa: Canada Communication Group, 1993. The Supreme Court of Canada has however so far deliberately refrained from making a decision on the issue. See *R. v. Pamajewon*, [1996] 2 S. C. R. 821; *Delgamuukw* v. *British Columbia*, [1997] 3 S. C. R. 1010. But in *Mitchell* v. *M.N.R.*, [2001] 1 S. C. R. 911, Binnie J., with Major J., explicitly evokes principles that could provide a basis for an Aboriginal right to self-government. He mentions the possibility of a mere "impairment" of Aboriginal sovereignty following the assertion of Crown sovereignty (par. 158) and of a "merged sovereignty and shared sovereignty" essential to the conciliation at the heart of section 35 of the *Constitution Act, 1982* (par. 167). See also *Campbell* v. *British Columbia*, [2000] 8 W.W.R. 600 (B.C.S.C.), in which the Court concludes that an aboriginal right to self-government is indeed part of positive law.

[13] Recognition of the "Aboriginal" rights of Aboriginal peoples is a central feature of British colonial common law, as formulated by the United States Supreme Court in the famous cases of *Johnson* v. *McIntosh*, 5 U. S. (8 Wheat.) 543 (1823) and *Worcester* v. *State of Georgia*, (1832) 31 U.S. 530. Thus, according to British co-

lonial law, while the external sovereignty of Indigenous peoples had been replaced by the title devolved to His Majesty for having "discovered" the land, Aboriginals were acknowledged to have retained preexisting rights as first occupants of the land. These rights, in particular customary land title, are considered to have survived the change in sovereignty and are therefore fully validated by state law, even though such law is not, in principle, the formal source of these rights. The Supreme Court of Canada belatedly decided that the Aboriginal rights doctrine also applies in Canada, and that its general foundations were similar in both former British colonies. See *Calder* v. *British Columbia*, [1973] S.C.R. 313. See also *R.* v. *Van Der Peet*, [1996] 2 S.C.R. 507.

[14] See section 35 of the *Constitution Act, 1982*. Sub-section (1) provides: "The existing aboriginal and treaty rights of the aboriginal peoples of Canada are hereby recognized and affirmed." The highest Canadian court has ruled that this provision now protects Aboriginal people from any unjustified infringement by state authorities of their aboriginal or treaty rights. See *R.* v. *Sparrow*, [1990] 1 S.C.R. 1075.

[15] R.S.C., Chapter I-5.

[16] The specific regimes are based either on legislation that enacts self-government agreements or on treaties establishing an autonomous Aboriginal government. In the case of agreements with treaty status, as is the case with the *Nisga'a Final Agreement*, Aboriginal governmental institutions have real constitutional protection under 35(1) of the *Constitution Act, 1982*. For a study of such specific regimes, see S. Grammond, *Aménager la coexistence: les peuples autochtones et le droit canadien*, Cowansville: Bruylant-Yvon Blais, 2003 at 279–353.

[17] The present composition of a "band" does not necessarily match the contours of the traditional group, tribe or band. See A. Émond, "Quels sont les partenaires autochtones avec lesquels Sa Majesté entretient une relation historique?", (1997) 76 *R. du B. Can.* 130 at 138–142.

[18] Thus, most administrative bylaws passed by a band council (see sections 81 and 83 of the *Indian Act*) can be revoked by the Minister (s. 82) or have to be approved by him or her before coming into effect (s. 83).

[19] *An Act for the gradual enfranchisement of Indians, the better management of Indian affairs*, S.C. 1869 c. 6, s. 10. However, this provision allowed traditional chiefs who were appointed for life to keep a seat on the council until they died.

[20] See SOR/2000-391. For a detailed history of federal legislation on this issue, see W. Daugherty and D. Madill, *Indian Government under Indian Act Legislation 1868–1951*, Part I, Ottawa: Indian Affairs and Northern Development, 1980. [Daugherty and Madill]

[21] As Daugherty and Madill (*Ibid.*, at 2) note,

> "the introduction of democratic, electoral regulations, which were seen at the time as a sign of progress and civilization, was one of the key features of the assimilation plan. The government thought that the introduction of elected government would lead Indians to abandon their traditional tribal institutions, which differed widely across the country and were seen as obstacles to the Indians' progress."

[22] In 1881, a senior official in the federal government pleaded in favour of the

introduction of the electoral system among Aboriginals because "a powerful civilizing tool would thereby be created, which would one day result in the elimination of the system of hereditary chiefs, the only bastion of ignorance and barbarism", in I. W. Powell, *Abrégé de rapports sur le système municipal projeté pour les bandes indiennes*, 1881, Ottawa at 155.

[23] On May 16, 1899, for example, the government decreed that the *Act's* electoral provisions would be applied to all of the communities in eastern Canada. There is no indication that the communities had agreed to this. See Daugherty and Madill, *supra* note 20 at 8.

[24] An example of this is the famous case of the Six Nations of Ohsweken, who protested before international organizations against the federal authorities' decision to impose an elected band council on them, and eliminate their traditional system of government. See in particular E. Wilson, *Apologies to the Iroquois*, Syracuse: Syracuse University Press, 1991 at 257–258. See also Daugherty and Madill, *supra* note 20 at 46–67.

[25] At that time, only 194 communities held elections under the Act. See Daugherty and Madill, *supra* note 20 at 99.

[26] See Daugherty and Madill, *supra* note 20 at 67–70.

[27] While some members of some bands were able to vote in federal elections between 1887 and 1896, it was only in 1960, ten years after the Inuit, that Aboriginals obtained the same electoral rights as other Canadian citizens at the federal level. In Québec, Aboriginals have been able to vote in provincial elections only since 1969. See *The Path to Electoral Equality*, Committee for Aboriginal Electoral Reform, Ottawa: Royal Commission on Electoral Reform and Party Financing, 1991 at 8. Generally, Aboriginal participation in elections is very low. During the elections in Québec on April 14, 2003, an average of only 29% of Aboriginals exercised their right to vote whereas the average rate of participation for the population as a whole was over 70%. See *Le Devoir*, Thursday, July 31, 2003 at A-2.

[28] Subsection 2(1) of the *Act* now explicitly recognizes that if there is no ministerial under section 74 making the *Act's* electoral provisions applicable, then the council is appointed according to the "custom of the band".

[29] This is the case of 196 communities. See Indian Affairs and Northern Development Canada, *Communities First: First Nations Governance*, http://www.ainc-inac.gc.ca/nr/prs/j-a2001/01136bk_e.html .

[30] See Daugherty and Madill, *supra* note 20 at 99.

[31] The ministerial order issued under section 74 of the *Act* makes the legislation's electoral provisions applicable to a community, but it can be abrogated, which entails *ipso facto* a return to customary practices. See *Sparvier* v. *Cowesses Indian Band No. 73*, [1993] 3 F.C.T.D. 142 at 149–150 [*Sparvier*]; *Gordon* v. *Canada*, [2001] F.C.T.D. No. 114, par. 12. Thus, 134 communities that had been subject to the electoral provisions of the *Act* were authorized to return to "customary" practices. However, the government did make withdrawal from the state regime conditional on the adoption of an "electoral code". See Indian Affairs and Northern Development Canada, *Communities First: First Nations Governance*, *supra* note 29.

[32] This information was provided to the author by officials at Indian Affairs and Northern Development Canada.

[33] *McLeod Lake Indian Band* v. *Chingee*, [1998] F.C.T.D. No. 1185, par. 8. [*McLeod Lake Indian Band*]. Hence, as is indicated in *Francis* v. *Mohawk Council of Kanesatake*, [2003] F.C.T.D. 115, [*Francis*] custom has two components: "The first involves «practices» which may either be «established» through repetitive acts in time, or through a single act such as the «adoption» of an electoral code" (para. 24), while the "second component of the definition of custom, therefore, involves a subjective element, which refers to the manifestation of the will of those interested in rules for determining the electoral process of band council membership to be bound by a given rule or practice" (para. 26).

[34] *Bigstone* v. *Big Eagle*, [1993] 1 C.N.L.R. 25 (F.C.T.D.) In *Francis, Ibid.,* Martineau J. says of broad consensus the "the practice pertaining to a particular issue or situation contemplated by that rule must be firmly established, generalized and followed consistently and conscientiously by a majority of the community" (para. 36). See also *Salt River First Nation No. 195 (Council)* v. *Salt River First No. 195*, [2003] F.C.T.D. No. 865, para. 42. [*Salt River*].

[35] *Francis, supra* note 33, para. 21; *McArthur* v. *Saskatchewan (Registrar, Department of Indian Affairs and Northern Development)*, (1992), 91 D.L.R. (4th) 666 (Sask. Q.B.).

[36] The Federal Court has highlighted the evolving nature of Aboriginal customs for the purposes of the *Indian Act*:

> "Also, custom by its nature is not frozen in time. It can and does change in response to changed circumstances. A band may choose to depart from oral tradition and set down its custom in written form. It may move from a hereditary to an electoral system. It may choose to adopt as its customary practices, practices and procedures that resemble the election procedures used to elect municipal or provincial governments. I cannot interpret the reference to «custom of the band» in subsection 2(1) as preventing a band from changing the custom according to which it governs itself from time to time in response to changing circumstances."

See *McLeod Lake Indian Band, supra* note 33, para. 10. See also *Francis, supra* note 33, para. 24–25.

[37] See, for example, *Salt River First Nation, supra* note 34 in which Rouleau J. says in paragraph 47 that "Election custom does not need to be codified or written in any form. Custom can be established by unwritten election practices followed consistently in prior elections without complaint from band members."

[38] *McLeod Lake Indian Band, supra* note 33, para. 10.

[39] Case law consistently recognizes that a simple proclamation on which there is broad consensus in the community can constitute a valid amendment of a community's regime. See, for example, *McLeod Lake Indian Band, supra* note 33.

[40] See *Napoleon* v. *Garbiit*, [1997] B.C.J. No. 1250 (B.C.S.C.), and *Francis, supra* note 33.

[41] The Federal Court recently reiterated that "it is the Act, and more particularly subsection 2(1) of the Act, which provides for recognition of the customary law under which the plaintiff, as Chief, and the defendants, as members of the Council of the Blood Tribe, each claim their offices» (para. 17), and had concluded that «the customary law of the Tribe has recognition as law by reason of federal statutory law and it is the Council so elected which has status in accord with the *Indian*

Act", see *Francis, supra* note 33, para. 17.

[42] For example, see *Gabriel* v. *Canatonquin et al.* [1980] 1 F.C. 792 (F.C.A.); *Sparvier, supra* note 31; *Parisier* v. *Ocean Man First Nation* [1996] F.C.T.D. No. 129; *Grand Rapids First Nation* v. *Nasikapow* [2000] F.C.T.D. No. 1896; *Francis, supra* note 33; *Roseau River Anishinabe First Nation* v. *Roseau River Anishinabe First Nation Council*, [2003] F.C.T.D. No. 251.

[43] P. Martin, *Les systèmes électoraux et les modes de scrutin,* Paris: Montchrestien, 1997 at 9 [our translation].

[44] *Figueroa* v. *Canada (Attorney General)* [2003] S.C.C. 37 at para. 30.

[45] We have to agree with O. Ihl, who says that "plebiscite is the symbol of the people's participation in government, the vote is synonymous with freedom and pluralism. This is sufficient, with the help of ritual, to make it the criterion, if not the guarantee, of a just organization of power." See O. Ihl, *Le vote*, Paris: Montchrestien, 1997 at 11 [our translation].

[46] Bold and Long formulate this criticism as follows: "Indian communities have engaged traditionally in an extensive consultation process in the selection of their leaders and all decisions affecting the group required a consensus by members. Under the democratic representative electoral system imposed on them by the Canadian government, however, leaders are generally elected by a minority of members, and the associated organization of delegated authority and hierarchical structures have relegated most members of the Indian community to the periphery of the decision-making process. Decisions are now made by Indian élites – elected and appointed", M. Bold and J. A. Long, "Tribal Philosophies and the Charter of Rights and Freedoms", in M. Bold and J. A. Long, Eds., *The Quest for Justice: Aboriginal Peoples and Aboriginal Rights*, Toronto: University of Toronto Press, 1985, 165 at 170.

[47] Study of precolonial consensualist political cultures tends to show that they were consistent with the "democratic" idea of legitimization of power by the consent of the political community. See D. Russell, *A People's Dream: Aboriginal Self-Government in Canada*, Vancouver: University Of British Columbia Press, 2000 at 100–101. [Russell].

[48] O. Duhamel and Y. Mény, *Dictionnaire constitutionnel,* Paris: P.U.F., 1992 at 207 [our translation].

[49] *Ibid* [our translation].

[50] See the Royal Commission on Aboriginal Peoples, *supra* note 2 at 151–152.

[51] Assembly of First Nations, *Reclaiming our Nationhood: Strengthening our Nation,* brief presented to the Royal Commission on Aboriginal Peoples, 1993, p. 16.

[52] *Ibid.*

[53] *Code de représentation de la Nation huronne-wendat*, Conseil de la Nation huronne-Wendat, June 2002, www.cnhw.qc.ca/affpolitiques/.

[54] In a brief submitted to the Royal Commission on Aboriginal Peoples, the Council of Elders said "The art of consensus decision making is dying. We are greatly concerned that Aboriginal people are increasingly equating 'democracy' with the act of voting ...[W]e are convinced that the practice of consensus decision making is essential to the culture of our peoples", Council of Elders, *A Negotiation Process for Off-Reserve Aboriginal Peoples in Ontario*, 1993, at 5, cited in Royal Commission on Aboriginal Peoples, *supra* note 2 at 149.

[55] Russell, *supra* note 47 at 103–104.

[56] Note that a community subject to the electoral provisions set out in section 74 of the *Indian Act* would not be authorized by the Minister to return to a community system unless it was an electoral system. The Minister's decision to revoke the order making the Act's provisions applicable is discretionary and the federal government has therefore adopted the policy of not using that power unless the community has committed itself to establishing an electoral system.

[57] Bill C-7, *An Act respecting leadership selection, administration and accountability of Indian bands, and to make amendments to other Acts*, Second Session, Thirty-seventh Parliament, 51-52 Elizabeth II, 2002–2003, as amended by the Standing Committee on Aboriginal Affairs, Northern Development and Natural Resources. See: http://www.parl.gc.ca/37/2/parlbus/chambus/house/bills/government/C-7/C-7_2/C-7_cover-E.html .

[58] See 4(1)(a) and 4(2) of the bill. If it failed to adopt such a code, the community would be subject to the general electoral regime set out in the *Act*.

[59] See 5(1)(b) of the bill.

[60] See 5(2)(b) and 5(3) of the bill.

[61] The amendment could occur before the new legislation comes into effect or in compliance with the amendment procedure set out in the code to be adopted by the community under the *Act*.

[62] The new legislation would nonetheless have reduced the communities' present "customary" independence because they would have been legally required to codify their practices, set out appeal mechanisms and adopt their electoral codes by referendum.

[63] See M. Coon-Come, "Approaching Change: Top Down or Bottom Up", speech made at the *Beyond the Indian Act* colloquium, Ottawa, April 17–18, 2002.

[64] See, among others, M. E. Turpel, "Aboriginal Peoples and the Charter: Interpretive Monopolies, Cultural Differences", (1989) *C.H.R.Y.B.* 3; D. Russell, *supra* note 47 at 103–130; Bold and Long, *supra* note 46; K. Wilkins, "But We Need the Eggs: The Royal Commission, the Charter of Rights and the Inherent Right of Aboriginal Government", (1999) 49 *U. of T.L.J.* 58 at 86–99. [Wilkins]. For a position with more nuances, see J. Borrows, "Contemporary Traditional Equality: the Effect of the *Charter* on First Nation Politics", (1994) 43 *U.N.B.L.J.* 19.

[65] See in particular C. E. S. Franks, "Rights and Self-government for Canada's Aboriginal Peoples" in Curtis Cook and Juan D. Lindau, Eds., *Aboriginal Rights and Self-Government*, (Montréal: McGill-Queens University Press, 2000), 101, at 128–133.

[66] Far from repudiating the modern state, Aboriginals often agree to essentially reproduce it in their self-government institutions. This is apparent in the *Nisga'a Final Agreement* and draft treaties currently being negotiated. The government institutions planned or established indeed have all of the essential characteristics of modern constitutionalism. See in particular the *Nisga'a Final Agreement,* Canada, British Columbia, Nisga'a Nation, 1998, Chapters 11 and 12.

[67] Russell writes (*supra* note 47 at 117–118 and 128–129):

> "Rights theory has a long history within the common law judicial system, and today it is firmly embedded with the Canadian psyche. However, Aboriginal people have been less enamoured of such notions. Ab-

original societies premised on an ethic of care and responsibility have traditionally been interested less in rights than in concepts of personal obligation",.

[68] An eloquent example can be seen in the long legal battle conducted by Aboriginals living off-reserve to have 77(1) of the *Indian Act*, which denied off-reserve band members the right in band council elections, declared unconstitutional for breach of equality rights guaranteed in the Canadian *Charter*. The Supreme Court of Canada ruled in their favour. See *Corbière* v. *Canada*, [1999] 2 S.C.R. 203. [*Corbière*]

[69] See for example some recent cases, such as: *Francis, supra* note 33; *Scrimbitt* v. *Sakimay Indian Band*, [2000] 1 F.C.T.D. 513; *Hall* v. *Dakota Tipi Indian Band*, [2000] F.C.T.D. No. 207; *Gros-Louis* v. *Huron-Wendat Nation Band Council*, [2000] F.C.T.D. No. 1529; *Sark* v. *Lennox Island Band of Indians*, [1999] F.C.T.D. No. 1025; and *Crow* v. *Blood Band*, (1996) 107 F.C.T.D. 270.

[70] See in particular H. Hogh, "Finding a Balance Between Ethnicity and Gender Among Inuit in Arctic Canada", in *Indigenous Women: the Right to a Voice*, International Working Group for Indigenous Affairs, 1998 at 75–82.

[71] So far, the courts have generally taken it for granted that the *Charter* applies to electoral customs without examining the issue in detail. See the case law summarized in *Francis, supra* note 33 at para. 77.

[72] *Blencoe* v. *British Columbia*, [2000] 2 S.C.R. 307 [*Blencoe*]; *Eldridge* v. *British Columbia*, [1997] 3 S.C.R. 624 [*Eldridge*]; *Slaight Communications Inc.* v. *Davidson*, [1989] S.C.R. 1038. Thus, a band council is subject to the *Charter* in the exercise of the powers conferred by the *Indian Act* in order to implement federal government policy as conveyed by the legislation. See in particular *Canada* v. *Gordon Band Council*, [2001] 1 F.C. 124 at para. 32.

[73] *Bone* v. *Sioux Valley Indian Band No. 290*, [1996] 3 F.C.T.D. 54; *Francis, supra* note 33 at para. 18.

[74] *Supra*, note 41.

[75] See for example K. McNeil, "Aboriginal Governments and the Canadian Charter of Rights and Freedoms", (1996) 34 *Osgoode Hall L.J.* 61 at 88–90, reprinted in K. McNeil, *Emerging Justice? Essays on Indigenous Rights in Canada and Australia*, Saskatoon: University of Saskatchewan Native Law Center, 2001 at 215. [McNeil].

[76] *Eldridge, supra* note 72 at para. 42.

[77] Indeed, there is no doubt that the Charter applies to the electoral provisions of the *Canada Elections Act* and Regulations. See *Corbière, supra* note 68.

[78] For example, section 25 prevents a challenge to section 2 of the *Act*, which validates customary codes, on the grounds that the provision would authorize treatment less favourable than that of the electoral regime flowing from section 74. It is also an obstacle to challenging the electoral code of a community on the grounds that the code is less advantageous than that of another community. The ability of every community governed by custom to adopt a distinctive code is an essential feature of the right mentioned in section 2 of the *Act*.

[79] See in particular: *Reference re: An Act to Amend the Education Act*, [1987] 1 S.C.R. 1148, and *Adler* v. *Ontario*, [1996] 3 S.C.R. 609. See also P. W. Hogg and M. E. Turpel, "Implementing Aboriginal Self-Government: Constitutional and

Jurisdictional Issues", (1995) 74 *R. du B. Can.* 187 at 213–215; Macklem, *supra* note 12 at 221–227; Royal Commission on Aboriginal Peoples, *supra* note 2 at 250–258. However, see also: McNeil, *supra* note 75 at 68–79 and 88–90, and Wilkins, *supra* note 64 at 108–114.

[80] Section 3 of the *Charter*, which guarantees Canadian citizens the right to vote, applies only to federal and provincial elections. See *Haig* v. *Canada*, [1993] 2 S.C.R. 995.

[81] See 15(1) of the Canadian *Charter*.

[82] See *Law* v. *Canada*, [1999] 1 S.C.R. 497.

[83] See *Corbière, supra*, note 68.

[84] In *R.* v. *Oakes*, [1986] 1 S.C.R. 103 at 136, the Supreme Court of Canada insisted on the fact that, when applying section 1, the "court must be guided by the values and principles essential to a free and democratic society", including "faith in social and political institutions which enhance the participation of individuals and groups in society".

[85] *Corbière , supra* note 68.

Legal Pluralism at Kahnawake?[1]

Andrée Lajoie, Henry Quillinan, Rod Macdonald and Guy Rocher[2]

Observation and analysis of Canadian and traditional institutions at Kahnawake have shown that, from a formal standpoint, there are multiple sources of governmental and non-governmental normativity, which constitute a highly complex, evolutionary pluralism. In recent years, this legal pluralism has lost some of its intensity through the transfer of legitimacy and normative effectiveness among the various legal orders, though the formal appearances of both intra- and extra-state pluralism have been kept intact. The dominance of one legal order over others, not to mention the effectiveness and even survival of a given legal order, seem to depend upon three factors: financial resources, external credibility and internal legitimacy. There are also similarities between Aboriginal legal systems and our own. Both wampums and our Canadian constitutional acts lack precision, call upon the same techniques of interpretation, and entail the same role for the interpreter in the production of norms. In both cases, there are similar normative limits linked to legitimacy, which is based on how closely the values that legal interpreters write into law match the dominant values in the community.

We have been visiting Kahnawake regularly between 1991 and 1998 to do research on the Mohawk concept of Aboriginal rights, though the work was slowed by the participation of some of the present authors in the work of the Dussault-Erasmus Commission. Initially, we thought that the concept would not be univocal and that it would vary not so much in accordance with individual opinions but depending on adherence to the Band Council or a longhouse, in other words, a traditional "government" as is found in most Aboriginal communities. However, in the preliminary stage of our research, we found that there was not one but three longhouses that set out norms intended to be exclusive: the Nation Office, the Longhouse at the Quarry, and the Longhouse at Mohawks' Trail. It immediately became clear to us that we were looking at an example of pluralism such as one might dream of inventing. The relationships that we were building every day with the various groups in the community would allow us to conduct parallel research through close observation and analysis of legal pluralism *in vivo*. At least, this was our hypothesis at first. Seven years of observation and nearly a thousand hours of interviews later, we have not rejected our hypothesis, far from it, in a sense. However, our notion of legal pluralism has changed, and its contours, which were based on experience in our legal universe, have been bent to accommodate other forms from a tradition that is nonetheless not as different from our own as its oral nature could lead one to think.

Thus, we first have to identify our initial theoretical choices with respect to pluralism (section 1). This will enable us to analyse legal practices at Kahnawake (section 2) and confirm, if applicable, the presence of a form of pluralism which remains to be described (section 3), and in conclusion show how this original system challenges our earlier notions of pluralism.

1. Theories of Pluralism

It might be said that, by definition, pluralism has several forms: it could be (successively?) social, political or legal.[3] We see an initial form of pluralism, namely the social form, as soon as a single society contains different value systems held by distinct groups. In the Western tradition, a pluralist society is considered to be one that accepts with tolerance the multiplicity of values implied at all times by the variety of points of view and interests of the various groups that make it up. In this sense, and in a state context, social pluralism seems to go hand in hand with political pluralism, the minimal form of which is the multiparty system.[4] However, it is possible to imagine a non-state society, and this is particularly relevant in Kahnawake's case, which contains a variety of currents representing different values without forming veritable parties. In either case, but by different paths, the conditions are sufficient to cross the border into legal pluralism. Where the border is located and what conditions must be fulfilled depend not only on the underlying theoretical framework, but also on the definition of law that is adopted.

From our point of view, legal pluralism has its source in social pluralism of values. It begins when a unified legal system attributes to a group a special regime based on the group's values or when such a group becomes semi-autonomous[5] and establishes a special regime in a new legal order distinct from the first. Based on this, we can identify two contemporary concepts of pluralism, which have been analysed by Jean-Guy Belley.[6] The first, moderate,[7] concept is based on the positivist definition of law, and limits itself to recognizing that there are social powers different from the state, whose means of coercion are often more effective than the state's. The second, radical,[8] concept challenges the state definition of law in favour of a pluralist and decentralized form of democracy itself. From the second point of view, not only is normative power shared between the state and other parallel legal orders, but also the concurrent legal orders are not hierarchized, so the state is decentralized and flattened, so to speak. In other words, the various social milieus create their own norms to shape social behaviour and their own institutions to strengthen and enforce the norms. According to this concept, there are few distinctions between legal norms and other social norms.[9] Clearly, what is in question here is the definition of law. Law is thus *implicit* and *inferential*, and includes "the general principles of law and tacit presuppositions that govern the actions of communities".[10] The norms, the varying legal weight of which is not important, emanate from various legal orders and come together without any predetermined hierarchy in the individual's subjective experience.[11]

In so far as subjective experience is reconstructed as the law itself and not as an indication that there are multiple legal orders, we will not take this approach. For us, law, which certainly exists outside of state frameworks and according to hierarchies that may be "flat" or highly accentuated depending on the case and society in question, remains a social, collective phenomenon. Though a person targeted by a legal order may resist normative rules, that person does not have the individual right to choose the shape or borders of any legal order. From our theoretical perspective,[12] our initial hypothesis about the legal pluralism at Kahnawake depended, thus, on the concomitant existence of several legal orders (the federal and Québec governments, Band Council and longhouses). In other words, it depended on the existence of institutions with more or less formal and differentiated bodies that, in at least a semi-autonomous manner and not necessarily within the state framework, set out, interpreted and applied norms of social behaviour, and claimed exclusive authority over the whole community. These roles, because they are integrated into a more complex world, are related to the concepts of pre-, co- and over-determination in «*systémale analysis*».[13]

From this point of view, which is consistent on another level with that of the researchers at the *Laboratoire d'anthropologie juridique de Paris I*,[14] law is not so much a set of specific rules but rather an inter-normative process of juridicization directed by factors linked to conditions essential for the cohesion and perpetuation of the group in question.[15] Étienne LeRoy and Mamadou Wane have used this perspective to develop a typology of Aboriginal legal systems in Africa.[16] Despite the geographical differences and probably because of features shared by all colonial situations, their typology seems to us to be especially useful for analysing the pluralist practices at Kahnawake.

The theory identifies four phases of pluralism in colonial contexts. The first is characterized by traditional law used by Aboriginal populations before the arrival of Europeans and is based on their specific visions of the world. In the second phase, colonization introduces a new form of law, in which customary law is dominant but in which the colonial government records customs or uses them in a foreign framework, thus adulterating the traditional law. In the third phase, local law replaces traditional law as the government's influence and state apparatus grows. The formation and legitimization of local law are essentially determined by the state, whereas the way it operates is left more or less up to local authorities. Such local law of state inspiration is characterized by the possibility of reinterpreting foreign legal categories in light of Aboriginal legal concepts.

The fourth phase results from a reaction to the forms of law imposed by the state in phases two and three, and is marked by popular law created outside of the state apparatus. It should be noted that such law is no longer really traditional, but rather a new creation, at least partially, in which traditional law is reinterpreted in a completely new context. The little we knew when we began our research on changes in the law at Kahnawake led us to rally to this point of view. For example, longhouses, traditional legal bodies, reappeared formally only in the 1970s, after having disappeared during a period in which the Canadian authorities subjected the community to phases very similar to those described by LeRoy and Wane. This is thus the hypothesis that we tested against the varied and changing Mohawk reality at Kahnawake.

2. Pluralism of Practices at Kahnawake

Before analysing the legal practices at Kahnawake (2.3), we will describe the Mohawk community (2.1) and our methodology (2.2).

2.1. The Mohawk Community at Kahnawake

Located in a suburb near Montréal,[17] Kahnawake has an estimated population of 6000–7000[18] living on around 10 km^2. The land was classified as a "reserve" in the nineteenth century,[19] and is officially governed, in the eyes of Canadian positive law, by a band council, which administers a budget that reached $32 million in the 1997–1998 fiscal year.[20]

As can easily be seen, the area is now very urbanized. This is made explicit by data in a report from the Kahnawake hospital.[21] The community has its own police force (the Peacekeepers), a municipal court, a local community services centre (CLSC), a social services centre, a hospital, a school board, a Catholic church and a Protestant congregation. The largely English-speaking community also has cultural facilities, such as the band council rooms, which are used as cinemas, concert halls and exhibition rooms, and a community newspaper and radio station, which face competition from *The Gazette*, CFCF and American television stations.[22] It also has several social associations (the Rotary and Moose clubs, and the Canadian Legion) and sports associations (curling, lacrosse, ice hockey, canoeing, kayaking clubs). Since there is little local public transit, the motor vehicle ownership rate is very high,[23] and in 1998 there were many stores: 12 corner stores, 7 grocery stores and 21 tobacco shops.

Kahnawake has features characteristic of urbanized societies, which may or may not be seen as advantages depending on the point of view but which clearly change traditional Aboriginal lifestyles in accordance with outside ideas. However, according to the hospital report, it also has the social problems that the Dussault-Erasmus Commission documented on most reserves.[24] The community has high alcoholism, multiple drug addiction, teenage pregnancy and crime (traffic, family, sexual and economic) rates in a context where there is also a high illiteracy rate and economic dependence. According to inside sources, this is the present state of the community.

Naturally, it was not always this way.

Kahnawake's present territory is located on land where nomadic Iroquois tribes hunted occasionally from time immemorial. Under the French regime, the land was part of the Seigneurie du Sault St. Louis, and was granted to the Jesuits by the King for the benefit of the Iroquois, who initially settled at La Prairie.[25] Yet, the Iroquois had not surrendered their rights, and they were not subject to foreign powers, as can be seen from a French memorandum on the Iroquois missions that was cited (in translation) by Jaenen[26] and confirmed in 1748 by a notarized act signed before witnesses by the Six Nations and La Galissonière.[27] Under the authority of their Confederation and respective longhouses, the Iroquois of the Six Nations, including the Mohawks of Kahnawake, thus had their own political organization long before the federal authorities established the reserve at the end of the nineteenth century.[28]

Have these traditional Aboriginal political institutions survived underground since the creation of the reserve and the introduction of the first band council? Did their activities vary in intensity over time? Did they disappear temporarily at different stages or for the whole time? We do not know the answers to these questions, which far exceed the scope of our research, to say nothing of our competencies.

However, given the way that some traditionalist Aboriginals read the current situation at Kahnawake, it is not surprising that the teachings of Louis Hall[29] and the events at Wounded Knee in the United States[30] led to the (re)emergence of a first official longhouse in 1973. This was the Nation Office, which was established as a counterweight to the band council, and which seems to have had over 70 active members and around 500 sympathizers in 1990, before it temporarily disappeared in 1994. The size of the membership at its height indicates that it had succeeded in leading almost the whole community. In 1976, the Longhouse at the Quarry separated from the Nation Office. Because it is very radical, the Longhouse at the Quarry's influence is more visible than one might think from the number of its members, for around its charismatic Chief Mihao, there were only about 30 members and 15 sympathizers in 1998. In 1991, the Longhouse at Mohawk's Trail split off under the leadership of Chief McComber, who took with him a small number of sympathizers, whose ranks have swollen since to around 20 members.[31]

Are these legal orders? Is this a case of complex intra- and inter-state pluralism, in which there is Canadian law and its components, including the band council, but also various longhouses, each constituting a legal order in itself? On the contrary, are there not only two legal orders: one White and the other Aboriginal? Or even a single one, namely that of the Canadian state, which would then disprove our pluralist hypothesis and confirm the official positivism? These are the questions that our research seeks to address by verifying the hypothesis we posited in the first section using methods we will now briefly describe.

2.2. Methodology

Naturally, our choice of methods was dictated by our theoretical framework, but the specific purpose and context of our research were even more determining. Our goal was to verify a pluralist hypothesis. This required identifying whether there were separate and parallel legal orders at Kahnawake. In other words, we had to see whether there were institutions that were sufficiently formal to be identified by the stakeholders in the community and that set out, interpreted and applied norms that were claimed to apply to all members of the community living on the reserve. Moreover, we hoped to verify the hypothesis in a community with an oral tradition that was also regulated from the outside by a state with formalized positive law.

We therefore chose three methods: classical interpretation of positive law, observation of the operation of Aboriginal institutions and group interviews.

2.2.1. Classical Interpretation of Positive Law

The purpose of the first method was to identify positive Canadian law from all sources applicable to inhabitants of Kahnawake, and more specifically to the operation of the band council. This entailed interpreting relevant texts in a classical manner, the limitations and gaps of which Pierre-André Côté has described in such detail[32] that we clearly do not need to review them here. The author of these lines is quite aware of the artificial nature of the interpretations that result from such analysis.[33].

The same cannot be said of the two other methods, namely observation and interviews, which have been borrowed from the social sciences. The technical aspects of these methods are less familiar to lawyers.

2.2.2. Observation of the Operation of the Institutions

We wanted to verify whether Aboriginal institutions were legal orders in the sense of institutionalist sociology of law, which is the theoretical option we chose. Observation of their operations was selected as the best method, particularly because our research team visited Kahnawake regularly to do research for another project on Aboriginal rights. We did not engage in participatory observation in the strict anthropological sense, but in direct observation specific to anthropology of *law*. Vanderlinden has described the requirements of this form of observation as long immersion in the society under study, perfect mastery (?) of its forms of expression and familiarization that can be achieved only over time.[34]

Vanderlinden warns of pitfalls, including cultural transcription of meaning and legal qualification of interpretations of observed actions. We believe that there are also problems related to changes in the behaviour of those observed owing to the simple fact that they are being observed, particularly given the identity of the observers as perceived by the observed.

In our case, the conditions for access to the four groups were different in each case. Andrée Lajoie's contacts with the Chief of the band council preceded the project, dating from a conference on Aboriginal constitutional claims at Queen's University in 1990. We were able to meet with the chiefs of the traditional longhouses the next year thanks to Cynthia Chataway, who was a Ph.D. student at Harvard University doing research in the community at the time and is now a professor at York University. Our grants and the team's participation in the Dussault-Erasmus Commission were known to and accepted by every group. Martha Montour, a Mohawk lawyer living in Kahnawake, was on the team of our Aboriginal rights project, and Henry Quillinan had been a liaison officer between the *Fédération des travailleurs et travailleuses du Québec* (FTQ) and Mohawks on construction sites. This also "coloured" our identity.

All of these factors could have generated a degree of self-censorship in the community. We will never know the content or degree of this, and it probably also came into play in the behaviour of both those observed and those interviewed. Indeed, "the difficulties inherent to this method [of observation] most often make it necessary to make allowances".[35] However, these problems would discourage only researchers claiming "scientific neutrality", which constructivism has been shown to be illusory.[36] We prefer to take responsibility for the limitations inherent to our methods by pointing them out to our readers, who will then be aware as we are of the scope of our results, which are also circumscribed by the framework of the interviews.

2.2.3. Interviews

In a society with an oral tradition in which, in principle, written works play a minor role, interviews are a research tool that complements direct observation. Like the latter, they are designed to shed light on the operation of the groups that members of the community acknowledge as legal orders according to our definition, which is based on the criteria of institutionalist sociology of law.

Our goal was neither to identify people's perceptions of the authority centres in the community nor, therefore, to survey a representative sample. We hoped to contact members of the band council and traditional longhouses who could tell us about how those bodies operate, and more specifically, about their functions and how they set out, interpret and apply exclusive normative corpuses. We therefore asked the leaders of the institutions to refer us to members of their groups so that they could give us the information. Thanks to their collaboration, we interviewed an initial group of 76 respondents, who were members of possible legal orders. The respondents were on lists provided by the band council chiefs (20 respondents) and the three longhouses (Nation Office (20 respondents), Longhouse at the Quarry (20 respondents) and Longhouse at Mohawks' Trail (16 respondents).[37]

A second group of interviewees included 20 "unaligned" residents of Kahnawake selected from the general population based on a pretest of 150 people. Two criteria had to be met: non-membership in and indifference to the bodies being studied, and an equal distribution by sex and age.[38] The purpose of creating a second group of informants was to obtain an outside analysis of the changes in the relative strengths of the various groups during the study from 1992–1998, and of the effectiveness of the various normative corpuses competing with one another at Kahnawake.

The semi-structured interviews[39] all concerned compliance with the corpus of the *Great Law of Peace*,[40] which is the normative foundation of the traditional orders; the survival of those norms in the face of intrusion by colonial society and law; their past and present incarnation in a traditional group or specific legal order; and the respective present effectiveness of the *Great Law of Peace* and Canadian law in various aspects of the individual and collective lives of the interviewees. In short, their topic was the establishment, interpretation and application of possibly competing corpuses of exclusive norms addressed to the community as a whole. Band council and longhouse respondents were interviewed by Henry Quillinan, and the unaligned respondents by people known to the team as unaligned and under a guarantee of confidentiality.[41] The respondents were interviewed three times: once in 1993, once in 1995 and once in 1997, so as to take into account changes in the groups and the power relations between them, and the no less changing processes of judicialization of norms and the institutions that convey them.

2.3. Legal Practices at Kahnawake

It is thus from this pluralist point of view and with these sociological and legal methods, which were chosen in accordance with the social and cultural context at Kahnawake, that we approach the analysis of the production of norms operating both at the level of the state, which is most present and operationalized by the band council, and at the level of the traditional longhouses, of which it must be verified whether they are legal orders and therefore entail a possible pluralism, in a form not yet described.

2.3.1. The Band Council and Canadian State Law

An average lawyer, not to mention a positivist, would recognize as applicable at Kahnawake only Canadian state law, of which the band council is the most visible arm. Moreover, even from a pluralist point of view, this is not a legal order to be overlooked when charting out local legal normativity. Indeed, the band council is only the tip of the iceberg of Canadian state institutions, and Canadian law is set out as wholly applicable, aside from some exceptions, to Kahnawake.

In order to see more clearly, we should begin, as always, with the constitutional division of jurisdiction, which gives the federal government jurisdiction over "Indians and lands reserved for the Indians",[42] according to the nineteenth-century formulation. This does not exclude application[43] of provincial laws of general scope, in virtue both of the general principles of constitutional law[44] and their incorporation in federal legislation itself.[45] Proof of this is the fact that in 1886, very soon after Confederation, the federal parliament legislated to adopt a general law concerning Indians, which provided for the legal regime of "bands" and set out the powers of their councils.[46] This was followed by orders in council to create individual reserves.

Three years later, it was in virtue of such an order in council that the Caughnawaga (as it was called at the time) reserve was created.[47] Its council, which was later restructured by decree under the *Indian Act*, has the regulatory powers delegated to all band councils.[48] Regulations created under the powers delegated by positive Canadian law are interpreted and applied by the band council, as are other federal norms, such as those contained in the *Indian Act*.

The band council even enforces them through a local court[49] and its own police force, the Peacekeepers.[50] In other words, in the area covered by the Kahnawake "reserve", the band council is a subordinate level of the Canadian government, which sets out, interprets and applies local and other norms, thereby exercising the regulatory powers delegated within the classical positivist pyramid under the superior and preponderant authority of federal legislation.[51] These powers are parallel to Québec legislation,[52] under the supreme authority of the constitutional *grundnorm* and consequently in compliance with constitutionalized Aboriginal rights,[53] as defined by Canadian courts.

Here we find LeRoy and Wane's third type of law,[54] namely, "local law" resulting from the development of the state and its accompanying administrative apparatus, which determines the way the law is formed, though its operation is controlled by local authorities. A feature of this form of law is the possibility for colonial law to be reinterpreted in light of Aboriginal ideas. It is thus a reversal of earlier times, when several versions of pre-colonial Iroquois law, the pre-existence of which has been established,[55] were codified under the colonizer's influence at the end of the nineteenth century and the beginning of the twentieth century.[56]

This is to say that at the end of an evolution in which we see the three first stages of LeRoy and Wane's schema, we find at Kahnawake not only a local legal order of state origin, but also, more generally, the Canadian legal order. In this sense, there is dual pluralism. First, there is Canadian federalism, which is already a certain, very moderate, form of pluralism. Next, there is the other form of pluralism, which is no less weak and involves devolution of powers to the band council, to which the unified Canadian state has assigned a special regime based on the values of the group that it represents.

However, taken in isolation, these forms of pluralism would not have been sufficient to confirm our hypothesis. In both cases, the pluralism is of the most benign intra-state sort. It involves a kind of recovery of control by powers with non-dominant values, and is designed to guarantee the unity of the Canadian state, if not its cohesion, and ward off the emergence of a more radical, extra-state pluralism.

Is the attempt successful or are we now witnessing the emergence of precisely the "popular law" of the fourth type described by LeRoy and Wane, which results in extra-state pluralism itself? The answer is not obvious, especially considering the fact[57] that the respondents designated by the band council never unanimously claimed to be governed solely by Canadian law. However, to circumscribe the issue a little better, we first have to look much more closely at the normative practices of the traditional longhouses.

2.3.2. The Traditional Longhouses and their Normative Practices

There are thus three longhouses at Kahnawake (2.3.2.1), which have many features in common, but differ from one another, especially over time. All of these aspects have to be considered, in addition to those to which we normally refer, to determine whether they are real legal orders (2.3.2.2).

2.3.2.1. Three Traditional Longhouses

Above, we briefly presented the three longhouses to which we will now return to see whether their operations involve setting out, interpreting and applying norms. We will draw our information from the findings compiled from our observations and the responses to the interviews, as well as from the respective versions of the *Great Law of Peace* that each longhouse gave us as a reference document.[58]

- #### The Nation Office

According to the members questioned in 1993, the Nation Office adopts norms that it sets out and applies under the authority of the *Great Law of Peace*, which is used as a constitution.[59] Its interpretative activities extend even to its constitution. The first to appear on the contemporary traditional political and normative scene in Kahnawake, this longhouse takes a very clear position on the normative exclusiveness of the *Great Law of Peace* and the bodies that the constitutional document institutes.

All of the respondents adhered to it in 1993. Indeed, even if they did not all have unshakeable faith in the founding myth of the Peacemaker and the Mohawk's civilizing mission[60] they all said that the *Great Law of Peace* contained political, social and religious norms binding on Mohawks since time immemorial. They said it was especially binding on the organization of clans, in which women play a key role, particularly with respect to appointing members of great peace and war councils. The great councils are responsible for setting out and applying norms composed of corresponding rights and obligations concerning an individual's membership in the Mohawk nation.[61] They also unanimously maintained that the norms and government bodies had survived colonization and were now incarnated in the Nation Office. All those with an opinion on the topic (17 out of 20 respondents) said that they governed themselves according to the general principles of the *Great Law of Peace* with respect to both private relationships with family members and members of the community, and even in relations with traditional government and Canadian administrative bodies.

Beginning in 1995 and growing in 1997, in the wake of the very painful consequences of the Oka crisis for this group, the admirable unanimity began to crumble. Though fewer believed in the founding myth, the respondents linked with the Nation Office still unanimously asserted that the old rules of Mohawk society had survived. However only a small majority said that its government bodies were still there (11 out of 20) and only 13 out of 20 said that they governed themselves according to a combination of the *Great Law of Peace* and Canadian law. They held that the bodies instituted by the *Great Law of Peace* were competent to interpret not only the norms they produced but also the *Great Law* itself.[62] Thus, belief in the founding myth dropped, as did the importance of the Confederation, which is considered by this longhouse to encompass six nations. Modernity was partially accepted, particularly with respect to science and medicine. The *Great Law* was construed as giving the Mohawks control over land to the south of Québec, in New

York State, the border of which was not recognized. It was also interpreted as classifying violence as one of several legitimate means of fighting enemies. The same bodies were responsible for applying norms, and sanctions included compensation and, in the most serious cases, exclusion.

- ### The Longhouse at the Quarry

The Longhouse at the Quarry is much more monolithic than the Nation Office. Its members' answers to our questions were unanimous and did not change from year to year. Indeed, in many respects their constant positions have remained those of the Nation Office in 1993, particularly with respect to the survival of Mohawk norms and government bodies, which they naturally consider to be incarnated in the Longhouse at the Quarry. They also unanimously agreed that they governed themselves according to a mixture of Canadian law and the precepts of the *Great Law of Peace*, despite an interpretation of the latter that might lead one to think the opposite.

Indeed, this interpretation[63] validates the founding myth, for it is consistent with the myth's most messianic aspects, in which the creator is present and the Mohawks are invested with a civilizing mission that completely rejects modernity. However, they considered that the Confederation of Five Nations no longer exists, and their land claims extend all the way down to Florida. Yet, this longhouse's interpretation of the *Great Law* does not justify violence or intervention in Canadian affairs. Norms are applied by the great councils set out in the *Great Law* and using traditional sanctions: compensation and exclusion.

- ### The Longhouse at Mohawk's Trail

Just as monolithic as the preceding longhouse, and just as unchanging in its positions, which are in fact almost identical, the Longhouse at Mohawk's Trail is different only in that more of its members believe in the founding myth, its interpretation of the *Great Law* is even more pacifist, and its land claims are limited to the area historically occupied by the Iroquois.

2.3.2.2. Three Legal Orders?

Are the longhouses, the normative activity of which we have just described, veritable legal orders and separate from one another? The answer to this question differs slightly depending on the time period.

- ### At the Beginning of the 1990s

When we began our observation and study, the three longhouses were distinct, complete legal orders, even though two of them could be considered embryonic at the time. All three had complete normative activities: they set out, interpreted and applied, through the great peace and war councils instituted by the *Great Law of Peace*, norms with exclusive scope that addressed the whole community.

However, we should note some particularities of the normative activities at the time, especially with respect to interpretation and effectiveness.

- **Interpretation**

If we begin by taking it as a given that the legal orders with which we are dealing do not contain internal institutional differentiation, and that their three normative functions (setting out, interpretation and application) are performed by a single body in each longhouse, namely the great peace council or the great war council depending on the situation, then we should not be surprised to find that the same people set out and interpret norms. Indeed, this has no consequences for these functions so long as what is in question is the interpretation of rules adopted by the councils themselves. However, the longhouses interpret not only their own respective norms, but also their shared constitution, the *Great Law of Peace*. The interpretations that we consulted contained major differences, and were among the features that make it possible to distinguish between the three legal orders constituted by the Nation Office, Longhouse at the Quarry and Longhouse at Mohawk's Trail. Again, this is not surprising to a lawyer familiar with the ways that courts of various levels of a federal state can interpret their shared constitution, for example with respect to jurisdiction. This is an example of the dialogue that exists in every community in which there is social pluralism. However, in the case of Kahnawake, each longhouse's different interpretation of the *Great Law of Peace* seems at first sight to also be a setting out of the *Law*.

This impression results from the oral tradition characteristic of Mohawk society, in which the *Great Law* was initially recorded on *wampums*.[64] The pictographs used to preserve legal provisions and treaties are not read like a book, but are rather like memory aids in the form of symbols that help to recall the commitments the sacred nature of which they symbolize. In these circumstances, a longhouse belonging to Mohawk society, the tradition of which is still oral but experiencing a transition imposed by immersion in contemporary Canadian society, interprets, adopts and sometimes even transcribes its version of the *Great Law of Peace* in a text. Is this not in fact a statement of the norms contained in the *Great Law*? Here there may be not only interpretation of the constitutional instrument by a body to which it applies and which it created, but also a merger (or perhaps confusion) of the functions themselves.

Unlike the internal norms adopted by each longhouse, those contained in the *Great Law of Peace* are held to have been proclaimed by the Peacemaker on behalf of the Creator, the Great Spirit. Yet is it not in fact the longhouse councils that proclaim them through their choice to have a written version of the document and through their oral interpretations, by setting out what has until now been only evoked? Stanley Fish[65] would certainly be pleased to see his theories confirmed in a traditional society! Without going so far as to deny that interpreters of legislation are unconstrained by the normative texts in question, which in this case is in a symbolic medium, we can draw a parallel with interpretations of our own *Constitution*. In the end, are *wampum* pictographs really less restrictive than some expressions that appear in the *Constitution* of Canada, which are nonetheless in written form, such as "freedom of expression", "free and democratic society" or even, and more relevantly, "Aboriginal rights"? Indeed, even if we were to conclude here (wrongly, we believe) that the functions of statement and interpretation are merged, and that the longhouses set out different "Great Laws of Peace", this would only strengthen their status as legal orders. It seems to us that the same problems do not arise when it comes to the relative effectiveness[66] of the norms that the longhouses produce. For, even though the norms are designed to be exclusive and are addressed to the whole community, support for and compliance with them depends on the group in question. This is an issue that has to be explored.

• Effectiveness

In the first period we are analysing, which lasted from the late 1980s to 1994, the Nation Office gained the support of a significant part of Kahnawake's population, which it almost managed to hegemonize during the Oka crisis in 1990. Its members governed in accordance with the *Great Law of Peace*, set out exclusive norms, addressed them to the whole community, and had almost enough legitimacy to completely replace the state authorities. A large minority of unaligned respondents said that they wholly or partly followed the traditional norms flowing from the *Great Law*, and some went even so far as to say that the ancient Mohawk government bodies were incarnated in the Nation Office.

The same could not be said for the two other longhouses, which never had more than a few dozen members and sympathizers, and which unaligned respondents did not consider to be repositories of the ancient rules. From the inside, however, the longhouses adopted missions that encompassed the whole community, maintained the exclusive nature of their norms and, even when they admitted to also being partly subject to Canadian legislation, always said that it was not their choice but out of obligation and realism. Technically, and seen from inside, they were complete legal orders, but outside perceptions did not make people as willing to spontaneously acknowledge that status as they were in the case of the Nation Office. The respective strength of the legal orders at Kahnawake, as is probably the case elsewhere, was thus linked in a way to their success and the effectiveness of their norms. In short, it was related to their legitimacy. By analysing these factors, we can also circumscribe their roles and that of the state legal order in the whole picture, and see whether we are looking at intra- or extra-state pluralism. The second period, which began in 1994, advanced our findings.

• From 1994

Effectiveness of norms and legitimacy of legal orders are at the heart of the changes that began in 1994. The Longhouse at the Quarry and Longhouse at Mohawks' Trail kept but did not increase their memberships and maintained their earlier positions on the founding myth, the survival of Mohawk government bodies and rules, the incarnation of the bodies in their respective longhouses, voluntary compliance with the precepts of the *Great Law of Peace*, and submission by obligation to Canadian law in all spheres of private and public life. However, beginning in 1994, though the Nation Office continued to assert the survival of Mohawk government bodies, only a small majority of respondents asserted that this was the case and that the bodies were incarnated in the Nation Office. Only a small minority said that they governed themselves according to the *Great Law of Peace* alone, even though submission to Canadian law was still seen as an obligation. While the other longhouses remained stable, not to say frozen, the local state legal order, namely the band council, moved in the opposite direction from that of the Nation Office. Until then, band council respondents had weak belief in the founding myth, unanimously agreed that traditional Mohawk rules and bodies had not survived, and generally said that they complied with Canadian law in all circumstances, though out of obligation also. However, beginning in 1994, they grew closer to traditionalist positions. Of course, their belief in the founding myth was no stronger, perhaps even weaker, but a small minority (3 and 4 out of 20 in 1995 and 1997, respectively) considered that the Mohawks' ancient rules had survived colonialism, even though they were not incarnated in any longhouse. Moreover, a majority (15 out of 20) in 1995 and all of the respondents in 1997 said that they were governed both by Canadian law, to which they submitted by obligation, and the precepts of the *Great Law of Peace*.

What had happened? On the political level, the Oka crisis profoundly shook the Nation Office which, having begun a process that it was unable to control to the community's satisfaction, first became more radical, and then divided in two after the death of Louis Hall, its chief for many years. The split was over ideology and interpretation of doctrine. The loss of a number of members and sympathizers, who were discouraged by the failure at Oka and the loss of the revenue that it would have produced, even resulted in the facilities closing for over a year. At the same time, the band council, which had been losing steam at first, rebuilt its power by managing the aftermath of the crisis so as to re-establish its outside credibility and internal legitimacy. With respect to the outside, it succeeded in inspiring trust in the federal government by proving that it had enough control over the "reserve" to enforce its decisions. Within the community, it opened public forums (a community newspaper and radio station) to even the most radical members of the longhouses and, especially, integrated traditionalist themes into its own discourse, as can be seen from our findings.

The reconciliation of the local arm of the state legal order and the traditional legal order that had been until then dominant, and the resulting marginalization of the other longhouses, was not without consequences for the production of law at Kahnawake. In particular, it had an impact on the presence in the community of a legal pluralism that we will now try to describe.

3. A complex and Evolving Pluralism

As we have pointed out, at Kahnawake there has been pluralism internal to the state legal order since the end of the nineteenth century. The band council is only an administrative arm exercising at Kahnawake powers analogous to those of municipalities and delegated by the Canadian legislatures. Both Canadian and Québec legislation of general scope apply to the "reserve". Federalism and administrative delegation combine to create an initial intra-state "pluralism" with normative, non-competing arms that are hierarchized in a Kelsenian pyramid crowned by the *Constitution* of Canada. The unity of the state is in no way threatened by this kind of integrating and reconciling pluralism. However, this is only the first feature of the present normative landscape, which dates from the 1970s. There is also another pluralism, this time extra-state. In it, three traditional longhouses are juxtaposed, each with the attributes of legal orders. In other words, they each set out, interpret and apply exclusive norms targeting the whole community. No hierarchical relationship exists among the three longhouses, and they compete with one another.

Despite the fact that they all refer to the *Great Law of Peace* as to a constitution, these are complete legal orders. Of course, a large part of their normative activity rests in stating an interpretation of the *Great Law of Peace* through a process characteristic of oral traditions, which consists in explaining the *wampum* pictographs. If this was the limit of their normativity, they would be only partial legal orders.[67] They would perform only two of the three functions essential to a legal order: interpretation and application.

Indeed, in such a case, the partial legal orders would be triplets, perhaps even Siamese triplets, for they would have a common trunk: the *Great Law of Peace*, whose mythical author, the Peacemaker, was sent to Earth by the Creator to re-establish order after humans had caused chaos following creation. He created the *Great Law of Peace* and thereby performed the function of establishing the norms. However, by setting out norms to supplement the *Great Law*, the longhouses participate in the establishment function also, thereby becoming complete legal orders that perform all of the functions that characterize such bodies.

Thus, there is no doubt. Formally, we are faced with several sources of state and non-state norms, which form a very complex pluralism. However, the pluralism is changing and has to be described as having two different stages. In Kahnawake's recent history, the first stage runs from the end of the 1970s, when the Nation Office and then the two other longhouses emerged on the normative scene, to the mid-1990s. The second begins in 1994, when the effects of the 1990 Oka crisis began to be felt. Particularly through the transfer of legitimacy and normative effectiveness between the various legal orders in question, the real legal pluralism that characterized the stages reduced the intensity while maintaining intact the formal appearances of complex intra- and extra-state pluralism throughout the whole period.

In the first stage, the Nation Office, the main Mohawk legal order, enjoyed growing legitimacy, which was reflected in recognition of its authority and the effectiveness of its norms throughout the community. The norms of the two other competing legal orders were binding on only small sub-groups of the community, though they targeted the whole. The normative scene was initially vague and piecemeal, but gradually became polarized between the band council and the Nation Office, which almost led to a successful popular takeover at the time of the Oka crisis. At that point, through the legal orders that we have described, a real legitimate extra-state pluralism existed at the same time as the formal extra-state pluralism. The "local" law of the band council coexisted with the "popular" law of the Nation Office,[68] which seemed to be on the verge of supplanting it.

In the second stage, the normative scene, which was then polarized, became more dispersed again. The prominence of the dominant traditional legal order decreased until it temporarily disappeared, the state legal order was consolidated, and "local" law conquered "popular" law. Was the triumph definitive or are we simply observing one of many swings in the power relationships? Despite the many years that we spent on it, perhaps our research captured only an episode, and a relatively short one, when we consider the Mohawks' history. We certainly do not want to be caught making determinist predictions.

However, we can review the conditions that were met, and which are perhaps necessary for the kind of normative reversal that began in 1994. The band council's reappropriation of control over Mohawk norms at Kahnawake initially involved a loss of the Nation Office's legitimacy within the community following the Oka failure and a large share of the population's disapproval of the methods used by the radical longhouse during the crisis. The Nation Office also lost some of its income because radical members left out of disappointment with the turn of events. Yet, the reappropriation would not have been possible if the band council, which distributes a large federal budget on the "reserve" and has the power to enforce its laws on the population, had not also built up its credibility in the eyes of the outside Canadian community, to which it belongs, by proving the effectiveness of its authority in the community at Kahnawake. Its effectiveness was in turn dependent on its legitimacy in the Mohawk community, to which it also belongs, which it gained by making ideological and other concessions to the traditionalists.

In short, the dominance, if not the effectiveness and even survival, of a legal order in a context of evolving pluralism seems to depend on three factors: financial resources, outside credibility and internal legitimacy. At Kahnawake, as elsewhere, these requirements were not always compatible because outside credibility and internal legitimacy are difficult to reconcile in the context of domination, particularly when the domination is colonial. If our observations are accurate, variations in these factors underlie the unpredictable evolution of the state legal order and local law towards confirmation of their still precarious status, or their possible replacement by a traditional legal order and popular law. It is very difficult to tell which scenario is likely to occur first in a pluralist environment that is by definition changing.

4. Conclusion

Beyond confirming our hypotheses, our findings suggest a surprising observation and an avenue of research. Let us begin with the observation: there are similarities where we least expected them between Aboriginal law and our own. First, the *wampums* and Canadian constitutional legislation resemble each other. They are both equally imprecise, give rise to the same interpretation mechanisms, and assign the same role to the interpreter in the production of law.

It suffices to compare the creation implied in the various written versions of the *wampums* symbolizing the *Great Law of Peace* with that recently demonstrated by the Supreme Court of Canada with respect to the preamble of the *Constitution Act, 1867*[69] to see that we are not exaggerating the similarity.

Moreover, in both Mohawk society and our own, this creativity seems to face the same kinds of limitations related to legitimacy based on the match between the values that the legislators convey in the law and the dominant values in the community. After the Oka crisis, the fate of those who had interpreted the *Great Law of Peace* as authorizing violence was no different from that of judges who err in their readings of dominant cultural values.[70] This means that hermeneutic theories, particularly «*systémale analysis*», have greater scope than that generally attributed to them. This is despite the fact that they are based on relationships to *texts* and situate in the interpretative community the limits of the interpretative creativity of law like other forms of written discourse.[71] As we suspected, «*systémale analysis*» is also valid in societies based on oral traditions, where the relationship to writing is replaced by a relationship to symbolic media.[72]

An avenue of research emerges from the theoretical contradictions to which we were led by analysing pluralism at Kahnawake. Probably because of its relationship with legitimacy, we have been led to place great importance on the effectiveness of law as a means of accounting for significant differences between legal orders that are nonetheless formally similar and consistent with the requirements of institutionalist theory. This almost makes effectiveness a constitutive feature of law.

APPENDIX

INTERVIEW GUIDE AND QUESTIONNAIRE

The interviews were broken into three themes about which we began by trying to talk freely with the respondents (open questions). The information thus provided was complemented by data gathered by asking specific questions (questionnaire), when necessary.

Interview

Theme 1 - The existence of Mohawk norms: the *Great Law of Peace*

1.   Objective
*   Confirm (infirm) the hypothesis that the *Great Law of Peace* is a set of binding norms.

2.   Procedure
*   Ask the respondent about the existence of binding Mohawk norms, whether or not they are contained in the *Great Law of Peace*;
*   Ask the respondent to identify these norms, their origins and their nature;
*   Ask the respondent about his or her degree of compliance with the norms flowing from the *Great Law of Peace*.

The answers of the unaligned respondents are used to weight the answers of the aligned respondents and provide a socio-political context.

3.   Questions
First: open question(s) that give the respondent complete latitude to express him or herself.
Second: specific complementary questions on various aspects of the *Great Law of Peace*.
Third: validation questions, which reformulate questions already asked and should obtain, in theory, answers identical to those already given.

Theme 2 – The bodies under study, and the setting out, interpretation and application of Mohawk norms

1.   Objective
*   Confirm (infirm) the hypothesis that one or more of the bodies in question sets out, interprets and applies binding Mohawk norms; assess the scope of the bodies' authority in the community

2.   Procedure
*   Ask the respondent about all aspects of the operation of the body under study and to which he or she belongs;

- Ask the respondent about his or her perception of the nature and vocation of the body under study and to which he or she belongs;
- Ask the respondent about his or her perception of the operation, nature and vocation of the bodies under study other than the one to which he or she belongs.

The answers of the unaligned respondents are used to weight the answers of the aligned respondents and to provide a socio-political context.

3.   Questions

First: open question(s) that give the respondent complete latitude to express him or herself.

Second: specific complementary questions on the operation of the bodies in question.

Third: validation questions, which reformulate questions already asked and should obtain, in theory, answers identical to those already given

Theme 3 – The relationship between Mohawk and Canadian norms

1.   Objective
- Confirm (infirm) the hypothesis that Mohawk and Canadian norms apply concurrently at Kahnawake;
- Confirm (infirm) the hypothesis that Mohawks adhere to, feel bound by and comply with Aboriginal norms more spontaneously than they do in the case of Canadian norms.

2.   Procedure
- Obtain information from respondents on their perceptions of the relationship between Mohawk and Canadian norms at Kahnawake;
- Obtain information from respondents on their reasons for complying with the respective norms.

3.   Questions
- Specific questions about the relationship between the norms of Mohawk law and Canadian law with respect to key aspects of family, social and political life, and about the respondents' attitudes to these norms.

QUESTIONNAIRE

Fifteen specific questions could be asked, depending on what had been mentioned or omitted in response to the open questions. The first five were designed to determine the respondents' degree of loyalty to the body to which they belonged. The other ten were designed to tell whether the bodies were legal orders. The questions were as follows:

1.   Do you believe in the creation story as told by the *Great Law of Peace*, in the roles of inspired men (shamans), and in traditional Mohawk medicine and magic?

2.   Do you believe that the Iroquois have a civilizing mission to make other

peoples aware of the precepts of the *Great Law of Peace* and to impose the precepts by force?

3. Do you believe that in ancient times five (or six) Iroquois nations united to form a confederation and that they adopted a series of binding political, legal and religious norms and the apparatus required to enforce them?

4. Do you believe that in ancient times the Mohawk nation adopted binding political, legal and religious norms made up of corresponding rights and obligations that were related to an individual's membership in the nation?

5. Do you believe that the social organization of the Mohawk nation was based on the clan, in which women played a key role, and which elected the members of the great peace and war councils, who were responsible for enacting and applying norms to which Mohawks had to submit, and for performing rites essential to life?

6. Do you believe that the norms of Mohawk society, or some of them, have survived contact with White society?

7. Do you believe that the government and legal bodies of Mohawk society have survived contact with White society?

8. Do you believe that these bodies are now incarnated in:
   a) the Mihao group
   b) the McComber group
   c) the Nation Office
   d) the Band Council

9. Do you believe that these bodies have ever been incarnated in:
   a) the Mihao group
   b) the McComber group
   c) the Nation Office
   d) the Band Council

10. In general, do you govern your actions in accordance with:
    a) the *Great Law of Peace*
    b) White people's law
    c) a combination of the two

11. In your relationships with members of your family, do you follow:
    a) the *Great Law of Peace*
    b) White people's law
    c) a combination of the two

12. In your relationships with members of the community, do you follow:
    a) the *Great Law of Peace*
    b) White people's law
    c) a combination of the two

13. In your relationships with the community's administrative bodies, do you follow:
    a) the *Great Law of Peace*
    b) White people's law
    d) a combination of the two

14. In your relationships with White administrative bodies, do you follow:
    a) the *Great Law of Peace*

      b)   White people's law
      c)   a combination of the two
15.   When you obey White people's law, is it:
      a)   by choice?
      b)   out of obligation?

---

[1] The research project the findings of which are reported here was designed and initiated with the collaboration of Alain Bissonnette. Unfortunately, he had to leave the project when he became Research Director of the International Centre for Human Rights and Democratic Development. The authors would like to thank the Social Sciences and Humanities Research Council (SSHRC) of Canada and the *Fonds pour la formation de chercheurs et l'aide à la recherche* (FCAR) for the grants they awarded for the research. The authors would also like to express their gratitude to the chiefs of the band council and the traditional longhouses, their members and more generally, the people of Kahnawake, without whose collaboration this project could not have been carried out.

[2] A. Lajoie and G. Rocher, professors, Centre de recherche en droit public, Faculty of Law, University of Montréal; H. Quillinan, Ph.D. Student, Faculty of Law, University of Montréal; R. Macdonald, Professor, Faculty of Law, McGill University.

[3] See A. Lajoie, "Synthèse introductive" in A. Lajoie, J. M. Brisson, S. Normand and A. Bissonnette, Eds., *Le statut juridique des peuples autochtones au Québec et le pluralisme*, Cowansville: Éditions Yvon Blais, 1996, 1 at 7–20 [Lajoie]; we summarize this introduction in the following paragraphs for reasons of clarity.

[4] R. A. Dahl, *Polyarchy: Participation and Opposition*, New Haven: Yale University Press, 1971.

[5] S. F. Moore, "Law and Social Change: The Semi-Autonomous Social Field as an Appropriate Subject of Study", (1973) 7 *Law and Society Review* 719.

[6] J. G. Belley, "L'État et la régulation juridique des sociétés globales. Pour une problématique du pluralisme juridique", (April 1986) 18 (1) *Sociologie et sociétés*, 11–32.

[7] M. Reinstein, Ed., *Max Weber on Law in Economy and Society*, Cambridge: Harvard University Press, 1954; J. Griffith, "What is Legal Pluralism", (1986) 24 *Journal of Legal Pluralism* 1. [Griffith].

[8] G. Gurvitch, *L'idée du droit social*, Paris: Sirey, 1932; J. Griffith, *ibid.*

[9] R. A. Macdonald, "Images du notariat et imagination du notaire", (1994) 1 *C.P. du N.* 1 at 47 and 48.

[10] R. A. Macdonald, "Pour la reconnaissance d'une normativité juridique implicite et 'inférentielle'", (April 1986) 18 (1) *Sociologie et sociétés* 47–58 [our translation].

[11] This point of view is also shared by J. Vanderlinden, "Vers une nouvelle conception du pluralisme juridique", (1993) 53 *Revue de la recherche juridique. Droit prospectif* 573 – 579.

[12] S. Romano, *L'ordre juridique*, Trans. L. François and P. Gothot, Paris: Dalloz, 1975 at 174; G. Rocher, "Pour une sociologie des ordres juridiques", (1988) 29

C. de D. 91.

[13] G. Timsit, "Sur l'engendrement du droit", (1988) *R.D.P.* 39–75; G. Timsit, *Les noms de la loi*, Paris: PUF, 1991.

[14] According to Alain Bissonnette, who was closely involved in the work of the *Laboratoire d'anthropologie juridique* and familiarized us with it, these researchers consider that law should not be approached as a concept but as a phenomenon. Thus, rather than trying to define what law is, they have chosen to study the phenomena of juridicization in various societies. For them, law is less a specific type of social relation than a specific description that each society gives to certain social relations. In other words, while legal facts are social facts, not all social facts are legal facts. A social fact becomes legal only as a result of specific social control, the purpose of which is to ensure the cohesion and perpetuation of the group in question. From this point of view, law is not a set of specific rules, but instead an inter-normative process.

[15] N. Rouland, *Anthropologie juridique*, "Droit fondamental" collection, Paris: PUF, 1988 at 147.

[16] É. LeRoy and M. Wane, "La formation des droits non-étatiques", in P. Touzard, Ed., *Encyclopédie juridique de l'Afrique*, Vol. 1: *L'état et le droit*, Abidjan: Nouvelles Éditions africaines, 1982 at 353.

[17] Kahnawake is about 10 kilometers from downtown Montréal.

[18] The Indian Register kept by the Department of Indian Affairs and Northern Development under sections 5, 11 and following of the *Indian Act*, R.S.C. (1985), c. I-5 currently contains the names of around 8600 members of the Kahnawake band, some of whom do not live on the reserve. Others are not on the band council list, which is kept according to the strictest citizenship criteria and contains only 6200 names. There are around 7000 people, federally registered as band members or not, living on the reserve according to departmental sources reported by newspapers. See M. Thibodeau, "Subventions en trop à Kahnawake?", *La Presse* (March 21, 1998) at A5. [Thibodeau].

[19] *Indian Act*, R.S.C. 1886, c. 43.

[20] Thibodeau, *supra*, note 18.

[21] D.R., J. MV. and J. H., "All About Kahnawake: An Answer to Joe Norton", *The Eastern Door*, November 13, 1994.

[22] According to D.R., J. MV. and J. H., *ibid.*, 99.7% of the population own radios and televisions, 80% own VCRs and 41% have stereo systems.

[23] Again according to D.R., J. MV. and J. H., *id.*, 95% of the men over the age of 18 have cars and 60% of the homes have ATVs or snowmobiles.

[24] Royal Commission on Aboriginal Peoples, *People to People, Nation to Nation: Highlights from the Report*, Ottawa: Department of Supply and Services, 1996 at 59–84.

[25] S. Normand, "Les droits des Amérindiens sur le territoire sous le Régime français", in A. Lajoie, J. M. Brisson, S. Normand and A. Bissonnette, *supra*, note 3, 107 at 134.

[26] "It must seem that the Iroquois recognize no masters. And although the French have posted the coat of arms of France among them before and after the English posted those of England, they nevertheless recognize no domination" in C. Jeanen, "The French Relationship with the Amerindians" in *Actes du IV Convengo Inter-*

nazionale dell'Associazione Italiana di Studi Canadesi, Universita di Messina, March 25–28, 1981 at 5–9.

[27] *Acte authentique des Six Nations Iroquoises sur leur indépendance,* November 2, 1748, signed at Château St. Louis, Québec City, and preserved in the Archives judiciaires de Québec, Dulaurent registry.

[28] See Lajoie, *supra,* note 3 at 14–16.

[29] Louis Hall, who died a few days before the interview that he had promised us, was the spiritual father of the Nation Office and Warriors. His teaching, rooted in Mohawk pride, conveyed an interpretation of the *Great Law of Peace* based on the Two Row Wampum. The Two Row Wampum is an Iroquois version of pluralism according to which Iroquois law and White law are two parallel sets of norms, hence the two rows, which coexist on the same land. Hall's teaching advocated armed resistance when necessary.

[30] Wounded Knee was where the United States Cavalry met with armed resistance from the Sioux when they tried to remove them from federal land. It symbolizes the revival of the Aboriginal movement in the United States in the 1970s.

[31] As is often the case in civilizations with oral traditions, we have no written source to validate this information, which was gathered through interviews and participatory observation in the community, the methodology of which is described below.

[32] P. A. Côté, *Interprétation des lois,* Second Edition, Cowansville: Éditions Yvon Blais, 1990.

[33] A. Lajoie, *Jugements de valeurs,* "Les Voies du droit" collection, Paris: PUF, 1997.

[34] J. Vanderlinden, *Anthropologie juridique,* "Connaissance du droit" collection, Paris: Dalloz, 1996 at 63–139.

[35] *Ibid.* at 69 [our translation].

[36] P. Watzlawick, "Préface", in P. Watzalawick, Ed., *L'invention de la réalité ou comment savons-nous ce que nous croyons savoir?,* Paris: Seuil, 1981 at 9–11; V. Villa, *La science du droit,* Paris: LGDJ, 1991; V. Villa, "La science juridique entre descriptivisme et constructivisme" in P. Amselek, Ed., *Théorie du droit et science,* Paris: PUF, 1994 at 281; See also, in a context similar to that of our study, J. P. Chauveau, J. P. Dozon, E. Le Bris, E. Le Roy, G. Salem and F. G. Snyder, "Rapport introductif aux journées d'études", in E. Le Bris, E. Le Roy and F. Leimdorfer, Eds., *Enjeux fonciers en Afrique noire,* Paris: Orstom/Karthala, 1982 at 17–43.

[37] The word *longhouse* designates a traditional Iroquois house used as a meeting place. By extension and metonymy, it has come to mean the body that meets there, just as in English the *House of Commons* has come to mean the body that sits there.

[38] A description of the five groups of respondents can be found in Appendix I [removed from English version].

[39] The interview guide and questionnaire can be found in Appendix II ['Appendix' in English version].

[40] As we indicate below (*infra,* note 58), there are several versions of the *Great Law of Peace,* and each longhouse has chosen a different interpretation. We will try to avoid adding our own, but it should be noted from the beginning that the *Great Law* is the foundation for the Iroquois nation. First, it concerns the founding

myth of the creation of the world and the Peacemaker, who was sent to earth by the Creator to re-establish order out of the chaos that humans had unleashed after creation. However, it also structures the political and social organization of the Iroquois nation and the correlative rights and obligations of the individuals who make up the nation, as well as establishes a code of spiritual practices necessary for communal life.

[41] These people are linked with institutions that are themselves unaligned (the CLSC, hospital, school board and credit union), and Henry Quillinan has remained in touch with them since the 1980s.

[42] *Constitution Act, 1867*, (U.K.), 30 & 31 Vict., c. 3, section 91(24).

[43] We should instead speak of "applicability" in the sense in which positivists consider law set out by a constitutionally valid source to be intrinsically applicable. In fact, and this time in terms of effectiveness, the concrete application of provincial law, including Québec law, on reserve land varies depending on the government in power, its conception of Aboriginal status and, as always, the power relations at the time.

[44] *Four B Manufacturing Ltd.* v. *United Garment Workers of America*, [1980] 1 S.C.R. 1031.

[45] *Indian Act, supra*, note 18, s. 88.

[46] *Indian Act, 1886, supra*, note 19.

[47] Order in Council, March 5, 1889, P.C. 466.

[48] *Indian Act, supra*, note 18, section 81. The powers concern public health, traffic, compliance with legislation, order, misconduct, urban planning, some farm issues, local business, games and sports, and other similar matters.

[49] The municipal court was created by *Kahnawake Band Council Resolution* C-432, 1989, adopted under section 107 of the *Indian Act, supra*, note 18.

[50] Initially created by *Kahnawake Band Council Resolution* 44/79-80, 1979 and amended by *Kahnawake Band Council Resolution* 71/91-92, 1991, the police force was later "integrated" into the set of municipal police forces in Québec by a series of Québec government decree: *Décret 1219-95 concernant le maintien d'un corps de police autochtone sur le territoire de Kahnawake*, (1995) 127 G.O. II, 4271; *Décret 433-96 concernant la prolongation de l'entente concernant les services de police sur le territoire de Kahnawake, signée le 11 septembre 1995*, (1996) 128 G.O. II, 2666; *Décret 621-97 concernant la prestation des services policiers autochtones dans la communauté de Kahnawake*, (1997) 129 G.O. II, 2990; *Décret 563-98 concernant la prestation des services policiers autochtones dans la communauté de Kahnawake*, (1998) 130 G.O. II, 2682.

[51] *Indian Act, supra*, note 18, s. 81, introductory paragraph.

[52] *Supra*, note 42 and 43.

[53] *Constitution Act, 1982*, Schedule B of *Canada Act 1982*, (U.K.) 1982, c. 11, s. 25 and 35.

[54] See *supra*, note 16 at 686.

[55] See *supra*, note 22, 23 and 24.

[56] P. Williams, *The Haudenosaunee Law,* study prepared for the Royal Commission on Aboriginal Peoples, Ottawa, 1993, Introduction at i. [Williams]; See also *supra*, note 55.

[57] Documented by their responses during our interviews. See Entretiens, Bloc III, p. 715.

[58] To our knowledge, there are at least seven written versions of the *Great Law of Peace*. G. Schaaf, "The Birth of Frontier Democracy from an Eagle's Eye View: From the Great Law of Peace to the Constitution of the United States", undated mimeograph, Tree of Peace Society, Akwasasne, consulted at the Nation Office at 5, lists six: (1) the Newhouse version, which is attributed to Seth Newhouse, a Canadian Mohawk, and was revised by Albert Cusick, an Onondaga from New York; (2) the Chiefs' version, compiled in 1900 by the chiefs of the Six Nations Reserve in Ontario and published by Duncan C. Scott in the *Proceedings and Transactions of the Royal Society of Canada* in 1911; (3) the Gibson version dictated in 1899 by Chief J. A. Gibson of the Six Nations Reserve to J. N. B. Newitt of the Smithsonian Institute, Washington, revised by chiefs A. Charles, John Buck and Joshua Buck between 1900 and 1914, and translated by W. N. Fenton of the Smithsonian Institute; (4) the Wallace version, which is a compilation of the first three versions and presented as a narrative by Dr. P. Wallace in *The White Roots of Peace*, Philadelphia, 1946; (5) the Buck version, which is a narrative in the Mohawk language by R. Buck that was transcribed and edited in English by the North American Indian Travelling College Staff, Cornwall, Ontario, in 1984 under the title *The Great Law, Traditional Teachings*; (6) the Mohawk version, a contemporary interpretation by J. C. Mohawk, former editor of *Akwasasne Notes*. We have also found a seventh version: the Hall version, published in September 1987 by the Iroquois Confederation and signed by Louis Hall. [Hall] It provides every article in both Mohawk and English. Note that versions 2, 3, 4 and 5, which were codified by or for colonizers, correspond to LeRoy and Wane's second type of customary law, while versions 1, 6 and 7 are popular law of the fourth type. At Kahnawake, the Nation Office uses the Hall version and has provided us with a copy of it, the Longhouse at Mohawks' Trail referred us to the Newhouse version, as did the Longhouse at the Quarry, though the latter said it preferred the oral version of its chief, Stuart Mihao.

[59] Hall version, *ibid.*

[60] According to the myth, the Creator or Great Spirit made an orderly world in which humans later unleashed chaos. The Creator sent the Peacemaker to re-establish order by revealing to the Mohawks the only code of conduct valid for every human in his or her relations with other living things. The code is to be used as a foundation for the civilizing mission the Mohawks have been assigned.

[61] The councils are composed of members of different clans, who are chosen by the clan mothers for their wisdom and skill as warriors. Council meetings are held in the presence of the clan mothers, and presided over by the Grand Chief. Their purpose is to make decisions and adopt rules necessary for governing the community.

[62] Later we will come back to the theoretical problems posed by the difficulty in distinguishing between the statement and interpretation of norms based on pictographs such as *wampums*, particularly when the interpretation is based in an oral tradition but recorded in a written text.

[63] Consistent with this longhouse's insistence on the dominance of the oral tradition, even over the Newhouse version, to which the respondents nonetheless

referred us, we have identified this interpretation in the teachings of the chief of this longhouse, to which Henry Quillinan has devoted much time.

[64] Defined by Paul Williams, *supra*, note 56 at 50, as a medium for communication and formalization of exchange.

[65] S. Fish, *Respecter le sens commun*, "La Pensée juridique moderne" collection, Paris: LGDJ, 1995; and especially S. Fish, *Is There a Text in this Class?*, Cambridge/London: Harvard University Press, 1980.

[66] Here, "effectiveness" is understood in its most common sense, in which it designates the attainment of the result apparently anticipated by those who state norms for their addressees. In other words, it means adherence, if not constant compliance and, implicitly, recognition of the authority of the originators of the norms.

[67] A. Lajoie, *Pouvoir disciplinaire et tests de dépistage de drogues en milieu de travail: illégalité ou pluralisme*, Cowansville: Éditions Yvon Blais, 1995 at 59–67.

[68] See É. LeRoy and M. Wane's classification, *supra*, note 16 at 686.

[69] *Reference re. Remuneration of Judges of the Provincial Court of Prince Edward Island* and *Reference re. Independence and Impartiality of Judges of the Provincial Court of Prince Edward Island*, [1998] 1 S.C.R. 3.

[70] See Lajoie, *supra*, note 3 at 186–191.

[71] *Ibid.*, at 140–167.

[72] R. Macdonald, "Legal Bilingualism", (1997) 42 *McGill L.J.* 119; A. Lajoie, *supra*, note 2 at 13–15 and 24; A. Lajoie and P. Verville, "Les traités d'alliance entre les Français et les Premières Nations sous le régime français" in A. Lajoie, J. M. Brisson, S. Normand and A. Bissonnette, quoted *supra*, note 3, 143 at 166 and 167.

Aboriginal Governance
with or without the Canadian *Charter*?

Ghislain Otis[1]

"Peoples are thus alive when they constantly transform their today into new customs..."[2]

1. Introduction

Among the still unresolved issues concerning application of the *Canadian Charter of Rights and Freedoms*,[3] the question of its enforceability on Aboriginal governments is probably the most complex in terms of law, and the most sensitive with respect to political philosophy. Indeed, this issue puts the spotlight on the underlying tension in the constitutional edifice between fundamental individual rights, which are the common heritage of all human beings, and the group rights of Aboriginal peoples, which are an exclusive heritage based on the principle of Aboriginality. In other words, this issue is about understanding how the *Constitution* had braided the universal with the individual as new Aboriginal governmental institutions emerge out of court decisions, territorial negotiations and self-government agreements.

There are a variety of legal regimes for organising and exercising power in Aboriginal communities. Such regimes range from band councils exercising the powers mentioned in the *Indian Act*[4] to the territorial government of Nunavut,[5] and includes the various institutions established through a growing number of self-government agreements.[6] This study focuses on the specific case of Aboriginal government institutions that are "recognized and affirmed" by section 35 of the *Constitution Act, 1982*,[7] that is, on institutions derived from aboriginal rights and those that are either confirmed or created by treaty.[8] This paper is intended as a contribution to the ongoing debate among legal scholars on the implications of sections 32[9] and 25[10] of the *Charter* with respect to these governments.

The Supreme Court of Canada has not yet unequivocally validated the thesis defended by the Royal Commission on Aboriginal peoples, and a clear majority of commentators, according to which existing Aboriginal rights under section 35 include a general right to self-government covering a wide range of powers relating to the affairs of a community holding such a right.[11] However, it is by no means inappropriate for the purpose of this paper to assume that the highest court will sooner or later acknowledge the inherent right to self-government.[12] As for Aboriginal governments whose powers are defined, confirmed or established by treaties, such as the *Nisga'a Final Agreement*,[13] they are likely to become a primary framework for new Aboriginal governance as land claim negotiations progress.[14]

A large body of scholarly work asserts that the *Charter* is completely[15] or very substantially inapplicable to an Aboriginal government acting pursuant to an Aboriginal or Treaty right. Is this the case? In this article, I argue that these Aboriginal governments only enjoy a limited immunity from *Charter* review based on the general principle of constitutional validation explicitly asserted in section 25 of the *Charter*. I will attempt to show that protecting Aboriginal difference is not inconsistent with construing section 32 of the *Charter* as extending to section 35 Aboriginal governments.

The absolute immunity thesis is first based on the fact that no explicit reference is made in section 32 of the *Charter*[16] to Aboriginal institutions flowing from Aboriginal or Treaty rights.[17] Absolute immunity is said to be reinforced by section 25, which, according to the proponents of this thesis, rules out any broad purposive interpretation of section 32 that would make it possible to include section 35 institutions in the *Charter's* ambit. I will therefore examine the meaning that should be given to the omission of Aboriginal institutions in the explicit definition of the *Charter's* scope. I will first argue that section 32 of the *Charter* can and should be read broadly so as to include section 35 Aboriginal governments. I will then explain why section 25 of the *Charter* by no means defeats such an extensive definition of governmental action for the purpose of applying the *Charter*. I will also attempt to show that legal commentators have so far failed to assess properly the scope of the *Charter* immunity provided by section 25 of the *Charter*.

Before reaching these rather technical legal issues, however, one must discuss the broader issue of the proper relationship, in the present-day context, between good governance, individual rights and freedoms, and Aboriginal difference. I will begin by questioning the widespread tendency among legal scholars to posit a fundamental tension, or even opposition, between Aboriginal cultures and the modern culture of fundamental individual rights and freedoms.

2. Good Governance, Individual Rights and Aboriginal Difference: Conflict or Symbiosis?

2.1. Fundamental Rights and Freedoms in the Era of "Good Governance"

The emergence of new Aboriginal governments means that, for a growing number of Aboriginal groups, the time has come to govern themselves as discrete human communities in the twenty-first century. Yet, today, "to govern" inevitably means coming to terms with the ideological and institutional universe of "good governance". In other words, it means taking care of a people's business in a time infused with a certain idea of good, just and efficient government.

The most neutral and generic meaning of the term "governance" refers to the procedures and institutions through which decisions are made and authority exercised within an organization. In a less neutral and more normative perspective, the notion of "good" governance was initially forged in management theory and was intended to improve the way private corporations were run.[18] In Canadian and international discourse today, the rhetoric of good governance has gradually permeated the political and institutional aspects of social life. It prescribes mechanisms, procedures and institutions through which citizens can exercise fundamental rights, fulfill obligations to one another and manage disputes peacefully. Governance is thus not mere "government". It is not an entity or body that dictates its will to the populace from the peak of an institutional pantheon, but a system in which communal concerns are subjects of ongoing deliberation, negotiation and arbitration involving both government and the governed. Government is thus regarded as just one of the components of a multi-hubbed network of stakeholders essential to a society's development.[19]

Regardless of its ideological bias, more or less embedded in economic liberalism,[20] good governance is a "child of democracy,"[21] and its minimum postulate is universal enjoyment of civil and political rights. Indeed, there is no intrinsic contradiction between good governance and social and economic rights as acknowledged by the United Nations which describe the rule of law and protection of fundamental rights, including social and economic rights, as necessary conditions for human development:

> "Good" or "democratic" governance also exists where government authorities are supported by and accountable to the will of the people. It exists where transparent and democratic institutions make it possible to participate fully in politics, and where the protection of human rights guarantees the right to expression, association and objection. Finally, it exists where the government and its institutions protect the poor and weakest, and promote the human development of all citizens.[22]

At first sight, "good" or "democratic" governance might seem like a fashionably named but essentially recycled version of classical legal and political notions such as the rule of law, democracy and human rights. However, captured in the dynamics of governance, human rights and freedoms take on a more clearly pragmatic and instrumental dimension. Good governance represents fundamental rights "in action", as practical tools for the management of economic and social development because they guarantee transparency, accountability and, at the end of the day, equitable effectiveness of government.[23] Based on the fact that no human society aspires to violence and poverty and on the observation that societies with democratic governance are less often prey to endemic violence and extreme poverty, the discourse of good governance is designed to provide operational, rather than philosophical, foundations for the universality of fundamental human rights.

However, does good governance, which corresponds, from this point of view, to a common human aspiration, accommodate cultural difference or distinctiveness? How does the universal logic of fundamental rights accord with the equally significant contemporary discourse of cultural diversity? These issues, which are faced by many non-occidental societies, are in fact at the heart of the encounter between Aboriginality and governance in Canada. Are individual rights and freedoms, viewed as essential ingredients of good governance, consistent with the legitimate aspirations of Aboriginal peoples wishing to develop without compromising their cultural identity?

2.2. The "Aboriginalist" Challenge to the Cultural Legitimacy of Fundamental Rights

When it discusses the effect of individual rights and freedoms on the exercise of Aboriginal political autonomy in Canada, dominant legal doctrine is steeped in a differentialism that leads some authors to postulate a kind of ontological conflict between Aboriginality and legal modernity, or at least a permanent potential for friction between Aboriginal cultural distinctiveness and individual rights and freedoms. Paradoxically, while commentators rightly denounce the Supreme Court of Canada's traditionalist dogma, which equates Aboriginal rights to pre-colonial customs,[24] they often cast doubt on the cultural legitimacy of individual rights and freedoms, which they regard as a serious threat to traditional tribal structures. Despite a few rhetorical references to the vitality and adaptability of Aboriginal cultures, a number of analysts depict two parallel worlds: on one hand, the western individualistic liberal culture, and on the other hand, a traditional Aboriginal culture infused with a philosophy of individual responsibility, communal harmony and solidarity.[25] Russell expresses this clearly:

> "Rights theory" has a long history within the common law judicial system, and today it is firmly embedded within the Canadian psyche. However, Aboriginal people have been less enamoured of such notions. Aboriginal societies, premised on an ethic of care and responsibility, have traditionally been interested less in rights than in concepts of personal obligation.[26]

According to Wilkins, there is a "profound incongruity between the rights regime in the *Charter* and the various traditions and shared understandings that Canada's Aboriginal peoples themselves regard as constitutive".[27] In the same vein, Turpel writes that "the collective or communal basis of Aboriginal life does not…have a parallel to individual rights: the conceptions of law are simply incommensurable".[28] McNeil considers that trying to apply to Aboriginal societies the dominant Canadian values underlying the *Charter of Rights* would be both colonialist and vain.[29] Differentialist detractors of individual rights like to describe pre-Columbian societies as consensual, egalitarian societies governed by essentially conciliatory customs that satisfied the legitimate aspirations of all their members.[30] Having retained this unique heritage over the centuries, today's Aboriginals would not feel the need for protection against a kind of power foreign to their cultural experience.[31] This radical critique of rights and freedoms draws on a romantic image of the "traditional self-governing communit[y]"[32] and advances, generally using hypothetical examples, that such customary communities would be tragically jeopardised by the adversarial and hierarchical group-individual relationships which are at the core individualistic charters of rights.[33]

Even when they do not posit such a contradiction between Aboriginal culture and the modern idea of subjective individual rights enforceable as against collective institutions, legal academics seem to think that the notion of Aboriginal good governance based on respect for rights and freedoms would, in a significant number of situations, pose a serious threat to Aboriginal difference.[34] This concern for the preservation of Aboriginal difference heavily influences legal arguments about the Canadian *Charter's* application to Aboriginal governments. It prompts some writers to advocate absolute immunity from *Charter* review for Aboriginal governments and causes others to minimise the *Charter* burden on those governments.

Are Aboriginals exiled from modernity? The differentialist analysis tends to turn its eyes away from the history of the Aboriginal condition. Because they fear being perceived as legitimising or trivialising the ravages of colonialism, legal analysts tend to overlook, or only reluctantly admit, the fact that while pre-colonial societies had forms of governance appropriate to the objective conditions in which they lived, those conditions have largely disappeared and cannot be revived.[35] Those who oppose the application of the *Charter*, as well as those who subordinate its application to Aboriginal difference, assume that individual rights and freedoms lack cultural normativity in an Aboriginal universe either steeped in traditions or aspiring to revive them. Yet, it would be wrong to take for granted that in their social, economic and political relations, today's Aboriginal men and women endorse any strong opposition between Aboriginality and modernity.

2.3. Aboriginal Claims to Individual Rights and Freedoms: Questioning or Reinterpreting Tradition

By demanding their own autonomous governments, Aboriginal communities expect to control institutions having all the trappings of the modern state. The ability of such institutions to unilaterally constrain individuals will be no less than that of other levels of government.[36] Aboriginal governments will typically be fashioned after state models and have little similarity to the kind of informal governance often ascribed to pre-colonial Aboriginal communities. While enabling communities to protect and promote their own identity, these governments will reinforce the subjection of Aboriginals to a collective power that will occasionally be inclined, like all governments, to impose its will to the detriment of fundamental rights.

At the same time, the actions and the current discourse of Aboriginal citizens suggest that Aboriginals, having experienced arbitrariness and discrimination firsthand, have no lower expectations than other citizens when it comes to governmental respect for their individual rights and freedoms. Observers tend to be oblivious of the fact that Aboriginal individuals, by repeatedly suing the Parliament of Canada for breach of the *Canadian Bill of Rights*,[37] have pioneered the development of a large body of case law concerning human rights.[38] Since the advent of the Canadian *Charter*, many Aboriginals have used it to challenge federal and provincial legislation and policies.[39] Are Aboriginal men and women less inclined, for reasons related to their distinct culture, to demand compliance with their *Charter* rights and freedoms from their Aboriginal brothers and sisters wielding governmental authority? Do they acknowledge that governmental power should be shielded by some cultural immunity when it rests in the hands of people from their own community? There are precedents that are not very compatible with the notion of Aboriginal cultural relativism that would make it legitimate to invoke rights and freedoms only against non-Aboriginal power.

The Canadian *Charter* has been used to challenge the electoral "customs" of a number of Aboriginal communities governed by the *Indian Act*.[40] It has been invoked by band councils to invalidate various actions,[41] with some councils claiming to be acting in accordance with ancestral values.[42] Aboriginal individuals have also resorted to federal and provincial human right statutes to seek redress from various Aboriginal authorities.[43] Well-known private litigation resulted in a head-on collision between an individual's claim to personal dignity and physical integrity and a group's claim to maintain its ancient practices.[44]

Naturally, these cases do not allow any categorical conclusion as to the exact degree that Aboriginals have appropriated fundamental rights values and culture. Yet such precedents could not be paternalistically dismissed by suggesting that non-Aboriginal lawyers have simply made technical use of fundamental rights on behalf of clients who were prevented by their cultural alienation from adhering to the values at stake in their cases.

Indeed, the Aboriginal elite's political and legal discourse, which used to feed the rhetoric on the *Charter's* cultural inappropriateness,[45] now makes it increasingly difficult to suggest that Aboriginal litigants using human rights arguments against Aboriginal governments are "cultural deviants" attracted by the sirens of a foreign ideology. While the major organisations representing Aboriginal women are notoriously committed to the *Charter*,[46] and Aboriginal women often consider that they are the ones who pay the price for experiments in criminal justice conducted in the name of Aboriginal customs,[47] it must be remembered that most Aboriginal leaders supported the defunct *Charlottetown Accord*, which explicitly required Aboriginal governments to comply with the *Charter*.[48] When modern treaties or self-government agreements are being negotiated, Aboriginal leaders and communities now accept that the Canadian *Charter* should apply to such governments.[49] They also consent to the adoption of Aboriginal charters that conform to the constitutional *Charter*, which they probably would not do if they deemed this *Charter* to be destructive of their identity or culture. Those who are tempted to suggest that the *Charter* is simply being forced down the Aboriginal people's throat by the federal government probably underestimate the present-day capacity of these people to resist governmental pressure when it comes to defending interests they consider central to their identity. Thus, the growing Aboriginal acceptance of *Charter* clauses must be contrasted with the hardening outright rejection of extinguishment clauses in modern treaties because such clauses are now regarded as a denial of the unique legal and cultural heritage of the Aboriginal peoples.[50]

In 1998, Aboriginal chiefs in Québec issued a declaration on the "Fundamental Principles of Peaceful Co-existence". In this declaration, they asserted their communities' rights to their own identities, cultures and traditions, but also proclaimed, in the first Article, that:

> The Aboriginal peoples of Québec have the right to full and effective enjoyment of all human rights and fundamental freedoms, both collective and individual, without hindrance or discrimination, as recognized by international and domestic law.[51]

Likewise, in debates at the United Nations, representatives of Canadian Aboriginals plead for the adoption of the present version of the *Draft Declaration on the Rights of Indigenous Peoples*.[52] The Declaration asserts the right of the Indigenous peoples to maintain their distinct identities,[53] but Article 33 subordinates Aboriginal laws and customs to "internationally recognized human rights standards."[54] A noteworthy feature of international human rights law is that it would impose even greater constraints on Aboriginal governments than the Canadian *Charter*.[55]

None of this reveals an opposition or some permanent tension between vibrant Aboriginal cultures and the quest for fundamental individual rights and freedoms. Indeed, it is even reasonable to think that, like other Canadians struggling to maintain their sense of distinctiveness in an ever-changing and confusing world, Aboriginals are willing to confront their traditional heritage with contemporary values. Naturally, the simultaneous reference to individual rights and special identity-based group rights highlights the dualism of Aboriginal claims, which are at once claims for both collective power and for individual protection. Because the process of balancing individual and group interests is neither an exact science nor a permanent arrangement, individual rights will sometimes prevail and will in other cases be trumped by the group's pressing concern. However, this is a dialectic experienced by every modern society that wishes to progress towards greater respect for individual dignity without sacrificing social peace, cultural development and community cohesiveness.

Acknowledging this does not amount to a denial of Aboriginal difference, which would be the ultimate deprivation. Instead, it is a recognition that while contemporary societies retain distinct cultural references and assert with unprecedented vigour their uniqueness in the face of feared standardisation, they increasingly draw on a common core of principles that often, but not always, produce generally similar answers to some of today's major challenges. This is what Mireille Delmas-Marty calls "pluralist universalism".[56]

Discourse and symbols that reinforce Aboriginal difference do not negate the convergence of societies towards a body of values that foster both cultural diversity and human dignity. Acknowledging the important part played by modernity in today's Aboriginality is an exercise in intellectual honesty, which social scientists have so far taken more seriously than legal scholars.[57] Simard rightly highlights the fact that the Aboriginal people do not escape the universal paradox of growing claims to distinctiveness combined with a modernity that reduces differences:

In fact, daily life leads to growing participation by Aboriginals in the surrounding society, with respect to customs, habitat, education, employment, leisure activities and the media, although the degree of integration varies from people living on isolated reserves to young professionals who are urbanized both in fact and in their attitudes. Yet there is no corresponding mental conversion to membership in the majority of ordinary Canadians, there is no psycho-cultural assimilation. On the contrary, the relative homogenisation of lifestyles gives rise to an even stronger desire for recognition and assertion of the Aboriginal "difference", prizing what contemporary imagination calls "traditional cultures"...the more we grow alike, the more highly we value what continues to make us different...[58]

It is legitimate for Aboriginals to value the preservation and even the flourishing of what makes them distinct.[59] The dynamics of stating this difference are however in a contemporary framework and, at the beginning of the twenty-first century, good governance prescribing respect for fundamental individual rights seems to be an objective condition for maintaining a plurality of vibrant living cultures. Is self-identification, that perpetual narrative of the history of the collective self-seeking to answer the question "who are we?", possible without reinterpreting what it means to be Aboriginal today? The cultural vitality of Aboriginal societies, that is their ability to fit the distinctiveness of their memory and their worldview into the reality of here and now, requires that they be able to reflect on their selves through deliberation and by confronting a pluralistic environment, and not through the ideological dogmatism of an immemorial identity that has to be "exhumed". Since no clan or sub-group has the exclusive right to determine a community's identity, the assertion of a truly accepted collective distinctiveness requires liberty, equality and security for the men and women claiming to belong to a cultural group.

The debate over the inclusion of sexual orientation in the *Nunavut Human Rights Act* vividly illustrates this close functional link between respect for some basic individual rights and freedoms and the dynamic process of Aboriginal collective self-identification. Inuit citizens opposing the protection of homosexuals from discrimination and those supporting it exercised their fundamental rights and freedoms when they engaged in a vigorous and open dialogue over what equality and individual dignity meant in today's Inuit society. The Act that was eventually passed by Nunavut legislature in November 2003 prohibits discrimination based on sexual orientation. However the statute embodies a compromise between the views of those who pressed for full recognition of any gender identity and those who relied on Inuit tradition to deny any legal basis for lesbian and gay rights.

These reflections on the relationship between good governance, fundamental individual rights and Aboriginal difference should be kept in mind when embarking upon the sometimes overly technical legal analysis of the effect of the Canadian *Charter* on Aboriginal governments. The purpose of the above discussion has not been to present the Canadian *Charter* as the best instrument for protecting individual rights and freedoms in Aboriginal societies. Indeed, it cannot be denied that a non-Aboriginal elite designed the *Charter*, and that the judges responsible for interpreting it also belong to that elite. This leads analysts to recommend that the Aboriginal people develop human rights instruments of their own. The drafting of Aboriginal charters of rights and freedoms designed to better accommodate the social, economic and cultural reality of Aboriginal communities, far from revealing a fundamental incompatibility between human rights and contemporary Aboriginal culture, will be a testimony to the widespread quest in contemporary societies for a just balance between the individual and the community.

3. Section 32 of the Charter: an Exhaustive List of Governmental Institutions or a General Principle of Good Governance?

3.1. Section 35 Governments: Aboriginal Powers Subject to the *Charter*

Legal analysis of the Canadian *Charter's* impact on the actions of Aboriginal governments begins by giving meaning to a textual omission. There is no doubt that only federal, provincial and territorial government institutions are mentioned in section 32 of the *Charter*, which defines the scope of application of the rights and freedoms that it guarantees. It is equally clear that governmental powers derived from an Aboriginal right cannot be subsumed under any of the levels of government explicitly designated in the *Charter*. Such powers are "inherent" in the sense that they flow, not from a federal or provincial grant, but from pre-colonial Aboriginal legal regimes that the constitution simply "recognizes and confirms" as part of Canadian law.[60]

The same goes for Aboriginal self-government as a Treaty right. Whether the treaty is the formal source of Aboriginal powers or whether it simply confirms and specifies the scope of an existing Aboriginal right, it does not make the Aboriginal government a federal, provincial or territorial entity. The *Charter* expressly binds the federal and provincial governments, which are parties to the treaty, which raises the question of whether government action that consists in agreeing to insert a clause into a treaty falls under the *Charter*. The courts will probably draw an analogy with collective agreements to which the Crown is party and that are subject to the *Charter*.[61] However, even though the *Charter* applies to federal or provincial approval of a treaty provision, the rule of non-abrogation set out in section 25 prevents, as will be shown in this article, the *Charter* from being used to annul the provisions of treaties or implementing legislation that create treaty rights or confirm Aboriginal rights.

As for Aboriginal governmental institutions with powers that are codified or granted by treaty, they can be said to act on behalf of neither the federal nor the provincial (or territorial) authorities. They cannot be described as an integral part of either federal or provincial (or territorial) governmental structures. Such governments are not under the control of federal or provincial (or territorial) authorities and their mission is not to implement government policy set out in federal or provincial (or territorial) legislation.[62] Moreover, because the Aboriginal powers are defined or created by treaty, they enjoy constitutional status and may not be unilaterally revoked by federal or provincial (or territorial) authorities.

The simple fact that the federal and provincial Crowns are party to a treaty is not sufficient to make an Aboriginal people a federal or provincial government body. If a situation arises where the sole legal source of Aboriginal self-government is a treaty, the Aboriginal government's powers are not simply delegated by other governments.[63] They are rather the result of a solemn accord with an Aboriginal people, which enjoys a unique legal status under the *Constitution*. Aboriginal peoples' power to sign treaties is inherent. It flows from the *sui generis* relation that Aboriginal nations have always had with the Crown and which entails, as a matter of fundamental public law, the ability to negotiate unique agreements with the government that are called "treaties".[64]

The signing and implementation of a treaty generally involve the executive and legislative powers of the governments mentioned in section 32 of the *Charter*. Legislators ratify the treaty and adopt implementing legislation in order to make treaty rights enforceable on government officials and third parties. Such legislation does not however make the Aboriginal government into a simple creature of the federal parliament or provincial legislature for the purposes of section 32 of the *Charter*. Its only purpose is to ensure that federal and provincial law will comply with Treaty rights including self-government rights. Thus, the courts are unlikely to endorse the argument advanced by Hogg and Turpel, according to which a treaty's implementing legislation may be sufficient to link Aboriginal governments to federal or provincial governmental action for the purpose of section 32.[65]

Treating section 35 Aboriginal governments as connected in any way to federal or provincial institutions must therefore be ruled out. Only a broad interpretation of section 32 based not on a technical reading of its wording, but on a generous vision of its role in the development of constitutional law and governance in Canada, will provide individuals subject to Aboriginal laws and authority with *Charter* protection.

The proponents of Aboriginal immunity, who regard the *Charter* as culturally inappropriate, are of the opinion that the list of institutions in section 32 is exhaustive and that, in any case, the drafters of the *Charter* did not have in mind governments such as those that emerged in the wake of section 35 of the *Constitution Act, 1982*.[66] They add that since Aboriginal peoples did not consent to the application of the *Charter* when it was inserted in the *Constitution*, it is incumbent on the courts to apply the rule of interpretation according to which any ambiguity in an Act should be resolved in favour of the rights of Aboriginal peoples, in other words, in favour of complete immunity from *Charter* scrutiny.[67]

In fact, the Supreme Court of Canada has not found that the *Charter's* domain is exhausted by the list of government institutions appearing in section 32, that is the legislative and executive branches of Canada, the provinces and the territories. The highest court, like lower jurisdictions, has thus applied the *Charter* to some court orders[68] even after having noted that courts are not among the institutions listed in section 32.[69] The Court has not tried to make judges into extensions or simple delegates of the "government" or "Parliament" referred to in section 32.[70] Instead, it has preferred a functional and remedial vision of the *Charter* by considering that a constitutional instrument designed to effectively safeguard rights and freedoms is by definition designed to constrain all bodies wielding governmental authority on behalf of political community.[71] While it is true that judges are clearly part of the Canadian state structure, it is also a fact that Aboriginal self-government recognized and confirmed by the *Constitution* of Canada is deployed within the Canadian legal system.

Moreover, the argument involving the limited role of Aboriginal leaders in the 1982 constitutional reform in fact raises the much wider and fundamental issue of the political legitimacy of Aboriginal peoples' unilateral incorporation in the state. As political communities, Aboriginals did not in general take part in the gradual building of the Canadian constitutional order that culminated in the enactment of the *Constitution Act, 1982*. This is a fact that certainly encumbrances the historical legitimacy of the Crown's sovereignty over them.[72] However, the legitimate quest for Aboriginal consent to the state [73] requires a global solution that will have to come from the political stakeholders. Judges would be ill advised to try to make up for the lack of formal Aboriginal endorsement of the *Charter* by purely and simply preventing Aboriginal Canadians from availing themselves of it. Why set aside the *Charter* but not other components central to the constitutional system to which Aboriginal peoples have also not formally consented, such as section 35 of the *Constitution Act, 1982,* which recognises their rights, and the *Constitution Act, 1867,* which substantially puts them beyond the reach of provincial laws?[74]

Indeed, the argument based on the absence of Aboriginal consent to the application of the *Charter*, and the claim that the *Charter's* effect on Aboriginal rights should be minimal, both assume that the political and collective rights of communities must, for the purpose of construing section 32, always take precedence over any concern for individual rights and freedoms. This is not consistent with the view of rights put forward so far by the Supreme Court of Canada. The Court has taken the view that under the *Constitution* aboriginal rights are "equal in importance and significance to the rights enshrined in the *Charter.*"[75] This vision of the relation between group and individual rights is more in accordance with conciliation and balance than with the idea of a total eclipse of the *Charter* by section 35 of the *Constitution Act, 1982*. The Court also asserts the need to harmonize Aboriginal rights with the "Canadian legal and constitutional structure."[76] That structure gives a central role to the *Charter*, which the highest court considers a "restatement of the fundamental values which guide and shape our democratic society and our legal system."[77]

In addition to seeing the *Constitution* as a whole tending towards harmony rather than as a lop-sided juxtaposition of disparate regimes,[78] recognizing and confirming Aboriginal and Treaty rights while making governmental institutions derived from them subject to the *Charter* is perfectly consistent with the way the recognition of Aboriginal rights has historically been intrinsically limited by the supremacy of certain fundamental values.[79] Of course, this judicially imposed internal limitation has long served to buttress colonialism by presupposing the moral superiority of European culture. However, it would be difficult today to suggest that the value of respect for rights and freedoms is so foreign to Aboriginal culture that it amounts to the destructive imposition of western values on Aboriginal peoples.

When properly placed in its context, section 32 of the *Charter* looks much more like the expression of a general principle of good governance in Canada than like a simple list that textually limits the sphere of enforceability of constitutional rights and freedoms.[80] Consequently, the crucial question for the purposes of section 32 should be whether the actions of an Aboriginal body acting pursuant to an Aboriginal or Treaty right amounts to the imposition on individuals of public power for the general good. If the answer is yes, then the *Charter* should be applicable *depending on how section 25 is interpreted.*

The institutions developed by Aboriginal communities may not always match the state model as a way of organizing power.[81] This fact should not however hinder the application of the *Charter* when the Aboriginal community exerts a genuine collective power with a legally binding impact on the individual. In other words, in order to identify the power relation that is targeted by section 32, we have to transcend formal considerations to consider the true essence of the relation in question.[82] However, it is also clear that the very wording of many of the rights set out in the *Charter* will preclude them from governing Aboriginal institutions.[83]

If section 32 has to be interpreted as reaching all government bodies recognized by the Canadian *Constitution*, and therefore as making the *Charter* binding on Aboriginal governments, what are we to make of section 33 which enables legislators to override provisions in sections 2 and 7—15 of the *Charter*?[84] It is plain that the wording of section 33 does not explicitly contemplate its application to Aboriginal legislators acting under an Aboriginal or Treaty right. Yet, like section 32, this provision lays down a fundamental principle of governance with respect to the proper relationship between the legislative and judicial branches in Canada. The necessary structural linkage of sections 32 and 33 requires a symmetrical purposive interpretation of these provisions, which means that section 33 empowers Aboriginal legislators, not specifically named in section 32 but to which the *Charter* nonetheless applies, to override rights and freedoms just like the legislators that are explicitly mentioned.[85] Nothing would justify unequal treatment for Aboriginal and non-Aboriginal legislators in this respect.

In its final report, the Royal Commission on Aboriginal Peoples writes that only "national" Aboriginal governments should be able to validly employ the override mechanism.[86] This position is based on the presumption, which has not yet been proven correct, that a local community cannot hold an Aboriginal right to self-government, and also, perhaps, on the unspoken fear that small communities would not be capable of making acceptable use of the mechanism. In fact, any Aboriginal institution that is functionally equivalent to Parliament or a legislature, whether local or national, should be able to turn to section 33. Just as it is incumbent on voters to hold their elected provincial and federal representatives accountable when they resort to a notwithstanding clause, it is the responsibility of Aboriginal citizens to be vigilant and ensure that their governments are accountable for policies that override individual rights or freedoms guaranteed by the *Charter*.

3.2. Applying the *Charter* by Way of Treaty

In order to dispel any doubt about the *Charter's* application to government institutions established by treaty, the Crown and the Aboriginal party may include provisions in the treaty itself imposing on such institutions the duty to exercise their powers in a manner consistent with the rights and freedoms set out in the *Charter*. This was done in Chapter 2 of the *Nisga'a Final Agreement*. Article 9 of the chapter states:

> The *Canadian Charter of Rights and Freedoms* applies to Nisga'a Government in respect of all matters within its authority, bearing in mind the free and democratic nature of Nisga'a Government as set out in this Agreement.[87]

If section 32 of the *Charter* already extends, independently of any stipulations to that effect, to section 35 Aboriginal government bodies, then the effect of such a clause can only be declaratory. But what if the opposite interpretation of section 32 were to prevail? What would then be the legal effect of a clause purporting to render *Charter* rights and freedoms nonetheless enforceable against the Aboriginal government? It is quite indisputable that the parties to a treaty cannot agree to expand the constitutional scope of the *Charter* beyond the institutions targeted by section 32. This can only be done through a formal constitutional amendment in accordance with the complex procedure provided for in Part V of the *Constitution Act, 1982*.

It does not follow, however, that Aboriginal authorities would be able to ignore a treaty clause requiring them to abide by the *Charter*. Since it is contained in an agreement that has the status of a treaty, such a clause is part of a solemn exchange of promises by which the parties agree on reciprocal obligations that are fully operative under Canadian public law.[88] Following negotiations in which the parties have agreed to mutual concessions, the Aboriginal party solemnly commits itself to complying with the *Charter* when it exercises the right to self-government, the scope and conditions of which are contained in the treaty. The commitment results in intrinsic limitations on the Aboriginal government prerogatives confirmed or protected by the treaty.

Writers generally assume, without delving into the issue, that the courts would uphold a *Charter* clause.[89] Wilkins, however, suggests that if self-government is an inherent Aboriginal right, then such consensual self-limitation of a constitutional right would be of dubious validity.[90] But if the Supreme Court of Canada has given effect to treaty provisions by which Aboriginal peoples purely and simply abandon their Aboriginal rights,[91] the courts should surely enforce a clause that simply provides a framework for the exercise of an Aboriginal or Treaty right, as long as the Aboriginal party has clearly consented to the said framework. The effect of such limitation is similar to that of provisions that have become standard in modern treaties whereby the exercise of hunting and fishing rights are made subject to the principles of conservation and public safety.

In other words, the clause pertaining to the *Charter's* application has the effect of incorporating the *Charter's* provisions into the treaty, which becomes the formal source of the obligation to respect the rights and freedoms of the individuals that are subject to the exercise of Aboriginal power. Assuming that the *Charter* does not apply *ex proprio vigore* under section 32, an unjustified infringement on a right or freedom would not technically be a violation of the *Constitution* of Canada. It would be an unlawful disregard for a limitation on the Aboriginal governmental power provided for in the treaty.

Wilkins argues that if consensual subjection to the *Charter* by referential incorporation were judged valid, then only the government parties would have legal standing to challenge an Aboriginal action for alleged non-compliance with the *Charter*.[92] If this were correct, only federal or provincial authorities would be able to hold the Aboriginal party accountable and, if required, seek redress for a failure to fulfil the commitment to obey the *Charter*. However, this argument obscures the fact that, by its very nature, a treaty provision that makes the *Charter* applicable has the purpose and the effect of conferring individual rights on members of the group to whom Aboriginal laws and action apply.

The creation of individual rights has indeed become a common feature of modern treaties. For example, in recent land claim agreements, the rights related to resource harvesting are often devolved to individuals who are the beneficiaries of a treaty,[93] which authorizes those individuals to personally challenge restrictions imposed on their treaty rights by government, including Aboriginal authorities.[94] The wholesale incorporation of the *Charter* into a treaty also extends to section 24 of this *Charter*, which explicitly guarantees that any person who believes that his or her rights have been infringed or denied has the right to seek a remedy from a court of competent jurisdiction.[95]

Despite the above arguments, the fact remains that opponents of the *Charter's* application to Aboriginal governments give section 25 decisive weight. According to them this provision counters any possibility of construing section 32 of the *Charter* so as to reach government action taken pursuant to Aboriginal or Treaty rights. The scope of the immunity flowing from section 25 must therefore be ascertained. In the next section, I argue that, when placed in its broader constitutional context, the constitutional validation principle expressed in section 25 does not support the absolute immunity thesis. After reviewing the various strands of academic opinion, I also propose an alternative interpretation of the constitutional validation principle.

4. The Scope of Immunity Conferred by Section 25: Review of Academic Opinion

The key passage of section 25 reads as follows:

> The guarantee in this Charter of certain rights and freedoms shall not be construed so as to abrogate or derogate from any aboriginal, treaty or other rights of the aboriginal peoples of Canada...

The French version provides:

> Le fait que la présente Charte garantit certains droits et libertés ne porte pas atteinte aux droits et libertés – ancestraux, issus de traités ou autres – des peuples autochtones du Canada...

There is unanimity on two essential points concerning this provision: (1) it does not in itself confer additional rights on Aboriginal peoples[96] but (2) it prevents the *Charter* from being used to invalidate an Aboriginal or Treaty right on the grounds that such a right constitutes a privilege that discriminates against non-Aboriginals. The result is protection against any attempt to deny, in the name of the equality, the right of the Aboriginal people to enjoy a unique legal and constitutional status that distinguishes them from other Canadians. This immunity is broadly equivalent to what Kymlicka calls "external" protection, that is, a bulwark against attempts by people who do not belong to the protected group to use the *Charter* to challenge the group's special rights.[97]

However, there is disagreement as to what extent section 25 also immunizes Aboriginal governments against *Charter* challenges that target not the special treatment inherent in the rights of the Aboriginal people, but the manner in which such group rights are exercised – what Kymlicka describes as "internal" restrictions – that is, constraints which the group imposes on its own members in the exercise of its Aboriginal or Treaty self-government powers.[98] While some argue that section 25 acts as a complete bar to any *Charter* review of Aboriginal governmental action, others suggest various ways of balancing *Charter* rights and Aboriginal difference without going so far as to recognize complete immunity. After commenting on the various shades of immunity advocated by commentators, I will argue that they fail to adequately capture the real nature and effect of section 25.

4.1. Absolute Immunity Based on the Rule of Non-Derogation

The argument according to which section 25 of the *Charter* provides Aboriginal governments with complete immunity is rather straightforward. It is based essentially on the word "derogate" in the English version of the provision. While the word "abrogate" protects the very existence of special Aboriginal rights against any challenge based on the *Charter* (external protection), the prohibition against applying the *Charter* so as to "derogate from" the rights of the Aboriginal people means, according to the proponents of absolute immunity, that the *Charter* can never have the effect of restricting or limiting the manner in which those rights can be exercised.[99] Thus, the word "derogate" is seen as protecting any government action based on an Aboriginal or Treaty right against a "limitation due to a partial conflict with some *Charter* right or freedom, for example, where an Aboriginal government exercising its right of self-government made a law that violated section 15 equality rights."[100] Thus it would completely block any attempt to expand the ambit of section 32 of the *Charter* to encompass Aboriginal governments. McNeil describes the immunising effect of the word "derogate" in section 25 as follows:

> The question which must be addressed is this: Would the application of the Charter to relations between Aboriginal individuals and their own governments amount to derogation from the right of self-government? Keeping in mind the nature of the right, I think the answer must be yes because any limitation on the exercise of the right necessarily involves a derogation from the right itself.[101]

The French version of section 25, invariably overlooked by commentators, does not at first sight seem incompatible with McNeil's argument since it provides that the constitutional guarantee of the rights and freedoms listed in the *Charter* "*ne porte pas atteinte*," in other words does not infringe or limit the rights of the Aboriginal people, including Aboriginal and Treaty rights. Using the Supreme Court of Canada's definition of an "infringement" – or "*atteinte* – of Aboriginal and Treaty rights for the purpose of section 35 of the *Constitution Act, 1982* , it would be possible to argue that a *Charter* right or freedom "*porte atteinte*" an Aboriginal or Treaty right whenever it results in a substantial restriction on the community's ability to exercise its right freely.[102] It cannot be denied that the obligation to comply with the *Charter's* requirements would in some cases limit a community's discretion as to how it will use its governmental powers. However, both versions of section 25 have to be taken into account and, as will be shown below, the rule of "non-derogation" found in the English version, which is not an absolute immunity rule when properly understood, is more precise and more accurately reflects the purpose of the provision than the French version. In this case, both versions should be given a common meaning based on a correct understanding of the non-derogation rule that appears in the English version.[103]

4.2. Qualified Immunity Based on Aboriginal Difference

Some writers take the view that section 32 of the *Charter* can be interpreted broadly so as to reach Aboriginal governments acting pursuant to Aboriginal or Treaty rights. While this leads them to reject the idea of an absolute immunity flowing from section 25, they nonetheless think that, in a potentially large number of cases, this provision does afford Aboriginal governments immunity from *Charter* scrutiny. According to those authors, section 25's role is to protect an Aboriginal government's ability to use its power for the purpose of reflecting, protecting or promoting Aboriginal difference. Section 25 would provide a qualified immunity, rather than an absolute one, because only specific government actions demonstrably related to Aboriginal difference would be sheltered from invalidation for failure to comply with the rights and freedoms guaranteed in the *Charter*.

Grammond thus suggests that section 25 imposes an obligation on anyone challenging Aboriginal governmental action for breach of the *Charter* to demonstrate that the impugned action is not related to Aboriginal difference, or to prove that Aboriginal difference is not fundamentally jeopardised by the *Charter* challenge.[104] For their part, Hogg and Turpel seem to consider that section 25 establishes a kind of Aboriginal "cultural exception" that prevents a *Charter* right or freedom from being interpreted in a manner that would trench on the Aboriginal community's power to protect, through its government, practices that belong to its distinct culture. Taking as an example the right to a lawyer in the criminal proceedings involving young offenders, these authors argue that section 25 would prevent a minor from using the *Charter* to defeat Aboriginal legislation that refuses him or her access to a lawyer in so far as the legislation is consistent with the community's traditions:

> If the juvenile justice system was reflecting Aboriginal culture and traditions, section 25 would shield such practices from attack based on the values expressed in the legal rights provisions of the *Charter*. In other words, the legal rights provisions would be given a new interpretation in light of Aboriginal traditions.[105]

If these authors have been understood correctly, they are not simply advocating an interpretation of the *Charter* that would be sensitive to possible tensions between individual rights and a certain view of Aboriginal values while in the end leaving to the judge the possibility of setting aside the argument based on Aboriginal difference. They apparently think that the application of *Charter* rights and freedoms is precluded if these rights and freedoms cannot be interpreted in a way that is compatible with Aboriginal difference. In its final report, the Royal Commission on Aboriginal Peoples appears to opt for a very similar reading of section 25.[106]

The merit of the qualified immunity thesis lies in its recognition that not every measure and initiative by an Aboriginal government necessarily promotes or reflects Aboriginal difference. However, it does not escape any of the usual pitfalls of doctrines that make a right, power or immunity dependent on the judicial definition of Aboriginal identity. Whether the operative constitutional criterion is "Aboriginal difference," the "core of Indianness"[107] or the "core of the people's identity,"[108] to give judges the responsibility for identifying Aboriginal difference in a legally binding manner is to risk stereotypical and simplistic definitions of Aboriginal identity. On the other hand, leaving Aboriginal authorities complete freedom to assess Aboriginal difference would amount to giving them discretion to "self-immunize" from the *Charter*.

The advocates of qualified immunity based on Aboriginal difference generally do not offer an in-depth study of the text and context of the section. Taking for granted that preserving Aboriginal difference is an essential purpose of the right to self-government protected by section 25, these authors seem to think that any significant constraint flowing from the *Charter* that hinders the achievement of that purpose constitutes a derogation prohibited by section 25. Consequently, there does not seem to be any fundamental difference between their interpretation of the word "derogate" and that of those who argue that the section gives complete immunity. The immunity they advocate is only partial because they ascribe a better-defined role to section 25, namely that of protecting Aboriginal difference whose confrontation with *Charter* rights and freedoms must be assessed on a case-by-case basis.

4.3. Section 25 is a Rule of Interpretation that Promotes Aboriginal Difference

According to another differentialist understanding of section 25, whose main proponent is Patrick Macklem, this provision is, when applied to an internal restriction, no more than a rule of interpretation that favours protection of Aboriginal difference. Thus, section 25 would require judges to make best efforts to define *Charter* rights and freedoms in a way that accommodates distinct Aboriginal cultures. However, if a *Charter* right or freedom does not lend itself to such cultural adaptation, then the Aboriginal government would not be able to use Aboriginal difference to avoid *Charter* constraints.[109] In short, according to this point of view, section 25 would result in complete immunity in the case of external challenges but would constitute a mere interpretative tool in the face of "internal" challenges, that is, when the *Charter* is used by a member of the community to question a measure taken by an Aboriginal government in the exercise of its powers. Contrary to the qualified immunity approach, this interpretation of section 25 therefore clearly opposes the idea that an Aboriginal group could force its members to choose, in the name of perpetuating Aboriginal difference, between enjoying Aboriginal or Treaty rights and exercising the individual rights and freedoms guaranteed to all Canadians.

This appears to be more or less the idea that federal authorities have of the role played by section 25. The Federal Policy Guide to Aboriginal Self-government states that all Canadians, including Aboriginals, must be able to invoke the *Charter* against their governments, but that section 25 is nonetheless designed to establish "a sensitive balance between individual rights and freedoms, and the unique values and traditions of Aboriginal peoples".[110]

These various interpretations of the protective effect of section 25 have emerged without their authors giving much importance to looking at this provision's place in our constitutional tradition. Aboriginal law specialists have in general wrongly assumed they could do without a thorough examination of the broader constitutional context in which section 25 operates. Wilkins is somewhat of an exception, for he makes a brief account of other constitutional provisions with are functionally equivalent to section 25. He tries to draw from his rather summary analysis confirmation of complete immunity for Aboriginal governments.[111] As will be seen below, this conclusion is at least questionable.

In fact, I am of the opinion that none of the approaches propounded so far by legal academics accurately describes the relationship between the *Charter* and the rights of Aboriginal peoples that is induced by section 25.

5. Section 25 in Context: Constitutional Validation as a General Doctrine

5.1. Section 25's Lack of Originality in Constitutional Law

It must be kept in mind that, in terms of legal technique, section 25 is by no means unique in our constitutional scheme. It has sister provisions in sections 21,[112] 22[113] and 29[114] of the *Charter*, and simply expresses a fundamental rule of internal consistency of the constitutional edifice. The rule is that when two constitutional provisions appear to conflict, they must nonetheless be able to coexist and each must be able to produce an effect regardless of when it was inserted into the supreme law.[115] The courts resolve such internal constitutional contradictions or tensions by ascribing each provision an exclusive scope of application then enabling every provision to be fully operative in its own normative sphere. In practice, the principle of *generalia specialibus non derogant* provides the most consistent explanation for the cohesive application within the constitutional structure of provisions and norms that are *a priori* irreconcilable.[116] Since inductive logic entails that a general rule cannot abrogate or derogate from an incompatible specific rule, the latter will therefore be maintained or validated by removing it from the normative scope of the former.

By making every provision operative in this way, courts have avoided concluding that one part of the *Constitution* implicitly abrogates or derogates from another. Indeed, the very nature of constitutional provisions is to entrench fundamental political compromises and to put in place a lasting framework for organizing and regulating the state's power. Moreover, formal constitution-making power is so strictly regulated and deployed so sparingly that judges cannot suppose that the drafters of the constitution made a "mistake" in enacting contradictory provisions and therefore undertake to "correct" that mistake by inferring from one part of the fundamental law a tacit intention to make another part of that law inoperative or to neutralize some essential aspect of it.

The existence of a general principle proscribing any effect that would result in the abrogation or derogation from one constitutional provision in relation to another was first stated by the Supreme Court of Canada in *Reference re. Bill 30, An Act to Amend the Education Act*.[117] In that case, the Government of Ontario asked the courts to rule on the constitutionality, in particular with respect to the *Charter*, of a legislative reform that would provide more complete funding for separate Catholic schools in the province. With respect to the *Charter's* applicability, the Court endorsed the Province of Ontario's argument that section 93 of the *Constitution Act, 1867*, under the terms of which the Catholic minority's educational rights and privileges are specifically protected, shielded the provincial legislation from any claim that it infringed the freedom of religion of non-Catholics or their equality rights under the *Charter*. The province's argument was also based on section 29 of the *Charter*, which, like section 25 with respect to the rights of the Aboriginal people, explicitly states that *Charter* provisions do not "abrogate or derogate from" (the French version says "*ne portent pas atteinte aux*") the specific rights of religious minorities.

Wilson J. explains that section 29 simply expresses, "for greater certainty" a general rule that is valid even when it is not explicitly formulated, namely that "It was never intended, in my opinion, that the *Charter* could be used to invalidate other provisions of the Constitution."[118] Since the special treatment that section 93 reserves for religious groups with the right to separate confessional schools "sits uncomfortably with the concept of equality embodied in the *Charter*," section 93 has to be shielded so as to protect "a fundamental part of the Confederation compromise."[119]

In *Gosselin (Tutor of) v. Québec,* [120] a case involving language minority rights, the Supreme Court of Canada reaffirmed that constitutional validation is an unwritten constitutional principle which is triggered whenever *Charter* equality rights are invoked in a way that conflicts with constitutional rights enjoyed by specific religious, linguistic or ethnic groups. Therefore, the fact that language minority rights guaranteed by section 23 of the *Charter* are not explicitly shielded from *Charter* abrogation or derogation was held to be irrelevant:

> The absence of a provision similar to s. 29 for minority language instruction therefore does not assist the appellants. Equality rights, while of immense importance, constitute just part of our constitutional fabric. In *Reference re Secession of Québec*, [1998] 2 S.C.R. 217, the protection of [page251] minorities was also identified as a key principle, manifested in part in minority language education rights (s. 23 of the *Canadian Charter*) denominational school rights (s. 93 of the *Constitution Act, 1867*) and aboriginal and treaty rights (ss. 25 of the *Canadian Charter* and 35 of the *Constitution Act, 1982*).[121]

The courts have held that a specific power, right or privilege is immune from *Charter* review whenever it falls within the protective fold of a "constitutional validation" found in the supreme law itself.

5.2. Constitutional Validation: a Rule of Non-Abrogation

In order for the rule of Non-Abrogation to come into play, the contradiction between a provision of the *Charter* and another constitutional provision must be such that the latter would become inoperative if the *Charter* remedy sought were granted. The purpose of the rule is to avoid, in the words of Supreme Court justices, having the *Charter* "abrogate"[122], "annul"[123] or "eliminate"[124] a right or power with constitutional status. McLachlin J. has phrased the test for immunity as follows: "The test is whether to accede to the *Charter* argument would amount to negating or removing a constitutional power. If so, the *Charter* does not apply."[125]

The entrenchment of religious and linguistic minority rights necessarily confers on Parliament or the legislatures the constitutional power to provide for differential treatment based on language or religion. Likewise, Parliament's specific jurisdiction over "Indians and Lands reserved for the Indians" would be meaningless without the ability to create statutory distinctions between Aboriginals and Non-Aboriginals. In this context, there is unavoidably a linkage between legislative power and constitutional rights or status. As a result, the rule of non-abrogation will prevent a *Charter*-based attack on constitutionally mandated legislation implementing special rights. As the Supreme Court of Canada explains in *Gosselin*:

> In advancing their claim, the appellants put aside the linkage between s. 73 of the *Charter of the French language* and s. 23 of the *Canadian Charter.* Section 23 may be part of the *Constitution*, they argue, but s. 73 is not, and like any other statute must comply with equality guarantees. ... We do not agree. The linkage is fundamental to an understanding of the constitutional issue. Otherwise, for example, any legislation under s. 91(24) of the *Constitution Act, 1867* ("Indians, and Lands reserved for the Indians") would be vulnerable to attack as race-based inequality, and denominational school legislation could be pried loose from its constitutional base and attacked on the ground of religious discrimination. Such an approach would, in effect, nullify any exercise of the constitutional power: *Adler*, at para. 39; *Reference re Bill 30, An Act to amend the Education Act (Ont.)*, [1987] 1 S.C.R. 1148, at 1197 and 1206.[126]

Consistent with constitutional validation as a general unwritten principle, the Supreme Court of Canada has ruled that the *Charter* does not apply to the parliamentary privilege that specifically allows the exclusion of "strangers" from a province's legislative chamber because it is a privilege with constitutional status.[127] The Assembly's specific constitutional power to keep out strangers would be neutralized if freedom of expression under para. 2(b) of the *Charter* gave to all members of the public a constitutional right to attend its proceedings.

The rule of non-abrogation will also afford direct protection to self-implementing constitutional rights, such as the right under section 17 of the *Charter* to use English or French in debates in Parliament, so that these rights could not be declared null or of no effect for breach of section 15 of the *Charter*.[128]

But the Supreme Court of Canada also states that the *Charter* cannot be applied in order to "derogate"[129] from a right provided for in the *Constitution*. This is precisely the terminology used in the English versions of *Charter* sections 21, 22, 25 and 29. According to these versions of the provisions, the *Charter* is prevented not only from abrogating but also from derogating from a constitutional right. It is therefore necessary to look closely at the difference between abrogation and derogation as conditions for constitutional validation.

5.3. Constitutional Validation: a Rule of Non-Derogation

As mentioned above, some authors argue that for the purposes of section 25 of the *Charter*, there is derogation from a constitutionally protected right or power as soon as the exercise of that right or power is subject to a *Charter* induced constraint. According to McNeil, for example, the only interpretation that could give the term "derogate" an operative effect different from the word "abrogate" would be the one that insulates from the *Charter* not only the existence of a special Aboriginal right or power (which is the rule of non-abrogation), but also any exercise of that right or power in a given case. He argues that the case law on the constitutional validation principle concerns only non-abrogation and is therefore not useful in making sense of the discrete non-derogation requirement laid down in section 25.[130]

However, this position seems untenable. It goes without saying that such an interpretation of the rule of non-derogation found in section 25 will not hold if the parties to a treaty solemnly assert that the *Charter*, including section 25, applies to the Aboriginal government.[131] We cannot assume that in such a case the parties would intend to play a zero-sum game by stipulating one thing and its exact opposite simultaneously, in other words by agreeing that the Aboriginal government would be bound by the *Charter* but also totally exempt from it through the non-derogation provision in section 25. To assert in a treaty that an Aboriginal group that governs itself in accordance with an Aboriginal or Treaty right is bound by the *Charter* but nonetheless enjoys the protection of section 25 is in fact to highlight the need for a coherent articulation of the group's rights and obligations. The need for a coherent approach to Aboriginal rights and duties is equally pressing in the absence of a treaty expressly addressing the issue of *Charter* application.

The argument that the rule of non-derogation yields absolute immunity from *Charter* scrutiny cannot be accepted because it disregards the real purpose of the reference to "derogation" in section 25 and similar provisions. It appears that the explicit protection from derogation is intended to defeat any attempt to bypass constitutional validation on the basis that the purpose or effect of a *Charter* challenge is not to annul a right guaranteed by the constitution but to define the rights of citizens under provincial or federal law.

This point is easier to understand if we look at Supreme Court of Canada decisions concerning the rights of religious and linguistic minorities. In *Adler*, the parents of children attending private religious schools challenged the constitutionality, under sections 2 and 15 of the *Charter*, of the Government of Ontario's failure to provide the same level of funding and free services to their schools as to separate Catholic schools and public secular schools. The plaintiffs in this case did not invoke sections 2 and 15 of the *Charter* to set aside or abrogate the rights guaranteed to the Catholic minority and secular schools in Ontario by section 93 of the *Constitution Act, 1867*. They simply resorted to the *Charter* as a means of obtaining under provincial law the same treatment as that provided to beneficiaries of section 93. But while they did not request the abrogation or suppression of rights conferred by that constitutional provision, they nonetheless asked the Court to use the *Charter* to *derogate* from a fundamental feature of section 93, which is that it reflects a historical compromise with respect to religious schools, of which the only beneficiaries are Protestants in Québec and Roman Catholics in other provinces including Ontario.[132] On behalf of the majority, Iacobucci J. writes:

> ...just as s. 23 is a comprehensive code with respect to minority language education rights, s. 93 is a comprehensive code with respect to denominational school rights. As a result, s. 2(*a*) of the *Charter* cannot be used to enlarge this comprehensive code. Given that the appellants cannot bring themselves within the terms of s. 93's guarantees, they have no claim to public funding for their schools.[133]

Therefore, using the *Charter* to extend such rights and freedoms to other Canadians would "unacceptably distort the meaning and scope of the educational guarantees."[134]

Likewise, the fact that under section 23 of the *Charter* only French and English-speaking minorities in Canada have the right to free public education in their own language is an intrinsic feature of the sensitive political balance that the provision is designed to achieve.[135] Consequently, it is impossible to derogate from this aspect of the special language rights regime by demanding that provincial law be changed to make similar benefits available to members of other linguistic groups on the basis of equality rights. To do so would not abrogate the linguistic rights of the minority since its members would retain their entrenched right to be educated in their language but it would fundamentally alter the very substance of such rights and impair their value as an integral part of their distinctive minority status.

In *Gosselin*, French-speaking parents relied on section 15 of the *Charter* in a bid to gain access to publicly funded English schools, a benefit they were denied under provincial law but which is afforded to members of the English language minority pursuant to section 23 of the *Charter*. They did not utilize the *Charter* to do away with or abrogate the Anglophones' constitutional rights but to secure the same treatment under provincial law[136]. But as the Court writes, the appellants were effectively attempting to use "equality guarantees to modify the categories of rights holders under s. 23".[137] This attempt was unanimously rejected by the Court, which took the view that providing equal access to all citizens to minority language schools would be inconsistent with "the carefully crafted compromise contained in s. 23 of the Canadian Charter of Rights and Freedom".[138] Because exclusivity is part and parcel of the compromise, it is a defining feature of language minority rights and is thus sheltered by the principle of constitutional validation.

Even if the Supreme Court of Canada does not make explicit the distinction between "abrogating" a right and "derogating" from its essential features, it is clear that the internal consistency of the constitutional edifice requires validation not only of the very existence of a right specifically protected under the constitution, but also of the fundamental characteristics or the essence of that right.

Applied to section 25, this interpretation is perfectly consistent with the English meaning of the word "derogate," which connotes not mere regulation of the exercise of a right, but a diminishment of or change in the very nature and substance of the right.[139] The notion of *"porter atteinte"* that appears in the French version can also convey the idea of cancelling or reducing a fundamental feature or the basic nature of a right.

5.4. The Limits of Constitutional Validation

If the *Constitution* clearly empowers a government body to adopt a given conduct, then using the *Charter* to prevent the body from adopting the conduct or to eliminate an essential feature of the constitutionally validated conduct would amount to the *Charter* abrogating or derogating from a clear constitutional empowerment. This is excluded by the rules of non-abrogation and non-derogation. However, in a case in which a government body adopts a standard or conduct that is not specifically validated by the *Constitution*, it will be impossible to claim that the *Charter's* application to the action nullifies or fundamentally alters what the *Constitution* itself considers valid.

Thus, once a government action falls beyond the sphere of a constitutional validation, the *Charter* will be binding on that action and will serve, if required, as a filter to expunge the effects or conditions of that action that infringe on individual rights and freedoms. This regulatory impact of the *Charter* on governmental actors, which is precisely its function in our constitutional democracy,[140] cannot in itself be considered to abrogate or derogate from any right or power. The Supreme Court of Canada recognizes the need to distinguish between "using the *Charter* to negate another constitutional provision and using the *Charter* to ensure that the exercise of a constitutional provision conforms with the *Charter*".[141]

The Court has highlighted the need to carefully circumscribe the scope of a constitutional validation in order to determine the limits of the *Charter* immunity deriving from such validation. In *Adler*, after having concluded that section 93 of the *Constitution Act, 1867* authorizes preferential treatment for Catholic and secular public schools, the majority rejects the idea that section 93 completely exempts a province from compliance with the *Charter* with respect to the public school system. Indeed, it is the preferential funding of public schools that is protected, and not the whole legislative and administrative system pertaining to public schools:

> Furthermore, it should be pointed out that all of this is not to say that no legislation in respect of public schools is subject to *Charter* scrutiny, just as this court's ruling in *Reference Re Bill 30* did not hold that no legislation in respect of separate schools was subject to *Charter* scrutiny. Rather, it is merely the fact of their existence, the fact that the government funds schools which are, in the words of the Lord Chancellor, in *Brophy, supra*, at p. 214, "designed for all the members of the community alike, whatever their creed" that is immune from *Charter* challenge. Whenever the government decides to go beyond the confines of this special

mandate, the *Charter* could be successfully invoked to strike down the legislation in question.[142]

Thus funding health services for public schools without providing equivalent services in private schools cannot be challenged because the difference in treatment is specifically validated by section 93.[143] This does not authorize the government to contravene the *Charter* when it develops legislation and regulations otherwise pertaining to public Catholic or secular schools. Likewise, if the government decides to create public religious schools other than Catholic schools, it will have to comply with the *Charter*, in particular with respect to equality of religions.[144]

What applies to the legislature in this case also applies to minority religious and linguistic educational institutions[145] created by legislation and protected by the *Constitution*. Since what is validated is their right to exist as separate institutions, and not a right to take specific action contrary to the *Charter* with respect to members of their minority group, such institutions are bound to respect *Charter* rights and freedoms in the exercise of their powers.[146] In *Hall (Litigation guardian of)* v. *Powers*, the Ontario Superior Court of Justice rejected the argument of a Catholic school board, according to which section 29 of the *Charter* prevented recourse to *Charter* equality rights in the case of a homosexual student who was excluded from an extracurricular activity.[147] While the religious and linguistic status of a minority institution will undoubtedly sometimes be a decisive factor in recognizing that the infringement of a right or freedom is justified under section one of the *Charter*, [148] it cannot be claimed that minority institutions have in-principle immunity from *Charter* scrutiny owing to the simple fact that the issue is related to their religious or linguistic identity.

The reasoning is valid in other contexts that require the delimitation of immunity resulting from constitutional validation.[149] Thus, the principle of federalism, which the Supreme Court of Canada has held to be a structural principle of the *Constitution*,[150] reinforces legislative pluralism, which is inherent in federal diversity.[151] Consequently, the sole fact that there are differences in provincial legislation on the same topic cannot be grounds for arguing that there is a violation of equality rights protected by section 15 of the *Charter*.[152] Since asymmetrical provincial legislation is a legitimate expression of provincial autonomy, and clearly authorized by the *Constitution*, it has to be protected against standardizing constraints flowing from the individualistic and egalitarian philosophy specific to the *Charter*.[153] Because asymmetry in provincial law-making is validated as a central feature of federalism, applying the *Charter* so as to suppress it would not abrogate provincial power but it would derogate from one of its essential characteristics.

On the other hand, it is clear that the *Charter* applies when rights and freedoms are not invoked to eliminate legislative differences among provincial communities in the federation. In the same manner, and subject to the same condition, the *Charter* applies to the manner in which a province exercises its constitutionally protected power to amend its internal constitution in accordance with its specific cultural or social context.[154]

These examples relating to provincial autonomy and cultural difference are particularly interesting when applied to Québec which, as the Supreme Court of Canada acknowledges, "possesses a distinct culture"[155] which federalism is designed to protect.[156] Québec's jurisdiction over areas such as civil law, cultural heritage, language and education are crucial to its difference. Yet the courts have not doubted that in exercising such jurisdiction, Québec is subject to the *Charter*. Cases like *Ford v. Québec*,[157] for example, show that a *Charter* constraint on the choice of means of promoting distinctive identities is not considered as an abrogation or derogation from a province's constitutional power or right to foster its cultural difference.

It follows that immunity will only operate if the enforcement of a *Charter* right or freedom would suppress an otherwise constitutionally valid right or power (rule of non-abrogation) or derogate from a characteristic that is part of the very definition of the right or power (rule of non-derogation). Aside from such situations, the rights and freedoms guaranteed by the *Charter*, subject to their internal or external limitations as provided in sections 1 to 33, can ground a challenge of any government action.

This is the broader constitutional context in which must be assessed the effect of section 25 of the *Charter* on an Aboriginal people's Aboriginal, Treaty or treaty-confirmed, right to self-government.

6. Constitutional Validation Applied to Aboriginal Governments

6.1. Section 25 as a Statement of Constitutional Validation

The above analysis shows that by stating that the rights and freedoms set out in the *Charter* can neither abrogate nor derogate from the rights of the Aboriginal people, section 25, like similar provisions in the *Charter*, simply expresses a general principle of constitutional law. Neither the underlying philosophy nor the purpose of this provision seems to have a claim to any uniqueness that would endow the rights of the Aboriginal people with greater immunity than that resulting from the constitutional validation approach described in the preceding section.

Like section 93 of the *Constitution Act, 1867* and section 23 of the *Charter*, section 35 of the *Constitution Act, 1982*, which confirms and recognizes the exclusive legal heritage of Aboriginal peoples in the form of Aboriginal and Treaty rights, does not conform with the universalist ideology reflected in the rights and freedoms guaranteed by the *Charter*. The Supreme Court of Canada has aptly underscored the ideological tension between "Aboriginalist" and universalist constitutional provisions:

> In the liberal enlightenment view, reflected in the American Bill of Rights and, more indirectly, in the *Charter*, rights are held by all people in society because each person is entitled to dignity and respect. Rights are general and universal; they are the way in which the "inherent dignity" of

each individual in society is respected...<u>Aboriginal</u> rights cannot, however, be defined on the basis of the philosophical precepts of the liberal enlightenment. Although equal in importance and significance to the rights enshrined in the *Charter*, aboriginal rights must be viewed differently from *Charter* rights because they are rights held only by aboriginal members of Canadian society. They arise from the fact that aboriginal people are <u>aboriginal</u>.[158]

First, we have to recognize the uniqueness of the rights of Aboriginal peoples because they not only differ from the individual rights set out in the *Charter* but also from the special rights of religious and linguistic minorities. In addition to being genuine group rights, Aboriginal and Treaty rights have the unparalleled feature of affording the constitutional basis for a fundamental realignment of power over land and communities in Canada. They are the constitutional vehicles for the present-day recognition of autonomous political communities legally connected to sovereign pre-colonial societies.[159]

However, even though they are very dissimilar to minority rights with respect to their normative justification, their source and contents, the rights recognized and confirmed in section 35 of the *Constitution Act, 1982* resemble minority rights in their relationship to liberal egalitarian philosophy.[160] The special legal regime of Aboriginal or Treaty rights, just like minority rights, attest to a desire to provide a way for distinct historical communities to thrive and co-exist within the Canadian polity.[161] These rights also share the characteristic of originating from historically founding moments or very specific political contexts rather than appearing in the supreme law as individual prerogatives that are inherent to human existence.

Just as the rights of linguistic and religious minorities have been described by the Supreme Court of Canada as resulting from "historical exigency,"[162] a "basic compact of Confederation"[163] or a "historically important compromise,"[164] recognition of the rights of Aboriginal peoples flows from the highly specific genesis of European colonization of North America, from inter-societal dynamics that gave rise to an original balance of power that forced the state to acknowledge the political necessity of reconciling its sovereignty with the pre-existence of the Aboriginal people.[165] Of course, as a matter of constitutional doctrine, the historical and political over-determination of Aboriginal and minority rights does not at all affect their importance and legitimacy, as can be seen from the explicit clauses in sections 25 and 29 of the *Charter*.

Thus, it seems difficult to argue that a sharp distinction between minority rights and the rights of the Aboriginal people warrants a markedly different application to the latter of the rules of non-abrogation and non-derogation applied in the Supreme Court of Canada decisions previously examined. According to the Supreme Court, a two-stage analysis is required to establish immunity for a right or power incompatible with the *Charter*. First, one has to identify the right or power targeted by an immunity claim and carefully determine its scope. Next, one has to ascertain whether applying the *Charter* would abrogate the right or power or derogate from one of its defining characteristics. For the purposes of the first stage, we have to apprehend the Aboriginal or Treaty right to self-government with a clear sense of its purposes. The general *raison d'être* of Aboriginal self-government undoubtedly includes the empowerment of Aboriginal peoples to express, protect and promote their distinctive culture.[166] Next, in the second stage, we have to ask whether applying the *Charter* would abrogate or derogate from the general right to express, protect and promote Aboriginal difference. The answer has to be no because the *Charter* typically has a mere regulatory effect that is not the same as an abrogation of or derogation from the right to self-government itself.

Requiring compliance with the *Charter* clearly does not abrogate the very existence of self-government. Even if the purpose of preserving aboriginal difference is one of the defining features of self-government, regulating the means of achieving that purpose does not suppress it so as to derogate from a central feature of self-government. The *Charter's* impact on Aboriginal institutions is no different from its effect on the constitutional power of Québec's Parliament to pass legislation adapted to its social, linguistic and cultural context, or to adopt a provincial constitution that reflects its own identity. The *Charter* also has the same effect on the actions of the institutions of religious and linguistic minorities, which certainly exist to strengthen the ability of such groups to protect and promote their unique identity.

The writers who favour an absolute Aboriginal immunity from *Charter* review, along with those advocating a qualified immunity based on Aboriginal difference, fear that the *Charter* will hinder the efforts of Aboriginal governments to perpetuate certain traditional values and practices or to breathe new life into customs which, although they may be irreconcilable with *Charter* rights and freedoms, Aboriginal authorities consider central to the group's cultural identity. Admittedly, it might be necessary to review some practices and customs that are not specifically validated by an Aboriginal or Treaty right in order to minimize their negative impact on individual rights or freedoms. On the other hand, it has to be recognized that governments are often able to achieve their objectives through other means that are in compliance with the *Charter*. Moreover, the limiting effect of the *Charter* should not be exaggerated, for it does not govern all facets of community life or all aspects of relationships between an individual and the group.[167] In addition, just as we should see no inherent contradiction between Aboriginal traditions and the values expressed in the *Charter*,[168] it is important to refrain from assuming that the setting aside of a given tradition-dictated measure is by definition an attack on the integrity or dignity of contemporary Aboriginal cultures that are penetrated by modernity. To do so would be to unwisely conflate tradition and Aboriginal difference.

Finally, unlike minority institutions, Aboriginal legislative authorities can avail themselves of section 33 of the *Charter*, which allows them to override individual rights and freedoms. This is the ultimate constitutional resource for resolving the most difficult confrontations between the collective will to promote a specific understanding of Aboriginal difference and individual claims to basic rights and freedoms. Since a *Charter* override lapses five years after its enactment,[169] the

Aboriginal community would have to maintain an ongoing debate about the present-day meaning and evolution of its difference.

Even if the protection provided by section 25 and the unwritten principle of constitutional validation is more limited than that contemplated by proponents of absolute immunity, or those who propose a qualified immunity based on Aboriginal difference, the non-abrogation and non-derogation rules remain very important for Aboriginal governments because they do safeguard some of their most vital interests.

6.2. Section 25 as a Protection for Essential Characteristics of Aboriginal Self-government

Aboriginal government institutions based on Aboriginal or Treaty rights are no less immune from *Charter* attacks on their very existence than are the linguistic and religious school bodies protected by the *Constitution*. Aboriginal land, cultural and political rights in Canada form the core of an exclusive legal heritage that fundamentally distinguishes the Aboriginal peoples as pre-existing political communities.[170] Aboriginal exclusivity inherent to Aboriginal and Treaty rights, and the fact that these rights reflect the special situation of the Aboriginal people, are the cornerstones of our constitutional arrangements. Without those essential features, Aboriginal and Treaty rights would lose their substance and section's 25 purpose is precisely to spare them that fate.

Likewise, the fact that an Aboriginal community, in the exercise of its Aboriginal or Treaty right, designs its own distinctive government structures cannot itself be challenged on the basis of an alleged right of all Canadians to be equal under or before the law. Any attempt to use the *Charter* to annul an Aboriginal law simply because it is perceived as less advantageous than a non-Aboriginal law or than a law of another Aboriginal people would fail. Just as it is a fundamental feature of federalism, legislative asymmetry is part and parcel of self-government for diverse Aboriginal peoples. Thus, the principle of diversity cannot be neutralized by the egalitarian values enshrined in the *Charter*.

Section 25's prohibition against derogating from fundamental aspects of the right to self-government, and therefore from Aboriginal exclusivity, will also prevent *Charter* challenges that are not intended to abrogate an Aboriginal right or power but to extend a similar right or power to non-Aboriginals. Thanks to section 25, the uniqueness of Aboriginal self-government could not be undermined in this fashion.

6.3. Section 25 as Validation of Specific Powers and Practices

Since the non-abrogation/non-derogation rule reiterated in section 25 of the *Charter* protects rights that are confirmed or created by treaty, the Aboriginal people can negotiate with competent governments to include in treaties specific aspects of self-government that will enjoy constitutional validation and thus be immune from *Charter* scrutiny. Interestingly, specific measures validated in this way do not strictly have to be related to Aboriginal difference. The parties need only create a Treaty right within the meaning of section 25 of the *Charter*.

The *Nisga'a Final Agreement* illustrates how immunity pursuant to section 25 of the *Charter* can be created through treaty negotiations. Because they are explicitly validated by treaty, the following powers of the Nisga'a authorities are immunized from any *Charter*-based abrogation or derogation: the power to control hunting and fishing on Nisga'a lands by requiring only non-Nisga'as to obtain a permit,[171] the power to regulate or even prohibit access by non-Nisga'as to Nisga'a fisheries,[172] and the power to restrict the right to vote and to run for elections to Nisga'as alone.[173] In *Campbell v. British Columbia*, the Supreme Court of British Columbia applied section 25 correctly by deciding that this provision precludes any recourse for non-Aboriginals wishing to use sections 3, 7 and 15 of the *Charter* to annul the special political rights that the *Agreement* accords to Nisga'a citizens.[174]

The *Agreement* also expressly states that the Nisga'a constitution adopted pursuant to the treaty will define the special role played by the elders in Nisga'a government.[175] This explicit power to give some members of the community unique prerogatives, in this case possibly because of their age, is protected by section 25 from any abrogation or derogation based on equality rights entrenched in the *Charter*. This example underscores the limitations of Macklem's thesis to the effect that section 25 has only an interpretative effect, rather than an immunizing impact, when applied to an internal restriction.[176] In the case at hand, the special rights of elders create a distinction among members of the community. It does not differentiate between Nisga'as and other Canadians. In short, it is an internal restriction, which only affects the relations between Nisga'a. From Macklem's point of view, in the case of such an internal restriction section 25 would require the judge to interpret section 15 of the *Charter* in such a way that it would not conflict with the Nisga'a law that gives elders special rights consistent with the treaty. If, however, the judge decided that the law contravened section 15, and could not be justified under section one of the *Charter*, he or she would then have to declare it to be without effect. Yet this is precisely what section 25 prohibits because the court would in fact be abrogating the special status of elders that is entrenched in the treaty.[177] Indeed, the idea that section 25 is only a rule of interpretation with regard to internal restrictions disregards the essential purpose of this kind of provision, which is precisely to prevent the validity of a measure authorized by a constitutional provision from being <u>evaluated</u> under another part of the fundamental law. What is proscribed is the very possibility that the judge could be forced to determine whether one constitutional standard is in compliance with another.[178]

By shielding the existence and intrinsic characteristics of Aboriginal and Treaty rights, section 25 of the *Charter* gives the parties to a treaty leverage in defining the very scope of the immunity it provides. However, does this section go so far as to allow governments and Aboriginal peoples to agree by treaty that an Aboriginal government has the "Treaty right" to exercise all its powers notwithstanding the rights and freedoms guaranteed by the *Charter*?[179] Using treaties to achieve such a permanent and massive neutralization of the *Charter* (which is highly unlikely, given the federal policy of that the *Charter* must apply) could not be easily reconciled with the interpretation of section 32 that makes the *Charter* applicable to Aboriginal governments. The intended work of section 25 seems to be the protection of specific Aboriginal or Treaty rights, not the wholesale abrogation of *Charter* rights and freedoms by way of treaty.[180] Moreover, a treaty purporting completely to override the *Charter* would contradict the equal importance that, according to the Supreme Court of Canada, the framers of the *Constitution Act, 1982* intended to accord to the *Charter* and the rights of the Aboriginal people.[181]

7. Conclusion

The interpretation of sections 25 and 32 of the *Charter* advocated in this paper makes it possible to invoke the *Charter* in many cases against Aboriginal authorities exercising a right to self-government recognized and confirmed by section 35 of the *Constitution Act, 1982*. Issues pertaining to *Charter* rights and freedoms therefore constitute an integral part of Aboriginal governance, though the special rights of the Aboriginal people are protected.

It does not mean, however, that the *Charter* should play a central role in the day-to-day governance of Aboriginal peoples. Aboriginal individuals may distrust the state's justice system and prefer the more or less formal processes developed by their communities to settle disputes. It would also be perfectly legitimate for Aboriginal citizens to resort to their people's own charter of rights instead of grounding their claim on the Canadian *Charter* whose role would thus be secondary and limited. This article only shows that invoking the constitutional instrument will be one of their options in a potentially pluralistic normative landscape.

Of course, like other governments whose policies and actions are subject to *Charter* scrutiny, Aboriginal authorities should have some leeway in attempting to strike a reasonable balance between the general interest and individual rights. Nothing in the *Charter* prevents judges from taking into account the specific context of Aboriginal communities when they interpret rights and reasonable limits on those rights under section one of the *Charter*. If the courts do not prove equal to the task of being sensitive to a dynamic understanding of Aboriginal difference, and there is sufficient consensus in a self-governing community that safeguarding Aboriginal difference demands decisive action in a given case, this community will be able to give the final word to its political institutions by having recourse, as often as deemed necessary, to the override provisions of section 33 of the *Charter*. There may be a political price to pay but it should not be higher than that exacted on non-aboriginal governments.

[1] Professor, Faculty of Law, Laval University. This paper is based on research done in connection with the *Autochtonie et gouvernance* project funded by *Valorisation recherche Québec*. The author would like to thank his colleagues Henri Brun and Christain Brunelle, who provided judicious comments on an earlier version of this paper. He would also like to thank Me Geneviève Motard, doctoral candidate at Laval University, who helped with the footnotes.

[2] F. Rosenzweig, *The Star of Redemption*, trans. By William Hallo, University of Notre Dame Press: London, 1985.

[3] Schedule B, *Canada Act 1982* (U.K.), 1982, c. 11, [hereinafter "the *Canadian Charter*" or "the *Charter*"].

[4] R.S.C., c. I-5, see in particular sections 81—86.

[5] *Nunavut Act*, S.C. 1993, c. 28.

[6] See for example: the *Kluane First Nation Land Claim Final Agreement*, Ottawa: Public Works and Government Services Canada, 2003 [the *Kluane Final Agreement*]; the *Kluane First Nation Self-Government Agreement*, Ottawa: Public Works and Government Services Canada, 2003 [the *Kluane Self-Government Agreement*]; the *Land Claims and Self-Government Agreement Among the Tlicho and the Government of the Northwest Territories and the Government of Canada*, Ottawa: Department of Indian Affairs and Northern Development, 2003 [the *Tlicho Agreement*]; the *Nisga'a Final Agreement*, published jointly by the Government of Canada, the Government of British Columbia and the Nisga'a Nation, April 27, 1999 [the *Nisga'a Final Agreement*]; the *Tr'ondele Hwech'in Self-Government Agreement*, Ottawa: Department of Indian Affairs and Northern Development, 1998; the *Selkirk First Nation Self-Government Agreement*, Ottawa: Department of Indian Affairs and Northern Development, 1998; the *Vuntut Gwitchin First Nation Self-Government Agreement*, Ottawa: Department of Indian Affairs and Northern Development, 1993; the *Teslin Tlingit Council Self-Government Agreement*, Ottawa: Department of Indian Affairs and Northern Development, 1993; the *Champagne and Aishihik First Nations Self-Government Agreement*, (Ottawa: Department of Indian Affairs and Northern Development, 1993); the *Nacho Nyak Dun First Nation Self-Government Agreement*, Ottawa: Department of Indian Affairs and Northern Development, 1993. See also: the *Yukon First Nations Self-Government Act*, S.C. 1994, c. 35.

[7] Section 35 of the *Constitution Act, 1982* reads as follows: "(1) The existing aboriginal and treaty rights of the aboriginal peoples of Canada are hereby recognized and affirmed. (2) In this Act, "aboriginal peoples of Canada" includes the Indian, Inuit and Métis peoples of Canada. (3) For greater certainty, in subsection (1) "treaty rights" includes rights that now exist by way of land claims agreements or may be so acquired. (4) Notwithstanding any other provision of the Act, the aboriginal and treaty rights referred to in subsection (1) are guaranteed equally to male and female persons."

[8] Under 35(3) of the *Constitution Act, 1982*, rights flowing from treaties include rights resulting from land claim agreements, which are generally known as "modern treaties".

[9] Section 32 of the *Charter* provides:
> "(1) This Charter applies (a) to the Parliament and government of Canada in respect of all matters within the authority of Parliament including all

matters relating to the Yukon Territory and Northwest Territories; and (b) to the legislature and government of each province in respect of all matters within the authority of the legislature of each province."

[10] The key passage of section 25 is: "The guarantee in this Charter of certain rights and freedoms shall not be construed so as to abrogate or derogate from any aboriginal, treaty or other rights of the aboriginal peoples of Canada". The French version reads: "*Le fait que la présente Charte garantit certains droits et libertés ne porte pas atteinte aux droits et libertés – ancestraux, issus de traités ou autres- des peuples autochtones du Canada...*"

[11] The Royal Commission on Aboriginal Peoples takes the view that section 35 recognises and affirms an existing Aboriginal right to self-government, see *Partners in Confederation: Aboriginal Peoples, Self-Government, and the Constitution*, Ottawa: the Royal Commission, 1993. Most writers consider that such an inherent right does indeed exist and should be acknowledged by the Supreme Court of Canada. See in particular: B. Slattery, "First Nations and the Constitution" (1992) 71 *Can. Bar Rev.* 261; K. McNeil, "Envisaging Constitutional Space for Aboriginal Governments" (1993) 19 *Queens L.J.* 951; P. Macklem, *Indigenous Difference and the Constitution of Canada*, Toronto: University of Toronto Press, 2001, [*Macklem*], at 107–131. However, see also: A. Émond, "Le sable dans l'engrenage du droit inhérent des autochtones à l'autonomie gouvernementale" (1996) 30 *R.J.T.* 89. So far, the Supreme Court of Canada has deliberately abstained from deciding the issue. See: *R.* v. *Pamajewon*, [1996] 2 S.C.R. 821; *Delgamuukw* v. *British Columbia*, [1997] 3 S.C.R. 1010 [*Delgamuukw*].

[12] In 1995, the Government of Canada adopted an official policy of recognition and negotiated implementation of Aboriginal peoples' inherent right to self-government. See: *Aboriginal Self-Government: Federal Policy Guide*, Ottawa: Public Works and Government Services Canada, 1995 [*Federal Policy Guide*]. In *Mitchell* v. *M.N.R.*, [2001] 1 S.C.R. 911 [*Mitchell*], Binnie J., with Major J., mentions principles that could provide a foundation for an Aboriginal right to self-government. He canvasses the possibility of a mere "impairment" of Aboriginal sovereignty upon assertion of European sovereignty (par. 158) and also of a "merged sovereignty and shared sovereignty" essential to the reconciliation at the heart of section 35 of the *Constitution Act, 1982* (par. 167). For a detailed analysis of *Mitchell*, see D. Moodie, "Thinking Outside the 20th Century Box: Revisiting Mitchell – Some Comments on the Politics of Judicial Law-Making in the Context of Aboriginal Self-Government" (2004) 35 *Ottawa L. R.* 2. In *Haida Nation v. British Columbia*, [2004] SCC 73, the Supreme Court of Canada uses language that can only strengthen the case for recognising the inherent right to self-government. It writes that "treaties serve to reconcile pre-existing Aboriginal sovereignty with assumed Crown sovereignty" and that the promise of section 35 is "realized and sovereignty claims reconciled through the process of honourable negotiations". See also *Campbell* v. *British Columbia*, [2000] 8 W.W.R. 600 (B.C.S.C.) [*Campbell*] in which the court concludes that an Aboriginal right to self-government already exists as a matter of law.

[13] *Supra* note 6. See the *Nisga'a Final Agreement Act*, S.C. 2000, c. 7.

[14] See for example: the *Entente de Principe d'ordre général entre les prmières nations de Mamuitun et de Nutashkuan et les gouvernements du Québec et du*

Canada, Secrétariat aux affaires autochtones, Québec, 2004; the *Sliammon First Nation Agreement-in-principle*, Canada, British Columbia, Sliammon First Nation, 2003; the *Tsawwassen First Nation Draft Agreement-in-principle*, Canada, British Columbia, Tsawwassen First Nation, 2003; the *Lheidli T'enneh First Nation Agreement-in-principle*, Canada, British Columbia, Lheidli T'enneh First Nation, 2003; the *Gwich'in and Inuvialuit Self-Government Agreement-in-principle for the Beaufort-Delta Region*, Ottawa: Department of Indian Affairs and Northern Development, 2003; the *Kluane Final Agreement*, *supra* note 6; the *Kluane Self-Government Agreement*, *supra* note 6; the *Tlicho Agreement*, *supra* note 6.

[15] However, there is no controversy over the fact that under section 35(4) of the *Constitution Act, 1982*, Aboriginal governments in exercising Aboriginal or Treaty rights must not discriminate on the basis of gender.

[16] It must be noted however that section 32(1) explicitly states that the *Charter* applies to Parliament in its areas of authority, "including all matters relating to the Yukon Territory and Northwest Territories". Since the territorial government of Nunavut derived from the Northwest Territories, there is virtually no doubt that this explicit reference now applies to the government institutions of Nunavut.

[17] The leading proponents of the absolute immunity thesis are K. McNeil, "Aboriginal Governments and the Canadian Charter of Rights and Freedoms" (1996) 34 *Osgoode Hall L.J.* 61 at 88-90, reprinted in K. McNeil, *Emerging Justice? Essays on Indigenous Rights in Canada and Australia*, Saskatoon: University of Saskatchewan Native Law Center, 2001 at 215 [*Emerging Justice?*]; K. Mac-Neil, "Aboriginal Governments and the Charter: Lessons from the United States" (2002) 17 *Can. J. Law & Soc.* 73 [*"Lessons from the United States"*]; K. Wilkins, "But We Need the Eggs: The Royal Commission, the Charter of Rights and the Inherent Right of Aboriginal Self-Government" (1999) 49 *U. Toronto L.J.* 53 [*Wilkins*]; and D. Russell, *A People's Dream: Aboriginal Self-Government in Canada*, Vancouver: University of British Columbia Press, 2000. [*Russell*]

[18] S. Montagne, "De la *pension governance* à la *corporate governance*" (2001) 63 *Revue d'économie financière* 53.

[19] P. Moreau-Defarges, *La gouvernance*, Paris : Presses universitaires de France, 2003 at 29-30 [Moreau-Defarges].

[20] Along with its origins in Anglo-American management, governance's challenge to the vertical nature of the relationship between power and civil society probably explains why some fear it can be used in the service of the neoliberal dogma of a minimal state and unbridled globalized market, and thus as an instrument for circumventing democratic legitimacy. See A. Lajoie, "Gouvernance et société civile" in D.M. Hayes, Ed., *Governance in the 21st Century/La gouvernance au 21e siècle*, Toronto: University of Toronto Press, 1999 at 149—152; L. Borot, *Gouvernance, Cités 9*, Paris: Presses universitaires de France, 2002 at 173-177.

[21] Moreau-Defarges, *supra* note 19 at 19.

[22] Programme de développement des Nations unies (PNUD) "La gouvernance démocratique: politique, pratique et propositions" Paris, Symposium sur l'accès aux financement internationaux, Agence intergouvernementale de la francophonie, Table ronde no. 3, November 20 and 21, 2003, at 1, online at: http://www. espace-economique-francophone.com/e/tr3_linda_maguire.pdf [our translation].

[23] Thus, Article 9 of the *Cotonou Agreement* defines good governance as follows:

"In the context of a political and institutional environment that upholds human rights, democratic principles and the rule of law, good governance is the transparent and accountable management of human, national, economic and financial resources for the purposes of equitable and sustainable development." See *Partnership Agreement between the members of the African, Caribbean and Pacific Group of States (ACP), of the one part, and the European Community and its Member States, of the other part, signed in Cotonou on 23 June 2000.* Online at: http://europa.eu.int/smartapi/cgi/sga_doc?smartapi!celexapi!prod!celexnumdoc&numdoc =22000a1215(01)&lg=en

[24] Legal academics have severely criticized the Court's essentialist and anachronistic approach. See, among others, Borrows, J., "The Trickster: Integral to a Distinctive Culture" (1997) 8 *Forum constitutionnel* 27; R.L. Barsh and J. Youngblood Henderson, "The Supreme Court's *Van der Peet* Trilogy: Naïve Imperialism and Ropes of Sand" (1997) 42 *R.D. McGill* 993; K. MacNeil, "Reduction by Definition: The Supreme Court's Treatment of Aboriginal Rights in 1996" (1997) 5 *Canada Watch* 60; G. Otis, "Opposing Aboriginality to Modernity: The Doctrine of Aboriginal Rights in Canada" (1997) 12 *B.J.C.S.* 182; L.I. Rotman, "Hunting for Answers in a Strange Kettle of Fish: Unilateralism, Paternalism and Fiduciary Rhetoric in *Badger* and *Van der Peet*" (1997) 8 *Forum constitutionnel* 40. See also: G. Mativat, *L'Amérindien dans la lorgnette des juges: le mémoir déformant de la justice*, Montréal : Recherches amérindiennes au Québec, 2003.

[25] J.J. Simard scathingly denounces what he terms the myth of the Indian as "the opposite of the White", "the reverse image of modernity", which reserves for "Whites" "individual assertion, critical thinking, cultural pluralism, democratic debates, and for Aboriginals a consensual, homogenous community and chiefs who exhale the substance of their people as soon as a microphone is placed under their noses". J.J. Simard, *La réduction: l'autochtone inventé et les amérindiens d'aujourd'hui,* Sillery, Québec: Septentrion, 2003, at 134 [our translation] [Simard].

[26] *Supra* note 17, at 117—118. See also at 128—129.

[27] *Supra* note 17, at 86.

[28] See M. E. Turpel, "Aboriginal Peoples and the Charter: Interpretive Monopolies, Cultural Differences" (1989) *C.H.R.Y.B.* 3 at 30.

[29] He writes: "Imposition of Canadian values and norms on the Aboriginal peoples perpetuates colonialism and – as our history teaches us so well – simply does not work." In "Lessons from the United States" *supra* note 17, at 104.

[30] See M. Bold and J.A. Long, "Tribal Philosophies and the Charter of Rights and Freedoms" in M. Bold and J.A. Long, Eds., *The Quest for Justice: Aboriginal Peoples and Aboriginal Rights*, Toronto: University of Toronto Press, 1985, 165, at 168—169. Franks rightly notes: "Many discussions of Aboriginal rights in Canada…claim that there was a golden age in the past where all members of the culture shared a blessed and nonalienated existence and the relationships between humans were conducted on a basis of civility and respect and ensured that the ideals embodied in fundamental rights were recognized." C.E.S. Franks, "Rights and Self-government for Canada's Aboriginal Peoples" in C. Cook and J.D. Lindau, Eds., *Aboriginal Rights and Self-Government: the Canadian and Mexican Experience in North American Perspective*, Montréal: McGill-Queens University

Press, 2000, 101, at 126. [Cook and Lindau].

[31] Wilkins, *supra* note 17 at 87—90.

[32] *Ibid.,* at 93.

[33] *Ibid.,* pp 81—99. Russell, *supra* note 17 at 103—130.

[34] For example, Macklem writes: "In my view, the Charter does pose a risk to the continuing vitality of Indigenous difference. The Charter enables litigants to constitutionally interrogate the rich complexity of Aboriginal societies according to a rigid analytic grid of individual right and state obligation." *Supra* note 11, at 195. A similar postulate underlies Grammond's analysis: S. Grammond, *Aménager la coexistence: les peuples autochtones et le droit canadien,* Brussels : Bruylant/ Yvon Blais, 2003, at 342—345.

[35] This does not mean that it is always impossible to be inspired by values considered traditional and still enduring in a community. For example, a persistent attachment to consensus can translate into specific ways of selecting political leaders. See G. Otis, "Élection, gouvernance traditionnelle et droits fondamentaux chez les peuples autochtones du Canada" (2004) 49 *R.D. McGill* 393.

[36] See for example the *Tlicho Agreement, supra* note 6, which provides in 7.4.1 that "the Tlicho government has the power to enact laws in relation to..."; likewise, the provisions of 13.0 of the *Kluane Self-Government Agreement, supra* note 6, specify the nature of the legislative powers of the Kluane First Nation; and, finally, Clause 1 of Chapter 11 of the *Nisga'a Final Agreement, supra* note 6, reads: "The Nisga'a Nation has the right to self-government, and the authority to make laws, as set out in this Agreement." See also the *Ta'an Kwach'an Council Final Agreement,* Ottawa: Public Works and Government Services Canada, 2002, cl. 24.1.2.1; the *Trondek Hwech'in Self-Government Agreement, supra* note 6; the *Little Salmon/Carmacks First Nation Self-Government Agreement,* Ottawa, Department of Indian Affairs and Northern Development, 1997.

[37] R.S.C. (1985).

[38] See for example: *R.* v. *Drybones,* [1970] S.C.R. 282; *Attorney General of Canada* v. *Lavell,* [1974] S.C.R. 1349; *Attorney General of Canada* v. *Canard,* [1976] 1 S.C.R. 170; *R.* v. *Jack,* [1985] 2 S.C.R. 332.

[39] Supreme Court of Canada decisions involving Aboriginal claims based on the *Canadian Charter* include *Native Women's Association of Canada* v. *Canada,* [1994] 3 S.C.R. 627; *Corbière* v. *Canada (Department of Indian Affairs and Northern Development),* [1999] 2 S.C.R. 203 [*Corbière*]; *Lovelace* v. *Ontario,* [2000] 1 S.C.R. 950. Cases in which Aboriginals have demanded that their individual rights and freedoms be respected are numerous, see for example: *R.* v. *Gladue,* [1999] 1 S.C.R. 688; *R.* v. *Williams,* [1998] 1 S.C.R. 1128; *R.* v. *Jones,* [1991] 3 S.C.R. 110; *R.* v. *Furtney,* [1991] 3 S.C.R. 89; *Tsilhqot'in Nation* v. *Attorney General of Canada,* [2004] B.C.C.A. 106; *Ardoch Algonquin First Nation* v. *Attorney General of Canada,* [2003] 1 F.C.A. 473 and (2003) 315 N.R. 76; *R.* v. *Carpenter,* [2002] B.C.C.A. 301; *R.* v. *Lamirande,* (2002) M.B.C.A. 41; *M.M.* v. *Roman Catholic Church of Canada,* (2001) M.B.C.A. 12.

[40] See *Francis* v. *Mohawk Council of Kanesatake,* [2003] F.C.T. 115; *Scrimbitt* v. *Sakimay Indian Band Council,* [2000] 1 F.C. 513; *Hall* v. *Dakota Tipi Indian Band,* [2000] F.C.T. 10139; *Gros-Louis* v. *Nation Huronne-Wendat (Conseil),* [2000] F.C.T. 11139; *Sark* v. *Lennox Island Band of Indians,* [1999] F.C.T. 10814; *Crow*

v. *Blood Band*, (1996) F.C.J. 119.

[41] See for example: *Edgar* v. *Kitasoo Band Council*, [2003] F.C.T. 166; *Horse Lake First Nation* v. *Horseman*, [2003] A.B.Q.B. 152; *R.* v. *Hatchard*, [1993] 1 C.N.L.R. 96 (Ont. Gen. Div.).

[42] *Sawridge Band* v. *Canada*, [1987] 2 F.C. 450.

[43] See *Azak* v. *Nisga'a Nation*, [2003] B.C.H.R.T. 79; *Jacob* v. *Mohawk Council of Kahnawake*, [1998] D.C.D.P. 2; *Schubenacadie Indian Band* v. *Canada*, [2000] 4 C.N.L.R. 275 (F.C.A.); *Canada (Human Rights Commission)* v. *Gordon Band Council*, [2001] 1 F.C. 124 (C.F.A.).

[44] *Thomas* v. *Norris*, [1992] 2 C.N.L.R. 139. See T. Isaac, "Individual Versus Collective Rights: Aboriginal People and the Significance of *Thomas* v. *Norris*" (1992) 21 *Man. L. J.* 618.

[45] See: Assembly of First Nations, *First Nations Circle on the Constitution: To the Source*, Commissioners' Report, Ottawa, 1992, at 61– 64, 78.

[46] Canadian Panel on Violence Against Women, *Changing the Landscape: Ending Violence, Achieving Equality*, Ottawa: Supplies and Services Canada, 1993; Native Women's Association of Canada, *Native Women and the Charter: A Discussion Paper*, Ottawa, 1992; T. Nahanee, "Dancing with a Gorilla: Aboriginal Women, Justice and the Charter" in the Royal Commission on Aboriginal Peoples, *Aboriginal Peoples and the Justice System: Report of the National Round Table on Aboriginal Justice Issues*, Ottawa: Supplies and Services Canada, 1992, at 359.

[47] See in particular H. Hogh, "Finding a Balance Between Ethnicity and Gender Among Inuit in Arctic Canada" in *Indigenous Women: the Right to a Voice*, International Work Group for Indigenous Affairs, 1998, at 75–82.

[48] Reprinted in A. Tremblay, *La réforme de la constitution au Canada,* Montréal: Thémis, 1995, at 464–495. The Accord provided that section 25 of the *Charter* would be amended by the addition of a subparagraph (c) specifying that "nothing in the Charter abrogates or derogates from…rights or freedoms relating to the exercise or protection of their languages, cultures or traditions". As will be seen from our analysis of section 25, this amendment would not have in practice changed the protection offered by the provision, which produces a limited immunizing effect with respect to the special rights of the Aboriginal people.

[49] See for example: the *Tlicho Agreement*, *supra* note 6, Article 2.15.1; the *Nisga'a Final Agreement*, *supra* note 6 Article 9; the *Gwich'in and Inuvialuit Self-Government Agreement-in-principle for the Beaufort-Delta Region*, *supra* note 14, Chapter 2, clause 2.9.1; the *Sioux Valley Dakota Nation Comprehensive Agreement-in-principle*, Canada, Sioux Valley Dakota Nation, 2001, Article 5.02(2); the *Entente de principe d'ordre général entre les premières nations de Mamuitun et de Nutashkuan et les gouvernements du Québec et du Canada*, *supra* note 14, Article 8.4.1.1.

[50] See in particular: the *Gwich'in and Inuvialuit Self-Government Agreement-in-principle for the Beaufort-Delta Region*, *supra* note 14, Chapter 4, Clause 3.3.3 (i) and Chapter 5, Clause 4.3.3., which reads: "The Inuvialuit Constitution shall: […] (i) provide for the protection of rights and freedoms for the Inuvialuit and others to whom Inuvialuit Laws apply which shall not be less than the rights and freedoms set out in the *Canadian Charter of Rights and Freedoms*". With respect to the opposition to extinguishment clauses in modern treaties, see, among others,

G. Otis and A. Émond, "L'identité autochtone dans les traités contemporains: de l'extinction à l'affirmation du titre ancestral" (1996) 41 *R.D. McGill* 543; Royal Commission on Aboriginal Peoples, *Treaty Making in the Spirit of Coexistence – An Alternative to Extinguishment*, Ottawa: Supplies and Services Canada, 1994.

[51] Assembly of First Nations in Québec and Labrador, *Les premières nations du Québec réaffirment les principes fondamentaux de co-existence pacifique*, Secretariat of the Assembly of First Nations in Québec and Labrador, May 19, 1998, at 1 [our translation].

[52] See: I. Bellier, "Dernières nouvelles du groupe de travail de l'ONU sur le projet de déclaration des droits des peuples autochtones" (2003) 32 *Recherches amérindiennes au Québec* 93.

[53] Article 8 of the Draft Declaration provides that "Indigenous peoples have the collective and individual right to maintain and develop their distinct identities and characteristics, including the right to identify themselves as indigenous and to be recognized as such." The *Draft Declaration on the Rights of Indigenous Peoples* is available at: http://www.ohchr.org/english/issues/indigenous/docs/crp1.doc

[54] *Ibid.* Moreover, Article 34 of the Draft Declaration states that "All the rights and freedoms recognized herein are equally guaranteed to male and female indigenous individuals." To get an idea of what it could in practice mean to subordinate Aboriginal powers to compliance with international treaties, see the recent report issued by the UNICEF Innocenti Research Centre, *Ensuring the Rights of Indigenous Children*, Innocenti Digest No. 11, Florence, Italy, 2004, in which it is written that "group claims that seek to maintain traditional acts otherwise deemed prejudicial to the child's dignity, health or development – this would be the cases, for instance, with female genital mutilation, non-consensual marriage or inhuman or degrading punishments for antisocial behaviour – contravene the rights of the individual and therefore cannot be legitimized as a right by the community. It is an operative principle under international law that the individual should receive the highest level of protection and, in the case of children, "the best interests of the child" (CRC Article 3) cannot be neglected or violated to safeguard the best interests of the group." Online at http://www.unicef-icdc.org/publications/pdf/digest11e.pdf With respect to the primacy of individual rights in the international normative scheme, see G. Otis and B. Melkevik, *Peuples autochtones et normes internationales,* (Cowansville: Yvon Blais, 1996), at 19–20.

[55] International instruments are more restrictive than the *Charter* with respect to the governments' power to override rights and freedoms. See A. Binette, "Le pouvoir dérogatoire de l'article 33 de la Charte canadienne des droits et libertés et la structure de la Constitution du Canada" (2003) *R. du B. Can.* (special issue) 107, at 125–128. International human rights law also includes a complex set of specific instruments that cover social, economic and cultural rights.

[56] Laurent Etre, "Concevoir, sans renoncer à nos différences, un universalisme pluraliste", interview with Mireille Delmas-Marty, *Le Monde*, Friday, March 19, 2004, Le Monde des livres, at VIII [our translation]; see also: M. Delmas-Marty and M.L. Izorche, "Marge nationale d'appréciation et internationalisation du droit: réflexions sur la validité formelle d'un droit commun pluraliste" 46 (2001) *McGill L.J.* 923.

[57] See in particular A. C. Cairns, *Citizens Plus: Aboriginal Peoples and the Cana-*

dian State, Vancouver: University of British Columbia Press, 2000 at 97—106.

[58] Simard, *supra* note 25 at 127—128; Y. Plasseraud, *L'identité*, Paris: Montchrestien, 2000 at 19 evokes in this respect "the metaphor of threatened organisms that secrete "differentiating antibodies" that rush to the rescue to fight against "progress's" mass and anthropic trends" [our translation].

[59] They are not alone in this in Canada. In a speech delivered at the Francophonie festival in Montréal in March 2004, Jean Charest, Premier of Québec, declared: "We will do everything to preserve our culture and we will always refuse to sell our identity", *Le Devoir*, Thursday, March 18, 2004 at A-3 [our translation].

[60] The Supreme Court of Canada recently noted the pre-colonial source of Aboriginal rights in the following terms:

> "In *Calder v. Attorney-General of British Columbia*, [1973] S.C.R. 313, the Court had recognized for the first time in the modern era that the Indian interest in their ancestral lands constituted a *legal* interest that predated European settlement. Recognition of Aboriginal rights could not, therefore, be treated merely as an act of grace and favour on the part of the Crown. These propositions, while brought to the fore in Canadian law relatively recently, are not new. Marshall C.J. of the United States ruled as early as 1823 that the legal rights of Indians in the lands they traditionally occupied prior to European colonization both pre-dated and survived the claims to sovereignty made by various European nations in the territories of the North American continent: *Johnson v. M'Intosh*…"

See *Wewaykum Indian Band* v. *Canada*, 2002 SCC 79, para. 75

[61] See *Lavigne* v. *Ontario Public Service Employees Union*, [1991] 2 S.C.R. 211. See also Macklem, *supra* note 11, at 201. In contrast, even though the *Charter* applies to government approval for a clause in a treaty, the principle of non-abrogation set out in section 25 prevents, as will be shown in this article, the *Charter* from being used to annul the provisions of treaties or implementing legislation that state Treaty rights or confirm ancestral Aboriginal rights.

[62] See *Slaight Communications Inc.* v. *Davidson*, [1989] 1 S.C.R. 1038; *McKinney* v. *University of Guelph*, [1990] 3 S.C.R. 229; *Eldridge* v. *British Columbia*, [1997] 3 S.C.R. 624 [*Eldridge*]; *Blencoe* v. *British Columbia (Human Rights Commission)*, [2000] 2 S.C.R. 307 [*Blencoe*].

[63] We cannot subscribe to Wilkins' opinion that a treaty that does not recognize a right as inherent is an instrument by which the federal government simply "confers" powers that, because they would derive purely from federal authority, would therefore be subject to the *Charter*. See *supra* note 17, at 61—62.

[64] In *R.* v. *Sioui*, [1990] 1 S.C.R. 1025 at 1056, the Supreme Court of Canada notes that: "The sui generis situation in which the Indians were placed had forced the European mother countries to acknowledge that they had sufficient autonomy for the valid creation of solemn agreements which were called "treaties", regardless of the strict meaning given to that word then and now by international law." In *R.* v. *Sundown*, [1999] 1 S.C.R. 393 at 24, the Court writes: "Treaties may appear to be no more than contracts. Yet they are far more. They are a solemn exchange of promises made by the Crown and various First Nations. They often formed the basis for peace and the expansion of European settlement."

[65] P. W. Hogg and M. E. Turpel, "Implementing Aboriginal Self-government: Constitutional and Jurisdictional Issues" (1995) 74: 2 *R. du B. Can.* 187, at 214. See also Russell, *supra* note 17, at 186—187. Wilkins considers that the reasoning by Hogg and Turpel is valid when a treaty is the source of a governmental power, but not when it only confirms a pre-existing Aboriginal right, *supra* note 17, at 73—75. This distinction between the two types of treaty does not appear to be tenable.

[66] *Wilkins*, *supra* note 17, at 64—71; *Emerging Justice?*, *supra* note 17, at 220—225. It seems that this was the position taken by the Court in *Hardy* v. *Westbank First Nation*, [2003] B.C.J. No. 2540 (B.C.S.C.). In that case, non-Aboriginals challenged the validity under the *Charter* of a self-government agreement between the federal government and the Westbank First Nation. The agreement provides that the Westbank First Nation's authorities can adopt legislation in a number of areas. The Court doubted the *Charter's* application to Westbank legislative institutions because, in the judge's opinion, those institutions would not be covered by the list in section 32: "Section 32 of the Charter effectively defines a "legislative assembly" and it does not include a government as envisaged by the Agreement," at par. 9.

[67] *Emerging Justice?*, *ibid*, at 222—223; Wilkins, *supra* note 17, at 77—78.

[68] *B.C.G.E.U.* v. *British Columbia (Attorney General)*, [1998] 2 S.C.R. 214 [*B.C.G.E.U.*]. The Court has however refused to apply the *Charter* to court orders issued to resolve entirely private disputes that involve no government action. See *SDGMR* v. *Dolphin Delivery Ltd.* [1986] 2 S.C.R. 573 [*Dolphin Delivery*]. See also L'Heureux-Dubé, J.'s reasons in *Young* v. *Young*, [1993] 4 S.C.R. 3 at 90—92 and in *P.(D.)* v. *S.(C.)*, [1993] 4 S.C.R. 141 at 107. See G. Otis, "Judicial Immunity from Charter Review: Myth or Reality?" (1989) 30 *C. de D.* 673; C. Beaulieu, *L'application de la Charte canadienne des droits et libertés au pouvoir judiciaire*, Cowansville: Yvon Blais, 1995; L. Huppé, *Le régime juridique du pouvoir judiciaire*, (Montréal : Wilson & Lafleur, 2000), at 195—200.

[69] *Dolphin Delivery*, *ibid*, at 600—601.

[70] This is the kind of reasoning attempted by Hogg. See P. W. Hogg, *Constitutional Law of Canada*, loose-leaf edition, Toronto: Carswell, 2004 at 34-17 and 34-18.

[71] In *B.C.G.E.U.*, *supra* note 68, the Court explains in pages 243—244 that a court order designed to ensure the orderly administration of justice and the vindication of criminal law is subject to the *Charter*:

> "The court is acting on its own motion and not at the instance of any private party. The motivation for the court's action is entirely "public" in nature, rather than "private". The criminal law is being applied to vindicate the rule of law and the fundamental freedoms protected by the *Charter*. At the same time, however, this branch of the criminal law, like any other, must comply with the fundamental standards established by the *Charter*."

[72] For a cogent analysis of the problem of political-legal legitimization of Canada's sovereignty over Aboriginal peoples, see M. Asch, "First Nations and the Derivation of Canada's Underlying Title: Comparing Perspectives on Legal Ideology" in Cook and Lindau, *supra* note 30, at 148—167.

[73] See in particular J. Tully, *Strange Multiplicity, Constitutionalism in an Age of Diversity*, Cambridge: Cambridge University Press, 1995 at 116—124.

[74] It can be added that the Supreme Court of Canada did not hesitate to rely on the rule of law to declare the *Charter* applicable to Québec institutions despite that province's opposition to the 1982 reform. See *Reference re Secession of Québec*, [1998] 2 S.C.R. 217, para. 47. [*Reference re. Secession of Québec*]. The same structural principle of the rule of law could probably be applied to deny legal effect to the failure to secure formal Aboriginal consent for the reform.

[75] *R.* v. *Van der Peet*, [1996] 2 S.C.R. 507, par. 19 [*Van der Peet*].

[76] *Ibid.*, at para. 49; *R.* v. *Gladstone*, [1996] 2 S.C.R. 723, par. 72 [*Gladstone*].

[77] *Hill* v. *Church of Scientology of Toronto*, [1995] 2 S.C.R. 1130, para. 92.

[78] Macklem also relies on the need to reconcile the *Charter* and Part II of the *Constitution Act, 1982* to conclude that the *Charter* is applicable to governments based on Aboriginal or Treaty rights. See *supra* note 11, at 208—209.

[79] B. Slattery, "Understanding Aboriginal Rights" (1987) 66 *Rev. du Bar. Can.* 727 at 738. *Mabo* v. *Queensland [No. 2]*, (1992) 175 C.L.R. 1 at 51; *Idewu Inasa* v. *Oshodi*, [1934] A.C. 99, at 105; *Mitchell, supra* note 12, par 141—142, Binnie, J.

[80] On this point, I therefore subscribe to the conclusion, albeit based on somewhat different reasoning, reached by the Royal Commission on Aboriginal Peoples. See the Report of the Royal Commission on Aboriginal Peoples, *Restructuring the Relationship*, Vol. 2, Canada Communication Group, 1996, at 255. See also B. Slattery, "First Nations and the Constitution: A Question of Trust" (1992) 71 *Rev. du Bar. Can.* 261 at 286, n. 82.

[81] *Emerging Justice?, supra* note 17, at 221.

[82] However, it is possible that the distinctiveness of Aboriginal institutions might sometimes make it impossible to apply a specific *Charter* right. For example, the legal protections listed in sections 8—14 of the *Charter* are based on the state model of criminal justice. If an Aboriginal people opt for a form of justice that does not similarly engage the underlying values of the *Charter*, it is quite possible that the *Charter's* relevance would be greatly reduced. See Grammond, *supra* note 34, at 337.

[83] This is true of sections 3, 4, 5, 6, 16, 17, 18, 19, 20 and 23 of the *Charter*.

[84] Section 33 of the *Charter* is as follows:

"(1) Parliament or the legislature of a province may expressly declare in an Act of Parliament or the legislature, as the case may be, that the Act or a provision thereof shall operate notwithstanding a provision included in section 2 or sections 7 to 15 of this Charter. (2) An Act or a provision of an Act in respect of which a declaration made under this section is in effect shall have such operation as it would have but for the provision of this Charter referred to in the declaration. (3) A declaration made under subsection (1) shall cease to have effect five years after it comes into force or on such earlier date as may be specified in the declaration. (4) Parliament or the legislature of a province may re-enact a declaration made under subsection (1). (5) Subsection (3) applies in respect of a re-enactment made under subsection (4)."

[85] See the *Royal Commission on Aboriginal Peoples, supra* note 80, at 255—256. See also Wilkins, *supra* note 17, at 100—101; *Emerging Justice?, supra* note 17, at 224—225.

[86] *Royal Commission on Aboriginal Peoples, Ibid.*, at 256.

[87] Article 8 of the same chapter reads: "This Agreement does not alter the Constitution of Canada, including: c) sections 25 and 35 of the *Constitution Act, 1982.*"

[88] *Simon* v. *The Queen*, [1985] 2 S.C.R. 387 at 401; *Sioui, supra* note 64, at 1063; *R.* v. *Badger*, [1996] 1 S.C.R. 771, para. 41; *R.* v. *Sundown*, [1999] 1 S.C.R. 393, para. 24.

[89] See in particular *Macklem, supra* note 11 at 201; T. Dickson, "Section 25 and Intercultural Judgment" (2003) 61 *U. of T. Fac. L. J.* 141; Grammond, *supra* note 34 at 339; "Lessons from the United States", *supra* note 17.

[90] See Wilkins, *supra* note 17, at 73, No. 81 and at 74, No. 85.

[91] See in particular *R.* v. *Howard*, [1994] 2 S.C.R. 299.

[92] The author writes: "only the parties to the agreement – not, for example, individuals whether community members or not – could enforce the Charter discipline against participating aboriginal governments", *supra* note 17 at 74, No. 85.

[93] See Article 24.3.1 of the *Agreement concerning James Bay and Northern Québec and Complementary Agreements,* Québec, Les publications du Québec, 1998: "Every native person shall have the right to hunt, fish and trap." Likewise, in the *Agreement between the Inuit of the Nunavut Settlement Area and Her Majesty the Queen in right of Canada*, Ottawa, Tungavik and the Department of Indian Affairs and Northern Development, 1993, the provisions concerning Inuit harvesting rights stipulate that "an Inuk shall have the right to harvest." See articles 5.6.1, 5.6.3 and 5.6.13.

[94] See for example *Kadlak* v. *Nunavut,* 2001 NUCJ 1, in which an Inuk successfully used his individual right to hunt for subsistence granted under the Nunavut Accord to have a decision made by the Nunavut authorities quashed.

[95] The referential incorporation of the *Charter* does not however make a given *Charter* provision applicable to Aboriginal governments if the wording or purpose of that provision is no way relevant to such governments (see for example sections 3, 4, 5, 6, 16, 17, 18, 19, 20 and 23).

[96] See in particular *Shubenacadie Indian Band* v. *Canada* [2000] 4 C.N.L.R. 275 (F.C.A.), par . 43; *Corbière, supra* note 39 at 248–249.

[97] W. Kymlicka, "Le nouveau débat sur les droits des minorités," in I. Schulte-Tenckhoff, *Altérité et droit: contributions à l'étude du rapport entre droit et culture*, Brussels : Bruylant, 2002, 91, at 99.

[98] *Ibid.*

[99] McNeil asserts: "…any limitation on the exercise of the right necessarily involves a derogation from the right itself" in *Emerging Justice?, supra* note 17, at 226. See also Wilkins, *supra* note 17, at 108–114; B. Wildsmith, *Aboriginal Peoples and Section 25 of the Canadian Charter of Rights and Freedoms*, Saskatoon: Native Law Center, 1988 at 51; W. Pentney, "The Rights of the Aboriginal People of Canada and the Constitution Act, 1982, Part I; the Interpretative Prism of Section 25" (1988) 22 *U.B.C. L. Rev.* 21 at 29.

[100] *Emerging Justice?, ibid.,* at 225.

[101] *Emerging Justice? ibid.,* at 226.

[102] *Gladstone, supra* note 76, para. 43; *R.* v. *Marshall*, [1999] 3 S.C.R. 456, para. 18.

[103] The version that is both the clearest and most consistent with the purpose of the provision, and which does not contradict the other version, will normally be

given preference. See *R.* v. *Turpin*, [1989] 1 S.C.R. 1296 at 1314; *Mahe* v. *Alberta*, [1990] 1 S.C.R. 342 at 370 [hereinafter *Mahe*]; *Harvey* v. *New Brunswick*, [1996] 2 S.C.R. 876 at 896—897.

[104] Grammond, *supra* note 34, at 342—345.

[105] Hogg and Turpel, *supra* note 65, at 215.

[106] *Royal Commission on Aboriginal Peoples, supra* note 80, at 256—257.

[107] Terms now preferred by the Supreme Court of Canada to describe the heart of federal jurisdiction over "Indians" pursuant to 91(24) of the *Constitution Act, 1867*, see *Delgamuukw, supra* note 11, para. 178.

[108] Terms used by the Supreme Court of Canada to identify customs and practices considered worthy of protection as Aboriginal rights recognized and confirmed in section 35 of the *Constitution Act, 1982*; see *Mitchell, supra* note 12, para. 12.

[109] See *Macklem, supra* note 11, at 226. See also Dickson, *supra* note 89, at 158—159. Grammond is apparently opposed to this reading of section 25 because he thinks that applying the *Charter* to "internal restrictions" would "lead to the general applicability of the Charter and [...] deprive section 25 of any useful meaning," *supra* note 34 at 342 [our translation].

[110] *Federal Policy Guide, supra* note 12, at 5.

[111] Wilkins, *supra* note 17, at 115—117.

[112] Section 21: "Nothing in sections 16 to 20 abrogates or derogates from any right, privilege or obligation with respect to the English and French languages, or either of them, that exists or is continued by virtue of any other provision of the Constitution of Canada."

[113] Section 22: " Nothing in sections 16 to 20 abrogates or derogates from any legal or customary right or privilege acquired or enjoyed either before or after the coming into force of this Charter with respect to any language that is not English or French."

[114] Section 29: "Nothing in this Charter abrogates or derogates from any rights or privileges guaranteed by or under the Constitution of Canada in respect of denominationalist, separate or dissentient schools."

[115] Brun and Tremblay write that "the provisions in the Constitution, whether old or new, are all on the same footing. They all have the same supralegislative value. They have to be interpreted and applied in relationship to one another. Each has to be given a meaning such that they can all operate concomitantly." In H. Brun and G. Tremblay, *Droit constitutionnel,* 4th Edition, Cowansville: Yvon Blais, 2002 at 209 [our translation].

[116] This rule is also often applied to give operative effect to two legislative provisions that are contradictory at first sight. See P. A. Côté, *Interpretation des lois,* 3rd Edition, Montréal: Thémis, 1999 at 455—456.

[117] *Reference re. An Act to Amend the Education Act* [1987] 1 S.C.R. 1148.

[118] *Ibid.,* at 1197.

[119] *Ibid.,* at 1197—1198. See also *Mahe, supra* note 103, at 369, where the Supreme Court of Canada writes that section 23 "is, if anything, an exception to the provisions of ss. 15 and 27 in that it accords these groups, the English and the French, special status in comparison to all other linguistic groups in Canada." Likewise, in *Adler* v. *Ontario*, [1996] 3 S.C.R. 609, para. 31—35 [*Adler*], Iacobucci J. establishes a parallel between section 93's effect on the application of the *Charter*

and that of section 23.

[120] *Gosselin (Tutor of) v. Québec* [2005] 1 S.C.R. 238 [*Gosselin*].

[121] *Ibid.*, at para. 27.

[122] *New Brunswick Broadcasting Co. v. Nova Scotia (Speaker of the House of Assembly),* [1993] 1 S.C.R. 319, at 389, (McLachlin J.). [*New Brunswick Broadcasting*].

[123] *Reference re. Bill 30, An Act to Amend the Education Act, supra* note 117 at 390, (Wilson J.)

[124] *New Brunswick Broadcasting, supra,* note 122, at 389 (McLachlin J.)

[125] *Ibid.,* at 390.

[126] *Gosselin, supra,* note 120, para. 13-14.

[127] *New Brunswick Broadcasting Co., supra,* note 122, at 389-390.

[128] The Supreme Court of Canada has also established that, since the *Charter* cannot contravene itself, the fact that only Canadian citizens benefit from democratic and mobility rights under sections 3 and 6 does not engage equality rights under section 15, even though the latter section prohibits discrimination on the basis of citizenship: <u>Canada (Minister of Employment and Immigration) v. Chiarelli</u> [1992] 1 S.C.R. 711; *Lavoie v. Canada,* [2002] 1 S.C.R. 769, par. 44, (Bastarache J.'s reasons, to which Gonthier, Iacobucci and Major, JJ. subscribe).

[129] *New Brunswick Broadcasting, supra,* note 122, at 391.

[130] *Emerging Justice?, supra* note 17, at 227.

[131] See, for example, the *Nisga'a Final Agreement, supra* note 13.

[132] The Supreme Court of Canada (*Reference re. Bill 30, An Act to Amend the Education Act, supra* note 117, at 1198—1199) endorses the opinion expressed by the Ontario Court of Appeal, according to which;

> These educational rights, granted specifically to the Protestants in Québec and the Roman Catholics in Ontario, make it impossible to treat all Canadians equally. The country was founded upon the recognition of special or unequal educational rights for specific religious groups in Ontario and Québec. The incorporation of the *Charter* into the *Constitution Act, 1982*, does not change the original Confederation bargain. A specific constitutional amendment would be required to accomplish that.

[133] *Ibid,.* at para. 35.

[134] *Adler, supra* note 119, para. 34.

[135] The Supreme Court of Canada has described section 23 of the Charter, rightly, as a "political compromise". See *Société des Acadiens du Nouveau-Brunswick v. Association of Parents for Fairness in Education,* [1986] 1 S.C.R. 549 at 578; *Reference re. Public Schools Act (Man.),* [1993] S.C.R. 839 at 851. Despite these origins, it does not follow that these rights call for a narrow interpretation that is at odds with their remedial purpose. See in particular: *R. v. Beaulac* [1999] 1 S.C.R. 768.

[136] The Court notes that, "As members of the French language majority in Québec, they seek to use the right to equality to access a right guaranteed in Québec only to the English language minority", *supra*, note 120, para. 10.

[137] *Ibid.,* at para. 22.

[138] *Ibid.,* at para. 2.

[139] "*Derogate*: 1. "to repeal or to abrogate in part; to destroy or impair the force or effect of; to lessen the extent of." In J. A. Simpson and E. S. C. Weiner, Eds., *Oxford English Dictionary*, Vol. 1, 2nd Edition, Oxford: Clarendon Press, 1989. "Derogation from a right is to prejudice or destroy it", see D. W. Walker, *Oxford Companion to Law,* Oxford: Clarendon Press, 1980, at 352.

[140] In *New Brunswick Broadcasting, supra* note 122, at 389, McLachlin writing for the majority says:

> The *Charter* has changed the balance of power between the legislative branch and the executive on the one hand, and the courts on the other hand, by requiring that all laws and government action must conform to the fundamental principles laid down in the *Charter*. As a practical matter, this means that, subject to the override provision in s. 33 of the *Charter*, the courts may be called upon to rule that laws and government acts are invalid. To this extent, the *Charter* has impinged on the supreme authority of the legislative branches.

[141] *Ibid.*, at 390—391, McLachlin J. In *Reference re. Bill 30, An Act to Amend the Education Act, supra* note 117 at 1207, Estey J. expressed this distinction in the following terms: "It is one thing to supervise and on a proper occasion curtail the exercise of a power to legislate; it is quite another thing to say that an entire power to legislate has been removed from the Constitution by the introduction of this judicial power of supervision."

[142] *Adler, supra* note 119, para. 49.

[143] The Court writes, *ibid.*, para. 54: "the provision of the health services to those qualified is simply a means to an end, a way to ensure access to education. Therefore, the SHSSP is simply a manifestation of the Ontario government's fulfilling its mandate to provide an education designed for all members of the community and is, thus, immune from *Charter* scrutiny."

[144] *Ibid.* at 648—649.

[145] Under section 23 of the *Charter*, the members of an official linguistic minority have, when their number warrants it, the right to a separate minority school board. See *Mahe, supra* note 102.

[146] There is every indication that a school board is a government body within the meaning of section 32 of the *Charter*. See in particular *Eldridge, supra* note 62; *Blencoe, supra* note 62. In *R.* v. *M.R.M.*, [1998] 3 S.C.R. 393, the Supreme Court of Canada presumed that the *Charter* applied to the actions of the vice-principal of a school. See also *Eaton* v. *Brant County Board of Education*, [1997] 1 S.C.R. 624.

[147] *Hall (Litigation guardian of)* v. *Powers* (2002) 59 O.R. (3d) 423, para. 39: the Court considered that the protection provided by section 93 of the *Constitution Act, 1867* and section 29 of the *Charter* "…does not mean that the Charter does not apply to separate schools generally."

[148] For example, the courts could consider it to be justified under section 1 of the *Charter* to restrict freedom of expression by making the use of French compulsory in a French language minority school, so long as the principle of proportionality is respected.

[149] In many cases, there is no constitutional validation for derogation from the *Charter*, and the *Charter* is fully enforceable against the exercise of a legislative

power. Thus, in *EGALE Canada Inc.* v. *Canada*, [2003] B/C/J/ no. 994, the British Columbia Court of Appeal rejected the argument that the exclusion of same-sex marriages was inherent in section 91(26) of the *Constitution Act, 1867* and therefore immune from *Charter* scrutiny.

[150] *Reference re. Secession of Québec, supra* note 74, para. 55—60.

[151] In the *Reference re. Secession of Québec*, the Supreme Court of Canada reiterated that "The principle of federalism recognizes the diversity of the component parts of Confederation, and the autonomy of provincial governments to develop their societies within their respective spheres of jurisdiction", *ibid.*, para. 58.

[152] *R.* v. *S. (S.)*, [1990] 2 S.C.R. 254, at 285; *Haig* v. *Canada*, [1993] 2 S.C.R. 995, at 1045.

[153] In *R.* v. *Advance Cutting & Coring Ltd.*, [2001] 3 S/C/R/ 209, Le Bel J. notes in para. 275 that "where the members of the federation differ in their cultural and historical experiences, the principle of federalism means that the application of the *Charter* in fields of provincial jurisdiction does not amount to a call for legislative uniformity."

[154] *Reference re. Prov. Electoral Boundaries (Sask.)*, [1991] 2 S.C.R. 158 at 179.

[155] *Reference re. Secesssion of Québec, supra*, note 74, para. 59

[156] *Ibid.*

[157] *Ford v. Québec* [1988] 2 S.C.R. 712.

[158] *Van Der Peet, supra* note 75, para. 18—19. The emphasis is Chief Justice Lamer's.

[159] The Supreme Court of Canada has distinguished the rights of the Aboriginal people from those of other non-dominant groups in Canada:

> In my view, the doctrine of aboriginal rights exists, and is recognized and affirmed by s. 35(1), because of one simple fact: when Europeans arrived in North America, aboriginal peoples <u>were already here</u>, living in communities on the land, and participating in distinctive cultures, as they had done for centuries. <u>It is this fact, and this fact above all others, which separates aboriginal peoples from all other minority groups in Canadian society and which mandates their special legal, and now constitutional, status.</u> (*Van Der Peet, ibid.*, para. 30 [our emphasis]); See also, *Mitchell, supra* note 12, para. 9.

[160] See in particular *Kymlicka, supra* note 97, at 91.

[161] In *Reference re. Québec Secession, supra* note 74, the Supreme Court of Canada clearly suggests that the rights of the Aboriginal people are rooted in a constitutional philosophy analogous to that underlying the protection of linguistic and religious minorities. In para. 82, the Court writes:

> Consistent with this long tradition of respect for minorities, which is at least as old as Canada itself, the framers of the *Constitution Act, 1982* included in s. 35 explicit protection for existing aboriginal and treaty rights, and in s. 25, a non-derogation clause in favour of the rights of aboriginal peoples. The "promise" of s. 35, as it was termed in *R. v. Sparrow, [1990] 1 S.C.R. 1075*, at p. 1083, recognized not only the ancient occupation of land by aboriginal peoples, but their contribution to the building of Canada, and the special commitments made to them by successive governments. The protection of these rights, so recently and arduously achieved,

whether looked at in their own right or as part of the larger concern with minorities, reflects an important underlying constitutional value. See also *Gosselin, supra*, note 120, para. 27.

[162] See *Greater Montréal Protestant School Board* v. *Québec (Attorney General)*, [1989] 1 S.C.R. 377, at 401, (Beetz J.); *Adler, supra* note 119, para. 30.

[163] *Reference re. An Act to Amend the Education Act, supra* note 117, at 1199.

[164] *Mitchell, supra* note 12.

[165] See in particular J. Webber, "Rapports de force, rapports de justice: la genèse d'une communauté normative entre colonisateurs et colonisés" in J.G. Belley, Ed., *Le droit soluble: contribution québécoise à l'étude de l'internormativité*, (Paris: L.G.D.J., 1996), at 113. For a judicial account of the specific historical context that led to the emergence of a *sui generis* political and legal relationship between the British colonizers and Aboriginal peoples, see in particular *Sioui, supra* note 64, at 1056.

[166] This is the premise that underlies all of Macklem's book, *supra* note 11.

[167] As *Franks, supra* note 30, writes at 134:

> Aboriginal communities face difficult choices in balancing the desires of traditionalists and modernists, in allocating scarce resources among competing demands, in coming to terms with the greater society in ensuring economic development while at the same time preserving their culture and important traditions. Human rights charters, including the Canadian Charter of Rights and Freedoms, do not tell governments how they should solve these problems and issues, any more than they tell individual citizens how they should run their private lives and businesses. What a charter of rights does is set the ground rules for these discussions and procedures, so that basic standards of equality and fairness are recognized and met by all parties.

[168] Some consensualist practices and institutions inspired by the past could strengthen the democratic philosophy that is the foundation of the *Charter*. See *Otis, supra* note 34, at 404–407.

[169] See 33(3) of the *Charter*.

[170] *Van Der Peet, supra* note 75, para. 27.

[171] See section 7 of Chapter 6 of *the Agreement*.

[172] See section 6 of Chapter 8 of *the Agreement*.

[173] See section 9(k) of Chapter 11 of *the Agreement*. See also *Campbell, supra* note 12.

[174] *Ibid.* in par. 158, Williamson J. writes about section 25, that "the purpose of this section is to shield the distinctive position of aboriginal peoples in Canada from being eroded or undermined by provisions of the Charter."

[175] See section 9(I) of Chapter 11 and pages 3 and 15 of Chapter 1 of *the Agreement*.

[176] *Macklem, supra* note 11, at 226.

[177] If, on the contrary, one argues that the judge has an obligation to apply the *Charter* in accordance with such rights, then the approach is no longer interpretative but purely and simply immunizing.

[178] On this point, Wildsmith correctly writes: "Section 25 is not a mere canon of interpretation whose force is spent once it is determined that the rights and free-

doms in the Charter cannot 'be construed so as not to abrogate or derogate' from the rights referred to in section 25"; see *Wildsmith, supra* note 99, at 2.

[179] Subject to the requirement of equality between men and women since section 25 cannot be invoked to defeat equal rights for men and women. Gender equality is constitutionally protected by section 35(4) of the *Constitution Act, 1982* and by section 28 of the *Charter*, which applies "notwithstanding anything in this Charter."

[180] Macklem comes to the same conclusion but, curiously, without taking into account the importance of section 25 in the analysis of this issue. See *supra* note 11, at 201–202.

[181] See *Van Der Peet, supra* note 75, par. 19.

The Integration of Aboriginal Values and Interests Into Canadian Judicial and Normative Discourse

A. Lajoie, E. Gélineau, I. Duplessis and G. Rocher[ ]

Much research remains to be done on the conditions that have to be met for courts and political decision makers to be able to integrate the values of minority groups into law. According to our recent findings, the Supreme Court of Canada looks favourably on private claims by minorities, such as gays and lesbians, and on the marginalized majority made up of women. It supports gender equality, protection from physical and symbolic violence, and use of private funds, but it draws the line at economic equality through public monies, and even more clearly at political and social power.[1] This observation allows us to distinguish between these types of "social" minorities and other "political" minorities, namely Québec kers and Aboriginals. Our hypothesis is that the Court is less receptive to the values and interests of the latter, but more likely to compensate them through public funds, including in the form of resources. This could be because their interests and values focus specifically on political power and land, which are reserved for specifically political negotiation. This article will explore these hypotheses based on an analysis of the ways that Aboriginal values and interests have been integrated into the formal legal system. For this, we have chosen to examine the two avenues by which the values transit. First, we will identify the values promoted by the discourse of groups representing Aboriginal interests,[2] and then we will see the paths by which the values, which originate in society, come into law through the courts, legislation and government (1). Next, we will identify the values that form the basis for the Court's discourse and those underlying the decisions of political actors, and then finally verify the degree to which they integrate Aboriginal values and interests (2).

1. Aboriginal Values and their Path Towards Law

First, we are going to identify the values asserted by the groups representing Aboriginal interests or invoked before the Supreme Court of Canada in cases concerning their interests. Next, we will describe the path they have taken towards the legal forum.

1.1. Values Present in the Discourse of Aboriginals

Our analysis of the values conveyed by Aboriginal discourse is based on briefs presented by Aboriginal stakeholders[3] in cases heard by the Supreme Court of Canada[4] and on interviews with representatives of the main Aboriginal groups active in Canada at the national level and in Québec.[5] We have identified a group of inter-related collective values that converge on a central core composed of *identity* in relationship with a belief in *Mother Earth* and *economic self-sufficiency*, as well as *land control* and *political self-determination*, in a context in which *respect for the environment and other peoples* leads to *sharing, tolerance* and *cooperation* with a view to *peace*. This relegates to the fringes other values that have only marginal support, and therefore cannot be considered real contradictions. Given the very strong inter-relations among all of these values in the discourse analysed, we will discuss them in the above order, which reflects their logic, rather than in accordance with the number of times each is explicitly mentioned.

1.1.2. Identity

Identity would have come first no matter what enumeration criteria we used. It is the foundation of both Aboriginal and Treaty rights, and more or less implicitly underlies all cases with which the courts have been seized in this area. It is also the value that was explicitly mentioned by the greatest number of interviewees and stakeholders.[6]

According to all those we interviewed[7] and many stakeholders[8], identity's connotations are primarily of the distinct, unique nature of Aboriginal peoples. Not only are Aboriginals neither Canadians nor Québec kers[9] (to such an extent that some groups reject Canadian citizenship, which is unilaterally granted,[10] though in contrast others demand it[11]), but also they are clearly distinct from one another. The Inuit are distinct from the Métis,[12] and both of those groups are different from 'Indians'.[13] Aboriginals themselves are divided into nations and communities that are distinct from one another.[14] These identities are different, particularly with respect to language, but are related through a common culture[15] and traditions, particularly spiritual traditions.[16] The common culture involves solidarity and community spirit,[17] but above all the relationship to Mother Earth[18] and the resources it provides through hunting, fishing and trade. These features are not frozen in folklore but lead by extension, from an evolutionary point of view, to other sources of development and, above all, economic self-sufficiency.[19]

1.1.3. Mother Earth and Economic Self-sufficiency

The oldest, and probably the strongest, link between Aboriginal identity and the values associated with it is located in its utterly central and specific relationship with the idea of Mother Earth, the source of life.

The majority of the groups interviewed and many stakeholders explicitly mentioned Mother Earth as a fundamental value with an inalienable global and symbolic dimension.[20] They made specific reference to its relationship to the traditional activities of hunting and fishing.[21]

However, far from freezing the relationship to the Earth in its traditional form, particularly before contact with the colonizers, a number of interviewees and stakeholders interpret it in a more modern sense and adapt it to contemporary economic development. What counts in the relationship with the Earth seems to be the fact that it produces food and possibilities for trade. It has always had these features, and they are now transferred onto real possibilities of collective economic self-sufficiency, in which the relationship with the Earth is only metaphorical.[22] One group even asserted that economic self-sufficiency is part of Aboriginal identity, which creates a link between Earth–land, and economic self-sufficiency–political self-determination.[23] This brings us to another aspect of the central core of integrated Aboriginal values to which we referred above and which we will now address.

1.1.4. Land Control and Political Self-determination

In Québec before the Conquest, the French colonizers' applied feudal law, which made no distinction between land ownership and control of territory, and it does not seem that this confusion has completely disappeared from common law, at least in Supreme Court of Canada decisions on "Indian title" and, more recently, "Aboriginal title". On the contrary, contemporary Aboriginal discourse incorporates this distinction, yet still asserts the links between a society's collective economic self-sufficiency and its political self-determination on its own land. This holds despite the economic changes that have marginalized the direct relationship between land ownership and economic self-sufficiency.

The very close links between all of these values are particularly well described by two stakeholders in a relatively recent case.[24] The point of contention, namely the establishment of a casino without the provincial authorization required under Canadian positive law, is a good illustration both of the replacement of traditional activities related to the land by contemporary economic activity that is nonetheless collective and of its link with economic self-sufficiency and political self-determination. Indeed, this link was highlighted by other interviewees and a stakeholder.[25] However, political self-determination is also valued in itself by a number of a groups who assert it very firmly as "already here" and reflected in the concrete exercise of sovereignty through Aboriginal institutions, which is a clear-cut fact that Canadian society has only to accept.[26] According to them, the source of self-determination is both stable occupation of an area[27] and a social organization that dates back to time immemorial.[28]

Yet the groups that expressed themselves on this issue do not seem to seek real independence from Canada,[29] though some of them target a very sophisticated form of intra-state pluralism through mutual legislative reference, in which the Canadian government would "voluntarily make some space" for Aboriginal normativity.[30] Others even more openly assert the most radical extra-state pluralism, illustrated by the two-row wampum[31] (which is conceptually not very different from the "independent Québec in a strong Canada" that is so dear to Yvon Deschamps, assuming that calling this a "concept" is not another oxymoron).

1.1.5. Respect, Tolerance, Cooperation, Sharing and Peace

Other values, which are less intimately related to the central core that we have just described, nonetheless follow from it and remain very closely linked with one another. First, there is respect, which is required for one's own identity and which has to be reconquered.[32] It involves collective equality,[33] as well as equality with others, such as other peoples, nations and governments,[34] and even the environment.[35]

This kind of respect leads to tolerance[36] and also cooperation (variously described as conciliation, working together, accommodation, partnership and balance[37]) and sharing through solidarity, particularly with respect to resources.[38] All of this is seen as leading to peace.[39]

1.1.6. Other Values

Other sets of values were occasionally mentioned by stakeholders in court cases involving arguments based on this type of values. The first has a collective nature like all the preceding ones. It is the protection–trust pair, which is linked to the concept of the Crown's fiduciary duty to Aboriginals.[40] The second is made up of the equality (or justice)–democracy–freedom of expression triad. The first two parts of the triad were initially invoked in the collective sense of equality among groups in a democracy.[41] In another context, the three parts were asserted together as classical individual values. This occurred when a party and stakeholder in a specific case concerning the rights of Aboriginal women[42] invoked these values to defend different points of view on equality between men and women. Aside from this exception, which should be considered a legal strategy, all of the values asserted by the Aboriginal groups interviewed and stakeholders in the cases examined seem very consistent and reflect unity based on a collective identity and desire for self-sufficiency and self-determination. Before looking at the fate of these values in Canadian law, we have to identify their paths towards the legal and political forums.

1.2. Paths Towards Legal and Political Forums

The number of decisions pertaining to Aboriginal law rendered by the Supreme Court of Canada since its creation, and the recent increase in such decisions could lead one to think that such recourse is the favourite strategy of Aboriginals. The reality is not so simple.

1.2.1. Court Decisions

An initial survey of decisions in Aboriginal law shows that, between 1880 and 1999, a total of 69 concerned Aboriginal interests.[43] Over half of the decisions were handed down in the last 20 years. Yet, this figure, which would place Aboriginals far in front of other groups that suffer discrimination,[44] is misleading in three ways. First, we have to subtract six decisions[45] in which none of the parties is Aboriginal, though the outcomes indirectly concern their interests. However, more important is the fact that out of the 63 remaining decisions, only 18 (28.5%) resulted from cases initiated by Aboriginal parties in the first instance.[46] The other cases are largely criminal proceedings brought by governments, especially concerning hunting and fishing rights. We should also note the distribution in space and time of the 18 proceedings brought by Aboriginals. None of them come from the eastern provinces, aside from one from Québec,[47] 11 come from British Columbia,[48] five from Ontario[49] and the last from a pan-Canadian organization.[50]

Finally, not only did the number grow in time, but so did, though less clearly, their proportion of all cases in this area over the same periods.[51] Thus, from the figures alone we can make a number of observations. Voluntary use of the courts by Aboriginals themselves is low or practically non-existent in the eastern provinces, it grows as one moves toward the west, and it has increased over time, at least in number. At least some light is shed on these findings by parallel information from the interviews that we conducted with Aboriginal groups active in Québec and at the national level in Canada.[52] Distrust of the courts is implicitly expressed in all of the discourse of the Québec and pan-Canadian Aboriginal associations that we interviewed and clearly admitted by some of them,[53] if not explicitly highlighted by others.[54] Only one of these groups was a plaintiff in a case that later reached the Supreme Court of Canada, but, as some wanted to point out,[55] it is almost always the governments that take them there.[56] They see court proceedings as a "last resort"[57] to be used when negotiations break down[58] or when the balance of power is not favourable.[59] Moreover, they use proceedings especially to obtain support in negotiations, to which the courts inevitably refer them.[60]

This is because the courts, while sometimes considered qualified to resolve disagreements between equal Aboriginal and Canadian governments, are not credited with the jurisdiction required to resolve conflicts internal to Aboriginal communities.[61] They are seen as poorly equipped and guided by the law to understand Aboriginal realities,[62] which are considered political and not judicial,[63] and it seems preferable to avoid justice that is expensive,[64] slow,[65] often ineffective,[66] and influenced by politics.[67]

Yet, even though some groups are aware that Aboriginal victories before the courts are more apparent than real, and therefore remain skeptical,[68] others note that the courts have recently become more open to Aboriginal issues,[69] particularly in western Canada,[70] perhaps because the practice of Aboriginal law has grown more in recent years.[71] Indeed, some who have refrained until now are thinking of using the courts in the future.[72] Yet, the preference of all of the Canadian and Québec groups interviewed is for negotiations as equals with the governments and, more generally, political and social action, which we will now discuss.

1.3. Political and Social Action

While it is not surprising to see a minority hesitating to entrust the outcome of its claims to the courts of the state that colonized it, it would be understandable if the same kind of misgivings arose with respect to negotiations in which it is difficult to imagine that the parties have equal weight. However, all of the groups interviewed prefer negotiations when the power relationship is favourable, which is something that remains to be achieved.

Despite some skepticism on the part of one group,[73] and another group's observation that there were growing difficulties,[74] all the groups favoured nation-to-nation[75] and government-to-government[76] negotiations,[77] not only at the federal and provincial levels, but also sometimes at the external, international level[78] and internal, regional and local levels.[79] The long-term goal of negotiations is self-determination but, pragmatically, they often concern more short-term goals, such as a ban on supersonic flights over hunting grounds,[80] implementation of specific policies and modalities of federal funding.[81] However, there are sometimes a large number of negotiations (for example, concerning justice, police, land management, membership in the community and sports and gaming regulations), which incrementally result in more complete self-determination.[82]

Yet, negotiations between such unequal parties, at least in terms of numbers,[83] cannot be useful to Aboriginals unless they can increase their weight by other means. All of the groups are perfectly aware of this and often work together both within Canada and internationally.

It seems that the most intense cooperation is channelled through the Assembly of First Nations (AFN). In Québec, the AFN cooperates with the Native Women's Association and *Regroupement des cercles d'amitié autochtones*, which have non-voting members on the AFN's council, and on an ad hoc basis depending on the issue with civil society groups in Québec, such as unions, grassroots solidarity groups and Jewish associations. The AFN also meets with other national organizations representing Aboriginal peoples, such as the Métis National Council, Inuit Tapirisat of Canada, and National Congress of Aboriginal People.[84] Naturally, some AFN member communities work together more closely than others.[85] Some communities are more reserved, especially when their objectives differ,[86] and still others simply prefer to establish their own links with other groups depending on the issue.[87]

Once cooperation is established, strategies can be deployed more effectively at the Canadian and international levels, and a wide range of communication and pressure tactics (including through the courts, international organizations, media, lobbying and demonstrations) can be combined to achieve the common goal of promoting the integration of Aboriginal values and interests in Canadian law, until self-determination is won.

Thus, within Canada, the groups interviewed use the courts for political purposes, but do not trust them with respect to strictly legal issues. This is particularly true of the Supreme Court of Canada because it influences governments and never fails to send the parties back to the bargaining table,[88] and human rights tribunals, which are seen as more favourable to Aboriginals.[89] However, Aboriginal groups also address the media for the same purposes.[90] They try to use the media to convey to the general population accurate information on the peaceful and reliable nature of their behaviour and practices, including through traditional[91] and contemporary[92] cultural works.

Despite the cost of these operations and the few resources of some groups,[93] it also seems useful to convey such information to the public using other communications strategies that increase interactions among the various means of ultimately influencing the negotiation process.[94] These strategies include giving talks at Bar association and judges' meetings,[95] and lobbying elected representatives.[96] Some prefer public demonstrations and mass movements,[97] but others are wary of that approach.[98]

The potential of international strategies is equally good. Most of the groups[99] (one group maintains links with the UN and some foreign countries, including France[100]) were explicitly in favour of using this avenue, which is not new. Indeed, the Mohawks tried to gain recognition as an international body with the same status as Canada at the time of the League of Nations.[101]

However, international activities have recently undergone a major development, notably with respect to the Working Group on Indigenous Populations instituted by the Sub-Commission on Prevention of Discrimination and Protection of Minorities, which is part of the UN Economic and Social Council's Commission on Human Rights.[102] Thanks to Isabelle Duplessis's participatory observation at and analysis of the Group's sixteenth session in July 1998,[103] we have been able to identify some of the international strategies that Canadian Aboriginals have used to position themselves in Canada's society so as to integrate their values and interests more effectively into Canadian law.

At first, Aboriginals used narrativism to reverse the power relationship to the state in which they are inserted. This involved the group concerned telling its own history from its own point of view rather than in the language of the dominant society. This strengthened the coherency of its collective identity (irenic function), and then "irritated" the legal system to change it to suit the group's interests (polemic function).[104]

Next, Aboriginals tried to write the collective rights entailed by recognition of their distinct narratives into the dominant discourse on human rights. This engaged them in the system of international legal rules infused with the dominant values of western societies, which take form in individual rights. At this point, they reached the limits of narrativism and had to begin legal arguments to propose an alternative to law as it stands. This has more than begun, as can be seen from their submissions to the Supreme Court of Canada.

However, it is through globalization of the socio-cultural system that Aboriginal issues have become international, thanks to Aboriginals' affiliation with environmentalists and their participation in International Labour Organization activities.[105] Since 1980, the focus has shifted away from nation-states, which has made it possible for Aboriginals to join international forums that used to be reserved for states, and to participate in the creation of an emerging international power composed of NGOs. In the new landscape, Aboriginals are no longer objects, but subjects of international law, though it is true that their status is special. The domestic practices of states such as Canada, where Aboriginals live in enclaves, are no longer sheltered from the eyes of the international community. The process, in combination of course with the *Charter*, has been so effective that in the 1980s the Supreme Court of Canada changed its position on Aboriginal law, and finally recognized the injustices that Aboriginals have suffered and the need to preserve their culture.[106]

In short, when it comes to promoting the integration of their values into Canadian law, Aboriginals prefer to take a political approached based on negotiation, which has the dual advantage of physically representing a relationship between bodies with the same status and not leading to a unilateral outcome. The courts, which are seen as untrustworthy and obsolete, though this attitude is more or less skillfully masked by the presence of Aboriginals in the judicial forum, are orchestrated in a political process in which other strategies are also involved, in particular strategies pertaining to the media and international relations. It remains to be seen how the respective reception of Aboriginal values and interests by political actors and Canadian courts validates the gamble implicit in these positions.

2. Reception of Aboriginal Values and Interests by the Courts and Political Players

By their very nature, the courts and political actors do not integrate dominant and other social values in the same way, and this goes for Aboriginal values as well. However, our analysis also shows that these two institutions have not been receptive to the same values, and the effects have not been the same on Aboriginal interests. We will report our findings on these two avenues of law production separately.

2.1. Reception by the Supreme Court

Analysis of the values affirmed in the 50 decisions pertaining to Aboriginal law in which the Court explicitly mentions or at least allows one to induce values[107] shows that it invoked most of those promoted by Aboriginals, though not always for the same purposes, as well as others specific to the Court itself. The first set of values includes Aboriginal identity and status, Mother Earth and economic development, respect and dignity, the protection–trust pair, and the justice–equality–democracy trio. The second set includes the economic interests of the society and property, Canadian sovereignty and rule of law. While these two sets support decisions that do not necessarily go in the same direction, they play a complementary role in the Court's integration of Aboriginal values into law.

2.2. Values Already Present in Aboriginal Discourse

2.2.1. Identity and Status

As in Aboriginal discourse, identity is the value that was mentioned most often in the Court's rulings: 21 times,[108] the great majority of which were in support of Aboriginal victories,[109] which should not be surprising given that Aboriginal identity is precisely what is used as the basis for the legal regime that Canadian law applies to them.

2.2.1.1. Mother Earth and Economic Development

It is mainly with respect to resource, and particularly wildlife, conservation that the Court implicitly invoked Mother Earth. Sometimes it mentioned these values to justify an Aboriginal defeat,[110] but more often it affirmed that these values were not challenged by the points at issue, which enabled it to then validate an Aboriginal victory.[111] The same goes for economic development of Aboriginal communities, which is used as a justification in Aboriginal victories, as ambiguous as they may be.[112]

2.2.1.2. Respect

Rarely invoked, respect for dignity[113] and physical integrity[114] appeared more often in Aboriginal appeals that had been dismissed.

2.2.1.3. Protection–Trust

As in the case of Aboriginal discourse, it was in appeals that were upheld and related to the Crown's fiduciary relationship to Aboriginal peoples that protection and trust were mentioned.[115] The results were mitigated and did not really favour either party.[116]

2.2.1.4. Justice–Equality–Democracy

Justice, while it does not often appear in Aboriginal discourse on values except as a near synonym of equality, is however mentioned many times in the Court's discourse[117] in decisions that are in great majority favourable to Aboriginals.[118] Equality maintains its collective nature in some decisions, which make up the majority of Aboriginal victories,[119] but it is often asserted as an individual value that favours neither one party nor the other.[120]

2.3. Values Specific to the Court

2.3.1. Society's Economic Interests and Property

With greater transparency than predicted, the Court explicitly invoked the economic interests of the provinces, the "Nation" (sic[121]) and more generally non-Aboriginals,[122] and even private property.[123] However, when it did so, it limited these interests in favour of Aboriginals, which might seem surprising at first, if it did not confirm one of our key initial hypotheses.

Indeed, we raised the possibility that the Court was ready to concede public monies (including resources) to political but not social minorities as compensation for not ruling in favour of land and political claims.[124]

As we will see in a moment, the political values specific to the Court play a complementary role in this respect.

2.3.2. Canadian Sovereignty and Rule of Law

The Court has invoked both rule of law[125] and Canadian sovereignty,[126] mostly to justify Aboriginal defeats, in particular in *Pamajewon*, in which the Court refused to rule on self-government because it considered the context too general.

2.4. Analysis of the Court's Integration of Aboriginal Values and Interests

An initial portrait of the Court's integration of Aboriginal values can thus be made by comparing those promoted by Aboriginals and those that the Court admits. Overall, the Court integrates into the law most of the values carried in Aboriginal discourse. Identity, protection of the environment and wildlife resources (which are part of the Mother Earth concept), and economic development (though not self-sufficiency as such) are core Aboriginal values, are admitted by the Court without modification of meaning and are used to validate a majority of Aboriginal victories. The same goes for respect and justice. The Court also affirms the protection–trust and equality of expression–democracy pairs, though less often and without clear results in favour of Aboriginals or their adversaries.

Moreover, our interviewees were partially right in their perception that the Court has been more open to Aboriginal claims in recent years. The proportion of Aboriginal victories, including partial victories, has been 54% since 1990, which is higher than the percentage since the Court's creation in 1875. Indeed, there was a major break between the first period from 1880 to 1939, in which the percentage of Aboriginal victories was 33%, and the second period, which began in 1964 after 25 years of silence from the Court on these issues and ended in 1990. During that period, 37.8% of such cases were Aboriginal victories. However, these apparently positive findings have to be contrasted with the values that are absent from the Court's discourse, as well as the use the Court makes of its own values.

First and foremost, the Aboriginal values most notably absent from the Court's discourse are political self-determination and control of land. These are political issues that, to our knowledge, the Court has mentioned only once, only to explicitly reject them. Next, among the values specific to the Court, we have to highlight the predominance of the economic interests of non-Aboriginals and the Canadian sovereignty–rule of law pair, as well as the contrasting and complementary effects of the Court's use of these values. Indeed, the Court does not use these two values in the same way or to the same effect. It mentions the economic interests of non-Aboriginals to limit them in order to support Aboriginal victories with respect to economic issues,[127] whereas, on the contrary, it unreservedly invokes Canadian sovereignty and rule of law to justify Aboriginal defeats, particularly with respect to the most important political rights.[128]

The difference in terms of treatment and results between decisions concerning political rights and other decisions is also very clear in the distribution of Aboriginal victories and defeats. Overall, the rulings in such cases are not in Aboriginals' favour since there are 38 defeats to 29 victories.[129] However, what is most revealing is analysis of the rights affected, namely, political, land and economic rights.[130] In terms of political rights, defeats are clearly predominant: eight[131] to four.[132] This is also the case with land rights: nine defeats[133] to three victories.[134] However, in economic matters,[135] there are more victories (22)[136] than defeats (21).[137]

This largely confirms our hypotheses on the Court's economic concessions to Aboriginals as compensation for their political claims. The Court dismisses the great majority of political appeals, and rules in favour only of rights linked to status, such as pertaining to Eskimos, off reserve "Indians" and Aboriginals in general with respect to non-Aboriginals.[138] It does not rule in favour of political control, particularly with respect to political participation, self-government and exemption from the jurisdiction of the Canadian state.[139] In contrast, it allows the majority of economic claims, including those related to tax exemptions[140] analogous to those it has rejected in the cases of women and gays and lesbians. However, these quantitative data do not provide us with a complete picture of the role that the Court plays in producing Aboriginal law or of the ideological process it uses.

In order to get a better picture of the situation, we have to look at the mechanism that the Court uses in Aboriginal cases,[141] in virtue of which it solemnly affirms a principle that integrates Aboriginal values and is favourable to their interests, only to deprive it of effect in the next breath in ways that depend on the circumstances. For example, it affirms an obligation of the government but denies that it has not been fulfilled in the case in question, or attributes a right but at the same time limits it to such an extent as to make it useless or freeze it in time to reduce its scope.[142] Thus, it takes back with one hand what it has not finished giving with the other in decisions concerning most of the values that it endorses: identity, Mother Earth and economic development, and even protection and trust.

Thus, as we have noted, there are many instances in Supreme Court of Canada decisions in which Aboriginal identity and culture are affirmed, mostly in support of decisions that are in principle favourable to Aboriginals. However, while appearing to assume the consequences of such identity by setting out the principle of taking Aboriginals' point of view into account in the determination of their rights,[143] the Court immediately decides that such taking into account is possible only in so far as Aboriginal perspectives are formulated in terms that comply with Canadian legal and constitutional structures and are reconcilable with Canadian sovereignty.[144] Moreover, when it comes to preserving the cultural dimension of Aboriginal identity through the exercise of ancestral rights, rather than more broadly confirming the real vectors of culture, namely customs and traditions, the Court reduces the scope of rights to practices that are only the external expression of such customs and traditions.[145] However, it is probably with respect to Aboriginal title, related to Mother Earth and economic development, that the Court's ideological procedures have the most serious consequences and are, despite their transparency, probably most effective.

From the time of its first decisions in the nineteenth century, the Supreme Court of Canada has limited the content of "Indian title", as it was then called, to a right of usufruct and occupation.[146] At first, the Court alternated between two limiting mechanisms every time Aboriginals raised the question: systematic refusal to discuss the issue or a "finding" that the right was extinguished.[147] Later, when the title (now called "Aboriginal") had evolved towards a right to occupation/possession "analogous" to common law property rights (fee simple),[148] the mechanisms changed also.

First, the Court supported reductionist positions on non-Aboriginal interests.[149] Then, probably impeded in the process and renouncing the attempt to completely define the scope of traditional title to the land in question,[150] it began to allow new means of using the same resources[151] and then extended the scope of land title to boundaries based on oral evidence.

Finally, this time basing its arguments on its paternalistic conception of Aboriginals' interests, it extended the permitted uses to those that are not incompatible with traditional use of the land in question.[152] Yet, this should not lead one to believe that incompatible uses are completely prohibited. Indeed, the Canadian government can use the land in such ways once Aboriginals have been forced to "retrocede" the title.[153] New collective economic activities that could replace traditional resource harvesting and the Mother Earth approach as means of ensuring Aboriginal economic self-sufficiency, for example casinos and gambling, are prohibited on the grounds that they contravene Canadian laws and sovereignty.[154]

Indeed, even the Crown's fiduciary obligation with respect to Aboriginals, which is so often repeated, does not escape the attenuating mechanisms that undermine the effectiveness of statements of principle. The principle is rarely applied because the government has never been found at fault in this respect, and the obligation is considered inapplicable in the implementation of treaties.[155]

In short, there is a clear dichotomy between the fates the Supreme Court of Canada reserves for Aboriginal political and economic rights. In fact, with respect to economic rights, it even almost manages to square the circle. It allows almost half of the appeals in the name of the very values promoted by Aboriginals, while paradoxically mentioning and limiting the interests of non-Aboriginals. However, it uses various mechanisms to reduce the practical scope of the rights that are generously confirmed in principle. When it comes to political rights, the picture is reversed. The strategy is to silence the key political value invoked by Aboriginals, namely self-determination, and to substitute those specific to the Court, such as Canadian sovereignty and rule of law. We know the consequences.

This reveals the complementary roles played by, on one hand, the values put forth by Aboriginals and endorsed by the Court and, on the other hand, the values specific to the Court. In the first case, the Court justifies the economic rights that it grants as compensation by affirming principles that it deprives of practical scope as soon as they seem likely to adversely affect the interests of non-Aboriginals. In the second case, it substitutes its own values for Aboriginal values of the same type in order to dismiss major political rights.

Not only are our hypotheses thus verified both quantitatively and qualitatively, but the distrust displayed by our interviewees with respect to the power of the courts does not seem altogether unfounded, at least with respect to the political rights most important to them.

It remains to be seen whether the behaviour of political players also justifies our Aboriginal interviewees' preference for political action. It seems that the answer, even though it is given by political actors (who are mainly federal to top it off), is not as clear as the question.

2.5. Reception by Political Actors

If we look at the number of self-government negotiations undertaken between Aboriginals and the Government of Canada, which was over 80 in 1998,[156] not including those with the provinces, it indeed seems that Aboriginal strategies favouring negotiation have struck a chord with their counterparts. In order to get a better idea of how these initiatives serve Aboriginal interests and how they integrate their values into law, we focussed our analysis on those that have recently led to concrete legal results in the form of an agreement or treaty: the Framework Agreement on First Nation Land Management, the agreements between Québec and the Mohawks of Kahnawake, the *Nisga'a Final Agreement* and the Agreement between the Inuit of the Nunavut Settlement Area and Her Majesty the Queen in Right of Canada. We will discuss them in this order, which reflects the growing degree of self-government that they embody.

2.5.1. The Framework Agreement on First Nation Land Management

The Framework Agreement,[157] which Canadian Aboriginal band councils are free to opt into, provides for the management of Aboriginal land by First Nations, who first have to adopt a land code applicable to their respective lands and covering the matters set out in the Agreement. Its potential territorial scope is thus huge and, given its economic importance, it is a limited but important step towards self-government.

In this we can read recognition of central Aboriginal values: Mother Earth and economic development, and identity and self-government. There is no need to demonstrate the concrete importance of swift, internal management of Aboriginal lands, which have until now been controlled from a distance by federal authorities, for the financial and banking aspects of economic development are linked to the creation of companies that require real estate credit. However, the symbolic importance of negotiation of a framework agreement is just as great, for it involves ratification by Parliament and incorporation into Canadian law as a bilateral instrument. This entails official recognition of the identity of the Aboriginal nations and marks an important step towards political self-determination.

Yet, we have to note that the material scope of the agreement concerns only land management, which is under federal jurisdiction and, despite its economic and symbolic importance, far from covering all of the competencies targeted by self-government, not to speak of political self-determination. Moreover, the imposition of matters that have to be covered by land codes clashes with the cultural dimension of Aboriginal identity in that some topics imposed on Aboriginal normativity, in particular alienation of land, go against basic Aboriginal values. It is too early to know whether and how these obstacles will be overcome,[158] but the experiment is certainly interesting and shows what can be achieved through negotiation.

2.5.2. The Statement of Understanding and Mutual Respect, Framework Agreement and Sectoral Agreements Between Québec and the Mohawks of Kahnawake

The same applies to the ten sectoral agreements that Guy Chevrette, then Minister Responsible for Aboriginal Affairs, and Joe Norton, then Grand Chief of the Kahnawake Band Council, have signed since the adoption in 1998 of a Statement of Understanding and Mutual Respect and of a Framework Agreement[159] designed to provide a context for sectoral agreements. Their preambles, which are integral parts of the instruments, refer to a number of key Aboriginal values, such as identity, self-determination, cooperation, economic development and control over land. In the Statement of Understanding, the parties declare: "With a strong sense of their respective culture, language, custom, laws and traditions, Kahnawake and Québec agree to negotiate with mutual respect for their national identities and each other's history and territorial occupation."

The sectoral agreements signed to date[160] concern three areas: law enforcement,[161] some civil law issues,[162] and certain economic issues.[163] The agreements have the same basic format but are adapted to the issues, all of which fall under provincial jurisdiction. They provide for either the future substitution of Mohawk norms for Québec law or a future coordination of both sources of norms on the Kahnawake reserve.

Our interviewee from the Kahnawake Band Council[164] describes this as a complex model of intrastate pluralism in which Québec makes space (of different dimensions, depending on the issue) in its legal system for Aboriginal norms. Self-government and, to an extent, political self-determination in these areas are recognized, while the surrender of ancestral rights is explicitly excluded, as is constitutionalization of the treaty within the meaning of section 35 of the *Constitution Act, 1982*.[165] Likewise, some economic interests are compensated through grants[166] and tax exemptions,[167] but in exchange the Kahnawake Band Council agrees to maintain certain services[168] and regulations[169] in clauses that in practice have effects analogous to that of the Framework Agreement on First Nation Land Management when it sets out the issues to which land codes must apply, though in the case of Kahnawake the constraints are not as heavy.

While in terms of territory these agreements cover less ground than the Framework Agreement on First Nation Land Management, their material scope is greater because they already target ten areas of application and can cover others as needs arise and consensus is reached. They are also different from the federal agreement on land management in that, in addition to confirming political rights, a number of them provide for economic advantages. However, they are also not given the status of a Treaty, constitutionalized in 1982. As we will see below, the Nisga'a treaty is not necessarily in the same situation.

2.5.3. The Nisga'a Final Agreement

The tripartite *Nisga'a Final Agreement*[170] provides for the exercise by the Nisga'a Nation of powers in areas that used to be under federal and provincial jurisdiction: culture, citizenship, health, social services, education, transportation, justice, police, etc. At first sight, this set of powers seems to have an even larger scope than the sum of all those that have so far been recognized at Kahnawake by the Québec authorities. Moreover, the fact that it is not just an agreement, but a Treaty within the meaning of section 35 of the *Constitution Act, 1982*, which does not distinguish between treaties prior to or later than that date, also implies its constitutionalization (but not an amendment of the *Constitution* itself). It is possible to conclude that not only does this text integrate the Aboriginal values of self-determination and economic development into Canadian law, but it also recognizes the Aboriginal identity of the Nisga'a as distinct from that of Canadians[171] and as the foundation of an inherent right to self-government, which is now permanent, as can be seen from the treaty's official title.

This said, we have to qualify the situation. First, the land on which the Nisga'a live is the subject of legal action by another Aboriginal nation, the Gitanyow, who claim 84% of it. Moreover, the treaty was signed and ratified subject to a clause according to which the court's future decision would be integrated, if necessary in the form of an attenuated interpretation, unless the parties come to a different agreement.

However, in addition to these perhaps temporary difficulties, there are other limitations, this time permanent. The first, which probably explains the preceding ones, is related to the fact that effective power is not given to all those living on the land but only to the Nisga'a, to the exclusion of other Aboriginals and non-Aboriginals, who have only consultative voices in some respects. The second equally important limitation concerns the treaty's rank in the hierarchy of norms. Federal and provincial laws will continue to apply to the Nisga'a in a residual manner. The Nisga'a's ancestral rights will be maintained only in so far as they are compatible with the treaty. Finally, there is an apparent reversal of situations. By granting the political rights of self-government, which include self-determination, the political actors are saving money because the Nisga'a will eventually lose their income and other tax exemptions.

2.5.4. The Agreement Between the Inuit of the Nunavut Settlement Area and Her Majesty the Queen in Right of Canada

In contrast, it is indeed to a territory, namely Nunavut, that the eponymous agreement applies.[172] The government that it has been creating since April 1, 1999 is a territorial government with authority over not only the Inuit, who account for the majority in Nunavut, but also all of the other inhabitants of the territory that was cut out of the former Northwest Territories. Moreover, the jurisdictions that it will eventually exercise after several years of development include all of the jurisdictions of domestic law that are generally associated with a state, with an initial focus on values that are important to Aboriginals, such as land and resource management and conservation, but excluding external competencies such as defence of the Canadian Arctic, foreign policy and, of course, external sovereignty in the sense of international public law. In addition to the limitations with respect to sovereignty and external jurisdictions, other qualifications have to be noted. The first concerns the status of the Agreement, which is not a treaty within the meaning of section 35 of the *Constitution Act, 1982* and therefore implies neither constitutionalization of its content nor intrinsic permanency. The second concerns the Inuit's surrender of their land claims in exchange for financial compensation. The third has to do with them remaining subject to general tax laws, except in cases explicitly provided for in the Agreement.

In short, negotiations have made it possible for the Aboriginal minority to attain objectives related to the exercise of political power far beyond the limits of what the courts were ready to offer. The political power is in the form of growing self-government, land management for all band councils that adopt a land code that complies with the requirements negotiated with the federal government, and normative power over a number of areas until now under provincial jurisdiction at Kahnawake, over areas under provincial and federal jurisdiction in the case of the Nisga'a, and extending to all domestic competencies in Nunavut.

These political gains are however not without drawbacks, the most serious of which concern the limitations imposed on self-determination itself, because the Canadian political players have deliberately not given Aboriginals all of the "winning conditions." Indeed, either power is granted over the land and its inhabitants, as in the case of Nunavut, or a real Treaty within the meaning of the *Constitution Act, 1982* is concluded, as with the Nisga'a. In the former case there has been a refusal to give the agreement the status of a Treaty, and in the latter case the power granted applies only to Nisga'a people and not to their land as such or to non-Nisga'as. Aboriginals have not been given their cake and allowed to eat it too. In both cases, Canadian sovereignty over the land is intact, particularly since care has been taken to confirm the residual application of federal and provincial Canadian laws, specifically those pertaining to taxation.

In fact, these political victories are accompanied by complementary economic measures that vary depending on the case. Québec gives the Mohawks of Kahnawake grants and tax exemptions, and Canada gives economic compensation to the Nisga'a and Nunavut in exchange for the surrender of land claims, though the Nisga'a take an economic step backwards by being taxed in exchange for increased political powers. Here also the line drawn by the basic interests of non-Aboriginals has not been crossed, and a certain "balance" between political and economic rights seems to have been sought and, from the dominant point of view, attained.

3. Conclusion

Rooted in identity, the values most often invoked by Aboriginals have two foci: the first links Mother Earth with resources and economic development, while the second links control over land with political self-determination. Only the first has been integrated into the Supreme Court of Canada's discourse to justify a near majority of Aboriginal victories in economic matters, victories that have been awarded at the expense of one of the other values specific to the Court, namely the economic interests of the non-Aboriginal majority, which have often been explicitly limited. Moreover, the same set of values has been behind the Aboriginals' rare political victories, which have however been limited to issues related to their identity and political status. However, the Court has constantly upheld its own values of rule of law and Canadian sovereignty against claims to political power.

As we have already pointed out, our initial hypothesis has thus been confirmed. The Supreme Court of Canada has not allowed the central political claims of Aboriginals but, probably in compensation, has shown itself to be more generous to them with respect to resources and public funds. The dividing line between what it grants to social minorities, such as gays, lesbians and (minoritized) women and what it has always refused them has been between the public and the private domains. In the case of the Aboriginal political minority, this dividing line has been moved inside the public sector and is now located between economic and political rights linked to status on the one hand, and real political power and land, on the other.

Undoubtedly aware of these tendencies, Aboriginals have just barely enough trust in the courts to use them to influence political players in negotiations. Indeed, negotiations are their preferred means within a political and social action strategy that mainly targets the media and international fora, but also uses lobbying, mass movements and demonstrations to a lesser degree. The gamble that political players would be more receptive to Aboriginal demands if the power relationship was tilted more in favour of Aboriginals through globalization of the socio-cultural system has been won, at least in part. For, while greater self-government has been granted to various Aboriginal groups, their two central political values, namely those concerning control over land and political self-determination, have never been integrated at the same time into a single legal instrument.

By maintaining residual application of Canadian federal and provincial laws, particularly those covering taxation powers, and by dissociating control over land from the definitive self-government linked with a Treaty within the meaning of section 35 of the *Constitution Act, 1982*, political players have found a trick as useful to Canadian sovereignty as the ineffective statements of principle that the Supreme Court of Canada favours for the same purposes. Indeed, the Nisga'a are the only ones who have signed a constitutionalized Treaty giving them definitive self-government, but their jurisdiction does not cover all those living on the land. In contrast, control over land has been granted to various degrees to band councils, to the Mohawks of Kahnawake and to Nunavut, but their agreements have not been given Treaty status.

The difference, and it is not insignificant, between the Court and the politicians with respect to Aboriginal claims lies in the location of the dividing line between what is granted and what is refused, and in the inverse role played by the processing of economic claims.

The courts draw the line between personal political rights linked to status and those that incarnate real political power, whereas political players draw it between domestic self-government and control over land. Potential external self-determination, which is in fact not the object of explicit claims, has never been integrated into any agreement or accord, let alone treaty.

As we predicted, the Supreme Court of Canada uses economic concessions as compensation for its refusal to accord political rights, whereas federal political authorities do the opposite. As soon as recognized political powers are general in scope, the economic concessions that Aboriginals used to enjoy, such as income and other tax exemptions, are eliminated in exchange, aside from a few explicit exceptions.

At first sight, these findings are not really surprising, aside from what they reveal about what is constant and even systematic in the choice of values and interests involved in the production of law. They are even less surprising with respect to the political players than with regard to the courts. Who would find it unusual for a state to mobilize its central bodies in the production of law to maintain its integrity? Have we ever known elected officials to want to preside over the dismemberment of what they represent? Have we not always known that the judges of the central court of a state are not really free to saw off the branch on which they sit?

However, the consistency of both bodies over so many years, and especially the refinement and complementarity of their approaches, does seem surprising, even to the best informed.

Indeed, it seems to us that the role that the Court plays in the production of law has never been so visible, except perhaps in the virtually uniformly centralizing nature of the decisions that make concrete the sharing of jurisdiction in the Canadian federation. This can be seen in the summary of over a century of decisions on Aboriginal issues, in which the overdetermination of the dominant values, namely those that are acceptable to at least the majority, in the Court's decisions seems uninterrupted even in its variations. This once more confirms the heuristic value of this concept and, more generally, «*analyse systémale*».[173] The political actors are not to be outdone. They so clearly use law as a tool for reproducing Canadian society and identity that their behaviour could be the basis for the anthropological theory that has guided our work in recent years,[174] if it were not for the fact that the theory is based on a study of the Aboriginal law of African societies.

In other words, nation states, even when they are federal and probably especially when they identify themselves with a reputation for multiculturalism, are nonetheless dominated through a process that owes much to the complementarity of the ways by which they produce law.

Appendix I

Aboriginal Interveners in Selected Decisions

Alphabetical List

Aboriginal Legal Services of Toronto Inc.
Alberta Committee on Indian Rights for Indian Women Inc.
Alliance of Tribal Councils
Anishnawbekwek of Ontario Inc.
Assembly of First Nations
Assembly of Manitoba Chiefs
Association of Iroquois and Allied Indians
Atikamekw-Sipi/Atikamekw Nation Council
Brant County Six Nations Indian Band
Samson Indian Band and Nation
Chief Abel Bosum et al.
Chief Donal R. Brant
Chief Robert Whiteduck on behalf of the Algonquin First Nation of Golden Lake
et al.
Chief Terry Buffalo et al.
Chief Henry Mianscum, Chief Peter Gull, Chief George Wapachee, Chief Sidney
Georgekish, Chief Rusty Cheezo, Chief Walter Hughboy, Chief Sam Tapiatic and
Chief Robbie Dick
Confederation of Indians of Québec
Confederacy of Treaty 6 First Nation
Congress of Aboriginal Peoples
Erminiskin Tribal Council
Council for Yukon Indians
Cree Bands of Mistassini, Waswanipi, Nemaska, Rupert House, Eastman, Old
Factory, Fort George and Great Whale River
Cree Board of Health and Social Services of James Bay
Cree Regional Authority
Cree School board
Delgamuukw
Federation of Saskatchewan Indians
Federation of Saskatchewan Indian Nations
First Nations Summit
Gary Potts et al.
Grand Chief Billy Diamond, Executive Chief Philip Awashish and Abel Kitche
Grand Council of the Cree
Howard Pamajewon, Roger Jones, Arnold Gardner, Jack Pitchenese and Allen
Gardner
Indian Association of Alberta
Indian Brotherhood of the Northwest Territories
Inuit Tapirisat of Canada

Lesser Slave Lake Indian Regional Council
Manitoba Indian Brotherhood Inc.
Mocreebec
Musqueam Nation
National Indian Brotherhood
Native Council of Canada
Native Council of Nova Scotia
Native Women's Association of Canada
Ontario Federation of Anglers and Hunters
Randy Kapashesit
Treaty 7 Tribal Council
Treaty Voice of Alberta
Union of British Columbia Indian Chiefs
Union of New Brunswick Indians
Union of Nova Scotia Indians
Union of Ontario Indians
United Indian Council
United Native Nations Society of British Columbia
Westbank First Nation
White Bear First Nation
Yukon Native Brotherhood

Appendix II

Selected Decisions

Selection criteria

We chose to analyse Supreme Court of Canada decisions from 1875 to 1999 that affect Aboriginals' rights and interests, including cases involving only non-Aboriginal parties. We excluded Supreme Court decisions that involved Aboriginal parties but concerned neither Aboriginal collective interests nor their identity. Since our goal was to analyse the discourse of the Supreme Court as an institution, and not to establish positive law, we have included Supreme Court decisions that met the above-mentioned criteria, even if they were later set aside by the Privy Council, and excluded decisions by lower courts, which were not the subject of our analysis.

Alphabetical list

R. v. *Adams*, [1996] 3 S.C.R. 101.
R. v. *Badger*, [1996] S.C.R. 771
Ontario v. *Bear Island Foundation,* [1991] 2 S.C.R. 570
Blueberry River Indian Band v. *Canada*, [1995] 4 S.C.R. 344
R. v. *Bonhomme*, (1918) D.L.R. 690
Calder v. *Attorney General for British Columbia*, [1973] S.C.R. 313

Cardinal v. *Attorney General for Alberta*, [1974] S.C.R. 695
Church v. *Fenton*, (1880) 5 S.C.R. 239
Corbière v. *Canada*, [1999] 2 S.C.R. 203
R. v. *Côté*, [1996] 3 S.C.R. 139
St. Mary's Indian Band v. *Cranbrook (City)*, [1997] 2 S.C.R. 657
Daniel v. *White and The Queen*, [1968] S.C.R. 517
Davey v. *Isaac*, [1977] 2 S.C.R. 897
Delgamuukw v. *British Columbia*, [1997] 3 S.C.R. 1010
Derrickson v. *Derrickson*, [1986] 1 S.C.R. 285
R. v. *Derriksan*, (1976) 71 D.L.R. (3ʳᵈ) 159.
Dick v. *The Queen*, [1985] 2 S.C.R. 309
R. v. *Drybones*, [1970] S.C.R. 282
Elk v. *R.*, [1980] 2 S.C.R. 166
R. v. *Easterbrook*, [1931] S.C.R. 210
Four B Manufacturing Co. Limited v. *United Garment Workers of America*, [1980] 1 S.C.R. 1031
Frank v. *The Queen*, [1978] 1 S.C.R. 95
R. v. *George*, (1966) 55 D.L.R. 386
Attorney General for Canada v. *Giroux*, (1916) 53 S.C.R. 172
R. v. *Gladstone*, [1996] 2 S.C.R. 723
R. v. *Gladue*, [1999] 1 S.C.R. 688
Guérin v. *The Queen*, [1984] 2 S.C.R. 335
R. v. *Horse*, [1988] 1 S.C.R. 187
Horseman v. *The Queen*, [1990] 1 S.C.R. 901
R. v. *Howard*, [1994] 2 S.C.R. 299
Jack et al. v. *The Queen*, [1980] 1 S.C.R. 294
Jack and Charlie v. *The Queen*, (1985) 4 D.L.R. (4ᵗʰ) 96
Kruger & Manuel v. *The Queen*, [1978] 1 S.C.R. 104
Attorney General for Canada v. *Lavell*, [1974] S.C.R. 1349
R. v. *Lewis*, [1996] 1 S.C.R. 921
R. v. *Marshall (1)*, [1999] 3 S.C.R. 456
R. v. *Marshall (2)*, [1999] 3 S.C.R. 533
R. v. *McKinney*, [1980] 1 S.C.R. 1031
Mitchell v. *Peguis Indian Band*, [1990] 2 S.C.R. 85
Moosehunter v. *The Queen*, [1981] 1 S.C.R. 282
R. v. *Mousseau*, [1980] 2 S.C.R. 89
Myran, Meeches et al. v. *The Queen*, [1976] 2 S.C.R. 137
Native Women's Association of Canada v. *Canada*, [1994] 3 S.C.R. 627
Natural Parents v. *British Columbia (Superintendent of Child Welfare)*, [1976] 2 S.C.R. 751
R. v. *Nikal*, [1996] 1 S.C.R. 1013
Nowegijick v. *The Queen*, [1983] 1 S.C.R. 29
Québec (Attorney General) v. *Canada (National Energy Board)*, [1994] 1 S.C.R. 159
Opetchesaht Indian Band v. *Canada*, [1997] 2 S.C.R. 119
R. v. *Pamajewon*, [1996] 2 S.C.R. 821
Paul (I) v. *Paul*, [1986] 1 S.C.R. 306

Canadian Pacific Ltd. v. *Paul (II) and The Queen*, [1988] 2 S.C.R. 654

Paulete et al. v. *The Queen*, [1977] 2 S.C.R. 628

Prince & Myron v. *The Queen*, [1964] S.C.R. 81

Re. Eskimos, [1939] S.C.R. 105

Roberts v. *Canada*, [1989] 1 S.C.R. 323

Ontario Mining Co. v. *Seybold*, (1901) 32 S.C.R. 1

Sigeareak E1-53 v. *The Queen*, [1966] S.C.R. 625

Sikyea v. *The Queen*, [1965] 2 C.C.C. 129

Simon v. *The Queen*, [1985] 2 S.C.R. 387

R. v. *Sioui*, [1990] 1 S.C.R. 1025

Smith v. *The Queen*, [1983] 1 S.C.R. 554

R. v. *N.T.C. Smokehouse Ltd.*, [1996] 2 S.C.R. 672

Sparrow v. *The Queen*, [1990] 1 S.C.R. 1075

St. Catherine's Milling & Lumber Co. v. *The Queen*, (1887) 13 S.C.R. 577

R. v. *Sundown*, [1999] 1 S.C.R. 393

R. v. *Sutherland, Wilson & Wilson*, [1980] 2 S.C.R. 451

R. v. *Van der Peet*, [1996] 2 S.C.R. 507

Westbank First Nation v. *B.C. Hydro and Power Authority*, [1999] 3 S.C.R. 134

R. v. *Williams*, [1992] 1 S.C.R. 877

Analysis by variable (key at end of table)

	Year	Decision	Party at the origin of the proceedings	Nature of the right in question	Result
*	1880	Church v. Fenton	--	P	--
*	1887	St. Catherine's Milling & Lumber Co. v. The Queen	--	L	D
	1901	Ontario Mining Co. v. Seybold	N-A	L	D
	1916	Attorney General for Canada v. Giroux	N-A	L	V
	1918	R. v. Bonhomme	N-A	L	D
*/**	1931	R. v. Easterbrook	--	L	D
*/**	1939	Re. Eskimos	--	P	V
	1964	Prince & Myron v. The Queen	N-A	E	V
	1965	Sikyea v. The Queen	N-A	E	D
**	1966	Sigeareak E1-53 v. The Queen	N-A	E	D
**	1966	R. v. George	N-A	E	D
**	1968	Daniel v. White and The Queen	N-A	E	D
	1970	R. v. Drybones	N-A	P	V
	1973	Calder v. Attorney General for British Columbia	A	L	D
	1974	Cardinal v. Attorney General for Alberta	N-A	E	D
**	1974	Attorney General for Canada v. Lavell	A	P	D
	1976	Myran, Meeches et al. v. The Queen	N-A	E	D
*/**	1976	Natural Parents v. British Columbia (Superintendent of Child Welfare)	--	P	D
	1976	R. v. Derriksan	N-A	E	D
	1977	Paulete et al. V. The Queen	N-A	L	D
	1977	Davey v. Isaac	A	P	D
**	1978	Kruger & Manuel v. The Queen	N-A	E	D
	1978	Frank v. The Queen	N-A	E	V

	Year	Case			
	1980	Jack et al. v. The Queen	N-A	E	D
**	1980	Four B Manufacturing Co. Limited v. United Garment Workers of America	A	P	D
**	1980	R. v. McKinney	N-A	E	D
**	1980	R. v. Mousseau	N-A	E	D
**	1980	Elk v. The Queen	N-A	E	D
	1980	R. v. Sutherland, Wilson & Wilson	N-A	E	V
	1981	Moosehunter v. The Queen	N-A	E	V
	1983	Nowegijick v. The Queen	A	E	V
*/**	1983	Smith v. The Queen	--	L	V
	1984	Guérin v. The Queen	A	E	V
	1985	Simon v. The Queen	N-A	E	V
**	1985	Dick v. The Queen	N-A	E	D
**	1985	Jack and Charlie v. The Queen	N-A	P	D
	1986	Derrickson v. Derrickson	A	E	V
	1986	Paul (I) v. Paul	A	E	V
	1988	R. v. Horse	N-A	E	D
	1988	Canadian Pacific Ltd. v. Paul (II) and The Queen	N-A	L	D
**	1989	Roberts v. Canada	A	L	--
	1990	Horseman v. The Queen	N-A	E	D
	1990	Sparrow v. The Queen	N-A	E	PV
	1990	R. v. Sioui	N-A	P	V
	1990	Mitchell v. Peguis Indian Band	N-A	E	V
**	1991	Ontario v. Bear Island Foundation	N-A	L	D
	1992	R. v. Williams	A	E	V
	1994	Québec (Attorney General) v. Canada (National Energy Board)	A	E	PV
**	1994	R. v. Howard	N-A	E	D
	1994	Native Women's Association of Canada v. Canada	A	P	D

	Year	Case			
	1995	Blueberry River Indian Band v. Canada	A	E	V
	1996	R. v. Badger	N-A	E	PV
	1996	R. v. Lewis	N-A	E	D
	1996	R. v. Nikal	N-A	E	V
	1996	R. v. Pamajewon	N-A	P	D
	1996	R. v. Van der Peet	N-A	E	D
	1996	R. v. Gladstone	N-A	E	V
	1996	R. v. N.T.C. Smokehouse Ltd.	N-A	E	D
	1996	R. v. Adams	N-A	E	V
	1996	R. v. Côté	N-A	E	V
	1997	Opetchesaht Indian Band v. Canada	A	L	D
	1997	St. Mary's Indian Band v. Cranbrook (City)	A	E	D
	1997	Delgamuukw v. British Columbia	A	L	PV
	1999	R. v. Sundown	N-A	E	V
	1999	R. v. Gladue	A	P	D
	1999	Corbière v. Canada	A	P	V
**	1999	Westbank First Nation v. B.C. Hydro and Power Authority	A	E	D
	1999	R. v. Marshall (I)	N-A	E	V
	1999	R. v. Marshall (II)	N-A	E	V

Key:

* = case involving no Aboriginal parties

** = decision in which no values were identified

A = Aboriginal individual, group or organization

N-A = Non-Aboriginal individual, group or organization

E = economic right

L = land right

P = political right

D = Aboriginal defeat

V = Aboriginal victory

PV = partial aboriginal victory

-- = does not apply to the decision in question

Appendix III

Groups Interviewed

A) Selection criteria

This list includes all of the groups representing the interests of Aboriginals that were active at the national level in Canada in 1997, except for the Native Council of Canada, with which we were unable to obtain a meeting. It also includes the principal groups representing the interests of Aboriginals in Québec at that time. This is to make up for the fact that, unlike their counterparts in other provinces, Québec Aboriginals have rarely been involved in Supreme Court of Canada cases concerning Aboriginal interests. Indeed, only one such case has been brought by an Aboriginal party from Québec. The names of the people interviewed from each group and the date of the interview appear in the alphabetical list of groups (B). The interview guide (C) is included after the list.

B) Alphabetical list of groups

Assembly of First Nations
    Ghislain Picard, Regional Chief, February 28, 1997
Grand Council of the Crees
    Violette Pichanos, Vice-Chairman, Deputy Grand Chief for the Grand Council, February 5, 1997
Huron-Wendat Nation Council
    Jean Picard, Grand Chief, July 6, 1997
Inuit Tapirisat of Canada
    Mary Sillit, Internal President, May 19, 1997
Kahnawake Band Council (Mohawks)
    Arnold Goodleaf, Director of Inter-governmental Relations, September 26, 1997
Kitigan Zibi Band Council (Algonquins)
    Jean-Guy Whiteduck, Council Chief, March 6, 1997
Mamuitun Tribal Council (Montagnais)
    Jean-Marie Picard, Director, May 23, 1997
Métis National Council
    Richard Maresty, Council Coordinator, May 8, 1997
Mohawk Nation Office
    Dale Dion, Member, Secretariat for the People of the Long House, July 23, 1997
Regroupement Mamit Innuat (Montagnais)
    Jean Malek, Director General, August 14, 1997

C) Interview guide

Identity and organization
    -    name

- membership
- objectives
- structures
- internal decision-making process
- related, supportive and associated groups, objective allies

Image
- Content of the group's self-image
- Aspects given priority, accentuated
- Secondary aspects, mentioned
- Values identified as related to priority aspects
- Values identified as related to hidden aspects

Interests
- Conscious interests
- Admitted conscious interests
- Hidden conscious interests

Audiences
- universal
- special

Strategies
- media, general and specialized strategies
- infiltration strategies
- alliance strategies
- other strategies

Targets of strategies (legitimacy)

□ Andrée Lajoie and Guy Rocher are professors at the *Centre de recherche en droit public* in the Faculty of Law at the University of Montréal, where Éric Gélineau is a PhD. Student and Isabelle Duplessis was a post-doc when this article was prepared. Ms Duplessis is now a legal officer at the UN.

[1] A. Lajoie, M. C. Gervais, E. Gélineau, R. Janda, "When Silence is no Longer Acquiescence: Gays and Lesbians under Canadian Law", (1999) 13 *R.C.D.S.* 101–126; A. Lajoie, M. C. Gervais, E. Gélineau, R. Janda, "Les valeurs des femmes dans le discours de la Cour suprême du Canada", forthcoming in *R.J.T.* in 2000; A. Lajoie, "I valori delle minoranze sociali nelle giurisprudenza costituzionale delle Corte suprema del Canada", forthcoming in *Lo sviluppo dei diritti fondamentali in Canada fra universalita e diversita culturale*, Ed. G. Rolla, Milan: Giuffre, 2000.

[2] We have used a "Harrissian" method that we described in Lajoie et. al., "Les représentations de 'société libre et démocratique' à la Cour Dickson, la rhétorique dans le discours judiciaire canadien", (1994) 32 *Osgoode Hall L. J.* 295–391.

[3] See Appendix I, Aboriginal Stakeholders in Selected Decisions.

[4] See Appendix II, Selected Decisions.

[5] See Appendix III, Groups Interviewed.

[6] It was mentioned a total of 40 times by interviewees and stakeholders. In contrast, Mother Earth–economic self-sufficiency, land–political self-determination, and other values were mentioned 27, 31 and 25 times, respectively.

[7] See Appendix III.

[8] Delgamuukw and First Nations Summit in *Van der Peet*, Federation of Saskatchewan Indian Nations in *Badger*, Assembly of First Nations in *Bear Island*. Note that given the large number of cases analysed and the repetition resulting from our methods, we will cite cases by the titles that are indicated in bold in Appendix II, Selected Decisions.

[9] Kitigan Zibi Band Council (Algonquins), in interview.

[10] Union of Ontario Indians in *Davey*.

[11] Grand Council of the Cree in *Nowegijick*.

[12] Inuit Tapirisat of Canada and Métis National Council, in interviews.

[13] *Ibid.*

[14] Assembly of First Nations, Mohawk Nation Office, Mamuitun Tribal Council (Montagnais), Regroupement Mamit Innuat (Montagnais) and Huron-Wendat Nation Council, in interviews; Wet'suwet'en in *Delgamuukw*.

[15] Inuit Tapirisat, Mamuitum Tribal Council (Montagnais), Mohawk Nation Office, Kitigan Zibi Band Council (Algonquins), Grand Council of the Cree and Assembly of First Nations, in interviews; the Assembly of First Nations in *Sparrow* and *Association des femmes autochtones*, Association of Iroquois and Allied Indians and appellant in *Bear Island*, Union of Ontario Indians in *Davey*, appellant in *Calder*, Delgamuukw in *Van der Peet*, respondents, Lesser Slave Lake Indian Regional Council and Aboriginal Legal Services of Toronto in *Corbière* and *Gladue*.

[16] Assembly of First Nations, in interview.

[17] Assembly of First Nations in *Sparrow* and *Bear Island*, Chief Abel Bosum in *Blueberry*, Delgamuukw in *Van der Peet*.

[18] Assembly of First Nations, Inuit Tapirisat of Canada, Grand Council of the Cree, in interviews; appellants in *Calder*; respondents in *Sundown*; (see also the groups mentioned *infra*, note 20 and 21).

[19] Huron-Wendat Nation Council, in interview; Delgamuukw in *Van der Peet* and *Pamajewon*; and Federation of Saskatchewan Indians, also in *Pamajewon*.

[20] Métis National Council, Inuit Tapirisat of Canada, Grand Council of the Cree, Kitigan Zibi Band Council (Algonquins) and Huron-Wendat Nation Council, in interviews; appellants in *Calder*, Union of Ontario Indians in *Davey*, National Indian Brotherhood in *Guérin* and *Sparrow*, Chief Paulet and Woodstock Indian Reserve Band and Council in *Paul*, Delgamuukw in *Van der Peet* and *Pamajewon*, Wet'suwet'en and appellants in *Delgamuukw*.

[21] Grand Council of the Cree and Huron-Wendat Nation Council, in interviews; National Indian Brotherhood in *Sparrow*, Treaty 7 Tribal Council and Delgamuukw in *Badger*.

[22] This perspective was especially well developed by the Huron-Wendat Nation Council in its interview, but it was also described by others: the Grand Council of the Cree, Kitigan Zibi Band Council (Algonquins), Mamuitun Tribal Council

(Montagnais) and Kahnawake Band Council, in interviews; as well as the National Indian Brotherhood in *Sparrow*, Delgamuukw in *Pamajewon* and Delgamuukw and First Nations Summit in *Van der Peet*.

[23] First Nations Summit in *Van der Peet*.

[24] Delgamuukw and Federation of Saskatchewan Indians in *Pamajewon*.

[25] Huron-Wendat Nation Council and Mamuitan Tribal Council (Montagnais), in interviews; the National Indian Brotherhood in *Sparrow;* and Wet'suwet'en in *Delgamuukw*.

[26] Grand Council of the Cree, Mohawk Nation Office, Kahnawake Band Council (Mohawks), Kitigan Zibi Band Council (Algonquins), Assembly of First Nations in interview and appellants in *Corbière*.

[27] Grand Council of the Cree, Mohawk Nation Office, Huron-Wendat Nation Council and Mamuitun Tribal Council (Montagnais), in interviews; Union of Ontario Indians in *Davey*, Association of Iroquois and Allied Indians and National Indian Brotherhood in *Bear Island*, Delgamuukw and Federation of Saskatchewan Indians in *Pamajewon*, Delgamuukw in *Van der Peet*, Atikamekw-Sipi/Atikamekw Nation Council in *Côté*, Lesser Slave Lake Indian Regional Council in *Corbière*.

[28] Indian Brotherhood and Delgamuukw in *Bear Island*, Lesser Slave Lake Indian Regional Council in *Corbière*, appellants in *Delgamuukw*.

[29] Grand Council of the Cree, Mohawk Nation Office, Kahnawake Band Council (Mohawks), and Kitigan Zibi Band Council (Algonquins), in interviews.

[30] Kahnawake Band Council (Mohawks), in interview.

[31] Mohawk Nation Office, in interview.

[32] Assembly of First Nations, Inuit Tapirisat of Canada and Regroupement Mamit Innuat (Montagnais) in interviews; respondents in *Corbière*.

[33] Musqueam Nation in *Blueberry*, Federation of Saskatchewan Indians in *Pamajewon*.

[34] Assembly of First Nations, Métis National Council, Kahnawake Band Council (Mohawks) and Kitigan Zibi Band Council, in interviews.

[35] Assembly of First Nations and Grand Council of the Cree, in interviews.

[36] Métis National Council, in interview.

[37] Assembly of First Nations, Métis National Council, Inuit Tapirisat of Canada, Kahnawake Band Council (Mohawks), Mohawk Nation Office and Mamuitum Tribal Council (Montagnais) in interviews; Union of Ontario Indians in *Davey* and First Nation Summit in *Van der Peet*.

[38] Assembly of First Nations, Métis National Council and Kahnawake Band Council (Mohawks).

[39] Mohawk Nation Office and Regroupement Mamit Innuat in interviews.

[40] Union of Ontario Indians in *Davey*, appellants and National Indian Brotherhood in *Guérin*, Federation of Saskatchewan Indians in *Badger*, appellants and Union of British Columbia Indian Chiefs in *Opetchesaht*, and Congress of Aboriginal People in *Corbière*.

[41] Respondents, United Native Nations Society of B.C. and Congress of Aboriginal People in *Corbière* and Aboriginal Legal Services of Toronto in *Gladue*.

[42] Assembly of First Nations in *Native Women's Association of Canada*; Native Women's Association of Canada in the eponymous case and in *Corbière*, Aborigi-

nal Legal Services of Toronto in *Corbière*.

[43] By this we mean the collective interests of Aboriginals, which are linked to their status and constitutional rights, and not the individual interest of an Aboriginal person since that would make him or her no different from other Canadians, particularly in criminal cases, where identity is not in question, and with respect to procedural issues.

[44] In comparison, since the Supreme Court of Canada's creation in 1875, 20 decisions have been rendered in cases concerning the collective interests of women, and six concerning gays and lesbians.

[45] See the decisions marked with asterisks in Appendix II. These cases concern quarrels over Aboriginal law that have arisen between other parties, such as the governments of Canada and the provinces, non-Aboriginal private companies, and private individuals.

[46] In comparison, five out of six (83%) cases concerning the interests of gays and lesbians were brought by gays or lesbians, and nine out of 20 (45%) cases concerning women's rights were brought by women. See the articles cited *supra*, note 1.

[47] *National Energy Board.*

[48] *Calder, Guérin, Roberts, Williams, Blueberry, Optetchesaht, Cranbrook, Delgamuukw, Paul I, Derrickson* and *Westbank.*

[49] *Lavell, Davey, Four B Manufacturing, Nowegijick* and *Corbière.*

[50] *Native Women's Association of Canada.*

[51] Before 1970 there were none (0%); between 1971 and 1980, there were 3 (20%); between 1981 and 1990, there were 7 (43.7%); and between 1991 and 2000 there were 8 (33.3%).

[52] See Appendix I.

[53] Regroupement Mamit Innuat (Montagnais) and Métis National Council.

[54] Inuit Tapirisat of Canada, Mohawk Nation Office and Kitigan Zibi Band Council (Algonquins).

[55] Métis National Council, Inuit Tapirisat of Canada and Kahnawake Band Council (Mohawks). The Grand Council of the Cree, which was the plaintiff in the only case that went to the Supreme Court of Canada, said in an interview in 1997 that it never wanted to go before the courts again (but it is there at this time).

[56] Kahnawake Band Council (Mohawks).

[57] Assembly of First Nations, Huron-Wendat Nation Council, Mamuitum Tribal Council (Montagnais) and Regroupement Mamit Innuat (Montagnais).

[58] Assembly of First Nations and Kitigan Zibi Band Council (Algonquins).

[59] Huron-Wendat Nation Council.

[60] Assembly of First Nations, Grand Council of the Cree and Mamuitun Tribal Council (Montagnais).

[61] Métis National Council.

[62] Kahnawake Band Council (Mohawks).

[63] Mohawk Nation Office.

[64] Kitigan Zibi Band Council (Algonquins), Mamuitun Tribal Council (Montagnais) and Huron-Wendat Nation Council.

[65] Kahnawake Band Council (Mohawks).

[66] Inuit Tapirisat of Canada and Regroupement Mamit Innuat (Montagnais).

[67] Mohawk Nation Office, Kitigan Zibi Band Council (Algonquins), Inuit Tapirisat

of Canada, Assembly of First Nations and Métis National Council.

[68] Regroupement Mamit Innuat (Montagnais).

[69] Assembly of First Nations, Kahnawake Band Council (Mohawks) and Huron-Wendat Nation Council.

[70] Métis National Council.

[71] Assembly of First Nations and Kahnawake Band Council (Mohawks).

[72] Métis National Council.

[73] Mohawk Nation Office.

[74] Huron-Wendat Nation Council.

[75] Assembly of First Nations, Métis National Council, Inuit Tapirisat of Canada and Mamuitun Tribal Council (Montagnais).

[76] Kahnawake Band Council (Mohawks).

[77] Assembly of First Nations, Huron-Wendat Nation Council, Mamuitun Tribal Council (Montagnais), Grand Council of the Cree, Inuit Tapirisat of Canada, Kahnawake Band Council (Mohawks) Kitigan Zibi Band Council (Algonquins) Mohawk Nation Office, Regroupement Mamit Innuat (Montagnais) and Métis National Council.

[78] Such as New York State in the case of the Mohawk Nation Office.

[79] Regroupement Mamit Innuat (Montagnais).

[80] Grand Council of the Cree.

[81] Regroupement Mamit Innuat (Montagnais).

[82] Kahnawake Band Council (Mohawks).

[83] In the last census, Aboriginal people accounted for 2.8% of the population of Canada, and 1.01% of the population of Québec.

[84] This organization represents "non-status" Aboriginals, in other words, Aboriginals whose names do not appear on the federal government's lists.

[85] Kahnawake Band Council (Mohawks) and Huron-Wendat Nation Council.

[86] Métis National Council.

[87] The Regroupement Mamit Innuat (Montagnais) sometimes works with the *Comité d'appui aux Nations Autochtones de Montréal*, the Québec human rights commission, and the Nitassinan, an organization that protects Aboriginal land rights.

[88] Assembly of First Nations and Grand Council of the Cree.

[89] Grand Council of the Cree and Métis National Council.

[90] Huron-Wendat Nation Council, Grand Council of the Cree, Mamuitun Tribal Council (Montagnais), Inuit Tapirisat of Canada, Kahnawake Band Council (Mohawks), Kitigan Zibi Band Council (Algonquins), Mohawk Nation Office and Regroupement Mamit Innuat (Montagnais).

[91] Kahnawake Band Council (Mohawks).

[92] Mamuitun Tribal Council (Montagnais).

[93] Huron-Wendat Nation Council.

[94] Mamuitun Tribal Council (Montagnais), Huron-Wendat Nation Council, Grand Council of the Cree, Inuit Tapirisat of Canada and Mohawk Nation Office.

[95] Assembly of First Nations.

[96] Inuit Tapirisat of Canada.

[97] Assembly of First Nations, Mohawk Nation Office and (according to Inuit information) the Federation of Saskatchewan Indians.

[98] Inuit Tapirisat of Canada.

[99] Assembly of First Nations, Grand Council of the Cree, Mohawk Nation Office, Kahnawake Band Council (Mohawks), Regroupement Mamit Innuat (Montagnais) and Kitigan Zibi Band Council (Algonquins).

[100] Kitigan Zibi Band Council (Algonquins).

[101] See Li Xiu Woo. *The Haudenosaunee (Iroquois) Confederacy Petition to the League of Nations: How Canada set the Precedent for Excluding Indigenous Peoples from International Law*, Master's thesis, Montréal: Département de sciences juridiques, UQAM, 2000.

[102] The Aboriginals of Canada who participated included the Grand Council of the Cree of Québec (Ted Moses), Indigenous World Association (Kenneth Deer), Mohawk Nation (Kenneth Deer), International Organization of Indigenous Resource Development (Wilton Littlechild), Innu Council of Nitassinan (Armand McKenzie), Akuitcho Territory Government (Sharon Venne) and Haudesonaunee Nation.

[103] Duplessis, I., "Quand les histoires se font globales: l'exemple de l'internationalisation des revendications autochtones" (2000) 40 (2) *Droit et Cultures*, 109-13. Here, we review the key findings of this work, which was done in the framework of our project and with the material support of our research team.

[104] On narrativism, see, among others, I. S. Papadopoulos, "Guerre et paix en droit et littérature", (1999) 42 *Revue interdisciplinaire d'études juridiques* (Brussels) 181–196; R. Delgado, "Storytelling for Oppositionists and Others: A Plea for Narrative", (1989) 87 *Michigan Law Review* 2411 and "Shadowboxing: An Essay on Power", (1992) 77 *Cornell Law Review* 813.

[105] I. Schulte-Tenchkoff, *La question des peuples autochtones*, Brussels: Bruylant, AXES/savoir collection, 1977.

[106] E. Gélineau et al., "Les conceptions canadiennes des droits ancestraux", (2004) 38 *R.J.T.* 487.

[107] Of the 69 decisions selected for analysis, 19 were based strictly on technical legal arguments that did not make it possible to identify allegiance to any value at all, except perhaps to legal positivism. See the decisions identified with a double asterisk (**) in Appendix II.

[108] *Prince, Sutherland, Moosehunter, Nowegijick, Simon, Mitchell, Williams, Nikal, Gladstone, Adams, Côté, Corbière, Marshall I and II, Delgamuukw, Sparrow, Van der Peet, Smokehouse, Cranbrook, Pamajewon,* and *Gladue.*

[109] The first 14 cases mentioned in the preceding footnote are Aboriginal victories. The 15th is a partial victory and the last six are defeats. We have defined defeats as appeals lost by Aboriginal parties against their interests. Victories are appeals completely won by Aboriginal parties in favour of their interests. Partial victories are defined as those that were apparently won but in reality had mitigated results. Examples of the last category are *Sparrow* (in which Aboriginal rights were acknowledged, but the Court refused to apply them to the facts and ordered a new trial), *National Energy Board* (in which the appeal was upheld but fiduciary duty was not recognized), and *Delgamuukw* (in which oral evidence was admitted, but the land claim was limited and sent back to negotiation).

[110] *Cardinal, Jack, Horseman,* and *Sparrow.*

[111] *Nikal, Adams, Gladstone, Sundown, Sioui and Marshall I and II,* and *Badger and Delgamuukw*, which were partial victories.

[112] *Giroux, Simon, Williams, Côté and Marshall I, as well as Delgamuukw*, which was a partial victory.

[113] *Van der Peet, Corbière.*

[114] *Myran.*

[115]. *St. Catherine's Milling, Seybold, Bonhomme, Calder, Paul II, Guérin, Sioui,* and *Marshall I.*

[116] The five first decisions mentioned in the preceding footnote were defeats, but the last three were victories.

[117] *Mitchell, Derrickson, Blueberry, Adams, Sundown, Corbière, Marshall I and II, Simon, Badger, Sparrow, National Energy Board, Cranbrook, Gladue,* and *Sikyea.*

[118] The first nine decisions mentioned in the preceding footnote are Aboriginal victories, the next three are partial victories and the last three defeats.

[119] *Cardinal, Nowegijick, Blueberry* and *Marshall I.*

[120] *Drybones, Kruger, Cranbrook,* and *Corbière.*

[121] *St. Catherine's Milling.*

[122] *Church, St. Catherine's Milling, Seybold, Sioui, Mitchell, Williams, Horse, Gladstone, Côté, Delgamuukw, Marshall II, Native Women's Association,* and *Smokehouse.*

[123] *Horse.*

[124] However, we have to admit that we were surprised to find that these values have been mentioned since the Court's first work in this area, and regularly to this day.

[125] *Sikyea, Paulete, Derriksan, Horseman, Lewis, Jack, Davey, Sparrow* and *Badger* (of which only the last two are victories, and even then only partial).

[126] *St. Catherine's Milling, Van der Peet, Smokehouse, Opetchesaht, Cardinal, Calder, Horseman, Native Women's Association, Lewis, Pamajewon* and *Gladstone* (of which only the last is an Aboriginal victory).

[127] Except in *Native Women's Association*, in which this value is mentioned, the decisions based on this value all affect economic rights, in particular with respect to hunting and fishing.

[128] *Pamajewon* (self-government), and *Davey* (traditional political rights).

[129] Excluding two decisions that were neither defeats nor victories for Aboriginals, namely, *Church* and *Roberts.*

[130] Excluding the same two decisions for the same reason.

[131] *Lavell, Native Women's Association* (political equality of Aboriginal men and women), *Davey* (traditional Aboriginal political rights), *Four B Manufacturing* (independence from provincial labour legislation), *Pamajewon* (independence from provincial gaming legislation), *Jack and Charlie* (religious freedom), *Gladue* (Aboriginal identity), to which we should add *Natural Parents* (Indian status, denied).

[132] *Re. Eskimos* (recognition of "Indian" status), *Drybones* (equality of Aboriginal and non-Aboriginal persons in criminal matters), *Corbière* (political rights of Aboriginals off reserve), *Drybones* (equality) and *Sioui* (freedom).

[133] *Bonhomme, Easterbrooke, Paulete, Paul II, Bear Island, Opetchesacht, Calder, St. Catherine's Milling, Seybold.*

[134] *Delgamuukw, Giroux* and *Smith.*

[135] These cases almost all concern hunting and fishing rights, except for five: two concerning income tax exemptions (*Williams* and *Nowegijick*) and three related to long-term leases or surrender of land (*Blueberry, Guérin* and *Mitchell*), all of which were Aboriginal victories.

[136] *Prince, Frank, Sutherland, Moosehunter, Williams, Nowegijick, Blueberry, Guérin, Mitchell, Simon, Nikal, Adams, Sundown, Marshall I* and *II, Derrickson, Paul I* and *National Energy Board*, including four partial victories: *Sparrow, Gladstone, Côté* and *Badger*.

[137] *Sikyea, Sigeareak, Daniel, Cardinal, Myran, Derriksan, Kruger, Jack, McKinney, Mousseau, Elk, Dick, Horse, Horseman, Howard, Lewis, Van der Peet, Smokehouse, Cranbrook, Westbank,* and *George*.

[138] *Eskimos, Drybones* and *Corbière*.

[139] *Four B Manufacturing, Native Women's Association* and *Pamajewon*.

[140] *Nowegijick,* and *Williams*.

[141] This same mechanism can also be seen in the way the Court treats the value "equality" in the context of women's claims to economic equality, and the value "dignity with respect to identity" in cases involving gays and lesbians. See the articles cited *supra*, note 1.

[142] See in the same sense, G. Otis, "Les sources des droits ancestraux des peuples autochtones", [1999] 40 *C. de D.* 591–617 [*Otis*].

[143] *Sparrow*.

[144] *Van der Peet* and, in the same sense, Otis, *supra* note 142 at 601–602.

[145] *Van der Peet* and, in the same sense, Otis, *supra* note 142 at 604 and following.

[146] *St. Catherine's Milling,* and *Seybold*.

[147] *St. Catherine's Milling, Seybold, Bonhomme, Kruger, Calder, Adams, Côté,* and *Delgamuukw*. (In the last three cases, the Court did not reject the title but did not examine it in the facts and sent the parties back to a superior court or negotiation.)

[148] *Delgamuukw*.

[149] *Côté*.

[150] Particularly in *Sparrow, Pamajewon, Van der Peet, Gladstone* and *Smokehouse*.

[151] *Van der Peet, Gladstone* and *Smokehouse*.

[152] *Delgamuukw*.

[153] *Ibid.* See, in the same sense, G. Otis, "Revendications foncières, "autochtonité" et liberté de religion au Canada", [1999] 40 *C. de D.* 741–790 at 767.

[154] *Pamajewon*.

[155] *Sikyea, George,* and *Horseman*.

[156] B. Watts, Assistant Deputy Minister, Aboriginal Affairs, *Review of Developments pertaining to the Promotion and Protection of Human Rights and Fundamental Freedoms of Indigenous Populations*, United Nations Working Group on Indigenous Populations at the United Nations in Geneva, Sixteenth Session, July 28, 1998.

[157] *Act providing for the ratification and bringing into effect of the Framework Agreement on First Nation Land Management*, S.C. 1999, c. 24.

[158] Our empirical research on these issues has barely begun and will continue into 2002.

[159] Signed on October 15, 1998 and available on the *Secrétariat aux Affaires autochtones* site: www.saa.gouv.qc.ca .

[160] The English-language originals were signed on March 30, 1999.

[161] The agreements on police services, administration of justice, liquor permits and professional combat sports.

[162] The agreements on registration of births, deaths and marriages, and on childcare.

[163] The agreements on economic development, fiscal matters related to consumer goods and services, fiscal matters related to tobacco, petroleum and alcohol products, and transport and user fees.

[164] Arnold Goodleaf, September 26, 1997.

[165] Schedule B to the *Canada Act 1982*, (U.K.) 1982, c. 11.

[166] In particular concerning economic development, roads, administration of justice, childcare and police services.

[167] The agreements on fiscal matters related to consumer goods and services, and fiscal matters related to tobacco, petroleum and alcohol products.

[168] In particular police services and roads.

[169] In particular on liquor permits, registration of births, deaths and marriages, professional sports and extreme fighting.

[170] *Nisga'a Final Agreement Act* [2000, c.7].

[171] Trudeau said, and Chrétien cannot deny it: "It's inconceivable, I think, that in a given society one section of the society have a treaty with the other section of the society" (http://www.yukoncollege.yk.ca/~agraham/nost202/trud1.htm).

[172] Agreement between the Inuit of the Nunavut Settlement Area and Her Majesty the Queen in Right of Canada, ratified by the *Act to amend the Nunavut Act and the Constitution Act, 1867,* S.C. 1998, c.15.

[173] G. Timsit, "Sur l'engendrement du droit," (1988) *R.D.P.* 39–75; *Les noms de la loi*, Paris: P.U.F., "Les voies du droit" collection, 1991; and A. Lajoie, *Jugements de valeurs*, Paris: P.U.F., "Les voies du droit" collection, 1997.

[174] See in general the work by the *Laboratoire d'anthropologie juridique de Paris I* and, more specifically, the summary on this in N. Rouland, *Anthropologie juridique*, Paris: P.U.F., "Droit fondamental" collection, 1988 at 147 and following.

Aboriginal Peoples' Quest for Identity and Self-Government[1]

Carole Lévesque[2]

1. Introduction

Any reflection on the idea of citizenship has to incorporate an examination of the diversity that characterizes modern societies. In Québec, Aboriginal peoples' quest for identity and self-government is a major component of this diversity. This quest has a history (Delâge 1997; Dupuis 1997; Lajoie et al. 1996; Vincent 1992) about which Québec kers still know too little. The foundations of this quest have primarily involved the Government of Canada, given Aboriginal peoples' legal and historical ties with the federal government (Forest 1996 and 1998); and the trajectories that this quest has taken include components and aims of which the general public is largely unaware. It also involves legal, status, identity and membership issues.

In the eyes of Québec kers, "Indians" have long been "foreigners" living in the backcountry in small, disorganized, marginal groups. Until recently, few Québec kers knew that these groups formed structured social units (known as bands) or that they were usually linked together within a regional unit called, depending on the period and speaker, a tribe, cultural group, regional band or regional group. Over time and especially since events such as the 1975 signing of the *James Bay and Northern Québec Agreement* by the Cree and Inuit and, more recently, the 1990 Oka crisis, Aboriginal issues have gained greater visibility and interest. Today, more people are aware that Québec is home to ten Aboriginal nations (as they call themselves), each of which is divided into one to nine bands (in other words, communities), and that every Aboriginal nation, as well as the Inuit people in Nunavik in northern Québec, has its own history and identity.[3]

In the last 30 years, Aboriginal peoples have stated their claims in many forums. They have had ancestral land rights recognized and they have built a historically unprecedented collective identity. In Aboriginal communities, a new civil society is gradually emerging out of that collective identity.

Aboriginal peoples' quest for identity and autonomy no longer takes the form of isolated battles. It has been transformed into a veritable political agenda in response to the successes, defeats and changes that are inevitable features of life in society. It is following many paths, which are certainly complementary but remain distinct from one another in terms of the challenges and issues they raise. Three of these paths are discussed briefly in the following pages: the assertion of an inherent right to self-determination; the recognition of land claims and ancestral and treaty-based rights; and the abolition of discrimination against Aboriginal women.

2. Assertion of an Inherent Right to Self-determination

There is a world of difference between the question that federal civil servants asked in the 1950s when they were wondering about the *possibility* that "Indians" could have rights (Gibbins and Ponting 1986; Frideres 1988) and the objective of creating a third level of government within the Canadian confederation, as recommended by the Royal Commission on Aboriginal Peoples (RCAP 1996). Kept at a distance for centuries, pushed onto reserves and deprived of basic rights, Aboriginal peoples have been the artisans of a real revolution by becoming powerful political actors in only a few generations.

The inherent right to self-government has not yet been enshrined in the *Constitution*, and notions of self-government diverge (Forest 2000). The federal government favours the devolution of administrative powers at the local level, while national Aboriginal organizations are promoting an autonomous government with constitutional powers. Yet, it is clear that this is a whole new game. Aboriginal peoples are now recognized as one of the founding peoples of Canadian Confederation.

Already, with the legal creation in the eastern Arctic in 1999 of the Territory of Nunavut (located north of the 60th parallel in the area formerly known as the Northwest Territories) and the current negotiations on the establishment of self-government in Nunavik (formerly called New Québec), significant advances have been made with respect to self-determination, although the areas in question are very isolated and their populations are mainly Aboriginal. In the southern part of Canada, where the country's population is concentrated and where Aboriginal and non-Aboriginal people live side by side, the situation is however much more complex. Aboriginal people are not only few in number, but also scattered.

Will the future political foundations of Aboriginal peoples' forms of government be ethnic or territorial? Will they be regional or provincial? Will Aboriginal peoples have two nationalities in the future, one Canadian and the other Aboriginal? Will the Canadian *Charter of Rights and Freedoms* coexist in the future with a *Charter* of Aboriginal Rights (see in particular Carens 1995 and Elkins 1994)? These many different avenues have been examined by both Aboriginal and government jurists and political scientists, but remain open questions for now. However, the fact that we are studying them today shows the gains that have been made, the rights that have been recognized and the changes that have marked relations between Aboriginal and non-Aboriginal people in recent decades, and it also shows how far the discussions have advanced. It was only 30 years ago that the federal government proposed to abolish any form of different status for Aboriginal peoples in Canada.[4]

With respect to Québec more specifically, the issue of the inherent right to self-determination has been raised in a different manner, first because this area is under the exclusive jurisdiction of the federal government but also because Québec's relations with Aboriginal groups are different from those of the other provinces. For example, Québec is the only province that recognizes Aboriginal Nations (everywhere else in Canada, Aboriginal groups are considered peoples). Moreover, in 1985, Premier René Lévesque led the adoption of a special motion recognizing the rights of Aboriginal peoples in Québec, and in particular the right to self-government within Québec (Dupuis 1997). This right to self-government was however framed in such a way as to not alter the integrity of the territory of Québec, which appears to be unacceptable to most Aboriginal Nations.

It is also clear that the sovereigntist agenda of the *Parti Québécois* is influencing relations with Aboriginal peoples in a particular way. A number of Aboriginal Nations have indicated their intention to ask to remain in Canada if Québec were to separate. It is far from clear, however, that there would be more legal protection for them in such a case.

3. Recognition of Land Claims and Ancestral and Treaty-based Rights

As Aboriginal issues have become more complex and consolidated, the amount of jurisprudence in this area has been strengthened and expanded over the years. Proof of increased legal interest in the area can be seen in the emergence of Aboriginal law as a field in itself, with not only national but also international scope. The fact that the Canadian *Constitution* has recognized Aboriginal ancestral rights since 1982[5] has also helped to orient this new area of study.

Dozens of cases have been resolved in the last 25 years. The case of the Cree and Inuit concerning the James Bay hydroelectric complex is not only the most well known, but also the most decisive, even though it clearly led to the extinguishment of the territorial rights of those two groups. However, in order to extinguish rights, it first had to be admitted that they might exist. The first modern treaty, which was also the first treaty in Québec's history—the *James Bay and Northern Québec Agreement*—did not however extinguish the parties' ancestral rights, at least from their point of view. This is part of the basis for the current Cree initiative to renegotiate the *Agreement*, particularly since it was signed before the *Constitution* was repatriated, and since the legal conditions prevailing in the early 1970s were less favourable to Aboriginal peoples than they have been since 1982.

Under the *Agreement*, the Cree and the Inuit[6] obtained harvesting rights within a new land regime, as well as various other rights, such as those related to developing and managing wildlife resources. However, more importantly, these groups won recognition as Aboriginal Nations in Québec and Canada and thereby acquired a renewed regional standing. Some may say that the price (the extinguishment of territorial rights) was too high, but that loss has not prevented the Cree from becoming the most powerful Aboriginal political group in Canada, and probably one of the most powerful in the world. Moreover, the *Agreement* already opened the door, 25 years ago, to a new mode of economic and social development based on self-management and empowerment. Since then, the agreements that the federal and Québec governments have signed with Aboriginal Nations and Aboriginal organizations in various fields, such as health, education, public security, employment and resource management, have been inspired by the progress made in this respect.

The *James Bay and Northern Québec Agreement* also marked the beginning of Québec's official and legal involvement in Aboriginal affairs. Until then, Québec had played a relatively minor role and had essentially remained in the shadow of the federal government. As Québec came to assert itself, not only with respect to the sovereigntist agenda but also as a distinct society within Canada, relations between the Aboriginal Nations and the Government of Québec developed, although the main stumbling block has obviously been land (except in the cases of the Cree, Inuit and Naskapis, whose agreements include land settlements). For example, the land claims of the Montagnais-Innus, Algonquians and Atikamekw, who have never signed treaties with Canada and are not party to the northern agreements, have been under negotiation for over 20 years.

There is also another stumbling block for relations between Québec and Aboriginal peoples. It concerns renewable and non-renewable resource development and management. While land claim issues were on the forefront of the scene in the 1970s and 1980s, resources can be considered the issue of the 1990s. And it is very likely that there will be many cases involving this issue in the years to come.

4. Abolition of Discrimination Against Aboriginal Women

With respect to citizenship, Aboriginal peoples in Québec (excluding the Inuit), like those in the rest of Canada, are set apart from birth from the rest of the population because of the special legal status they are accorded under the *Indian Act*.[7] The federal legislation dates from the end of the nineteenth century. Amended in 1876, 1951 and 1985, it determines who is a "registered Indian" (in other words, a "status Indian"), and by extension who is not (in other words, who is a "non-status Indian"). Since Indians are considered wards of the state, the *Act* includes a series of protectionist measures according to which duly registered Indians can live on a reserve, have the right to education, health care and shelter at the state's expense, and are exempt from income tax when they work on reserve (Dupuis 1991; Lévesque 1989). On the other hand, a registered Indian is bound from birth to death by the decisions of the Department of Indian Affairs. He or she is a minor in the eyes of the law and is today still subject to a series of legal constraints and measures that limit his or her rights and freedoms as a citizen.[8]

Until the last amendment of the *Act* in 1985, the majority of non-status Indians were in fact Indian women who had lost their status as a result of a provision of the *Act*, because they had married a non-Indian. This legal provision was all the more discriminatory in that it also provided that a non-Indian woman who married a registered Indian automatically became a status Indian. Thus, in addition to turning Aboriginals into second-class, dominated citizens, the very wording of the *Act* created a second level of domination by legitimizing a hierarchy between men and women, recognizing only paternal filiation and refusing Indian women married to non-aboriginals the right to live on a reserve, and consequently to have access to basic services. It was only after a 20-year struggle by Aboriginal women's associations in Canada—in particular the Québec Native Women's Association—and a number of court cases, that Bill C-31 was adopted in 1985, resulting in the abolishment of the provisions legitimizing such sex discrimination. From then on, some excluded women and their mixed-race descendents were able to reintegrate into their original bands, and sometimes even go back to live on the reserve.

Since Indian groups began asserting their presence in the public arena in the 1960s, the *Indian Act* has been a primary focus. The *Act* reflects the colonizing policies and civic abuses to which Aboriginals have been subject for centuries. However, it also reflects the views of a society (ours) that has historically given little importance to women. When Indian women began fighting against the sex discrimination that negatively affected their identity, they came up against both a legislative and a civic brick wall, since Indian men opposed any partial amendment of the *Indian Act*.

Two main arguments were invoked by the band chiefs who refused to recognize the women's claims. The first was that the *Indian Act* had to undergo a complete rewriting before there could be any initiative to amend one of its components. It was suggested that the women should wait until the legislation was overhauled before they took action. The second argument suggested that collective rights claims should take precedence over individual rights claims.

Despite this opposition, and in keeping with clauses in the Canadian *Charter of Rights and Freedoms*, the women finally won and the *Act* was amended in 1985. However, correcting the legislation was not sufficient to eliminate all discrimination against women. After the adoption of *Bill C-31*, its implementing measures still had to be defined. The Minister of Indian Affairs divested himself of that responsibility by transferring it to the band councils, the creation and powers of which are also set out in the *Indian Act*. Thus, band councils are now in charge of developing membership codes that set the conditions for formerly excluded women to return to their reserves (AFAQ 1993). In other words, the bands are responsible for defining their own criteria for including or excluding those women and their descendents.

The selection of these criteria is not a simple matter. Indeed, the return to the reserve is complicated, even if it involves only two or three additional families, because homes on the reserve are already overpopulated and resources are insufficient. While some reserves have nonetheless found harmonious solutions to the problem, others have established criteria based on racial considerations, such as the proportion of Aboriginal blood, thereby perpetuating an unacceptable form of discrimination.

5. Conclusion

It is certainly not enough to look at the issue of the identity and citizenship of Aboriginal peoples from the viewpoint of rights alone. We also have to ask how such political and legal gains are translated into daily life. One example of these consequences has been shown in our discussion of the situation of Indian women. Discrimination does not end immediately when there is a law, even if this law serves as a legal mechanism that can be invoked in cases of abuse. Indeed, it is in how the legislation is applied that most difficulties arise.

In their fight for recognition of their rights, Aboriginal women have faced new dilemmas. Not only were they speaking up for the first time, but also their struggle (which is continuing in some cases) was particularly difficult within the Aboriginal milieu. Consequently, awareness was triggered, first among Aboriginal women but also with time among Aboriginal men, of the need to improve relations with one another and to promote family and community integration (AFAQ 1992). This movement, which attracted much less media attention than the big legal battles, has also helped to consolidate a collective identity with a more social than political scope.

Today, there is a feeling of belonging to a global Aboriginal community, and this feeling is becoming stronger. It is expressed in a sense of attachment to one's village of origin and Aboriginal Nation, but it is also felt at the national and international levels. Aboriginal identity now transcends borders.

References

- AFAQ – Association des Femmes Autochtones du Québec (1992). *Bâtir l'avenir en toute égalité.* Montréal, 21 p.
- Carens, Joseph H. (1995). *Citizenship and Aboriginal Self-Government.* Document prepared for the Royal Commission on Aboriginal Peoples. Toronto, 48 p.
- Delâge, Denys (1997). "Autochtones, Canadiens, Québécois," in L. Turgeon et al., eds., *Les espaces de l'identité*: 281-301. Les Presses de l'Université Laval, Québec.
- Dupuis, Renée (1991). *La question indienne au Canada.* Collection Boréal Express, Montréal.
  -- (1997). *Tribus, peuples et nations. Les nouveaux enjeux des revendications autochtones au Canada.* Les Éditions du Boréal, Montréal.
- Elkins, David (1994). *Aboriginal Citizenship and Federalism: Exploring Non-Territorial Models.* Document prepared for the Royal Commission on Aboriginal Peoples. Vancouver, 57 p.
- Forest, Pierre-Gerlier (1996). "Les relations politiques entre le Québec et les peuples autochtones depuis la Révolution tranquille," in U. Kempf and R. M. Nischik, eds., *Zeitschrift für Kanada-Studien*: 81-91. Verlag Dr Wißner, Augsburg.

-- (1998). "Les politiques autochtones au Canada," in M. Tremblay, ed., *Les politiques publiques canadiennes*: 264-304. Les Presses de l'Université Laval, Québec.

-- (2000). *Les aspects politiques de l'arrêt Corbière*. Notes préparées à l'occasion du colloque du Ministère des Affaires indiennes et du Nord canadien portant sur la décision de la Cour Suprême dans l'affaire Corbière c. Canada (1999). [Quoted with the author's permission.]

- Frideres, James (1988). *Native Peoples in Canada. Contemporary Conflicts*. Prentice-Hall, Scarborough.

- Gibbins, R. and J. R. Ponting (1986). "Historical Overview and Background," in R. Ponting, ed., *Arduous Journey. Canadian Indians and Decolonization*: 18-56. McClelland and Stewart, Toronto.

- Gouvernement du Québec (1998). *Partenariat. Développement. Actions. Les orientations du gouvernement québécois en regard des affaires autochtones*. Gouvernement du Québec, Québec.

- Lajoie, Andrée et al. (1996). *Le statut juridique des peuples autochtones au Québec et le pluralisme*. Les Éditions Yvon Blais Inc., Cowansville.

- Lévesque, Carole (1989). "Regards sur les femmes autochtones: les étapes d'une lutte politique et sociale," *Cahiers de recherche féministe*: 111-126.

-- (1990). "D'ombre et de lumière: l'Association des Femmes Autochtones du Québec," *Nouvelles Pratiques sociales* 3 (2): 71-83.

- QNWA – Québec Native Women Association (1993). *Taking our Rightful Place*. Brief submitted to the Royal Commission on Aboriginal Peoples. Montréal, 31.

- RCAP – Royal Commission on Aboriginal Peoples (1996). *Report of the Royal Commission on Aboriginal Peoples*. Department of Supply and Services, Ottawa, 5 volumes.

- Vincent, Sylvie (1992). "La révélation d'une force politique: les Autochtones," in D. Daigle and G. Rocher, eds., *Le Québec en jeu. Comprendre les grands défis*: 749-790. Les Presses de l'Université de Montréal, Montréal.

---

[1] This paper has been originally produced in French: Lévesque Carole, "La quête identitaire et autonomiste des Autochtones», in Y. Boisvert, J. Hamel et M. Molgat (eds) : *Vivre la citoyenneté. Identité, appartenance et participation,* Montréal : Éditions Liber, Coll. Éthique Publique, 2000 at 109-118.

[2] Professor, INRS-Urbanisation, Culture et Société

[3] The Cree live in the James Bay area, which they call *Eeyou Istchee*. The Montagnais-Innus are found mainly on the North Shore. The Mohawks live in the south of the province. Abitibi-Témiscamingue and the Ottawa Valley are home to the Algonquins; and the Atikamekw live in the upper St. Maurice River area. The Huron-Wendats live at Wendake, near Québec City; the Abenakis live at Odanak, near Sorel; and land is reserved for the Malecites in the Lower St. Lawrence area near Rivière-du-Loup. The Naskapis live at Kawawachikamach, some 15 kilometres from the former mining town of Schefferville. The Micmacs live in

the Gaspé Peninsula.

[4] In a 1969 White Paper, the federal government announced a definitive solution to the "Indian problem". The government was facing growing demands from Aboriginal groups claiming rights to the lands where they were living in degrading socioeconomic conditions. Pressed to deal with a problem that negatively affected its image and proved the ineffectiveness of its policies and programs for Aboriginal peoples, the government proposed, among other things, to abolish the *Indian Act* and any special status for "Indians" in order to make them fully Canadian. The Indian chiefs of the time reacted strongly against the White Paper and responded by publishing the *Red Paper* in 1971. Despite the many negative aspects of the *Indian Act*, they did not want to give up their special status without obtaining guarantees in return and without engaging in negotiations on recognition of their rights (Vincent 1992).

[5] Ancestral rights are rights based on legal recognition of the occupation of land by Aboriginal peoples prior to the arrival of Europeans. The rights in question may pertain to land, but they can also apply to hunting or fishing activities if it can be proven that they were ancestral practices or customs (Dupuis 1997).

[6] In the wake of the *James Bay and Northern Québec Agreement*, the Naskapis, whose territory was also affected by the construction of the James Bay hydroelectric complex, signed the *Northeastern Québec Agreement* in 1978.

[7] The only exception to the rule is in the case of the *James Bay and Northern Québec Agreement* (as with the *Northeastern Québec Agreement*). These agreements have precedence over the *Indian Act*.

[8] For example, Aboriginal people won the right to vote in federal elections only in 1960, and not until 1969 in provincial elections.

Aboriginal Peoples' Right to Self-Government: A Phoenix that Will Rise from its Ashes

Alain Bissonnette[1]

This article argues that despite the failure of the Charlottetown Accord, Aboriginal peoples' right to self determination will continue to be discussed, negotiated and implemented under both domestic and international law. The first part of the article deals with the main provisions of the Charlottetown Accord and, in light of legal anthropology, explains the reasons for its rejection, in particular by a significant number of Aboriginal peoples. The second part describes the present state of international law with respect to the claims of Aboriginal peoples; it underlines the fact that the norms of international law draw upon a logic and symbolism which, from the perspective of culture, are not truly universal.

1. Introduction

The Charlottetown Accord[2] is dead; long live Aboriginal peoples' right to self-government! While it might bring a laugh, this declaration is not a joke. In fact, the *Constitution* of Canada perhaps already recognizes the right, at least implicitly.[3] In any case, it will continue to be discussed, negotiated and implemented. Thus, it would be useful to understand the reasons for the failure of the Charlottetown Accord and identify current trends in international law pertaining to Aboriginal rights.

2. The Failure of the Charlottetown Accord

Rejected by Canadians, the Charlottetown Accord was an interconnected set of provisions none of which could be isolated from the others without compromising the overall balance. Aboriginal people's inherent right to self-government was one of the key components. In Québec, a number of influential people criticized this aspect of the Accord. In particular, the Editor of *le Devoir* wrote that by acknowledging the right, the Charlottetown Accord was choosing separate development. The notion of separate development led her to an analogy with apartheid, and she argued that Aboriginal governments would be founded on a racial bases.[4]

Let us analyse the Accord again briefly to review its content and clarify the reasons for its failure.

2.1. The Content of the *Accord*

The Charlottetown Accord contained a number of provisions directly or indirectly concerning the rights of Aboriginal peoples. In addition to formal recognition of Aboriginal peoples' inherent right to self-government and a commitment to negotiate agreements with respect to the exercise of that right, the Accord included provisions designed to protect Aboriginal rights and traditions.

If the Accord had been adopted, a new section 35.1(1) would have been integrated into the *Constitution Act, 1982*:

> The Aboriginal peoples of Canada have the inherent right of self-government within Canada.

The term "inherent" was used to qualify the right to self-government. Thus, the right was considered to belong essentially to Aboriginal peoples, and to be an attribute from which they could not be separated. This qualification of the right was also echoed in the Canada clause, in which it was stipulated that all interpretations of the Canadian *Constitution* had to be consistent with various fundamental features, including:

> The Aboriginal peoples of Canada, being the first peoples to govern this land, have the right to promote their languages, cultures and traditions and to ensure the integrity of their societies, and their governments constitute one of the three orders of government in Canada.[5]

Recognition of Aboriginal governments as one of the three levels of government in Canada was also inscribed in a provision that would have been incorporated into a new section 35.1(2) of the *Constitution Act, 1982*. The provision would certainly have made it possible to avoid lumping Aboriginal governments together with municipalities, for example, or any other institution exercising power delegated by Parliament or the provincial legislatures. Unlike such governments, those of Aboriginal peoples could have claimed a form of real sovereignty under the Canadian *Constitution*.[6]

However, the Accord did not specify the scope of the probable sovereignty of Aboriginal governments. Indeed, with respect to Aboriginal self-government, there was no clearly identified distribution of jurisdictions between the three levels of government in Canada. Nonetheless, there were provisions for three things. First, no later amendment pertaining to the distribution of jurisdictions between the federal and provincial levels could infringe on the rights or freedoms of Aboriginal peoples.[7] Second, the context in which the inherent right to self-government could be exercised was specified:

> The exercise of the right referred to in subsection (1) includes the authority of duly constituted legislative bodies of the Aboriginal peoples, each within its own jurisdiction, (a) to safeguard and develop their languages,

cultures, economies, identities, institutions and traditions, and (b) to develop, maintain and strengthen their relationship with their lands, waters and environment, so as to determine and control their development as peoples according to their own values and priorities and to ensure the integrity of their societies.[8]

Third, the legislative bodies of Aboriginal peoples would have been able to set aside the laws of the other governments within their own jurisdiction if they adopted legislation to that effect.[9]

The Accord did not define a "duly constituted" Aboriginal legislative body or the precise scope of its jurisdiction. One could assume that every Aboriginal people could, in virtue of its inherent right to self-government, create its own style of legislative body in compliance with procedures that ensure that the will of its members is expressed. The scope of the jurisdiction of the legislative body would probably be a function of the issue and the specific needs of the group in question since the relevant constitutional provision indicated that such peoples had to be able to "determine and control their development" and "ensure the integrity of their societies".

According to this analysis of the context statement included in the Accord, it would not have been absolutely necessary for agreements to be concluded with the other governments in order to identify legislative bodies and set out their jurisdictions. However, this would certainly have been useful, if only to avoid interminable debates before the courts. Moreover, the Accord contained a formal commitment to negotiate the implementation of the right to self-government in good faith:

> The government of Canada, the provincial and territorial governments and the Aboriginal peoples of Canada, including the Indian, Inuit and Métis peoples of Canada, in the various regions and communities shall negotiate in good faith the implementation of the right of self-government, including issues of jurisdiction, lands and resources, and economic and fiscal arrangements, with the objective of concluding agreements elaborating relationships between governments of Aboriginal peoples and the government of Canada and provincial or territorial governments.[10]

This constitutional provision would have guaranteed Aboriginal peoples that the agenda for negotiations would include all of the issues that are essential to the notion of self-government: legislative jurisdiction, land and resources, and economic and fiscal arrangements. The Accord also provided that only the representatives of governments of the Aboriginal peoples in question could have initiated such negotiations.[11] Thus, no Aboriginal community could have been obliged to do so. The five-year period of grace before it would have been possible to invoke the inherent right to self-government before the courts was certainly intended to incite the parties to engage in negotiations during that time.[12] However, even after the five years, a court seized with an issue concerning the scope of the inherent right to self-government or a claim of such a right would have had to examine the parties' efforts to resolve the dispute. Among other things, the court would have been able to "order the parties to take such steps as may be appropriate in the circumstances to effect a negotiated resolution".[13]

The Accord also made provisions for cases in which the negotiations resulted in the creation of Treaty rights:

> Where an agreement negotiated under this section (a) is set out in a treaty or land claims agreement, or in an amendment to a treaty including a land claims agreement, or (b) contains a declaration that the rights of the Aboriginal peoples set out in the agreement are treaty rights, the rights of the Aboriginal peoples set out in the agreement are treaty rights under subsection 35 (1).[14]

The desire to be able to consider rights related to the exercise of the right to self-government as Treaty rights can of course be explained by the history of relations between Aboriginal peoples and representatives of the Crown. However, it can also be explained by the constitutional status accorded to these rights, at least since 1982. Finally, note that the specific purpose of a number of provisions in the Accord was also to protect those rights.[15]

The following is a summary of the key provisions concerning Aboriginal self-government in the Accord. Now, let us try to identify the reasons why not only the Canadian electorate as a whole but also a large percentage of the people who claim to belong to an Aboriginal nation finally spoke against adopting the Accord.

2.2. The Reasons for its Failure

We propose two hypotheses to explain the rejection of the Accord by a large proportion of the Aboriginal population. The first is that Aboriginal peoples refer to their own legal notions when they seek to have their rights recognized by Canada. The second is that many people of Aboriginal origin fear that possible Aboriginal governments would ride roughshod over their individual rights. These two apparently contradictory hypotheses can both be verified, but within different parts of the Aboriginal population.

With respect to legal notions specific to Aboriginal peoples, or at least those that are different from those of Western legal discourse, note simply that if we look at world history, it is clear that there have been and still are many different political and legal systems. Even when a political and legal system is used in many different places in the world, the ways that state structures are employed varies considerably depending on the basic philosophy and specific objectives of the stakeholders. For example, the state organization of power is not exactly the same under a communist regime and under a regime that takes Islam as a general interpretation of the world. Moreover, within states, various semi-autonomous groups use the state's political and legal institutions and mechanisms to achieve their own goals, even though such institutions and mechanisms are designed to regulate relations within the group and in society as a whole.

This leads us to reflect on how we should interpret such diversity. Indeed, diversity and difference can themselves be interpreted in many different ways. Here, we will evoke only one possibility: an approach that has been developed over the last 20 years by researchers at the *Laboratoire d'anthropologie juridique* in Paris. According to the *Laboratoire*'s researchers, law should not be approached as a concept but as a phenomenon.[16] Thus, instead of trying to define what law is, we should study juridicization phenomena in various societies, and ethnography, ethnology and anthropology of law are all steps in this study. Ethnography entails gathering and describing data that a society defines as pertaining to law at the levels of discourse, practices and concepts. Ethnology of law is based on interpretation of the articulations that link these three levels with the general functioning of the society in question. Finally, anthropology of law consists in trying to discover the general structures of human culture in relation to juridicization phenomena.

Anthropologists of law thus look at law as a juridicization phenomenon, rather than as a concept. For them, law is less a specific type of social relation than a specific description that each society chooses to give to certain social relations. In other words, while legal facts are social facts, not all social facts are legal facts. Social facts become legal only by passing through a specific social filter or control designed to ensure the cohesion and perpetuation of the group in question. From this point of view, law is not a set of specific rules, but an inter-normative process:

$$\text{Social Facts } X \ \frac{\text{Social Control}}{\text{Reproduction of the Group}} = \text{Legal Facts}$$

Of course, social facts can vary over time within a society. Likewise, the kind of control can also vary, as can what a semi-autonomous group considers necessary for its cohesion and perpetuation. Naturally, what a society considers to be legal facts will vary in consequence.

Moreover, different societies are based on very different principles. While there is a risk of caricature, it is possible to suggest a typology. Some societies reject social divisions and have a generalizing structure in which the various aspects of social life are based on a consistent whole (e.g., hunter-gatherer societies in which there is no specialization of power and in which the interpretation of the world is often based on the group's own mythology). Other societies recognize social divisions, but ensure cohesion by seeing the differences as necessary complementarity. Finally, other societies, in which there are marked differences and extreme social division, nonetheless define themselves as egalitarian and united. (In such societies, the state most often incarnates unity despite disparities, and ensures equality in some areas despite social divisions.)[17]

361

Once more, a society's basic foundations are based on its specific vision of itself and the world, and can give rise to a very wide variety of juridicization phenomena because the foundations determine how the society handles changes, be they technological, political or philosophical. In accordance with its basic principles, every society uses a specific type of social control and will define what is essential to its cohesion and perpetuation in its own way. Thus, similar changes can result in the juridicization of very different social facts, among other things because not only do founding systems vary, but so does the specific vision that each society has of itself and the world.

We now have some fundamental concepts in mind: the phenomena of internormativity, different basic systems, and different ways of thinking. Now, let us look at the levels of observation chosen by researchers linked with the *Laboratoire d'anthropologie juridique* in Paris. There are three: discourse, practices and ideas. Discourse includes explicit written and verbal statements, such as legislation, codes, customs, speeches, judgments and maxims. In general, in the West, lawyers limit their analysis to such discourse, preferably written. However, the practices and actions of individuals and groups are often different from the norms expressed in legal discourse. Thus, not only discourse has to be taken into account, but also practices. Sometimes practices predetermine discourse, which is another reason why they are important. Stakeholders use ideas, beliefs and symbolic constructions to give meaning to their actions and discourse. Note that there are generally many different ideas in societies and that it is between the various ideas that are located the issues that determine what should or should not be judicialized in the society.

Thus, we now have some basic concepts and methodological guidelines that we can use to analyse reality. Let us look at a few categories of legal systems analysed from a dynamic perspective. The examples come from the specific context of contemporary Africa, which has been marked by both colonization and decolonization.

Étienne LeRoy and Mamadou Wane suggest the following typology:[18]

> A system marked by traditional rights practiced by an Aboriginal people prior to contact with Europeans and inspired by the vision of that Aboriginal people. Colonization brought with it economic changes, migrations of certain strata of the population, and religious and cultural conversions. Little by little, this neutralized the original system.
>
> A system marked by customary rights, which appear during the period of colonial administration, and in which customs are recorded and used in a foreign system, thereby leading to a distortion of traditional rights and marginalization of Aboriginal power. It should be noted that the colonial administrators themselves often interpret Aboriginal customs, and that new forms of decision-making and social control are introduced into Aboriginal practices. Consequently, this period often

coincides with a gradual but increasing absorption of traditional rights by the foreign system.

A system marked by local laws, in other words, "a legal system appearing as the influence of the state and its administrative apparatus grow, and essentially formed and legitimized by the state, while the mode of operation is more or less left up to local authorities, in accordance with true administrative decentralization."[19] The system is designed by the state, but the foreign legal categories can be reinterpreted in light of Aboriginal legal concepts. Local laws are thus ambiguous because the dominated group intervenes directly to adapt the system to its own needs, but the dominators continue to maintain or increase their control over the Aboriginal society.

A system characterized by popular law, in which laws are formed outside of state structures. It should be noted that the norms are not generally traditional, but rather new creations in which traditional laws are reinterpreted in a completely new context.

Clearly, the main purpose of this typology is simply to help think about and better understand social reality. In this respect, according to Étienne LeRoy, the ambitions of anthropologists of law force them to approach the subject of their research like archaeologists the site of Troy: by stratigraphy. "Under the surface there may be a number of deep layers. We have to explain the relationships between the layers in different sites and the reasons why they have accumulated."[20] Moreover, anthropologists of law have to "apply the rigor of a scientist to the specific vision of each social stakeholder."[21]

How can this way of approaching legal phenomena help us to identify the reasons for the failure of the Charlottetown Accord? This approach at least allows us to see that the mechanisms for recognizing and implementing Aboriginal self-government cannot be reduced to the formulas produced by the political representatives who negotiated the Accord. Indeed, the representatives may have been trying to create a new legal regime within Canadian constitutional law that would have made it possible to reinterpret the dominant legal categories in light of Aboriginal legal notions. The attempt was certainly commendable, but as LeRoy and Wane's typology shows, this type of regime remains self-contradictory in that it allows Aboriginals to adapt the dominant legal system but does not exempt them from its control, particularly when the fundamental values of Canadian society are in question. For example, the Accord allowed federal and provincial governments to challenge the laws of Aboriginal peoples and any Aboriginal exercise of the inherent right to self-government if considered incompatible with federal and provincial legislation essential to maintenance of peace, order and good government in Canada.

No aboriginal law or any other exercise of the inherent right of self-government under section 35.1 may be inconsistent with federal or provincial laws that are essential to the preservation of peace, order and good government in Canada. [22]

This approach also shows that within Aboriginal populations, various stakeholders may invoke different lines of reasoning. The most obvious example is of course that of the Mohawks, who constantly affirm their sovereignty but do not seek formal recognition from the Government of Canada. Canadian Aboriginals probably cannot claim that their traditional rights have survived until today in the same form as before the Europeans arrived. However, a large proportion of them reject the approach recommended by the artisans of the Accord, and controversy has arisen among such Aboriginal critics over how state apparatus should be related to local authority.

Finally, there are also major disagreements among people who accept the idea of a state regime permitting local adaptation. There are two things at stake for those who hold this point of view: a position of intermediate authority between the state and local power, and recourse to human rights when faced with the right to self-government, particularly when those who exercise the right invoke their people's traditions. Of course, this pertains to the debates concerning application of the *Canadian Charter of Rights and Freedoms* to Aboriginal peoples' inherent right to self-government. It illustrates the opposition between people who are basically in favour of local adaptation of the Canadian constitutional regime, but do not agree on the exact degree of adaptation.

The proposed section 32(1)(c) of the *Constitution Act, 1982* stipulated that the *Canadian Charter of Rights and Freedoms* would apply to the governments of the Aboriginal peoples of Canada:

> This Charter applies...to all legislative bodies and governments of the Aboriginal peoples of Canada in respect of all matters within the authority of their respective legislative bodies.

The *Accord* also contained a series of provisions designed to protect Aboriginal peoples. For example, there was a protective clause concerning the freedom of movement and establishment guaranteed in sections 6(2) and 6(3) of the *Canadian Charter of Rights and Freedoms*. The clause, which would have become the new section 35.5(1) of the *Constitution Act, 1982*, stipulated:

> Subsections 6(2) and (3) of the Canadian Charter of Rights and Freedoms do not preclude a legislative body or government of the Aboriginal peoples of Canada from exercising authority pursuant to this Part through affirmative action measures that have as their object the amelioration of conditions of individuals or groups who are socially or economically disadvantaged or the protection and advancement of aboriginal languages and cultures.

A general Notwithstanding Clause was also included in what would have become the new section 25 of the *Constitution Act, 1982*. It would have ensured that the rights and freedoms guaranteed by the *Canadian Charter of Rights and Freedoms* could not infringe on the ancestral or treaty rights of Aboriginal peoples, or on their rights and freedoms "relating to the exercise or protection of their languages, cultures or traditions." According to a number of analysts, this provision was compatible with the guarantee of equal rights for people of both sexes. The guarantee of equal rights for both sexes of Aboriginal persons was inscribed in the *Constitution* of Canada in 1983, when section 35(4) was added to Part II of the *Constitution Act, 1982*. The section provides that:

> Notwithstanding any other provision of this Act, the aboriginal and treaty rights referred to in subsection (1) are guaranteed equally to male and female persons.

With the Charlottetown Accord, the constitutional guarantee of equal rights for both sexes would have remained in effect and continued to apply to all of the *Constitution Act, 1982*, including the rights included in the *Canadian Charter of Rights and Freedoms*. The legal text of the Accord clarified this affirmation by inscribing the rule in a new provision that read as follows:

> Notwithstanding any other provision of this Act, the rights of the Aboriginal peoples of Canada referred to in this Part are guaranteed equally to male and female persons.[23]

Thus, according to the Accord, all ancestral and treaty rights, including the inherent right to self-government, would be subject to the guarantee of equal rights for male and female persons. Aboriginal governments would have been able to use the notwithstanding clause[24] to legislate that a law or provision applied despite section 2 and sections 7 to 15 of the *Canadian Charter of Rights and Freedoms*, but the clause could not have been used to violate the guarantee of equal rights for men and women.

Application of the *Canadian Charter of Rights and Freedoms* to Aboriginal governments was subject to the Canada clause and in particular to the fact that, according to that provision, the Aboriginal peoples of Canada have the right to promote their languages, cultures and traditions. In order to protect their identity and promote their cultural development, Aboriginal peoples probably would have had to weigh their right to promote their cultures and traditions against the guarantee of equal rights for men and women in every specific case.

Finally, while the provisions on the right to vote and run in legislative elections in the *Canadian Charter of Rights and Freedoms* did not apply to the legislative bodies of Aboriginal peoples, it would probably not have been possible for them to prohibit women from voting in an election. To do so would be a violation of the guarantee of equal rights for men and women that is consecrated in sections 35.7 and 28 of the *Constitution Act, 1982*.

A number of representatives of Aboriginal women rejected the Accord because they thought it would have made it possible to violate human rights. A number of representatives of Aboriginal associations rejected the Accord because they considered that it would have made it possible to violate their right to self-government. The compromise between these two extremes, which was in fact contained in the Accord itself, did not manage to rally the support of enough people.

We have suggested two hypotheses to explain why the Accord failed. There are probably others that should also be verified. While constitutional debates have been on hold in Canada for some time, we should not be led to believe that all discussion on the right to self-government is now prohibited. On one hand, it is absolutely certain that Aboriginal peoples will try to implement this right by various means. On the other hand, since the United Nations declared 1995-2004 the International Decade of the World's Indigenous People (followed by a Second International Decade, authorized in December of 2004[25]), we should anticipate that discussions on this topic will continue with even more intensity. Thus, it is in our interest to be informed about current trends in international law in this area.

3. Aboriginal Self-government in Light of Human and Peoples Rights

In this part, we will begin by trying to describe the notion of Aboriginal self-government in relation to human and peoples' rights in general, and then we will try to identify the limits of those rights when they are placed in a context of cultural diversity.[26]

3.1. A Review of the Situation

How is the notion of Aboriginal self-government defined if human and peoples' rights are taken as a starting point? We will base our answer to this question on two sources. The first is theoretical and made up of articles written by eminent theorists on international relations. The second is normative, and is in fact contained in the *Indigenous and Tribal Peoples Convention* adopted by the International Labour Organization in 1989.[27]

In his discussion of the relationship between minority, peoples' and human rights, Ian Brownie[28] says that the rights of minorities and peoples are human rights and that, while the latter have long been oriented towards individual rights alone, over time it has become apparent that respecting individual rights does not provide sufficient protection for group rights. Consequently, we have begun discussing the rights of groups, such as minorities and peoples, and, according to Brownie, we have come to accept the idea that every community with a distinct nature has the right to see its distinctiveness reflected in the institutions by which it is governed. Moreover, again according to Brownie, peoples can now exercise their rights to self-determination without having to establish a new state because they can simply use a form of self-government that he considers satisfactory.

When we try to apply these ideas to the specific situation of Aboriginal peoples, one of the questions that arises is whether implementing self-government, in particular by the creation or recognition of their own governments, would be discriminatory. This is a fundamental issue because human rights emphasize the right to equality not only between peoples but also between individuals. If a given state were to recognize Aboriginal self-government or create mechanisms promoting such self-determination, would it not be using racial criteria to identify different categories of citizens? Would it not at least lead to unequal treatment of Aboriginal individuals and other citizens?

According to Brownie, international human and peoples' rights law makes it possible to protect the cultural identity of a group without using discriminatory measures. He is of the opinion that racial criteria can be avoided by basing the distinction on the history and culture of Aboriginal peoples, and the fact that according to their own traditions they used and occupied a specific area where they were governed in their own way. He even adds that, supposing that such criteria could be employed, the measures implemented cannot be considered discriminatory if they are linked to objective facts, target a reasonable goal and infringe on the rights of other citizens as little as possible. In the case of Aboriginal peoples, the objective facts are their autonomy, and occupation of land that is now under state jurisdiction. A reasonable objective would surely be to give them appropriate protection against assimilation and greater equality with respect to other citizens, since these populations have hardly ever been represented in the state. Finally, the means of achieving these ends while infringing as little as possible on the rights of other citizens is probably to promote negotiations that take the interests of every party into account in order to come to compromises that are fair and equitable for all.

Assuming that it is possible to adopt non-discriminatory measures promoting the self-government of Aboriginal peoples, let us see what they might look like.

According to Richard Falk,[29] the measures should enable Aboriginal peoples to protect and regulate their communal life, create national and international support networks and promote human and peoples rights in direct reference to their specific situation. The measures should also allow Aboriginal peoples to lodge complaints and make claims in international forums, protect their special relationship with the land, and obtain compensation in the form of new lands and resources, and special means for promoting economic, social and cultural development. Finally, the measures should provide for mechanisms to resolve disputes arising out of conflicts among the bodies and pertaining to the rights of the various groups under the jurisdiction of the state in question. According to Falk, all of these features should be implemented in collaboration with the main stakeholders.

We believe that the *Indigenous and Tribal Peoples Convention* has created a legal regime specific to Aboriginal peoples that meets most of Falk's requirements but at the same time complies with the conditions that prevent it from being considered discriminatory.

First, let us see how it meets Falk's requirements. It gives the stakeholders the right "to exercise control, to the extent possible, over their own economic, social and cultural development", "to decide their own priorities for the process of development" when there are consequences for their way of life, and to "participate in the formulation, implementation and evaluation of plans and programmes for national and regional development which may affect them directly".[30] It also gives Indigenous and Tribal peoples the "right to retain their own customs and institutions, where these are not incompatible with fundamental rights defined by the national legal system and with internationally recognised human rights".[31] Next, it requires states to facilitate contact and cooperation among Indigenous and Tribal peoples.[32] Indeed, its primary objective is to enable such peoples to "enjoy the full measure of human rights and fundamental freedoms without hindrance or discrimination"[33] through two types of measures: measures ensuring that the peoples have "an equal footing from the rights and opportunities which national laws and regulations grant to other members of the population",[34] and special measures adopted as required for "safeguarding the persons, institutions, property, labour, cultures and environment of the peoples concerned".[35]

Naturally, the states that ratify the *Convention* will be accountable for how they implement it.[36] They will also have to take into account the special relationship such peoples have to their land, give them the property rights to and possession of the land they occupy,[37] and grant them the right to participate in the use, management and conservation of the natural resources on their lands.[38] The states will also have to create appropriate procedures within their national legal systems to be able to settle the land claims of these peoples.[39] Moreover, they will have to ensure the "full realisation of the social, economic and cultural rights of these peoples" while respecting their specific identity.[40] Finally, the states that ratify the *Convention* will be responsible for "developing, with the participation of the peoples concerned, co-ordinated and systematic action to protect the rights of these peoples and to guarantee respect for their integrity".[41]

The list probably seems rather long, but it shows that all of the characteristics suggested by Falk are indeed contained in this legal regime specific to Aboriginal peoples.

Now, let us see why the measures permitted by *ILO Convention No. 169* run little risk of being judged discriminatory. First, the very definition of the peoples in question includes no racial criterion. Instead, it is based on their specific history, which is an aspect that is often also reflected in their legal status within states, and on their specific social, cultural and economic conditions.[42] Next, it explicitly targets a reasonable goal, namely to ensure that the members of such peoples have full equality within states where they are only very inadequately represented, and also to protect them from cultural assimilation. Finally, *Convention No. 169* explicitly stipulates that the "nature and scope of the measures to be taken to give effect to this Convention shall be determined in a flexible manner, having regard to the conditions characteristic of each country".[43]

Naturally, one might think that this last provision is designed mainly to give states enough leeway to persuade them to adhere to the *Convention*. However, one might also see in it a concern (if not a will) to ensure that state measures really favour Indigenous and Tribal peoples but at the same time infringe as little as possible on the rights of other citizens. In any case, the general inspiration for the *Convention* is human rights and fundamental freedoms, and the *Convention's* mechanisms for protecting Indigenous and Tribal peoples often take the form of legislation. Thus, the judges of the state's legal system rule on the most serious conflicts, and there is little doubt that they will conscientiously take the rights of the stakeholders and other citizens into account.

Far from promoting reprehensible discrimination, the ILO's *Indigenous and Tribal Peoples Convention* will establish what is sometimes called the new concept of human and peoples' rights. Indeed, is its purpose not to protect both individuals and groups, not only through law applicable to all, but also by making it possible to avoid uniformity when necessary? This objective and the means for attaining it are part of the struggle for access to equality, and are based essentially on recognition of a fundamental human fact: cultural diversity.

In the general field of human and peoples' rights, *Convention No. 169* is certainly a great achievement. However, we cannot spend too much time celebrating because when we examine it from the point of view of cultural diversity, this admirable accomplishment has clear limitations.

3.2. Unavoidable Cultural Diversity

Now we would like to quickly sketch out why use of the *Indigenous and Tribal Peoples Convention* is limited. We will begin by situating human and peoples' rights with respect to other legal constraints, and then by identifying some of the issues flowing from the problems addressed by *Convention No. 169*.

When we examine human and peoples' rights in relation to other legal constraints, we need simply note the historical and cultural dimensions of this special conception of the relationships that should be established between the state and individuals. The logic and mythology of human and peoples' rights arose in the West, and the areas where such rights are really implemented today are limited to North America, Europe, Japan and Australia. Many claim that these rights have universal scope that goes beyond the culture that gave birth to them, but it remains that in practice, many of the world's peoples, including some in North America and Australia, do not identify themselves with the language and values conveyed by human rights. Such peoples have their own ideas and languages for speaking of the sharing and exercise of power.[44]

This said, the very great merit of *ILO Convention No. 169* is that it has made a fundamental contribution to the Western human rights tradition: it has added a community-based aspect.[45] While human rights instruments are generally designed to regulate the relationship between state power and individuals taken in isolation, the *Convention* introduces the community between these two, at least with re-spect to Indigenous and Tribal peoples. The *Convention* calls on the community to participate in implementation of the measures permitted under its provisions. If such participation is really ensured, we can already predict that representatives of Indigenous and Tribal peoples will use the protection they are offered to reassert their own concepts about what is just, necessary and reasonable.

However, as we said above, *Convention No. 169* gives states a lot of discretion as to the nature and scope of the measures that they are required to take. In short, *Convention No. 169* institutes a difficult situation in which different stakeholders, sometimes with conflicting ideas, seek to impose their own views and turn the situation to their own interest. This explains the stakes that every party has in the issues raised by the *Convention*.

For example, let us consider recognition of the right to Indigenous and Tribal self-government. *Convention No. 169* gives Indigenous and Tribal peoples the "right to retain their own customs and institutions", but it adds "where these are not incompatible with fundamental rights defined by the national legal system and with internationally recognised human rights".[46] Moreover, it requires that, when necessary, procedures be established to "resolve conflicts which may arise in the application of this principle".[47] This shows very clearly that the customs and insti-tutions of Indigenous and Aboriginal peoples are surrounded by two systems that remain, at least partially, foreign to them. Indeed, neither national legal systems nor international human and peoples' rights have fully acknowledged the ideas, discourse and practices that such peoples consider essential to the existence and maintenance of their identity.[48]

It seems clear that one of the stakes underlying the whole issue of Aboriginal self-government is inscribed in the interpretations of Aboriginal institutions that will be employed to resolve disputes arising over compatibility with rights considered fundamental in the Western tradition. The crucial factors include not only the cri-teria that will guide the interpretations, but also the choice of interpreters. In other words, to what extent will cultural diversity really be taken into account?

Another issue underlying recognition of Aboriginal peoples' right to self-gov-ernment seems even more fundamental. In Canada at least, Aboriginal peoples seek not only to have the state respect the rights that it recognizes or that the international community calls on it to recognize, but also to assert and exercise their own sovereignty. In other words, they want to define the nature and scope of their rights themselves in reference to their own traditions. However, generally, these traditions are completely outside of the discourse and logic of the state legal regime, even when the latter claims to respect human rights and fundamental freedoms. The fact that Aboriginal traditions share only part of the heritage of Western civilization does not mean that they are absolutely incompatible with our conception of human and peoples' rights. Moreover, by lifting the veil from this fact, which is too often obscured, we can see that the real debate, which causes many representatives of Aboriginal peoples to find themselves in conflict with government leaders, concerns effective control not only of the symbols and rules of interpretation, but also of power and the various resources that enable one to exercise it effectively.

Conflicts over control of such power can lead to sudden spikes of violence. In Québec, we are well aware of this, for the summer of 1990 was an unpleasant eye-opener. Of course, while it is fairly easy to accept that conflict is sometimes beneficial in a society, violence has to be limited as much as possible. How can this be done in the special case of the problems surrounding relations with Aboriginal communities? The answer probably lies in creating the possibility of intercultural dialogue everywhere in order to design new mechanisms for reconciling the parties and to foster the emergence of new shared legitimacy.

Major discussions on these issues are underway in the Working Group on Indigenous Populations. Created in 1982[49] following a recommendation by José R. Martinez Cobo in his *Study of the Problem of Discrimination Against Indigenous Populations*,[50] the Working Group is composed of five people representing the five major regions of the world. It meets for two weeks every year, generally at the end of July at the *Palais des Nations* in Geneva. Representatives of Aboriginal peoples are invited to every Working Group session so that they can report on the situation of Aboriginal peoples' rights in the world and contribute to the preparation of a draft *Universal Declaration of Indigenous Rights*. Around 500 people participate in Working Group sessions every year. Participants include representatives of states, United Nations-accredited non-governmental organizations and many Aboriginal organizations. In 1993, the International Year of the World's Indigenous People, Irene Erika Daes, Chairperson of the Working Group, submitted a draft *Universal Declaration of Indigenous Rights* to the highest authorities at the United Nations, including the General Assembly. This draft *Declaration* has been the subject of intense negotiations in intervening years. As we now enter the Second International Decade of the World's Indigenous People, the hope remains that this document will make its way to the General Assembly for adoption.[51] Hopefully, work of the recently established UN Permanent Forum on Indigenous Issues will also push forward this agenda.[52]

Let us briefly review the topics currently covered by the draft *Universal Declaration of Indigenous Rights*:

- Aboriginal peoples' right to self-determination;
- Their right to be protected against ethnocide;
- Their individual and collective rights to own, possess and use land and resources that they traditionally occupy and use;
- Their right to not have their lands taken from them without their free, informed consent in an agreement or treaty;
- Their right to claim both the surface and underground resources of their land, and their right to equitable compensation when such resources have been confiscated without their permission;

- Through representatives that they themselves have chosen, their right to participate fully in state government, and the making and implementation of decisions concerning all national and international issues that could change their lives and destiny;
- Their collective right to self-government with respect to their own internal and local affairs;
- Their right to maintain and develop cooperative cultural, social and commercial relationships with other Aboriginal peoples outside of state borders, and the obligation for the states concerned to adopt measures facilitating such contacts;
- Their right to access acceptable and equitable procedures to resolve disputes arising with states; depending on the case, the procedures may include negotiation, mediation, arbitration, national court procedures and regional and international mechanisms for examining complaints related to human rights.[53]

The draft *Declaration* is not yet an international legal instrument, but it certainly shows that the participants in the United Nations Working Group on Indigenous Populations are trying to establish a new order. The draft *Declaration's* keystone is a sincere hope for and real faith in human and peoples' rights. The *Declaration* is based on three ideas: first, the need to preserve the cultural identity of these peoples; next, the adoption of legal procedures to give such groups access to equality, in other words, normative dualism; and finally, the concrete implementation of the first two ideas by the conclusion of mutually acceptable agreements between states and these peoples.

Naturally, he who speaks of cultural identity runs a strong risk of uttering clichés and even stereotypes with little relation to reality. Statism has no place here. The rules of social and cultural dynamics are very often opaque to the main actors and stakeholders. In any case, Aboriginal peoples everywhere in the world are the repositories of traditions, languages and values that are different from those of the states by which they are governed. From generation to generation, despite the changes that have occurred or that are desired, Aboriginal peoples maintain a similar attitude towards certain activities that are considered traditional, continue to use their mother tongue along with other languages and still seek alliances based on their own traditions. Moreover, Aboriginal peoples, like any other group, try to control certain aspects that they believe have the greatest influence over their cultural identity. These aspects include land and land management, economic and political structures, and the legal system. Aboriginal peoples claim a form of autonomy in these areas based on their own ideas about development. Some see this as simply a reproduction of the reserve system, but in fact it is actually a better way to achieve equality through dual norms. In other words, the special treatment demanded by Aboriginal peoples should in no way prevent access to all of the rights, resources and institutions of the dominant society. This concept of duality has been widely employed in the Third World on the international scene and by women's groups and stigmatized minorities in our own society at the national level.[54] Aboriginal peoples use it likewise, and rightly.

Clearly, these two principles have to be made concrete someday if we really want to achieve results. Right or wrong, Aboriginal peoples favour signing specific agreements with states on these issues. Naturally, it is possible to object that consecrating a right in a piece of legislation or constitutional text determines only some of the social practices of a given group. However, in their situation, the absence of such norms is even more dangerous in that the dominant trend is very obviously to their disadvantage. In other words, the mutually acceptable agreements signed with states are only a necessary but not sufficient preliminary. The path that remains to be mapped and followed will depend not only on texts, but also on the practices of the parties.

Until it becomes concrete in a veritable international agreement that states can ratify, the draft *Universal Declaration of Indigenous Rights* will have no legal value in the classical sense. However, as we have seen in the case of international development law, a norm that cannot be enforced can still be effective. Moreover, representatives of Aboriginal peoples already refer to the draft *Declaration* when negotiating with states and when judging the behaviour of the same states in the international forum. One thing is certain: currently, representatives of Aboriginal peoples and states engage in dialogue on the international scene, where belief persists that in the medium term there will be both new means of respecting both the rights of Aboriginal peoples and human rights, and new legitimacy based on respect for diversity. Given this, there is no doubt that the legendary phoenix will rise again from its ashes.

---

[1] 1992 Holder of the Gordon F. Henderson Chair in Human Rights, Human Rights Research and Education Centre, University of Ottawa

[2] In order to analyse the *Accord*, which Canadian voters finally rejected, we will refer to its legal text and the articles that, had they been adopted, would have been incorporated into either the *Constitution Act, 1867* or the *Constitution Act, 1982.*

[3] See B. Slattery, "First Nations and the Constitution: A Question of Trust", (1992) 71 *Canadian Bar Review* at 261–293.

[4] L. Bissonnette, "Le tabou de Charlottetown", *Le Devoir*, Montréal, October 13, 1992 at A-10.

[5] This would have been incorporated into a new article 2(1) of the *Constitution Act, 1867*. A number of analysts pointed out that there were differences between the French and English versions of the proposed text. While the English text used the present participle and portrayed Aboriginal peoples as the first to govern the land: "...the Aboriginal peoples of Canada, *being* the first peoples to govern this land..."; the French version instead used the past tense and omitted the reference to the status of the peoples: "...les peuples autochtones du Canada, qui ont été les premiers gouvernants du territoire..."

[6] It should be noted that the vocabulary currently used by the political representatives of Canadian Aboriginal peoples refers to US law, in which it is recognized that American Indian nations have inherent sovereignty. See, among others, C. F. Wilkinson, *American Indians, Time and Law: Native Societies in a Modern Constitutional Society,* New Haven: Yale University Press, 1987.

[7] This would have been incorporated into a new section 127 of the *Constitution Act, 1867*.

[8] This would have been incorporated into a new section 35.1(3) of the *Constitution Act, 1982*.

[9] This would have been incorporated into a new section 35.4(1) of the *Constitution Act, 1982*.

[10] This would have been incorporated into a new section 35.2(1) of the *Constitution Act, 1982*.

[11] This was provided for in what would have been the new section 35.2(2) of the *Constitution Act, 1982*.

[12] The corresponding provision would have been incorporated into a new section 35.3(1) of the *Constitution Act, 1982*.

[13] This was according to what would have been the new section 35.1(4) of the *Constitution Act, 1982*.

[14] This would have been incorporated into a new section 35.2(6) of the *Constitution Act, 1982*.

[15] The *Accord* included a number of provisions designed to protect ancestral and treaty rights from effects flowing from new constitutional provisions. For example, the *Accord* included new sections 2(3) and 2(4), and a new section 127, which would have been incorporated into the *Constitution Act, 1867*, and new sections 25, 35.1(5), 35.2(7), 35.8 and 45.1, which would have been incorporated into the *Constitution Act, 1982*.

[16] Here we are inspired directly by the pages devoted to this topic in N. Rouland, *Anthropologie juridique*, Paris: Presses universitaires de France, 1988 at 121–151 [*Rouland 1988*]. See also Laboratoire d'anthropologie juridique de Paris, *Recherches-Publications 1977–1982*; and N. Rouland, *Aux confins du droit: anthropologie juridique de la modernité*, Paris: Éditions Odile Jacob, 1991. [Rouland 1991]

[17] An important methodological remark is required here: "As soon as the basic values diverge…or contradict one another…, observers have to situate themselves in several *topoï* (i.e., locations of different visions of the world), each with its own logic, and the observers have to describe what the *topoï* have in common in language that has its own logic but without destroying the logic of each specific law." É. LeRoy, "Juristique et anthropologie: un pari sur l'avenir", (1990) 29 *Journal of Legal Pluralism* 5–21 at 11 [our translation] [*LeRoy*].

[18] É. LeRoy and M. Wane, "La formation des droits non-étatiques", in *Encyclopédie juridique de l'Afrique*, Vol. 1, Dakar: Nouvelles Éditions africaines, 1982 at 353–391.

[19] É. LeRoy, quoted in *Rouland 1988, supra*, note 16 at 365 [our translation].

[20] *LeRoy, supra* note 17 at 16 [our translation].

[21] *Ibid.*, at 18 [our translation].

[22] This would have been incorporated into a new article 35.4(2) of the *Constitution Act, 1982*.

[23] This would have been incorporated into a new section 35.7 of the *Constitution Act, 1982*.

[24] This would have become the new section 33.1 of the *Constitution Act, 1982*.

[25] Resolution Adopted by the General Assembly (59/174): *Second International Decade of the World's Indigenous People*.

[26] The analyses that made it possible to write this part were originally performed for the Royal Commission on Aboriginal Peoples, to which we submitted a study entitled *Les droits des peuples autochtones: d'hier à demain* in June 1992. We would like to thank the Commission for allowing us to use the analyses here.

[27] The *Convention*, which is generally known as *ILO Convention No. 169*, was adopted with the collaboration of the UN, FAO, WHO, Inter-American Indigenous Institute and UNESCO. As set out in its Article 38, the *Convention* came into effect in 1991, one year after two members of the ILO ratified it (Norway on June 19, 1990, and Mexico on September 15, 1990). Two other countries have also ratified it since then: Columbia (August 7, 1991) and Bolivia (December 11, 1991).

[28] See I. Brownie, "The Rights of Peoples in Modern International Law" in J. Crawford, Ed., *The Rights of Peoples*, Oxford: Clarendon Press, 1988 at 1–16. (Mr. Brownie is Professor of International Public Law at Oxford University.)

[29] See R. Falk, "The Rights of Peoples (In Particular Indigenous Peoples)" in J. Crawford, Ed., *Ibid.*, at 17–37. (Mr. Falk is Professor of International Public Law at Princeton University.)

[30] See Article 7.1 of the *Convention*.

[31] See Article 8.2 of the *Convention*.

[32] See Article 32 of the *Convention*.

[33] See Article 3 of the *Convention*.

[34] See Article 2.2 of the *Convention*.

[35] See Article 4.1 of the *Convention*.

[36] See Article 22 of the ILO Constitution.

[37] See Article 14.1 of the *Convention*.

[38] See Article 15.1 of the *Convention*.

[39] See Article 14.3 of the *Convention*.

[40] See Article 2.2(b) of the *Convention*.

[41] See Article 2.1 of the *Convention*. Note that *Convention No. 169* should not be interpreted as preventing the peoples in question from taking advantage of rights and benefits flowing from other national or international legal instruments (Article 35). In other words, it should be considered a minimal charter. Various commentaries on the advantages and disadvantages to Aboriginal peoples of using the *Convention* have already been published. Among others, see R. L. Barsh, "An Advocate's Guide to the Convention on Indigenous and Tribal Peoples", (1990) 15 *Oklahoma City University Law Review* 209; N. Lerner, "The 1989 ILO Convention on Indigenous Populations: New Standards?", [1990] *Israel Yearbook on Human Rights* 223–241; N. Lerner, *Group Rights and Discrimination in International Law*, Dordrecht Nijhoff Publishers, 1991 at 105–110; and R. Stavenhagen, *The Ethnic Question: Conflicts, Development and Human Rights*, Tokyo: United Nations University Press, 1990 at 93–119.

[42] Article 1(a) and (b) of the *Convention*.

[43] Article 34 of the *Convention*.

[44] See the indispensable works by N. Rouland, *Aux confins du droit: Anthropologie juridique de la modernité, supra*, note 16 at 199 and ff; and *Anthropologie juridique, supra*, note 16. See also É. LeRoy, "Les fondements anthropologiques des droits de l'homme: crise de l'universalisme et post modernité", (1992) XVII-48 *Revue de Droit prospectif* at 139–160; and M. E. Turpel, "Aboriginal Peoples

and the Canadian Charter: Interpretive Monopolies, Cultural Difference", (1989–1990) 6 *Annuaire canadien des droits de la personne* at 3–45.

[45] The community-based aspect is also found in the *African Charter on Human and Peoples' Rights*.

[46] Article 8.2 of the *Convention*.

[47] *Ibid.*

[48] For example, see a very interesting case study on the Mohawks by E. J. Dickson-Gilmore, "La renaissance de la Grande Loi de la Paix: conceptions traditionnelles de la justice au sein de la Nation mohawk de Kahnawake", (1991) XXI(1–2) *Recherches amérindiennes au Québec* at 29–43.

[49] By Economic and Social Council Resolution 1982/43. See D. Sanders, "The UN Working Group on Indigenous Populations", [1989] *Human Rights Quarterly* 406–433.

[50] *Conclusions, Propositions and Recommendations*, E/CN.4/Sub.2/1986/7/Add.4, para. 8 at 4.

[51] A Programme of Action for the Second Decade can be accessed at: http://www.un.org/esa/socdev/unpfii/en/second_programme_of_action.htm. Under 'Areas of Action', 'Human Rights', the United Nations Permanent Forum on Indigenous Issues states that:

> The finalization of negotiations on the draft declaration on the rights of indigenous peoples and its adoption early in the Decade should be a priority for the Second Decade.

[52] Reports on Sessions of the Permanent Forum on Indigenous Issues can be accessed at: http://www.un.org/esa/socdev/unpfii/en/sessions.html. For earlier discussions on the need to work toward agreement on the draft *Declaration*, see *Report on the Working Group on Indigenous Populations on its ninth session*, Economic and Social Council, United Nations, E/CN.4/Sub.2/1991/Rev.1 at 53 and *Report on the Working Group on Indigenous Populations on its tenth session*, Economic and Social Council, United Nations, E/CN.4/Sub.2/1992/33 at 32.

[53] *Ibid.* See also R. N. Clinton, "The Rights of Indigenous Peoples as Collective Group Rights", (1990) 32 *Arizona Law Review* 739–747; D. Sanders, "Draft Universal Declaration on the Rights of Indigenous Peoples", [1992] 2 *Canadian Native Law Reporter* 1–5; and R. Stavenhagen, *supra*, note 39.

[54] See L. Noël, *L'intolérance: une problématique générale*, Montréal: Boréal, 1989 at 218–265. Concerning Third World countries, see G. Feuer and H. Cassan, *Le droit international du développement*, Paris: Dalloz, 1985 at 33–34, where they write:

> "Very early, developing countries asked that international law give them a special legal regime appropriate to their situation. From this point of view, they challenged the principle of the equality of every state before international law. They also helped to give rise to what is now the *summa divisio* of international development law, namely the existence of two categories of states: developed countries on one hand and developing countries on the other. This *duality of statuses* leads to a *duality of norms*, and produces legal consequences that are clearly defined by the formula in the Tokyo Round agreements, namely "differential and more favourable treatment" for developing countries. This principle is quite naturally

applied with respect to the right to aide, as well as to commercial law and technology transfer. Thus we can now consider it as one of the main lines by which international development law is guided today." [Our translation.]

Index

Acknowledgements

The articles in this text were originally published in French by, or produced under the supervision of, the following publishers and organizations. We gratefully acknowledge these sources.

Sylvie Vincent, "The Uepishtikueiau Narrative: The Arrival of the French at the site of Québec City according to Innu Oral Tradition", was originally produced under the supervision of the Institut éducatif et culturel montagnais. The map reproduced in this text was originally produced by Ashini Goupil, of Wendake, Québec.

Denys Delâge, "Aboriginal Influence on the Canadians and French at the Time of New France", was originally published as "L'influence des Amérindiens sur les Canadiens et les Français au temps de la Nouvelle France" (1992) 2 (ndeg. 2, automne) *L'acculturation, Lekton* 103.

Denys Delâge and Jean-Phillippe Warren, "The Meeting of Bourgeois and Aboriginal Ethics: Modernity, Postmodernity and Aboriginality", was originally published as "Modernité, postmodernité et amérindianité" (2001) 31 (3) *Recherches amérindiennes au Québec* 83.

Bernard Saladin d'Anglure, "The Construction of Shamanic Identity among the Inuit of Nunavut and Nunavik", was originally published as "La construction de l'identité chamanique chez les Inuit du Nunavut et du Nunavik" (2001) 25 (1-2) *Etudes Inuit Studies* 195.

Bernard Saladin d'Anglure, "The Inuit 'Third Gender'", was originally published as "Le troisième sexe" (1992) 245 *La Recherche* 836.

Bernard Saladin d'Anglure, "The Whale Hunting Among the Inuit of the Canadian Arctic", was originally published in Sophie Bobé (ed.), *Baleines, un enjeu écologique*, collection Monde/Nature extrême, Les Éditions Autrement, Paris, p. 88.

Mylène Jaccoud, "Aboriginal Criminal Justice: From Imposed Justice to Power Transfer", was originally published as "La justice pénale et les Autochtones: D'une justice imposée au transfert de pouvoirs" (2002) 17 (2) *Canadian Journal of Law and Society* 107.

Ghislain Otis, "Elections, Traditional Aboriginal Governance and the Charter", was originally published as "Élection, gouvernance traditionnelle et droits fondamentaux chez les peuples autochtones du Canada" (2004) 49 (2) *McGill Law Journal* 393.

Andrée Lajoie, Henry Quillinan, Rod Macdonald and Guy Rocher, "Legal Pluralism at Kahnawake", was originally published as "Pluralisme juridique à Kahnawake?" (1998) 39 (4) *Cahiers de droit* 681.

Ghislain Otis, "Aboriginal Governance with or without the Canadian Charter?", was published in 2006 by the *Ottawa Law Review*.

Andrée Lajoie, Eric Gelineau, Isabelle Duplessis and Guy Rocher, "The Integration of Aboriginal values and Interests Into Canadian Judicial and Normative Discourse", was originally published as "L'intégration des valeurs et des intérêts autochtones dans le discours judiciaire et normatif canadien" (2000) 38 (1) *Osgoode Hall Law Journal* 143.

Carole Lévesque, "Aboriginal Peoples' Quest for Identity and Self-Government", was originally published as "La quête autonomiste et identitaire des autochtones", in Y. Boisvert, J. Hamel et M. Molgat (eds.), *Vivre la citoyenneté. Identité, appartenance et participation* (Montréal: Liber, 2000) 109-118.

Alain Bissonnette, "Aboriginal Peoples' Right to Self-Government: A Phoenix that Will Rise from its Ashes", was originally published as "Le droit à l'autonomie gouvernementale des peuples autochtones : un phénix qui renaîtra de ses cendres" (1993) 24 *Revue Générale de Droit* 5.

MEMBER OF SCABRINI GROUP

Québec, Canada
2006